William Tyndale

GVLIELMVS: TINDALVS MARTYR.
OLIM EX AVLA MAGD:

Hac ut luce tuas dispergam Roma tenebras
Sponte ex torris ero Sponte Sacrificium

REFERT HÆC TABELLA QVOD SOLVM POTVIT ARS GVILHELMI TYNDAIL, HVIVS OLIM AVLÆ ALVMNI, SIMVL
ET ORNAMENTI, QVI POST FÆLICES PVRIORIS THEOLOGIÆ PRIMITIAS HIC DEPOSITAS ANTVEPIÆ IN NO=
VO TESTAMENTO NEC NON PENTATEVCHO IN VERNACVLAM TRANFERENDO OPERAM NAVAVIT, ANGLIS
SVIS EO VSQ SALVTIFERAM, VT INDE NON IMMERITO ANGLIÆ APOSTOLVS AVDIRET MARTYRIO WILFORDÆ PROPE
BRVXELLAS CORONATVS·Aº· 1536, VIR SI VEL ADVERSARIO (PROCVRATORI NEMPE IMPERTORIS GENERALI) CREDAMVS PERDOCTVS PIVS ET BONVS.

WILLIAM TYNDALE

A Biography

DAVID DANIELL

YALE UNIVERSITY PRESS
New Haven & London

Designed by Gillian Malpass
Set in Linotron Bembo by Best-set Typesetter Ltd., Hong Kong
Printed and bound at the Bath Press, Avon, Great Britain

Library of Congress Cataloging-in-Publication Data
Daniell, David.
William Tyndale : a biography / by David Daniell.
Includes bibliographical references and index.
ISBN 0-300-06132-3
1. Tyndale, William, d. 1536.   2. Reforamtion–England–Biography.
I. Title.
BR350. T8D33   1994
270.6′092–dc20
[B]   94-17509
CIP

A catalogue record for this book is available from
The British Library

Frontispiece: Anon., *William Tyndale,*
mid-sixteenth century (?).
Reproduced by kind permission of
the Principal of Hertford College, Oxford.

To Andy

CONTENTS

ACKNOWLEDGEMENTS

Many people have contributed to the making of this book. I want first of all to thank Tyndale enthusiasts across the world, a band that seems to increase daily, whose inspiring letters and phone calls have meant a great deal in the two years of its writing. I have felt 'compassed with so great a multitude of witnesses' as Tyndale puts it in Hebrews 12, and I am sorry that it is not possible to mention all by name.

I am especially grateful for specialist help in London. In the Library of University College London, John Spiers has been unfailingly re-sourceful and prompt with advice, with suggestions and even with books in hand, showing a patience with me that cannot have been easy amid the minute-by-minute demands from queues of students. Dr Michael Weitzman of the Department of Hebrew Studies at University College has illuminated my understanding of the Hebrew Bible with great wisdom and, again, patience, in many sessions. In the later stages Vanessa Champion-Smith did excellent research.

Professor Gerald Hammond of the University of Manchester gave much-needed encouragement and advice throughout the writing, and made his expertise freely available. Dr Anthea Hume of the University of Reading gave me permission to use her unpublished 1961 doctoral thesis, 'A Study of the Writings of the English Protestant Exiles, 1525–35': as will be apparent, her pioneering work has influenced my thinking at many points and I am glad to express in this book my particular appreciation. Miss Joan Johnson, the Gloucestershire historian, and Dr Joseph Bettey of the University of Bristol answered my questions by return of post.

For help with pictures I am glad to thank Vanessa Champion-Smith again and Tim Davies, Robert Ireland, Gertrude Starink, Andrew Valentine and the Revd. Dr Morris West.

I owe a special debt of thanks to Sue Thurgood, who worked under the greatest pressure to get the final text in order and presentable, twice. Without the initiative, skills and patience of Gillian Malpass at Yale University Press this book would not have happened.

The specialist knowledge of my elder son, Chris, saved me from many historical follies and his interest throughout has been an inspiration. I have also been rescued by his computer skills. The book is dedicated to my younger son, Andy, who set out on a different, but parallel, intellectual voyage. My deepest debt is to my wife, Dorothy, who has lived with Tyndale as well as me for two years: without her nothing at all would be possible.

Leverstock Green
May 1994

INTRODUCTION

William Tyndale gave us our English Bible. The sages assembled by King James to prepare the Authorised Version of 1611, so often praised for unlikely corporate inspiration, took over Tyndale's work. Nine-tenths of the Authorised Version's New Testament is Tyndale's. The same is true of the first half of the Old Testament, which is as far as he was able to get before he was executed outside Brussels in 1536.

Very many of the treasures which have enriched the lives and language of English speakers since the 1530s were made by Tyndale: a long list of common phrases like 'the salt of the earth' or 'let there be light' or 'the spirit is willing'; the haunting phrasing in parables like the Prodigal Son, 'this thy brother was dead, and is alive again: and was lost, and is found'; the gospel stories of Christmas ('there were shepherds abiding in the field') through to the events of the Passion in Jerusalem and the Resurrection: in the Old Testament, the telling of Creation and of Adam and Eve, right through the history told there to the Exile in Babylon. All these things came as something new to the men and women of Tyndale's time in the 1520s and 1530s. That was because Tyndale translated them, for the first time, from their original texts in Greek and Hebrew, into English; and then printed them in pocket volumes for everyone to own. Apart from manuscript translations into English from the Latin, made at the time of Chaucer, and linked with the Lollards, the Bible had been only in that Latin translation made a thousand years before, and few could understand it. Tyndale, before he left England for his life's work, said to a learned man, 'If God spare my life, ere many years I will cause a boy that driveth the plough shall know more of the Scripture than thou dost.' He succeeded.

The outlines of Tyndale's life have been generally known: the years at Oxford and in Gloucestershire, the fruitless attempt to get the

Bishop of London to support him, the exile to Germany and the Netherlands; the cargoes of Testaments smuggled into England; his arrest in Antwerp, imprisonment and, charged with heresy, burning. There has not been a full-scale study of him for nearly sixty years, since J.F. Mozley's biography of 1937, itself based on that by Robert Demaus in 1871 (Brian Edwards's excellent *God's Outlaw* of 1976 is a semi-fictionalised account). There is need for something more modern, especially as the quincentenary of Tyndale's birth in 1494 is widely celebrated.

There have always been those who unfashionably recognised something of his worth: but at the end of the twentieth century his achievement begins to look substantially greater than has ever been understood. William Tyndale was a most remarkable scholar and linguist, whose eight languages included skill in Greek and Hebrew far above the ordinary for an Englishman of the time—indeed, Hebrew was virtually unknown in England. His unsurpassed ability was to work as a translator with the sounds and rhythms as well as the senses of English, to create unforgettable words, phrases, paragraphs and chapters, and to do so in a way that, again unusually for the time, is still, even today, direct and living: newspaper headlines still quote Tyndale, though unknowingly, and he has reached more people than even Shakespeare. At the centre of it all for him was his root in the deepest heart of New Testament theology, a faith of the sort that can, and did, move mountains. Tyndale as theologian, making a Reformation theology that was just becoming discernibly English when he was killed, has been at best neglected and at worst twisted out of shape. Tyndale as conscious craftsman has been not just neglected, but denied: yet the evidence of the book that follows makes it beyond challenge that he used, as a master, the skill in the selection and arrangement of words which he partly learned at school and university, and partly developed from pioneering work by Erasmus. These things are shown in his treatises, but, together with his understanding of languages, they make the core of his Bible work. For him, an English translation of the Bible had to be as accurate to the original languages, Greek and Hebrew, as scholarship could make it; and it had to make sense. There are times when the original Greek, and for good reason even more the Hebrew, are baffling. A weak translator goes for paraphrase, or worse, for philological purity, and hang the sense (as the Authorised Version did often with the Prophets, for example, in those books lacking Tyndale as a base). Tyndale is clear. With a difficult word or phrase, he understands the alternatives presented by technical semantics, or changes of tone or feeling, and goes for what makes sense. In the pages that follow we shall watch that process again and again.

In doing all this, he made a language for England. It is a commonplace of Reformation history that Martin Luther seized the chance of
advanced Greek studies to make a New Testament in German that gave
a disunited Germany a language for the time; it has not been noised
abroad sufficiently clearly that Tyndale did something even greater for
England. As used to be said with pride, the English rapidly became a
People of the Book. To try to understand the literature, philosophy, art,
politics and society of the centuries from the sixteenth to the early
twentieth without knowledge of the Bible is to be crippled.

That Book was made by Tyndale in the language people spoke, not
as the scholars wrote. At a time when English was struggling to find a
form that was neither Latin nor French, Tyndale gave the nation a
Bible language that was English in words, word-order and lilt. He
invented some words (for example, 'scapegoat') and the great Oxford
English Dictionary has mis-attributed, and thus also mis-dated, a
number of his first uses. But more importantly, he made phrases which
have gone deep into English-speaking consciousness. For example, for
the Hebrew grammatical form of the possessive known as the construct, he greatly extended the English 'the + noun + of + the +
noun' ('the birds of the air, the fish of the sea'), which has lived on for
slightly heightened moments ever since and is rich in our literature
(where would D.H. Lawrence have been without it?). Further, the
English word-order is subject-verb-object: English with its independent roots does not, in its native form, have, wherever possible,
what Latin, which can be, when the need arises, brief, but being still,
as so often transmitted, legal in its necessity, a complexity which
escalates from a syntax which is basically subordinating, like this rather
ridiculous sentence. In some places, English did go down that road
in the next centuries; but not where most people knew their God.
Here is Tyndale: 'And they heard the voice of the Lord God as he
walked in the garden in the cool of the day. And Adam hid himself and
his wife from the face of the Lord God. And the Lord God called
Adam and said unto him, Where art thou?' Or 'The third day Abraham
lifted up his eyes and saw the place afar off, and said unto his young
men: bide here with the ass. I and the lad will go yonder and worship
and come again to you.' Or, 'And they brought their ships to land, and
forsook all, and followed him.' Most of those words are monosyllables.
Tyndale transmitted an English strength which is the opposite of Latin,
seen in the difference between 'high' and 'elevated', 'gift' and 'dona-
tion', 'many' and 'multitudinous'. Polysyllabic Latin can be dramatically
powerful, as in Macbeth's distraught 'the multitudinous seas incar-
nadine', but Macbeth suddenly clarifies that to 'making the green one
red'. When in her sleep Lady Macbeth's conscience at last speaks, she

says 'Yet who would have thought the old man to have had so much blood in him'; a chilling line made more so by the monosyllables.

There is a great deal of work to be done on Tyndale, in every area of his life, but particularly the Bible translations. This book is offered to give strength to such studies. He has been most unfairly neglected. In the tide of books and articles on so many aspects of our literature, history, theology and language, a flood that rises every year, there have been some that discuss Tyndale, work which is here gladly acknowledged. But very little has yet been done on him. Analysis of his rhetorical skills as a translator has barely begun. An admirable Tyndale Project based in Washington, D.C., will in the next years produce, in four finely edited scholarly volumes, the works of Tyndale. But those 'complete works' do not include the Bible translations. It is a matter of increasing grief that Tyndale lives in modern scholarship upside-down, so that attention is given to *The Practice of Prelates*, a book that would not greatly be missed, and almost none is given to Tyndale as translator, apart from a very few Hebrew and Greek scholars and historians of the Bible who shine like a city that is set on a hill. It remains curious, to put it mildly, that the gravitational pull of Sir Thomas More has been allowed to distort Tyndale's orbit, especially as More's dealings with Tyndale were coloured by near-rabid hatred. More had fine qualities, but they did not show when he attacked the reformers. Study of Tyndale is necessary to scholars of More, as More wrote so many black columns against Tyndale; Tyndale's reply was one short book. More is not vital to the study of Tyndale, whose world is elsewhere. People who have read Tyndale's Bible still speak of him as of an ordinary neighbour; nobody speaks like that of More.

Something should be said here about sources. Tyndale himself reveals little. There are documents, such as Stephen Vaughan's letters to Cromwell from Antwerp, which are valuable. Occasionally, friends like John Frith make a reference to him. More gives some facts, though they have to be challenged; he was not above romancing. A prime source is John Foxe; and with him comes a problem. This is not of his unreliability; work by historians checking this shows an increasing awareness that Foxe can be trusted more than has often been allowed.[1] Nor is it mainly from that influential prejudice that accepts as a historian, for example, Eustace Chapuys, the pro-Catherine official of the Emperor Charles V and a collector of Court gossip at the time of her rival Anne Boleyn, and dismisses Foxe, who painstakingly gave a lifetime to the assembly and printing of official documents and letters (which vast store still exists) as a Protestant propagandist, irritating as that is. No: the problem is Foxe's very success. John Foxe began as a

Marian exile with a small Latin book of recent English religious history printed in Strasburg in 1554. He followed that in 1559 with a big folio of 750 pages in six books taking the story further, but again in Latin. In the eighteen months after his return to England he assembled and on 20 March 1563 published the first *Acts and Monuments* ('Foxe's Book of Martyrs') in English, a bigger folio of nearly 1,800 pages, taking the story of religious persecution back to AD 1000 and across Europe, and printing for English historians, among much else, the complete episcopal registers of Norwich, London, Canterbury and Lichfield, as well as private manuscripts. Seven years later he published the second English edition of *Acts and Monuments*, now in two gigantic folio volumes, making 2,300 very large pages covered in type (often very small), taking the story back to the Apostles and printing vastly more documentation. In spite of the size, however, in order to make room for all the new documents that had come to his hand, he had to cut material from the first edition. It will be seen that there is immediately a problem for the modern student, as both editions have to be consulted at once—a difficulty increased thirty-fold by the chaotic chronology of each volume. His general principle, sound enough in its way, is to be an obituarist; the story of X or Y is told at their deaths and the indexes of such main entries are reliable. There is also, however, much additional material, scattered sometimes scores of pages apart, which is not indexed. A modern researcher needs a modern, properly edited edition. There isn't one. Best available in libraries are versions of a Victorian eight-volume set where the 'editing', though well-intentioned, includes interference with the text in the matter of punctuation (a pepper-pot of commas and semi-colons has been shaken over every page, with distressing effects) and arrangement, as what is printed is Foxe's second, 1570, version: input from the earlier 1563 edition (often of great value, and otherwise lost) is reduced to a grudging footnote inviting the reader to look there. As it can be much more easily consulted, I have thought it best in this book to follow that set, rather than transcribe from rare copies of various Foxe editions (though that has been done, where necessary); to take quotations from it, and give references to it. So in the notes to what follows 'Foxe IV', for example, means the fourth volume of that eight-volume set. It first appeared between 1843 and 1849, introduced and edited by George Townsend. It was printed again, in another edition for all practical purposes identical, this time from J. Pratt and J. Stoughton, which appeared in 1877: this tended to be standard in libraries until 1965, when AMS Press Inc. of New York issued a facsimile of Townsend's eight volumes. The multiplicity does not matter too much: volume division and pagination are the same in all. Some of Foxe's unpublished material was assembled in the eighteenth century by John Strype, with his own additions, in an arrangement in various sets of volumes that is only slightly easier to use.

Something of the same interference afflicts the works of Tyndale. All he wrote (and some he didn't) except the Bible translations, were assembled by Henry Walter for the Parker Society in 1848 and soon after, in three rather depressing volumes. Again, intrusive commas and semi-colons (the latter not even invented in Tyndale's time) are thick on the page, and Walter could not always use the best edition. Again, because they are the only volumes available, they have been quoted and referred to here. He did not number his three volumes, so in the notes below 'PS 176' means a reference to the relevant Parker Society volume.

Quotations from Luther are from the great Weimar fifty-eight volume edition. It has been thought best to give the sixteenth-century German without modernising. This might seem 'at first chop', as Tyndale would say, a bizarre decision, when all English works here are in modernised spelling: but it has felt safest to put in front of the reader what Tyndale had in front of him.

Finally, as this book was going to press, the British Library announced that it is buying for one million pounds the copy of Tyndale's 1526 Worms New Testament which has been since the late eighteenth century in the possession of Bristol Baptist College. This precious little book is unique in two ways. The pages are quite richly decorated (not by Peter Schoeffer, the work-a-day German printer); and it is the only complete survivor of Tyndale's original print-run of 3,000—some would say, 6,000. It is hoped that in London very many people, as week follows week, will be able to gaze on this jewel in the crown of England's Bible, and give thanks for Tyndale's skill in giving us the Word of God in a language that still speaks directly to the heart.

Part 1

THE MAKING OF THE TRANSLATOR

Chapter 1

GLOUCESTERSHIRE

Tyndale Families

For many centuries there have been Tyndales in Essex, Northampton-shire, Norfolk and especially in Gloucestershire, where England faces Wales across the wide valley of the River Severn. Tyndales have lived in that county since at least the middle of the fourteenth century. A branch of those Gloucestershire Tyndales took the name of Hutchins as well: it includes William Tyndale, translator.[1]

There is no documentary evidence of him at all until he took his Oxford BA in his late teens. No record exists of when or where he was born, but there have been strong local traditions and a few meagre facts about his family in mid-Gloucestershire. The most likely year of his birth, 1494, is a computation from factors in such family records as are felt to be firm and his University of Oxford record. The most likely region of his origin is within a few miles of Dursley, between Bristol and Gloucester, on the western edge of the Cotswold hills.

It is a domestic but also in its way a dramatic landscape. Below Dursley, five miles to the west and close to the Severn, lies the village of Berkeley. The Norman castle there—where William the Conqueror had been crowned, the barons assembled before Runnymede and Edward II was shamefully murdered—still dominates that three-mile-wide stretch below the Cotswold hills, running north-east and south-west for ten miles alongside the Severn, a fertile area of arable and dairy farms known as the Vale of Berkeley. One and a half miles west of Dursley, looking out from its hill over Berkeley, lies Stinchcombe. Melksham Court outside Stinchcombe (the present fine Tudor house was built later) is the most likely place of William Tyndale's family at the time of his birth, though it is not known for certain where he was born. Tebota Hochyns was tenant of Melksham Court at the end of the fifteenth century, and her tenancy passed to Richard Tyndale in the early 1500s, though it is uncertain whether he was her son or husband or more distantly related. Richard, possibly with Tebota as wife, had, among others, two sons, a Thomas and a William, who, when Richard died in January 1506/7, inherited jointly the Hochyns tenancy. It seems that that particular William married Alice Hunt of the farm called Hunt's Court beside the village of North Nibley, two miles south-east of Stinchcombe, giving rise to the later belief that the translator originated from Hunt's Court. That William, however, was still alive in the 1540s. The church at North Nibley is still thought, not impossibly, to be where William the translator was baptised, wherever in the Stinchcombe area he was born. Overlooking the village of North Nibley is the commanding height of Nibley Knoll, on which in 1866 there was erected a striking monument to William Tyndale the translator, a tall tower visible for many miles across the Severn valley, familiar to all who have walked the long-distance path, the Cotswold Way.

Three miles north of Stinchcombe, beside the Severn, is the village of Slimbridge. In a house a mile and a half south-west of Slimbridge known as Hurst Farm lived an able and successful man named Edward Tyndale, who, according to a separate strand of information, was brother to William the translator. There exist two letters dated 1533 from the Bishop of London, John Stokesley, probably sent to Henry VIII's secretary, Thomas Cromwell, asking (with a sweetener of cash accompanying the second letter) that a certain Gloucestershire farm be given to an old servant of his, and not to the rival claimant, who 'hath a kinsman called Edward Tyndale, brother to Tyndale the arch-heretic'.[2] It may be that in 1533 Stokesley felt that he could score a point with Cromwell by smearing Edward's name in that way. Stokesley, as the final chapters of this book will show, is the most likely person to have orchestrated the secret plot against William Tyndale which led to his betrayal, capture, imprisonment for sixteen months, trial and execution. Stokesley knew that Edward was a powerful man in the area, for since 1509 he, Stokesley, had been rector of Slimbridge. The parish had a curate (possibly two) and Stokesley was a pluralist, with at least two other livings, so he probably never visited the parish. He had, however, also been Fellow and Tutor of Magdalen Collge since 1495, Vice-President of that college from 1505—and Principal of Magdalen Hall in 1498. Magdalen Hall, then so intimately connected with Magdalen College as to be inside it, was William Tyndale's Oxford institution from about 1506 to about 1516. Stokesley, we may feel, may have known a good deal about the Gloucestershire Tyndale clan.

The Tyndale properties were not small; William Tyndale belonged to a family which included reasonably wealthy merchants and landowners, and they, with the Church, were the holders of local power. The notion that William Tyndale crept out of humble origins, a small country mouse from an unimpressive clan, and then dared to challenge the great and well-connected lions of London, is not true: indeed, it should perhaps be reversed. Cuthbert Tunstall, Bishop of London, was said to have been born the illegitimate son of a squire in a remote Yorkshire hamlet; Thomas Cromwell was the son of a London brewer; and Thomas More's grandfather was a London baker.[3] The Tyndales, successful people in one of England's most prosperous counties, could hold their heads high. By 1522, the Tyndale family had risen to positions of real affluence and influence.[4]

Edward Tyndale—like another brother John, he did not use the name Hutchins—was a significant man in Gloucestershire. The Marquess of Berkeley had died in 1492 and, apparently in spite, bequeathed his estates not to his brother but to the Crown, and a local receiver of rents and other payments due to the Crown from the Berkeley lands was appointed. Such a crown steward was a powerful man, largely taking over the local authority which the Berkeley family had recently dissipated. The lords of Berkeley, it was said, could walk to London without leaving their own lands. An early crown steward was Sir John Walsh of Little Sodbury Manor, who was to be William Tyndale's first employer. His successor from 1519 was Edward Tyndale. Later, in 1529, Edward received a grant of the lease of the manor of Hurst in Slimbridge. He later held, as Demaus explains, 'by grant from the Abbot of Tewkesbury, the Manor of the Pull, or Pull Court, in the parish of Bushley in Worcester, and that of Burnet juxta Keynsham, in the county of Somerset. His will, which was proved in London in 1546, shows him to have been a man of substance . . .'[5] At one time or another he had responsibilities in the three counties of Gloucestershire, Worcestershire and Somerset. At the Dissolution he was appointed auditor and Steward of Tewkesbury Abbey, again succeeding Sir John Walsh in the post. He was wealthy as well as able, and, like Walsh and the Tyndale brother John, he was sympathetic to the cause of reform. In the early 1520s only Thomas held land: Edward's strength was in trade.[6]

The name Tyndale suggests a northern origin, from the Tyne regions of Northumberland. In a letter of 1663 a descendant of Edward expressed the notion that the Vale of Berkeley clan grew from a certain Tyndale who came from the north in the Wars of the Roses, settling in Gloucestershire where he changed his name to Hutchins for safety, only revealing his true name to his children on his deathbed. That

Restoration embroidery might, however, contain a thread of truth, in the idea of ultimate northern origins. The most likely reason for the keeping of the addition of Hutchins to Tyndale is that it commemorated the inheritance brought in through marriage. Hutchins and its variants is a Gloucestershire name still common in the Stinchcombe area. In the sixteenth century the name Tyndale seems to have had a better ring to it in loftier London circles than Hutchins: in the 1530s, when Sir Thomas More wished to sneer at William Tyndale, he called him Hutchins.

William the translator belonged to an extensive clan of significant Gloucestershire people, well regarded locally over a wide area and known in London. His childhood, in those circumstances, may be imagined. Lacking any hard information about young William Tyndale, imagining, regrettably, is all that can be done. Life then for a small child in that part of rural Gloucestershire would be full. Agriculture was prosperous, as was trade, especially in wool and cloth: the houses and gardens were good and well planned, local fairs and events flourished, and main trade-routes from all parts of the north were funnelled through that strip of land east of the Severn. The ways went on to the south and west, then via Bristol to London or to the further western coasts. From Bristol, trade could reach southern Ireland, the south of Europe and even Africa. From Southampton, it could go to London and northern Europe. Pilgrim routes to Hereford and Worcester were heavily used, crossing the country.[7] News and influences from far abroad would soon be known. It would be very wrong to think of Tyndale's birthplace as 'remote', if that means cut off from the activities of the widest world.[8] The local education was good: it is likely that as a young child Tyndale had some schooling at Wotton-under-Edge, four miles south-west of Stinchcombe, where there was an excellent grammar-school, which had been founded in 1384 by the dowager Lady Berkeley.

Tyndale reveals only one tiny fact about his childhood. In *The Obedience of a Christian Man* he wrote: '. . . except my memory fail me and that I have forgotten what I read when I was a child thou shalt find in the English chronicle how that king Adelstone caused the holy scripture to be translated into the tongue that then was in England and how the prelates exhorted him thereto.'[9] The *Obedience* is packed with rhetorical devices, and here are the figures of *Recordatio* (calling to memory) and *Testatio* (confirming by one's own experience) with the device of postulating a possible lapse of memory about what is commonly understood (as in the modern 'Two and two make four: at least I seem to recall they did when I was at school'). Tyndale is pressing the point that the Scriptures in English have been part of the nation's life for centuries. What 'English chronicle' he was reading is problematic, if he means something specific. Athelstan followed the example of his grandfather Alfred in his enthusiasm for learning and the education of the nation, and William of Malmesbury's account of him in his twelfth-century *De gestis regum* would seem to support Tyndale. This might have been the chronicle of English kings that the young Tyndale was reading. We have no idea what age 'when I was a child' means: his Latin must have been reasonably good by then to enable him to read William of Malmesbury. As he had been librarian of Malmesbury Abbey, a dozen miles to the south-east, he could have been read as a local chronicler in Wotton-under-Edge Grammar School.[10]

Gloucestershire in 1500

There are several things about William Tyndale's upbringing, however, that may be remarked. One is the landscape. The Cotswolds are civilised hills, settled successfully from the most ancient times, their sheltered valleys full of crops and their hills full of sheep, their towns and villages centres of thriving industry by clear, fast-running streams, graceful with friendly and attractive buildings of the local stone that glows in the sunshine. The long western escarpment of the Cotswolds looks over the wide Severn valley to the hills and mountains of Wales. Some of those Cotswold hills give spectacular views; north up the Severn to the Malvern Hills and far beyond, west across the Severn and deep into Wales, south as the Severn winds to the region round Bristol. Stinchcombe Hill is itself a famous viewpoint, from which it is said that seven counties can be seen. William Tyndale as a boy would have been used to a short climb giving views of the longest range. He would have grown up with the idea, moreover, of the presence of people across the Severn valley having another, and very different, language. He would assuredly have heard much Welsh spoken in the normal trading of the district.

It may be fanciful, but it is interesting to consider that some of the greatest users of the English language have been on the edges of other cultures and other tongues. Chaucer, for example, an official working in the Pool of London, spent many of his hours talking to sailors of many nationalities who had been across the known world. Shakespeare grew up in what was effectively a border town, where English stolidity met Celtic fire in an important market-centre; Stratford-upon-Avon, though set on Warwickshire loam, is close enough to Wales for him to have known the people and their language well. He put different kinds of Welsh men and women in his plays with a variety of amused affection (Fluellen, Sir John Evans, Glendower and his daughter who speaks only Welsh) not found in his Scots, Irish, French, Spanish, Italian or German characters. Tyndale grew up to be a remarkable linguist, noted in Europe for knowing seven languages as well as English, like a native. From Gloucestershire several generations of English merchants had been travelling to the Low Countries and France and further afield, as far as Italy and Spain; their foreign counterparts had from long before taken to coming to Gloucestershire to buy the strong, white wool of the Cotswold sheep, in fleeces as well in the best of the spring and autumn clips, for themselves.[11] The trade was refined when it was recognised that, instead of raw wool, woollen cloth would be more profitable still. By the time of Tyndale's boyhood, villages like Dursley, with good water for fulling and dyeing, were manufacturing cloth for export far abroad, with a corresponding increase in foreign links: young William would have grown up with the idea of languages. He became no dry philologist: part of his genius as a translator was his gift for knowing how ordinary people used language at slightly heightened moments, and translating at that level ('Am I my brother's keeper?', 'the burden and heat of the day', 'the signs of the times', 'a law unto themselves'). The proverb of the time 'As sure as God's in Gloucestershire' might have been a reference to the fact that in the late Middle Ages about a third of the county belonged to the Church, yet it might also have commented on the natural wealth and human prosperity there. Gloucestershire was a good place to live, secure, self-supporting, with wide communications. For the place of origin of William Tyndale it is not fanciful to add to that domestic solidity which he had in his Gloucestershire childhood the availability of distant prospects, including the awareness of the particularity of languages as they were daily used.

It is also possible now to say something more about the livelihood of the people in the Vale of Berkeley among whom William Tyndale grew up. Gloucestershire in 1500 had a population of about 50,000, most of it rural.[12] The strong development in the county of the many local centres of the rural cloth-making industry, of which the Vale of Berkeley was especially significant, depended partly on the fast-flowing streams coming down from the Cotswolds. Many of the small communities were beside the main road down England from the North and Midlands on the way to Bristol and Exeter, and could use the Severn as a waterway as well. That development paralleled the beginning of the centuries-long change of power from the great Church and lay houses to people of the middle rank, in local and in national affairs.

Such people 'took for granted that they could run the country better than all the lords and kings in the world, because for the most they actually did organise most activities at the grass roots (where 95 per cent of the population lived), where it counted.'[13] The networks of communication across the county and outside were strong. The population was intensely aware of itself and of its routes of connection. Within the Vale of Berkeley were something like 150 households, involving about thirty families.[14] Working in cloth supported half that population. Cloth-working involved fourteen separate crafts.

> Counting the labour of women and children, more hours were spent growing wool, preparing it, processing it into finished cloth, taking it to local, national and international markets, than were spent in any other activity, with the possible exception of sleeping . . . Shepherds stood at one end of the chain, merchants, tailors and consumers at the other. In between were shearers, packers, loaders, carriers, unloaders, market officials, wool merchants, mill-owners and workers, clothiers, sea-captains and sailors, winders and spinners, cardmakers, carders, weavers, fullers, dyers . . . Cloth brought more wealth into the region than anything else from 1300 to 1840 . . .[15]

In all this, Edward Tyndale was the most powerful man in the Vale, furthering the newer industrial enterprise of the older Berkeley families: and the fourth brother, John Tyndale, organised the production of cloth in the Vale, and its sale in London. It is not surprising that William Tyndale later found support in London from a cloth-merchant whose name, Humphrey Monmouth, suggests neighbourhood to the Severn.[16] John Tewkesbury, one of the first to be burned for distributing Tyndale's Testaments, whose name suggests connection with the abbey town just to the north, was a leather-seller, an adjunct of cloth-working. Not for nothing did William Tyndale, exiled in Cologne, Worms and Antwerp use the international trade-routes of the cloth-merchants to get his books into England, smuggled in bales of cloth.

Since the days of the Oxford man John Wyclif, Master of Balliol (who in 1378 met Parliament at Gloucester) the textile areas of the Vale of Severn had been one of the main regions of 'Lollardy'. This was originally an imprecise pejorative term (rather like the modern 'commie') for Wyclif's followers and their descendants. They based the theology of their personal faith on the Bible and set store by it translated into the vernacular; from that came their attacks on the more corrupt practices of the Church. The great interlacing allegorical poem by William Langland, *Piers Plowman*, mostly written at the time of Wyclif, between 1360 and 1390, and like him critical of much in the practice of the Church, is set in the Vale of Berkeley and also a little further north in the Malvern Hills. Even severe persecution in the early fifteenth century had not wiped out the anti-clerical movement, and cloth-workers and Lollardy had long been linked in England.[17] In Tyndale's time it was 'clothmen' who carried the Word as well as the product from village to village in Essex and Kent,[18] as well as Oxford-shire and Gloucester. They went to the craft halls and wool marts of the clothing centres of London, which acted as exchanges of ideas as well as cloth.[19] After William Tyndale's work abroad from 1525, 'the Word' included not just verbal teaching, nor scraps of manuscript from a Lollard Bible, nor written collections of texts, but 'heretical' printed matter, sheets of printed Bibles, or whole Testaments.

Dialect Influences on Tyndale

Such traffic across counties and into London had one other effect of which we can speak with some confidence. Tyndale's Bible translations have an extraordinary power to address all English-speakers, not just across all the dialects of Britain but over the whole globe, so that present-day Hebrew scholars in North London are as touched by him as are crofters in the Outer Hebrides, and the most rural Ameri-cans are as moved as urban Australians. Considering that local forms (for example, 'Americanisms' in England) can still be so sensitively felt in spite of the shrinking globe, Tyndale's achievement of a language which speaks to the world is astonishing. It is even more remarkable when one considers how different were local dialects all over England in 1500. Tyndale's base was the speech of the Vale of Berkeley, which, from the records of a historian a hundred years later is known to have been, like all such localised speech, distinctive in sound, syntax and vocabulary.[20] Occasionally, a Gloucestershire form is admitted to his printed page, like 'toot-hill' in his translation of Genesis in chapter 31, for a hill used for a look-out.[21] Baffling words like 'back' or 'ixion' for birds, 'perleyed' for small-eyed or 'fellowship' in the sense of 'I pray you'[22] are probably local terms otherwise unrecorded. But these are rare. Much more significant was his understanding, which he shared with Shakespeare, that basing his sentences on the elements of the language with which he grew up, using a neutral word-order and English rather than Latin forms, would make something widely com-prehensible. Two illustrations might help the point. First, the weight which Tyndale gave to certain regular, local, English words. 'Elder', for example, was his final choice for his translation of the Greek word *presbuteros* for the Christian minister, a rendering close to the Greek of the New Testament but causing ferocious offence to the Church hierarchy, who wanted no differentiation from *hieros*, priest, which the New Testament uses for the Jewish officer: the enmity such matters caused was enough to make the books containing them publicly burned. Yet 'elder' is right not only for the Greek, *presbuteros*, but for the person singled out because of wisdom and experience to minister to the local congregation (another 'heretical' word). This is a point where Tyndale's Greek scholarship, his New Testament theology, and his understanding of how an English neighbourhood works, come together. In Stinchcombe and North Nibley the village elder would be someone who 'had earned the title by helping and advising his neighbours in thoroughly practical ways.'[23] Tyndale's understanding of the down-to-earth matters of behaviour, the commonsense expression of his theology, the existential ways in which faith should produce works, was one of the ways in which he was always marked off from Luther, and those who argue for Gloucestershire making Tyndale, far more than Luther ever did, have here a point.[24] Several pages of the *Obedience* are given to the explanation of local meanings of common sayings.[25] Such common practicalities of everyday life, however, experienced by 99 per cent of Englishmen at many levels of local society, were invisible to the bishops, who saw only heresy.

The second local linguistic effect was the ancient skill of the people in encapsulating wisdom in brief and trenchant form. All crafts had—and still have—their own cant terms, just as all English dialects had—and still have—their own vocabulary. The combination of speech-forms peculiar to the Vale of Berkeley, with its national and international connections, and to the work of cloth-making, with its comprehensive involvement of most people in a district, produced at least the possibility of a written English which reflected everyday speech in a slightly heightened form; and that is precisely what we find in Tyndale as translator of the Bible. These near-proverbial statements ('Ask and it shall be given you. Seek and ye shall find. Knock and it shall be opened unto you'[26]) act as proverbs do, in passing on practical wisdom, like the carpenter's 'Measure twice and cut once', from group to group and generation to generation. The sayings themselves are crafted, in rhythm and often near-rhyme. Something of the long history of proverbs can be seen in the rich medieval, sometimes multilingual, collections which have survived.[27] Such assemblies of general sayings would be used both in preaching and the learning of grammar and rhetoric[28]. Well-rounded forms of expression and alter-

native ways of saying things were bases of the arts of rhetoric, re-
established in sixteenth-century schools under the influence, mostly, of
Erasmus. As important, possibly more important however, were the
local proverbs, keeping an idea or an instruction with its feet on the
ground. Take the local North Nibley proverb 'When Westridge Wood
is motley, then 'tis time to sow barley'.[29] The intention is to fix
memory, often in the landscape, like using 'Westridge Wood'. The
Renaissance rediscovery of the classical arts of memory, whereby ideas
are mentally placed in parts of a space such as a body or a room for
later systematic recall, has usually been explained as coming from Italy
to the intellectual élite of the later sixteenth century. Yet the activity
of placing wisdom about the permanent landscape has for a long
time been part of country living. Tyndale's remarkable ability to make
the Greek and Hebrew of the Bible speak in English has one of
its origins, at least, in the local speech of his childhood, in the
clothworking villages of Stinchcombe, North Nibley and Slimbridge:
and Westridge Wood belonged to the Tyndale family.[30] Many forces
combined to help Tyndale make his distinctive clarity: Oxford logical
and rhetorical training; knowledge of Latin, Greek, German, French,
Hebrew, Spanish, Italian (and probably with some ability in other
languages including Welsh) with the interest and skill in translating
them into English; the business life of the craft halls of London; the
technical artifices of preaching. These were consciously used. The
unconscious ground, if one can so call it, was the language spoken
in the Vale of Berkeley by his parents, brothers, friends, neighbours,
by officials and labourers, priests and ploughboys. This was from
middle England in the largest possible sense.[31] He translated Greek and
Hebrew into what he knew best, into what he had taken in with his
mother's milk.

   Tyndale wrote little about literature in English, three or four mentions of the tale of Robin Hood being about the sum of his references,
always in a derogatory context. Ever since Sir Philip Sidney at the end
of the sixteenth century derided English poetry (judging by Italian and
classical standards only) it has often been fashionable to say, with
Sidney, that there was hardly any older literature at all, and what there
was was very poor, with only a handful of exceptions such as Chaucer's
Troilus and Criseide ('Yet had he great wants') and the poems of
Surrey—Sidney's very exceptions are dominated by Italy. Sidney was
looking to a rebirth of English poetry and had to denounce the older
stuff. The eclogues in *The Shepherd's Calendar* are praised by Sidney, but
Spenser's technique of 'framing of his style to an old rustic language I

dare not allow, since neither Theocritus in Greek, Virgil in Latin, nor Sannazaro in Italian did effect it'.[32]

Writing in English

For a very particular reason connected with Tyndale, it is worth looking more closely at what was being written in English while he was at Oxford. A good deal of semi-legal Church material was increasingly written in English in those decades—not only visitation returns and churchwardens' accounts, but wills—until almost all of such things were in English. As literature, seventy years before Sidney wrote his *Apology for Poetry* and eighty before George Puttenham his *The Art of English Poesy*, there was Alexander Barclay's *Ship of Fools* of 1509—but that was a translation from the German. There were some poems from Barclay, and from Stephen Hawes. Possibly at that time came the morality play *Everyman*—another translation. There were racy, vivid poems by the gifted John Skelton, praised by Caxton and by Erasmus (who called him 'the light and glory of England's letters'), and his play *Magnyfycence*. And that is all, we are told. Little of it, not even Skelton, is read much today, though *Everyman* is sometimes performed. The English printers of the time were following Caxton's earlier lead and producing grand older works for aristocratic readers, with much fine reprinting of Chaucer, then nearly a century and a half old. A popular work printed as Tyndale was leaving Oxford was Sir Thomas More's *Utopia*—at Louvain, in Latin. More's hero, Hythlodaeus (an invented Greek name ironically meaning 'someone who talks nonsense') sets out on his travels taking with him a trunkful of books, but not one of them is English, and not one printed by Caxton. Hythlodaeus's 'non-sense' is the most up-to-date humanism and all his books are Greek, even to the denial of Latin authors apart from some Cicero and Seneca. The Utopians fall upon the Greek language and the art of printing and are wholly satisfied, needing nothing else.

The denial of a strong native tradition in the early sixteenth century is a myth that needs to be challenged. Eyes dazzled by Italian sunshine, itself flooding ancient Greece and Rome, have not only failed to look at the English poetry and prose, but often denied it any critical worth. True, few now read Barclay and Hawes—perhaps that is why they are always officially mentioned; the Scottish poets Gavin Douglas and William Dunbar are beyond the border; the native chivalric tradition represented by Lord Berners is difficult to find in print. Yet the common picture is surely distorted. There is space here only for two small examples of a possible native wealth still largely ignored. The miraculously effective short prayers, the 'collects', in Cranmer's *Book of Common Prayer* of forty years later did not come from nowhere; they were the latest flowering of a long English tradition of devotional writing of great skill and beauty.[33] Creating the harmony and balance of the short phrases of such writing was a craft that must have been known to Tyndale, as he uses it again and again: as, for example, at the opening of John 14: 'I go to prepare a place for you. And if I go to prepare a place for you, I will come again, and receive you even unto myself, that where I am, there may ye be also.' Furthermore, it is at first sight an odd fact that when the Antwerp printers very early in the sixteenth century woke up to a possible large English market one of the first books printed for sale in England (in about 1502) included 'The Nut-Brown Maid', that mysterious poem of love-dialogue ('For in my mind of all mankind/I love but you alone'). It is as English as Robin Hood, or as Shakespeare's *As You Like It* of a hundred years later, with which it has something in common. Nothing is known about its origins or circulation; yet a foreign printer of Tyndale's time felt it would add to the English saleability of his book, a miscellany of antiquarian, legal and administrative matter, and general facts, including recipes, known as *Arnold's Chronicle*. The English and Scottish ballad tradition is well-documented, of course, and even Sidney recognised the force in poetry of a tale, 'which holdeth children from play, and old men from the chimney corner';[34] but we have only what has survived, in manuscript or print, and there is no catalogue of what has disappeared. 'The Nut Brown Maid' is not quite a ballad, neither in its psychology nor its form. What else so very English was so strong at the time is simply not in the common understanding of our literary history.[35] Again, the craft lies in the making of short effective lines— making a poem, as it were, out of extended proverbs at moments of heightened psychology, a technique Tyndale is well aware of, in his translation of parables, for example, or the account of the temptation of Jesus at the start of Matthew 4: 'Man shall not live by bread only... Thou shalt not tempt thy Lord God... Thou shalt worship the Lord thy God...'

We have no knowledge of anything more than casual observation by Tyndale of poetry or music. He was dismissive of the ballads of Robin Hood; but again, those remarks, and others like them, are made in the process of strong argument about what was used to fill people's minds in order to point up the startling absence of Scripture, the Word of God, in the Church's teaching.[36] He noted children making descant, a word he uses several times.[37] Though there are few references, this is not to argue that Tyndale did not understand poetry or music. To take an example: it has been a commonplace of comment on the eight-eenth-century poet Alexander Pope to say that he had no ear for music; not only does this turn out on investigation to have originated in a deliberate slander by an envious rival, but no-one who attends at all to the poetic effects that Pope can achieve with his heroic couplets can surely doubt for a moment that the ear which tuned them was not only musical, but remarkably so.[38] Similarly, though Tyndale's mind was not apparently filled with poetry and he did not write poems, being angry with his co-translator William Roye who did,[39] and though he barely refers to music, no-one who is alert to the effects he achieves with the sounds and rhythms of English should doubt that he had a remarkable poetic and musical ear. To local Gloucestershire forms of speech we must add as an influence an awareness of a native tradition of writing. That is a matter quite unexplored, on which much work remains to be done.

Chapter 2

TYNDALE'S OXFORD

Magdalen and its School

The first hard fact that exists about William Tyndale is when he was eighteen, and even then it is about William Hychyns. The registers of the University of Oxford record him taking his BA on 4 July 1512; being licensed MA on 26 June 1515; and created MA on 2 July 1515, all from Magdalen Hall.[1] He went to Oxford in about 1506.

The present Magdalen College was founded in 1448 by William Waynflete, Bishop of Winchester and former Provost of Eton, on a site between Merton Street and High Street, west of the present Examination Schools. Eight years later he began the work which would lead to the foundation on the fine site by the Cherwell: building started in 1467 and the College was first occupied in about 1480. Waynflete made his College a place of educational reform, sorely needed in Oxford. In other colleges the traditional long arts course, the essential route to the even longer work for degrees in theology, law and medicine, was often poorly taught, usually by recent graduates paid so badly that incentive and morale were impossibly low. Waynflete made a rational whole of the work of undergraduates ('Demies', thirty of them), graduates ('Fellows', forty) and other senior teachers ('Readers' in key subjects), and paid them well. 'He also allowed the admission of twenty *commensales* (Commoners), the sons of noble and powerful friends of the College.'[2] He endowed a chapel with four chaplains, eight clerks and sixteen choristers: and he founded a school, with a master and an usher, to ensure a real grounding in the humanities. Elsewhere, grammar—which meant Latin language and literature—was assumed before entry, but was sometimes tested only by a prepared passage which could have been learned parrot-fashion.

Three great English schools, Winchester, Eton and Magdalen, had been founded in the hundred years before the first students went to Magdalen College, all based on the idea (ultimately derived from William of Wykeham) of linking school, college and university.[3] Waynflete's Magdalen School, with its grammar master, was founded about 1480, and was always intended 'to train up Demies for the College'.[4] This it did with success, as Magdalen men presently became pre-eminent in the world of the new learning: William Grocyn became the first official teacher of Greek in Oxford. His pupil Richard Croke was first Public Orator and Reader in Greek at Cambridge. Thomas Wolsey, who went on to found what became Christ Church Oxford and a school at Ipswich, among other things, began as master of Magdalen School and was probably a pupil. Richard Fox who founded Corpus Christi College in 1516 and established the first public Greek Lecture in England, was probably a Magdalen man. So was John Colet.[5] Magdalen was the temporary home of Erasmus in Oxford. The list can continue and must now include William Tyndale, linguist extraordinary, whose scholarly understanding of the implications of the new learning for the expression of the Word of God was founded at Magdalen Hall, and whose work reached immeasurably more people than all of those great figures put together.

The rooms that made up Magdalen Hall had a curious and developing relation to the College, being from the first a separate charitable institution paying rent to the College, but presently with independent standing as a community of undergraduates with a principal appointed by the College; eventually, in the fullness of time and through strange procedures, evolving into the present Hertford College.[6] (Thus both Magdalen and Hertford correctly claim Tyndale as their own.) The special legacy of Magdalen School, however, was not in its institution so much as its educational innovation. We should assume a close pedagogic link between Magdalen College, Magdalen Hall and Magdalen School. The first known Master, John Anwykyll, published in about 1483 a new method of teaching Latin, his *Compendium totius Grammatice ex Laurentio Valla Servio et Perotto*, based on the work of Valla, the Italian humanist, Servius, the fourth-century grammarian and commentator on Virgil, and Perotti, the exponent of the new Italian grammar. Anwykyll's book contains in the same volume material of great interest in English, and Anwykyll may have been the original author of *Parvula* (*c.* 1481), the first Latin grammar in English.[7] Others followed, related either to Magdalen—as with John Stanbridge—or to Dean Colet's St Paul's School. At Magdalen School, a succession of fine, humane grammarians began the movement towards teaching Latin by way of English. After Anwykyll, John Stanbridge and later Robert Whittington, produced *Vulgaria*, that is,

Latin textbooks, with the rules and exercises in colloquial English as well as Latin. A grammar school was to teach Latin as a spoken as well as a written language, and in the eight or nine years a pupil would spend with Latin before university, he would acquire what he needed to express himself in daily life. This all paved the way for that further revolution which appeared in the printed grammar written by another Magdalen man, William Lily, appointed first master of St Paul's School. Lily's grammar of 1515, with input from Erasmus and Colet, was still standard (by law) a century later and set the style for a further three centuries. It was reactionary in the sense that it contained little English, but it constantly pointed in the direction of literature. What young William Tyndale experienced at Magdalen Hall, it seems, was the learning of Latin starting to be humanised in two ways: in the device of reference to great Latin literature, and in the incorporation of English phrases. If William Tyndale was taught using one of the *Vulgaria* that were coming into use, he would have found in them collections of trenchant and everyday English phrases with their Latin equivalent, roughly grouped together to make miniature essays and very close to the proverbial English from Gloucestershire.[8] Here is a passage from the *Vulgaria* of Robert Whittington, an early pupil at Magdalen School: 'It cometh to thee by nature to be a dullard, therefore it were pity to put thee from thy inheritance. It is clerkely spoken [learnedly said] of you, a man might as soon pick mary [marrow] out of a mattock as drive three good latin words out of your foretop.' This the language of Falstaff and Sir Toby Belch.[9] More work needs to be done on those two elements, the proverbial English phrases and the classical literary references, in schoolboy education in grammar as it affected a writer like Tyndale.[10]

It is possible to reconstruct the work done, form by form, about a dozen years after Tyndale was a schoolboy, as Wolsey ordained it for his school at Ipswich, in a curriculum parallel to that at Magdalen. Wolsey had been briefly the master of Magdalen School, having also very probably been a pupil there under John Anwykyll and his succesor John Stanbridge. In the First Form,

> the boys learn the eight parts of speech and the pronunciation of Latin . . . In the Second they learn to speak Latin and do easy sentences into Latin and write them out fair . . . In the Third Form Aesop and Terence are read and Lily's Nouns studied: in the Fourth, Virgil and Lily's Principal Parts of Verbs. The Fifth are to read select leters of Cicero; the Sixth Form 'seems to call for some history, whether Sallust or Caesar'. In the Seventh the boys read

Horace's *Epistles* or Ovid's *Metamorphoses* or *Fasti*; they compose verses or letters, practising the turning of verse into prose and back again into verse, and learn by heart, just before going to sleep, passages to be said next day. In the Eighth Class they study the science of Grammar proper in Donatus or Valla and deal with some set book thoroughly. Letters and compositions are to be practised . . . The ease of Aesop and the usefulness of Terence (as an aid in conversation), the necessity of reading Virgil *voce ben sonora* to bring out the majesty of his poetry. . .[11]

Anwykyll had published a selection of sentences and dialogues from Terence, *Vulgari quedam abs Terentio in anglicam linguam traducta* in 1483 (the second part of which was the *Compendium totius Grammaticae* noticed above) and Wolsey had found Magdalen School studying it when he arrived as master, and may well have used it himself as a pupil there.

In that proverbial 'ease' of Aesop; in the 'usefulness' of the street-dialogues in the comedies of Terence; and in the 'majesty' of the sound of Virgil, may be detected a good deal of the groundwork of the later writing of William Tyndale as, for example, in the opening of the third chapter of Genesis in his translation:

But the serpent was subtler than all the beasts of the field which the Lord God had made, and said unto the woman. Ah sir, that God hath said, ye shall not eat of all manner trees in the garden. And the woman said unto the serpent, of the fruit of the trees in the garden we may eat, but of the fruit of the tree that is in the midst of the garden (said God) see that ye eat not, and see that ye touch it not, lest ye die. Then said the serpent unto the woman: tush ye shall not die . . .[12]

Yet we have to acknowledge that we are only seeing glimpses of what was taught. In 1513, when a second usher was appointed to the Hall, he was admitted Bachelor 'with this condition . . . that he should not at any time teach his scholars Ovid 'de arte amandi', or Pamphilus 'de amore'.[13]

The timetable seems to have been parallel to that of the University, with early school from 6 to 9, breakfast, school from 9.45 to 11, dinner, and school from 1 to 5, all probably in four or five days of the week, with frequent whole-day or half-day holidays. Many of the boys would have lived at home with their parents in the town, and all the pupils would be to some extent outside the stricter discipline of the college, where, for example, nothing but Latin would be spoken.[14] Classrooms would have been, as well as smoky, very noisy places, as 'reading' automatically meant reading aloud, as it did for some time to come: the 'punies', as the later Elizabethans were to call them, conning their lessons, would be vocal. A picture of the lives of Magdalen schoolboys comes through the *Vulgaria*, one anonymous and one each from Stanbridge and Whittington, in which we can hear their small-talk and bickering and feel their hunger and cold—though not downright misery.

For some of William Tyndale's time at Magdalen Hall, the Master was Thomas Brynknell, described later by Wood as 'a person of great literature and a most skilfull interpreter of Holy Writ'.[15] (Much work remains to be done on the influence of schoolmasters early in the century on the later development of English prose.[16]) Brynknell may have been responsible for giving Tyndale 'the knowledge of tongues and other liberal arts' reported by Foxe. Brynknell was favoured by Wolsey—'such respect had the Cardinal for him that by his means he was selected by the King as the most considerable person to write against Luther',[17] in 1521; but his orthodoxy would not have welcomed Tyndale's further activity, the private reading of Scripture to certain students and fellows, as also reported by Foxe. While Wolsey had himself been Master in 1498, for one month his usher had been John Stokesley, later Bishop of London after Cuthbert Tunstall. It was Wolsey's time in the post that led to his own rapid rise, when in the middle of his two-term tenure, in 1498, the Marquess of Dorset had the schoolmaster [Wolsey] as well his own three sons home for Christmas. Stokesley went on to become Vice-President of the college during Tyndale's time at Magdalen Hall. Tyndale cannot have been ignorant of strife surrounding Stokesely: in 1507 Fox, the Bishop of Winchester, Visitor of Magdalen College and School, came officially to investigate trouble. Stokesely 'was accused by the rival faction of numerous crimes and misdemeanours, ranging from disobedience to the President to adultery with the wife of the Organist and baptizing a cat in order to discover a treasure by magic.'[18] Stokesley was largely exonerated by the visitation, on grounds that the accusations were gossip (unsubstantiated hostile witness was to be, under Stokesely when Bishop, a standard procedure when burning heretics). A gifted man, Stokesley caused strong reactions all his life. Later, in 1535, he was the most likely figure behind Henry Phillips, the evil betrayer of Tyndale. It is uncomfortable to think that nearly thirty years before, the persecuting bishop and the dying Tyndale had shared the same plot of ground in Oxford. It is speculation, but worth a moment's thought, that Stokesley's hatred of Tyndale might have been founded then. Stokesley became rector of Slimbridge in 1509, though it is possible that he never went there. In 1501, an ex-Master of Magdalen, Richard Jackson, then Bishop of Worcester, had been persuaded by the college to appropriate part of the revenues of the Rectory of Slimbridge to Magdalen. Later, as Bishop of London, as has been seen, Stokesley wrote, probably to Cromwell, to divert an appointment away from the family of 'Tyndale the arch-heretic'. The Tyndale family might have officially expressed local hostility to the mis-use of their funds.

The strong likelihood is that William Tyndale went to Magdalen School in 1506, at the age of twelve, for that grounding in Latin which was essential for later undergraduate work and for any higher profession thereafter. That is not automatically to say that he had no Latin before; local schools at that time could do a good job teaching Latin grammar and it could be that Tyndale attended the grammar school at Wotton-under-Edge and profited from that.

Tyndale's Oxford

On its well-watered, richly wooded site, Tyndale's Oxford was freshly beautiful, the 'towery city and branchy between towers' of Gerard Manley Hopkins's imagery, 'cuckoo-echoing, bell-swarmed, lark-charmed, roof-racked, river-rounded.'[19] The university church of St Mary's had been restored, Merton Tower had been built, the new colleges of Lincoln, All Souls and Magdalen itself were open. The glorious Divinity School had been completed less than twenty years before he went up; it had originally been funded by 'Good Duke Humphrey', as was his spacious library above, to house what had followed his original benefaction. Magdalen's superbly graceful tower had been opened in 1504, just before Tyndale arrived; it was dedicated with a concert on its roof and the choristers then first began to greet the dawn of May morning, a ceremony possibly paid for by an endowment from the rectory of Slimbridge, Gloucestershire.

Between 1400 and 1500, the Oxford to which Tyndale went had, to a large extent, taken over from the University of Paris the leading role in Europe.[20] For a hundred years before Tyndale's time, great Oxford sages like Scotus and Ockham—and even the heretic Master of Balliol, Wyclif—had been read in many countries, but it is increasingly clear that continental libraries also held manuscripts by Oxford arts men, particularly logicians and the earliest scientists, in significant bulk. The University of Oxford had considerably influenced the late medieval northern European world of learning. On the other hand, the human-

ist new learning, the study of Greek as well as Latin, using the re-
discovered texts outside the more usual Virgil or Cicero, which was
taking so strong a hold in academies beyond northern Italy, was slow
to become official in Oxford. Though students were free to read, and
even lecture on, such writers as Sallust or Terence, required reading for
an Oxford arts student in 1500 differed little from that of a century
earlier.[21] Oxford was fortunate in that in the mid-fifteenth century its
university library received many works by classical authors and contemporary humanists, particularly in medicine and the arts. Those were
donated by a great patron of studies, the youngest son of Henry IV, the
Duke of Gloucester—and Duke Humphrey's Library has remained a
core of what later became the Bodleian. Yet in the Faculty of Arts,
Oxford's singularity at the turn of the century remained as it had been
for a hundred years in the length and complexity of its course as well
as in the dominance of linguistic logic and the deference paid to
Scotist philosophy.[22] In spite of Oxford's reputation abroad, few continental students came to Oxford to study arts. The Continent, one
might say, was further away from Tyndale in Oxford than it had been
in cloth-trading Gloucestershire.

How many students were in Oxford in Tyndale's time is a statistic
very difficult to compute. There were, when he went up, about a
dozen colleges (including Merton, University, Balliol, Exeter, Lincoln,
Queen's, New College, All Souls, Oriel and Magdalen) and many
halls, with students in perhaps a score of university schools. Possibly a
general estimate of between one and three thousand students of all
kinds is not too wide of the mark, though numbers were always
changing, from poverty or illness or the closing of institutions because
of plague; many dropped out before taking a degree, and perhaps even
more died. The age range was likely to have been great, though most
undergraduates probably began in middle to late teens: Thomas Wolsey,
'the boy bachelor' at the age of fifteen, was unusual enough to be
remarked.[23] We might feel safe in estimating that Tyndale began his
undergraduate studies in October 1508 at the age of fourteen in an
institution containing a thousand students. His work would occupy
twelve terms: he is recorded as taking his BA in July 1512.

Undergraduates reading for their first degree in a medieval university did not need, and were not likely to own, books. They heard
lectures in which a master or a bachelor read out a prescribed text
sentence by sentence and explained and commented on each one as he
went along.[24] For degrees in the higher faculties, taken after the arts
BA, and especially theology, taken after MA, books were essential. A
student was expected to have access by buying or borrowing books, or

paying for them to be copied, or borrowing an exemplar and copying it himself. Though printed books were on sale in England from the latter part of the fifteenth century, they were expensive and not all were relevant to the arts curriculum.

As well as donating valuable books, Duke Humphrey had been sufficiently interested in the arts in the University of Oxford to suggest changes in the curriculum, and a new course in the seven liberal arts for the BA and three philosophies for the MA was established in 1431 to give more emphasis to the study of rhetoric and the literature of classical antiquity.[25] This course was still in force in Tyndale's day, and it meant that Tyndale would have spent his time for the BA listening to lectures on the *trivium* (grammar, rhetoric, logic) and the *quadrivium* (arithmetic, music, geometry and astronomy) given by masters or bachelors on the days prescribed. These lectures were becoming increasingly rare—in Tyndale's time it could have been as few, it seems, as four a term. The lectures given by the masters would have been on the material necessary to the course, and those by the bachelors on textual sources, with a minimum of commentary;[26] there would have been other lectures on subjects outside the curriculum. The set texts, it seems, were traditional: for the BA, Priscian, Aristotle, Boethius, Euclid, Ptolemy,[27] though there was a possibility of Ovid's *Metamorphoses* or Virgil's poetry in the first year. For the MA, the three philosophies, natural, moral and metaphysical, were taught over eight terms, and were almost wholly dependent on Aristotle.[28] It is, however, impossible to be certain what was taught, or even prescribed, at any particular time. It has been noted how odd the 1431 revision was in several ways, for example giving only three terms to logic at a time when the dominance of logic in the Oxford arts course is confirmed across Europe and by the university itself.[29] There is a dismaying absence of documentation. What evidence can be collected, for example from surviving manuscripts or, later, books, sometimes containing notes of lectures heard, or from other occasional material, suggests that texts not mentioned in the statutes were heard by students and recognised by the faculty, and conversely prescribed texts were not heard. Lectures were given on a core of traditional material around which there grew a corpus of acceptable commentary.[30] In continental universities in the fifteenth century, surviving manuscripts and books show how much the work of Oxford scholars was studied, and not by any means the familiar and expected names only. There is evidence of a large substratum of now little-regarded work, sometimes in manuscripts unassigned to an author, which makes confidence about what was studied in Oxford even more difficult.

Academic fashions throughout Europe could produce violent controversy; it was a rare university of any standing that could stand aloof
from continental theories and their warring partisans, a situation familiar at the close of the twentieth century in the world of literary theory.
Oxford seems not to have taken part with any passion in the controversies between the two philosophical and interpretative schools, the
realist *via antiqua* and the nominalist *via moderna*, which is all the more
surprising as two of the leaders of each faction, Scotus and Ockham,
were Oxford men. The issue which split the university of Freiburg
down the middle so that in 1490 the faculty of arts had to introduce
new statutes providing for separate teaching of both *viae*, seems to have
produced less heat in Oxford, whence much of the fuel for the
controversy came. (Perhaps the enervating summer afternoons of low-
lying, marshy Oxford were an unregarded cause of wisdom.) As happened in later centuries, Oxford went its own rather ponderous way,
letting the continental universities get on with their flashy quarrels. In
the faculty of arts Oxford still taught a curriculum which remained
long and complicated, dominated by linguistic logic, deferring to
Scotus and the *via antiqua*, as it had done for a hundred years before,
and would do long after. (In the first-year curriculum leading to the
classical degree known as 'Greats', strong traces of the *trivium* and the
quadrivium, in logic, arithmetic and geometry, for example, survived
well into the twentieth century.)

Tyndale at Oxford would have found all too familiar the lean
'hollow', moneyless, unbeneficed Clerk of Oxenford in Chaucer's
General Prologue to his *Canterbury Tales* of one hundred and thirty
years before, with his preference for twenty books of Aristotle rather
than rich robes, and his careful formal speech and love of learning and
teaching. The Clerk had gone into logic long before: Tyndale's occasional remarks about the education he received in his years at Oxford
make it sound dusty and barren, as mostly it probably was. Somewhere, presumably while at Oxford, he acquired good Greek as well as
improving his Latin. In the study of rhetoric he may have sharpened
his (already probably acute) sense of what words can do. For much of
the rest he seems to have felt scorn. We have no idea what, at this
stage, his ambitions were, or what governed his judgement. It is surely
sentimental to see him, as hagiographers have done, already as an
undergraduate condemning the threadbare Aristotle by the light of the
full gospel of Christ, though that is certainly something he did twenty
years later, in for example, *The Obedience of a Christian Man*. By that
time he had translated the Greek New Testament into English, and
been very deeply stirred by Paul's Epistle to the Romans and Luther's

exposition of it. On the other hand, there is increasing evidence that he came to Oxford from a Vale of Berkeley in which lived people who were not unaware of what the core of the New Testament contained; and though Oxford had condemned as a heretic its own Wyclif, more than a century before for, among things, giving the people a vernacular Bible, his memory was still green.

Indeed, in Tyndale's time Oxford theology, as opposed to philosophy, for all its dry logical base, had available a current of rejection of the 'frogs and toads, croaking in the swamp' of continental speculation, an independence which could have been partly a legacy of Wyclif. Theology in Oxford, though a science, and though it was in the university of Scotus and Ockham, was considered a practical science, which could be applied and diffused through sermons.[31] About half of the thousand or so theologians known to have been at Oxford between 1440 and 1500 were monks or friars, and about four-fifths of the other half were fellows of colleges. So nine-tenths of theology students belonged therefore to the institution-supported, privileged section of Oxford's population.[32] What was in reality being preached at the parish level throughout England was a matter of persistent Lollard complaint throughout the century.[33] But as well as formally trying to guard against Wycliffite heresy,[34] the university's intention was to keep the communities quietly working, not to generate intellectually brilliant free-floating scholar-gypsies unattached to any institutional base. The system may not have produced many preachers able to feed all the needs of the hungrier sheep in the parishes, but in its customary way, pressing stolidly on in the tracks it had always used, Oxford got on with the business it knew best, mixing the intellectual and the practical, absorbing its eccentrics as far as possible into the system. A mid-century oddity such as Reginald Pecock was ahead of his time, and though successively Bishop of St Asaph and of Chichester, his individualism was too great for the Church at large. His *The Rule of Christian Religion* of 1456 contains in chapter 19 an eloquent plea for interpreting Scripture afresh, guided by contemporary reason rather than authorities.[35] Pecock had begun by countering Wycliffite ideas with writings in English which were a mixture of orthodox theology of the time, a Thomist insistence on the primacy of the intellect and the results of pastoral experience—a very Oxford mixture; he had been a Fellow of Oriel. He ended his life in 1461 condemned as a heretic, imprisoned and denied his books, though his views had not changed. He was too individual for comfort.[36] Yet by the end of the century, individualism was commonplace,[37] and the university could absorb Grocyn on Greek literature—and Colet on Romans.

There was in Oxford just before Tyndale arrived a detectable theological movement against the barrenness that a secular-based scholasticism could cause. Some Oxford thinkers had been abroad, to Germany and especially to northern Italy. Some came back from Florence with strange neo-Platonic notions learned from Ficino, but some, among them William Grocyn, Thomas Linacre and William Latimer, also with good Greek refined at the new Italian academies, and, even more importantly, with manuscripts and, later, printed books, in Greek, which still adorn the older college libraries. It had been possible to learn to read Greek at Oxford since about 1462,[38] but a time in Italy was necessary for real ability. The way had been paved for the Oxford humanists by such Englishmen as John Free and William Sellyng, and a handful of foreign scholars who visited England such as Stefano Surigone, Emanuel of Constantinople and John Serbopoulos.[39] Grocyn returned to Oxford to give the first lectures on Greek literature in the university in the 1490s. These influenced for life his godson, William Lily, later appointed by Dean Colet as the first High Master of his new St Paul's School, and affected the future course of English education for ever after. The so-called battle between such 'Grecians', and the supposedly reactionary 'Trojans' who opposed the innovations, has probably been a little exaggerated for effect.[40] Nevertheless, Tyndale came to a university where, partly under the North Italian influence, literary and theological, and especially scriptural, matters had shown signs of beginning to stir again with a little of the life they had had under the energetic Wyclif. Erasmus's crucial Greek New Testament did not appear until Tyndale was an MA. But already in his earliest undergraduate time fourth-century Jerome, as a model of plain biblical learning, was in places preferred to the efflorations of later speculative Fathers; and Colet found it arrogant of Aquinas, no less, to have 'defined everything'.

Colet's Oxford Lectures

Which brings us to twenty-nine year-old John Colet, newly returned from over three years in Italy and Paris, and his 1496–9 Oxford lectures on Paul's Epistles. For a non-theologian to give well-attended lectures on Scripture, and for him to treat systematically the *content* of the central documents of the New Testament, rather than the *Sentences* of Peter Lombard or something similar, marked some sort of change in the Oxford climate. Since the mid-nineteenth century, however, there has grown a mythology of the effect those lectures especially, and the 'Oxford Reformers' in general, had on English and European theology, and thus the history of the time. The wise and moderate Erasmus, no less, attended the lectures, and the legend has had it that they affected him as a Damascus-road experience, then and there revealing to him, it has been claimed, the need for a Greek New Testament. Had Colet's lectures, and their influence on Erasmus, and the gentle support of Sir Thomas More been more fully heeded, the Reformation might, it was said, have travelled a better, broader, less violent road. In those hours in an Oxford lecture-room in the last days of the century, we were assured, Colet gave to the world again the historical Paul, with his essential epistles now stripped of all the enormous accretion of centuries of false allegorical and scholastic commentary, and nothing presented but the vital literal meaning, to understand which, it was implied, the Greek was essential. Scripture 'has the sense that appears on the surface; nor is one thing said and another meant, but the very thing is meant which is said and the sense is wholly literal'—a sentence which apparently rang like a trumpet-call down the ages, for the lectures had, fortunately, survived. If that mythology is right, then Tyndale came to an Oxford already electric with revolutionary rejection of all but the historical 'bare text' of Scripture, and Scripture in the original Greek at that. The ancient dragon of the four-fold method of interpretation—literal, allegorical, tropological and anagogical[41]—applied to every Scripture word, had been slain in Oxford by the young and vigorous Colet. England could breathe the clean air of the Apostle again.

It has been a seductive and influential scheme ever since Frederic Seebohm's *The Oxford Reformers* of 1867.[42] That book was rapidly absorbed into popular histories and in 1914 achieved the classic status of inclusion, shorn of many notes and the appendices, in Everyman's Library, Dent's series of pocket-book editions of what were thought to be the world's best books. Seebohm linked Colet closely with Erasmus and Thomas More in a supposed joint endeavour to try to establish a non-violent, un-doctrinaire groundwork for reform in the Church in England. In the centuries before Seebohm's book, Colet had been seen as the founder of a school, St Paul's, and one of the more obscure heralds of what eventually became the Reformation. After that publication, he was a pioneer, right at the front of a campaign to make the coming Reformation into something it did not turn out to be. Colet's nostrum was the historical Paul, his Epistles 'the earnest words of a living man addressed to living men,'[43] to be taken only literally, and in Greek.

The problems with this version of Colet are so big that they are impossible to overcome. In spite of his time in Italy, Colet only began to try to learn Greek twenty years after those Oxford lectures, on the appearance of Erasmus's Greek New Testament in 1516.[44] He found the language too daunting and gave up. On his death in 1519 he was still ignorant of Greek. It would, moreover, have been more unusual than we can imagine for him to have considered Greek essential for exposition of the New Testament. The Council of Trent, even as late as 1563, represented the majority view in considering the Latin Vulgate as not only 'authentic' but replacing the original in every respect.[45] Until Erasmus himself had learned classical Greek so painfully after he had left England the first time, and then printed his Greek New Testament in Basle in 1516, discrepancies between the Vulgate and the Greek would not have been regarded. In any case, the evidence sugests that Erasmus learned Greek, as was normal for those few who did, in order to read secular Greek literature—of which, until Aldus Manutius set up his press in Venice in 1494—there would be precious little for them to read. Colet knew no Greek. Secondly, the manuscripts of Colet's work on Paul that Seebohm used date, in fact, from between ten and twenty years after the original Oxford lectures, and as they incorporate later revisions are not reliable as hard evidence of what Colet said in 1496–9.[46] Thirdly, although the earliest record of Colet's thought in his lecture-manuscripts is 1505–6, there is some evidence in a letter Colet wrote in 1499 to Dr Richard Kidderminster, Abbot of Winchcombe (in Gloucestershire), and from notes later worked up by Erasmus into a short book called 'Disputantiuncula', of what Colet thought about the exegesis of Scripture in that year. The latter work, published in a volume of shorter works in 1503 and often thereafter, comes out of an account of an extended discussion begun at an Oxford dinner party some time late in 1499 between Erasmus, Colet and others, about a theological crux in interpreting Christ's agony in the garden. From that account, and from Erasmus's letters of the time, a picture of Colet emerges that is some way from that given in the modern mythology. In private letters, Erasmus, though admiring Colet's fine mind and spiritual integrity, is privately scornful of a Greekless exegete. In the published discussion, Colet emerges as denying that a passage had more meanings than one—not denying the familiar fourfold sense of Scripture, but, cornered for a moment by Erasmus, denying the ancient and useful formula of *duplex sensus literalis*, that the literal sense itself could have more meanings than one.

The issue is complex.[47] Clearly Colet's interest in Biblical interpretation included much that was allegorical, and to present him in those Oxford lectures as a kind of John the Baptist of some new messianic 'bare text' scholarship is simply wrong; the famous quotation above, about 'the sense that appears on the surface', is in fact from Colet on the Hierarchies of Pseudo-Dionysius, of which the surviving manuscripts were written between 1512 and 1516 when Colet was in London.[48] Seebohm, for his own purposes, gave his readers, as Colet's 'historical' Apostle, a Paul who is unrecognisable, being mainly a moralist. In this work of 'rediscovering' Colet, Frederic Seebohm was addressing the mid-nineteenth-century Church of England, a new Broad Church. He was speaking to what later became the Modernist movement. His readers were to think back to what the English Reformation might have been if Colet, More and Erasmus had been heeded. Behind Seebohm's chapters is the unexpressed ideal of how it would have been if Tyndale (whom Seebohm mentions only in passing and not as a translator) had not armed an extreme popular front in England with a polemic New Testament, and if the searing and destructive dogmatics of such foreigners as Luther had not invaded our shores. His Colet studied the Scriptures in a wholly new light and cut away centuries of allegorising irrelevance simply in order to reveal the ethical teaching of Jesus and the 'essential and eternal thing' in Christianity, its 'moral sense'.[49]

As an account of the New Testament it will not do. As an account of Colet it will not do, either. Certainly Colet lectured—in Latin, let us not forget—on Paul's Epistles, an unusual thing for a young man to do; and certainly he used the grammatical methods of the Italian humanists and the early Patristic writers instead of the dialectical methods of the Scholastics;[50] and certainly Erasmus, brought to England by the young nobleman he was tutoring for cash, William, Lord Mountjoy, went to Oxford to meet Colet and there heard some of a winter's lectures. Erasmus wrote to Colet his usual flattering letter, but in his later posthumous tribute he gave the lectures only eight lines out of 357.[51] Nowhere does he say that it was while he was in Oxford that he, Erasmus, recognised the need for a properly edited printed Greek New Testament.[52] Indeed, Erasmus's vocation to devote himself to sacred studies was slow to develop even when he was learning Greek in France or the Netherlands between 1500 and 1505.[53] No-one in England in 1499 thought of Colet as excelling in biblical exegesis, and surviving accounts by contemporaries who attended the lectures do not record anything revolutionary—Erasmus's flattery in letters is his usual manner.[54] What can be reconstructed is that Colet's lectures explained the moral lessons of the text, and as much of the literal sense as was necessary, with neither reference to the standard authorities, nor speculative questions.[55] The Bible, Colet implied, was not an enormous assembly of propositions to be logically reconciled into dogma. He understood that access to the inner meaning of the sacred texts must require something more than appeals to reason and the apparatus of scholarship.[56] That something more, expressed by a real Paul not a speculative system, is a spiritual meaning, drawn from the heart of the New Testament, at the centre of which is Christ's redemptive sacrifice. It was not Colet's method in such writing to make public manifestos (his later sermons as Dean of St Paul's after 1504 are in a different vein); much of his attractiveness lies in the quietness, even privateness, of his theology, drawn from practical, pastoral considerations and the very human muddles in the quest for a moral education in which he finds himself—all the characteristic Oxford mixture of the previous hundred years.

Accepting that we do not have the original lectures as given, it may still be assumed that the new quality in those early lectures on 1 Corinthians and Romans lay in his understanding of the centrality of Scripture, the implication that a man did not have to have studied the classics in order to understand Scripture. That he chose Paul and Romans indicates a desire to help his hearers get to the heart of New Testament (as opposed to scholastic) theology. The lecturer had both a penetrating mind and a devout heart; in the popularity of the lectures might be seen the beginning of a movement in Oxford towards an emphasis on Scripture associated with the Christian life. In those senses he can be considered a pioneer.[57] As Foxe wrote about Colet: 'After he came from Italy and Paris, he first began to read the epistles of St Paul openly in Oxford, instead of Scotus and Aquinas.'[58] But though we can find him saying *Vita eterna erit ex justicia fidei sola*, 'Eternal life will come from the righteousness of faith alone', his emphasis is quite the opposite of the reformers' views—leaving even Augustine, never mind Paul, far behind, and following Aquinas to say that a man is justified not by faith alone, but by faith and works, whereas Luther insisted that Paul said that man is not made righteous by his works, but the righteousness is imputed at his conversion as a result of his faith.

To what extent this came to influence Tyndale cannot be known. If the dates are correct, Colet had left Oxford by the time Tyndale arrived, a likelihood which diminishes the speculation that young Tyndale heard Colet lecture. Tyndale referred only once to Colet. In the *Answer to More* of 1531, he replied to More's remark that 'The bishop of London was wise, virtuous, and cunning [i.e. knowing]' with 'For all those three, yet he would have made the old dean Colet of St Paul's an heretic for translating the Paternoster in English, had not the bishop of Canterbury holp the dean.' To score a point against More's own point-scoring praise of a reactionary bishop, Tyndale is using Colet as an example of the trouble even the Dean of St Paul's could get into for translating a few verses of the New Testament into the vernacular. Colet had preached frequently and at length on the Lord's Prayer in English. His published version is brief—and well within the Church's permission. The story originated with Erasmus, and is, as is usual with him, more tangled than at first appears.[59] It should be noted that Tyndale does not say that in his day Oxford still thrilled to the memory of Colet on Romans.

Tyndale and Oxford Theology

On the contrary, Tyndale was scornful of his experience of theology in Oxford, which could not be studied until the whole arts course, MA on top of BA, had been taken. A student could not get to it, he wrote, until he had been brainwashed by years of statutory immersion in scholasticism. In a passage in *The Practice of Prelates* of 1530, marked in the margin 'The use of universities', he wrote: 'And in the universities they have ordained that no man shall look in the Scripture until he be noselled [nursed] in heathen learning eight or nine years and armed with false principles with which he is clean shut out of the understanding of scripture.' He is in the process of arguing that the heart of the Christian faith has been removed by the Church: 'the promises and testament, which the sacrament of Christ's body and blood did preach daily unto the people, that they put out of knowledge'. Not only do the universities teach heathen writers instead: they bind the scholars.

> And at his first coming unto university he is sworn that he shall not defame the university, whatsoever he seeth. And when he taketh first degree, he is sworn that he shall hold none opinion condemned by the church: but what such opinions be, that he shall not know. And then when they be admitted to study divinity, because the scripture is locked up with such false expositions, and with false principles of natural philosophy, that they cannot enter in, they go about the outside, and dispute all their lives about words and vain opinions, pertaining as much unto the healing of a man's heel, as health of his soul: provided yet alway, lest God give his singular grace unto any person, that none may preach except he be admitted of the bishops.[60]

A year later, writing *The Exposition of the First Epistle of Saint John*, he remembered the folly of Oxford disputations. He is working up to his sarcastic point that 'our holy father proveth the authority of scripture by his decrees, for the scripture is not authentic but as his decrees admit it', in order to make his decrees 'shine and appear glorious' by alleging that scripture makes 'fools stark mad'. His recollection is:

> I heard a great clerk in Oxford stand half an hour in a pulpit, to prove that Christ was a true prophet by the testimony of John the Baptist, and another half hour to prove John the Baptist a true prophet by the authority of Christ: as we say, Claw me, claw thee: and as every thief might lightly prove himself a true man in bearing record to another as false as he and taking record of the same again.[61]

In the same year, 1531, answering Sir Thomas More, he remembered an Oxford dispute about the nature of the sacramental wafer, 'whether it were bread or none, some affirming that the flour, with long lying in water, was turned to starch, and had lost its nature'.[62] (For Tyndale, the essence is the faith of the communicant.)

The recollection most damning to the *mores* of university theology, however, comes in the *Obedience* (though he does not say it happened at Oxford).

> I was once at the creating of doctors of divinity where the opponent brought the same reason to prove that the widow had more merit than the virgin: because she had greater pain forasmuch as she had once proved the pleasures of matrimony. Ego nego domine doctor said the respondent, for though the virgin have not proved yet she imagineth that the pleasure is greater than it is indeed, and therefore is more moved, and hath greater temptation and greater pain.[63]

This is part of his argument that allegories and similitudes can lead to wanderings far from the truth of Christ. Citing 1 Timothy 6, he writes:

> . . . they are not content with the wholesome words of our Lord Jesus Christ and doctrines of godliness: and therefore know nothing, but waste their brains about questions and strife of words, whereof spring envy, strife and railing of men with corrupt minds, destitute of the truth.[64]

Tyndale may have spent a dozen years in Oxford (and then gone on to Cambridge). Unlike many, he persevered. The unflattering picture he gives of the study of theology, and of the preparation for it in the Arts Faculty, does not enable us to breathe much of a living spirit into the bare bones of the record of his student life. However, there may have been one part of the arts work that did in fact touch his mind closely. Meanwhile, here is Foxe:

> William Tyndale, the faithful minister and constant martyr of Christ, was born about the borders of Wales, and brought up from a child in the university of Oxford, where he, by long continuance, grew up, and increased as well in the knowledge of tongues and other liberal arts as especially in the knowledge of the scriptures, whereunto his mind was singularly addicted: insomuch that he, lying then in Magdalen hall, read privily to certain students and fellows of Magdalen college some parcel of divinity, instructing them in the knowledge and truth of the scriptures. His manners also and conversation being correspondent to the same, were such, that all they that knew him, reputed and esteemed him to be a man of most virtuous disposition, and of life unspotted.
>
> Thus he, in the university of Oxford, increasing more and more in learning, and proceeding in degrees of the schools, removed from thence to the university of Cambridge . . .[65]

The point about his virtuous disposition is supported even by his enemy More, who called him well known in his earlier life 'for a man of right good living, studious and well learned in scripture, and in divers places in England was very well liked and did great good with preaching.'[66] Foxe agrees with Edward Hall in his Chronicle of 1548: 'Such as best knew him reported him to be a very sober man, born upon the borders of Wales, and brought in the University of Oxford and in life and conversation unreprovable . . .'[67] Hall then goes on to elaborate, in a confusingly rambling sentence, a story about Tyndale responding to Luther even while at Oxford, and among other things 'lamenting the ignorant state that his native country of England was in' and, therefore, answering the call of God, 'he translated into English the New Testament'. Hall makes the origin of this vocation Tyndale resolving to search the Scriptures to see whether what Luther said in 'certain works against the Bishop of Rome' was true or not, apparently while still in Oxford. There is much that is not known about Tyndale in Oxford. What Hall seems to be saying is unlikely, as Luther did not start confronting the Roman Church publicly until 1517 and Tyndale took his MA in 1515. Later in Tyndale's story a former pupil of his, John Tisen, appears, who is in the university records as taking the degree of Bachelor of Civil Law in 1524.[68] Tyndale was probably teaching in the university as a Master of Arts, and could, theoretically, have been still there in 1517 when Luther opened his attack on Rome.

Hall, however, is summarising—his paragraph, in 'the XVII year of Henry VIII' begins with Tyndale's execution. He does in a rough way support Foxe's point about Tyndale with the 'knowledge and truth of the scriptures'.

If Hall and Foxe are right in the general direction of Tyndale's unofficial reading of the Scriptures, the question is what such Scriptures would have been. After March 1516, the word could have meant Erasmus's *Novum instrumentum*, with Erasmus's new Latin translation supported by the Greek New Testament, both printed for the first time. This would add point to the general sense in both Hall and Foxe of Tyndale opening up something new. Before March 1516, 'scriptures' would have to mean the Latin Vulgate or a version of the forbidden Wyclif Bible. In that case, what was Tyndale doing that was new? One answer could simply be—reading them. That is to say, reading Romans in the spirit of Colet fifteen or so years before, for what Paul said and not for what centuries of commentators had said he said. Much work needs to be done here in a neglected field, that of trying to evaluate, in the time of Tyndale's residence in Oxford, how much of a movement there was towards taking books of the Bible neat, if one may so put it. Colet had found a new and living Paul in Romans and 1 Corinthians. Though as has been seen there is no record of the immediate effect of that (apart from Erasmus's lavish remarks for his own purpose), it does not follow that the tenor of his work was forgotten. Just as there is no real knowledge yet of what was, and what was not actually taught, only an approximation to an intended syllabus, so there is no real knowledge of what went on in Wyclif's university in the hundred and twenty-five years after his death. Out in the real world, away from the university, in Gloucestershire, in Essex, in Kent, Lollardy in Tyndale's time had a full-bodied understanding of what effect all the Scriptures might have if only they could be read. It is unlikely that this originally Wycliffite 'heresy' was now non-existent in Wyclif's own place, however alert the authorities were to prevent it appearing in official places. In any case, not only was there often so little formally going on in term-time that there was ample time for contacts with friends from home, as it might have been cloth-workers passing through; but in the long three-month vacation Tyndale would have almost certainly been back in Gloucestershire.

Tyndale and Oxford Rhetoric

It might be useful at this point to consider a part of Tyndale's Arts training which could have been more valuable to him than the rest.

Foxe speaks of him as one who 'increased as well in the knowledge of tongues, and other liberal arts, as especially in the knowledge of the scriptures'. There is a double hint here: first, that Oxford benefited Tyndale more than he admitted. Perhaps it should be remembered that each of the references he made was in a polemic work, supporting an argument that essential truth had been abandoned and demonstrating some of the evidences of that. The second hint in Foxe is that 'tongues . . . liberal arts . . . and scriptures' belonged together. 'Tongues' is no problem—learning good Latin and Greek was possible and vital to him: he could theoretically also have learned French and German. 'Liberal arts' means the *trivium* and *quadrivium*. The latter (arithmetic, music, geometry and astronomy) is not suggestive for Tyndale's later work. The former (grammar, logic and rhetoric) would have been more helpful for a translator. Grammar and logic, particularly as taught at Oxford at the time, would probably not be especially inspiring, except as they supported rhetoric, which might have been in a rather different case.

Tyndale was studying rhetoric at Oxford too soon to have benefited from the developments inspired by Erasmus. Throughout Europe, stimulated by him, and in the mid-sixteenth century by Peter Ramus, and by the wide availability of printed texts, interest grew in rhetoric and methods of teaching it, and in particular its relation to poetics. Leonard Cox's *The Art or Craft of Rhetoric* (1529), Thomas Wilson's *The Art of Rhetoric* (1560), Robert Rainolde's *A Book called the Foundation of Rhetoric* (1563), George Puttenham's *The Art of English Poesy* (1589) and Sir Philip Sidney's *Apology for Poetry* (c. 1583) were all in their different ways milestones on a road to a fully English consciousness about the making of poetry. Rhetoric and poetry were both broadly the arts of persuasion, to some extent dependent on grammar and logic. Lyric poetry related to one of the subjects of the *quadrivium*, music.

A poetic and musical sensitivity would have been enhanced by his formal training in rhetoric at Oxford, however dull it might seem today. To take another illustration: because a popular writer like Dickens has given pictures of what it was like to be a schoolboy that are gloomy or worse, and because Shakespeare for dramatic purposes made unflattering references to school, it has been popularly assumed that Shakespeare's schooldays at Stratford were as tedious, as numbing, indeed as destructive, as those endured by Toots in Dickens's *Dombey and Son*. Yet so far from being such a broken relic of educational tyranny, Shakespeare went on from that upstairs room in Stratford to constant and steady intellectual and artistic growth—all the seeds planted in his school flourished. One has only to think of Shakespeare's

affection for, and developing use of, Ovid, throughout his working
life, to understand that far from being the rural clod animated by a
single, and freakish, divine bolt of lightning, as even his admirers in the
eighteenth and nineteenth centuries found him, Shakespeare was,
though unusual, the product of a widespread educational method—
and his own foundations were so well laid that he achieved all he did
without going on to university, as all his contemporary poets and
dramatists had done.

Rhetoric, the art of persuasion, was the ancient craft of choosing
and placing words. Roughly speaking, at the time Tyndale went to
Magdalen Hall, rhetoric was learned through the works of the classical
masters of that craft, especially Cicero's *De inventione* and Quintilian's
Institutio oratoria, and a book wrongly thought to have been by Cicero,
the *Rhetorica ad Herennium*. In the year, and the very month, July 1512,
that Tyndale took his BA, Erasmus published a book he had written
in England, in Latin, intended for the boys at John Colet's innova-
tive school, St Paul's. This intelligent and attractive work extended
Quintilian in one direction especially, in that it helped the young
orator (that is to say, in effect, writer) with the process of *amplificatio*,
invention by amplification.[69] This book especially, the *De utraque
verborum ac rerum copia* of 1512, usually known today as *De copia*,
became the inspiration, with other work of Erasmus, for a great deal
of the educational innovation for the two generations of schoolboys
that followed, to the extent that a wise critic could remark of the link
between sixteenth-century education and high artistic achievement,
'Without Erasmus, no Shakespeare'.[70] *De copia*, which is in good and
readable Latin, is about methods of varying the form of expression,
being 'copious' in fact. A famous practice lesson gives no fewer than
one hundred and fifty ways of saying 'Your letter has delighted me very
much.' It teaches the use of all the verbal muscles in order to avoid any
hint of flabbiness. The book's aim was to license and encourage not
only the invention which aided coherence of argument, but copiousness, enlargement, amplitude of mind and phrase. The scholar was to
discover how much both mind and phrase could do, with a view to
choosing the various ways which gave the most wisdom and pleasure.
The first meaning of 'copy' (now obsolete) was fullness, abundance.
Shakespeare knew it, and used it well in a speech in an early play in
which a wife who thinks herself wronged is telling how she chided her
husband for his presumed infidelity:

It was the copy of our conference.
In bed, he slept not for my urging it;

At board, he fed not for my urging it;
Alone, it was the subject of my theme;
In company, I often glanced at it;
Still did I tell him it was vile and bad.[71]

Here, the rhetorical scheme is part of the copiousness of the invention as well as part of the characterisation—the husband has apparently gone mad; the wife is told she might have overdone things a little.

Following Quintilian, tropes are thought of as words in other than their normal significance, like metaphor, and figures as schemes of thought or words. Erasmus tends to use 'figures' for both, and an index in a modern English translation gives eighty-five in Latin and twenty-five in Greek. The split in the title, *utraque verborum ac rerum*, 'both words and things', in fact goes beyond that simple division. The *verba* element stands for the minor units of style: *res* for the more general handling of the subject.[72]

Another, far less attractive school text, a treatise by Rudolph Agricola, *De inventione dialectica libri tres*, was printed in Louvain in 1515, although finished in 1480. Agricola had much less general impact than Erasmus, but he influenced theoreticians in the sixteenth century in something of a similar direction, towards comprehensiveness. There were other treatises and school textbooks on rhetoric, often continually reprinted, though none so successful as Erasmus's *De copia*.

Though it came out just as his undergraduate studies were over, Tyndale could hardly have missed *De copia*. It was immensely popular throughout England (running through one hundred and fifty editions before 1572). Nor would he have wanted to ignore something so practically helpful in the business of handling words and assembling an argument. Erasmus's theme is, in effect, transformation, which is at root what Tyndale as a translator was doing. Not so much the sort of transformation that turns an English chronicle into a Shakespearean history play, as that which turns New Testament Greek-coloured-by-Hebrew into rhythmic and unforgettable English. Whether Tyndale read *De copia*, as a point of hard fact, we do not know, though evidence in, for example, his *Obedience* suggests that he must have done.[73] Erasmus was a figure never far from Tyndale's mind, at least from when he went down from Oxford. At Cambridge, if he did go there, he would have been where Erasmus had until recently taught. Tyndale translated Erasmus's *Enchiridion militis christiani* and his 1516 Greek New Testament (the latter twice) and referred a number of times to him.[74] The point to be made here is that Tyndale, like

Shakespeare, did not stop growing in the skills of his craft, and with Tyndale as with Shakespeare, there is a continual development in the enlargement of mind and phrase—and equally continual reading. Tyndale's rhetorical skills did not stop when he became BA. One of the constants throughout all his writing is his special interest in how languages work. He knows how common people manage to express what it is not permitted to say, as in the section in the *Obedience* noted above ('And of him that is betrayed and wotteth not how we say, He hath been at shrift'[75]). He records how the Church used Latin as a form of magic, how some Greek words are best translated, what a mysterious Egyptian word might mean, how Hebrew grammar functions—his concern with the latter being so immediate that he put it first in introducing his revised, 1534, New Testament (see below, p. 317), to get across to the close reader why some of his renderings seem unfamiliar: it is because he has noted that hidden in some Greek expressions lies a controlling Hebrew form (necessarily undetectable in the Latin, though he takes that implication as read). He expects a great deal of linguistic awareness from his ploughboy—rightly so, it might be said, if that young man were working the fields of the Vale of Berkeley. The ordinary man-in-the-field, 'who runs may read', is expected to be alert. Discussing allegory in *De copia*, Erasmus wrote, '. . . things should not be written in such a way that everyone understands everything, but so that they are forced to investigate certain things, and learn.'[76] Tyndale wanted everyone to understand, and also to learn.

The notion that Tyndale was a conscious craftsman, using the tools of his trade with the expertise and pleasure of a modern designer of aircraft engines, has often been absent from discussion of him. In an influential essay written in 1938, Gavin Bone, of St John's College Oxford, concluded that there was 'no vestige of literariness' in Tyndale's writings: 'In all his works there is no trace of writing for effect'. The essay concludes with a sigh of relief that, thanks to Tyndale, we do not have 'a self-consciously written Bible . . . It is an ironical thing that any essay should come to be written on Tindale the literary artist.'[77] Thirty-three years later the Merton Professor at Oxford came to Tyndale's rescue: in a lecture given at University College London, Norman Davies elaborated some of the devices he could see Tyndale consciously using. He concluded, 'effect in the sense of getting results was what Tyndale wanted, and he used most of the resources of the rhetorician . . . to achieve it'.[78] Even Davies, however original, alert and illuminating he is, does not go far enough into the effect of classical rhetorical training on Tyndale. As can be seen below in the account of the *Obedience*, Tyndale was, in fact, very far from the 'natural' artless scribbler some would, even now, have him. Just as the evidence of the extraordinary efflorescence of all English writing from the 1580s points to a fascination with the developed skills of organising words learned at school ('Without Erasmus, no Shakespeare'), so surely one must not try to explain Tyndale's unusual power as somehow independent of consciousness. The age was preoccupied with language skills, and schools were founded to develop them. Wolsey's school at Ipswich, like Colet's at St Paul's (which had virtually identical curricula), worked very precisely on the principles of Erasmus. In each case authors were fundamental, to be used as models for oral and written composition, founded on the observation and use of the figures and tropes of rhetoric.[79] The Elizabethan schoolboys who went on to write remarkable poetry in English—and there were so many of them—worked from Cicero's apparently mechanical lists of figures of speech and Erasmus's exercises, but they clearly relished that combination of technicality and potential for invention which schoolboys in any age can love. Their dedicated enthusiasm must have had something of the same excited single-mindedness with which schoolboys earlier this century would make intricate scale-drawings and models of the workings of complex engines, and today master the technicalities of unfamiliarly advanced computers with the nonchalance of ducks entering water. At the end of Elizabeth's reign, and under James, for over two dozen years it seemed that no-one could write badly, and most wrote with brilliance. Before Erasmus and the sixteenth-century revolution, however, the intention of rhetoric was less towards making good poets than making wise servants of the state. The Ciceronian orator was one who could advise and persuade by his eloquence in great causes towards a goal of wisdom (a concern of the greater poets as well, of course). Quintilian's interest was more with the expression of private virtue. But the art of making a case from a strongly-held virtuous position, for the general good, is a rough summary of classical rhetoric as Tyndale would have learned to apply it at Oxford.

Tyndale wrote in English. Most writing of his time was in Latin. The two most famous books in Europe, Sir Thomas More's fantasy known now as *Utopia*, and Erasmus's *The Praise of Folly*, were in Latin. To be a scholar and not to write in Latin was odd to the point of standing condemned; both John Wyclif and Reginald Pecock had suffered in that way. All university work and most printed books were in Latin; in 1605, of six thousand volumes in the Oxford University Library, only sixty were in English.[80] Colet's now-famous lectures were in Latin. Erasmus, so influential on his three visits to England, sharing the life of warm households, debating, staying in Magdalen,

inspiring and being inspired, teaching Greek as Lady Margaret Reader
at Cambridge, listening, commenting, writing letters, maintaining his
friendships, spoke not a word of English. When Caxton set up his press
at Westminster in 1476 there were already presses in seventy European
towns in eight European countries. All these produced books almost
exclusively in Latin; Caxton printed books in English for wealthy
general readers, not scholars. The effort across Europe to dignify and
use the vernaculars, largely at first through books intended for pastime,
was slow to produce much—though the quantity can only be judged
by what has survived, and many early books must have been read to
pieces. From before printing, some ordinary manuscripts (as opposed
to lavish ones made for wealthy patrons) survived. Tyndale could have
read in manuscript *Piers Plowman* (unlike the many editions of
Chaucer, it was not in print until 1550). Reginald Pecock's *The
Repressor of Over Much Blaming of the Clergy* of the early 1450s was in
manuscript in English, as were several chronicles, and Fortescue's
Monarchia. The popular collection of tales in manuscript, the Latin
Gesta romanorum, was translated and frequently copied, as was the
English version of the similar *Legenda aurea*, now *The Golden Legend*.
Caxton at his press knew what his rich readers wanted, and gave them
in print and in English much Chaucer, Gower's collection of love-
stories known as the *Confessio amantis*, Malory's *Le morte d'Arthur* and
a good deal else. His *Golden Legend* in print contained, incidentally,
some Bible passages in English from Latin. Fifty years later, while
Tyndale was at Oxford, the other London printers (very few in
number) had a steady output, also including much Chaucer, Lydgate's
Fall of Princes, Mandeville's extraordinary *Travels*, Barclay's *Ship of Fools*,
and an increasing number of devotional handbooks. Printers in Antwerp were beginning to do well with English books in England.
Alongside original works in English can be detected the first trickle of
printed translations which was to become such a mighty flood later in
the century. Yet, admirable though all this new activity was, the natural
language for anything serious or official was still Latin.

   As has been suggested, the impetus for Tyndale to write in English
when he began to do so had several origins: the expressive everyday
phrases of the Vale of Berkeley, and the Lollard pastoral concern that
the Word of God should be in the vernacular; with, as will be seen
in a later chapter, the example of Luther. In the Oxford of Tyndale's
time should be now added the first signs, hardly more than the
tiniest seedling of what might be called a rhetorical nationalism. The
important treatises on rhetoric of later in the century, Cox, Rainolde,
Wilson, Puttenham and the rest—and above all, Sidney—were written

not just to defend but actively to promote poetry and prose in the vernacular on the most correct classical and Italian models. Puttenham, on an early page of his *Art of English Poesie* of 1589 (the title suddenly looks more interesting) wrote in a way which echoes Tyndale on the vernacular Bible in The *Obedience* in 1528:

> And if the art of Poesy be still appertaining to utterance why may not the same be with us as well as them, our language being no less copious pithy and significative as theirs, our conceits the same, and our wits no less apt to devise and imitate than theirs were? If again Art be but a certain order of rules prescribed by reason and gathered by experience, why should not Poesy be vulgar Art with us as well as with the Greeks and Latins, our language admitting no fewer rules and nice diversities than theirs?[81]

Tyndale was there first, fifty and more years before, making his passionate plea for the vernacular as the best rhetorical vehicle for the very best 'poesy' (which word means 'making', as Sidney stressed), the word of God. The printed texts in Tyndale's Oxford were all, without exception, in Latin—Cicero, Quintilian, Aristotle, the Bible, all the schoolbooks, all the academic commentaries—with one or two newly available books in Greek. All his compositions as a schoolboy under-graduate and graduate would be in Latin, like the lectures and disputations he gave. Yet from somewhere, possibly even while he was at Oxford, came the impulse to translate the technical rhetorical skills he had learned into English use, for the benefit of the English people. In this he was, as in so much else, ahead of his time.

For Tyndale's consciousness of his craft, learned at Oxford from classical models, there is one piece of evidence which has been over-looked. In the first prologue to his Pentateuch, Tyndale tells how, some years after leaving Oxford, he set out from Gloucestershire for London to try to gain the support of the Bishop of London for his work of translating the New Testament from Greek into English. He took with him, he said, 'an oration of Isocrates which I had translated out of Greek into English' (the greater significance of this will appear in the next chapter).[82] Isocrates, a great Athenian orator of the fourth century BC, was the founder of a school of rhetoric. His emphasis was on unusually clear, written style, rather than on practical spoken oratory, and his wide influence extended to Cicero and thus into modern prose. His 'Areopagiticus' lies behind Milton's 'Areopagitica', and he is 'that old man eloquent' in one of that poet's sonnets.[83] Which of Isocrates' many orations Tyndale translated we cannot now know, though it is in order to speculate. The point here is five-fold. First, that in about 1522 Tyndale was awake enough to the world of classical literature to offer to senior London scholars and friends of Erasmus a translation of an important Greek stylist. Second, he had unusually good Greek, as Isocrates is difficult. Third, his gesture to the London scholars is partly about rhetoric; he is setting out his stall as someone who knows the highest rhetorical authority, expecting that that would be recognised. Fourth, part of that stall would have been a demonstration that since Oxford he has kept up his study, and has up-to-date knowledge of contemporary translation theory. And fifth, he shows that he is a scholar with knowledge of, and access to, uncommon books. Much has been made of Thomas More's continuance of his studies after his Oxford days. Because of More's higher profile it is known that he learned Greek from Grocyn and was a good Latinist, and we are to admire him because in London after Oxford, while working in his lucrative commercial law practice, he found time to lecture on Augustine's *City of God*. We do not know who taught Tyndale Greek; and he, far less loudly sung about, was also a good Latinist. Tyndale, working as a tutor and translator of Erasmus, demonstrated through the Isocrates translation that his Oxford experience had helped to make him one of the few very able scholars of Greek and Latin in the country, and, more importantly, a conscious craftsman.

Chapter 3

CAMBRIDGE,
AND GLOUCESTERSHIRE AGAIN

Tyndale at Cambridge?

Foxe concludes his paragraph about Tyndale at Oxford noting that 'spying his time, [he] removed from thence to the university of Cambridge, where, after he had likewise made his abode a certain space, being now further ripened in the knowledge of God's word, leaving that university also . . .'[1] This is the only reference to Tyndale at Cambridge, which may have been some time, shorter or longer, between 1517 and 1521. He himself did not mention the younger university. In view of what is so often said about Lutherans in Cambridge in the early 1520s, the idea of Tyndale spending a period there seems so natural that it can surely only be an accident that his name does not appear in the records. Luther, it is said, was read and discussed by scholars in Cambridge so openly that copies of his books were burned there at the end of the year in 1520, a full six months before the famous first bonfire in London. Such official discouragement did not stop the discussion, which often took place in an inn, the White Horse, 'which for despite of them,' wrote Foxe, 'to bring God's word into contempt, was called Germany. This house especially was chosen because many of them of John's, the King's College and the Queen's College, came in on the back side.'[2] Legend has developed the story. A distinguished modern historian of the Reformation may here represent many who have written glowingly about these gatherings:

> The great majority of the men who led the first generation of English Protestants were in residence at Cambridge during the years when the White Horse meetings were in progress. This is true of Tyndale, Joye, Roy, Barnes, Coverdale, Bilney, Latimer, Cranmer, Frith, Lambert, Ridley, Rowland Taylor, Thomas Arthur, Matthew Parker and many others who preached, wrote, accepted high office or embraced martyrdom in the cause.[3]

What an assembly of saints! What debates must the White Horse have known! The names peal down the centuries. Unfortunately, as that cautious first sentence tells us, the hard evidence that any of them, in Cambridge, were ever in the same place at the same time, never mind together in the snug of a Tudor pub, is minimal. There is a certain rightness in having Tyndale's name leading all the rest; but even if it were certain that he was in Cambridge in about 1520, which it is not, there is not a scrap of witness that he even knew where the White Horse was.[4] Some on that list heard others preach, it is true. Robert Barnes, prior of the Cambridge Augustinians, who was later martyred, preached a sermon on Christmas Eve 1525 which was well noted. Foxe says that 'good Master Bilney with others' had before that converted him to Christ, but is vague on particulars of place or time.[5] Not all in the list were up at the same time. Certainly there was some scholarly interest in Luther in Cambridge in the 1520s, and it does appear striking that so many Protestant leaders were there. There is no doubt that Tyndale knew the Cambridge men Joye, Roy, Barnes, Coverdale and Frith, but that was when he was abroad. Roy he chose as a helper in Cologne and Worms; Joye lived in Antwerp; Barnes, if he spent time with Tyndale, came to him either in Hamburg or via Luther at Wittenberg; Coverdale joined him to help with the Pentateuch in Hamburg: Frith he knew in London. Tyndale did not need to have been in Cambridge to know them. Granted, counterbalancing those Cambridge friends and helpers, the only certain names from his Oxford days are John Tisen, whom, Tyndale says, he tutored at Magdalen; and probably John Frith. Tisen later helped shamefully in Tyndale's betrayal. (Oxford, it seems, specialised in his later persecutors, like Tisen, Tunstall, Stokesley, More and the egregious Henry Phillips.) It is interesting that Cambridge supplied his friends, because Oxford as well as London was a centre of Lutheran interest; the Oxford bookseller John Dorne sold, between 29 January and late December 1520, a dozen books by Luther;[6] and there were enough in London in May 1521 for the grand burning at St Paul's Cross, an occasion 'where, before an enormous crowd, Wolsey took the chair under a canopy of cloth of gold, attended by a brilliant throng of peers, bishops and foreign ambassadors.'[7] Some years before, from August 1511 to January 1514 Cambridge, of course, had had as its first teacher of Greek the great Erasmus himself, and some of his work on his Greek New Testament was done there: that _Novum instrumentum_, with its new Latin version and parallel Greek, was influential, as is revealed in the correspondence of the Cambridge lawyer Thomas Bilney, for whom the reading of that Latin text was a turning-point—

though it is not known if the experience happened while he was at Cambridge.[8]

Why should Tyndale, after leaving Oxford, have gone to Cambridge? He could have gone because he felt it might be easier to concentrate there—Cambridge was inferior to Oxford in both size and reputation. Erasmus had found it tranquil to the point of boredom among the utterly undistinguished Scotists he lived with at Queens'. He lectured on Greek to small, unexcited classes. Privately he was writing a great deal. He sent to Colet in September 1511 a booklet, *De ratione studii*. In October he finished a Latin transcription of Basil's commentary on Isaiah, in December a further translation of more of Lucian, a work begun with Thomas More. Early in 1512 he wrote *De copia*, and in that year began comparing texts for his Greek New Testament, and worked on Jerome. He prepared a new and enlarged *Adagia*, edited Seneca, translated two works of Plutarch, and wrote a boring commentary on the extremely boring *Disticha catonis*. Before he left Cambridge, he published—anonymously—his venomous attack on Pope Julius II, *Julius exclusus*.[9] Though he was frequently ill in Cambridge, he made his time there very productive. Perhaps the idea of Cambridge suggested to Tyndale a scholarly but quiet place in which to collect himself; he might even have begun his work on Erasmus's Greek Testament there. Indeed, he might have gone there to improve his Greek, as in 1518 Richard Croke, who had been Professor of Greek at Leipsig, had returned to Cambridge and begun to lecture on that language. In 1519, Wolsey had established a chair of Greek studies in Oxford: a means of further establishing the subject, though it had been taught there for half a century.[10] Even so, Cambridge had the edge. Tyndale might have gone to Cambridge to study divinity, or even to be ordained. Foxe says that he was 'further ripened in the study of God's word'. He also uses the odd phrase 'spying the time' for Tyndale removing from Oxford to Cambridge. That might mean that he saw how openly Lutheran it was possible to be in Cambridge, or that he foresaw increasing hostility in Oxford, or both.

Foxe gives a colourful story at the tail of his account of Wolsey, after the Cardinal's sudden death and burial at the end of November 1530 (his body 'did so stink . . . such a tempest with such a stench there arose'). Wolsey had founded a new college in Oxford [i.e. Cardinal College, later Christ Church]

for the furniture whereof he had gathered together all the best learned he could hear of, amongst which number were these; Clarke, Tyndale, Sommer, Frith, and Taverner, with others. These, holding an assembly together in the college, were accounted to be heretics (as they called them), and thereupon were cast into a prison of the college where salt-fish lay, through the stink whereof the most part of them were infected; and the said Clark, being a tender young man, and the most singular in learning amongst them all, died in the same prison; and others in other places in the town also, of the same infection deceased.[11]

Some University records give the name of Tyndale as a Fellow of Christ Church.[12] This is as shadowy as his sojourn in Cambridge. There may be some underlying truth: Tyndale's abilities would have been worth catching for the new college; Magdalen had recently led the way in the reform of grammatical studies of Latin, and had been an important stimulus to humanist studies in the university. Wolsey had taught grammar at Magdalen school; though that was before Tyndale was there, such an obviously gifted scholar as Tyndale would have a later reputation as one to be considered. In 1525, when Wolsey's Cardinal College was founded, however, Tyndale was in Germany. The story of the imprisonment is fishy, to say the least—unless it represents some whiff of a story of persecution of Tyndale and other 'heretics' in Oxford, conflated by Foxe to the mention of smelliness and Wolsey. In 1528 a ruthless search for Tyndale's New Testament in Oxford as well as London was the cause of imprisonment of some canons of Wolsey's college, including John Frith, but by that time William Tyndale himself had been four years overseas. Foxe, and others, probably passed on a confused report in linking Tyndale with Christ Church. It does seem that while he was at Oxford, and even for some years after, such 'heretics' were unmolested there.

The conflict at Oxford arose rather because the reactionaries who opposed the new learning violently attacked the 'Grecians': it seems that they took to calling themselves 'Trojans'. One of these attacks, probably part of the general discrediting of Erasmus led by Henry Standish, a vocal and powerful Franciscan who had earlier challenged Colet, was a sermon of such intolerance, calling the lecturers in Greek 'archdevils' and the students of Greek 'underdevils' among other things, that it provoked a strong letter to the Oxford authorities from Sir Thomas More, who was then nearby with the King at Abingdon. He begged them to restrain that 'Trojan' faction, who were 'cavorting, guffawing and monkeying around in the pulpit' in the middle of the university. In fact, the Chancellor of the university, William Warham, Archbishop of Canterbury, was one of Erasmus's most cherished patrons. The 'Trojans' were in a weak position, which is perhaps why they were so noisy. And if they did call themselves 'Priam' or 'Hector' or 'Paris' as More alleged, then they cannot have been too hostile to all the conceits of classical scholarship.[13] Part of More's defence of secular learning in that letter, interestingly, is that knowledge of human nature and the human situation is the foundation of the study of theology. But it was not a theological issue.

Tyndale was familiar with those skirmishes, and a dozen years later recalled them to More's memory:

> Remember ye not how within this thirty years and far less, and yet dureth unto this day, the old barking curs, Duns' disciples and like draff [refuse, dregs], called Scotists, the children of darkness, raged in every pulpit against Greek, Latin and Hebrew, and what sorrow the schoolmasters, that taught the true Latin tongue, had with them, some [i.e. preachers], beating the pulpit with their fists for madness, and roaring out with open and foaming mouth, that if there were but one Terence or Virgil in the world, and that same in their sleeves, and a fire before them, they would burn them therein, though it should cost them their lives; affirming that all good learning decayed and was utterly lost, since men gave them unto the Latin tongue?[14]

Those Oxford battles were not about Scripture—or not overtly: hostility to the re-establishment of the Greek New Testament was in the background. In Cambridge, however, things were different. Foxe tells how Robert Barnes established 'Terence, Plautus, and Cicero' at the Augustinian priory, and with the aid of 'copia verborum et rerum' [presumably Erasmus's *De copia*] 'he caused the house shortly to flourish with good letters'. From there he went on to promote the study of

> Paul's Epistles, and put by Duns and Dorbel . . . and only because he would have Christ there taught, and his holy word, he turned their unsavoury problems and fruitless disputations to other better matter of the holy Scripture . . .

This influenced others in the university. Presently, after 'that good Master Bilney, with others . . . converted him wholly unto Christ',

> the first sermon that ever he preached of this truth, was the Sunday before Christmas-day, at St Edward's church, belonging to Trinity Hall in Cambridge, by the Peas-market, whose theme was the epistle of the same Sunday, 'Gaudete in Domino,' &c.; and so postilled [commented upon] the whole epistle, following Scripture

and Luther's Postil; and for that sermon he was immediately accused of heresy by two fellows of the King's Hall. Then the godly learned in Christ both of Pembroke-hall, St John's, Peter-house, Queen's college, the King's college, Gunwell-hall, and Benet college, showed themselves, and flocked together in open sight, both in the schools, and at open sermons at St Mary's, and at the Augustines, and at other disputations; and then they conferred continually together.[15]

This happened in 1525, long after Tyndale would have left. Yet it does suggest a university in which the very heart of New Testament teaching, the nature of Christ in Paul's Epistles, was the chief issue, something not imaginable in Oxford at that time (or any time since, come to that). Foxe's phrase, 'spying the time', with his remark that Tyndale was 'further ripened in the knowledge of God's word', may contain the kernel of truth that Cambridge attracted Tyndale for purely scriptural reasons.

Tyndale in Gloucestershire Again

Foxe's paragraph continues: '. . . leaving that university also, he resorted to one Master Welch, a knight of Gloucestershire, and was there schoolmaster to his children, and in good favour with his master.'[16] Tyndale returned to Gloucestershire to be in one of the important houses of the district. In the next two years his connections were again of the closest with significant landowners, working with the Crown and the Church. Sir John Walsh in 1522 was recorded as having considerable wealth in goods and lands extending over a wide area of Gloucestershire.[17] Sir John, then between thirty and thirty-five, living at Little Sodbury Manor, a fine Cotswold house a dozen miles south of Stinchcombe, was a senior figure in the county. A distinguished man who had been Crown Steward for the Berkeley estate (a position he had handed over in 1519 to Edward Tyndale, William's brother[18]) and auditor and Steward of Tewkesbury Abbey (which post, again, he handed over to Edward Tyndale in 1536 at the Dissolution), he was twice High Sheriff of Gloucestershire. He had been at Court, a young man close to the eighteen-year-old Henry VIII at the coronation in 1509. Henry did not forget him, and a royal progress with Queen Anne in 1535 included honouring the Walshes with a royal visit to Little Sodbury on the night of 23 August 1535.[19] The progress took in towns in Berkshire, Oxfordshire, Gloucestershire, Wiltshire and Hampshire, and ended on 19 September with the consecration of three reforming bishops in Winchester Cathedral. The route included

Tewkesbury, Gloucester, Berkeley, Little Sodbury and, of particular importance for the Walshes, Acton Court at Iron Acton, a village six miles west of Little Sodbury, and the home of Sir Nicholas Poyntz. Henry and Anne stayed at Acton Court from Saturday 21 August to Monday 23 August, after which they went on for a night to the Walshes at Little Sodbury.

Nicholas Poyntz was then twenty-six: three years before he had been with the King and his fiancée Anne at Calais from 25 to 29 October 1532 at the interview with Francis I. It is sometimes said that the delay in sailing home provided the couple, kept indoors by bad weather for some days, with the opportunity for what had been put off for six years, and that there they first consummated their love.[20] Politically the meeting paved the way for Henry and Anne to marry. Anne had that cause at least for remembering Nicholas Poyntz, and the royal visit no doubt acknowledged it. (Holbein's fine portrait drawing of 'Sir Nicholas Poyntz of Acton Court' in the Royal Collection shows in profile a handsome young courtier of some personal authority). For his part, Nicholas marked the importance of the occasion by adding an east range to his house, sumptuously decorated inside, to receive them. The Poyntz family had had connections with the Tudor court since the 1470s. In 1479 Robert Poyntz, Nicholas's grandfather, married a niece of Edward IV's queen: as a courtier he survived Richard III's reign, and was knighted at Bosworth Field in 1485. He entertained Henry VII at Acton Court on 23 May 1486 while that king was on a royal progress to Bristol. He was a fairly high-ranking courtier, and with his son Anthony attended the Field of the Cloth of Gold in 1520. Anthony's son Nicholas now received King Henry and Queen Anne: but the cause was probably rather more than a sense of royal favour and family histories. There are strong indications that Nicholas was of the reform camp. Thomas Cromwell, since January the King's viceregent in spirituals, had joined the progress at Winchcombe a month before, and stayed with it for two months. He was using the occasion to begin his work of visitation of the monasteries. Under Queen Anne, with Cromwell present, and culminating in the consecration of reform bishops, the progress had an 'evangelical' flavour—even the visit to Little Sodbury; for Sir John Walsh had married Anne Poyntz, sister to Sir Anthony and aunt to Sir Nicholas. Sir John and Lady Anne had been on the side of reform at least since they had taken in as tutor over a dozen years before the young scholar from Oxford, and possibly Cambridge, William Tyndale.

When Tyndale arrived, the two Walsh boys were very young, possibly under seven. They would not make too many demands on his professional time. Though the manor then had a private chapel, Tyndale was firmly tutor to the children, it seems, and not chaplain to the family.[21] He was probably ordained priest before he arrived: Mozley prints details of records in Hereford which seem to point to William and his brother John being ordained to minor orders; but it is not yet known for certain when and where William became a priest, only that he did.[22] Little Sodbury Manor, as Demaus wrote in 1871, 'is charmingly situated on the south-western slope of the Cotswolds, and enjoys a magnificent prospect over the richly-wooded vale of the Severn, to the distant hills of Wales'.[23] Tyndale would have found the setting familiar: the house looks out from below Camp Hill much as Melksham Court does below Stinchcombe Hill, both facing west across the Severn. There is no reason why he could not have known Little Sodbury Manor, and the Walshes, from long before; it is only a dozen miles south of Stinchcombe, roughly on the way to Bristol, which is itself only fifteen miles further. His brother Edward shared professional interests with Sir John. The manor, attractive in its Cotswold stone walls and roofs, was, and still is, a large and rambling assembly of added-on rooms round a fine hall, set in trees and gardens with a small lake. The hall itself, oak-beamed and panelled, with a large fireplace, was an impressive place to dine, as Tyndale did as one of the family. The room that tradition has given him to sleep and work in is an attic looking out to the hill in which the curved oak beams of the ceilings reach almost to the floor. On the hillside a few stone steps away from the manor lay the little Walsh private chapel, dedicated to St Adeline. She was the patron saint of weavers and an object of gratitude for the local success of the cloth trade. (It is the only church in England so dedicated.) In 1859 the ruins of it were pulled down and some of the materials used to build a small church on the same plan, now with a tower, in the village of Little Sodbury below. The small wooden pulpit from the original chapel, having spent over a century in a local farmhouse and traditionally said to have been used by Tyndale, has been set up there.

Perhaps unexpectedly, Tyndale began to have a name in the district as a preacher. Foxe, commenting on him later in London, wrote that he preached 'according as he had done in the country before, and especially about the town of Bristol, and also in the said town, in the common place called St Austin's Green'.[24] That was a central open space in front of the Augustinian priory, still there but now called College Green. We would give much to know about those preachings (and very much more to have copies of his sermons). Foxe's phrases 'about the town' and 'in the common place' suggest that he was an open-air field preacher in the late medieval manner. Though the text of his sermon would probably have been from the Bible in Latin, as being more familiar to many of his hearers, his sermon would have been in English. (From Chaucer's repellent Pardoner preaching in English, a hundred and fifty years before, on the repeated Latin phrase *radix malorum est cupiditas*, through John Fisher, Bishop of Rochester in the 1520s, to John Donne, Dean of St Paul's in the early seventeenth century, our literature has many prominent examples of such sermons.) Thousands of volumes of them, now never opened, are in the vaults of the great libraries. They would have had an intricate pattern of ideas in logical steps, which can be set out on the page in clear summary of heads and subheads, a skeleton which gives shape and coherence to the whole. Thus John Colet's *Convocation Sermon* can be set out under the main headings of Exordium (introduction); The Text (Romans 12:2); and Peroration (conclusion),[25] with subheadings again subdivided in patterns including, twice, eleven further divisions. The sermons of John Fisher show the same schemes;[26] and as will be seen, the printed treatises of William Tyndale do the same. Unlike all the other regular clergy, however, Tyndale could have made his subject-matter not only the very heart of Scripture, in, for example, Paul's Epistle to the Romans: but Paul to the Romans in English, and probably from Paul's own original Greek to boot. Lollards had kept alive the Wyclif Bible, in spite of the Constitutions of Oxford of 1408 which expressly forbade the translation of any part of Scripture into English by any man on his own authority, under pain of punishment as a heretic.[27] Some who heard Tyndale preach would have had access to a complete manuscript Bible, for Lollardy was not confined to the poor. Others would have seen parts, or even scraps. The Bible in English was not unknown. Significantly, there is today slowly-growing evidence of a common oral pool of English sentences and short passages from the New Testament, phrases used like proverbs; not only common sayings like 'the patience of Job' from James 5, or 'Abraham's bosom' from Luke 16, but more theologically pointed ones like 'the wages of sin is death' from Romans 6, or 'it is God that justifieth, who is that condemneth?' from Romans 8, or 'whoever knowledgeth that Jesus is the son of God, God dwelleth in him and he in God' from 1 John 4.[28] Such common phrases, however, valuable as they were, were always from the Latin. Tyndale, working from the Greek, would first of all give his hearers something new that would need from them a little adjustment, rather like, in the late twentieth century, getting used to saying 'Beijing' instead of 'Peking'. So the Lollard Bible's sentence from Romans 5, 'But God commendeth his charity in us; for if when were

yet sinners, after the time Christ was dead for us . . .' became, as
Tyndale worked from the Greek, 'But God setteth out his love that he
hath to us, seeing that while we were yet sinners, Christ died for
us . . .' It is as if a fuzzy, out-of-focus picture had suddenly become
sharp.

A second, more important point, and one often neglected, is that
Tyndale would be using not just single texts, but the whole New
Testament. Modern champions of the Catholic position like to support
a view of the Reformation, that it was entirely a political imposition
by a ruthless minority in power against both the traditions and the
wishes of the pious lay people of England, with the claim that, if
matters had not been interfered with, the Church in its reforming
wisdom would have got round to issuing a vernacular Bible in its own
time. That may or may not be so: it seems extremely unlikely. As we
shall see in a later chapter, the argument is weakened when such
historians give examples of that process already visible in the fifteenth
and sixteenth centuries, which produces constructions of the Gospels
with very little relation to what was written by Matthew, Mark, Luke
or John; or small sections in English of the Latin New Testament, as
separate from each other as stained-glass windows at opposite ends of
a building.[29] Some reforming politicians can be made out to be
ruthless self-seeking thugs, no doubt, just as some Catholic politicians
can. The energy which affected every human life in Northern Europe,
however, came from a different place. It was not the result of political
imposition. It came from the discovery of the Word of God as originally written, from Matthew—indeed, from Genesis—to Revelation,
in the language of the people. Moreover, it could be read and understood, without censorship by the Church or mediation through the
Church, as it was written to be read, as a coherent, cross-referring
whole. Such reading produced a totally different view of everyday
Christianity: the weekly, daily, even hourly ceremonies so lovingly
catalogued by some Catholic revisionists are not there; Purgatory is not
there; there is no aural confession and penance. Two supports of the
Church's wealth and power collapsed. Instead, there was simply individual faith in Christ as Saviour, found in Scripture. That and only that
'justified' the sinner, whose root failings were now in the face of God,
not the bishops or the pope.

Extrapolating back from Tyndale's printed work in Germany less
than two years later, it seems that Tyndale would almost certainly have
been preaching in Gloucestershire in a compelling, systematic way that
whole New Testament, focused on Paul, and expositing as the heart of
Paul justification by faith. He would not have needed Luther to find

that: study of the Greek New Testament would have given it to him. Precisely when he knew his calling to translate the New Testament from Greek for everyone we do not know. It did not need to have come in a flash of divine vision. Foxe's sentence about his Oxford days, that he 'read privily to certain students and fellows of Magdalen college some parcel of divinity; instructing them in the knowledge and truth of the scriptures' suggests private seminars on the Greek New Testament, private because translating the Bible into English was illegal. For that, he must by then have had, first, leadership in the college in knowledge of Greek, and secondly, access to Erasmus's *Novum instrumentum*, from 1516. These things, his Greek and his Testament, would not have been lost on the journey to south Gloucestershire; far from it. His attic room in the manor must have been a quiet place for intensive further study, conveniently far from the household noises, and the children. Some writers have suggested that Tyndale, leaving Oxford, and possibly Cambridge, fell into a bad situation; even the sympathetic Mozley regretted that Tyndale had 'to bury himself in a remote village in order to teach little boys . . . No man in his senses would go from Cambridge to a Gloucestershire country house, if he wished to translate the New Testament.'[30] There is another way of looking at it: that Tyndale knew that he had a lot of work to do alone with the Greek New Testament. At Little Sodbury Manor, living comfortably with possibly already supportive employers and light duties, receiving a salary and full maintenance, with freedom to come and go, and booksellers selling Erasmus and others not far away in Bristol or Oxford,[31] his position could be considered to have been ideal, to the point of having been specifically arranged by him, as he and his locally influential brothers might have made agreement with the Walshes.

Erasmus's Novum instrumentum

Modern New Testament scholars who slip a copy of Nestlé's Greek New Testament in a pocket to read at a bus stop might find it hard to grasp what facing Erasmus's great book entails. Nestlé has as well as small size, clear type, necessary *apparatus criticus*, some cross-references and chapter and verse numbers. Erasmus's very large, very heavy folio contains in its bulk three elements. At the front, hundreds of pages of parallel columns of Greek and Erasmus's Latin of the whole New Testament. The Greek is printed in the unfortunate cursive fount developed in Europe from Aldus's first making of it. There are no variant readings, no divisions into verses, nor even chapters. There is no indication at the top of the column beyond the title of the New

Testament book, so finding one's way is not easy. Only when a second Latin column was added in 1527, giving the Vulgate, were chapter numbers added in the margins. The second element in the whole book is the long series of essays in Latin, one third of the whole volume, printed after the New Testament, entitled the *Annotations*. These are not 'notes' in the modern sense, but quite separate discussions (the *Annotations* were sometimes printed as a separate volume) more in the spirit of the *Adages*, or even *The Praise of Folly*, than scholarly annotations. Always readable, they are sometimes short comments on a word or phrase in the text, and sometimes quite long essays arising from, or associated with, the original. Keying is to the Latin, with Greek quoted. Erasmus praised in *De copia* the schoolboy habit of composing half in Latin and half in Greek,[32] and he is clearly at home here.

But note that he keys to the Latin, to his own Latin. For to put the Greek text first is to get this volume very wrong. Erasmus's chief aim was to correct the Vulgate; to make a new Latin text from the Greek that would avoid, and correct, the Vulgate's many mistakes. *That* is the *Novum instrumentum*; the Greek is there to to explain his Latin, for whoever can follow. The quality of learned mockery in the *Annotations*, paralleling the tone of *The Praise of Folly*, is aimed at those who relied on the Vulgate as it stood, especially those without Greek—and Colet, who is praised in the preface, is necessarily among those condemned. The Greek text was corrected, not always wisely, in successive editions. At the same time as editions passed the *Annotations* increased mightily, in a fashion familiar in the Renaissance (as in the *Essays* of Montaigne). The increase was largely in comment on the Gospels, as Erasmus defended his *philosophia Christi*. In other words, this complex volume gives two sets of commentaries on the new Latin, one Erasmus's carefully-edited Greek text and the other his *Annotations*. Against the old Latin 'so-called *Testamentum*' is his *Novum instrumentum*, the new Latin. Indeed, the long title-page does not even mention that the Greek is being printed, and for the first time.

It was the new Latin that caused outrage in conservative circles. For example, in Erasmus, Christ thanked the Father for revealing the secrets of the Kingdom not to babes but to fools (*stulti*). After 1519, John's Gospel opens with the Word as *sermo* instead of *verbum* as the Vulgate. Worse, in the *Annotations* Erasmus emphasised the errors in the Vulgate and mocked honoured scholastic authorities whom he had found inadequate. There is a legend that Erasmus worked with Froben his printer at break neck speed in 1516 in order to get ahead in the market. It was known that the Spanish scholars producing at Alcalá ('Complutum' in Latin) who were working on a Polyglot printing of a complete Bible in Hebrew, Greek, Aramaic and Latin. But though their New Testament was set up in type by January 1514, the magnificent Complutensian Polyglot was not on sale until 1522. The legend, partly resulting from Erasmus's own explanation of haste, perhaps as a cover for possible errors, has been used to condemn the enterprise; in fact, all the parts of Erasmus's volume show care and accuracy. Some evidence of the importance of Erasmus's Latin for the early reformers is given by the fact that on four occasions (in 1538, 1548, 1549 and 1550) Tyndale's 1534 New Testament was printed with Erasmus's Latin on the page in a parallel column. Erasmus's Latin broke a thousand-year chain, the unchallengeability of Jerome's Vulgate text. But his Greek was the real breaker of chains. Luther was able to see that the Greek made a new German possible. Tyndale did even more, and found in the Greek an English which is still, nearly five hundred years later, modern.

Disturbance in Gloucestershire

Mozley's 'remote village' does injustice to those cultural connections possible in Gloucestershire at the time noted above, especially with the support of landed gentry. The call to devote his life to the printing of the Scriptures in English might have come to Tyndale as a slowly growing conviction over some years. Some part in it may have been taken by the uncomfortable events he now found himself experiencing.

Tyndale sat at the Walsh's table as a modern scholar of Latin and Greek. Sir John and his wife were hospitable to the good and the great of the county, most of whom were churchmen, and, though elevated, were hardly scholars at all, and certainly not modern. However humble of bearing Tyndale might have been, there was bound to be some suspicion of this local young man, who had been away to Oxford and had come back so clever, from Magdalen of all places, with its reputation for advanced thinking about Latin and Greek and interest in alarming texts in those languages. What happened to Tyndale is best understood through the words of a man identified by Demaus, with justification, as Richard Webb of Chipping Sodbury, who had been servant to Hugh Latimer.[33] Much later, Webb, in London, gave Foxe a story about the burning alive of a woman in Chipping Sodbury in 1508. Foxe goes to some pains to acknowledge Webb as his personal source for that story, and Webb himself had heard the tale many times from his father, 'who was both a papist, and present at the same time'. Foxe defends that source because of the spectacular end to the story:

a maddened bull escaped from the butcher, ran amok in the crowd coming from a burning of a heretic woman, and, 'touching neither man nor child' went straight to the bishop's chancellor (who was there to see that execution was done) and gored him to instant death. If Webb reliably told Foxe this story in London in early 1560, he could have given him from local gossip the following story about Tyndale. Like the account of the miraculously targeting bull, it has the air of a tale often told. The account is clearest in the 1563 edition of Foxe, probably as Webb spoke it:

> Master Tyndale . . . being in good favour with his master, sat most commonly at his own table [i.e. his master's], having resort to him many times divers great beneficed men, as Abbots, Deans, Archdeacons, and other divers doctors and learned men. Amongst whom commonly was talk of learning, as well of Luther and Erasmus Roterodamus as of the opinions in the scripture. The said Master Tyndall being learned and which had been a student of divinity in Cambridge, and had therein taken degree of school, did many times therein show his mind and learning, wherein as those men and Tyndall did vary in opinions and judgments, then Master Tyndall would show them on the book the places, by open and manifest scripture, the which continued for a certain season, diverse and sundry times until in the continuance thereof those great beneficed doctors waxed weary and bare a secret grudge in their hearts against Master Tyndall. So upon a time some of those beneficed doctors, had master Welch and the Lady his wife, at a supper or banquet, there having among them talk at will without any gainsaying, and the supper or banquet being done, and Master Welch and the Lady his wife come home. They called for Master Tyndall, and talked with him of such communication as had been, where they came from, and of their opinions. Master Tyndall thereunto made answer agreeable to the truth of God's word, and in reproving of their false opinions. The Lady Welch, being a stout [resolute] woman, and as master Tyndall did report her to be wise, being there no more but they three, Master Welch, his wife and Master Tyndall. Well, said she, there was such a doctor, he may dispend [spend] £200 by the year, another one hundred pound, and another three hundred pound, and what think ye, were it reason that we should believe you before them so great, learned and beneficed men?[34]

That story ends there. No reply was possible. But Tyndale took his time, and did indeed make a most effective response. Foxe goes on to say that while he was in the Walsh household, he translated Erasmus's famous little book, the *Enchiridion*:

> But then he did translate into English a book called as I remember *Enchiridion militis Christiani.* The which being translated, delivered to his master and Lady. And after they had read that book, those great prelates were no more so often called to the house, nor when they came, had the cheer nor countenance as they were wont to have, the which they did well perceive, and that it was by the means and incensing of Master Tyndale, and at the last came no more there.

It might be thought that there could have been nothing in the Walshes' possession of a copy of the *Enchiridion* that might have caused the 'doctorly prelates' as Foxe calls them in the 1563 edition, no longer to be welcome. Erasmus was not generally known at that time as a 'heretical' writer, he himself reported that only one Cambridge college rejected his biblical teaching.[35] The local 'prelates' could have been ignorant and bigoted; Webb's story might support that. The book is not anti-prelatical, though Erasmus is as always strong in his attack on popular but scripturally peripheral Church practices, like the worship of saints and their images and relics. Not surprisingly given his miserable experience at a monastery, in similar vein to *The Praise of Folly* and other works he has nothing good to say about monks—they

> live in idleness, and be fed of other men's liberality, possessing that amongst themself in common, which they never laboured or sweated for (yet I speak nothing of them that be vicious).

Evil monks, he says, in this typical passage, are more evil than evil laymen; the good are about the same. . . .[36] Yet attacking corruption in the monasteries was no new thing at all (we need only think of Chaucer's *Canterbury Tales* and Langland's *Piers Plowman* of a century and a half before) and some at least of the 'doctorly prelates' would probably have been a good deal more specific. Erasmus's book is original in its moral directness and strong appeal to Scripture as well as classical writers and the Fathers, but in its assumption that lay Christians are so important it is more oblique in its attack on the Church than openly subversive. Foxe's implication is that reading the book changed the Walsh's minds. Perhaps Erasmus's final directions, for example, for avoiding such vices as lust, avarice, ambition, pride and haughtiness struck the flank of the 'prelates' too squarely. (Foxe, writing in the early 1560s, could just have been governed by hindsight, in that in 1558 the suspicion of Erasmus was hardened by his writings being forbidden by Pope Paul IV.) It is more likely that Tyndale's gift of the translation awoke the Walshes to the quality of the priest they had in their household, a man of God not only of some originality in his scholarship and understanding of the absolute importance of the Scriptures, but also in those things being in tune with advanced continental thinking within the Church about reform from the inside. What Sir John and his Lady saw, no doubt amplified by Tyndale on the spot, took them some steps towards the new reform position.

The Enchiridion *and its English Translation*

Erasmus wrote his *Enchiridion militis Christiani* in 1501, at the request of a friend of a friend. The mixture of Greek and Latin of the title had a long history. *Enchiridion* is a Greek word meaning 'in the hand'; it is one of the Greek words for a hand-knife or dagger: it had been used since classical times (by Pliny, for example, and Augustine, and was not infrequent in the sixteenth century) as a title for a hand-book, a 'manual', something 'handsome' as the fifteenth and early sixteenth centuries had it, meaning ready at hand, and applied to a document giving essential information about a matter. Attaching it to the idea of a Christian as soldier or knight, Erasmus uses Paul's well-known imagery in Ephesians 6 about putting on the armour of God:

> Finally my brethren, be strong in the Lord, and in the power of his might. Put on the armour of God, that ye may stand steadfast against the crafty assaults of the devil. For we wrestle not against flesh and blood: but against rule, against power, and against worldly rulers of the darkness of this world, against spiritual wickedness for heavenly things. . .
>
> Stand therefore and your loins girt about with verity, having on the breastplate of righteousness, and shod with shoes prepared by the gospel of peace. Above all take to you the shield of faith, wherewith ye may quench all the fiery darts of the wicked. And take the helmet of salvation and the sword of the spirit, which is the word of God.[37]

In his *Enchiridion*, Erasmus gives defences by which the Christian could prepare himself for the inevitable encounters with the world and the Devil.

> These be the most special things which will make thee sure from pleasures and enticings of the flesh. First of all circumspect and diligent avoiding of all occasions . . . Secondly moderation of eating and drinking and of sleep. Temperance and abstinence from pleas-

ures, yea from such as be lawful and permitted. The regard of thine own death, and the contemplation of the death of Christ . . .[38]

The specific weapons of attack are virtue, with knowledge of the classics and of the works of the Church Fathers, and above all understanding Scripture, particularly through the latest methods of exegesis of the New Testament—to put it shortly, not through allegory. Erasmus is original and undogmatic, unusually so for the fashion of the times; he also wrote this 'method of morals' for a layman.

Some years later he gave an explanation how the book was written. It was in answer to a plea from 'a lady of singular piety' whose irreligious husband, Johann Poopenruyter of Nurnberg, known to Erasmus, was not only openly adulterous and generally loose-living, but apt to be violent to her when she did mention religion. (Sir John and Lady Walsh would not possibly take that as relevant to themselves.) The wife was anxious about her spouse's salvation and so through an intermediary asked Erasmus 'to set down some . . . sense of religion, without his perceiving that it was done at the insistence of his wife . . . I consented to the request and put down some observations suitable to the occasion'.[39] It was written in Tournehem in the Pas de Calais, and first published in February 1503 in Antwerp, a year and a half later. It sold reasonably well: a revision in 1518, dedicated to Abbot Volz of the Benedictine community at 'Hughes Court', Hugshofen near Schlettstadt, and now prefaced by a letter to him, suddenly began to sell very well indeed, as the news of Luther's open challenge in his Ninety-five Theses in 1517 had stirred Europe with religious controversy.

In all, this slim book of under forty leaves in quarto ran through over fifty Latin editions in Erasmus's lifetime, and was translated in that time into Czech, German, English, French, Dutch and Spanish. In the 1520s alone, there were

> three Latin editions and one German in 1520, six Latin and another German in 1521, eight Latin in 1522, and . . . in 1523 . . . ten Latin and two Dutch editions . . . two Latin editions in 1524, a French and a German in 1525, one Latin edition each in 1525, 1526, 1527, and 1528, with a Spanish edition in 1527 and two in 1528, three Latin editions and one French in 1529 . . .[40]

Tyndale would have been hard put to it to miss it. In English, after the first edition in 1533, there were ten editions in the next forty years (then one in 1765 and no more until 1904).

Erasmus's book was neither, as the time might have expected, a firework-display of scholastic metaphysics, nor a mystical treatise—nor even a traditional book of meditation: all three would have been inappropriate to his declared purpose. *Enchiridion* is a practical book about being a Christian in the world. The pious lady's errant husband is a layman, and Erasmus tells him he could—indeed, should—have a vocation as a Christian. In place of clerical authority stands Scripture, particularly the New Testament, and especially the Gospels and the letters of Paul to the Romans and Corinthians, without elaborate glossing or fanciful allegorising, and to be used spiritually as showing the way of a Christian in ordinary life. Erasmus could include some classical writers, and the earlier Fathers, who were looking in the same moral direction, for their own sakes, and because they were taken as underpinning the understanding of Scripture. One can see the attraction for Tyndale: Scripture for the lay wayfarer, who has through reading the New Testament in particular the authority he needs to live the Christian life.

The Christian knight's two chief weapons, above all, Erasmus says in the second chapter, are prayer and knowledge, especially knowledge of Scripture, which is to be studied continually. After explanation of the nature of man, drawn from Paul, come twenty-one 'rules' by which the Christian knight overcomes the enemy, starting, because 'faith is the only gate unto Christ', with affirmation of him and of the New Testament. The second rule begins 'Let the first point be therefore that thou doubt in no wise of the promises of god. The next that thou go unto the way of life, not slothfully, not fearfully: but with sure purpose, with all thy heart, with a confident mind . . .'[41] It might be Tyndale writing. Further rules develop the importance of 'inner religion', and show, by contrast, the vanity of external religious practices for their own sakes.

> One saluteth Christopher every day, but not except he behold his image . . . Another worshippeth one Rochus, but why? because he believeth that he will keep away the pestilence from his body. Another mumbleth certain prayers to Barbara or George, lest he should fall into his enemies' hands. This man fasteth to saint Apollonia, lest his teeth should ache. That man visiteth the image of holy Job, because he would be without scabs . . .[42]
>
> Honourest thou the bones of Paul hid in a shrine, and honourest thou not the mind of Paul hid in his writings? Magnifiest thou a piece of his carcase shining through a glass, and regardest not thou the whole mind of Paul shining through his letters?[43]

Again, it might be Tyndale, in his *Obedience of a Christian Man*.

External ceremonies, writes Erasmus, are not bad in themselves, and can even be useful, but they are always in danger of taking over and producing a legalism like Judaism, from which Christ has set mankind free. That liberty was defined by Paul for Christians as the state of being one in Christ, with love for our neighbours. There is very little in *Enchiridion* about the sacraments: saying masses, baptism and confession are mentioned, for example, in chapter 13, the fifth rule, but in a way which reduces their sacramental nature. The rules thereafter develop the power of reading the New Testament as a force against common vices, particularly a final selection of the Seven Deadly Sins. *Enchiridion* is a theological book in the special sense that all the theology emanated from Scripture and from nowhere else. The medieval seduction of theology by philosophy has here its counter-movement. In all his writing, Erasmus presses his *philosophia Christi*, which sounds scholastic: but it is declared in his continued work of editing Greek texts of the New Testament, and his expositions of New Testament books. It is in much of his scheme of educational reform, where pupils were to learn the nuts and bolts of language through short, vivid down-to-earth passages where ethical and moral matters were embodied. The classical authors would provide techniques of study, and background information, which would then bring the New Testament forcefully to life: skill in the ancient languages would help this, but was not essential. Just as the Church implied that the truths of Christ could not be grasped without mountains of complicated and burdensome labour, almost necessarily only available to the occupants of religious houses, so by contrast here the Holy Spirit will illuminate the simplicity of the *philosophia Christi* to the simplest souls—who should in any case have the Scriptures in their own vernacular. As he wrote in an influential passage in his *Paraclesis*, prefacing his Greek New Testament,

> Christ wishes his mysteries to be published as widely as possible. I would wish even all women to read the gospel and the epistles of St Paul, and I wish that they were translated into all languages of all Christian people, that they might be read and known, not merely by the Scotch and the Irish, but even by the Turks and the Saracens. I wish that the husbandman may sing parts of them at his plow, that the weaver may warble them at his shuttle, that the traveller may with their narratives beguile the wearinesss of the way.[44]

Erasmus begins to appear more and more a man after Tyndale's own heart. The famous remark that Erasmus laid the egg which Luther hatched suggests the force of his presence as pre-reformer. Alexander Pope, in about 1709, towards the end of his *Essay on Criticism* wrote:

> With *Tyranny*, then *Superstition* join'd,
> As that the *Body*, this enslav'd the *Mind*;
> Much was *Believ'd*, but little *understood*,
> And to be *dull* was constru'd to be *good*;
> A *second* Deluge Learning thus o'er-run.
> And the *Monks* finish'd what the *Goths* begun.
>   At length, *Erasmus*, that *great, injur'd* Name,
> (The *Glory* of the Priesthood, and the *Shame!*)
> *Stemm'd* the *wild Torrent* of a *barb'rous Age*,
> And drove those *Holy Vandals* off the Stage.[45]

And the Popes, of course, were Catholic—and lest that remark should get a prize for being the most blindingly obvious, I hasten to add that I mean not the pontiffs but the poet Alexander and his parents. By the early eighteenth century, even in 'the old religion' Erasmus stood for what was obviously great and good.

Yet something in the *Enchiridion* is missing. In stirring to action a Christian knight, Erasmus was addressing, as much as the licentious arms-manufacturer Johann Poppenruyter of Nurnberg and his over-pious wife, himself. He was seeing himself rising to arms, against the Devil on behalf of Christ, as well as against the obfuscations of the Church and its barbarous Latin. He hit a note which had been struck in Europe before from northern Italy to the Netherlands, and in England from Wyclif to Colet; but he now sounded it in such a way that most of Europe heard it at once. A famous preacher in Antwerp, it is said, based all his sermons during the year 1514–16 on passages from the book, and Luther's sermons and letters of 1516 echo it.[46] Albrecht Dürer made in 1513 his famous engraving *Knight, Death and the Devil* and explained that it was called up by the *Enchiridion*: the marvellous power of the horse and single-minded strength of the rider remain an inspiration to this day. Like Erasmus, Dürer broke new ground; his innovation was that the Knight's foes are not 'real' but, as Erasmus had noted, *terricula et phantasmata* ('fearful things and fanta-sies'), to be ignored, something Virgil's Aeneas had to do 'in the first entering of hell'.[47]

Dürer's engraving is magnificent; yet Erasmus did not exhibit Death or the Devil with such particularity as Dürer did. Moreover, though he used in the *Enchiridion* the name 'Christ' a very great deal, Christ is a rather pale figure in the book. It is a masterpiece of humanist piety, straight, not satirical like its rivals in popularity, *The Praise of Folly*, and More's *Utopia*. In 1535 Thomas Lupset, advising his young reader not to meddle with Church matters, still recommended the *Enchiridion* as a book that 'in a few leaves containeth an infinite knowledge of goodness'. Yet though Erasmus was girding himself up, as well as his knight, to fight, armed with the New Testament, his punches were pulled. The activity of Christ in the Gospels, his special work of salvation so strongly detailed there and in the Epistles of Paul, is largely missing. Christologically, where Luther thunders, Erasmus makes a sweet sound: what to Tyndale was an impregnable stronghold feels in the *Enchiridion* like a summer pavilion. Moreover, though he wanted lay people to study Scripture continually, and famously longed for Scriptures in the vernacular, all he himself wrote was in Latin— beautiful Latin, to be sure, and even in that, a blow against the scholastic and educational barbarians. Yet he never went all the way into a lay person's common language with anything he did. Indeed, it is possible that just as More blocked requests for an English translation of *Utopia*, 'lest it might fall into the hands of the simple and unlearned who might misunderstand and take harm from it',[48] so Erasmus was in no hurry to see even his most famous work, the *Moriae encomium*, in English. When the vernacular Bible was available in England in the fourteenth century, and in Germany, France and England in particular in the first decades of the sixteenth century, it produced movements infinitely more highly charged than a wish for a simple, ethical *philosophia Christi*. Those movements, officially branded 'heresy', were powerful enough to suggest to the ordinary worshipper in Europe, whose soul's salvation and spiritual welfare depended automatically on the Church, as they had done for hundreds of years, that there was in fact an alternative. Erasmus, for all his importance, did not have that great charge: Luther and Tyndale did.

Not only is there no fully realised Christ or Devil in Erasmus's book for the Christian knight: there is a touch of irony about it all, with a feeling of the writer cultivating a faintly superior ambiguity: as if to be dogmatic, for example about the full theology of the work of Christ, was to be rather distasteful, below the best, élite, humanist heights.[49] This ironic self-mockery is common to both Erasmus and More, and it is to be noted in the portraits of Erasmus, those for example by Quentin Matsys and by Holbein.[50] By contrast, Tyndale (of whom we have no certain contemporary portrait) is in his writing ferociously single-minded; the matter in hand, the immediate access of the soul to God without intermediary, is far too important for hints of faintly ironic superiority. To compare Tyndale's few accounts of himself (as in the prologue to his Pentateuch, for example) with Erasmus's explanation of how he came to write the *Enchiridion* is to make the point clear. Tyndale is as four-square as a carpenter's tool. But in Erasmus's account of the origins of his book there is a touch of the sort of layering of ironies found in the games with *personae*, and with the reader, played by Jonathan Swift (as there is quite often when Erasmus writes about himself). Did Erasmus seriously believe that a successful, vigorous, amoral, independent arms-trader might by some chance engineered by his pious wife settle down and study a rambling, rather disorganised Latin monologue on virtue, illuminated by reference to the best classical-humanist texts and the earlier Fathers, and as a result solemnly leave his mistress and his energetic ways for his wife's extreme piety? Even that assumes that the man could read and understand Latin. Erasmus himself said that he made his book 'for myself only, and for a certain friend of mine being utterly unlearned'.[51] Is the Johann Poppenruyter story to be taken seriously or not? The self-deprecating ambiguity about the purpose of the book is disconcerting. We recall Swift's wry complaint about his *Gulliver's Travels*, in the person of Gulliver, that 'after above six months' warning, I cannot learn that my book hath produced one single effect according to mine intentions . . .'[52] Swift could afford to tease, especially as the point of his mock travel-book was to vex. Erasmus could not, for souls were at stake. And Erasmus notes that the man is now 'much deeper drowned . . . than he was . . .'

The English Enchiridion

An English edition of the *Enchiridion* appeared in 1533, followed by a close revision in 1534. Both were 'printed at London by Wynkyn de Worde' in Fleet Street: neither gives the name of the translator. Tyndale left Little Sodbury some time in 1523 or early 1524 at the latest; the translation of the *Enchiridion* that Foxe says he presented to his master and mistress must have been in manuscript, unless there was an English edition printed before 1533—indeed, before 1523—which has since perished. It remains possible that he gave them a printed book, though any commercial print-run would have meant that enough copies would have been made for the hope that if not the volumes, some reference to them at least, might have survived. English translations of at least nine works by Erasmus, probably all slim octavos, extremely vulnerable to the numerous enemies of books, have disappeared. No record remains of an *Enchiridion* in English before 1533. What happened to the work Tyndale presented to the Walshes is not known.

The position is thus: on the one hand, there is Foxe making some capital out of his statement that Tyndale translated the work at Little

Sodbury, which must mean around 1522; on the other, an unattri-buted translation appears in London in 1533, with a revision in 1534. There is no means of joining up the two statements. Analysis of stylistic habits, in the English *Enchiridion* and in Tyndale, produces no clear result. Both writers use quite vivid illustrations from daily life: but that was standard in the tradition of classical exhortation as well as preaching. Stylistically, even though both write on a scriptural base, the sage and the translator show no common ground that is definitive, as the most recent editor of the English translation has very thoroughly demonstrated. 'The internal evidence for Tyndale's authorship of the 1533 *Enchiridion* is no more conclusive than the external evidence. There is a disappointing lack of correspondence between the scriptural references in the *Enchiridion* and in Tyndale's known biblical transla-tions.'[53] Comparison of the translation of Erasmus's frequent Scripture quotations (from the New Testament alone, ninety-odd from Matthew, some sixty from 1 Corinthians and about fifty from Romans) with Tyndale's translations is hampered, of course, by the fact that Erasmus is using the Latin Vulgate and Tyndale is using the Greek and Hebrew. Stylistic comparison of the English *Enchiridion* and Tyndale's non-biblical prose might reveal a little more similarity.[54] But lacking such a detailed comparison, which is not possible without future computer-generated concordances of all the works, it is impossible to tell on stylistic grounds only whether Tyndale did translate that English *Enchiridion* which Wynkyn de Worde printed. Various tests do not produce clear results. It could be that in trying to solve the problem the right questions are not yet being asked. There may be more to be learned about the Gloucestershire 'doctorly prelates' and the curious withdrawal of the Walshes' hospitality to them. A search for local Gloucestershire significance in some words or proverbs in the printed English *Enchridion* might be revealing. In her edition, the recent editor carefully notes the score of words in the *Enchiridion* which are in fact found first in Tyndale, the first use mis-dated by the Oxford English Dictionary. Patient work might reveal a local vocabulary in the printed translation: it must be said that a quick impression gives a sense that it did not originate in Gloucestershire. One unusual and obsolete word is interesting: the printed *Enchiridion* translator uses 'nyggyshe', mean-ing 'stingy', or 'niggardly', in chapter 21 (and there are two cognate words, 'nyggardes' and 'nyggishnes' elsewhere). The word 'nyggyshe' has a first use in the Oxford Dictionary attributed to Nicholas Udall in 1542 instead of the *Enchiridion* in 1533. It is not, apparently, a word Tyndale uses. It may, or may not, have local importance somewhere (Udall was a Hampshire man). Further computer-generated studies might also recognise the particularities of apprentice-work in Tyndale as a translator. Again, evidence of any effects of current theories of translation in Tyndale and in the English *Enchiridion* might repay study. We must hope for further light.

We might also hope for a convincing candidate for the translator other than Tyndale, who would possibly show reason for having been influenced by Tyndale. Such a man might be Nicholas Udall, user of 'nyggyshe', who a decade later became a significant translator of Erasmus into English. An Oxford man, for a while he was a fellow and tutor at Corpus Christi College; through his known purchase of Lutheran books from Thomas Garret, an Oxford bookseller who sympathised with Lutheran doctrines, in about 1525, Udall became known as one of the earliest adherents of Protestant theology among Oxford tutors. He was appointed headmaster of Eton in 1534, and is best known today for the creation of what is called the first comedy in English, *Ralph Roister Doister*, strongly based on the Latin playwright Terence, in the 1540s or 1550s. Udall might have found translating Erasmus's *Enchiridion* in the early 1530s a profitable exercise, not only to help him secure that prize headmastership at the age of twenty-eight, but because various sins of the flesh were attractive enough to him to cause his dismissal from Eton seven years later.[55] (He became a canon of Windsor, and finally headmaster of Westminster School.) In the 1540s, he translated with others, under Catherine Parr's patronage, the two volumes of the *Paraphrases of the New Testament* of Erasmus. The first volume, a very thick large folio of a thousand pages, was largely his: he finished translating Luke, the longest paraphrase, in 1545, and translated Matthew and Acts later. Thomas Key translated Mark. John was begun by no less a personage than Princess Mary, later Queen Mary, but she soon turned the work over to her chaplain.[56] In September 1542 he published the first English version of the third and fourth books of Erasmus's *Apophthegms*. When Udall in the *Paraphrases* quotes the New Testament in English, as he frequently does, he uses the Great Bible version, Coverdale's light revision of the work of Tyndale: it is thus startling to find here the work of Princess Mary Tudor. Udall could be thought to have known more of Tyndale's writing up to 1533.[57] Perhaps more experimental speculation such as this could be illuminating on the, at present, unbridgeable gap between Tyndale's gift to the Walshes and Wynkyn de Worde. There have been attempts that are interesting, but without support of any evidence, to make the printing of Tyndale's translation 'part of Cromwell's campaign to justify the possible break with Rome'.[58] For the present, the best that can be said is that Tyndale probably translated the *Enchiridion* at Little Sodbury, and presented his employers with a manuscript copy. His translation has disappeared: it may have influenced the one printed ten years later.

There remain two further questions. First, what, if anything is known about Tyndale's attitude to Erasmus in 1522? Was it likely that Tyndale, down from Oxford (and possibly Cambridge) might have turned to this Latin book as being important enough for him to spend considerable time translating it? In the year 1520 the Oxford book-seller John Dorne sold over one hundred and sixty items edited or written by Erasmus (all in Latin, of course, and almost all printed abroad).[59] In provincial England among the very few scattered learned clergy and courtiers who were in touch with the latest European and humanist thought, particularly on education, there would be some knowledge of the great deal that he had written, which by 1540, four years after his death, filled twelve large printed folio volumes. Particularly, his *Moriae encomium*, printed in Paris in 1509 (not translated in English as *The Praise of Folly* until 1549) was celebrated across Europe, as were his collections of proverbs, the *Adagia*, in various forms, beginning, again in Paris, in 1500. Indeed, one particular educational tool, the *Colloquiorum formulae*, first from Basle in 1516, was the most popular book of the century, with ninety editions to 1546. Though it is important not to exaggerate Erasmus's influence across England, beyond the humanist élite circle,[60] Foxe does record in his 1563 edition dinner-table conversation at Little Sodbury being 'as well of Luther and Erasmus Roterodamus, as of opinions in the Scripture . . .' By 1522, Tyndale might well have been working already with his Greek New Testament. The *Enchiridion*, being a short, handy, Scripture-based call to Christian morality in lay people, moderately critical of practices of the Church, by someone so well-known for sharp writing, someone moreover whose scholarly credentials were wonderfully impressive in the fields that were beginning to matter at the time—classical litera-ture, the earlier fathers, the Italian humanists, the essential New Testa-ment text—by a man who was himself a teacher and model of the very art of writing, would almost present itself to Tyndale's hand to be worked on. Tyndale was, however, critical of Erasmus at various points in his own writing (see, for example, in 'W.T. To the Reader' at the beginning of his Pentateuch[61]). Erasmus, fine Greek scholar and editor, was, to the hard men among the reformers, felt to be a fence-sitter when the issue was *sola fides* and the Scripture-based call for reform from outside the Church. Tyndale did draw his readers' attention to Erasmus's *Paraclesis* and *Paraphrase of Matthew* at the end of his preface to the reader introducing his *Obedience of a Christian Man*. On these grounds, it may be said that in 1522 Tyndale was well aware of the *Enchiridion*.

The second question takes us forward six years or so to 1528, and Tyndale's London benefactor, Humphrey Monmouth. This part of the story, four years after Tyndale sailed for Germany, will occupy a later chapter. Here we note that when Monmouth petitioned the King's Council on 19 May 1528, after his arrest for possession of heretical books, he included the remarks that Tyndale

> left me an English book, called *Enchiridion*. The which book the Abbess of Dennye desired it of me, and I sent it to her . . . Another book I had of the same copy: a friar of Greenwich desired it of me, and I gave it him. I think my Lord of Rochester hath it . . .

After mentioning other books in English, by Luther, he notes

> And all those books . . . lay openly in my house for the space of two years or more, that every man might read on them that would, at their pleasure. I never heard priest, nor friar, nor lay man find any great fault in them.

After he had heard Tunstall, Bishop of London, preach against Tyndale in 1526, he burned everything that he had of Tyndale's, including letters and sermons, 'with divers copies of books, that my servant did write . . .', adding that the servant who made the copies witnessed the burning.[62] That these 'books' included books in manuscript is obvious, and there is nothing strange in that. The question which teases a modern biographer is about how many copies of Tyndale's manuscript English *Enchiridion* there were. One went to the Walshes; one must have travelled with Tyndale to London, and possibly on to Germany. One was left with Humphrey Monmouth, and a copy of that was made by Monmouth's scribe for the Abbess of Denny, and another for a friar of Greenwich. The copies in Monmouth's house clearly interested 'priest . . . friar . . . [and] lay man', and the requested duplicates may well have fathered further copies. The more copies there were, by that much the more likely it becomes that it was a manuscript of Tyndale's version that arrived at Wynkyn de Worde's print-shop alongside St Bride's, Fleet Street, in November 1533.

Local Conflict

The 'doctorly prelates' in Gloucestershire, meanwhile, did not take kindly to the loss of Sir John and Lady Walsh's excellent hospitality at Little Sodbury. They plotted against Tyndale, who—rather than their own conservatism and ignorance, of course—was the cause of their loss of status with an important man and their equally grievous loss of good food and wine. They reported to the bishop's chancellor what he had said, and invented what he had inconveniently not said, to make it all add up to a charge of heresy. Tyndale was scathing in his account some seven years later, in 'W.T. To the Reader', the first preface to his Pentateuch of 1530.

> ... when I was so turmoiled in the country where I was that I could no longer there dwell (the process whereof were too long here to rehearse) I this wise thought in myself, this I suffer because the priests of the country be unlearned, as God it knoweth there are a full ignorant sort which have seen no more Latin than that they read in their portesses and missals which yet many of them can scarcely read, (except it be Albertus *de secretis mulierum* in which yet, though they be never so sorrily learned, they pore day and night, and make notes therein and all to teach the midwives as they say, and Linwode a book of constitutions to gather tithes, mortuaries, offerings, customs, and other pillage, which they call, not theirs, but God's part and the duty of holy church, to discharge their consciences withal: for they are bound that they shall not diminish, but increase all things unto the uttermost of their powers) and therefore (because they are thus unlearned, thought I) when they come together to the ale house, which is their preaching place, they affirm that my sayings are heresy. And besides that they add to of their own heads which I never spake, as the manner is to prolong the tale to short the time withal, and accused me secretly to the chancellor and other the bishop's officers.[63]

Foxe fills out the story in a passage which, in the 1563 edition, bears the marks of the continued verbatim narrative of Richard Webb:

> After that, when there was a sitting of the bishop's commisary or chancellor. And warning was given to the priests to appear, Master Tyndall was also warned to be there. And whether he had knowledge by their threatening, or that he did suspect that they would lay to his charge it is not now perfectly in my mind, but thus he told me, that he doubted their examinations, so that he in his going thitherwards prayed in his mind heartily to God to strengthen him to stand fast to the truth of his word, so he being there before them, they laid sore to his charge, saying he was an heretic in Sophistry, an heretic in Logic, an heretic in his divinity, and so continueth. But they said unto him, you bear yourself boldly of the Gentlemen here

in this country, but you shall be otherwise talked with. Then Master Tyndal answered them. I am content that you bring me where you will into any country within England, giving me ten pounds a year to live with. So you bind me to nothing, but to teach children and preach. Then they had nothing more to say to him, and thus he departed, and went home to his master again.[64]

Inside this account are two separate activities: the general antagonism and malice of local clergy, at various levels; and an official enquiry into him as reported heretic, which he was 'warned' to attend. The clergy who accused him, 'the priests' who were 'there', were present, if silent, when the chancellor interrogated him. Whether the absurd notions of heresy in sophistry and in logic as well as divinity came from the chancellor, from the malevolent and ignorant clerics, or from Foxe's informant, we cannot know. The chancellor, however, does not seem to have behaved with any dignity. This officer was one who acted for a bishop, holding courts for him to decide cases tried in ecclesiastical law; a powerful office and a useful step upwards. He would, for example, be required to attend to make sure that a heretic was properly burned alive, as in Richard Webb's story of the bull in Chipping Sodbury, and as was to happen at the end of Tyndale's life. Tyndale's own account, from the prologue to the Pentateuch, continues as follows:

And indeed, when I came before the chancellor, he threatened me grievously, and reviled me, and rated me as though I had been a dog, and laid to my charge whereof there could be none accuser brought forth (as their manner is not to bring forth the accuser) and yet all the priests of the country were the same day there.[65]

That nothing official happened further suggests that Tyndale won the day. The chancellor would not want to make himself in bad odour with the powerful families of Walsh and Poyntz, by banishing Sir John's servant, though had Tyndale truly been found a heretic, no doubt even that could have been arranged. Tyndale was not found a heretic. His appeal would have been to the New Testament, with which that chancellor, at least, was intelligent enough not to argue—he was John Bell, afterwards Bishop of Worcester. He saved his face by threatening and scolding severely, and, Tyndale suggests, quite intemperately. Tyndale's mild reply ('I am content . . .') would leave little room for further action, as well as asserting his own independence: he was a teacher and not a chaplain.

The encounter between Tyndale and chancellor seems to have been famous. Thomas More knew enough of it to mis-report it in his first shot in his campaign against Tyndale five or six years later, his *Dialogue* of June 1529. He doubles the 'examinations', and makes Tyndale yield the day, changing his tune to fit his accusers' requirements and swearing the changes on oath.

> Tyndale was taken for a man of sober and honest living, and looked and preached holily, saving that it sometimes savoured so shrewdly of heresy, that he was once or twice examined thereof. But yet, because he glossed these his words with a better sense, and said and swore that he meant no harm, folk were glad to take all for the best.[66]

The patronising tone of that last sentence is characteristic of More's strategy at that point in his attack. Tyndale in his *Answer* retorted that he made no oath, and was never asked for one.[67]

Tyndale had scotched the snake, not killed it. His local opponents were not likely to leave it at that. Indeed, he was specifically warned of the effect of further opening the Scriptures. Richard Webb's narrative continues:

> There dwelt not far off an old doctor, that had been archchancellor to a bishop, the which was of old familiar acquaintance with Master Tyndall, who also favoured him well: to whom Master Tyndall went, and opened his mind upon divers questions of the scriptures; for he durst boldly open unto him his mind. That ancient doctor said: Do you not know that the pope is the very antichrist, which the scripture speaketh of? But beware what ye say, for if ye shall be perceived to be of that opinion, it will cost you your life: and said, I have been an officer of his, but I have given it up, and defy him and all his works.[68]

Mozley reasonably conjectures that the 'old doctor' was William Latimer, the friend of Erasmus and of More, who had been teaching in Oxford while Tyndale was there, and who in his retirement held two livings in north-east Gloucestershire.[69] The advice was kindly meant, but it did not fit with Tyndale's growing realisation that the root of the matter was the clergy's ignorance of the New Testament—'this I suffer because the priests of the country be unlearned', as we saw him express it above. Those with any knowledge of Latin would be glossing and allegorising a few texts of Scripture, twisting them into the curious shapes that the Church's centuries-old tradition of exegesis expected—and using the Latin Scriptures, of course, which in places differed markedly (and conveniently) from the Greek originals.[70] But the proportion of clergy who could understand the Latin they read was very small. While Tyndale was in Little Sodbury, William Warham, Archbishop of Canterbury, was complaining of the monks who performed the services that they were 'wholly ignorant of what they read'.[71] Even in 'God's Gloucestershire', thirty years later, investigation under the reforming Bishop Hooper famously reveals details not only of the 'negligence and ungodly behaviour of the ministers of Gloucestershire' but 'inhospitable, non-resident, inefficient, drunken and evil-living incumbents, who were to be found in every deanery'. The vicar of Wotton-under-Edge had to answer a charge of forging a will.[72] Their ignorance was great.

> Of the unsatisfactory clergy in 1551, nine did not know how many commandments there were, 33 did not know where they appeared in the Bible (the gospel of St Matthew was a favourite guess) and 168 could not repeat them. Concerning the Creed, 10 could not repeat it and 216 were unable to prove it: a large number of these said that they were perfectly satisfied that it was right because the king and Mother Church said so. Most extraordinary of all, perhaps, were the results of the Lord's Prayer part of the examination: 39 did not know where it appeared in the Bible, 34 did not know who was its author, and 10 actually proved unable to recite it.[73]

On 10 August 1551 John Trigg of Dursley was given penance 'that is upon Sunday next coming [he] shall be in his shirt only, standing upon a form, and there shall openly say that I suffer this penance because I can not say one of the commandments of all-mighty God, but I am more like an ethnic than a Christian man'. John Cooke of Wotton-under-Edge was presented for adultery, and said 'Be that as be may, I know the law is for me to have children by adultery. I would wish Moses' law to be again'.[74] These things happened a quarter of a century after Tyndale left England.

Earlier, in London, things had been just as bad. Immediately on his consecration as Bishop of London in November 1530, Stokesley investigated his curates 'in letters and in their capacity and suitability for those things which pertain to the cure of souls'. In one result, of fifty-six men examined, twenty-two were barred from practising in the London diocese on account of their ignorance. Two of these were MAs and two were canons of Waltham Abbey. Six more were allowed to remain 'provided that they studied and later convinced the bishop of their competence'.[75]

Until it was available in English as a whole book, the humble layman and woman had even less chance of knowing what the New

Testament said: it might have been in Chinese for all the sense the Latin made, though some scattered New Testament phrases circulated as proverbs in English, and a few might have seen parts of a Lollard Bible. Tyndale saw that what was needed was a New Testament in English from the Greek. Richard Webb's narrative concludes, famously:

> And soon after, Master Tyndall happened to be in the company of a learned man, and in communing and disputing with him drove him to that issue that the learned man said, we were better be without God's law than the pope's: Maister Tyndall hearing that, answered him, I defy the Pope and all his laws, and said, if God spare my life ere many years, I will cause a boy that driveth the plough, shall know more of the scripture than thou dost.[76]

The words echo Erasmus in his *Paraclesis*. Tyndale's problem was finding a high enough authority to work under, to exempt him from the fatal charge of heresy under the Constitutions of Oxford. Thoughts of Erasmus directed Tyndale's mind to London.

Part 2

GREEK INTO ENGLISH

Chapter 4

TO LONDON

Tyndale himself continues the story in the first preface to his Pentateuch. He had recognised the need for the Scriptures in the mother
tongue. His own bad experiences had been 'because the priests of the
country be unlearned', unable to expound Scripture to the laity,
whose needs were desperate. Everyone should be able to see 'the
process, order, and meaning' of the Bible.

> As I this thought, the bishop of London came to my remembrance
> whom Erasmus (whose tongue maketh of little gnats great elephants
> and lifteth up above the stars whosoever giveth him a little exhi-
> bition) praiseth exceedingly among other in his annotations on
> the new testament for his learning . . . And even in the bishop of
> London's house I intended to have done it . . .'[1]

The bishop of London since 1522 had been Cuthert Tunstall. As
Tyndale was aware, Erasmus used flattery, sometimes to excess. He
needed somewhere comfortable to live, food and like-minded company, as everyone does, and he rarely had a regular salary: buttering the
great might make patronage come more easily. Such conventional
praise of Tunstall from Erasmus, carefully exaggerated (and not in the
Annotations) was not to be taken too seriously: it seems to have been
part of an ironic game he played with the good and the great. Erasmus
does praise this man, though not in the *Annotations*.[2]

It was not naive of Tyndale as scholar and fellow 'Grecian' to
approach Tunstall, probably in the summer of 1523. Cuthbert Tunstall
had been at Oxford with More, Colet and Linacre, a dozen years
before Tyndale, and then gone on to Cambridge. He had studied in
Padua, where Linacre and Grocyn had been, from about 1499 to 1505
or 1506. Among his friends in Italy were, as well as Aldus Manutius
(the founder of the influential Aldine press at Venice) the English

classical scholar William Latimer.[3] If Latimer was the old doctor who received a visit from Tyndale in Gloucestershire twenty years later, in about 1522, then perhaps it was he put who the name of Cuthbert Tunstall into Tyndale's 'remembrance'. Tyndale might have known (perhaps again from Latimer) that Tunstall had helped Erasmus with the second edition of his Greek New Testament, working on it with him at Brussels, Ghent and Bruges during the later months of 1516 and the first half of 1517. Tunstall had lent Erasmus a Greek New Testament manuscript, had consulted Greek codices for him in cases of doubt, and suggested a number of emendations.[4] For William Tyndale, Tunstall would be the ideal patron: a significant Greek scholar, at the forefront of making editions of the New Testament, holding an office which would give Tyndale the necessary authority to override the Constitutions of Oxford. Moreover, London was where the printers were and the metropolis was the centre of the web of communications in Britain, for the easier dissemination of his finished translation.

The true nature of Tunstall, a moderate, learned man, is now quite difficult to grasp. Almost a saint to what one might call the Catholic humanists, almost an ogre to the pious reformed, he warrants neither label. He was generally a considerate and considering cleric and politician who shunned the certainties at either extreme, and moved in a reasonable way through the difficulties that presented themselves in his long life. Eleven years old when the Battle of Bosworth was fought and Henry VII was crowned, he ended his days under Elizabeth, at the age of eighty-five, having seen five reigns. Respected in Europe as a mathematician as well as classicist; diplomatic emissary, adviser to generals and governors; Bishop of London, and then of Durham, at times of particular religious conflict; named on the title-pages of the fourth and sixth editions of the Great Bible (still largely Tyndale's work), he was praised for eloquence and wit. And, one must note, humaneness. In the eight years that he was Bishop of London, no heretic was burned (books were a different matter). It was his successor Stokesley who, from 1530 when he took over the bishopric from Tunstall, started again the burning of people alive: as we shall see below, both Bayfield and Tewkesbury, who had abjured under Tunstall, relapsed under Stokesley and were executed by him. 'The county of Durham, while he [Tunstall] was bishop from 1530, saw no burnings in the nation-wide persecutions under Mary.'[5] He is recorded with praise even on Thomas More's tomb, where he is 'Tunstall . . . than whom the world contains today scarcely anyone more learned, sagacious or good'.[6] Tunstall's book on arithmetic was dedicated to More. In the opening lines of *Utopia*, no less, after perfunctory mentions of

Henry VIII and Prince Charles of Castile, the rest of the paragraph is given to Tunstall:

> An excellent person . . . his learning and moral character . . . are too remarkable for me to describe adequately, and too well known to need describing at all.[7]

The oblique manner is typical of the book: the praise is empty, Tunstall's worth being carefully *not* expressed. It is to be matched with the mock letter to Busleiden a few pages before, referring to 'Thomas More—who is, I'm sure you'll agree, one of the glories of our age'.[8] With Erasmus leading, between all the friends there is a game of flavouring the customary flattery with a pinch of mockery: yet Tunstall does come across as an Englishman of unusual learning at a time when that was rare.

It was not foolish of Tyndale the scholar to approach Tunstall. It was innocent of him, politically, however, not to expect that news of him as a trouble-maker from Gloucestershire with radical proposals had not preceded him. With the best intentions, William Latimer might have written from Gloucestershire to his old friend Tunstall. Any one of the senior clergy in Gloucestershire might have 'had a word', as the Establishment phrase still has it, with an emissary of the current bishop. Stokesley himself, soon to take over his job, and with access to the goings-on in the Vale of Berkeley, might have dropped something in Tunstall's ear.

> Then thought I, if I might come to this man's service, I were happy. And so I gat me to London, and, through the acquaintance of my master [Sir John Walsh] came to sir Harry Gilford, the king's grace's controller, and brought him an oration of Isocrates which I had translated out of Greek into English, and desired him to speak unto my lord of London [Tunstall] for me, which he also did as he shewed me, and willed me to write an epistle to my lord, and to go to him myself which I also did, and delivered my epistle to a servant of his own, one William Hebilthwayte, a man of mine old acquaint-ance. But God which knoweth what is within hypocrites, saw that I was beguiled, and that that counsel was not the next way unto my purpose. And therefore he gat me no favour in my lord's [Tunstall's] sight.
>
> Whereupon my lord answered me, his house was full, he had more than he could well find, and advised me to seek in London, where he said I could not lack a service . . . I . . . understood at the last . . . that there was no room in my lord of London's palace to translate the new testament . . .[9]

Not for the last time, Tyndale was too trusting. The otherwise unknown William Hebilthwayte, of 'old acquaintance' (possibly from
Oxford days) did him no good at all, and might have done harm. In
Tyndale's narrative two things come across: first, the sense of the
deviousness of influences around the palace, for which Tyndale was
quite unprepared; and second, that, for all that he was rebuffing him,
Tunstall treated Tyndale not unharshly. Whether Tunstall gave Tyndale
an audience, wrote him a letter or sent a message is not clear: but the
tone of his reply is considerate; he did not bark at him, accuse him
or forbid him to work in London. He courteously recommended
a course of action, and indicated that he understood the value of
Tyndale's intentions ('he said I could not lack a service'). Tyndale later
called Tunstall a 'still Saturn, that so seldom speaketh, but walketh up
and down all day musing, a ducking hypocrite made to dissemble'.[10]
That sounds like personal recollection, and it may be that when
Tyndale went to London House, Tunstall's large palace close to the
north-west end of Old St Paul's,[11] the Bishop signalled his importance
as a man at the centre of affairs. Tyndale was close to Tunstall's palace
probably not long after 15 April 1523, when the Bishop had addressed
at its opening the only Parliament summoned under Wolsey's supremacy (the previous Parliament had met in 1515, the next would
not be until 1529). On that occasion, Tunstall had spoken for a full
hour on the nature of kingship and Parliament. He was praised for his
speech by King Henry, who had been present. Weeks later Tunstall
was, according to the Venetian ambassador, 'constantly occupied from
morning till night on account of this Parliament';[12] this would account
for Tunstall's house being full. Tyndale's timing was perhaps unfortunate. The summoning of the Parliament had been a desperate throw by
Wolsey, demanding money effectively for his own schemes of advance-
ment. It lasted four months, at the end of which he had only half of
what he wanted. Wolsey was, in Mozley's words, 'the best-hated man
in the kingdom'.[13]

Tunstall as a churchman was embroiled in the highest politics,
officially opening this contentious Parliament, already himself Lord
Privy Seal, stepping carefully through a political minefield. It is remarkable, therefore, that though he snubbed Tyndale he did not, at
that stage, do more: his mind seems to have been more open to the
idea of a printed vernacular New Testament from the Greek than it
was a few years later. By then, of course, the enterprise of Bible-
printing was heavily tainted with the name and work of Luther, and
root-and-branch opposition to all such 'heresy' was organised by
Wolsey to please the Pope.

Sir Henry Guildford, to whom Tyndale first applied, was a lively, active courtier in his thirties, close to the King. He was Master of the Horse and Controller of the Royal Household. At Henry's coronation Guildford was twenty, and a favourite with the new young King, given to putting on elaborate performances for the Court. The Tyndale link must have been through Sir John Walsh, who at about the same age revelled as another close companion around the newly crowned King. (It was Guildford who had organised the famous sudden arrival of Robin Hood and his companions into the chamber of the startled Queen on 18 January 1510: she had had the presence of mind to quell her fright and be graciously welcoming, happily, as 'Robin Hood' revealed himself as—surprise, surprise—the King.[14]) In Tyndale's account of his arrival in London, what should again be noted, however, is what it was that he took with him, to demonstrate his ability as a translator of Greek, that is, 'an oration of Isocrates'. This was to be given to the courtier Guildford, who was also a classical scholar who certainly corresponded with Erasmus, and possibly with Cuthbert Tunstall. The significance of this has not yet been fully noticed. Such a translation indicates several things of importance, as suggested above, not least that Tyndale's classical Greek was very good.

'An Oration of Isocrates'

Isocrates' older fellow-orator, Gorgias (485–375 BC), refined his techniques of persuasion to the point where he could teach his pupils to argue either side of a case, and even how to make the worse or weaker cause appear the better or stronger.[15] Isocrates set himself against such moral irresponsibility and claimed for rhetoric an altogether higher and nobler role. He made rhetoric the basis of education in the Greek world, and thus in the Roman world, and thus eventually in 'the west'. Isocrates wrote to Alexander the Great setting out his loftier claims, which embraced the 'art of speech'—the latter word there being *logos*. For that he made exceptional claims: that study of it would, he wrote, produce virtue, enlarge the mind, and create philosophers or statesmen full of eloquent wisdom. One can see at once the attraction of Isocrates's mind for someone like Tyndale who had the Greek of the first chapter of John's Gospel in his head, with its meditation on the incarnation of the *logos*.

Isocrates established his work of integration in the school he opened a little before Plato founded his Academy in about 385 BC.[16] This integrating of rhetoric and lofty ideals was then undone by Socrates, a dislocation which was recorded by Plato. Socrates' own analysis and criticism of Isocrates became itself an influential book on rhetoric by Socrates' pupil Aristotle. In Rome, it was Cicero who reinstated the highest claims for the work of the orator. Thus, for Tyndale to be offering a work of Isocrates is for him to be showing himself to be going back to the fountainhead of a system of rhetoric thought of as a main source of virtue. Interestingly, twenty years after Tyndale's journey to London, the Cambridge Greek scholar and humanist Roger Ascham, tutor to Princess Elizabeth, singled out Isocrates for special attention. The Greek that was done with his royal pupil, the future queen, seems to have been confined to Isocrates and the New Testament: we notice again the high level of Greek knowledge, and the conjunction of the two texts which Tyndale had in his head when he went to London.

The greatest of Isocrates' orations in both structure and expression is the *Panegyricus* or 'festival oration' written about 380 BC. We do not know which oration Tyndale took with him, but this has a claim to special attention, and there would be some appropriateness. Its message is that all Greeks should unite against the barbarians—of interest to Tyndale, perhaps, from inside the camp of the somewhat beleaguered English 'Grecians'. Moreover, the leadership, says Isocrates here, belongs to Athens. His declaration that only Athens herself united all the widespread Greek traditions and cultures might be thought to warm the heart of a bishop of London entangled with interference from Wolsey in the north and from Rome. Isocrates in this oration makes resonant claims for the greatness of Athenian speech, which would be appropriate for Tyndale's declared hope of uniting the whole nation, clerical and lay alike, through knowledge of the Scriptures in English, the language of London, and not Latin, the language of Rome.

Structurally, the *Panegyricus* oration shows a unity of elevated theme and method, and is best taken whole. But the passage just mentioned, about the greatness of the speech of Athens, is worth considering a little further. Isocrates was famous for very long sentences—a glance at a text by his fellow-orator Demosthenes marks the comparison. Isocrates' passage about the speech of Athens is one long sentence. Yet it is triumphantly clear. To make that clarity, he uses a system of statements and dependent clauses, with special work done by the patterning of the verbs. It is possible to set out that sentence in English in diagram form, making the logical pattern immediately visible: such a diagram is given at the end of this book in Appendix C. With it, as Appendices A and B, are similar diagrams setting out in B the thought-pattern of part of Tyndale's most important original book, *The Obedience of a Christian Man* (1530), and in A, the pattern of the whole of *The Parable of the Wicked Mammon*. Tyndale's sentences are not quite as long as Isocrates's, and it is not being claimed here that we are dealing with a source. Yet the method of that particular kind of logical development, basically learned at Oxford, practised in preaching, reaching rich fruition in the *Obedience* well over a dozen years after Oxford, could well have owed something to Isocrates, to the *Panegyricus*, and even to that long sentence commending the mother tongue.[17]

Tyndale's translation has disappeared; it is most unlikely that it will ever turn up in unknown Guildford (or Tunstall) papers. It must be assumed that he made it in Gloucestershire. Isocrates was in print in Greek in an edition of the *Orationes* published in Milan in 1493, which includes the *Panegyricus*. He was included in a three-volume collection of Greek orators printed by Aldus Manutius in Venice in 1513, which also includes the *Panegyricus*. (The *Panegyricus* does not seem to have been printed on its own in Greek until 1786, and not on its own in English until 1848.) In other words, on the one hand Tyndale records that he made a translation, and on the other there are the two available printed editions—and once again there is no means of joining up the two statements. Did he have a copy of the Milan or Venice editions with him in his attic room at Little Sodbury? Or did he stay in Oxford to use the university library? That held the 1493 Milan edition and Aldus's collection of orators—or at least it did in 1843, as shown by the printed catalogue of that year. The university library also had Isocrates in Latin in manuscript, though it seems not including the *Panegyricus*, given to the university by Duke Humphrey between 1435 and 1444. Both New College and Queen's have copies of the Milan 1493 Greek edition. New College also has a manuscript written by Ioannes Serbopoulos at Reading Abbey in 1494, containing two of the orations (again not the *Panegyricus*).[18] When the various Isocrates manuscripts and printed books arrived in Oxford, and from what source, is now almost impossible to establish. The majority of New College's Greek manuscripts and printed books came in the bequest of Cardinal Pole, who died in 1558; whether the bequest included that particular Serbopoulos manuscript is unknown; other Oxford men (Grocyn and Linacre, earlier) also had manuscripts from him.[19]

It is all guesswork. We do not know any details, and most probably never shall. Yet we can hold to the evidence we have: the Isocrates translation tells us that Tyndale had good Greek before he arrived in London; and no-one could translate Isocrates and remain unaware of the tropes and figures of rhetoric, or unregarding of that rhetoric being the vehicle of high ideal purposes, all with the persuasive power of the familiar complex logical development. Moreover, even if it was not the *Panegyricus* that Tyndale took, the translation of any oration of Isocrates represents a formidable amount of work. In the 1493 Milan edition the *Panegyricus* occupies thirty-nine large folio pages of Greek, and others are not much less. For comparison: this is easily the length of Mark's Gospel with half of Luke as well; or the Epistles to the Romans and 1 and 2 Corinthians combined. Tyndale would also be demonstrating his skill as a translator into English. The sixteenth century was the great age of the arrival of ancient texts in English, to very fruitful effect. From Douglas's *Aeneid*, through Golding's Ovid to North's Plutarch, Chapman's Homer and Holland's Livy, to name the first that come to mind, the aim is not just to make the classical text available: it is also to demonstrate that English can be noble enough, and flexible enough, to carry the freight. That Golding's Ovid, North's Plutarch and Chapman's Homer went into the creation of English works able even to rival the great originals, the plays of Shakespeare, suggests what was happening to the language. Such 'Englishing' of texts was not the production of Latin and Greek cribs. Just as Erasmus was introducing to schoolboys a Latin that was not barbarous, so the translators were reaching for, and helping to make, an English that was noble. They were demonstrating, consciously and carefully, what English could do. That was a craft where Tyndale was superbly a master. We must not forget the fact that, some time before 1522, so early in the century, he was the first recorded translator of Isocrates into English. It was not until 1534 that the first printed English translation of an oration was published, by Sir Thomas Elyot, as *The Doctrinal of Princes*: it was of the *Ad Nicoclem*, the oration that tends to occur most frequently in the Greek selections.

The Theories of Translation

Tyndale would also be demonstrating his practice as a translator, a matter of keen interest to scholars and alert readers. From classical times, the art of translating was a natural sister of grammar, with rhetoric as a member of the family. Necessity was the mother of this particular invention: the Hebrew Bible needed to live in a Greek, and then Latin, world. Christianity needed Latin after its original Aramaic and Greek. Philosophy, medicine and agriculture went from Greek and Latin to far afield. At the level of grammar, the bare fact is the transposition of single words. With rhetoric arrives the possibility of clothing the bare fact with various styles, from various intentions. Instantly, a hugely important rift appears. Do you translate word for word or sense for sense? Horace translated the opening lines of Homer's *Odyssey* both ways, instructively. Cicero wanted to observe Latin idiom, and translate not word for word but figure by figure. Interpreters of Virgil ranged from strictly word for word at one extreme to the wholly allegorical at the other.[20] Jerome, for his own high reasons, translated the Bible into the Latin which became the Vulgate, word for word, on the grounds that a sacred text should not be interfered with. One result of that was the overly-philological attempt at accuracy which plagues parts of the Authorised Version's major prophets, where verse after verse is incomprehensible in English ('The heart also of the rash shall understand knowledge . . . The vile person shall no more be called liberal'[21]). In classrooms from classical times there grew a combination of comment, paraphrase, translation and gloss which in its opportunity for mixture avoided doctrinaire solutions, and was clearly the broad way forward. Whether that combination would be suitable across the territory where precision was felt to be imperative, as in legal, medical, philosophical and above all religious texts, had to be worked out. Translators of the Bible used all four almost from the earliest times. What has usefully been called 'stencil translation'[22] had a tendency to take over in, for example, philosophy, where the terms used often hardened from some generality into words that were technical and exclusive. The great task came with the rise of the European vernaculars, accompanying the growth of printing. Here was a new opportunity, to make the classical texts, so unreachably higher, live fully in the vulgar tongues. The matter was discussed for centuries, from the sixteenth onwards, and is still rumbling in prefaces today. Perhaps the highest statement of the total approach a translator should have is made by Chapman in 1598:

> The worth of a skilful and worthy translator is to observe the sentences, figures and forms of speech proposed in his author, his true sense and height, and to adorn them with figures and forms of oration fitted to the original in the same tongue to which they are translated: and these things I would gladly have made the questions of whatsoever my labours have deserved.[23]

The high Renaissance translator was no harmless drudge or lowly artisan; he was an artist and inventor, able to alter both the past and the future, to change the ways of a nation.[24]

The English *Enchiridion* may not be Tyndale's, and the Isocrates is missing. But though we cannot use those, we can note here for the future that William Tyndale brought to the work of translating an unusually thorough and almost alarmingly single-minded grasp of all the technical skills involved, and then used them to do two things. First, to understand the Greek and Hebrew of the original Bible texts as well as it was then humanly possible to do. Secondly, to write an English that above all, and at all times, made sense. Comparison of some knottier moments in Paul or the Old Testament, in the Authorised Version attempts and in Tyndale, shows that at once. As we shall see, Tyndale makes some sense of the almost completely baffling descriptions of the furnishings of the Temple in the later chapters of Exodus, in 1 Kings 6 and 7, and 2 Chronicles 3 and 4. Elsewhere, when Hebrew poetry produces nonsense if taken literally, Tyndale's quest for sense can help him to inspired renderings. On top of this is his extraordinary gift for uniting the skill of making sense of an original with the music of spoken English at its best ('Lay not thy hands upon the child neither do anything at all unto him, for now I know that thou fearest God . . .' 'Art thou he that shall come, or shall we look for another?'[25]).

Printed Vernacular Translations

And so in London I abode almost a year, and marked the course of the world . . . and saw things whereof I defer to speak at this time and understood at the last not only that there was no room in my lord of London's palace to translate the New Testament, but also that there was no place to do it in all England, as experience doth now openly declare.[26]

So Tyndale concludes the story in the prologue to his Pentateuch. It is all the information we have of those twelve months except for the bare facts from Foxe that he preached in St Dunstan's in Fleet Street, and came to know the merchant Sir Henry Monmouth.

It had dawned on Tyndale that England was to remain without a printed vernacular translation of the Bible. Worse, it was to continue to be the one European country in that position. The first printed translation of the Bible in German had been published in Strasburg in 1466, nearly sixty years before Tyndale arrived in London. A second version followed in about 1470, and by 1483 there had been nine. By the time of Luther's New Testament in 1522, there had been fourteen separate identifiable printed German vernacular Bibles, several depending on the earlier ones, to be sure, but demonstrating an active market. In addition, there had been several Psalters and four Bibles in Low German, the western dialect. All these were from the Vulgate. The earlier ones, printing a manuscript version of about 1350, resembled the first Wyclif Bible in England in being not always comprehensible. As books they were not, it must be said, objects of beauty: the description of them as 'huge cubes of board and paper, almost impossible to carry and even to use' is accurate.[27] Yet they do show that a German Bible was expected to sell well. Luther improved the looks as well as the comprehensibility. His first Testaments and Bibles were still big, however: it was Tyndale who began with smart, small, but very readable pocket-sized volumes, with his New Testaments and Pentateuch. A fuller account of Luther's 'September Testament' of 1522 and its wide influence will appear in a later chapter: we note here that by the time Tyndale went to London, in addition to the earlier vernacular German Bibles, most of the Bible had been translated into German from Greek and Hebrew by Luther, in large print-runs and frequent reprints. Several other German printed translations of parts of the Bible between 1521 and 1524 had appeared but were quickly swamped by Luther's superior version.

The first printed Bible translation in French dates from about 1474, a New Testament several times reprinted, with a condensed version of the whole Bible in 1498 also reprinted. The New Testament, almost certainly the work of Jacques le Fèvre d'Étaples, which appeared in 1523, was later placed on the Roman Catholic Index of prohibited books for its Protestant tone, though it was largely from the Vulgate, with only some input from Erasmus's Greek. In Italy, the real home of vernacular printing, the first Italian printed Bible (from Latin) appeared in 1471, reprinted several times. The idea of a printed Italian Bible from Greek and Hebrew was for some time in the air; a New Testament from Erasmus's Greek did not appear until 1530. In Spain, a Catalan translation of the whole Bible was printed in 1478 and parts appeared in Spanish and Portuguese before 1500, and after; the first Spanish New Testament from the Greek was not until 1543. The first printed New Testament in Czech appeared in 1475, with a Bible in 1488. A Dutch complete Bible was printed in 1477, and another in 1478 by Peter Quentell of Cologne. In Scandinavia, as in the Netherlands, the impact of Luther's translation was strong, leading to a Danish New Testament in 1524, and work on a Swedish translation.

Where, in all this, was English? Tyndale must have been puzzled as well as grieved as it became clear that 'there was no place to do it in all England'. Not only had England missed generations of printed vernaculars in the previous fifty years, the recent double impact of Erasmus's 1516 *Novum instrumentum* and Luther's ground-breaking 1522 New Testament, felt in every European country, stopped at the English Channel. There were scholars in England—not many, but enough—like himself, with sufficiently good Greek to turn Erasmus's edition into English. Someone like Cuthbert Tunstall might have been expected to jump at the chance offered by Tyndale. What was wrong? Possibly Tunstall's snub could be put down to his own day-to-day political pressures. Yet in spite of the Bishop's assurance that Tyndale would find a place in London, he did not. There was no-one who would support the work. Why that was, is a difficult matter to evaluate now. Tyndale was only a few years ahead of the trend in London; a dozen years later Henry VIII allowed a complete Bible in English to be 'set forth with the king's own gracious licence': that was 'Matthew's Bible', two-thirds of which was by then the work of Tyndale himself. The English Greek scholars were also mostly churchmen, of course, and the Catholic Church was terrified of losing control; but what was different about England, when for sixty years there had been vernacular Bibles in Europe, with a new strong scholarly wave of translating from the Greek now rolling in? There were the Constitutions of Oxford. To translate the Bible into the vernacular remained illegal—in England alone. They could have been overturned, given the will. Was it the legacy of Wyclif that was still so powerful? Were the Lollards, at all levels of society, maintaining the Wycliffite anti-prelatical, anti-ceremonial, pro-vernacular-Bible tenets of Wyclif stronger than was officially acknowledged, even in the early 1520s? Within a few years, Lollards were again to be vigorously attacked as heretics, but that persecution had probably not started when Tyndale confronted Tunstall. The immediate answer was Luther. Luther's 1522 German New Testament was the subject of a critique drawn up in 1523 at the request of Duke Georg of Saxony, which listed in it hundreds of 'heretical errors and lies'. In the three years between the Diet of Worms and Tyndale arriving in London, there had been much fear of the sudden spread of Lutheranism, a fear actively encouraged by Wolsey: that it would bring anarchy, schism and the dislocation of authority. Lutheran books had been publicly burned in Cambridge and in London. Lutherans as well as Lollards were now sought out for punishment.

A less instant answer, however, and one that becomes increasingly fashionable among some English historians, is that Luther's ideas and methods, such as vernacular translation from the original languages, had to be stamped out because they interfered from outside with a process already well under way in which the English Church was reforming itself from within. Left to herself, so the argument goes, Mother Church would in her own time, have removed the more outrageous evidences of corruption (like selling indulgences to raise money for the opulence of St Peter's in Rome) and allowed the ordinary Christians in the parishes to continue undisturbed the strong and vigorous tradition of their valued and necessary spiritual experiences, ceremony by ceremony, day by day, mass by mass, from the first Sunday in Advent to the twenty-fifth Sunday after Trinity, from baptism through all the constellation of rituals to last rites. It is an idealised, indeed erroneous, picture. For one thing, it omits most of the Christian experience as found in the New Testament. For another, it does not notice that the Church's tyrannical defence of its own absoluteness ensured its downfall. For a third here follows an extract from the preface to the Rheims New Testament translated into English from the Vulgate in 1582, the Catholic answer to the demand for a vernacular Bible:

> Yet we must not imagine that in the primitive Church . . . the translated Bibles into the vulgar tongues, were in the hands of every husbandman, artificer, prentice, boys, girls, mistress, maid, man . . . No, in those better times men were neither so ill, nor so curious of themselves, so to abuse the blessed book of Christ . . . The poor ploughman, could then in labouring the ground, sing the hymns and psalms either in known or unknown languages, as they heard them in the holy Church, though they could neither read nor know the sense, meaning and mysteries of the same . . .[28]

Many of the arguments put forward by Catholic revisionists will be, and are, challenged.[29] One in particular concerns us here. There is a very basic need of ordinary Christians to know what the Bible, all the Bible, says, in their own tongue. By 1520 that had been supplied, often generations earlier, in every European country except England. It is suggested that the English Church would eventually have given the laity an English New Testament, smoothly absorbed into all the ceremonies and devotions, without the harsh disruption of the Lutheran Reformation. On the one hand, that evidence from the Rheims New Testament, sixty years later, shows that the laity were going to have to wait a very long time indeed—and then be given the Word not from the Greek and Hebrew, but the Latin Vulgate put into English. On the other, the claim that is made, that the process could be seen to have already begun, needs examining carefully.

Printed English Gospels before Tyndale?

The argument that the Church already had a tradition of giving the people the Bible for devotional use, and, coming from within the

Church, such an English Bible would have avoided all the doctrinal disturbance that happened,[30] is a little curious, as the Bible in English brings its own disturbance to the sort of condition the Church was in. More than curious, indeed seriously alarming, is the implication of the illustration of the process already in action, of Gospels, printed in English, already available, from before 1500. In England in the late Middle Ages, as well as the Wycliffite Bibles, there were small portions of the Gospels and other parts of the Bible in manuscript for liturgical or devotional reading, often with extensive commentary, in several forms including Primers or Books of Hours.[31] They were technically prohibited under the Constitutions of Oxford of 1408, unless approved by a bishop. In 1410, Thomas Arundel, Archbishop of Canterbury, the originator of the Constitutions of two years before which forbade the translation of any part of the Bible into English, himself approved a compilation by Nicholas Love, a kind known as a 'Mirror of the Life of Christ', where a few brief passages were arranged to make a sort of harmony of the four Gospels. Nicholas Love was the Prior of the Carthusian Monastery of Mount Grace de Ingleby in Yorkshire. His book was a translation from a Latin work popular all over Europe, the *Meditationes vitae Christi* attributed to the Augustinian Cardinal Bonaventura. Medieval lives of Christ were of various kinds, with very short, simple biblical paraphrases at one extreme, through homilies, to emotional reflections, for devotional use, hung on the briefest of references to the Gospel texts. Bonaventura's *Meditationes* belongs to the latter kind. It does not pretend to be a hard-edged life of Christ, though the many headings may suggest that. Nicholas Love both cut and added to the original. His aim, he said, was to be more accessible than the original, and he was anxious that 'the blessed life of Jesu should be written in English'. It was written to supersede the Lollard translations of the Gospels, and attracted anti-Lollard scribal remarks.[32] Archbishop Arundel's approval was for the reading by the devout, and it was popular among the orthodox. It was printed by Caxton in 1486, and again in 1490 under its Latin title, *Speculum vitae Christi*, by Pynson probably in 1495, and by Wynkyn de Worde in 1517 and 1523. Twenty-three copies are known today.[33] It is claimed that this book is an example of the printed New Testament in English circulating before Tyndale.[34] If that claim is true, then it is of course most important.

Gospel harmonies are a very ancient form which loosely conflate incidents in the four Gospels to give one harmonious narrative. They were originally in Latin, and from the ninth century in Europe in the vernacular. Printed harmonies appeared first in Latin at the end of the fifteenth century: there are about fifteen from 1470 until 1535 (and many thereafter), all printed in Europe and all but two concentrating on the Passion story. After Love's *Mirror*, the next printed harmony in English did not appear until 1584, a version with a commentary by Calvin. If Love's book is a true Gospel harmony printed in English, then it does indeed alter the picture of the Reformation in England, and disrupt our traditional view of the importance of Tyndale.

Let us look at what is in the *Mirror*. It consists of sixty-four chapters, divided into the seven days of the week under their Latin names; each chapter has a title referring in the main to events in the life of Christ. For example, chapters 16, 17 and 18 are headed 'How our lord Jesu began to teach and gather disciples', 'Of the miracle done at the bridal of water turned into wine', and 'Of the excellent sermon of our Lord Jesu in the hill'. This seems promising. Turn up the latter chapter, however, expecting the Sermon on the Mount, the three chapters of Matthew (5, 6 and 7), and what appears is very unlike the New Testament. Love begins his chapter 16 by explaining that Jesus led his disciples up a hill 'and there he made them a long sermon full of fruit'. And that is all. After 'fruit' he goes at once to Augustine, notes the importance of poverty, and then gives many pages to quoting the fathers on the *Pater Noster*, with occasional phrases from that prayer given in English. It is, I am sure, useful for meditation, but it is not what is in the Gospels.

The seventh chapter, 'Of the circumcision of our Lord Jesus' (a matter dealt with in half a dozen words in Luke) consists of many pages of Mary's feelings and words, as, for example:

> Dear Son, if thou wilt that I cease of weeping, cease also thy weeping: for I may not but I weep, what time that I see thee weep. And so through the compassion of the mother the child ceased of sobbing and weeping. And then his mother, wiping his face and kissing him and putting the pap in his mouth, comforted him in all the manners that she might . . .

It is touching, but it is not in the New Testament.

'Jesus came from Nazareth of Galilee and was baptised of John in Jordan', says Mark's Gospel: twelve words in the Greek. Here is the *Mirror*:

> After that twenty-nine years were complete in which our Lord Jesu had lived in penance and abjection, as it is said, in the beginning of his thirtieth year, he spake to his mother and said: Dear mother, it is now time that I go to glorify and make known my father, and also

to show my self to the world, and to work the salvation of man's
soul, as my father hath ordained and sent me in to this world for this
end. Wherefore, good mother, be of good comfort, for I shall soon
come again to thee. And therwith that sovereign master of meekness, kneeling down to his mother, asked lowly her blessing. And
she also kneeling and clipping him derworthly [dearly] in her arms,
with weeping, said thus: My blessed son, as thou wilt go now with
thy father's blessing and mine, think on me and have in mind soon
to come again. And so reverently taking leave at his mother, and also
his supposed father Joseph, he took his way from Nazareth toward
Jordan, and so forth till he came to the water Jordan, where John
baptized the people at that time . . .

Or consider, to take a further example at random, the *Mirror* version
of a story which appears in Matthew 26, Mark 14, Luke 7 and John
12, about the woman who anointed Jesus's feet or head with precious
ointment. Nicholas Love gives several pages to it. After a sketchy
account of what happened, full attention is given—the marginal note
has 'Nota verba Magdalena intima'—to Mary Magdalen's long address
to Jesus. Not a word of this speech is in the Gospels. A glance at
Matthew 26, Mark 14, Luke 7 or John 12, will show that—and it is
thanks to the Reformation translations that we can make that glance.
The Gospels do not say that the woman who anointed Jesus's feet was
Mary Magdalen. The only name given is in John 12, and there it is
Mary the sister of Lazarus and Martha. It is a late Church tradition that
identifies the woman with the ointment as Mary Magdalen, and argues
how many Maries there were. By this, Mary Magdalen becomes the
type of the reformed fallen woman, and the occasion for 'verba . . .
intima' to Jesus. This is part of what she says:

> Good lord, put me not from you and forsake not my repentance: for
> other refuge I wole not have, for I love you sovereignly above all
> other: wherefore, good lord, forsake ye not me, but punish ye
> me at your will: nevertheless I ask algate [nevertheless] mercy. And
> herewith, with great trust of his mercy and inward affection of his
> love, she kissed his feet oft: and sadly weeping and shedding tears so
> thick that she washed his feet with them . . .

There is nothing in the book that can truly be termed a Gospel
harmony. As can be seen, it gives a mixture of paraphrase of some basic
events and very free comment. Most of what is printed even as
narrative is not in the Gospels at all. Before any mention of the start
of Jesus's ministry, many pages are given to a rhapsody on 'the Manner

of living of the blessed virgin maiden Mary', as the second chapter is entitled, a mixture of Mary's private thoughts and comment from the Fathers. In these first fifteen chapters of Love's book the bare bones of a few verses from Luke 1 and 2 show through: but Mary is the subject. The chapters are fiction—devout fiction, to be sure, but not from the Bible.

Half the book, as was traditional both with Gospel harmonies and medieval lives of Christ, is given to the Crucifixion. But most of those pages in Love is extensive maternal contemplation. Many pages are given to the deeds and long speeches of Mary at the Cross, which are not, of course, in the Gospels. Whenever Mary can be presented, she is there with some vividness. The outline of the Gospel story of Jesus is just visible there, but Jesus is secondary. The emphasis throughout the book is on Mary, to the extent that it is her suffering, and her words, that occupy page after page. Christ is seen, movingly, in relation to those who knew him on earth: movingly, but fictitiously. (The woman who touched Jesus's hem becomes Martha.) It is no doubt excellent Catholic piety, and suitable for devotions of a certain kind, but it absolutely not what is in the Gospels. Nicholas Love's book does give a simple outline of the Gospel story, in English: the very basic events only. Nothing at all of the teaching of Christ, and few of the incidents, are present. Moreover, not only is hardly anything of the Gospels there: most of what is printed in Love's *Mirror* is not in the Gospels at all.

It is tendentious to maintain that such books point the way to the probability that the Church would 'sooner or later' have given the laity the New Testament in the vernacular; that the 'devotional mood which dominated English religious reading' at the time would have produced an English version of the New Testament 'without the doctrinal uncertainty and conflict which in fact ensued'.[35] To say that, is simply to register how very far the Church of the time (and such historians of our time) are from the New Testament. One of the most recent historians writes:

> The ban on English versions of the New Testament had to a large extent been ameliorated by the production of Nicholas Love's translation of the *Meditationes vitae Christi* [i.e., the *Mirror*], for that work was essentially an expanded Gospel harmony, and went a long way towards satisfying lay eagerness for knowledge of the Gospels.[36]

That remark takes the breath away in its assumption of what 'knowledge of the Gospels' means. For what is missing from books like Love's *Mirror*, of course, is the other nine-tenths, the doctrinal heart, of the

Gospels. This is something that has not until this point been brought into the debate about the English Reformation. There is nothing in the *Mirror* of the Gospel doctrines, and of course no hint of the writing of Paul and others in the epistles and in Revelation, all the very bedrock of Christian theology. Only when the whole Bible, as given originally in Greek and Hebrew, was printed in English could it be seen that the Bible preceded the Church and gave it all its authority. Only then could not only New Testament theology but also that system of internal reference—within the New Testament itself, within the Old Testament itself, and so fully linking the two—be visible to everybody.

Catholic revisionist historians miss the vital point. The Gospels-as-pap represents no New Testament theology. The Church would never permit a complete printed New Testament in English from the Greek, because in that New Testament can be found neither the Seven Sacraments nor the doctrine of purgatory, two chief sources of the Church's power. The recent remark 'there was nothing in the character of religion in late medieval England which could *only* or even *best* have been developed within Protestantism',[37] only points to how far religion in late medieval England was from mainstream Christianity. An elementary working knowledge of the Bible, the ultimate root of the Christian faith, could only have been developed within Protestantism. 'When all is said and done, the Reformation was a violent disruption, not the natural fulfilment, of most of what was vigorous in late medieval piety and religious practice.'[38] Such piety and practice, in many ways admirable, we must reply, was imprisoned in a little world of recent Church tradition, while the vast continents of historic Bible revelation, towered over by the mountain range of Paul's theology, were forbidden territory: no 'natural fulfilment' would ever set foot there. 'On the eve of the Reformation there were probably over 50,000 Books of Hours or Primers in circulation among the English laity. No other book commanded anything like such readership . . .'[39] That is no doubt true, but it ignores the fact that during the English Reformation, lay men and women were so hungry for the Bible in English that they were often prepared to die for it. Nobody was burned alive for 'The Little Hours of the Virgin'.

Printing in England in the 1520s

Compared to all continental countries, England had few printers. Caxton, who had died in 1491, had successfully produced for fifteen years interesting books for discerning and wealthy readers. His successors, which effectively means Richard Pynson and Wynkyn de Worde, though prolific over several decades, were not able, not minded, and most importantly not permitted, to rival their brethren in Europe by producing finely-turned-out books. No Greek book was printed in England. No-one in London could have produced the physical form of Luther's folio 'September Testament', with its fine binding, paper, text and illustrations, and all for a florin; a volume which sold so well that reprints appeared before the end of the year. By 1533, eleven years later, no fewer than eighty-five editions had been printed. Pynson and de Worde could not have produced a vernacular Bible, one suspects: and Caxton would not. All three printers would have been too tightly aware of controls by clerics and Court to let them even ask for release from the Constitutions of Oxford. The thought of Caxton printing a version of the Wyclif Bible, parallel to the process that happened in every continental country in the years he was working in London, is like trying to imagine the Library of Congress in the 1950s publishing a deluxe edition of the Communist Manifesto. Caxton issued Chaucer, lavishly, and Gower, and Malory, but not Langland's *Piers Plowman*. The nearest he came to the Bible was in the stories (in English, from Latin) in the collection *The Golden Legend*. Nothing Lollard, or remotely doctrinal, there.

Caxton, Pynson, de Worde—that is almost all. Yet, as noticed above, by 1476, when Caxton first set up his press at Westminster, there were already presses abroad in seventy European towns in eight European countries. 'We know the names of a thousand printers operating before the year 1500, and the titles of about 30,000 books which they produced . . . Between 1517 and 1520 Luther's thirty publications probably sold well over 300,000 copies.'[40] In London, when Tyndale arrived there, the two printers, Pynson and de Worde, were responsible for over 70 per cent of the English output; imports from foreign presses accounted for 17 per cent; other printers made only 10 per cent of books.[41] It is a fairly miserable story. Printers came and went, like T. Berthelet, H. Pepwell or J. Rastell; sometimes working their presses, sometimes not. When Tyndale was preaching in St Dunstan's in Fleet Street, Wynkyn de Worde's press was down the hill towards Ludgate, in the shadow of St Bride's church, and there were only possibly four others apart from Pynson doing occasional work. The quality was about good enough for schoolbooks or practical manuals, but never anything to write home about. The strategy was to have a rapid turnover of small cheap popular books, and, in de Worde's case, not to fuss about aesthetics. After Caxton's death in 1491, some of his

better volumes had been quickly reprinted in Antwerp and exported
to London, claiming that market for better quality. For the London
presses could not in any way rival the skills, resources and funds to
produce the fine books like those coming out of Paris, Rouen, Venice
and even Antwerp. Beautifully made books were part of the continental craft, and their successful printers profited at such centres of international trading and shipping as Cologne, Basel, Paris, Valencia, Seville
and Naples.[42]

Tyndale in London

> And so in London I abode almost a year, and marked the course of
> the world, and heard our praters, I would say our preachers how
> they boasted themselves and their high authority, and beheld the
> pomp of our prelates, and how busied they were as they yet are, to
> set peace and unity in the world (though it be not possible for them
> that walk in darkness to continue long in peace, for they cannot but
> either stumble or dash themselves at one thing or another that shall
> clean unquiet all together) and saw things whereof I defer to speak
> at this time . . .[43]

Foxe in his account of Tyndale was able to expand Tyndale's own
account of his year in London.[44] He quotes the prologue to the
Pentateuch as above, and then continues:

> And therefore, finding no place for his purpose within the realm,
> and having, by God's providence, some aid and provision minis-
> tered unto him by Humphrey Mummuth . . . and certain other
> good men, he took his leave of the realm, and departed into
> Germany . . .[45]

Foxe wrote under the date 1530, six years on from Tyndale's stay in
London, when 'the Lutheran threat' had produced aggressive, and by
now lethal, opposition from Cuthbert Tunstall's successor as Bishop of
London, John Stokesley. In May 1528 Monmouth, a leading London
businessman (a draper, connected with the cloth trade, whose name
suggests origins on the Gloucestershire border) was sent for and interrogated by Thomas More, and put in the Tower. He petitioned the
King, through Wolsey, in a letter dated 19 May 1528. Foxe bases his
information on a document, a letter from Monmouth himself, recalling events.[46] Foxe's heading is 'The Trouble of Humphrey Mummuth,
Alderman of London'.

> Master Humphrey Mummuth was a right godly and sincere alder-
> man of London, who, in the days of Cardinal Wolsey, was troubled

and put into the Tower, for the gospel of Christ, and for maintaining them that favoured the same.

Stokesely, then bishop of London, ministered articles unto him, to the number of four and twenty: as for adhering to Luther and his opinions; for having and reading heretical books and treatises; for giving exhibition to William Tyndale, Roy, and such others; for helping them over the sea to Luther; for administering privy help to translate, as well the Testament as other books into English; for eating flesh in Lent; for affirming faith only to justify; for derogating from men's constitutions; for not praying to saints, not allowing pilgrimage, auricular confession, the pope's pardons: briefly, for being an advancer of all Martin Luther's opinions, &c.

He, being of these articles examined, and cast into the Tower, at last was compelled to make his suit or purgation, writing to the aforesaid cardinal, then lord chancellor, and the whole council, out of the Tower; in the contents whereof he answered to the criminous accusation of them that charged him with certain books received from beyond the sea; also for his acquaintance with Master Tyndale. Whereupon he said, that he denied not but that, four years then past, he had heard the said Tyndale preach two or three sermons at St Dunstan's in the West . . .

At this point we may take up Monmouth's own account:

Upon four years and a half past, and more, I heard the foresaid Sir William preach two or three sermons at St Dunstan's in the West, in London; and after that I chanced to meet him, and with communication I examined what living he had. He said he had none at all, but he trusted to be with my Lord of London [i.e. Tunstall] in his service. And therefore I had the better fantasy [inclination] to him. And afterward he went to my Lord and spake to him, as he told me, and my L. of London answered him, that he had Chaplains enough, and he said to him, would have no more at that time. And so the Priest came to me again, and besought me to help him, and so I took him into my house for half a year, where he lived like a good priest, as me thought. He studied most part of the day and of the night, at his book; and he would eat but sodden meat by his good will, nor drink but small single beer.[47] I never saw him wear linen about him in the space he was with me.[48]

Meagre as this is, it is valuable as being all we have beyond Tyndale's own words about his year in London. How often Tyndale preached in St Dunstan's is not known: nor how he came to be invited there: nor what he lived on before Monmouth heard him and then met him.

'Four years and a half past' gives us a date for the sermons at the end of 1523. Tyndale appears then to have been waiting for the summons to Tunstall's palace. Mozley reports a useful theory that Lady Walsh's relatives, the Poyntz family, may have had a hand in the invitation to preach at St Dunstan's. The then rector was Thomas Green MA: Tyndale may have known him at Oxford or Cambridge, or have been introduced by Thomas Poyntz, who was buried at St Dunstan's forty years later, despite the fact that his family home was in Essex. Green was a member of the Grocer's Company, and he may have been known to Monmouth.[49] He might have been a Gloucestershire man—something made Monmouth (probably also from Gloucestershire) leave his home parish of All Hallows, Barking, on Sundays to attend St Dunstan's three miles away, where he heard Tyndale preach. We might suspect that St Dunstan's was a church moving to some reformed ideas about the gospel, and possibly one of the London Lollard communities. Monmouth had been a 'Scripture-man' for ten years (see below): not all such were Lollards, but what were called 'known men' existed in Monmouth's own Drapers' Company[50]—the connection between Lollardy and the cloth trade again showing itself.

Foxe prints a story about Monmouth as follows:

Of this Humphrey Mummuth we read of a notable example of christian patience, in the sermons of Master Latimer,[51] which the said Latimer heard in Cambridge from master George Stafford, reader of the divinity lecture in the university; who, expounding the place of St Paul to the Romans, that we shall overcome our enemy with well doing, and so heap hot coals upon his head, &c.,[52] brought in an example, saying, that he knew in London a great rich merchant (meaning this Humphrey Mummuth) who had a very poor neighbour; yet for all his poverty he loved him very well, and lent him money at his need, and let him come to his table whensoever he would. It was even at that time when Dr Colet was in trouble, and should have been burned, if God had not turned the king's heart to the contrary. Now the rich man began to be a Scripture-man; he began to smell the gospel. The poor man was a papist still.

It chanced on a time, when the rich man talked of the gospel, sitting at his table, where he reproved popery, and such kind of things; the poor man, being there present, took a great displeasure against the rich man, insomuch that he would come no more to his house, he would borrow no more money of him, as he was wont to do before times, yea, and conceived such hatred and malice against

him, that he went and accused him before the bishops. Now the
rich man, not knowing of any such displeasure, offered many times
to talk with him, and to set him at quiet. It would not be. The poor
man had such a stomach, that he would not vouchsafe to speak with
him. If he met the rich man in the street, he would go out of his
way. One time it happened that he met him so in a narrow street,
that he could not avoid, but come near him; yet for all that, this
poor man (I say) had such a stomach against the rich man, that he
was minded to go forward, and not to speak with him. The rich
man, perceiving that, caught him by the hand, and asked him,
saying, 'Neighbour! what is come into your heart to take such
displeasure with me? What have I done against you? Tell me, and I
will be ready at all times to make you amends.'

Finally, he spake so gently, so charitably, so lovingly and friendly,
that it wrought so in the poor man's heart, that by and by he fell
down upon his knees, and asked him forgiveness. The rich man
forgave him, and so took him again to his favour, and they loved as
well as ever they did afore.[53]

The reference to Colet is interesting. He was said to have been accused
of heresy between 1512 and 1514 because of a translation of the Lord's
Prayer into English. The story came from Erasmus who had an axe to
grind, and it was mentioned by Tyndale in his *Answer unto Sir Thomas
More's Dialogue*,[54] and much expanded by John Bale, the Protestant
playwright and historian. It is fiction—Erasmus does not come out
well—for on the one hand the Church at that time was actively
promoting knowledge of the Lord's Prayer in English; and on the other
Colet at the time was going in the opposite direction, busily persecuting heretics.[55] One of those might already have been Monmouth, for
the poor man has informed the bishops of his host's heresy. Latimer's
sermon was delivered in 1555, over thirty years later, and matters have
a way of being improved in the telling, as can be seen from the
reference to Colet. Nevertheless, the story gives a firm idea of
Monmouth as a good man, and one who would be sympathetic to
evangelical preaching. The odd form of the story as parable, 'the poor
man', 'the rich man', and so on, might be not only in conscious
imitation of the Gospels, but because Monmouth was still alive, and
well-known in Cambridge and London circles.

What Tyndale preached we can never know—Monmouth, under
pressure four and a half years later, in May 1528, burned Tyndale's
sermons. It is legitimate to speculate that they came out of the study
of 'his book' that occupied him day and night at Monmouth's house.

The most likely book to have been so studied is Erasmus's *Novum instrumentum*, as we imagined him working on it at Little Sodbury. By now, here in London, Tyndale has behind him the translation of Isocrates and Erasmus's *Enchiridion*; his Greek and Latin are at a high pitch. To appeal so to Humphrey Monmouth his sermons must have been Scripture expositions; one can suppose little else from Tyndale. But how much at this stage did Tyndale know of Luther, and further, if he knew enough, how much was he expressing sympathy with him? Tyndale was living in Monmouth's house, and Monmouth's name was probably known to the Church authorities. If the tale is true, 'the poor man' had acted as informer, some years before Luther's decisive Ninety-five Theses of 1517.

By 1520, however, enough of Luther's tracts had reached London for a correspondent writing from London in that year to note that 'as for news there is none but of late there was heretics here which did take Luther's opinions.'[56] The native 'Scripture-men' could not but be fired by the incendiary events in Europe, where the understanding was so rapidly spreading of a new Christianity, where men might find their salvation through faith alone, in Christ alone, discovered through Scripture alone.[57] The Gloucestershire 'doctorly prelates' had discussed Luther in Little Sodbury; some time between July 1520 and the beginning of March 1521, Wolsey had forbidden the importation and reading of Luther's books. Tyndale may have arrived in London in 1523 tainted by Gloucestershire rumour: he had then given himself away on the need for a vernacular Bible to the Bishop himself, no less.[58] Tyndale lived in peace in the city for six months. There is no record of any London moves against Tyndale before he went abroad, either on the older, more Lollard base (as would fit Monmouth at that stage) or the newer, Lutheran grounds.

An expatriate community of Germans lived in London in the Steelyard, which was north of the Thames, just below London Bridge (where Cannon Street station now stands), the centre for Hanseatic merchants in London. The name came from *Staalhof*, a sample-yard, and had nothing to do with steel. In 1523 or 1524, they may not have been under particular suspicion. In 1525 Monmouth was able to use one of them, Hans Collenbeke, to take money to Tyndale in Hamburg. There was no reason why they should not have had with them in the Steelyard not only Lutheran tracts but copies of Luther's 'September Testament' of 1522: indeed, it is highly likely. Thomas More's raid on their premises found Lutheran books and took them away for a ceremonial burning. Christians in London were not polarised. Many, and probably most, were aware of some loosening of traditional belief in the ways of the Church, and conscious of new ideas coming in quickly from Germany. There was no doubt a confused feeling that there might be no harm in subscribing to both beliefs, in the absolute Church and in Luther's *sola fides*. Evidence from wills may support this.[59] One of the routes of the new ideas would be through the Steelyard. Tyndale could easily have seen a 'September Testament' there. He would know what could be done in the work of translation and printing in Germany. From now on he had German thoughts.

Chapter 5

COLOGNE, 1525

Tyndale probably set out from England in April 1524. He had a little
money from Henry Monmouth and from London merchants.[1] Where
in Germany he began, is unknown. Mozley had an ingenious theory
that allowed Tyndale a brief stay in Hamburg before going to
Wittenberg for over a year, with a brief time back in Hamburg in the
spring of 1525. The three great trading ports of north-east Europe
were Hamburg, Antwerp and Cologne, and if Tyndale were to succeed
in making books in Europe for distribution in England, he would have
to expect to be in, or close to, one of them. All three cities had
printers: Cologne and Antwerp had many. Both Antwerp and Cologne
had thriving English business communities, and Tyndale was later to
settle permanently in Antwerp. We next hear of him, however, on the
Rhine at Cologne. Why he began work in Cologne we do not know.
With a helper, he set to work overseeing the printing of an English
New Testament in the printing-house of Peter Quentell.

This is a moment, most probably in the summer of 1525, at which
to pause. Tyndale, after snubs, set-backs and delays in England, and
sojourns at unknown places in Germany, can now stand in a prosperous print-shop and watch, coming off a press, sheets of a translation of
the New Testament from Greek into English. 'The prologue. I have
here translated . . .' the first sheet begins, '. . . (brethren and sisters most
dear and tenderly beloved in Christ) the new Testament for your
spiritual edifying, consolation and solace.' Presently comes, 'The gospel
of S. Mathew, The first chapter', and soon after 'When Jesus was born
in Bethlehem . . .' When it was that he did the work of translation we
cannot know. He would have had to have given Peter Quentell the
complete book before printing could start.

He had with him an assistant, an apostate friar, William Roye,
from the Observant house at Greenwich. Roye had matriculated at

Wittenberg on 10 June 1525, and his presence as Tyndale's assistant suggests that they met in that university, a further point in favour of Mozley's theory. Roye seems to have been reasonably competent, but he was not Tyndale's first choice as assistant. Three years later, in the preface to *The Parable of the Wicked Mammon*, Tyndale wrote of this time, 'While I abode [awaited] a faithful companion which now hath taken another voyage upon him, to preach Christ where (I suppose) he was never yet preached . . . one William Roye . . . came unto me and offered his help . . .' Who that first choice was we do not know. We can speculate about an Oxford—or Cambridge—fellow-student, competent in Greek, or a London friend with the necessary scholarship: it could well have been Miles Coverdale, who did join him later; but it has to remain speculation. Roye was by no means ideal. He seems to have been adequate in intellect but specious and unstable in character, and relations between them were not good. In the preface to *The Wicked Mammon*, Tyndale wrote of him, 'a man somewhat crafty when he cometh unto new acquaintance and before he be thorough known and namely when all is spent . . . his tongue is able not only to make fools stark mad, but also to deceive the wisest, that is at the first sight and acquaintance.'[2] When the time came for them to part, Tyndale reports, he took his leave and 'bade him farewell for our two lives, and (as men say) a day longer'.

Meanwhile, Tyndale and Roye were working together in Cologne. The printing had reached as far as Matthew 22, in the middle of what would later be verse 12, at the foot of the next page following signature H, when it was broken off. The Cologne authorities were about to arrest the two Englishmen and impound their work. Tyndale and Roye escaped and fled up the Rhine to Worms, taking their work with them. The agent of the interruption was a Cologne scholar-writer called John Dobneck, whose Latin name was Cochlaeus. Work of his in several large volumes was also being printed at Peter Quentell's press, and he came to know the workers in the print shop. While they were drunk (a condition he may have encouraged), they boasted to him

that whether the King and Cardinal of England [Wolsey] would or not, all England would in short time be Lutheran. He heard also that there were two Englishmen lurking there, learned, skilful in languages, and fluent . . . [and] that three thousand copies of the Lutheran New Testament, translated into the English language, were in the press, and already were advanced as far as the letter K, in *ordine quaternionum*.[3]

Cochlaeus went secretly to a powerful senator of Cologne, Herman Rinck, who was a friend of Henry VIII, and told him the whole business. Rinck obtained from the senate a prohibition against the printers, and himself set out to impound what he could, with incomplete success. Cochlaeus told how 'the two English apostates, snatching away with them the quarto sheets printed, fled by ship, going up the Rhine to Worms'. Cochlaeus, never one to hold himself back, always remained impressed with what he had done and his published writings, printed in 1533, in 1538 and in 1549, contain three separate accounts of those events.

What Tyndale and Roye had begun, with a fine Cologne printer, was a quite elaborate English New Testament, in quarto. The first Gospel is prefaced by a full-page woodcut of St Matthew dipping his pen in an ink-pot held by a young angel. There are large illuminations at all the chapter-divisions, which are particularly heavy, and biblical cross-references in the inside margins. In the outside margins are almost continuous expository comments with a system of asterisks and pointing hands in the text. The pages that have survived are handsome. They are also familiar to anyone who has even glanced at Luther's 'September Bible'. Here are similar woodcuts. Here, as in Luther's 1522 volume, are several pages of prologue setting out the approach to the New Testament. The list of the New Testament books is identical in form and order and even page setting: in both they are numbered 1–23 from Matthew to 3 John; then, unnumbered and set apart, are Hebrews, James, Jude and Revelation. The prologue and biblical text look like a translation of Luther. Tyndale's book is smaller than Luther's impressive folio, and anonymous, but otherwise it does seem that Tyndale's first attempt at a printed New Testament is the Luther-in-English that Cochlaeus described and modern commentators have labelled.[4]

Cochlaeus related that the printers had got at least as far as signature K. That would finish Matthew and take the work well into Mark. There is indeed evidence that possibly large numbers of quarto sheets from Quentell's shop, perhaps sewn but not of course bound, containing the translation of Matthew and Mark, with the prologue and marginal notes, in fact reached England. There are mentions of an edition of those two Evangelists, alongside the New Testament completed the following year.[5] All that has survived, however, is to Matthew 22, in a single copy in the Grenville collection in the British Library. Cochlaeus's description of the work by 'the two English apostates' as 'the Lutheran New Testament, translated into the English language', though it has in modern times been seized on as a fair description, needs serious qualification. Certainly the prologue, as we shall see presently, contains a lot of Luther. Most of the theology there is Luther's. Whole paragraphs are taken from his *Vorrhede* (prologue). Tyndale, however, goes his own way. He moves in and out, translating Luther directly for sentences at a time, and then modifying the German with his own words. He omits much. Above all, he adds much. His own fresh material makes his prologue twice as long. That prologue is also more important, as, circulating in sheets, it made the first English Protestant tract, giving to English people Lutheran ideas in print for the first time.

Tyndale's First Translation

We shall begin, however, not with that prologue, but with Tyndale's translation of Matthew, almost complete (nearly twenty-two out of twenty-eight chapters). Since this work is the first from him, and because Tyndale is first of all a Bible translator, we shall begin with analysis in some detail.

The marginal glosses are heavily, though not at all exclusively, dependent on Luther's. At first sight, so is the text. The first page, with its heavy Gothic titles, large illumination, solid blocks of marginal notes and vertical list, looks like a very close copy of Luther indeed. But this is appearance only, Luther begins 'Dis ist das buch von der gepurt Jhesu Christi der do ist ein son Davids des sons Abraham'. Sure enough, Tyndale begins 'This is the book . . .', where the Greek simply begins *Biblos*, 'Book . . .', as does the Vulgate, *Liber*. . . . Peter Quentell the printer and his assistants may have had Luther's page in front of them and made it again in a slightly smaller format. That does not mean that Tyndale did. If he had followed Luther for the rest of that first sentence he would have written 'of the birth of Jesus Christ he who is a son of David the son of Abraham'. That he did not do. He wrote:

> This is the book of the generation of Jesus Christ the son of David,
> The son also of Abraham.
> Abraham begat Isaac:
> Isaac begat Jacob:
> Jacob begat Judas and his brethren . . .

If anything, Tyndale is closer to the Vulgate, especially in the omission of the definite article where the Greek and Luther have 'the Isaak, the Jacob, the Juda' and so on right down the list. The Greek, the Vulgate and Tyndale agree that 'Judas' not 'Juda' as in Luther begat Phares. Tyndale alone carries that 'Judas' back to the name of the man Jacob begat, for clarity; not being troubled in English by the inconsistency produced by inflected endings, where the Greek has to have *Ioudan* for object and *Ioudas* for subject. Tyndale follows the Greek single word, *eggenese* (Latin *genuit*), and gives 'begat', where Luther every time gives *hat geporn*, so that Tyndale's 'Isaac begat Jacob' is in Luther 'Isaac hatt geporn den Jacob', 'Isaac had borne the Jacob'.

Such minute details begin to allow us to see from the very beginning that Tyndale is his own man. The marginal notes are to some extent a different matter; but in the text of Scripture, what at first looks like straightforward following of Luther can be seen to be no such thing. Much of the likeness is a matter of the particularly striking printing-house style. Peter Quentell's aggressive impact, particularly in chapter openings, was unlike English printers of the time. The externals are all very much Luther. The heart of the matter, however, is Tyndale's own.

Tyndale Translating the Greek

On close examination, the same effect appears again and again. He follows Luther, but only when he chooses to do so. His primary source is the Greek. The most celebrated chapters of Matthew are 5, 6 and 7, the Sermon on the Mount. Here, translated a little too literally, is the opening, in Luther:

> But when he the people saw, ascended he up a mountain, and sat himself, and his disciples stepped to him, and he opened his mouth, taught them, and said, Blessed are, they that spiritually poor are, because the heavenly kingdom is theirs, Blessed are, they that grief carry, because they shall consoled be . . .

Certainly Tyndale begins, as Luther does, 'When he saw the people . . .', where the Greek and Latin, have 'Seeing the crowd', with a sense of irregularity, even of 'mob', which 'the people' does not give. Tyndale goes on, 'he went up into a mountain, and when he was set, his disciples came unto him, and he opened his mouth, and taught them saying: Blessed are the poor in spirit: for theirs is the kingdom of heaven. Blessed are they that mourn: for they shall be comforted . . .' The familar words, taken into the Authorised Version virtually unchanged, sing with an English rhythm, making a poem which reflects the poetic, shaped, quality of the original Greek. A case can be made throughout the Sermon on the Mount for Tyndale's dependence on the Greek alone, the Vulgate Latin alone, the German alone, or all three together. What is characteristic of Tyndale, and what matters, is his clarity, his determination to put nothing in the way of being understood. Tyndale's 'they that mourn', (Greek, 'the mourners') is more open even than Luther's strong notion of carrying grief. Perhaps Tyndale's 'Blessed are the pure in heart: for they shall see God' (only one word more than the Greek) is clearer than Luther's 'Blessed are those who are from heart pure, because they will look at God'. It is puzzling that Tyndale should open up the simple, and not uncommon, Greek *eirenopoioi*, meaning 'peacemakers', into 'the maintainers of peace', against the Vulgate Latin and Luther's text. Luther's marginal note on his *friedfertig* (peacable), however, led Tyndale to that shading. In his revision of 1534, he reverted properly to 'peacemakers'.

Tyndale Translating Luther

It would be foolish to try to build a final case for Tyndale's independence of Luther from a few passages, suggestive though they might be. Take the last sentence of Matthew's Christmas story in the middle of chapter 2, for example. For the departure of the wise men, the Greek has, translated literally, 'And being solemnly [or divinely] warned in sleep [or by a dream] not to return [bend back] towards Herod, by another way they returned to their own place [spot]'. The Vulgate is not happy with the oracular verb, and paraphrases, roughly, into 'And having accepted a response in sleep', and then has 'through another way they were turned back into their region.' Luther has, literally, 'And God told them in a dream, that they should not again to Herod turn, and they went through another way again into their land'. Tyndale's solutions are interesting. He has: 'And after they were warned in their sleep, that they should not go again to Herod, they returned into their own country another way.' The syntax is neater than Luther's, and is close to the Greek. So is the vocabulary. Tyndale's 'warned in their sleep' is right for the Greek (and not dependent on the Latin), and wholly unlike Luther's 'And God told them in a dream'—Tyndale is most obviously not copying Luther. It is Tyndale's alone of the four versions which provides the familiar cadence from Christmas readings, 'they returned into their own country another way', which went into the Authorised Version and far beyond. 'Their own country' is important, but it is 'another way' which needs the stress which comes from being at the end. Moreover, we are already hearing the effect of that characteristic Tyndalian ear for rhythm, the recognition that 'another way into their own country', which all the other versions have, including the Greek, comes to a more limping end in English. This is because of the light stress at the end of 'country': 'into their own country another way', makes a cadence—as much through the break between 'country' and 'another'—for the whole paragraph.

There are occasions when Tyndale quite unmistakably follows Luther. In chapter 2, the Greek, followed by the Vulgate, begins the quotation from Jeremiah 31 with 'A voice was heard in Rama . . .' Luther has 'Auff dem gebirge hat man ein geschrey gehoret . . .' ('On the mountains was a cry heard . . .') which Tyndale follows, though preferring the Greek *phone*, 'voice'—'On the hills was a voice heard . . .' There Tyndale, like Luther, has offered something understandable. With similar intention, no doubt, at the end of chapter 4, where the Greek tells of great crowds following from 'Galilee and Decapolis and Jerusalem and Judaea and from beyond Jordan', Luther translates the Greek of 'Decapolis' and gives 'ten towns', which Tyndale also does, with 'ten cities'. In chapter 8, the centurion in the Greek says 'I say to this', that is, 'to this man', which the Vulgate follows with 'et dico huic'. Luther has 'ich sage zu eynem' ('I say to one'), and Tyndale follows. Later in chapter 8, Luther makes the devils in the men in the tombs begin their cry 'Ach Jesu du son gottis . . .', though the Greek begins 'What have we to do with thee'. Tyndale follows with 'they cried out saying: O Jesu the son of God . . .' The same happens towards the end of chapter 9 with the calling of the two blind men, where the Greek has 'Have mercy on us, son of David', but Luther 'Ach du son David, erbarm dich unser', exactly followed by Tyndale's 'O thou son of David, have mercy on us.' 'And when ye come into an house, salute the same', say both Luther and Tyndale in chapter 10, where the Greek has 'salute it'. Near the beginning of chapter 14, for the Greek 'Herodias the wife of Philip his brother,' both Luther and Tyndale have 'his brother Philip's wife'. In chapter 21, the people in Tyndale shout 'Hosianna' as they do in Luther, where the Greek and Vulgate have 'Hosanna'.

A number of other examples can be found of Tyndale using what he finds good in Luther. He is doing the work to which he has felt himself called, translating the Scriptures into English, and like any good translator he will use what help he can. This is a very different matter from a slavish following. There are more, and many more, examples of Tyndale following the Greek and differing from Luther, or not taking Luther's obvious hint, because he prefers to put into English what is in the Greek. To take a small example from chapter 21, Tyndale has 'the chief priests and the seniors of the people', after the Vulgate's *seniores populi*, itself after the Greek *presbuteroi tou laou*. There Luther has 'die Elltisten im volk': Tyndale was later to change 'seniors', here and elsewhere, to 'elders', which is Luther's word. If Tyndale were following Luther alone, he would have taken 'elders' there. To take another example: 'And when you pray', says Luther in chapter 6, 'you shall not much blabber, like the heathen . . .' 'But when ye pray', writes Tyndale, 'babble not much as the gentiles do . . .': *multum loqui* is the unadventurous Vulgate. Perhaps Luther's *plappern* suggested Tyndale's 'babble'; but the Greek is onomatopoeic enough, *battalogesete*, a word made from the name, *Battos*, of a stammering king. And Tyndale gives the more correct 'gentiles'.

Tyndale and Erasmus's Latin

One other stream of influence, which so far seems no more than a trickle, is Erasmus's Latin, the chief point of the *Novum instrumentum*. There is need for much more study of this, for one or two readings in the Cologne Matthew do seem to support Tyndale's use of it. In the genealogical list at the beginning of chapter 1, the Greek and the Vulgate say that Solomon's mother was 'of' Uria. Tyndale spells out 'the wife of ury', and Erasmus hasa '*uxor Uriae*'. In chapter 2, Tyndale has, of the wise men, 'they were warned in their sleep', closer to Erasmus's *admoniti* than the other versions. At two moments in the Beatitudes at the start of Matthew 5, Tyndale catches a lighter tone, possibly from Erasmus. With 'theirs is the kingdom of heaven', Erasmus's *illorum* matches the Greek: it is contrary to Luther's heavier construction (the Vulgate is heavier still). The same pattern is seen in Tyndale's 'inherit'. (Perhaps these simply tells us that Erasmus knew what he was doing with the Greek.) Early in chapter 11, Tyndale's 'happy is he that is not hurt by me' looks likely to have been influenced by Erasmus's *offensus*, representing a knock, a harmful injury, personal offence. More illustrations can be found.[6]

Tyndale's English

Tyndale had more than adequate Greek. Detailed analysis throughout the whole Testament of all Tyndale's work of translation, word by word, has yet to be done. The Matthew chapters printed in Cologne went unchanged into the complete New Testament printed in Worms in the following months, and such work of analysis would be demanding—but essential for a definitive answer to the question of his primary dependence. Yet something much more important is happening; the English into which Tyndale is translating has a special quality for the time, being the simple, direct form of the spoken language, with a dignity and harmony that make it perfect for what it is doing. Tyndale is in the process of giving us a Bible language. Luther is often praised for having given, in the 'September Bible', a language to the emerging German nation. In his Bible translations, Tyndale's conscious use of everyday words, without inversions, in a neutral word-order, and his wonderful ear for rhythmic patterns, gave to English not only a Bible language, but a new prose. England was blessed as a nation in that the language of its principal book, as the Bible in English rapidly became, was the fountain from which flowed the lucidity, suppleness and expressive range of the greatest prose thereafter.

These are qualities of this extended example from Matthew 20 in the Cologne fragment—which should ideally be read aloud:

> For the kingdom of heaven is like unto an householder which went out early in the morning to hire labourers into his vineyard. And he agreed with the labourers for a penny a day, and sent them into his vineyard. And he went out about the third hour, and saw other standing idle in the market-place, and said unto them: go ye also into my vineyard, and whatsoever is right, I will give you. And they went their way. Again he went out about the sixth and ninth hour, and did likewise. And he went out about the eleventh hour, and found other standing idle, and said unto them why stand ye here all the day idle? They said unto him: because no man hath hired us. He said unto them: go ye also into my vineyard, and whatsoever shall be right, that shall ye receive.
>
> When even was come, the lord of the vineyard, said unto his steward: call the labourers, and give them their hire, beginning at the last till thou come to the first. And they which were hired about the eleventh hour, came and received every man a penny. Then came the first, supposing that they should receive more, and they likewise received every man a penny. And when they had received it, they grudged against the good man of the house, saying: These last have wrought but one hour, and thou hast made them equal unto us which have borne the burden and heat of the day.
>
> He answered to one of them, saying: friend I do thee no wrong. Didst thou not agree with me for a penny? Take that which is thy duty [due], and go thy way. I will give unto this last, as much as to thee. Is it not lawful for me to do as me listeth, with mine own? Is thine eye evil because I am good? So the last shall be first, and the first shall be last. For many are called, and few be chosen.

The Cologne Marginal Notes

In the outside margins of those twenty-two chapters of Matthew printed in Cologne, there are ninety marginal notes, more to the page than in any other text of Tyndale's, sometimes by a long way—the finished New Testament printed in Worms the following year has no notes at all; the 1530 Genesis only six in the whole book. The first thing to be said about Tyndale's notes here is that they are entirely expository. They are Lutheran, but not sensational. Modern readers who have heard about Tyndale's margins and their 'salty' notes and come looking for titillation will be disappointed, and no doubt bored. The first one comes with the first line of Matthew: 'Abraham and David are first rehearsed, because that Christ was chiefly promised unto them'. The second, just below and taking half the column, is

> Saint Matthew leaveth out certain generations, & describeth Christ's lineage from Solomon, after the law of Moses, but Luke describeth it according to nature, from Nathan Solomon's brother. For the law calleth them a man's children which his brother begat of his wife left behind him after his death. Deut.25.c.

Both are exact translations of the equivalent notes in Luther. By Luther's normal standard, they are rather short. Next in the first chapter, where Joseph does not wish to defame Mary, the note is translated by Tyndale,

> That is he would not put her to open shame, as he well might have done ['als er wol macht hatte', 'as he well had the might', which is not quite the same, and indeed is curiously literal] by the law. Also Matthew rejoiceth of the goodness of Joseph, which for love's sake did remit of his right [again, not quite the German, which is 'das er sich auch seynes rechten und liebe . . .' 'that he himself also his right and love . . .'].

Luther's third note in this chapter only appears in the second and third editions of his German New Testament, and Tyndale reproduces it, which gives us a useful clue about his working habits. (We can see him and his helper surrounded by open books, including at least two editions of Luther's New Testament.) In English it takes twenty lines, and crosses the page- and chapter-break: it comments on Matthew's statement that Joseph 'knew her not, till she had brought forth her first son', explaining that Scripture usage does not mean that 'Joseph knew our lady afterward' (for 'our lady' Luther has *Maria*). He makes a linguistic reference to Genesis 8 and the raven: that is, when Scripture says that Noah's raven, sent from the ark, 'came not again till the water was drunk up and the earth dried', it does not mean 'he came again afterward'.

In this first chapter, Tyndale adds three short notes of his own. Mary was found with child 'by the holy ghost'. Tyndale glosses, 'That is to say by the working and power of the holy ghost'. The name given to the child, Jesus, is glossed 'Jesus is as much as to say as a saver, for he only saveth all men from their sins by his mercies without their deserving'. The prophecy ending 'God with us' Tyndale glosses 'Christ bringeth god. Where Christ is there is god: and where Christ is not, there is not god'.

Of the ninety notes, thirty are by Tyndale alone. He omits eight of Luther's, uses two which only appear in the second and third editions and expands and alters five. Once again, a detailed study is needed of how Luther's notes are translated or occasionally altered, and what might be the difference in content and manner between Luther's and Tyndale's. While awaiting the result of such investigation, we note first that Tyndale's own notes are usually explanatory: in chapter 2, 'Jewry is the land. Juda is that tribe or kindred that dwelt therein'; in chapter 3, 'Locusts are more than our grasshoppers . . .'; in chapter 5, 'Jot is as much to say as the least letter. For so is the least letter that the greeks or the Hebrews have called'; in chapter 6, 'Furnace. Men heat their furnaces and ovens with such things in those countries'; in chapter 8, 'Centurion is a captain of an hundred men, whom I call sometimes centurion, but for the most part an under-captain'; in chapter 10, 'Beyond the sea commonly they have as well brasen money as gold and silver', and so on. Many of them, however, take philological or cultural explanation further. Commenting on his own reading of 'hurt' in chapter 11, he writes: 'Hurted and offended throughout all the New Testament betokeneth to decay and fail in the faith. For many when they saw that Christ was but a carpenter's son as they supposed, and he himself also a carpenter, and his mother, and kin, of so low degree. Moreover when they saw him put to so vile a death, fell clean from the faith, and could not believe.'

Tyndale's longest note is to 'Thou art Peter. And upon this rock . . .' in chapter 16. Neither Tyndale nor Luther, whom he greatly expands, take the opportunity of doing what a modern reader might expect, and at least comment on the importance of that text for the Roman Church. There it is Peter, erroneously labelled the first pope, on whom everything is founded: thus 'the keys of the kingdom' are given to the pope, to use to bind and loose. What the Greek says is that it is Peter's

confession that is 'the rock'. The keys go to each believer who confesses that Jesus is 'the Christ, the son of the living god'. Indeed
Tyndale avoids Luther's occasional open anti-clerical and anti-papal
stabs. In chapter 5, at Jesus's words 'Whosoever breaketh one of these
least commandments . . .', Tyndale's note 'This do they which say that
these Christ's commandments are not commandments but counsels', is
taken from Luther, who has 'Thus the papists say. . .' The long note on
Peter and the rock, which continues on the 'keys of the kingdom'
passage, is worth giving in full, as the flavour of it is characteristic of
many of Tyndale's later Old Testament and New Testament notes,
though few are so long. He starts from Luther's note which simply says
that Peter means 'rock' and that all Christians are Peters:

> Peter in the greek signifieth a stone in English. This confession [i.e.
> of faith] is the rock. Now is simon bar-jona, or simon jonas' son,
> called Peter, because of his confession. Whosoever then thiswise
> confesseth of Christ, the same is called Peter. Now is this confession
> come to all that are true christian. Then is every christian man and
> woman Peter. Read Bede, Augustine and Jerome, of the manner of
> loosing and binding and note how Jerome checketh the presump-
> tion of the pharisees in his time, which yet had not so monstrous
> interpretations as our new gods have feigned. Read Erasmus's anno-
> tations [i.e. to the new Testament]. It was not for naught that Christ
> bade beware of the leaven of the pharisees. Nothing is so sweet that
> they make not sour with their traditions. The evangelion, that joyful
> tidings, is now bitterer than the old law, Christ's burden is heavier
> than the yoke of Moses, our condition and estate is ten times more
> grievous than was ever the jews'. The pharisees have so leavened
> Christ's sweet bread.

The tone is learned and sorrowful. Such readers as that note had in
England late in 1525, as sheets secretly passed from hand to hand like
samizdat literature, would recognise the burden laid by the Church,
and have no difficulty with who the modern Pharisees were. The
bomb hiding in that text, of course, is that 'every Christian man and
woman is Peter'.

The Cologne Prologue: Tyndale and Luther

Luther's *Vorrhede* to his 1522 New Testament translated, altered, cut and
above all added to, was the first printed Lutheran document in English
to reach England. It warrants careful study. What in Luther's Bible is

barely seven pages was expanded by Tyndale into a full fourteen. To summarise: Tyndale explains why a translation is necessary; what the Old Testament and New Testament are; what 'Gospel' and 'law' mean, following Paul; and what is sin. There are effectively, as so often in expositions in this period, three parts: Tyndale's own welcome to the reader and account of the need for a translation; Luther's New Testament theology, heavily Pauline and much expanded by Tyndale; and a curious six-page conclusion about man's depravity.

Tyndale largely expands Luther; but he equally largely cuts him. In losing Luther's final pages, he ignores the celebrated last page of all, present in all Luther's Wittenberg editions until 1534, setting out 'which are the correct and most vital books of the New Testament'. These, according to Luther, are the Gospel of John and his first Epistle, Paul's Epistles, especially Romans, Galatians and Ephesians, and the first Epistle of Peter. Tyndale is not interested in a two-tier New Testament and may well have been glad once in Worms to abandon Peter Quentell's Lutheran table whereby the Gospels and everything by Paul, Peter and John is numbered and special, and everything else— Hebrews, James, Jude and Revelation—is to be set aside, un-numbered and literally printed apart. Luther's famous description of the Epistle of James as 'an epistle of straw' is thus ignored. Luther objected to James because it seemed to distract from the absolute nature of faith, allowing in a little bit of works as well. Tyndale, as shown later by his preface to James in his 1534 New Testament, is not only wiser and more gener-ous—he is also more true to the New Testament. He understands that you cannot choose which bits of it to have. His life was dedicated to the English reformers' proposition that the words of the Bible, and especially the 'hard places' as they were called, could only be inter-preted by the Bible itself, taken whole.

He begins on his own with a direct and personal paragraph:

> I have here translated (brethren and sisters most dear and tenderly beloved in Christ) the new Testament for your spiritual edifying, consolation, and solace: Exhorting instantly and beseeching those that are better seen in the tongues than I, and that have higher gifts of grace to interpret the sense of the scripture and meaning of the spirit, than I, to consider and ponder my labour, and that with the spirit of meekness. And if they perceive in any places that I have not attained the very sense of the tongue, or meaning of the scripture, or have not given the right English word, that they put to their hands to amend it, remembering that so is their duty to do. For we have not received the gifts of god for ourselves only, or for to hide

them, but for to bestow them unto the honouring of god and christ,
and edifying of the congregation, which is the body of christ.

This is the first undisputed writing of Tyndale that still exists. It is
wholly characteristic in its clarity, its scholarly concern, its eagerness to
explain and even its warmth. It is unlike Luther's lofty opening, 'es wer
wol recht und billich, das dis buch . . .' ('it were indeed right and just,
that this book . . .'). We should note that the first sentences from
Tyndale are about the craft and skill of translating. It is possible, and
today most frequently done, to write about Tyndale as polemicist,
as propagandist, as political reformer, as moralist, as theologian, as
historian, as enemy of the institutions of the Church: yet he first
presents himself as a working translator of the Scriptures. It cannot be
right to see him as being anything else more important than that. He
translated two-thirds of the Bible so well that his translations endured
until today, a labour so great that that list of secondary definitions must
surely dwindle by comparison.

Tyndale, still independent of Luther, continues:

> The causes that moved me to translate, I thought better that other
> should imagine than that I should rehearse them. Moreover I sup-
> posed it superfluous, for who is so blind to ask why light should be
> showed to them that walk in darkness, where they cannot but
> stumble, and where to stumble is the danger of eternal damnation,
> other [or] so despiteful that he would envy any man (I speak not his
> brother) so necessary a thing, or so bedlam mad to affirm that good
> is the natural cause of evil, and darkness to proceed out of light,
> and that lying should be grounded in truth and verity, and not
> rather clean contrary, that light destroyeth darkness, and verity
> reproveth all manner lying.

That is Tyndale's first page; it is possible for a late twentieth-century
reader to see it as unexceptional, even mild, and even rather over-
obvious, and begin to patronise Tyndale. Yet the page, printed in
English in 1525, contained high explosive. Inside the reasonableness of
tone, stating the need for a New Testament in English as, to borrow a
phrase, a truth universally acknowledged; a truth so obvious that it
would be superfluous to explain, and only those who were blind or
malicious or mad could deny it, as it would be mad to say that the
Bible in English would cause evil, darkness and lying—inside that
mildness was found an attack on the Church so dangerous that it could
only be countered by the most vicious burnings, of books and men
and women. These first sentences of Tyndale have a calm that suggests

that Tyndale himself does not understand yet that his work, and he himself, will be answered with hatred and burning.

There is worse 'heresy'. A quality of the passages of this prologue where Tyndale speaks as himself, not translating Luther, is that they are made of Bible phrases. Thus in the second paragraph above, he quotes Luke (his opening sentence); Isaiah (the 'walk in darkness' phrase), John's Gospel and Epistles (the two 'darkness' sections) and Paul in Ephesians ('Exhorting . . . that have higher gifts . . .'). The last sentence of the first paragraph is in fact entirely a paraphrase of Paul, being the substance of parts of 1 Corinthians 14 or Ephesians 1 and 4—the sentence goes easily back into Greek. At its heart is the central New Testament doctrine of equality of sharing the received gifts of God so that everyone benefits, 'everyone' being 'the congregation, which is the body of Christ'. That, in England, was damnable heresy, as was every Christian man and woman being Peter. If Tyndale is saying in print that the body of Christ is everyone, without distinction—no laity, no priests, no bishops, no pope, if everyone is equal in Christ—then the gathering of Christians together is a congregation of equals, not a church of divisions and hierarchies, where priest and bishop and pope are essential. So Tyndale translated the Greek New Testament word *ekklesia* as 'congregation'. Philologically, he was correct: Erasmus, no less, had done the same before him. Theologically he was correct, too, as the New Testament understands the gathering of believers as a congregation of equals with no distinctions of rank, something that does not exist in the Kingdom of Heaven. Bishops (in Greek, 'overseers') and ministers (in Greek, 'presbyters', that is 'elders') are administrative ministers (the word means 'servants'), not the sole agents of God's powers priests and bishops had become. No matter that the last words of Tyndale's first paragraph, 'the congregation, which is the body of Christ' is an accurate translation of the last sentence of Ephesians 1, 'te ekklesia, etis estin to soma autou' ('the congregation, which is his body'). To the English bishops, the heresy was twofold: the implied equality and the pernicious word 'congregation' instead of 'church'. The bishops saw that this idea, which they took as basically Lutheran rather than scriptural, could make the whole Church structure fall apart. That indeed, is what it did, and quickly.

Though it never prefaced a New Testament, Tyndale regarded his prologue as important enough to expand and print separately in 1531 as *The Pathway to Holy Scripture*. That volume was attacked in England and denounced as heretical. Here we are concerned with the original prologue: Tyndale used Luther as a springboard: we note his manner of addressing the sort of understanding he believes his readers to have, and the kind of knowledge he realises they need. His second page, and third paragraph, begins:

> After it had pleased god to put in my mind, and also to give me grace to translate this fore-rehearsed new testament into our english tongue, howsoever we have done it. I supposed it very necessary to put you in remembrance of certain points, which are: that ye well understand what these words mean. The Old testament. The New testament. The law. The gospel. Moses. Christ. Nature. Grace. Working and believing. Deeds and faith, lest we ascribe to the one that which belongeth to the other, and make of Christ Moses, of the gospel the law, despise grace and rob faith: and fall from meek learning into idle despitions, brawling and scolding about words.[7]

Tyndale now takes up Luther, and while condensing him a little, follows him closely for over a page and a half, as he briefly defines the Old Testament and the New, and then explains at greater length 'Evangelion (that we call the gospel) . . .' This 'is a Greek word and signifieth good, merry, glad and joyful tidings, that maketh a man's heart glad, and maketh him sing, dance and leap for joy'. Luther's rhetorical pattern, in an ancient tradition, presents Christ as 'the right David', who has fought with the Goliath of sin, death and the Devil (a characteristic trio of Luther) and overcome them: as the woman's seed that in Genesis 3 has trodden underfoot the Devil's head, 'that is to say, sin, death, hell and all his power': and as the seed of Abraham, bringing blessing to all generations through faith in him, delivering from sin, death and Hell. Luther refers to Paul, in Romans 1, to introduce the Genesis 3 reference, and in Galatians 3 to clarify the seed of Abraham' point. He ends the section with a quotation from John 11, 'He that believeth on me shall never more die', as Tyndale gives it. At this point, Tyndale leaves Luther's *Vorrhede*, and does not return. (Luther, meanwhile, develops the promise to David in '2 Samuel 17' [he means 2 Samuel 7] about his house and kingdom being established for ever, with support from Micah and Hosea. He then gives his remaining five paragraphs to the differences between Moses and Christ.)

Tyndale, now on his own again, goes back to the original list given when he first took up Luther, and proceeds to expound over six pages, to the next section, the other parts of the doctrine of justification by faith, beginning with law. As he puts it, 'the law and the gospel may never be separate', and it is essential to Tyndale to set the definition of 'evangelion', taken verbatim from Luther, in relation to law. Though he is swimming alone, Luther is never far away. The doctrines expounded over the next six pages by Tyndale alone are fully from Luther (and ultimately from Paul). Justification is not by outward deeds, because by nature men are convicted to eternal damnation by the law. But, 'when the gospel is preached to us, he [God] openeth our hearts, and giveth us grace to believe and putteth the spirit of Christ in us, and we know him as our father most merciful . . . the blood of Christ hath obtained all things for us of god.'[8] Luther's presence can sometimes be felt in the wording: Luther's phrase 'low bottom and ground of the heart' tends to recur. But though the matter is strongly Lutheran, the manner is very much Tyndale's own.

This prologue is one of Tyndale's most important documents. It is, as it were, his first manifesto. Though it belongs to his early, predominantly Lutheran, phase, it also demonstrates his originality, that readiness to strike out on his own which is a mark of all he does. This Prologue is almost entirely theological exposition of Scripture: the short opening passages that are not are about the necessity of reading Scripture. A modern reader looks in vain for reforming politics or antipapal polemics. Because it is so important, space will be given here to examining it in more detail than will be given later to other writings of Tyndale that are not translations of the Bible. Though it involves some fairly heavy analysis, this is necessary in order to remove some serious misconceptions about these pages—principally that they are artless, not to say formless.

The Cologne Prologue: Tyndale Alone

In these central six pages, he can be seen going his own way in three strikingly important ways. First, he expounds the New Testament theology with a determination to be above all things clear to his readers. Secondly, some of these six pages are most interesting stylistically. His central theme, the twin poles that 'the law and the gospel may never be separate', is matched by the way he can set up a scheme of balanced sentences: 'I must therefore have always the law in my sight . . . I must also have the promises before mine eyes . . .' This balancing will be found to be part of a larger governing shape. The third thing that Tyndale does in some of these pages is to build much of what he says out of the New Testament. Thus, his first page on his own begins with 'the gospel of John in the first chapter', and returns twice to quote from there, interweaving, and commenting on, three quotations from Paul. The change of tone from Luther is striking. It is more than the switch from largely Old Testament to wholly New Testament references. Tyndale's pages are less dogmatically presented than Luther's, yet from them a reader can learn what the New Testament says. (An even more significant implication will arise from this third point presently.)

Some of the clarity is achieved by the organisation: the units are short and relate to each other. Some of it comes from his striking avoidance of complicated or technical abstract words, going for plain vocabulary, as concrete as possible: 'I must also have the promises before mine eyes & see the mercy, favour and good will of God upon me.'[9] 'With the law he condemneth himself and all his deeds, and giveth all the praise to god.'[10] This concreteness becomes especially vigorous in the images, 'yet are we full of the natural poison . . . our nature is to do sin, as is the nature of a serpent to sting . . . as an adder, a toad or a snake is hated of man . . . the fruit maketh not the tree evil . . .'[11] It is noticeable that throughout the prologue such images are all in sections describing the natural man and his natural tendency to sin, matching the concrete, the incarnate, to natural experience.

The balancing of the sentences fits his desire always to give the doctrine whole. 'When the law hath passed upon us and condemned us to death . . . then have we in Christ grace . . . promises of life . . . In the old testament are many promises, which are nothing else but the evangelion or gospel, to save those that believed them, from the vengeance of the law'.[12] There is a steady tick-tock of the two experiences, the Law and the Gospel. Tyndale in these pages hardly ever mentions the one without the other. This twofold quality is in the very structure. The subjects of the six pages are, in order, the antithetical Law and Gospel, and then the antithetical Nature and Grace. His first page and a half shows that the Law demands: Gospel gives; summarised as: Law and Gospel may never be separated. The second antithesis, Nature and Grace, covers two and a half pages. Between those two bigger sections come pages organised as two plus one, which is repeated. Two kinds of person are deceived, those who think to be justified through outward deeds, those given to 'all manner vices' who say 'God is merciful'. Then he states what true faith is. Again, the justiciary does not glorify God, the sensual does not fear God. He states what the true Christian man is. Nature is of man (with the natural images we noticed above). The acceptance of grace is the work of Christ. The summary explains righteousness, mistaken by the Jews, concluding with a vivid image: 'As when the temporal law oft times condemneth the thief or murderer and bringeth him to execution, so that he seeth nothing before him but present death, and then cometh good tidings, a charter from the king and delivereth him' (sig. B2).

The whole might be expressed:

Law
Gospel
    summary: may never be separated
                Deceived 1 deeds
                Deceived 2 vices
                    true faith
                Deceived 1 not glorify God
                Deceived 2 not fear God
                    true Christian
Nature
Grace
    summary: righteousness.

Though it has not been fashionable to say so, such rhetorical organisation is characteristic of most of Tyndale's writing. It owes much to an Oxford training of the time, and to late medieval habits of preaching, developed in Tudor times by men like Colet. The aim is not to dazzle with verbal arabesques and flourishes, but to be clear to the humblest hearer.

There are other marks of artifice. Tyndale's double portrait of the deceived, miniature pictures of characters like ghosts of a future *Pilgrim's Progress*, have taken the place of 'Moses, Christ' as an antithesis in Luther's original list. When he comes to the opposition 'Nature, Grace' the writing expresses contrasts in itself. The 'Nature' paragraph,[13] as we noted, contains brief natural images; but these together make a picture. What has come 'through the fault of Adam' is seen through a serpent (and its poison) and a tree (and its fruit) throughout the paragraph, in a familiar iconography. That icon is something fixed. The next paragraph, beginning 'By grace . . .' shows us 'plucked out' of that picture, and moved to be 'grafted in Christ the root of all goodness. In Christ god loved us as his elect and chosen before the world began . . .' There follows a soaring sentence of ten phrases, each beginning with 'and', which may be set out thus:

and reserved us unto the knowledge of his son
and of his holy gospel,
and when the gospel is preached to us he openeth our hearts,
and giveth us grace to believe
and putteth the spirit of Christ in us,
and we know him as our father most merciful,

and consent to the law,
and love it inwardly in our heart,
and desire to fulfil it,
and sorrow because we cannot,
which will . . . is sufficient . . .

The work of Christ, in the experience of salvation, goes on and on through existential verbs, arranged in threes after the 'and when'— 'openeth, giveth, putteth/know, consent, love/desire, sorrow, is sufficient . . .' The verbs, like even more miniature figures in a tiny *Pilgrim's Progress*, tell the whole story of Christ's work with a believer.

The foundation of those present and future verbs is something past:

the blood of Christ hath made satisfaction for the rest;
the blood of Christ hath obtained all things for us of god:

making it secure:

Christ is our
             satisfaction
             redeemer
             deliverer
             saviour
                       from vengeance and wrath.

It makes a sort of four-two win for Christ over vengeance and wrath. The final command is not to attend mass or do penance but the very Lutheran work of 'Observe and mark in the epistles of Paul, and Peter, and in the gospel and epistles of John what Christ is unto us'.[14] That paragraph is made of New Testament phrases—the mind that composed it is steeped in Paul and John, or phrases from them, in English.

'Faith, love, works' says the margin against the next sentence: and Tyndale does not want to disentangle them. He has come to the final words in his original list, 'Working and believing. Deeds and faith . . .' (the latter a mirror of the former). He uses the few lines there to lead to the longer summary of 'Righteousness', which demonstrates many mis-takings of works in the light of all that has gone before, Law and Gospel, Nature and Grace. Even Peter and Paul sighed after righteousness. Paul 'cried out saying "Oh wretched man that I am: who shall deliver me from this body of death?"'—a cry in Romans 7 which went through Tyndale's New Testaments, with one variation, into the Authorised Version and today.

The Cologne Prologue: Use of Scripture

Which brings us to the third quality of these pages, the making of the text a tapestry of Scripture. 'He that believeth on me', Tyndale writes, 'shall never more die.' 'The law was given by Moses: but grace and verity by Jesus Christ.' It takes a moment to recognise that these quotations from John 11 and 1 at the start of the six pages (at the top of the fourth page of the prologue) are the first printed New Testament passages from the Greek to appear in English. He translates from John 1 again, lower down the page—'This is he of whose abundance, or fulness, all we have received, grace for grace, or favour for favour.' In mid-page, he quotes Paul from 2 Corinthians 3 saying that the Law is 'the ministration of death', contrasted presently with the Gospel as 'the ministration of life . . . the ministration of the spirit, and of righteousness'. Tyndale, like Luther, quotes from the Gospel and first Epistle of John and the major Epistles of Paul.

This writing about the Gospel in the first page and a half is almost entirely made of the New Testament: the quotations do not stick out like sultanas in a scone—they are part of the verbal mixture, in which the New Testament is used more in paraphrase than in precise renderings. The sense is exact, but the words are often used as if from memory. Indeed, that may be exactly what is happening. Comparing the New Testament quotations with the two later Tyndale translations, the Cologne 1525 and Worms 1526, and the 1534 revision, shows something odd. The quotation from John 1 which begins the section, 'The law was given by Moses: but grace and verity by Jesus Christ', does not match the version in the Worms New Testament, where it is 'favour and verity', changed again in 1534 to 'grace and truth'. 'Ministration of righteousness' becomes 'administration . . .' Of course, Tyndale, like all good translators, constantly revised, and it may be such a process that we are seeing. On the other hand, consider a particularly Pauline passage in this prologue such as

> As affirmeth Paul saying: which loved us in his beloved before creation of the world. For the love that god hath to Christ, he loveth us, and not for our own sakes. Christ is made lord over all, and is called in scripture god's mercy stool; whoever flieth to Christ, can neither hear nor receive of God any other thing save mercy.[15]

It is at the same time both impeccable New Testament theology and quite hard to pin down. The address is direct, the texture exactly like Paul in English as he would be found in Tyndale's two translations; but where is it from? The last part echoes Romans 10 and other places. The 'mercy stool' reference is to Romans 3. (The history of that particular coinage will be considered later.)

It seems possible that Tyndale is putting together some central New Testament texts from memory. Memory of what? It has been customary to say that Tyndale did not use the Wycliffite versions. But the revised Wyclif version, which we now call Wyclif B, has for John 1 'For the law was given by Moses: but grace and truth is made by Jesus Christ', and for Paul 'ministration of death . . . ministration of the spirit . . . ministry of righteousness . . .' Had the Wyclif B version gradually established a form of words for some key texts in English which were in common use? It is imaginable. That other sentence from John, in Wyclif B, however, is 'and of the plenty of him we all han taken', which is pidgin, not English (Tyndale translates it 'and of his fulness all we have received'). It mirrors the Latin which it is translating. Yet that, of course, is what the first quotations in Tyndale are doing as well. It is not too difficult to conceive that the Vulgate's phrase in John 1, 'quia lex per Moysen data est, gratia et veritas per Jesum Christum facta est', had existed in an English version for some time as 'for the law was given by Moses, but grace and truth were made by Jesus Christ'. It is, after all, a key text. Was the same, however, true of the 'God's mercy stool' phrase, which seems to have come from Luther's 'gnade stuel'? Or of Paul's cry from Romans 7, noted above? There Wyclif B has for Tyndale's 'O wretched man that I am' the very different 'I an unsely man', itself a curious form of the Vulgate's 'Infelix ego homo!' Tyndale's drawn-out syntax there is very good for the Greek *talaiporos* with its sense of laborious hardship in misery. It is highly unlikely that before Erasmus's 1516 Greek New Testament or Luther's New Testament of September 1522 similar English phrases were part of some common pool from the Greek. It is very possible, however, and indeed likely, that, as on the one hand, up to the 1520s when Tyndale was tutoring, studying and preaching, there was some re-establishment of the theology of the New Testament, particularly focused on Paul; so on the other, those men and women who understood that New Testament theology was the ground of the work of reform, had already available a pool of texts in English from the Vulgate. (They would extend a late medieval tradition of making such short English passages, though for devotional use within the Church rather than for theological use to challenge it, as we saw in the previous chapter.) One would give a great deal to be able to study Tyndale's sermons in Bristol and in London. The existence of such a pool would do nothing to diminish his achievement, of course, which was to turn into English the whole New Testament from the Greek. Much more study of the question of which New Testament texts in English, in the sense of quotable sentences, were circulating in the early 1500s needs to be done.

Some help might again come from a parallel study of proverbs. At the very learned end of the culture, model apophthegms were published at the beginning of the century by Erasmus, and at the end of the century by Bacon. In making his theological manifesto a catena of New Testament quotations and echoes in English, Tyndale was behaving like any hard-pressed man of the time, joining together formulaic statements to try to express what was felt to be almost inexpressible, whether it were a personal philosophy in proverbs or the mystery of salvation in the New Testament.

It is tempting make a bold suggestion that a good deal of the first part of Tyndale's Prologue was not written in Cologne, and was not even at first written to preface a New Testament, but was a long-considered statement of his understanding of the gospel of Christ as expressed by Paul, presented in English texts that were already in a common pool, now reinforced by contact with Luther and stitched on to his own address to readers at the beginning, with some quotation from the *Vorrhede*. Literary (and biblical) scholars might say that to disintegrate the composition of a text like this is a technique over a hundred years out of date: yet there is evidence, beyond that already given, and one further and even bolder, suggestion, which point in that direction.

Tyndale's own six-page exposition of Luther's list of essentials concludes with a long sentence which ends 'commending his weakness unto god in the blood of our saviour Jesus Christ'. It is a convenient period, and the Prologue could have ended there. Instead, comes an inset heading 'Here shall ye see compendiously and plainly set out the order and practice of everything afore rehearsed'. Then follow five pages which are not a précis of what has gone before, but a full and harsh statement of some New Testament doctrines of our bondage to Satan, through Adam's fall, until Christ, bringing faith, sets us at liberty. Christ gave himself and was an example. Works, however elevated, do not qualify us for heaven: Christ's blood obtained that for us. The law binds us: Christ looses us; it is his doing.

The tone is remarkably different. The familar sequence of echoes and quotations from the New Testament has gone. The references in the first pages are largely to the Old Testament. The form of address, even when revisiting the 'fault of Adam' matter from his earlier 'Nature' paragraph, is now ferocious. He begins:

The fault of Adam hath made us heirs of the vengeance and wrath of god, and heirs of eternal damnation. And hath brought us into captivity and bondage under the devil. And the devil is our lord, and our ruler, our head, our governor, our prince, yea and our god. And our will is locked and knit faster unto the will of the devil, than could an hundred thousand chains bind a man unto a post. Unto the devil's will consent we, with all our hearts, with all our minds, with all our might, power, strength, will and lust. With what poisoned, deadly, and venomous hate, hateth a man his enemy? With how great malice of mind inwardly do we slay and murder? With what violence and rage, yea and with how fervent lust commit we advoutry [adultery], fornication and such like uncleanness? With what pleasure and delectation inwardly serveth a glutton his belly?[16]

The biblical echo, 'with all our hearts, with all our minds . . .' is the command in Deuteronomy 6 to love God, but horribly inverted. For a whole page there is a terrible picture of the total depravity of man. 'Man's wit, reason and will, are so fast glued, yea nailed and chained unto the will of the devil . . .' It is as if suddenly the sun has gone in, and a dark cloud of St Augustine covers the writing. More, even the glimpse of the sun has an odd Christology about it: 'His blood, his death, his patience, in suffering rebukes and wrong, his prayers and fasting, his meekness and fulfilling the utmost point of the law, appeased the wrath of god . . .' Christ's meekness is mentioned at 2 Corinthians 10, his patience only in a doubtful phrase, not by an Apostle, in Revelation 1. Christ's prayers and fasting are not the ground of the theology of Peter or Paul. Indeed, the qualities and activities in that paragraph—patience, prayers, fasting, meekness—are truly New Testament only in the sense that they are what was expected of members of the earliest congregations, rather than part of the work of Christ. The emphasis is on more human activity and applied to Christ it has the feel of older, more scholastic, even monkish, writing.

Moreover, the theology does not fit the Tyndale of the earlier section. There, what appeases the wrath of God, as in the New Testament, is Christ's blood and death as in Romans 5 and elsewhere. That he also appeased the wrath because he 'fulfilled the utmost point of the law' is hard to locate in Paul or Peter, or even the more likely Epistle to the Hebrews. When the New Testament uses 'fulfil', it is usually referring to Christ fulfilling the Scripture. The nearest, perhaps, is a sentence in Romans 10, 'For Christ is the end of the law, to justify all that believe' as Tyndale had it, though there is nothing there about the wrath of God. The overwhelming New Testament application of the Greek word for law, *nomos*, itself translating as the Septuagint did the core Hebrew word *torah*, is to the believer's relation to the Law, not Christ's. True, Matthew 5 gives Christ saying that 'one jot or one tittle' of the law shall not pass till all be fulfilled by him: but that is countering any notion of licence, rather than announcing that his work is to appease a wrathful god.

What has happened? It might seem that Tyndale had returned to Luther's *Vorrhede*, but that is not so. It has long been left behind. These pages, do however, smell strongly of Luther: the vivid image of the man bound to a post by more than a hundred thousand chains has a neurotic quality in its excess not a hundred miles from Luther at times; the long strings of legal words ('our redeemer, deliverer, reconciler, mediator, intercessor, advocate, attorney, solicitor . . .' (sig. B3); the repeated *hertz von grund* phrase (though something similar appears in the 'Tyndale only' passages above); the issue of living chaste as an illustration of works, with its attendant claim of being no nearer heaven 'than a whore of the stews (if she repent)'; even the phrasing of a long quotation from Romans 8 on sig. B4—all these, and more, seem to suggest dependence on some writing by Luther not yet identified.[17] (Luther wrote a great deal before 1525, and most of his writing is not yet in English.) On the other hand, though the Old Testament quotations are typical of Luther, the New Testament references are untypically wide, being to Matthew, Mark, Luke, one to John, one to 1 Peter and several to Paul. They are noticeably closer to Tyndale's Worms translation, though sometimes not exactly matching. Their very range suggests something beyond a common pool of proof-texts.

The inset subheading, 'Here shall ye see compendiously . . .' does mark a break. The formula is fairly frequent in books of the time, and perhaps need not be taken too seriously. The mystery remains, about five pages which on many grounds (not all covered here) do not quite share the qualities of Tyndale's six solo pages. There may be behind them a different writing of Luther's: but even if that were so, the translating and adapting does not quite match Tyndale's usual grace. A bold suggestion here follows: that unlike Tyndale's solo six pages, the final five pages were written after most, or all, the New Testament had been translated, but not printed—using the reasonable assumption that Tyndale and Roye would not have started with Quentell until the whole work was in manuscript. This would mean that well-known texts (presumably from a common pool) would be less in evidence (as they are), and lead to a higher rate of accurate relation to the finished New Testament (as happens). The rather rougher manner of translation might be explained as being the work not of William Tyndale but of William Roye. In 1527 Roye published a translation of a short German book (see chapter 6, below), and in 1529 a translation by Luther of 1 Corinthians 7, on marriage. In both he referred to working with Tyndale on the New Testament. Neither translation has yet been studied in the detail required for certainty here, but the immediate impression is that Roye's work of translating from German is generally cruder than Tyndale's, the images and colloquialisms (usually introduced) being coarser and the syntax rather more muddied. These attributes would fit the qualities of that part of the prologue— just as there is nothing in those last five pages which quite sings in Tyndale's voice.[18] (It may be also that Roye contributed some of the marginal notes in Cologne. This would account for certain infelicities, observed for example in the second note to Matthew 1, above.) There would be nothing unusual in such an occurrence. We may be assured that Tyndale felt that his authority over the whole enterprise was secure.

A page from the end of the prologue to the Cologne New Testament fragment, on sigature B4, contains the longest New Testament quotation, a passage from Romans 8. Though it is not exactly as in the Worms 1526 translation, it is noticeably close, with at least one shared unique reading ('angel' for the Greek 'angels'). This printed in English for the first time, possibly a year ahead of the Worms translation, speaks of Tyndale's presence in the whole:

> Who shall separate us from the love that god loveth us withal? . . .
> Shall tribulation? Anguish? Persecution? Shall hunger? Nakedness?
> Shall a sword? Nay, I am sure that neither death, nor life, neither
> angel, neither rule, nor power, neither present things, nor things to
> come, neither high nor low, neither any creature is able to separate
> us from the love of god which is in christ Jesu our lord.

Chapter 6

WORMS, 1526

The 1526 New Testament

The small city of Worms, with its Roman Cathedral and eight-hundred-year-old history of meetings of the Diet, so recently linked wth Luther's name, was hospitable to 'the English apostates' who had fled from Cologne. Tyndale, assisted by Roye, successfully completed the printing of the translation of the whole New Testament at the press of Peter Schoeffer, probably early in 1526. It was a simple, small, octavo (roughly hymn-book size), without prologue or marginal notes, with simple chapter-breaks, printed in exceptionally clear Bastard type (*Schwabacher*) with small illuminations at the start of each book.[1] It is little else but seven hundred pages of text. Of a print-run said to be either three or six thousand, two copies survive, one imperfect. Neither has a title-page, but we know from Tyndale's remarks in the preface to *The Parable of the Wicked Mammon* that he did not put his name to the book, following the counsel of Christ to do 'good deeds secretly and to be content with the conscience of well doing'. The date on a title-page might have been late 1525, or more probably 1526. Copies were brought to England and were already being sold openly, for example by 'Master Garrett, Curate of All Hallows in Honey Lane London' by early February 1526.

It was Tyndale's revision of this New Testament eight years later in 1534 which not only went forward into later Renaissance Bibles, most notably the Authorised Version, but is still dominant, even today. Yet the 1534 Testament, important as it is, is a revision. We must not lose sight of the extraordinary quality of that first printed New Testament in English, as it was welcomed and read in London and southern and eastern England. Here was suddenly the complete New Testament, all twenty-seven books, the four Gospels, the Acts, the twenty-one Epistles and Revelation, in very portable form, clearly printed.

Here was the original Greek, in English. The bare text itself was complete, and without an iota of allegorising commentary. Everything that had been originally written was here, to be read freely without addition or subtraction. The only constraints were the implicit command to read it, and in reading to relate one text to another, even one book to another, so that the high theology of Paul in the Epistles could be understood in relation to the words and work of Jesus in the Gospels.

It was the Greek in English, the common *koine* of the first-century Mediterranean in the common spoken language of England. Phrase after phrase after phrase came from English life as lived in the 1520s by English people: 'A city that is set on an hill cannot be hid . . . No man can serve two masters . . . Ask and it shall be given you. Seek and ye shall find. Knock and it shall be opened unto you . . . and the floods came, and the winds blew . . . as sheep having no shepherd . . . give unto one of these little ones to drink, a cup of cold water only . . .' These phrases, here taken at random from the earlier chapters of Matthew, would have been on the sheets of the abandoned Cologne edition and possibly were therefore already familiar to some readers. But here were no longer scattered fragments, but the whole thing, the precious first-century documents in which the Christian faith was first formulated, in modern English.

What still strikes a late-twentieth-century reader is how modern it is. There are occasional words that have been lost to common use since 1526, like 'noosell' for nurture, or have changed their meaning, like 'naughty' for valueless, or 'haunt' for remain. But both vocabulary and syntax are not only recognisable today, they still belong to today's language. This seems to be for two reasons. First, Tyndale goes for clear, everyday, spoken, English. Because it was largely the current language of his day, it remains largely a current language of ours. He is not out to make antiquarian effects, as the Authorised Version did, for partly political reasons. The result is that Tyndale usually feels more modern than the Authorised Version, though that revision was made nearly a century later. The second reason is that Tyndale makes a language for the Word of God which speaks to the heart: 'And all that heard it wondered, at those things which were told them of the shepherds. But Mary kept all those sayings, and pondered them in her heart.' (Luke 2.) That is the end of one of the Christmas stories. Such phrases have gone deep into the consciousness of English-speakers ever since. The twelve words of the second sentence, only slightly changed in the Authorised Version, have been rightly loved. (Tyndale has kept the Greek's 'sayings', where the Authorised Version repeats 'things'.)

His 'pondered' is his own. It not only matches and extends 'wondered'; it does something original and important. Luther in the 'September Bible' has *bewiget* (weighed), which is too evaluative. The Vulgate's *conferens* (basically, brought together), which translates the main meaning of the Greek verb *sunballousa*, conveys thoughtfulness. But Tyndale has gone for what makes the best sense for his ordinary English readers, knowing that it should not need explaining to people what it is for a woman to ponder sayings in her heart.

To take another example. The meditative nature of the fourth Gospel demands a particular kind of technique of translation. Here the Greek must be allowed its proper value all the time—it will do much of its own stylistic work in English if left unhindered. Greek experts can find fault sometimes with Tyndale's grasp of certain verb tenses or of the true function, from time to time, of the little particles which are characteristic of the language. Occasionally things are not quite right. In the opening paragraph of John 14, the printer, by a common scribal error, has dropped a line which in the original seems repeated. In the Greek Jesus says 'I go to prepare a place for you' and then 'If I go to prepare a place for you . . .' There are things that we today would want different. For 'In my Father's house are many mansions' Tyndale has taken over the Vulgate's word *mansiones* for the Greek *monai*, meaning 'places to stay' (from the Greek verb *meno*, to stay or remain), where we might have expected something like 'dwelling-places'. The word was, however, taken straight into the Authorised Version, as was, effectively, the whole chapter—indeed, the whole Gospel: and a late-twentieth-century reader still understands clearly enough what Jesus is saying.

Yet we have cause to be eternally grateful for Tyndale's genius with our own language. There, at the opening of John 14, Jesus explains to his disciples that he will soon be taken from them. 'Whither I go ye know, and the way ye know:'—that is, he will be taken away after having been with them for several years. The opening sentences are full of the most weighty promise. 'I go to prepare a place for you. I will come again, and receive you unto myself . . .' The meaning is as profound as one can find anywhere, but the Greek is simple, with short fluid sentences. The only thing to do in translating is to weigh each Greek word and find a simple form of English. It is no place for unexpected colour in the translating, for straining at special effects. Tyndale begins his chapter, 'And he said unto his disciples: Let not your hearts be troubled . . .' That is the Greek in English. The Greek has effectively two elements—the 'letting not be troubled' and 'your hearts'. Each is clear and serious and recognisable as belonging to profound experience. To have a troubled heart is, for example, a more sorrowful thing than having a troubled mind. Being commanded not to let your heart be troubled, even when hearing spiritual mysteries, is something coming from a special kind of wisdom. By letting the Greek speak, he has allowed the possibility of the weight of glory. Twentieth-century translators have not been so humble. Apparently imagining that the phrase 'a troubled heart' was somehow either not understandable or not relevant to experience, the translators of one modern version give that opening as 'Do not be worried or upset', as if the disciples were being told by Jesus to cheer up after having missed a bus.[2]

Tyndale has also grasped how narrative must be kept moving. To illustrate, consider the teaching and parable of Jesus in part of Luke 14 below. Note the monosyllables of the spoken language, 'the poor, the maimed, the lame and the blind' (not, as someone might try to make it, 'the impecunious, the disfigured, the limping with the addition of the sightless') and the running-forward rhythm of that phrase. Indeed, monosyllables dominate—'The first said unto him: I have bought a farm, and I must needs go and see it'. The parables share with the teaching a tone of absolute clarity. Polysyllables, like 'recompense', are placed at the end for weight: 'lest they bid thee again, and make thee recompense'. In the parable, the similar rhythmic effect of disyllables and polysyllables is striking: 'Come, for all things are ready... I pray thee have me excused... Then was the good man of the house displeased... lord it is done as thou commandest...' Such technique adds power to the unexpected word 'compel' at the end.

> Then said he also to him that bade him to dinner: when thou makest a dinner or a supper: call not thy friends, nor thy brethren neither thy kinsmen nor yet rich neighbours: lest they bid thee again, and make thee recompense. But when thou makest a feast, call the poor, the maimed, the lame and the blind, and thou shalt be happy, for they cannot recompense thee. But thou shalt be recompensed at the resurrection of the just men.
>
> When one of them that sat at meat also heard that, he said unto him: happy is he that eateth bread in the kingdom of God. Then said he to him. A certain man ordered a great supper, and bade many, and sent his servant at supper time, to say to them that were bidden, come: for all things are ready. And they all at once began to make excuse. The first said unto him: I have bought a farm, and I must needs go and see it, I pray thee have me excused. And another said: I have bought five yoke of oxen, and I must go to prove them, I pray thee have me excused. The third said: I have married a wife,

and therefore I cannot come. The servant went again, and brought his master word thereof.

Then was the good man of the house displeased, and said to his servant: Go out quickly into the streets and quarters of the city, and bring in hither the poor and the maimed and the halt and the blind. And the servant said: lord it is done as thou commandest, and yet there is room. And the lord said to the servant: Go out into the high ways and hedges, and compel them to come in, that my house may be filled. For I say unto you, that none of those men which were bidden, shall taste of my supper. (Luke 14.)

To see Tyndale at work with strong Greek narrative is to watch a translator who knows how epic stories are told.

And at the ninth hour, Jesus cried with a loud voice, saying: Eloi, Eloi, lama sabaththani, which is, if it be interpreted: my god, my god, why hast thou forsaken me? And some of them that stood by when they heard that said: behold, he calleth for Helias. And one ran, and filled a sponge full of vinegar, and put it on a reed, and gave it to him to drink, saying: let him alone, let us see whether Helias will come and take him down. (Mark 15.)

('Sabaththani' is a misprint for 'Sabachthani'.) Tyndale has turned Greek participial phrases, like 'one running' into English clauses, 'one ran'. So 'being interpreted' becomes 'if it be interpreted'; 'those standing by' becomes 'that stood by'; 'hearing' becomes 'when they heard that'. This keeps more of the sequence of finite verbs, 'cried', 'be interpreted', 'hast forsaken', which lead at the heart of the action to the force of 'stood', 'heard', 'said', 'calleth', 'ran', 'filled', 'put' and 'gave'. Tyndale's double 'filled a sponge full' catches the Greek sense in *gemisas* of not just 'full' but 'freighted'. It is not in the Latin or Luther. But like the strong simple verbs, it has the manner of the greatest stories.

A different kind of New Testament narrative begins in the Greek of Acts 21, where 'we' suddenly replaces 'they' for the last eight chapters of that book, recording Luke's eyewitness account. It is his journal of the happenings in Jerusalem which led to Paul's appeal to Caesar, and of his resulting eventful journey to Rome. The sense of reportage is strong.

And we found a ship ready to sail unto Phenices, and went aboard and set forth. Then appeared unto us Cyprus, and we left it on the left hand, and sailed unto Syria, and came unto Tyre. For there the ship unladed her burden . . . and they all brought us on our way, with their wives and children, till we were come out of the city. And we kneeled down in the shore and prayed . . .

Here the looser, even more casual, run of the sentences and clauses, marked by the repeated 'and' with 'then' and 'till', gives the proper sense of journal notes.

In other words, Tyndale is sharply aware of the variety of registers in the whole New Testament, within particular books, and even within chapters. The narrative of a parable is differently formed, shows a different craft, from the language of high and dramatic event, and different again from a more informal journal. This is one happy result of his preference for the common spoken language. Appeal to Latin, so characteristic of the Authorised Version, tends to flatten differences, and make one special kind of language for everything, something a little antiquated, a little removed, and feeling therefore, for the New Testament, rather artificially holy. There is nothing artificial about 'And there were two evil doers led with him to be slain. And when they were come to the place, which is called Calvary, there they crucified him, and the evil doers, one on the right hand, and the other on the left hand.' (Luke 23.) The heart of the English, as of the continental, theological Reformation was the discovery of the theology of Paul. Central to Tyndale's insistence on the need for the Scriptures in English was his grasp that Paul had to be understood in relation to each reader's salvation, and he needed there, above all, to be clear. Paul presents the translator with special problems, when his thinking is dense and allusive, and the surface of the sense hard to follow. To illustrate Tyndale at work, consider the celebrated passage of Paul being both pastoral and metaphoric, at the end of his Epistle to the Ephesians, in chapter 6. The Christians of Ephesus, as Paul well knew from first-hand experience, were subject to pressures from the local magic cults. He begins 'Finally, my brethren be strong in the Lord, and the power of his might.' Three different words are needed for the idea of strength. The Greek of the first, *endunamousthe,* 'acquire strength', is related to the noun *dunamis,* which has given us dynamic, dynamo and so on. The second, *kratei,* is one of a group of *krat-* words all expressing power, might and especially rule or sway or dominion. The third, *ischuos,* is strength or might in the sense of bodily strength. The sentence is so familiar in English that it is hard to remember that Tyndale made it. The Vulgate gave him *potentia* for the second, but *virtutis* for the third. Luther's three words are *bekrefftiget, macht* and *stercke* (revised in 1546 to *seyd stark . . . der Macht seiner Staerke,* doubling the first

word). Tyndale has thought about rhythm. (Modern translators seem to
trouble less: one has 'Finally, find your strength in the Lord, in his
mighty power'.[3]) Which might we think preferable, since the words
could be interchangeable, 'the might of his power' or 'the power of his
might'? The strength of the closing-off made by the final 't' in 'might',
Tyndale seems to have understood, outweighs his frequent preference
for closing a sentence or phrase with a disyllable. 'Put on the armour
of god, that ye may stand steadfast against the crafty assaults of the
devil. For we wrestle not against flesh and blood: but against rule,
against power, and against worldly rulers of the darkness of this world,
against spiritual wickedness in heavenly things.' The Authorised Version
has 'Put on the whole armour of God, that ye may be able to stand
against the wiles of the devil. For we wrestle not against flesh and
blood, but against principalities, against powers, against the rulers of
the darkness of this world, against spiritual wickedness in high places.'
'Whole armour' is better for the sense of full armour in the Greek
panoplia. Paul's general drift about what is being fought against is
graspable, though somewhat mysterious in detail if we do not know
the Ephesian cults. But Tyndale's determination to be clear is well
demonstrated. There is more hand-to-hand in Tyndale's combat. Standing steadfast against crafty assaults, though it is different from the 'being
able' which the Authorised Version has correctly brought in from
the Greek, leads to nouns which yield more sense. The Authorised
Version has gone back to the Vulgate's *principes et potestates* to produce
something grand but surely vague. The words 'principalities and
powers' may mean something to demonologists (and King James wrote
a book on the subject) but what Tyndale felt were wanted were words
with their feet more on the ground, 'rule' and 'power': and with
'worldly rulers' he was understanding the Greek better than the
Authorised Version did, as he was with 'in heavenly things'.

Paul in the Epistle to the Romans develops an argument from the
faith of Abraham who 'contrary to hope, believed in hope, that he
should be the father of many nations . . .'. Such faith 'was reckoned to
him for righteousness'; something that was not for Abraham also, 'but
also for us . . . so we believe on him that raised up Jesus our Lord from
death'. The last sentence of that chapter 4 is 'Which was delivered for
our sins, and rose again for to justify us'.

Chapter 5 begins: 'Because therefore that we are justified by faith,
we are at peace with god through our lord Jesus Christ: by whom we
have a way in through faith, unto this favour wherein we stand and
rejoice in hope of the praise that shall be given of God.' We might
expect Tyndale, translating a passage so famously linked with Luther,

to draw specially on Luther's 'September Bible'. He does not do so. Indeed, he characteristically goes his own way with 'we are at peace with god' where Greek, Latin and German all say 'have peace with'. Perhaps Luther's *Eingang* suggested Tyndale's 'a way in'—or perhaps not. The Greek is a touch complicated, *prosagogen* suggesting a privileged approach or entrance—the Vulgate gives *accessum*. But 'a way in . . . unto this favour wherein we stand' is as clear as could be and Tyndale must have felt that it was not a moment for ultra-sophistication. 'Favour' is his also, acceptable for the Greek, where Vulgate and Luther have 'grace' (in 1534 he changed it to 'grace'). 'The praise that shall be given of god' is also his own, extending the Greek's 'the glory of God' to defeat ambiguity, as the Vulgate and Luther are made to do, in different ways.

Many more than a few pages are needed to do any kind of justice to Tyndale's first New Testament. The point to establish is that Tyndale was so visibly his own man. He knew what he was doing. The 1526 New Testament has occasional infelicities, but it is triumphantly the work of a Greek scholar who knew that language well, of a skilled translator who could draw on the Latin of the Vulgate and Erasmus, and German, for help when needed, but above all of a writer of English who was determined to be clear, however hard the work of being clear might be. The word of God must speak directly in a way that can be understood by a reader alone. The bare text, if given whole, will interpret itself.

Finally, here is Tyndale translating Paul at his most argumentative and trenchant, in the middle of Romans 7—as complicated a passage as can be found in the New Testament.

> What shall we say then? Is the law sin? God forbid: but I knew not what sin meant and but by the law [corrected in 1534 by dropping the 'and']. For I had not known what lust had meant, except the law had said, thou shalt not lust. But sin took occasion by means of the commandment, and wrought in me all manner of concupiscence. For verily without the law, sin was dead. I once lived without law. But when the commandment came, sin revived, and I was dead. And the very same commandment which was ordained unto life, was found to be to me an occasion of death. For sin took occasion by the means of the commandment and so deceived me, and by the self commandment slew me. Wherefore the law is holy, and the commandment holy, just and good.

'God forbid' throughout these Romans passages is Tyndale's, and it went through to the Authorised Version and far beyond. The Greek is an idiom of the order of 'let it not happen!' The Vulgate has *Absit* (Go away!) and Luther *das sey ferne* (be that far away).

The tone of the passage is one of control. By 'lust' Tyndale means as the Greek does a bad form of desire; he uses the Anglo-Saxon form in preference to the Vulgate's *concupiscentiam*, but turns to that word for the extension of lust into the wider 'all manner of . . .' The Authorised Version manages by strange alterations—making the second 'lust' into 'covet', quite against the Greek: complicating Tyndale's 'I once lived without law' into 'For I was alive without the law once'; and unnecessarily putting a scattering of words into italics, not to mention doubling the marks of punctuation—to make the reasoning that much more cloudy. Tyndale knows Paul's argument and is conveying it as lucidly as he can, and for that the reader is grateful.

Sophistical pedantry can still find damnable fault with Tyndale's Greek on occasions and dismiss the whole—as he himself remarked in the Prologue to the Pentateuch, condemn as heresy his failure to dot an 'i'. But sophistical pedantry does not live in most English-speakers' minds, mouths and hearts for nearly five centuries. 'The signs of the times', 'the spirit is willing', 'Live and move and have our being', 'fight the good fight'—the list of such near-proverbial phrases is endless. More important is that greater effect whereby the teaching and work of Jesus reached men and women entire, complete in all four Gospels: and with it the further writing and record of Luke in Acts, of Paul, Peter, James, the two Johns, Jude and the author of the Epistle to the Hebrews, also entire and complete and in a pellucidly direct English. The boy that driveth the plough had got his Scripture. With this volume, Tyndale gave us a Bible language.

William Roye

What part William Roye had in the work remains conjecture. Two heads are better than one. It might be safe to assume that both sat with Erasmus's Greek Testament, with its new parallel Latin, in front of them, with Luther's 'September Bible', also its second and third editions, and the Vulgate, also open; and Greek, Latin and German dictionaries to hand: and that Roye wrote down for the printer what Tyndale decided. Friar Roye was not without ability. Tyndale records in the preface to *The Wicked Mammon* that Roye supplied necessary help 'both to write and help me compare the texts together'. As with the Cologne fragment, so in this 1526 New Testament, no-one's name appears on the title-page. But it was Tyndale's work, and known as that. As the Cologne prologue begins 'I have here translated . . .' and goes on 'The causes that moved me . . .' so the epilogue to this 1526 Testament also speaks in the first person singular: 'I have interpreted it, as far forth as god gave me the gift of knowledge, and understanding . . .'

Roye does at least seem to have understood something about the man he was working for. There are references in two of his own five books which make that clear. In his *Brief Dialogue between A Christian Father and his Stubborn Son* printed in Strasburg on 31 August 1527 he wrote 'It is not unknown to you all . . . how that this last year, the new testament of our saviour, was delivered unto you, through the faithful and diligent study of one of our nation . . . named William Hitchyns, unto whom I was . . . as help fellow, and partaker of his labours.'[4] Two years later, in two additional paragraphs to the prologue to his translation of Luther on the seventh chapter of First Corinthians (a great Lutheran defence of marriage) printed in 1529, Roye defends his use of a different word from that in 'our English text'. He notes that he does not want to appear to be setting up in rivalry, as 'our Pharisees' will be quick to suggest, leading them to 'speak evil . . . of me and of the good man which did it translate. . . .'[5]

Tyndale himself, however, twice gives what is possibly a rather different view of Roye. In the 1534 New Testament, the first prologue, 'W.T. Unto the Reader', refers to him beginning his revision (of the 1526 Testament) by weeding out of it many faults, 'which lack of help at the beginning, and oversight, did sow therein'. That remark could be made to suggest that Roye's presence was not valuable. It might mean that the translation was begun in Cologne (or before) without him, and he was recruited (or volunteered) to help. More specifically, as seen above, two years later, in 1528, in *The Parable of the Wicked Mammon*, the first book to have his name on the title-page, Tyndale devotes nearly half his Prologue to an attack on Roye's character.[6] He writes that he took pains to warn a fellow friar of Roye's, Jerome Barlow, who had come out from England in the spring of 1527, to be careful with Roye: 'which Jerome with all diligence I warned of Roye's boldness and exhorted him to beware of him and to walk quietly and with all patience.' His advice was not taken. 'Nevertheless when he was come to Argentine [Strasburg] William Roye . . . gat him to him and set him a work to make rhymes, while he himself translated a dialogue out of Latin into English, in whose prologue he promiseth more a great deal than I fear me he will ever pay.' The 'rhymes' were Barlow's knowledgeable scurrilous poem attacking Wolsey, *Rede me and be not wroth . . .* , a violent piece of work printed in Strasburg in 1528. No names were on the title-page. Tyndale apparently heard that he was said to be the author. For Tyndale to be even thought of as writer of such 'railing rhymes' could only do damage, not just to the new Protestant cause, but also to God's Word: for it was also common knowledge that Roye had helped with the New Testament in Cologne and Worms. The English exiles on the Continent were few enough for gossip to suggest that the verses had been made by Roye and another person. To feel the force of Tyndale's attack on Roye, we have to remember that up to 1528 the only Protestant works printed in English and coming into England were Tyndale's New Testament and his translation of Luther on Romans, his *Mammon* and his *Obedience*, Roye's *Brief Dialogue* and Barlow's *Rede me . . .* Of the three writers, Tyndale and Roye were known as the principals.

In the preface to *Mammon* Tyndale is using one of the few defences he has. He nowhere denies that Roye assisted with the New Testament work, allowing the common claim to stand. What he has to do is to make sure that he himself is strongly removed from any smears-by-association, either with regard to the published New Testament work, or, just as importantly, to the Old Testament work most probably then under Tyndale's hand. For Roye damagingly remarked in his *Brief Dialogue* that he, Roye, had 'partly translated certain books of the Old Testament', work that Tyndale would be widely known to be than undertaking. No doubt Roye was translating from the Latin rather than the Hebrew: no trace of any such work has survived. But it would be one more thread to bind Tyndale to the tuppence-coloured *Rede me . . .* So Tyndale detaches himself by affirming that the man is a specious rogue, and leaves it at that. For the dignity, and above all the authority, of the Word of God, no less, is at stake.[7] This makes the ground of Tyndale's character-attack very different from what a late-twentieth-century reader might assume. He is defending the capacity of the Word of God left untramelled to justify its own authority. Tyndale is effectively asserting that the language of the fairground devalues the only currency God has. It is not for nothing that the passage against Roye prefaces his exposition of that parable wherein he tackles systematically the issue of works as subsidiary to faith. Roye's untrustworthiness and trivial works show him seriously lacking in faith.

Examination of Roye's writing does not improve the picture. His *Brief Dialogue* is a translation of a small book for the instruction of children printed in Strasburg in 1527 by Wolfgang Capito, the pastor of New St Peter's, Strasburg, who was a close friend and colleague of Martin Bucer and in 1532 married the widow of the German scholar and reformer, Oecolampadius. Whether Roye worked also from the

Latin version that then existed, or entirely from the German text, is not known. But enough can be drawn from his handling of that text to show that Roye had a mind of some immediate spirit and ingenuity (he gets literary advantage out of reversing the characters, so that the stubborn son catechizes the Christian father) but cruder craft than Tyndale, coarsening the colloquialisms he introduces, confusing the syntax of the original, leaning towards polysyllabic neologistic Latinisms like 'preordination' and 'exterial' and showing some intellectual disorder.[8] The *Rede me* . . . poem was known to contemporaries as *The Burial of the Mass*, and as such represented the English model of an existing strain of German satire. But the poem moves away from the account of the death of the Mass (which, it says, robbed the clergy of great profit) to become a work in the line of native English late-medieval and early Tudor satire denouncing the evils of the times. Even the focus on Wolsey, 'an individual who seemed in his own person to epitomise all the most appalling vices of church and state',[9] was a common one, familiar from satires by John Skelton, in much the same running metres. How much of the work was Roye's beyond the initial suggestion is unknown. It is virtually empty of theology. It varies between vapid incompetence and occasional Skeltonic sharpness, so perhaps two hands were at work. It was popular in England for what it was, but Tyndale felt, surely rightly, that the mind that bent itself to the great work of turning the Greek New Testament into English should not be seen to be scrabbling in the mud. He himself would presently, and in the *Obedience* especially, pound similar targets with a whole front line of properly aimed heavy artillery. For the moment, he felt betrayed by Roye's shallowness of mind. (He was not to know that Roye would be burnt for heresy, it seems, in Portugal in 1531.[10])

A Bare Text

In 1868 Bishop Westcott wrote of Tyndale that 'His influence decided that our Bible should be popular and not literary, speaking in a simple dialect, and that so by its simplicity it should be endowed with permanence.'[11] That this, God-given as it was, was the product of great labour under greater difficulties, Tyndale makes clear in his three-page epilogue to his 1526 New Testament, 'To the Reader'. He explains that he knows that there is room for improvement. On the one hand he had no English model, either of translation or of commentary—he is a pioneer: '. . . that the rudeness of the work now at the first time, offend them [that are learned Christianly] not: but that they consider how that I had no man to counterfeit, neither was holp with English of any that had interpreted the same, or such like thing in the scripture before time.' On the other, he was actively hindered: 'Moreover, even very necessity and cumbrance (God is record) above strength, which I will not rehearse, lest we should seem to boast ourselves, caused that many things are lacking, which necessarily are required. Count it as a thing not having his full shape, but as it were born afore his time, even as a thing begun rather than finished.' 'In time to come (if god have appointed us thereto)' he will revise by pruning and filling out where necessary, and so on—he gives a short list of what he knows needs to be done.[12] There follow three pages of errata, giving seventy literals to be corrected. Many escaped, like the 'Wehdder' of Matthew 21, an ommission of 'ypocrites' in Matthew 23, 'whith in him' of Luke 4, and the peculiar 'And they had no leisure wong for to eat' in Mark 6.

Though the impact of this New Testament was, and is still, so splendid in its accuracy and its clear, memorable English, there are occasional things which might have been done better. The dropped line in the first paragraph of John 14 may not have been wholly in Tyndale's control. What was in his power was the awkwardness of rhythm which sometimes startles: in Matthew 13, the excellent 'And the children of the kingdom, they are the good seed' is answered not by what he gave in 1534, 'And the tares are the children of the wicked' but by 'The evil man's children are the tares', which jolts oddly to an anticlimax. In Matthew 18, Peter does not ask, 'Master, how oft shall I forgive my brother, if he sin against me, seven times?' as in the 1534 revision, but the overloaded 'master, how oft shall my brother trespass against me, and I shall forgive him? shall I forgive him seven times?' In the discussion of the 1534 revision, it will be seen that there are scores, and indeed hundreds, of improvements, the products of greater finesse with English, of greater knowledge of Greek, and particularly of the impact of Tyndale's Hebrew studies. On the other hand, it is possible to list some forty instances where the change was not for the better. One of the clearest is in Matthew 19, where Jesus lists the commandments to the young enquirer. Here is the 1534 version:

> The other said to him, Which? And Jesus said: break no wedlock, kill not, steal not: bear not false witness: honour father and mother: and love thy neighbour as thyself. And the young man said unto him: I have observed all these things from my youth, what lack I yet?

And here the 1526

> He said: Which? And Jesus said: Thou shalt not kill. Thou shalt not break wedlock: Thou shalt not steal: Thou shalt not bear false witness:

Honour thy father and mother: And thou shalt love thine neighbour
as thyself. The young man said unto him: I have observed all these
things from my youth: what have I more to do?

We do not know what the words 'very necessity and cumbrance
(God is record) above strength' in the epilogue refer. They might be
about the inadequacies of William Roye, with whom Tyndale was
apparently stuck until the end of the work. Peter Schoeffer, though
bearing a distinguished name (his father had been a celebrated printer
in Mayence), and a good Protestant printer of German Bibles, as well
as general books (one on mining, for instance), may not have been
ideal for a New Testament in English. There might have been difficulties for two Englishmen in the small city of Worms. Reference books
may have been hard to come by. Monmouth's money might not have
been adequate. This is guesswork. But what that last page and a half of
the epilogue expresses, supported by the list of errata and the other
faults in the text, is stress. The most likely explanation of the cause of
the apology as well as the blemishes is that after the experience in
Cologne, Tyndale felt himself under threat. In Cologne he had seemed
safe, and was not. In Worms, though a Lutheran city, he might still be
prevented. The important thing was to get the book out and across the
sea and on sale in England. This seems the most convincing reason for
the omission of the prologue and marginal notes. He might have
received word from people in England who possessed sheets of Matthew from Cologne that such Lutheran matter would not help; we
have no evidence. Peter Schoeffer, in all his Worms printing, tended to
produce octavos, with some folios: the necessity for Tyndale to abandon the Cologne quarto size to fit in with Schoeffer's working habits
could have contributed to the decision to make a bare text, quickly.

The first half of the epilogue consists of four paragraphs which
summarise the Cologne prologue. Tyndale begins:

> Give diligence Reader (I exhort thee) that thou come with a pure
> mind, and as the scripture saith with a single eye, unto the words of
> health, and of eternal life: by the which (if we repent and believe
> them) we are born anew, created afresh, and enjoy the fruits of the
> blood of Christ. Which blood crieth not for vengeance, as the blood
> of Abel: but hath purchased life, love, favour, grace, blessing, and
> whatever is promised in the scriptures . . .

The third and fourth paragraphs distinguish the Law and the Gospel,
while simply pointing to the necessity of the Law. Though he does not
refer there to Paul, the fourth paragraph is thoroughly Pauline, in its
contrast of the law, leading to repentance, and the promises 'unto the

mercy of god and his truth, and so shalt thou not despair: but shalt feel god as a kind and a merciful father.'

These one-and-a-half pages make a miniature instruction-manual for reading the New Testament. Read, 'repent and believe the gospel as saith Christ in the first of Mark', and begin life anew. 'And his spirit shall dwell in thee, and shall be strong in thee: and the promises shall be given thee at the last . . . and all threatenings shall be forgiven thee for Christ's blood's sake, to whom commit thyself altogether, without respect, either of thy good deeds or of thy bad.' Repentance and belief is all. Works count for nothing in Christ's blood, as the last phrase shows. Repentance and belief come from reading, which brings salvation. This is sound New Testament doctrine: boil that book down, and this is what you get. All Tyndale is doing is giving a distillation of the seven hundred pages which have gone before. For that to work, you have to take the entire book, not snippets, and the whole book, not later constructions. The second paragraph explains: 'Mark the plain and manifest places of the scriptures, and in doubtful places, see thou add no interpretation contrary to them: but (as Paul saith) let all be conformable and agreeing to the faith.' There is strikingly no reference to the Church, to what the pope, the bishops or the priests teach; nor to the ceremonies of the Church as necessities for salvation; nor to the tomes of casuistry erected on each syllable of Scripture down the centuries; nor to the element, taught as essential, of doing good works, especially in giving money to priests, monks and friars. All you need is this New Testament and a believing heart.

Thus Tyndale is not being perverse in translating the New Testament word for the Christian minister, *presbuteros*, as 'senior', reserving 'priest' for the occasional Greek *iereus*, the Jewish religious official. In Greek, a *presbuteros* is 'a more senior man'—it is the comparative of the word for an old man. (In 1534, Tyndale changed his reading to 'elder'.) The group of Christians together, called by the New Testament *ekklesia*, he calls, correctly, a 'congregation': the Greek word means 'an assembly', ultimately those called together by the town crier. *Congregatio* had been used by Erasmus in his parallel Latin translation for the Greek *ekklesia* wherever it occurred. Tyndale avoids 'church' because it is not what the New Testament says. The Greek verb *metanoeo* means, precisely, 'repent', that is turn the mind, and so Tyndale gives 'repent', and not 'do penance'. The Greek verb *exomologeo* has a primary sense of 'acknowledge, admit', and 'acknowledge' is what Tyndale usually prints, rather than 'confess'. The Greek word *agape* is one of several words for 'love', so Tyndale prints 'love' (as in 1 Corinthians 13) and not 'charity'. In other words, he is making the New Testament refer inwardly to itself, as he instructs his readers to do, and not outwardly to the enormous secondary construction of late-mediaeval practices of the Church: priests and penance and confession and charity. Interpretation, as he explains in the second paragraph of the epilogue, has to be so that 'all is conformable and agreeing to the faith' of the New Testament. He cannot possibly have been unaware that those words in particular undercut the entire sacramental structure of the thousand-year Church throughout Europe, Asia and north Africa. It was the Greek New Testament that was doing the undercutting.

A Compendious Introduction to Romans, with A Treatise of the Paternoster

Also from Peter Schoeffer of Worms in 1526 or early 1527[13] came another theological book in English, a thin octavo of twenty-two leaves, again in Bastard (*schwabacher*) type, entitled *A compendious introduction, prologue or preface unto the epistle of Paul to the Romans*. There was no name on the title-page, but it was known in England as Tyndale's, and an expanded version appeared as the introduction to Romans in Tyndale's 1534 New Testament. Only one copy now exists, in the Bodleian Library.[14] It was the second Protestant tract in English, and like the 1525 prologue, it is based on Luther, in this case his *Vorrhede auf die Epistel Sanct Paulus zu den Romern*, 'Prologue to the Epistle of St Paul to the Romans' in all the editions of his German New Testament. It was a key document for the reformers throughout Europe, being 'probably Luther's finest exposition of the doctrine of justification by faith'.[15] As in the Cologne Prologue, Tyndale feels able to weave in and out of Luther, freely adding phrases, sentences or whole paragraphs while translating. In this he was helped by a Latin version of Luther's German made in 1524 by Justus Jonas, who also freely uses Luther, often expanding his sentences to twice the original length. Tyndale, however, is not a slave to either. He feels free to take what he needs from German or Latin in order, above all, to make the doctrine clear.[16]

> We have a chance in all this to see Tyndale at work as a writer and translator, and are struck by the energy with which he searches on the one hand for clear explanations and amplifications of difficult concepts, and on the other for images with which to increase vividness. His handling of Luther displays a concern to put over the Lutheran doctrines with intelligibility and power.[17]

Tyndale can be watched flying solo, for example on the theme of regeneration. When Luther expounds Paul's fourth chapter—faith is justified without works (although it does not remain without them): man is helpless in the sway of evil, the Law and the Gospel play their roles; good works follow; God is absolute sovereign—Tyndale adds a longish paragraph, of which the second sentence is

> For how is it possible to do anything well in the sight of God, while we are yet in bondage and captivity under the devil, and the devil possesseth us altogether and holdeth our hearts, so that we can not once consent unto the will of God.[18]

The intensity of that is carefully built, with cumulative clauses and a rounded shape which effectively makes the Devil a double filling (bondage, possession) in a God sandwich (sight of God, will of God). Like Luther, Tyndale refers to 'the thunder of the law', but unlike Luther he brings with it 'the pleasant rain of the gospel'. Later, Tyndale brings home Luther's general idea of original sin in an added first-person passage of some existential power, about the difference between not hurting an enemy and being able to love him, refusing money and being able to stop loving riches, and 'To abstain from adultery as concerning the outward deed can I do of mine own strength, but not to desire in mine heart is as unpossible unto me as it is to choose whether I will hunger or thirst, and yet so the law requireth.'[19] To the spiritual man, writes Luther, outward works can be spiritual, like Peter fishing. Tyndale adds 'the very wiping of shoes, and suchlike'. Tyndale does not follow Luther's, or Jonas's, anticlericalism, where both attack Rome explicity, being content with unspecific reference to 'those who beguile the simple with the traditions of men'.[20]

The last nine pages of the little book ('to fill up the leaf withal') are Tyndale's 'treatise' on the Lord's Prayer, freely adapted from one of Luther's expositions of it, in this case a *kurtz begreiff* or summary of a longer exposition on the Prayer.[21] Tyndale writes his own two-and-a-half-page introduction, with familiar images of the sinner as sick and longing after health, and how 'no crafty subtlety of the devil' can 'separate us from the love of God in Christ Jesus'. A striking passage towards the end is pure Tyndale: 'I pass over with silence, how without all fruit, yea with how terrible ignorance the lay and unlearned people say the pater noster and also the creed in the Latin tongue.'[22] The main text is a fair translation of Luther, a little dialogue between the Sinner and God, where Luther is expanding the biblical text, and Tyndale is expanding Luther, adding about a quarter as much again in extensions of ideas and sentences.

Tyndale's second book from Peter Schoeffer, this *Compendious Introduction* was attacked in England as the work of Tyndale and Roye, especially in a letter from Robert Ridley, Tunstall's secretary, to Tunstall.[23] To have Roye associated was, as we saw, damaging for Tyndale. English information was often significantly wrong, intentionally or no. The same letter of Robert Ridley, refers, apparently specifically, to Tyndale and Roye's New Testament, which is fair enough, but also to what can only be a complete Matthew and Mark done in Cologne. On this subject there has been much throwing about of brains, not least by Mozley.[24] Ridley does however say in his letter that he has not the books in front of him. He mistakenly gives the 1526 Worms New Testament a prologue. He quotes nothing from the supposed earlier Mark. Just as Tunstall later, as we shall see, even on a special occasion made gross errors about the book he was attacking, which suggests that he did not do the checking himself,[25] so Ridley is probably recalling observation by someone else, and may himself not have seen the translations. It does not matter. Tyndale's 'lay and unlearned people' did, and they now had the complete New Testament in their own tongue.

Part 3

PERSECUTION AND POLEMICS

Chapter 7

THE WICKED MAMMON

We next hear of Tyndale in Antwerp, that tight, thriving city of trade and commercial enterprise. We do not know when he left Worms or where he was in the two years between the issuing of the Worms New Testament and the *Compendious Introduction* in 1526 and 8 May 1528 when his next book, *The Parable of the Wicked Mammon*, was printed in Antwerp. One thread of evidence has him in Hamburg with Miles Coverdale at some point, but that is associated with the translation of the Pentateuch, and probably belongs later in the story. Whether he can be thought realistically to have spent time with Luther at Wittenberg is discussed later.

Antwerp had good printers and an export trade of books to England. Though knowledge of English in Antwerp was poor, and there was poor regard for the language, the printers worked through Dutch and German stationers in London.[1] Antwerp had a powerful English community of merchants, and it is not surprising to find Tyndale at the time of his arrest nine years later, in 1535, living in the English House in Antwerp: that may have been his address from as early as 1526. He was certainly in Antwerp at those key moments in 1531 when Stephen Vaughan met him on Cromwell's behalf, though Vaughan had been told that he was in Frankfurt, Hamburg or Marburg; such information was perhaps cover. He must have travelled; but Antwerp would be a good place in which to settle and be inconspicuous. All his books from now on were printed in Antwerp, and it was a printer in that city who pirated his New Testament. Antwerp was one of Europe's centres of Christian humanism as well as 'heretical' printing. It was the place where not only Tyndale's Pentateuch and revised New Testament appeared, but George Joye's translations of the Psalms and some Prophets (from Latin). It was where the first complete Bible in English was printed, Coverdale's translation of 1535, and the first Bible in English to be licensed, 'Matthew's Bible' of 1537.

The Parable of the Wicked Mammon was the first of Tyndale's extended
treatises; it is an exposition of the New Testament teaching that faith
is more important than works. It is loosely based on a sermon by
Luther, about the puzzling 'wicked mammon' parable in Luke 16,
better known today as 'the unjust steward', in which a servant accused
of embezzlement is unscrupulous in getting back into his master's
favour and is commended. Tyndale makes it a means of approaching a
theological problem. We are supposed to do good works—look no
further than Matthew 25, 'I was an hungered, and ye gave me meat: I
was thirsty, and ye gave me drink . . .', and so on; yet works, though
important, do not bring eternal life. Luther and Tyndale emphasise that
the teaching in the New Testament is that true works only come
naturally from true faith, as fruit comes from the tree. Moreover, the
mistaken reliance on works leads to the superstitious dependence on
ritual, something fostered by the Church simply for its own profit: at
the hour of death, we are saved by faith in the promises of God, as
Tyndale puts it, and not by a holy candle.

The book is a clearly-printed black-letter octavo of seventy-two
leaves, and thus, in form, pocket-size and roughly like a slim version
of the 1526 Worms New Testament. The colophon states that it was
'printed the viij. day of May. Anno M.D. xxviij', and gives a false name
for the printer. It is the first of ten quite well-printed English Lutheran
books appearing between 1527 and 1535 from 'Hans Luft of Marburg',
who was in reality Johannes Hoochstraten of Antwerp.[2] Hans Luft was
certainly a printer of the time, but he was in Wittenberg and particularly successful with Luther's own works. Such concealing devices were
increasingly common. Hoochstraten called himself various names, including 'Peter Congeth at Parishe', 'Joannes Philoponos at Malborow',
and 'Adam Anomymous, Basel'.[3] Several printers suggestively located
themselves in 'Utopia', or, for fully Lutheran pieces, even 'Rome, at St
Peter's court'.[4] The pages of *Mammon* have few ornaments and no
marginal notes; 'The Principal notes of the book' are printed on two
leaves at the end. There is no title-page as such. Instead, on the first
side of the first leaf, is the following:

> That faith the mother of all good works justifieth us, before we can
> bring forth any good work: as the husband marrieth his wife before
> he can have any lawful children by her. Furthermore as the husband
> marrieth not his wife, that she should continue unfruitful as before,
> and as she was in the state of virginity (wherein it was impossible for
> her to bear fruit) but contrariwise to make her fruitful: even so faith
> justifieth us not, that is to say, marrieth us not to God, that we

should continue unfruitful as before, but that he should put the seed of his holy spirit in us (as saint John in his first epistle calleth it) and to make us fruitful. For saith Paul Ephes.2 By grace are ye made safe through faith, and that not of your selves: for it is the gift of God and cometh not of the works, lest any man should boast himself. For we are his workmanship created in Christ Jesu unto good works, which God hath ordained that we should walk in them.

This is the 'title' of what was now the sixth Lutheran work in English, little books smuggled into England, after the sheets of the 1525 Cologne New Testament. The second was Tyndale's own 1526 complete Testament from Worms, the third Tyndale's *Compendious Introduction to Romans*, the fourth Roye's *Brief Dialogue* and the fifth *Read me and be not wroth*, by Jerome but apparently encouraged by Roye. This new long 'title' is a trumpet-call. It is Lutheran, declaratory, and made of the New Testament—the last third of it is Paul in Tyndale's own 1526 translation. The 'title' is in its way sensational. We could expect a book so announced to have had a powerful impact in England, and that is what we shall find.

Prologue to The Parable of the Wicked Mammon

It is the first book of the six with an attribution. The first four leaves are a prologue headed 'William Tyndale otherwise called hychins to the reader'. He must have thought he had a pressing reason to declare himself. In a revealing narrative in the first two pages of the preface, half of the whole, he tells us first his previous position.

> The cause why I set my name before this little treatise and have not rather done it in the new testament is that then I followed the counsel of Christ which exhorteth men Matt. vi. to do their good deeds secretly and to be content with the conscience of well doing, and that God seeth us, and patiently to abide the reward of the last day, which Christ hath purchased for us and now would I fain have done like wise but am compelled otherwise to do.

The compelling reason, however, comes out of unhappiness. When the work at Worms on the 1526 New Testament was finished, his slippery assistant William Roye went on to Strasburg and apparently made a fool of himself in print. Tyndale had to dissociate himself publicly. He did it by telling the story, and then by setting those events against the New Testament, and particularly the teaching of Paul. So far, so clear. William Roye, having been an incompatible but adequate assistant to

take the place of the unknown helper who did not arrive, left him
when the work was done, early in 1526, and, having dubiously made
new friends and some money, went off to Strasburg 'where he
professeth wonderful faculties and maketh boast of no small things . . .'
The real trouble began in May of the following year, 1527.

> A year after that, and now twelve months before the printing of this
> work, came one Jerome a brother of Greenwich also through
> Worms to Argentine [Strasburg], saying that he intended to be
> Christ's disciple another while, and to keep (as nigh as God would
> give him grace) the profession of his baptism, and to get his living
> with his hands, and to live no longer idly and of the sweat and
> labour of those captives which they had taught not to believe in
> Christ: but in cut shoes and russet coats.

Like Roye, Jerome had been a Franciscan friar in the reformed
order of Observants in their monastery at Greenwich. Jerome was
apparently saying that his Christian conscience could no longer allow
him to live idly on the backs of monastery servants taught to believe
not in Christ but in the sign of having been on a pilgrimage ('cut
shoes') and in the monastic institution ('russet coats'). Though warned,
Jerome set to work with Roye, to make the anti-Wolsey rhymes: the
first printing of *Rede me and be not wroth* opens with an emblem of
Wolsey, in which his cardinal's hat is coloured red, and the six axes in
the design have drops of red blood falling from them. Tyndale's attack
on Roye did not come from peevish bad temper, as has been asserted.[5]
It is not for nothing that the passage against Roye prefaces his exposition of the parable wherein he tackles systematically the issue of
works as subsidiary to faith: Roye's bad works show him lacking in
faith, and untrustworthy.

The Parable

The book proper, opens with Jesus's parable from Luke 16, set in
larger, bolder type. Tyndale follows his own 1526 translation (apart
from two or three minor changes in punctuation).

> There was a certain rich man which had a steward that was accused
> unto him that he had wasted his goods. And he called him and said
> unto him. How is it that I hear this of thee? Give accounts of thy
> stewardship. For thou mayest be no longer my steward. The steward
> said within himself: what shall I do? for my master will take away
> from me my stewardship. I cannot dig, and to beg, I am ashamed.

I woot [know] what to do, that when I am put out of my steward-
ship, they may receive me into their houses.

Then called he all his master's debtors, and said unto the first,
how much owest thou unto my master? And he said, an hundred
tons of oil, and he said to him. Take thy bill, and sit down quickly,
and write fifty. Then said he to another, what owest thou? And he
said, an hundred quarters of wheat. He said to him. Take thy bill,
and write fourscore. And the lord commended the unjust steward,
because he had done wisely. For the children of this world, are in
their kind, wiser than the children of light. And I say also unto you,
make friends of the wicked mammon, that when ye shall have need,
they may receive you into everlasting habitation.

What follows in the book divides into three large sections, with
systematic sub-sections. One of the important apsects of this treatise, as
of others of Tyndale, neglected until now, is the logical step-by-step
way the argument is developed.[6] The first main section is about faith
and works—how faith has to come first, and alone justifies. The
second, arising from a brief discussion of the meaning of 'mammon'
(an Aramaic word meaning 'riches') and particularly 'unrighteous
mammon', so-called 'principally because it is not bestowed and ministered unto our neighbours' need', plunges into the problem of why we
should follow an unjust steward, who waits wisely on his own
unrighteousness: if only the righteous were so wise to work, pray or
study. There follow twenty-nine pages of lavish quotation from Matthew 5, 6 and 7 (the Sermon on the Mount) and elsewhere in the
Gospels, with digressions into Paul and John's Epistles, making the
New Testament speak for itself on the point that true wisdom should
follow true faith in Christ, with a page on the power of Scripture.
The final section starts with the New Testament understanding that
we are naturally damned but God sends his spirit to open our eyes
to his mercy. In that case, Tyndale asks, what are good works, what
is their intent, and how do they serve? He lists the principal ones
as commended by Scripture—fasting, watching, prayer and almsgiving—concluding with thirty-eight pages of Scripture doctrine and
illustration.

The method, as it would have been in the preaching of the time, is
of a rather simple systematic argument under headings, filled out with
repetition and illustration of the basic truths of the New Testament—
our sinfulness, Christ's promises, our faith in him alone saving us—
making a kind of layering. Tyndale is following Luther, but as usual
making the matter very much his own, particularly in the reiteration

of the central fact. This, says Tyndale, is the gospel, and he lays over that statement another of what the gospel is, and another and another and another. This is not a twentieth-century method; but such accumulation immerses the reader in the New Testament. It is impossible to come away from this book not knowing a good deal of the Gospels, and of what Christ and Paul taught, side-lit from John and Peter. It is likely that in writing it Tyndale had in mind that for some readers these pages could have been a first encounter with New Testament words in English, and a first exposition of the New Testament doctrine of faith before works. Accumulation of New Testament reference and quotation has a confirming effect. Tyndale, as a reformer, understood that Scripture, separately in both Testaments and then taken together whole, comments on and proves Scripture. Later, the force of Scripture leads Tyndale to attack what is unscriptural in current Church practice, but not here as often as in later books such as the *Obedience*.

His one-and-a-half-page introduction to the whole argument announces that as people have been falsely led to trust in works, he will set out the true New Testament teaching. To show a little of the ordering of his ideas, here is the first main section of the three main parts, on faith and works, set out to show how it also divides into three, and into three again, like this:

I. Faith comes first and alone justifies.
   A. Faith alone brings life: the law, death.
      1. God cannot but fulfil his promises.
      2. Paul and Christ declare goodness necessary before good works result.
      3. The law cannot justify, only the promises.
   B. Scripture enjoins good works.
      1. Matthew 25, 'I was an hungred . . .'
      2. These only come from faith.
      3. Scripture ascribes both faith and works to God only.
   C. The outward works show the inward goodness.
      1. Righteousness is by faith, shown by works: profit is not to result.
      2. Eternal life follows faith and good living, and cannot be earned.
      3. God (not saints) receives us in heaven: works should be aimed at the poor, not saints.

(The complete systematic scheme will be found at the end of this book in Appendix A.)

Tyndale's source is Luther, specifically a sermon printed twice, in identical texts, at Wittenberg in 1522, *Ein Sermon von dem unrechten Mammon Lu. XVI.*[7] Luther gives partly an exposition of the parable,

> it is, more essentially, a discussion of the relationship between faith and works, in the light not only of Luke XVI but also of many other New Testament passages which seem to imply that works will win salvation and heaven for man. Luther maintains, first, that faith alone justifies, second, that true faith will always reveal itself in good works done freely and without thought of reward, and, third, that it is not the saints, but God, who receives men into heaven.[8]

We see at once that this is only the first of Tyndale's three main sections. Tyndale has greatly expanded Luther, as he had done before with the Prologue to the Cologne New Testament and the *Compendious Introduction to Romans*, but here the enlargement is much greater. Luther's printed sermon occupies only six leaves in quarto; Tyndale has six times as much. As before, the expansion is in two ways: the filling-out of Luther's rather stark sentences, often with human experience; and the addition of much new material. Here, in the *Wicked Mammon*, both ways are themselves much extended: Tyndale, as he learns his craft of scriptural translation and exposition, develops his own strengths, and leaves Luther increasingly behind. Here he grounds Luther's theology in everyday experience, opening up the German statements of doctrine to describe over and over again what it is like to be human and experience the unmerited gift of faith. Moreover, Tyndale alone sets out the whole parable—Luther's text is only the final verse, 'make friends of the wicked mammon, that when ye shall have need, they may receive you into everlasting habitations'. Luther preached often, and many sermons have survived: the Weimar edition prints sixty-four for the year 1522, a not uncommon number. Many were printed at the time. This one, however, had at least five editions in 1522 and one in 1523, printed in Wittenberg, and probably as well in Augsburg, Basle and Erfurt. It was a well-known statement of the primacy of faith, and in translating it Tyndale was showing himself to be firmly in the Lutheran mainstream. At the same time, he was not just translating it: his *Wicked Mammon* is an *English* Lutheran work, existentially illuminated—and five times the length.

Tyndale's increasing freedom can be felt everywhere. For Luther's three introductory paragraphs, he prints one of his own, beginning 'Forasmuch as ... many have ...', a direct echo of his translation of the opening of Luke's Gospel. Because many have 'enforced to draw people from the true faith', he begins (a statement then expanded with biblical quotation, continuing 'and brought them in belief that they shall be justified in the sight of God by the goodness of their own works, and have corrupted the pure word of God, to confirm their Aristotle withal . . .', a point again developed), 'wherefore I have taken in hand . . .'; a phrase that again imitates Luke's opening sentence,

> to expound this gospel, and certain other places of the new Testament; and (as far forth as God shall lend me grace) to bring the scripture unto the right sense, and to dig again the wells of Abraham, and to purge and cleanse them of the earth of worldly wisdom, wherewith these Philistines have stopped them. Which grace grant me God, for the love that he hath unto his son, Jesus our Lord, unto the glory of his name. Amen.

After this information, Tyndale greatly expands Luther's brief introductory quotations of four texts from Romans to prove that faith alone justifies, and amplifies the German to expound at length over six sides a number of other texts on faith, the law and the gospel. Tyndale is going out of his way at the very beginning to explain law and gospel, expecting to reach readers who would find it all very new. Luther had already by August 1522, the month of the sermon, been copious on the subject. By 1528 there had been nothing at all printed in English with such radical theology, apart from Tyndale's 1525 Cologne prologue, and his Worms *Compendious Introduction*. Tyndale, we must also notice, is behaving like a good Erasmian rhetorician, using the figure *amplificatio*. His own thirty-eight-line introductory paragraph, plus thirty-line parable (replacing Luther's thirty-three lines) is all one sentence, amplifying in balanced sections the contrast between the teachings of the schoolmen and of Scripture. Now, as the treatise begins, his first point reproduces Luther's proof from Paul that faith alone justifies, and then amplifies it extensively, layer by scriptural layer. Tyndale uses *amplificatio* in two particular directions, scriptural and existential. In both those he is being properly Erasmian. An appeal to ancient texts linked with illustration from everyday life in the same remark or in adjacent sentences in good clear Latin is how Erasmus advised a student to write, as in *De copia*, and how he himself worked, as in the *Enchiridion*. Yet Tyndale is his own man: he is writing good clear English, which Erasmus would not appreciate, and his texts are all from Scripture, a source which Erasmus noticeably avoided (we nowhere have Erasmus on Romans). Tyndale both takes Luther's Scripture references further and makes his everyday illustrations move Luther's bald statements into fuller humanity. Thus, to show the latter work in action, where Luther, on his first page, remarks 'Gleich wie er leyplich muss zuuor gesundt seyn ehe ehr arbeytt und gesund werck thutt' ('Just as a sick man must previously be made bodily whole before he can do the work of a whole man'), Tyndale takes that idea and elaborates it:

> even as a sick man must first be healed or made whole, ere he can do the deeds of an whole man, and as the blind man must first have sight given him ere he can see: and he that hath his feet in fetters, gyves or stocks must first be loosed or he can go, walk or run, and even as they which thou readest of in the Gospel that they were possessed of the devils, could not laud God till the devils were cast out . . .[9]

Unlike Erasmus, however, all Tyndale's amplificatory pictures of human life have one common theme—the healing release that comes from the work of Christ in a body. Where Luther explains that the effect of faith on the human heart is to make a man renewed and reborn and live in a new way, Tyndale amplifies as follows:

> Therefore it [faith] is mighty in operation, full of virtue and ever working, which also reneweth a man, and begetteth him afresh, altereth him, changeth him, and turneth him altogether into a new nature and conversation, so that a man feeleth his heart altogether altered and changed, and far otherwise disposed than before, and hath power to love that which before he could not but hate, and delighteth in that which before he abhorred, and hateth that which before he could not but love. And it setteth the soul at liberty and maketh her free to follow the will of God, and doth to the soul even as health doth unto the body, after that a man is pined and wasted away with a long soking [consuming] disease. The legs cannot bear him, he cannot lift up his hands to help himself, his taste is corrupt, sugar is bitter in his mouth, his stomach abhorreth longing after sibbersause and swash [bland food and pig-swill], at which his whole stomach is ready to cast his gorge. When health cometh, she changeth and altereth him clean, giveth him strength in all his members and lust to do of his own accord that which before he could not do neither could suffer that any man exhorted him to do, and hath now lust in wholesome things, and his members are free and at liberty and have power to do of their own accord all things which belong to an whole man to do, which afore they had no power to do, but were in captivity and bondage. So likewise in all things doth right faith to the soul.[10]

Here, after the opening line freely rendering Luther, Tyndale has made a soaring set of variations on the theme of joyful release from illness. Later in the treatise, little pictures from home life begin to be seen: in the course of three of his own paragraphs on, as so often, the nature of the law and the promises, Tyndale notes the way the law reveals, and even causes, wrath: 'when the mother commandeth her child, but even to rock the cradle, it grudgeth [complains], the commandment doth but utter the poison that lay hid, and setteth him at bate with his mother and maketh him believe she loveth him not.'[11]

Soon after, the reception of the idea of faith to those who have not heard of it before is 'as when a man telleth a story or a thing done in a strange land, that pertaineth not to them at all. Which yet they believe and tell as a true thing.'[12] A full parallel text, Luther alongside Tyndale, would show that Tyndale adds to Luther's words, over and over again, description of the effect of the gift of faith on personality, a genuine alteration, something visible. He is recording a conversion experience, a transformation. His method is to craft as carefully as ever, with short parallel units in a swift rhythm, patterns of sound through alliteration and assonance, and so on: but there can be felt through it all strong feeling 'in our hearts' about what it is to receive Christ and be converted. The nature of the experience and its intensity are both clear.

> And when the gospel is preached unto us we believe the mercy of God, and in believing we receive the spirit of God, which is the earnest of eternal life, and we are in eternal life already, and feel already in our hearts the sweetness thereof, and are overcome with the kindness of God and Christ and therefore love the will of God, and of love are ready to work freely, and not to obtain that which is given us freely and whereof we are heirs already.[13]

That is Tyndale not Luther. The most remarkable of all Tyndale's additions to Luther is what develops from the example he chooses in order to show that outward deeds are signs of inward faith. This is the story in Luke 7 about Simon the Pharisee who invited Jesus to his house, and the woman 'who was a sinner' who there anointed Jesus's feet and was told her sins were forgiven and that her faith had saved her (as we saw above,[14] named in late Church tradition as Mary Magdalen, though the Gospels do not say so). This simple example becomes what has been rightly described as a 'cascading passage', where 'its irrepressible torrent of clauses accurately reflects the subject matter'—'like Mary's love, the clauses themselves "could not abide nor hold, but must break out"'.[15] The subject is the reality of works produced by the intensity of feeling at the presence of Christ and faith. The illustration fills three pages of *Wicked Mammon*. Tyndale writes:

Take for an ensample Mary, that anointed Christ's feet . . . [Tyndale then reproduces Luke's story in full from his own 1526 translation, beginning with Simon 'which bade Christ to his house', ending with Jesus's words 'To whom less is forgiven . . .' Tyndale sums up 'Deeds are the fruits of love; and love is the fruit of faith.' He goes on:] But Mary had a strong faith, and therefore burning love, and notable deeds done with exceeding profound and deep meekness. On the one hand she saw herself clearly in the law, both in what danger she was in, and her cruel bondage under sin, her horrible damnation and also the fearful sentence and judgement of God upon sinners. On the other side she saw the gospel of Christ preached, and in the promises she saw with eagles eyes the exceed-ing abundant mercy of God, that passeth all utterance of speech, which is set forth in Christ for all meek sinners. Which knowledge their sins. And she believed the word of God mightily and glorified God over his mercy and truth, and being overcome and over-whelmed with the unspeakable yea and incomprehensible abundant riches of the kindness of God, did inflame and burn in love, yea was so swollen in love, that she could not abide nor hold, but must break out, and was so drunk in love that she regarded no thing, but even to utter the fervent and burning love of her heart only. She had no respect to herself, though she was never so great and notable a sinner, neither to the curious hypocrisy of the Pharisees which ever disdain weak sinners, neither the costliness of her ointment, but with all humbleness did run unto his feet. Washed them with tears of her eyes, and wiped them with the hairs of her head, and anointed them with her precious ointment, yea and would no doubt have run into the ground under his feet to have uttered her love toward him, yea would have descended down into hell, if it had been possible.[16]

The passage responds to rhetorical analysis, revealing as well as alliteration, three-fold parison, *repetitio*. Yet it is also personal and more immediate than anything in Luther's sermon. It bears comparison, also, with the passage quoted above from Nicholas Love's *Mirror*: there Mary expressed her own feelings in direct speech; we are meant to believe that such words were part of Luke's Gospel story, from which of course they are many miles distant. Here Tyndale, by contrast, is amplifying the text to demonstrate the power of love to produce deeds. Nicholas Love and Tyndale share the using of the Gospel to write for the heart. In every other way they are polar opposites, in that Nicholas Love creates his own words for Mary as if they were in the Gospel, full of feeling for devotion and humbled imitation, and all enclosed within the Church. Tyndale, having given Luke's text in full, comments on it, drawing attention to the direct and amazing force of faith upon a sinner at a moment of conversion—an experience enabled by the text alone.

This passage, quoting in full and developing the story in Luke 7, how the inward goodness prompted by love and inspired by faith produces genuine and not feigned good works, is not in Luther. It is typical of the double *amplificatio* that Tyndale uses: on the one hand greatly enlarging Luther's scripture reference, even to longer quotation, and on the other, grounding the meaning of the doctrine in human behaviour. The sub-sections are of different lengths: that which we have labelled II.A, for example, is of only a few lines, as (directly translating Luther) Tyndale explains the word 'mammon'. The last sub-sections of the second and third parts are many pages long (twenty-six in the first, and thirty in the second) and are made up entirely of detailed quotation from, and comment on, the New Testament, from Matthew, Luke and John, with Romans, I and 2 Corinthians, Hebrews, John and Peter's first Epistles, and James's, as well. The Old Testament, the few times that it is mentioned, is seen only through the New, as the classic examples of faith from Abraham and Rahab are reached through James 2 and Hebrews 11, as is a mention of Pharaoh, implicitly. It is, as noted, impossible to come away from this volume not knowing many of the key texts of the New Testament, in English. One of the ways in which Tyndale differs from Luther is in his desire always to instruct, to make things as clear as they can be made. In the Scripture passages that make the last section of all, Tyndale moves right away from the parable of the unjust steward and quotes and expounds many texts that at first sight suggest that good works should be done in order to gain heaven, such as 'If thou wilt enter into life, keep the commandments Matt. xix'. These twenty-six original pages deserve much more attention than there is space for here as, rooted in the words of Christ, they make clear how wrong it is to make works the passport to heaven. Good works do not deserve heaven, or justify the doer, since justification and heaven are given for the sake of Christ's blood. Good works are urged because they are the will of God.[17] Matthew's Gospel alone makes this irrefutable. In this submersion in the New Testament Tyndale differs from Luther, who more frequently elsewhere takes his Scripture from the Old, though not here. This, of course, was one reason for ascribing the last section of the 1525 Cologne prologue to Luther translated by someone other than Tyndale: when Tyndale is flying solo, as it were, and writing to instruct, his mind rightly reaches for the New Testament alone. One of the purposes of this book must have been to penetrate English minds with the essence of the New Testament. In its first following of Luther it is Lutheran: yet most of it is original and Tyndalian, if that word means an entire book immersed in the New Testament.

His other use of *amplificatio* is in the much stronger sense of human life. When he begins his third main part with a steady look at good works, they are not simply the standard late medieval trio of fasting, almsgiving and pilgrimage. He begins 'Good works are all things that are done within the laws of God, in which God is honoured and for which thanks are given to God'[18] A few lines later he expresses vividly how fasting, like modern slimming regimes, can so easily distort.

> Some fast from meat and drink, and yet so tangle themselves in worldly business that they cannot once think on God. Some abstain from butter, some from eggs, some from all manner of white meats, some this day, some that day, some in the honour of this saint, some of that, and every man for a sundry purpose. Some for the tooth ache, some for the head ache, for fevers, pestilence, for sudden death, for hanging, drowning, and to be delivered from the pains of hell.

The running, jolting rhythm of that last sentence is excellent, like an ambling horse: the awkwardness of the breaks matches the folly of the treatments, until the last nine words run away into extreme absurdity. But he goes on, 'some are so mad that they fast one of the Thursdays between the two saint Mary days in the worship of that saint whose day is hallowed between christmas and candlemas, and that to be delivered of the pestilence.'[19] Some pages later, explaining that 'all works are good which are done within the law of God', he is blunt: 'and understand that thou in doing them pleasest God, whatsoever thou doest within the law of God, as when thou makest water. And trust me if either wind or water were stopped thou shouldest feel what a precious thing it were to do either of both, and what thanks ought to be given God therefore.'[20] Such basic reality extends in the next sentence to the essential point that 'as touching to please God, there is no work better than another . . . whether thou be an apostle or a shoe maker . . . Thou art a kitchen page and washest thy masters dishes, another is an Apostle and preacheth the word of God . . . Now if thou compare deed to deed there is difference betwixt washing of dishes and preaching of the word of God. But as touching to please God none at all.'[21] In other words, 'there is nothing to exclude the simplest layman from the upper reaches of the spiritual life';[22] no wonder the English prelates had to destroy this book and those who loved it.

There are over two dozen places in the book where images of daily life as it is lived come as sudden shafts of sunlight: the child complaining when asked to rock the baby's cradle, an actor coming back as someone else, a sick person loathing slops, someone finding the cause of a lunar eclipse, a father speaking to his child, 'he that loveth not my dog, loveth not me', a child warned from the attraction of fire and water, taverners altering their wines, a servant washing dishes. This is a piece of literature quite without pretence to be elevated. Caxton would not have considered it for printing for his wealthy, upper-echelon customers. Indeed, Tyndale, explaining the commonality of works in Christ ('Let every man of whatsoever craft or occupation he be of . . . refer his craft and occupation unto the common wealth, and serve his brethren as he would do Christ himself'[23]) gives a list of crafts or occupations which accurately describes his readers: 'whether brewer baker tailor victualler merchant or husbandman'. Again, it is no wonder that the super-elevated Sir Thomas More sneered, and worse. These are people for whom the Gospel was too good: the good news must be kept from them.[24]

Tyndale can be polemic. Explaining that the world does not understand God and that Socrates, Plato and Aristotle do not reveal him, he presents the common Church view, asking 'How can he be a divine, and wotteth not what is *subjectum in theologia?*' Early in the book he explains that God's 'son's blood is stronger than all the sins and wickedness of the whole world',

> . . . and thereunto commit thyself . . . (namely at the hour of death) . . . Or else perisheth thou though thou hast a thousand holy candles about thee, a hundred tons of holy water, a ship-ful of pardons, a cloth sack full of friars' coats and all the ceremonies in the world and all the good works, deservings and merits of all the men in the world, be they or were they never so holy.[25]

Tyndale's Prologue to *Wicked Mammon* ends with powerful attack on Antichrist—it is he that can come on again in different name and clothes, like an actor—in a long paragraph identified, by means of Christ's attack on Pharisees as hypocrites, with 'our prelates', 'There is difference in the names between a pope, a cardinal, a bishop, and so forth, and to say a scribe, a Pharisee, a senior and so forth, but the thing is all one.'

The old Antichrists brought Christ unto Pilate saying, by our law he ought to die . . . They do all things of a good zeal, they say, they love you so well, that they had rather burn you than that you should have fellowship with Christ . . . Some man will ask peradventure why I take the labour to make this work inasmuch as they will burn it, seeing they burnt the gospel? I answer, in burning the New Testament they did none other thing than that I looked for: not more shall they do, if they burn me also, if it be God's will it shall so be.

Nevertheless in translating the New Testament I did my duty, and so do I now, and will do as much more as God hath ordained me to do . . . If God's word bear record unto it and thou feelest in thine heart that it be so, be of good comfort and give God thanks.[26]

Printing in Antwerp

Printing was of far greater importance in the Low Countries than in England. Up to December 1500, just under 2,000 books were issued there, compared with about 360 in England.[27] In the first decades of the sixteenth century there were some sixty printers in Antwerp, capable of producing work of high quality for a growing English market, and printing in Latin, German, French, Danish, Italian, Spanish, Greek and Hebrew.[28] The large printing-houses, which had rich resources, skilled technical staffs, and learned translators and editors, could produce books cheaply, efficiently and quickly.[29] Much of the output was good, trade, run-of-the-mill stuff and sometimes slightly below, like the first piracy of Tyndale's New Testament in 1526 from Christoffel van Ruremund, also called von Endhoven, in squint-producing sextodecimo. Though the English authorities issued proclamations against books by Luther, Tyndale and Roye (and presently others) not all copies were destroyed, though there was early in 1527 a burning of Tyndale's New Testaments even in Antwerp itself[30]— it is intriguing to think that Tyndale might even have watched. Hoochstraten, who began printing in Antwerp in 1525, at first specialised in Latin theology, but seems to have had some connections with Lutheran circles, especially in Scandinavia. He showed courage. He printed two forbidden Dutch books in 1526 and 1528 under the name of 'Adam Anonymous, Basel'.[31] He printed the ten 'Hans Luft of Marburg' books in semi-black-letter type, workmanlike rather than beautiful. All ten have woodcut initials in common and often share one or two title-page compartments. Printing 'religious' books in

English for smuggling was dangerous, as the word easily meant 'seditious', but it was obviously lucrative.

Since historians regularly announce that Tyndale's work was attacked because of its inflammatory marginal notes, it should stated here that in Tyndale's lifetime editions of *The Parable of the Wicked Mammon* had no marginal notes at all, after the prologue. A few pages at the back of the book give short notes keyed to pages, notes like 'The law death, and the promises life' or 'The promises justify' or 'The talent, Matt.xxv', which act as a kind of index. When there are notes in the margin, they work in a way typical of all Tyndale's treatises. Thus, there are eight marginal notes to the preface, and they make a sort of rough summary: '2 Tim. ii. With God's word ought a man to rebuke wickedness and not with railing rhymes'; 'Antichrist is as much as to say, as against Christ and is nothing but a preacher of false doctrine'; 'Antichrist was ever'; 'Antichrist when he is spied goeth out of the play and disguises himself and then cometh in again'; 'Antichrist is a spiritual thing and cannot be seen but in the light of God's word'; 'The prelates have a burning zeal to their ghostly children'; 'Try all doctrine by God's word' and 'Believe nothing except God's word bear record, that it is true'. These are points which summarise the text. Before we have read the prologue, skimming the margins gives the argument, useful in finding one's way around. As usual, it is instructive to watch the accumulation of notes, now placed in the margin, in editions after Tyndale's death, until by the time of John Daye's edition in 1573 they are averaging five or six on each page. It is these which Walter printed in the Parker Society text. Even so, the zealous searcher after offence in the margins will be disappointed.

Mammon's Reception

The Parable of the Wicked Mammon was published on the 8 May 1528, and it probably began to circulate in England not long after. When the Lutheran-hunting authorities—Tunstall, Warham, Wolsey himself—intercepted copies, they were violent. Archbishop Warham's council of divines found over two dozen heresies in it. A little later, Sir Thomas More called it a 'very *mammona iniquitatis*, a very treasury and wellspring of wickedness . . . the wicked book of *Mammon*'[32] On 18 June 1528, Wolsey instructed the English ambassador to the Low Countries, John Hackett, to demand from the Regent the handing-over of three heretics, believed to have been Tyndale, Roye and an English merchant called Richard Herman, who was a citizen of Antwerp, who had heretical books for sale. The Regent replied that not even the Emperor had powers of extradition, but a search would be made for the three and their books, and they would, if found, be tried. Only if they were found guilty would they be sent to England, or punished on the spot. The investigators only succeeded in finding one, the merchant Herman, whom they imprisoned, in June. Early in the autumn they were still looking, for Tyndale and Roye, and for evidence against Herman. Mozley prints letters from Herman Rinck which give a picture of the confusion the authorities were in, using information that was too meagre, wrong, out of date or all three. After repeated demands for more evidence from England, the Regent's court, receiving little or nothing from Wolsey, gave up on the whole of Hackett's case, and released Herman on 5 February 1529.

Tyndale's *Wicked Mammon*, coming on top of his Worms 1526 New Testament and its Endhoven Antwerp pirating the same year, his *Compendious Introduction*, and (Roye and) Barlowe's *Rede Me . . .* , had stirred up much persecution in England. Many of those mentioned by Foxe were examined or punished, or usually both, for possessing, usually with Tyndale's Testament, 'a book called the Wicked Mammon'. Foxe does not always follow a strict chronological order, to put it mildly, and tends to print documents as they come to hand, making it difficult to get an immediate picture of the rolling, rising tide of persecution in England month by month, from May 1528. Nevertheless, it is clear enough, first, that Tyndale's *Wicked Mammon* had an immediate impact in England, and was read and owned fairly widely among what we can call evangelicals, often tradesmen and merchants:[33] and second, that it continued to be influential and was still prohibited, and hunted out, years later. Foxe gives fuller details of the examination of some of those who owned a copy, particularly if they became martyrs. Thus 'John Tewkesbury, Leatherseller, of London, Martyr'[34] (Strype, using Foxe's papers, calls him a haberdasher[35]) who was converted by the reading of Tyndale's Testament and the *Wicked Mammon*, was twice examined in April 1529, by Tunstall and other bishops and later by More at his house in Chelsea, where he was elaborately tortured.[36] From there he was sent to the Tower and was racked 'till he was almost lame'. (He had abjured, but later recanted and was burned alive by Stokesley.) In his first examination, he was so expert in 'the doctrine of justification and all other articles of his faith . . . that Tunstall, and all his learned men, were ashamed that a leather-seller should so dispute with them, and with such power of the Scriptures and heavenly wisdom, that they were not able to resist him'. Foxe gives several pages to the interrogations and what followed. Tewkesbury was first examined by Tunstall, with the Bishop of St Asaph and the Abbot of Westminster, entirely on detailed articles of heresy 'extracted out of the Book of "The Wicked Mammon"'. He was first asked if 'he would stand to the contents of the book named The Wicked Mammon' to which he replied that he would. Tewkesbury, throughout the documentation, which Foxe prints from Tunstall's register, comes across as an honest, faithful, Christian man—a mixture of Bunyan's Faithful and Mr Standfast—holding firmly to what he has experienced. When a passage of the book, from the section on alms, was put to him,

> Now seest thou what alms-deeds meaneth, and wherefore it serveth. He that seeketh with his alms more than to be merciful, to be a neighbour to succour his brother's need, to do his duty to his brother, to give his brother what he owed him, the same is blind, and seeth not what it is to be a Christian man[37]

(which is an edited version of the passage in Tyndale), Tewkesbury replied 'that he findeth no fault throughout all the book, but that all the book is good, and it hath given him great comfort and light to his conscience.'[38] The first examination was on nineteen articles, of which these are typical: 'First, that Antichrist is not an outward thing, that is to say, a man that should suddenly appear with wonders, as your forefathers talked of him, but Antichrist is a spiritual thing— Whereunto he answered and said, that he findeth no fault in it.' 'Again, it was demanded of him touching the article, whether faith only justifieth a man? To this he said, that if he should look to deserve heaven by works, he should do wickedly; for works follow faith, and Christ redeemed us all, with the merits of his passion.' Or, '"We are damned by nature, as a toad is a toad by nature, and a serpent is a serpent by nature." To that he answered, that it is true, as it is in the book.' The next examination, before Tunstall and the Bishops of Ely, Lincoln, Bath and Wells, and others, produced another five articles of heresy, as 'Item, "We desire one another to pray for us. That done, we must put our neighbour in remembrance of his duty, and that he trust not on his holiness."—To this he answered, 'Take it as ye will; I will take it well enough"'. Again and again, Tewkesbury answers that he finds no fault, or no ill, in it, a sentiment surely hard not to agree with.

Later detailed attacks on the *Wicked Mammon* allow us to watch the process of destruction, invariably by the manipulation of evidence to reveal heresy. Quoted phrases are left incomplete, summaries are subtly false, and ideas are imported. Archbishop Warham, on 24 May 1530, with his bishops, issued 'A Public Instrument . . . for the abolishing of the Scripture and other Books to be read in English', which opens with 'Heresies and Errors collected by the Bishops out of the Book of

Tyndale, named "The Wicked Mammon"'. Foxe prints the twenty-nine articles of heresy, and adds his own comments.[39] The very first article is 'Faith only justifieth', on which Foxe comments, 'This article being a principle of the Scripture, and the ground of our salvation, is plain enough by St Paul and the whole body of the Scripture; neither can any man make this a heresy, but they must make St Paul a heretic, and show themselves enemies unto the promises of grace, and to the cross of Christ.'

Against almost every Article, Foxe simply writes 'Read the place', or 'The words of Tyndale be these', indicating distortion. For example, Article VII, 'Christ with all his works did not deserve heaven': Foxe prints Tyndale's passage,[40] which not only gives impeccable Christology, ignored by the Article, but shows that the damage is done simply by cutting Tyndale's phrase short: what Tyndale wrote was '. . . Christ did not deserve heaven (for that was his already) . . .' By supplying contexts, correcting wording, completing statements and, above all, appealing directly to Scripture, Foxe shows the extent of the manipulation needed to make charges of heresy. Before printing the full passage after Articles II and III ('The law maketh us to hate God, because we be born under the power of the devil', and 'It is impossible for us to consent to the will of God'), Foxe writes, 'The place of Tyndale from which these articles be wrested, is in the "Wicked Mammon" as followeth: which place I beseech thee indifferently to read, and then to judge.'[41]

A modern biographer of More calls *The Parable of the Wicked Mammon* 'fierce', adding that 'it exalted justification by faith and held the standard Lutheran position that good works were sinful if they were done with a view to reward', saying no more about it.[42] Even apart from that travesty of the content of Tyndale's book, we may wonder what is the more 'fierce': printing the New Testament accurately in English, protesting when the word of God is burned, and setting out the New Testament doctrine of faith with much quotation—or imprisoning, humiliating, repeatedly torturing and finally burning alive men and women.

Chapter 8

TYNDALE AND ENGLISH POLITICS

English Readers and Persecution

We need now to go back in time a little and catch up with events in England, and look at those who were buying and studying Tyndale's writings. The second wave of the campaign against Luther and his books in England had been publicly marked by the demonstration in St Paul's on 11 February 1526, when Fisher preached his second sermon against Luther, and Robert Barnes and the Steelyard merchants cast their faggots on the pile of Luther's books hastily assembled for burning—among them German New Testaments and German Pentateuchs which Thomas More had taken during his raid on the Steelyard.

That was an extension of the pursuit of Lollards which the bishops had been engaged in for over a hundred years, seizing the fragments of manuscript Bibles, forcing the owners to recant, even burning them at the stake. In the next month, March 1526, a new, significant factor— from the authorities' position, a devastating one—was added with the discovery that copies were in circulation of a smart, printed, complete New Testament in English. It had no name on the title-page. It was coming in from abroad, in large numbers, without overmuch secrecy at first, joining a steady flow of books in English imported from Antwerp and elsewhere to the half-dozen London booksellers, the costs of this book's transport apparently defrayed by well-wishers on both sides of the Channel. Other agents in the south and east of England distributed it to eager readers. What was on the title-page is unknown, as of the two surviving copies, one lacks the first seventy pages and the other is complete except for the title-page.[1] However, it cannot have mentioned Tyndale's name. Cochlaeus had reported (to Wolsey, and the King and More) the two unnamed English apostates fleeing to Worms, but it is unlikely that the title-page gave a printer's name and place, and there is no colophon at the end of the surviving copies. The books arrived as neat, complete, probably unbound octavo volumes, the pages noticeably smaller than the Cologne sheets, making the whole book easy to carry in a pocket. They probably announced themselves simply as the New Testament. They had neither prologue nor glosses, going straight to 'The Gospell of S. Matthew. The first Chapter', and ending after 'The revelation Of Sanct Jhon The xxii Chapter' with 'Theende of the newe testiment', three pages of expository afterword 'To the Reder.' and two pages of printer's errata.

A month or two later, in the summer of 1526, the bishops met, under Wolsey, and agreed that the 'untrue translations' should be burned, 'with further sharp correction and punishment against the keepers and readers of the same'.[2] Tunstall issued an injunction to his archdeacons on 24 October 1526, which said the New Testament was the joint work of Tyndale and Roye,[3] and summoned the booksellers on the following day and warned them. Two days after that, Tunstall preached his famous sermon at St Paul's claiming to have found two thousand errors. Some copies of the New Testament in English were burned.[4]

By November 1526 the volumes of Tyndale's own careful Worms New Testament had apparently been joined in England by some of the three thousand volumes printed by Christopher von Endhoven at Antwerp: these were, it seems, awkwardly small sextodecimos, inadequately proof-read. Even assuming the lower figure of three thousand for the print-run from Worms,[5] adding the three thousand Endhoven piracies and probable sheets from Cologne, and even granting the inconspicuous way they were circulated, we can see that Wolsey might have felt that he was getting reports of a flood. He began to think he might stop the flow at its source. On the 21 November 1526 the English ambassador to the Low Countries, Sir John Hackett, received instructions from Wolsey to act against printers or booksellers there involved in the production and distribution of the English New Testaments, and in mid-January 1527 there were enough collected for burnings in Antwerp and Bergen-op-Zoom—the letter from Robert Ridley of 24 February mentions 'many hundreds' of New Testaments 'burnt beyond the sea'.[6] In May 1527 Archbishop Warham put into action a scheme for buying up the New Testaments in order to destroy them, 'as well those with the glosses joined unto them as those without the glosses' and one of his bishops, Nix of Norwich, wrote on 14 June 1527 to congratulate him on doing 'a gracious and a blessed deed' for which God would highly reward him.[7]

Burning New Testaments, however unthinkable, is one thing: burning people alive is 'sharp correction and punishment' on a horrifyingly different scale. Burning heretical books at the pope's command was a means of purifying the Church: burning the heretics themselves was even more virtuous, as it was declared to be a means of purifying their grossly-diseased souls to allow them to reach Heaven. Lollards had suffered such martyrdom for many decades, and from 1530 it would be used against Lutherans. But buying up books and making bonfires of them seem to have been the limits of the campaign for about eighteen months after Tyndale's New Testaments first began to arrive in England in March 1526. It is likely that Wolsey's men could not discover who were the distributors. Thinking of the print-runs in Worms and Antwerp, and the efficiency of distributors, printers, booksellers and general traders in Germany and the Low Countries, including the large extent of the cloth trade, it is probably right to think of Tyndale's New Testament having owners and readers by the late summer of 1527 numbering many hundreds, even possibly thousands, throughout the south and east of England (and there was at least one large consigment early in 1527 from Zeeland to St Andrews and Edinburgh[8]). Such readers would undoubtedly be concentrated in London, and in Cambridge and Oxford.

In November 1527 the campaign moved into a new phase. In Cambridge Thomas Bilney was arrested and appeared before Wolsey, not for the first time. 'Little Bilney', as Hugh Latimer called him, was a fellow of Trinity Hall in his early thirties, 'profiting in all kind of liberal science, even unto the profession of both laws'. Foxe's long account of Bilney begins by putting everything in as happening all at once, like a medieval painting of a saint's life (it has all the customary Foxe marks of being taken down verbatim from the spoken memories of his obituarist) making a kaleidoscope of fragments from which it is possible to glimpse a whole picture.

> This godly man, being a bachelor of law, was but of little stature and very slender of body; and of a strait and temperate diet; and given to good letters; and very fervent and studious in the Scriptures, as appeared by his sermons, his converting of sinners, his preaching at the lazar cots [leper houses], wrapping them in sheets, helping them of that they wanted, if [hoping] they would convert to Christ; laborious and painful to [going to great pains for] the desperates; a preacher to the prisoners and comfortless; a great doer in Cambridge, and a great preacher in Suffolk and Norfolk [9]

In Latimer's words he was 'meek and charitable, a simple good soul, not fit for this world', which fits the picture of the visitor to the foul

and malodorous hospitals and prisons. He had studied Erasmus's
Novum instrumentum, and in the Latin version there he had found for
himself Paul's doctrine of justification by faith, with profound effect.
'Immediately, I seemed unto myself inwardly to feel a marvellous
comfort and quietness, insomuch as my bruised bones leaped for
joy.'[10] He had great effect on two leaders in Cambridge, Robert Barnes
and Hugh Latimer, and others, with far-reaching consequences. Like
Luther, Bilney found that this inward experience went with an understanding of the pointlessness of a religion based only on outward
observances. Yet his deviations were few and slight: he held the orthodox position on the central doctrines of papal supremacy and the
authority of the Church, on transubstantiation and confession. He
wanted reform from the inside, and like Erasmus he felt free to attack
the worship of images and saints. In July 1525 he was licensed to
preach throughout the diocese of Ely, but went further afield. He
disputed with a friar at Ipswich about the worship of saints. Famously
(Foxe has a picture of the event) he was hauled out of the pulpit in
mid-sermon at a church in Norwich (twice, in fact). Some time in
1526 he was questioned by Wolsey on his views on the worship of
saints, and made to take an oath, which he did gladly, that he did not
hold and would not disseminate the doctrines of Martin Luther.

Bilney's arrest in November 1527 led to much greater trouble for
him, and heralded an onslaught. Wolsey handed him over, with his
associate Thomas Arthur, to Tunstall in London. Foxe records the
respectful correspondence between Tunstall and Bilney, and the trial.
Bilney remained puzzled about why he was being accused of heresy.
During questioning he said that Luther was 'a wicked and detestable
heretic', and detached himself from the charge of preaching Luther's
doctrines. No doubt the questions were carefully placed; he seemed
curiously unable to make his interrogators understand distinctions that
he himself found clear, in spite of his legal training. In the bishops'
world of absolutes Bilney was a heretic, and Tunstall declared him so,
refusing to hear witnesses in his defence.[11] Persuaded by friends, Bilney
recanted, though insisting that he did not understand why he should
feel guilty. In agonies of bewilderment and doubt, he was imprisoned
in the Tower for twelve months from December 1527. He reaffirmed
his recantation and in November 1528 Wolsey allowed him to return
to Cambridge, though he was in a parlous mental state and his friends
tried to make sure that he was not left alone. It is possible that Thomas
Bilney's innocent scrupulousness, or things said by Thomas Arthur
under interrogation in December 1527, may, however unwittingly,
have given Wolsey through Tunstall the clues he needed in the search

for distributors and owners of Tyndale's New Testaments. Certainly in February 1528 the Bishop was able to launch a new offensive, much bigger than before, and very effective. For six months he sought out Lollards and Lutherans, with a systematic visitation of the whole diocese (his jurisdiction then included the county of Essex). Even by mid-March his prisons were overflowing. The depositions of the prisoners taken in this campaign provide the first profile of the likely readership of that first New Testament.

As might be expected, it matches pretty well that of known Lollards. 'Usually', notes Mozley, 'they abjured and were put to punishment.'[12] Foxe records groups of people accused in 1527 and 1528, and after, for 'the cause of the gospel'. Valuable as they are, his records are incomplete; some few more of his documents were printed by Strype in his *Ecclesiastical Memorials* of 1721, and much still remains in the Foxe papers still unpublished. Foxe's emotional colouring can be high. In the Victorian edition that is the best now generally available, his chronology is at times almost impossible to follow. Some scheme, however, can be found.[13] For this time, for example, he lists twenty-eight people 'about London, Colchester, and other places also' including Richard Necton (probably Robert Necton the bookseller), a priest, a parson, a curate, and 'William Butcher, whose father's grandfather was burned for the same religion'.[14] Richard, or Robert, Necton, had been described earlier by Foxe, as one of those later betrayed by George Constantine, who 'showed to the aforesaid sir Thomas More, chancellor, the ship-man's name that had them, and the marks of the fardels [large packages], by which the books afterwards were taken and burned'.[15] Constantine had been one of those in Cambridge who took reformist views. He went to Antwerp, where he was known to Tyndale and Joye. He was seized on a visit to England to distribute books and interrogated by More. To escape punishment for heresy he gave the names of associates abroad and the shipmen who carried the books. He then escaped, arriving in Antwerp in December 1531; he died in 1559.

So betrayed, Necton was committed to Newgate and died in prison. Richard Bayfield, 'monk of Bury', had bought two English Testaments at Christmas 1527.[16] In his earler account of Bayfield, Foxe had recorded the influence on him of Robert Barnes, and other laymen.

Doctor Barnes gave him a New Testament in Latin, and the other two gave him Tyndale's Testament in English, with a book called 'The Wicked Mammon', and 'The Obedience of a Christian Man': wherein he prospered so mightily in two years' space, that he was cast into the prison of his house [i.e. the Abbey of Bury], there sore whipped, with a gag in his mouth, and then stocked; and so continued in the same torment three quarters of a year before Dr. Barnes could get him out . . . This Bayfield . . . was beneficial to Master Tyndale and Master Frith, for he . . . sold all their works. [He was tortured] to accuse others who had bought his books. He accused none . . .[17]

Foxe gives a useful 'catalogue of the books brought in by Richard Bayfield'. It is largely of several biblical commentaries each by Luther, Oecolampadius, Zwingli, Pomeran [Bugenhagen], Lambert, Melancthon, Bucer and a dozen more, and

> An Answer of Tyndale unto Sir Thomas More; a Disputation of Purgatory made by John Frith in English; a Prologue to the fifth Book of Moses, called Deuteronomy; the first Book of Moses, called Genesis; a Prologue to the third book of Moses called Leviticus; a Prologue to the Fourth Book of Moses, called Numbers; a Prologue to the second Book of Moses, called Exodus; the Practise of Prelates [by Tyndale]; the New Testament in English, with an Introduction to the Romans [the *Compendious Introduction*]; the Parable of the Wicked Mammon; the Obedience of a Christian Man,

and five other small Protestant books in English, including Joye's Primer, Barlow's *Proper Dialogue* and the *Examination of Thorpe*.[18] The list tells its own interesting tale, not least in the separateness of the books of the Pentateuch. This was the time when Humphrey Monmouth, the merchant friend of Tyndale, and alderman of London, was investigated by Sir Thomas More, and imprisoned. All eight members of a family called Wily were arrested, including 'Lucy Wily, and Agnes Wily, two young girls . . . as Katherine Wily did lie in child-bed, the other wives, with the two girls, were found eating all together of a broth made with the forepart of a rack of mutton'. The eve of St Peter's day, 28 June, was a fast day. Foxe adds 'Item, The aforesaid John Wily the elder had a primer in English in his house, and other books'.[19]

In Tunstall's last two years as Bishop of London (1528–30), he had had to deal with heresy in three particular areas. He was not entirely his own master in these dealings, as he was acting as Wolsey's deputy and having to work with the narrow-minded Longland, Bishop of Lincoln (a huge diocese), and others. The first was the Cambridge group, epecially Barnes, Bilney, Arthur and Bayfield, and including

George Joye, who was ordered to appear but managed, after 'dancing a cold attendance' at the Bishop of Lincoln's palace in London (he assumed it was he and not Wolsey who had summoned him) managed to slip away to the continent. There he wrote a defence of his views, as a booklet addressed to John Ashwell Prior of Newnham Abbey beside Bedford, the source of the charges against him. It was printed by Martin de Keyser in Antwerp on 10 June 1531. It is, considering the circumstances, a good-tempered and even amusing account of his adventures as well as his beliefs.[20]

The heresy of the Cambridge men did not include rejecting the Pope's authority, or sacramental issues: they denounced prayers to saints and affirmed, from reading the New Testament, justification by faith alone. A second group was based largely on Colchester, inheriting the Lollard tradition of working with a vernacular Bible and rejecting the Catholic doctrine of the Eucharist. A large number of men and women were charged, and many brought to London; some of their confessions and recantations are among the Foxe papers and were printed by Strype.[21] The third group were investigated by Tunstall at the instigation of Longland, as a result of the latter's alarm at the large number of heretical books coming into Oxford. On 21 February 1528, Thomas Garrad or Garrett, who had certainly distributed books, was arrested near Bristol, and Longland asked Tunstall to interrogate him, with a bookseller named Gough, Bilney's friend Dr Forman, Jeffrey Lome, Forman's curate, in Foxe's words 'sometime usher of St Anthony's School' (More's old school in Threadneedle Street), 'Sigar Nicholson, Stationer of Cambridge' and 'John Raimund, a Dutchman, For causing fifteen hundred of Tyndale's New Testaments to be printed at Antwerp, and for bringing five hundred into England'.[22] (The latter was John van Ruremond, the brother of Christoffel van Ruremond, also known as Christopher van Endhoven, the Antwerp printer.) Foxe's list goes on to include 'Paul Luther, Friar, and Warden of the House at Ware', a 'Merchant Tailor', several priests, a 'Holy Water Clerk', two tilers (the building trade, like the cloth trade, seems to have had historic connections with dissent) and 'John Tyndale . . . For sending five marks to his brother William Tyndale beyond the sea, and for receiving and keeping with him certain letters from his brother'.[23] John Tyndale also appears in the account of a cloth-maker named Boswell. On 28 February 1528 he was in the Colchester Hall, London, with cloth to sell, when 'one John Tyndale of London, merchant, dwelling about the well with the two buckets towards Austin Friars, chanced to come in'. Boswell asked him to buy cloth, but he refused, as he was unlikely to sell it again because of high unemployment arising from government policies. Boswell was sent to Wolsey for examination as he had 'named a person in London', but it is not recorded what happened.[24] Wolsey also imprisoned in the Tower Thomas Alwaye, who bought 'English Testaments and certain other books prohibited', and after over a year handed him over to Tunstall and Longland; they imposed heavy penances, and Longland made sure he would never earn a living again.[25]

Some time before August 1528, a group of young scholars at Wolsey's own Cardinal College in Oxford, specially brought over by Wolsey from Cambridge and elsewhere for their excellence ('most picked young men, of grave judgement and sharp wits') including John Frith (and, according to Foxe, Tyndale) were arrested and imprisoned. Foxe has two goes at the story, the second explaining that they were accused by 'Dr London; Dr Higdon, dean of the said college; and Dr Cottesford, commissary [bishop's officer]'. This is another version of the 'salt-fish' story previously noted.[26] The young men, 'holding an assembly together in the college . . . accounted to be heretics' because they were 'conferring together upon the abuses of religion . . . [were] . . . cast into a prison, within a deep cave under the ground of the same college, where the salt fish was laid . . . so that with the filthy stench thereof, they were all infected . . .' The youngest and cleverest, Clark, 'being a tender young man', was the first to die.[27]

England, 1529–31

Throughout 1529, as Foxe records, persecution continued. John Tewkesbury, 'leatherseller' (or haberdasher) of London 'was converted by the reading of Tyndale's Testament and the *Wicked Mammon*. He had the Bible written' (that is, in manuscript; presumably a Wycliffite version).[28] Foxe gives a long account of his disputation 'with such power of the Scriptures and heavenly wisdom' that Tunstall and all his learned men were ashamed, and of his torture at Sir Thomas More's house at Chelsea, as recounted above.[29] Foxe says that his examination began on 21 April 1529, and he was given penance on 8 May, being 'enforced through infirmity. . . to retract and abjure his doctrine'. (Foxe has probably brought the date of Tewkesbury's interrogation forward two years.) Edward Freese, a painter, was imprisoned for painting on cloths for the new inn in Colchester 'certain sentences of Scripture: and by that he was plainly known to be one of them that they call heretics': he was imprisoned at the Bishop's house at Fulham with 'one Johnson and his wife: Wylie, and his wife and son'.[30] Mistress Alice Dolly was accused by her servant Elizabeth Wighthill and Dr

London. Robert West, priest of St Andrew Undershaft, abjured and did penance.[31] Paul Luther, Grey Friar; Robert Whaplod, merchant tailor; Nicholas White of Rye, Richard Kitchen, priest; William Wegen, priest; William Hale, holy-water clerk, and William Blomfield, monk of Bury, all abjured within the diocese of London in 1529.

Then the scene suddenly darkened. In January or February, a priest named Thomas Hitton, who had been on the Continent and was probably known personally to the English refugees at Antwerp, was seized in Kent for preaching heresy. At his examination he confessed that he had smuggled a New Testament and a Primer in from abroad. After imprisonment he was condemned by Archbishop Warham, and the Bishop Fisher of Rochester, and on 23 February burned alive at Maidstone. He was the reformers' first English martyr. The English refugees at Antwerp were deeply shocked. Joye introduced a new saint into the calendar in his *Ortulus* printed soon after, so that 23 February celebrates 'Saint Thomas', that is, Hitton. When More in his *Dialogue* taunted Tyndale with the remark that he had never heard of a heretic who wouldn't perjure himself to save his life, Tyndale in his *Answer* cited Hitton, and referred to him elsewhere.[32] The original remark ill became More, already active with such venom to eradicate those with different opinions. His further retort to Tyndale's *Answer* was to tell a demeaning fable of Hitton's arrest ('for pilfering . . . certain linen clothes that were hanging on a hedge') and list his supposed heresies at some length, not forgetting the ever-present compulsive fantasies about priests and marriage: 'The man meant by likelihood that it was good enough to wed upon a cushion when the dogs be abed, as their priests wed I wene where their persons be known. For else they let not to wed openly at church, and take the whole parish for witness of their beastly bitchery.'[33] So you see, writes More, that Tyndale has no great cause to glory in this new saint: he should scrape his name out of the calendar, and 'restore the blessed bishop saint Polycarp'. More concludes his waspish account of Hitton, saying that he learned his 'false faith and heresies' from 'Tyndale's holy books, and now the spirit of error and lying, hath taken his wretched soul with him straight from the short fire to the fire everlasting. And this is lo sir Thomas Hitton the devil's stinking martyr, of whose burning Tyndale must make boast.' That last remark defies comment.

Charles Lamb wrote that More's account of Hitton was 'penned with a wit and malice hyper-satanic'.[34] Mozley remarks: 'There was indeed a nobler side to More: but he never showed it to the reformers.'[35] Sir Thomas More had been made Chancellor on the 25 October 1529: Wolsey had surrendered the Great Seal eight days before and been exiled to the north. On 21 February 1530 Tunstall was translated to the See of Durham, a position of far more wealth for him.[36] The Bishop of London from November 1530 was the more sinister John Stokesley. Wolsey began in August 1530 to put into action his moves for a spectacular return, starting with enthronement at York as Archbishop in November. But he was arrested and died three days later, on the morning of 29 November 1530.

Meanwhile, in 1530, betrayals and arrests at a humbler level continued. Simon Wisdom of Burford had 'three books in English, one was the gospels in English, another was the psalter, the third was the Sum of the Holy Scripture in English'. Persecution was often set in motion on grounds little more than gossip. John Eaton and Cecily his wife were persecuted by Longland for, *inter alia*, being noticed by 'certain in the parish' holding down their heads in church, and not looking at the Sacrament, and for saying in a butcher's house at the sound of the bells, 'What a clampering of bells is here!' John Eaton had 'Jesus's Gospels in English'. James Algar or Ayer had been heard to declare the priesthood of all believers and to deny purgatory; and had answered Dr Algonby's reference to 'Thou art Peter' (Matthew 16) with 'that which followeth in the gospel after, "Get thee after me Satan" etc.' John French of Long Witham denied the Church's doctrine on two of the sacraments. Longland persecuted ten people, listed by Foxe, for hearing the Scriptures read in English. John Ryburn, arrested in August 1530, was testified against by his sisters, wife and father: he believed that the service in church should be in English. Foxe gives a summary list of 'all such as were forced to abjure in King Henry's days, after the first beginning of Luther', over a hundred names from London and the Colchester area.[37] A further eight are listed later.[38] In 1531, in London alone, Foxe give details of thirty who abjured, often adding their trades and professions—skinner, glazier, serving man, tailor, harper, bookbinder, weaver, priest—many for having the New Testament in English or other books from Antwerp. Here is 'Christopher, a Dutchman of Antwerp' (Christopher van Ruremond of Endhoven) 'for selling certain New Testaments in English to John Row aforesaid (bookbinder) was put in prison at Westminster, and there died.'[39] (This tells us that the Endhoven piracies of Tyndale, at least, were imported unbound.)

Stokesley reintroduced into London, and elsewhere, the burning of men and women alive for heresy, which had not been seen for over a dozen years. Under him, in the spring of 1531, Thomas Bilney and Richard Bayfield were rearrested. Bilney was burned on 19 August, Bayfield at the end of November. Thomas Dusgate or Benet was burnt in Devonshire in January 1532. James Bainham, John Bent and Thomas Harding were burned in the spring of 1532. Andrew Hewet was burned on 4 July 1533, with John Frith. Elizabeth Barton, 'the Maid of Kent', and her conspirators, were burned in April 1534. There were others, probably at least four.[40]

We should pause at some of these names. ('The Maid of Kent' does not come into Tyndale's story, though at More's downfall a supposed association with her was damaging to Sir Thomas.) Bilney's time of freedom had tormented his conscience, as he accused himself of betraying his principles. In 1530 he began field preaching again in Norfolk, and gave the anchoress at Norwich a copy of Tyndale's New Testament. He was soon picked up by the officers of the Bishop of Norwich, condemned, degraded (reduced from the priesthood), handed over by the bishop's chancellor to the secular arm, and burned at the Lollard's pit in Norwich. Bilney's case was very well known. The poet John Skelton in his 'A Replication Against Certain Young Scholars Abjured of Late, Etc' had suggested that Bilney had been so careless as to laugh when carrying his faggot.[41] Skelton wrote at Wolsey's command: there is evidence that he and Thomas More were two sides of the same attack.[42] More's insistent denigration of heretics included a good deal of highly-coloured writing against Bilney, at first in the *Dialogue*, and then after Bilney's death in the *Confutation*. In the preface to the latter, More began the fiction, on the basis of what he had been told, that Bilney had 'unto God confessed and asked his mercy, that he had so grievously erred in that point (on the peace and unity of the Church), and so sore offended him in contemning his church'.[43] Against that, it appears on the one hand that Bilney had so little of any substance to recant: on the other, that Matthew Parker (Archbishop of Canterbury under Elizabeth), who was an eye-witness of Bilney's death, denied it.

Bayfield, another Cambridge man, had abjured before Tunstall in 1528, and then fled abroad. He greatly helped Tyndale and Frith, and three times took great loads of books over to London, twice via East Anglia, and once to St Katherine's docks in London, where they were seized by More. He was betrayed on his last venture, through information extracted by More from George Constantine. More writes in the preface to the *Confutation* of 'Richard Bayfield, late a monk and a priest, which fell to heresy and was abjured, and after that like a dog returning to his vomit, and being fled over the sea, and sending from thence Tyndale's heresies thither with many mischievous sorts of books'. More objects to Bayfield continuing to bring in books while 'suing for remission and pardon': he objects much more to Bayfield

> when being both a priest and a monk, he went about two wives, one in Brabant, another in England. What he meant I cannot make you sure, whether he would be sure of the one if the other should hap to refuse him, or that he would have them both, the one here, the tother there, or else both in one place, the one because he was a priest, the tother because he was a monk. Of Bayfield's burning hath Tyndale no great cause to glory.[44]

James Bainham became an even greater *cause célèbre*. He was a gentleman of the Inns of Court, who in December 1531 was found by Stokesley in possession of all five books by Tyndale, and books by Frith and Joye. In February 1532 he abjured, carrying a faggot and paying a fine of £20, but like Bilney suffered very greatly in his conscience. On a Sunday morning in March, as Foxe has it, 'he came to St Austin's, with the New Testament in his hand in English, and the Obedience of a Christian Man (Tyndale's book, rather than an abstract principle) in his bosom, and stood there before the people in his pew, there declaring openly, with weeping tears, that he had denied God . . .'[45] Foxe gives a good deal of space to documenting Bainham's case, and he gives a strong account of his burning: but what has caused alarm has been his double mention of Thomas More's personal violence against him—'he cast him in prison in his own house, and whipped him at the tree in his garden, called the tree of Troth, and after sent him to the Tower to be racked: and so he was, sir Thomas More being present himself, till in a manner he had lamed him . . .'[46] Before his death he was again tortured, not least in the Tower, 'where he lay a fortnight, scourged with whips, to make him revoke his opinions'.[47] Argument over the truth of Foxe's report about More has consisted largely in ignoring it, or denying it even as a possibility; this is not the place to enter that quagmire. More rejoiced in Bainham's death—the man was only a chatterer, he said, and, with other heretics, 'as they be as well worthy, the temporality doth burn them. And after the fire of Smithfield, hell doth receive them where the wretches burn for ever'.[48] It must be said that from More's writing alone the evidence of personal disturbance at this time is great, and that, linked with his fanatical, even frenzied, loathing for someone showing even the merest suggestion of heresy, does perhaps make a reader think a little about the qualities normally expected in a saint of the Catholic Church.

Smuggling

By 1526 and Tyndale's first Testament, the transport of books across the Channel for sale in England had been commonplace for half a century. In London, the chief but not the only port to receive such continental imports, there were a few booksellers, possibly no more than half a dozen. An Act of Parliament of 1483, not repealed until 1533, gave preference to imported books. More books were printed abroad, and at home, each year, and more sold. The metropolitan booksellers, native Londoners such as Henry Pepwell or Robert Necton, or Flemings like Peter Kaetz or Francis Byrckman, who were agents of the rising Antwerp book trade, were able, effectively, to import what they liked. Luther in Latin was in demand, in spite of official bans and two ceremonial burnings, in 1521 and 1526. The booksellers sold Latin to learned readers, and English to an increasing general public. School-books—Latin grammars for Dean Colet's St Paul's School nearby—Latin technical books (one on the valuation of gold and silver suggests developing north-European wealth), finely-printed Latin service books with the Sarum usage, fanciful Latin travel-books, books in English of hygiene or homecraft, almanacs and what would later be called ency-clopaedias, all and many more came in ships from Antwerp to London booksellers in the first half of the 1520s.[49] On the whole, foreign-printed books were better, and in greater demand, from France as well as Germany, the Netherlands, northern Italy, Switzerland and Spain. Antwerp was the great centre. Books by Luther and Tyndale would be smuggled in, and available in bookshops, as well as privately through dealers and fellow-believers.

Smuggling was efficient. Attempts at controls, forbidding people to receive books on a long list headed by the works of Tyndale, clearly did not work, for all the evidence points to there being increasing numbers of readers of contraband books year by year—in spite of punishments for people caught. Bales of cloth (the commonest method) would be secretly marked, containing well-hidden flat printed sheets.

> Barrels or casks, apparently full of wine or oil, might secrete water-tight boxes holding dangerous propaganda. Cargoes of wheat or grain, hides or skins were not always made up exclusively of these items. Flour sacks often held carefully packed contraband books strategically placed in the meal. Chests with false sides or bases, hidden receptacles or secret compartments brought over documents . . .[50]

A modern Catholic historian paints a powerful picture:

Already toward the end of March 1526, along the arteries leading to London, through ports and rivers and creeks along the eastern seaboard and across the heaths and marshes of East Anglia the explosive copies of the first printed English New Testament were being smuggled.

> . . . there comes a power
> Into this scatter'd kingdom; who already,
> Wise in our negligence, have secret feet
> In some of our best ports, and are at point
> To show their open banner.
> (*King Lear, III.i.30–4*)

The English protestant reformation was entering a radically new phase. Bursting its containment of learned Latin enclaves and clerical outposts, it was carrying the war into the marketplace and would soon arm the common man with an ageless weapon of religious revolution.[51]

What would be remarkable about the smuggled Tyndale cargoes was their bulk. If the figure of six thousand for the print-run of the Worms New Testament is true, then it was very unusual. In Venice, Aldus, to get his Greek editions off the ground thirty years earlier, had raised the number of copies of each edition to 1,000, intead of the 100, 250 or at most 500 previously considered best.[52] German printers tended to go for a large number of titles—in fifteen years, Heinrich Quentell (father of Peter) in Cologne produced four hundred items—rather than big print-runs. From about 1480 to about 1520, an average print-run of books in Europe seems to have been between 1,000 and 1,500.[53] True, Bibles commanded bigger runs, but even Luther's 'September Testament' only had a first run of 4,000 copies. If the figure for Tyndale's first New Testament can be trusted, then it says a great deal about the translator's confidence, his understanding of the demand in England. His years in Oxford, and possibly Cambridge, and then back in Gloucestershire, had opened his eyes to the need: his months in London had, it seems, helped him to quantify it. The high print-run made a big financial risk for Peter Schoeffer, who was not one of the great German printers. Tyndale must have been very sure. What happened to that edition he could not have foreseen; but the evidence shows that even taking into account the destruction of some copies, he had not, in fact, overestimated the demand; for example, this New Testament was five times printed in Antwerp in pirate editions for sale in England between 1527 and 1534, a trade that was only stopped when Tyndale protested in the preface to his 1534 New Testament; each piracy must have sold out to justify the next, and all were overtaken by Tyndale's 1534 revision. Perhaps six thousand is, after all, exaggeration. Cautious scholars suggest three thousand.[54] Even so, it was a confident printing and shipment for a revolutionary little book, almost bare of decoration and cramped in page-setting, even dull—nothing here of Luther's lavish Cranach-designed pages of pictures and ornaments.

The point is worth stressing because of a declared difficulty in assessing the numbers of 'heretics' in England in the mid-1520s. The Cambridge Lutheran academics, though they have had a high profile, can be reduced to not very many. The Oxford ones discovered in 1528, mostly at Cardinal College, even on Foxe's count amount to five, one of whom (Tyndale) can be discounted. In London, the heretical book trade, probably under Dr Robert Forman's leadership, accounted for a few more. It is possible, with this sort of accounting, to claim that English Lutherans amounted to less than fifty people, many of them probably harmless academics going through a phase, and the rest merchants, no doubt after profit. Similarly, although there were more Lollards than Lutherans, work has been done to show that the clamp-downs on Lollards in the 1520s, in London, the south-east and the midlands, although producing figures in the hundreds, were also turning up the same names, suggesting a much smaller core. In other words, the long-held Protestant view, from 'propagandists' like Foxe, that there was a strong popular desire for reform in England under Henry VIII, can be found to be wrong; that whatever colour they wore, the 'heresies' cannot produce more than a few hundred people—and can therefore be discounted as a force in English history. Recent Catholic revisionists assure us that this is so.[55] No doubt the strength of anti-clericalism was formerly exaggerated: but it was still formidable, at all levels of society ('even among such important people as courtiers and Crown lawyers'[56]) and the Church was busily sealing its own doom by its reactionary aggression: why was it so alarmed? It is, moreover, possible to challenge the revisionist position and produce, for example, three thousand names of English Protestants between 1525 and 1558, they being only the ones with an unusually high profile, enough to be registered.[57] (When the seminal revisionist book, under the title *The Reformation and the English People*, devotes to the Marian persecution of reformers only seven words, one has perhaps to wonder a little.[58]) To all this, the size of Tyndale's print-run is relevant, whether six thousand or three thousand. Tyndale was a 'simple' man in his Christian trust of Tunstall as friend of Erasmus, or of Henry

Phillips, fatally, as sympathetic friend. But he was unmistakably street-wise when it came to translating, printing, distributing, selling—and reading—his Testaments. He must have been sure of his market.

What happened next shocked Tyndale deeply. He never recovered. If, in his eleven years on the Continent, he made several changes of direction in his thought as he worked (somewhat away from Luther, for example, towards Zwingli, or possibly into a more thorough-going covenant theology), nothing was so sharp an alteration as came when he began to gather what was happening to his first New Testaments in London. Cuthbert Tunstall, no less, was ordering them all to be gathered in; at St Paul's, after an intemperate sermon by him denouncing them, copies were ceremonially piled up and burned. It is from this event that Tyndale's anti-clerical attacks can be dated, including some marginal notes.

Book-Burning in England

The leader of the Cambridge Lutherans, the academic Robert Barnes, had preached the sermon at Christmas 1525 noticed above. When rival academics brought it to the ears of Wolsey, it caused him serious trouble. In February 1526 Barnes was summoned to London to appear before the Cardinal, with his Cambridge friend Miles Coverdale among those helping his defence. The charge was being a Lutheran. At the time of his arrest in Cambridge, the town had been searched for prohibited books, but there had been enough warning for the owners (Foxe says there were thirty of them) to hide the wanted volumes, even though the search-party went 'directly to the place where the books lay (whereby it was perceived that there were some privy spies among that small company)'.[59] Foxe gives a vivid account of Barnes before Wolsey, and goes on to tell the unhappy story of the persecution of Barnes over the next years. The point here is that anti-Lutheran campaigns by Wolsey were rekindling early in 1526.

Wolsey as Legate used his power on 26 and 27 January 1526, with Henry's approval, and accompanied by Sir Thomas More, to make a raid in London on the Steelyard, and seized five Germans 'to be examined for Luther's books and Lollardy'.[60] He then initiated another grand ceremony in St Paul's Cathedral on 11 February 1526, at which he himself presided, sitting in splendour on a high scaffold with, it is said, thirty-six bishops, abbots and priors.[61] The Bishop of Rochester, John Fisher, preached the sermon, taking a second opportunity to deliver an attack on Luther. Robert Barnes and the five Germans abjured, and did public penance, carrying their faggots, which they then threw on a fire, followed by 'heretical', that is, Lutheran books. A new phase in the war against Luther had begun, attacking local people and books, though it is said that there was for a while difficulty in finding enough books to burn.[62]

Tyndale's New Testaments began arriving in England in March 1526.[63] Enough were in circulation by the early autumn for Tunstall, now back in England after his third embassy, this time in Spain, to be alarmed. On October 24 he wrote a monition (in Latin) to the City authorities to search out and confiscate Tyndale's New Testaments, and other books.

> Many children of iniquity, maintainers of Luther's sect, blinded through extreme wickedness, wandering from the way of truth and the Catholic faith, have craftily translated the New Testament into our English tongue, intermeddling therewith many heretical articles and erroneous opinions, seducing the common people; attempting by their wicked and perverse interpretations to profane the majesty of Scripture, which hitherto had remained undefiled, and craftily to abuse the most holy word of God, and the true sense of the same. Of this translation there are many books printed, some with glosses and some without, containing in the English tongue that pestiferous and pernicious poison, dispersed in our diocese of London.[64]

The following day the London civic authorities resolved that every alderman should examine those in their respective wards 'on and concerning certain books of heresies'.[65]

'Many books printed' seems to support the notion of a large print-run: 'some with glosses and some without' confirms the circulation of unbound sheets of the 1525 Cologne Testament. But we must note that the Cuthbert Tunstall who said to Tyndale less than two years before that he was sure he would get a place in London to do his translation into English of the New Testament is now calling that very work 'pestiferous and pernicious poison'. The climate has changed. Now Wolsey, having quickly mobilised the full apparatus of Church and State, was organising the official horror of heresy. As early as October 1524, if not before, the task of vetting all imported books for their heretical views had been assigned not only to Wolsey but also to Warham, Tunstall and Fisher.[66] On 3 November Archbishop Warham wrote to his suffragan bishops in almost the exact words of Tunstall's monition: it looks like an orchestrated attack, led by Wolsey.[67] There is evidence of a meeting of 'prelates and learned men' where Tyndale's Testament was 'accursed and damned . . . and commanded to be burned', some time before February 1527, when Robert Ridley, Tunstall's chaplain, metioned it. Wolsey would have called such a meeting. Cochlaeus had not been reluctant in 1525 to pass on the news of the heretic Testament-printers in Cologne to Wolsey himself. So Wolsey would have been on the look-out for English Testaments, and had a strategy in place.

Tunstall was a co-worker with Wolsey in what was, until Henry's break with Rome nearly ten years later, royal policy; but Tunstall was also, irritatingly for him, under Wolsey. There are signs of friction. The Bishop of London resented the Cardinal's interference in promoting heresy-hunts in his diocese.[68] Perhaps Tunstall was trying to assert his authority. He too preached at St Paul's against a heretic in Germany, on 24 October 1526, and organised his own book-burning of that heretic's work. The heretic was Tyndale, the book his New Testament, copies of which were burned a few days later at St Paul's, probably the following Sunday, 28 October.[69] The day after the sermon, 25 October, he summoned the booksellers of London to a chapel in the palace of the Bishop of Norwich, near Charing Cross, and warned them again against importing Lutheran books, whether Latin or English.[70]

Tunstall's sermon has not survived, but there are several accounts of it, from different camps. It seems to have been an exposition of the errors in Tyndale's translation. It is usually reported by modern historians that Tunstall spoke of two thousand errors: he can hardly have enumerated them without putting his audience to sleep—or enraging them—so he must have given examples and then generalised. (As a response, in fact, rage may have been closer to the surface than has been assumed. There is evidence that the Church's official malevolence to the English New Testament caused distress.) Four years later Tyndale, in his *The Practice of Prelates* of 1530 wrote of Tunstall as the Bishop of Durham's secretary—Wolsey held the bishopric of Durham with the archbishopric of York, 1523–9—and then as Bishop of London.

> And as for the bishopric of Durham, to say the very truth, he could not of good congruity but reward his old chaplain, and one of the chief of all his secretaries withal . . . which, for what service done in Christ's gospel came he to the bishopric of London; or what such service did he therein? He burnt the New Testament, calling it Doctrinam peregrinam, 'strange learning'.[71]

Those five incontestable words, 'He burnt the New Testament', express Tyndale's shock. Books had been burned in Europe and in England. The Papal Bull of 15 June 1520, *Exsurge Domine*, which condemned forty-one propositions of Luther as heretical, also ordered the faithful to burn Luther's books wherever they could be found, a command which was carried out in Rome on the same day, in Louvain on 8 October, and in Cologne on 12 November.[72] Luther replied in kind, and on the morning of 10 December 1520, in a field between the city wall of Wittenberg and the river Elbe, he burned the books of canon law and the papal decretals and a copy of the Bull on a bonfire, watched by citizens and members of the university. The event, seen as retaliation, was widely reported. Tunstall was in Worms early in 1521 (he left on 11 April, five days before Luther arrived for the Diet) and on the 21 January wrote to Wolsey regretting that 'some idle fellow' had translated into Latin for wide circulation Luther's declaration made at the time of the bonfire, that what he burned was erroneous. This was Luther's *De captivitate Babylonica,* his most hard-hitting attack on the Church. Tunstall enclosed a copy and asked Wolsey to burn it, as he did not want to seem to be helping the spread of Luther's writings in English.[73] He suggested that Wolsey should call the booksellers together and forbid them to import, sell or translate Luther's books. Two months later, the Pope commended Wolsey's prohibition but suggested that 'a general bonfire would be more satisfactory',[74] and two months after that, on 12 May 1521, Wolsey's first elaborate ceremony of burning Luther's books at St Paul's took place. There may have been a Cambridge burning before. All such burnings are to be seen in part as moves in the desperate game of alliances in those weeks. Would the Emperor Charles side with the Pope against Luther? Would Henry VIII then ally himself with Charles? Then the day after the Diet of Worms, on 19 April 1521, the Emperor announced his intention 'that all the books of Martin, wheresover found, should be burnt, and he himself punished as a notorious heretic . . .'[75] So Wolsey's London burning three weeks later was a very visible gesture of England's alliance with the Pope and Emperor. It was, according to the Venetian ambassador, rather hastily arranged in only four or five days. There had been burnings of Luther's books just before in Venice and Naples.[76] The flames were a signal in international politics, as they consumed whatever could be collected in time of Luther's books.

Tunstall burned the *New Testament.* This was why Tyndale was so shocked. He was right to be so. There was a difference in scale, as well as, what was so much worse, a difference in essence. To be known as a heretic author was to run the risk of having your careful theological labours destroyed. But to burn God's word itself, carefully translated by a scholar from the original Greek into English that all men and women could receive, was havoc of a different order. Hasty historians in the last hundred years have spoken of Tunstall as finding cause for his attack in Tyndale's marginal notes,[77] which have always been well-known among such writers for their bitterness. That case is spoiled by the fact that there are no marginal notes at all in Tyndale's 1526 New Testament. True, if the unbound sheets of Matthew's Gospel as far as chapter 21 printed in Cologne are in mind, then yes, there are marginal notes there. Again, however, the case collapses, for as we saw they are not 'bitter' at all, being without exception informative glosses on scriptural words or phrases, though necessarily, as such, stinging, as in 'Peter' being every Christian man and woman. Indeed, as also saw, Tyndale has omitted the anti-papal and anti-clerical remarks of his model, Luther's 1522 New Testament. Tunstall's attack can only have been on Tyndale's rendering of the New Testament text itself. Two thousand errors in a volume of 680 pages gives an average rate of three per page. Some of these would be words to which the most serious offence could be taken by the Church, like 'congregation' for 'church', 'love' for 'charity', and 'repent' for 'do penance'. Some of them (in point of fact, not many) would be mistakes Tyndale himself later corrected. Most of them would be exceedingly trivial. Tyndale himself wrote later of the heresy of failing to dot an 'i'.[78]

The shock for Tyndale was double. That an English bishop should burn an English New Testament; and that that bishop should be Cuthbert Tunstall, Erasmus's friend, who had worked with Erasmus in Bruges on his edition of the Greek New Testament, even supplying him with information on Greek New Testament texts. Tunstall was himself a Greek scholar who would know very well, better than most, that Tyndale's English was faithful to the Greek, even and especially in matters like 'congregation', 'love' and 'repent'. Tunstall would know better than almost any other man in England that Erasmus in his *Novum instrumentum*, with his new Latin translation from the Greek, was often startling, giving *sermo* instead of the Vulgate's *verbum* for the Greek *logos* at the crucial opening of the fourth Gospel—and *congregatio* for the Greek *ekklesia* throughout. Tunstall, whose name would shortly appear on the title-pages approving two editions of the Great Bible, was playing politics, being a puppet of the Pope through Wolsey and the King, betraying his Christian humanist learning at the direction of the Church, needing to be receiving Wolsey's favour. The word 'hypocrite', with or without 'ducking', does not seem too strong for him.[79] Tyndale's shock, in fact, does him credit. Burning Lutheran tracts is one thing, however brutal the collecting of them and the symbolism. To burn God's word for politics was to Tyndale barbarous.

And to many others, it seems. There is detectable in London a reaction of puzzlement. Politically, the Church, led by Wolsey, was in fact making a great mistake, sowing the dragons' teeth which would before long yield destruction, and not just through Henry's divorce and the break with Rome. Luther had torn down thousand-year-old walls hiding the Bible. The bishops in England were building them higher. London men and women were not going to be soothed with the sops of Nicholas Love, the best the Church could manage, with the addition of the Lord's Prayer in English. Luther was giving the German people the Epistle to the Romans, raw, and all the rest of the New Testament. Henry Monmouth in his letter to Wolsey from the Tower wrote that he was present at Tunstall's sermon. 'That before he heard the Bishop of London say at Paul's Cross, that William Tyndale had translated the New Testament in English, and done it noughtily, he never suspected or knew any evil by him.'[80] The Cambridge scholar John Lambert, in his long answer in 1538 to the bishops' forty-five articles against him (printed in full by Foxe), wrote:

> Moreover I was at Paul's cross, when the New Testament, imprinted of late beyond the sea, was first forefended; and truly my heart lamented greatly to hear a great man preaching against it, who showed forth certain things that he noted for hideous errors to be in it, that I, yea and not only I, but likewise did many others, think verily to be none. But (alack for pity!) malice cannot say well. God help us all, and amend it.[81]

Lambert, and, it seems 'many others' saw Tunstall's malice, and grieved.

The fullest information we have about the entire process of the official attack on Tyndale's 1526 New Testament is in *Read me and be not wroth*. This doggerel is never worth much attention, except that, as has been said, it is only one of six Protestant works, four of which were by Tyndale, circulating in English before 1528. Jerome Barlow might well have heard Tunstall's sermon and seen the burning. 'Watkin' asks 'Who caused it so to be done?' 'Jeffrey' replies:

> In sooth the bishop of London
> With the cardinal's authority
> Which at Paul's Cross earnestly
> Denounced it to be heresy
> That the gospel should come to light
> Calling them heretics execrable
> Which caused the gospel venerable
> To come into laymen's sight.

> He declared there in his furiousness
> That he found errors more and less
> Above three thousand in the translation.
> Howbeit when all came to pass
> I daresay unable he was
> Of one error to make probation.[82]

He went on to say that 'common women/shall as soon come to heaven/As those that live perfectly' and 'In a certain prologue . . . a whore . . . shall sooner come to salvation/By merits of Christ's passion/Than an outward holy liver', to which 'Watkin' replies that it is in Matthew 21, as it is (in Tyndale 'Jesus [addressing the chief priests and the elders of the people] said unto them: verily I say unto you, that the publicans and the harlots shall come into the kingdom of God before you'). Through the rhyming, we do get a picture of a furious Tunstall who has worked himself up to violent indignation on the principle of 'argument weak, shout here', and who possibly knows that he is betraying himself. Locating a key verse of Matthew 21 in 'a certain prologue' is peculiar for one who worked with Erasmus. Perhaps Tunstall did not after all know his New Testament well. In that case, who found the two thousand errors? In Roye and Barlow, they have now risen to three thousand. Tunstall in his fury might have said both numbers, for a certain effect.

The poem expresses no doubt that behind everything is Wolsey, but it makes two further points of special interest. The first is that 'the man in the red cap' had to be persuaded to move against the maker of the English translation. At first 'He spake the words of Pilate/Saying I find no fault therein' until he asked an assembly of the bishops. 'Then answered bishop Caiaphas/That a great part better it was/The gospel to be condemned . . .' Caiaphas was of course the Jewish high priest who presided at the trial of Jesus. Who he is Roye and Barlow leave in no doubt as the margin notes 'Hoc est London episcopus', 'this is the Bishop of London'. Here is evidence of the meeting 'sometime before February 1527' mentioned by Ridley that we saw above. The second point is that the chief indictment of Wolsey in the poem, above all others to which he laid himself open, and hammered as the refrain of stanza after stanza, is the charge of 'burning God's word, the holy testament'.

New Testament Readers

Of that 1526 edition, how many arrived we do not know. Strype's invaluable eighteenth-century *Ecclesiastical Memorials* gives a picture of some of the traffic. John Pykas, a baker of Colchester, bought in 1526 in Colchester, 'of a Lombard of London, a New Testament in English, and paid for it four shillings': Barnes sold to two men a Testament for 3s. 2d. 'and desired them that they would keep it close'. Robert Necton 'sold five of the said New Testaments to Sir William Furboshore Singing man, in Stowmarket in Suffolk, for seven or eight groats apiece. He also sold to Sir Richard Bayfell two New Testaments unbound . . . for the which he paid 3s. 4d. A Dutchman (i.e. a German) now in Fleet prison would have sold Robert Necton two or three hundred of the New Testaments, some 'of the biggest' and others 'of the small volume', at 9d. apiece. (The latter sound like sextodecimo Endhoven pirate editions.) How many were burned, and how many were thoroughly read, we also do not know, though evidence suggests that such a risky purchase was eagerly devoured, and, unbound, probably read and shared till it was in pieces. A few years later, the depositions printed by Foxe of prisoners burned at the stake as heretics for possessing Tyndale's Testament, reveal that they were brought to the light of the Gospel through reading that book. At this point, however, an unexpected element of comedy is brought in with a story in Hall's *Chronicle* of 1548. (It must be understood that Antwerp was the great clearing-house of books for export to England and that Tyndale's printing in Worms would reach England through that port.) In the summer of 1529 Cuthbert Tunstall was on the Continent negotiating the treaty of Cambrai, as Hall explains in some detail. He digresses as follows:

Here it is to be remembered, that at this present time [i.c. 1528], William Tyndale had newly translated and imprinted the New Testament in English, and the bishop of London not pleased with the translation thereof, debated with himself, how he might compass and devise, to destroy that false and erroneous translation, (as he said). And so it happened that one Augustine Packington, a mercer and merchant of London, and of a great honesty, the same time was in Antwerp, where the bishop then was, and this Packington was a man that highly favoured William Tyndale, but to the bishop utterly showed himself to the contrary. The bishop desirous to have his purpose brought to pass, communed of the New Testaments, and how gladly he would buy them. Packington then hearing that he wished for, said unto the bishop. My Lord if it be your pleasure, I can in this matter do more I dare say, than most of the merchants of England that are here, for I know the Dutch men and strangers that have brought them of Tyndale, and have them here to sell, so that if it be your lordship's pleasure, to pay for them, I will then assure you, to have every book of them, that is imprinted and is here unsold. The bishop thinking that he had God by the toe, when indeed he had (as after he thought) the Devil by the fist, said, gentle Master Packington, do your diligence and get them and with all my heart I will pay for them, whatsoever they cost you, for the books are erroneous and naughts [nothings] and I intend surely to destroy them all, and to burn them at Paul's Cross. Augustine Packington came to William Tyndale and said, William I know thou art a poor man, and hast a heap of New Testaments, and books by thee, for the which though hast both endangered thy friends, and beggared thyself, and I have now gotten thee a merchant, which with ready money shall dispatch thee of all that thou hast, if you think it so profitable for yourself. Who is the merchant said Tyndale? The bishop of London said Packington. O that is because he will burn them said Tyndale, yea marry quoth Packinton. I am the gladder said Tyndale, for these two benefits shall come thereo, I shall get money of him for these books, to bring myself out of debt, (and the whole world shall cry out upon the burning of God's word). And the overplus of the money, that shall remain to me, shall make me more studious, to correct the said New Testament, and so newly to imprint the same once again, and I trust the second will much better like you, than ever did the first: And so forward went the bargain, the bishop had the books, Packington had the thanks, and Tyndale had the money

Afterward, when more New Testaments were printed, they came thick and threefold into England, the bishop of London hearing that still there were so many New Testaments abroad, sent for Augustine Packington and said unto him: Sir how cometh this, that there are so many New Testaments abroad, and you promised and assured me, that you had bought all? Then said Packington, I promise you that I bought all that then was to be had: but I perceive they have made more sense, and it will never be better, as long as they have the letters and stamps, therefore it were best for your lordship, to buy the stamps too, and then are you sure: the bishop smiled at him and said, well Packington well, and so ended this matter.[83]

Mozley is right to say that the tale has lost nothing in the telling, and that it doesn't even agree with itself about who owns the books that are being sold.[84] By 1529 Tyndale's outlawed books included also *The Parable of the Wicked Mammon* and *The Obedience of a Christian Man*, and somewhere down the line they were also no doubt bought for burning. Even so, there is a ring of truth to the basic idea of buying up in bulk (though not of Tyndale agreeing to sell New Testaments for burning); especially when we recall that Packington as a mercer would be a dealer in fine textiles at the wealthier end of the cloth trade.

Tyndale in Hamburg

During that summer of 1528, at the end of June, Wolsey asked the Regent in the Low Countries to hunt for Tyndale and Roye, as we saw above in telling of *Mammon*,[85] without success. Between September 1528 and early 1529 rumours reached Rinck and West that Tyndale was to be found in Antwerp, Cologne and Frankfurt. Between the Antwerp printings of the *Obedience* in October 1528 and the Pentateuch in January 1530, where, in fact, should we think of Tyndale living? Wherever it was, he was working on the Pentateuch, his Hebrew now good enough for fine work of translation. There is an extraordinary story, given by Foxe only in his second (1570) edition, about the period from late 1528 to early 1530.

> At what time Tyndale had translated the fifth book of Moses called Deuteronomy, minding to print the same at Hamborough [Hamburg], he sailed thereward [from Antwerp]: where by the way, upon the coast of Holland, he suffered shipwreck, by the which he lost all his books, writings and copies, and so was compelled to begin all again new, to his hindrance and doubling of his labours. Thus having lost by that ship both money, his copies and time, he came in another ship to Hamborough, where at his appointment Master Coverdale tarried for him, and helped him in the translating the whole five books of Moses, from Easter [March 1529] till December, in the house of a worshipful widow, Mistress Margaret van Emmerson, Anno 1529, a great sweating sickness being the same time in the town. So having dispatched his business at Hamborough, he returned afterward to Antwerp again.[86]

It is understandable that Tyndale should think of leaving Antwerp as Wolsey's long arm was reaching for him. It used to be argued that Foxe was romancing, on the several grounds that Coverdale was not recorded in Hamburg and that Hamburg had no printers. Mozley gives good reasons to counter both, and adds the results of research into the von Emmerson family, and into the epidemic of sweating sickness, to support Foxe.

It looks very much as if Tyndale was indeed in Hamburg at that time. There were certainly printers there, including a great one, the younger George Richloff of Lübeck thirty-five miles away, then opening a printing-shop in Hamburg. Tyndale would also be drawn to the city by the presence of possibly an old acquaintance, Johannes Bugenhagen, Luther's close associate (he who had written to the English reformers the letter of encouragement), who had been rector of the town church at Wittenberg when Tyndale could have been there learning Hebrew. In July 1528 Bugenhagen had been invited to supervise the reform of the Church in Hamburg; Tyndale would be going to a reforming city: by February 1529, the work of reform was complete. He would be safe there.

And what of Miles Coverdale? Then at the age of forty-two, a Yorkshireman (from the city of York), he had been at Cambridge and influenced by Robert Barnes, whom he supported, making a parallel progress 'from Erasmus through Colet to Luther'.[87] John Bale described him in those years as 'a young man of friendly and upright nature and very gentle spirit . . . The spirit of God . . . in him . . . is a still small voice comforting wavering hearts. His style is charming and gentle, flowing limpidly along; it moves and instructs and delights'.[88] He would go on, of course, in October 1535 to give his nation the first complete Bible in English, in two recensions, the second being the April 1539 'Great Bible' (from which the Psalms were taken into the Book of Common Prayer, used daily in the Church of England until the late twentieth century). In 1528, however, having ceased to be a monk, and preaching in Essex against the Mass, image-worship and ear-confession, Coverdale found trouble for himself steadily approaching and later that year fled to the Continent, where he stayed for about seven years. It is quite possible that he went to Hamburg at the invitation of Tyndale, to assist with the work on the Pentateuch. Though his knowledge of Greek and Hebrew was small, Coverdale's ability to digest recent translations in Latin, German and French would be useful. It is just possible that Coverdale was also the mysterious friend from England who Tyndale hoped would be a helper in Cologne, as he explains in the preface to *Mammon*.[89] It is certain that Coverdale was with Tyndale in Antwerp in 1534 and 1535, and there is no reason at all why Foxe should not be right about Coverdale being in Hamburg and working with Tyndale there.

So what about the shipwreck? Foxe's account is the only reference to it. Tyndale does not mention it. That does not mean that it did not happen. Tyndale's stories about his own life—about university, about experiences in Gloucestershire, about failing to get patronage in London—have all a larger frame, a bigger point. Oxford 'theology' was grotesque folly; ignorant and bigoted rural men were entrusted with the holy office; the Bishop of London kept England, alone in Europe, in darkness, not permitting the light of the Word in the mother tongue. By contrast, the moral of the shipwreck story is simply Tyndale's own heroic determination, and therefore it is not to be mentioned. Several years' work, presumably ('writings'), with his necessary books including manuscripts ('and copies') were lost. The labour and cost of reassembling such primary materials as a Hebrew text and lexicons and grammars and a Septuagint, and secondary sources like Pagninus and Luther, would have been permeated with an overwhelming frustration and even despair, not to mention grief at the destruction of irreplaceable work. Yet in the history of such disasters it is noteworthy that writers, painters and musicians have all reported their sense that the result was even better—starting again with courage seemed to bring a new clarity. The most grievous thing for us is the loss of time. Had Richloff started printing Tyndale's Pentateuch in Hamburg late in 1528, the translator could have gone much further, and finished the historical books of the Old Testament and been well into the poetry and the prophets before 1535 and his arrest. As it is, we only have the Pentateuch with his oversight, itself a revision if the shipwreck story is true, and the historical books printed in 1537 after his death.

In August 1529 the scene in England changed. Henry needed his divorce, and called on the universities throughout Europe for their support. A Parliament had been assembled. The implications of the question were immense, and for a while the heat was off the hunting of Lutherans and Lollards. Wolsey had other things to occupy him, trying to hold the Emperor, whose aunt was the wronged Queen Catherine, the Pope, and his own hopes of the papal throne, in the same hand as service to his King. At a lower level, this meant that Antwerp was not so immediately dangerous, and is likely that Tyndale returned there later that year from Hamburg. He would have been safer in Germany, but Antwerp was where the connection was with England, where goods were dispatched to England, and refugees from England welcomed. Edward Hall's story of Tunstall and Packington and that merchant's buying of Tyndale's books for burning took place in Antwerp. Tunstall and More had been with Hackett in Cambrai negotiating peace early in August 1529, and were now presumably on their way home, putting Tunstall in the same city as Tyndale. Early autumn 1529 is just early enough for Tyndale's return (though Tyndale's agreement to sell Testaments for burning is unlikely). We must allow a little flexibility. Foxe has said that Tyndale stayed in Hamburg in the house of Margaret von Emmerson until December 1529. The first book of the Pentateuch, Genesis, came off Hoochstraten's press in Antwerp on 17 January 1530.

Tyndale was then in Antwerp for the rest of his time of freedom, about four and a half years. He stayed, it seems, at the English House, long ago demolished—there are now only a few old streets and the Cathedral remaining in that area. This was a residence of English merchants, some of whom were becoming sympathetic to the growing cause of reform. They had their own chaplain, who four years later was John Rogers, a priest of orthodox beliefs who soon became a supporter of Tyndale. After Tyndale's death Rogers published in 1537, under the name of Thomas Matthew, Tyndale's translations in that first English Bible to be licensed by the King. Rogers was the first of the almost three hundred martyrs burned by Mary after her accession in 1553.

The Practice of Prelates

Tyndale probably wrote in the English House at Antwerp the last of his non-biblical books (apart from the *Answer to More*). This was a short book, entitled *The Practice of Prelates. Whether the King's grace may be separated from his queen because she was his brother's wife*, and printed by Hoochstraten as if from 'Marburg'. It is a book fierce against the prelates, and against Tyndale's sense of international conspiracy seen particularly through the fact of Wolsey's upward climb, riding on top of the rise of the Pope to absolute power. Tyndale considers the lawfulness of putting away a wife, and concludes that Henry cannot divorce Catherine. He sees the practice of the prelates in promoting divorce to enable Henry possibly to marry the French king's sister— something to their advantage. Such choking entanglement is presented throughout the book as the Pope's ivy strangling the nation's tree. As well as its more customary meaning today of the exercise of a profession, 'practice' carries even more its older meaning, now almost lost, of scheming through trickery—the poisoned and dying Laertes says 'The foul practice hath turned itself on me' (*Hamlet* V.ii.309);[90] and 'This is practice, Gloucester,' says Goneril to the fallen and dying Edmund (*King Lear* V.iii.151). 'By the law of war thou wast not bound to answer/An unknown opposite . . .' Shakespeare clearly associated the word with trickery that is lethal.

The book is not long. In reprintings later in the century it was shorter by as much as a quarter. King Henry, we are told, was much angered by it, understandably. Elizabethan editors and printers including John Day found it necessary to omit much of the last section where Tyndale argues learnedly against Henry's divorce of Catherine, because it questioned the legitimacy of his marriage to Anne, the mother of Queen Elizabeth. That, as it happens, is not the most forceful part of the book: the exposition of passages of Leviticus do not come alive in the way that the accounts of the practices of the prelates do elsewhere in the book. Here the swingeing attacks produce stinging rhythms, even in the short prologue, where he explains that just as the old scribes and Pharisees played politics against Christ, so the modern ones do the same against 'heretics', who are the preachers of Christ. 'And ye elders of the people, fear ye God also . . .' begins a paragraph.

As we have learned to expect, the organisation of the whole is logical, developing through twenty points, a technique that adds to the power of the passion. There are few marginal notes (later versions, including the Parker Society edition, are as usual misleading). The mixture of biblical truth about Peter, the betrayal by the prelates, appointed to preach Christ, the history of the papacy and its grounding in money, and so on, rises to heights at the attacks on the current practices of prelates, making lists which mount in force: 'they come from stewardships in gentlemen's houses, and from surveying of great men's lands, lords' secrets, kings' councils, ambassadorship, from war and ministering all worldly matters, yea, worldly mischief.'[91] In that climax the balanced alliteration of 'w' and 'm', 'war and ministering . . . worldly matters . . . worldly mischief' does a good deal of work. A little later he builds to one of his stronger sarcasms. Several pages are given to Charlemagne, half of the account being of his lusts, and particularly a fantastic legend about the corpse of his dead whore, the power of an enchanted ring, a well, and a monastery, to allow him to conclude 'And there he lieth and is a saint as right is . . .'[92] Soon after that is the famous passage about the folly of the university system, divinity students being 'noselled [nurtured] in heathen learning eight or nine year' and shut out of Scripture and made to swear on oath not to preach what the Church does not approve, though not knowing what that is, and not being appointed without a bishop.[93]

A neat little Chaucerian picture follows, to show the insidious infiltration of the Church at every level.

And little master parson after the same manner if he come into an house, and the wife be snout-fair, he will root himself there by one craft or other: either by using such pastime as the good man doth, or in being beneficial by one way or other, or he will lend him, and so bring him into his danger [dependence] that he cannot thrust him out when he would, but must be compelled to bear him, and to let him be homely, whether he will or no.[94]

That might be part of the Shipman's Tale, or Summoner's Tale. The phrase 'snout-fair' is Tyndale's coinage: it was taken up frequently in the following two centuries.

A longer section illustrating practice by the bishops in England's history leads to the dominant matter of the last half, the power of 'Thomas Wolfsee' (Wolsey) telling the inside story of his despicable craftiness, and pulling no punches—though all necessarily based on hearsay.

And in like manner played he with the ladies and gentlemen. Whosoever of them was great, with her was he familiar, and to her gave he gifts: yea and where St Thomas of Canterbury was wont to come after, Thomas cardinal went oft before, preventing his prince, and perverted the order of that holy man. If any were subtle-witted, and meet for his purpose, her made he sworn to betray the queen likewise, and tell him what she said or did. I know one that departed the court for no other cause, than that she would no longer betray her mistress.[95]

National and international matters are detailed by Tyndale as utterly corrupted by Wolsey, making a context for the final sarcastic tirade about why the Queen should be divorced. As well as 'Wolfsee', Longland the Bishop of Lincoln, and Stokesley, feature in these pages: all three had been connected with Magdalen Hall two decades before.

Though Tyndale's discussion of the divorce comes only in the last pages, his mention of it in the book's title is right, as it is his response to the issue. Living on the Continent, he is aware that reformed opinion there is that the marriage had to stand, even though the marriage was probably invalid. Writing for English readers, he knows that reformers like Latimer argue that it was no marriage at all, and ought to be broken. His entangling himself in the jungle of arguments of Leviticus 18, forbidding marriage with a brother's wife, versus Deuteronomy 25, ordering 'Levirate' marriage (in which a widow continues the male line by marrying her dead husband's brother) is one of his least successful pieces of writing. He is unusually unclear, coming out in a muffled way for the Leviticus text but only as it might apply to the lifetime of the first husband—a less than ringing call. Only let England realise the political dangers of divorce, he writes. He sees ahead nothing but infamy worse than what the Church has already caused his nation. The matter of the King's divorce, his whole book implies, can only be understood as a further example of the internationally widespread 'practice' of the Church, seen at its most blatant in Wolsey. He knows that Wolsey has retired to the north, but sees that move as only the latest move in his customary deviousness: he will be back.

Tyndale is at his best in this book when he is closest to the Gospels. The text proper, after the prologue, begins:

> Our Saviour Jesus Christ answered Pilate, that his kingdom was not of this world. And (Matthew, in the tenth) he saith, The disciple is not greater than his master . . . Wherefore if Christ's kingdom be not of this world, nor any of his disciples may be otherwise than he was: then Christ's vicars, which minister his kingdom here in his bodily absence, and have the oversight of his flock, may be none emperors, kings, dukes, lords, knights, temporal judges, or any temporal officer, or under false names have any such dominion, or minister any such office as requireth violence.[96]

The paragraph begins with Christ and ends with a list of great offices, a rhetorical scheme he uses often in this book as a symbol of the sheer volume of the interaction of Church and State. The symbol of the one against the many runs through his arguments from that base: what began with Christ alone, and should continue with Christ with the Christian soul alone, or among the Christian equals of the congregation, has become a gigantic international hierarchy with absolute worldly power. The device of extending a sentence beyond an expected end, to give a sense of power almost out of control, is frequent. He writes at his most passionate in the prologue, in every sentence of which the Bible translator can be felt. Both qualities can be seen in this paragraph from the prologue:

> And let all men be they never so great hearken unto this and let this be an answer unto them. Wicked king Ahab said unto the prophet Elias, Art thou he that troublest Israel? And Elias answered, It is not I that trouble Israel, but thou and thy father's household, in that ye have forsaken the commandments of the Lord and follow idols. Even so the preachers of the truth, which rebuke sin, are not the troublers of realms and commonwealths, but they that do wickedly: and namely high prelates and mighty princes, which walk without the fear of God, and live abominably, corrupting the common people with their ensample. They be they that bring the wrath of

God on all realms, and trouble all commonwealths with war, dearth, poverty, pestilence, evil luck, and all misfortune.[97]

The penultimate sentence, beginning with the concrete 'preachers', contrasts with the shadowy 'they that do wickedly'. But the sentence has not ended; it runs on through seven further ideas—prelates, princes, without fear of God, abominably, corrupting, common people, example. The last sentence balances 'bring wrath . . . realms' and 'trouble . . . commonwealths' and then runs on in a list to a climax with a variant on Tyndale's customary dactyl a heavy stress followed by two light stresses—'(mis)fortune'. So the paragraph has begun with Elias (Elijah) one-to-one with 'wicked king Ahab' has ended with two elaborations of evil.

The exchange between Ahab and Elias is also interesting because it is almost word for word the translation of 1 Kings 18 which will eventually appear in 'Matthew's Bible'.[98] Tyndale has already published the Pentateuch, but is clearly already looking far ahead. He has made the translation here, from the Hebrew of 'the third book of the Kings'. The story of the prophet known as Elijah in the last chapters of what we know as 1 Kings was important for the religious exiles. They identified with the fearless man of God who was so hunted in his own country that he retreated far away, and there in solitude complained to his God that 'I only am left, and they seek my soul to have it too'.[99] God, however, was not in the wind, earthquake or fire of tempestuous events, but in 'a small still voice' asking 'what doest thou here, Eliah?' (Tyndale's phrases). The command of God was to political involvement—'Go and anoint Hazael to be king of Siria . . . and Jehu the son of Namsi anoint to be king over Israel . . .' Moreover, God declared that the office of prophet was not doomed: 'And Eliseus the son of Saphat of Abel Mehulah anoint to be prophet in thy room . . . And thereto I have left me seven thousand in Israel, of which never man bowed his knees unto Baal nor kissed him with his mouth.' How far ahead he sees in his Hebrew studies in Antwerp in 1530 we cannot now know: but it appears that he translated, and published, the short book of the prophet Jonah, some time in 1531.

The Prophet Jonah

The strange story of Jonah tells also of a prophet's retreat and refusal, and the challenge he should be facing in the name of his God. Rather than take the word of God to the alien Nineveh, whose people might even receive it and repent, Jonah set out to flee to the end of the world (beyond Gibraltar) and had to be brought back by a miraculous storm and whale. His preaching was successful, and to his disgust the city, from the king to the animals, repented. Jonah sat outside and sulked. A miraculous vine brought him shade, and was then destroyed, and a 'fervent east wind' caused him extreme suffering in the heat. How, asked God, could Jonah be so selfishly angry over the loss of the vine, which he had done nothing to make, and not understand 'should not I have compassion on Nineve that great city, wherein there is a multitude of people, even above an hundred thousand that know not their right hand from their left, besides much cattle?'[100]

The four small chapters of this short book were important for the reformers. Luther had himself translated it separately in 1526, on his way to his whole Bible in 1534. There were many separate Latin and vernacular versions throughout reformed Europe. Tyndale did nothing particularly odd in singling it out from far ahead in the Hebrew Bible, a late prophecy worked on while he had still only just finished the Pentateuch, we must assume. It was sometimes though of as a historical book as the prophet Jonah the son of Amittai is first mentioned towards the end of 2 Kings 14. Christ himself, as was often noticed, showed how to read Scripture aright with reference to this very story (Matthew 12, Luke 11), allowing it to be an allegory of his own resurrection. Added to that was the pointed message of the call to preach repentance to a sinful nation, massively effective in spite of the lamentable weakness of the messenger.

The usual dating of 1531 for Tyndale's translation depends on a reference in More's *Confutation of Tyndale's Answer* of 1532. Early in the preface to that mammoth work More sets out seventeen 'books . . . of these evil sects . . .', seven by Tyndale. They issue from the followers of Luther, 'the new sects sprongen out of his, which like the children of the viper would now gnaw out of their mother's belly. . . First Tyndale's New Testament father of them all by reason of his false translating. . .' Then More lists the Romans introduction, the *Wicked Mammon*, the *Obedience* and the *Exposition of the first epistle of Saint John*, followed by books by Joye, Fish, Roye and *The examination of Thorpe* 'put forth as it is said by George Constantine.' 'Then we have Jonas made out by Tyndale, a book that who so delight therein shall stand in peril that Jonas was never so swallowed up with the whale, as by the delight of that book: a man's soul may be so swallowed up by the devil, that he shall never have the grace to get out again.'[101]

A letter from the English merchant Stephen Vaughan in Antwerp (of whom more below) to Thomas Cromwell dated 19 June 1531 mentions that 'the prophets Isaiah and Jonas are put forth in the English tongue, and passeth any man's power to stop them from coming forth'.[102] This gives a date of May 1531, it is assumed, as the translation of Isaiah by George Joye was printed by Martin de Keyser of Antwerp, according to the colophon, on 10 May 1531. The translation of Jonah is also from the press of Martin de Keyser, and also in octavo, and also in Bastard type except for the words of the first line of the title page which are in textura, and it is clearly a twin volume to Joye's Isaiah, even to the parallel theme: Joye has on his title-page 'Despise not the doctrine and warning of the Prophet of God'. The prologue was a number of times reprinted, but the translation of Jonah was for a long time thought lost, until in 1861 it was discovered by Lord Arthur Hervey in his family library, bound as a pamphlet with eight other Reformation tracts of the early 1530s, including *The prayer and complaint of the plowman*, *A proper dialogue between a gentleman and a husbandman*, and *The Testament of Master William Tracie*. It is now in the British Library. The title occupies twenty-three lines, and contains no translator's name. Thirty-eight pages of prologue (without marginal notes, which were added in the 1570s by John Day) then lead to seven pages of translation (again without notes), the first headed, in a different type, the familiar 'W.T. unto the Christian reader'. The long prologue is solid and worthy rather than lively, and carries the reformers' message that Scripture, now released from being shut up by the papal church, contains the call to preach to the English, with terrible consequences if, as before in the times of Gildas and Wyclif, the nation hardens its heart.

The translation probably is, as the 'W.T.' indicates, by Tyndale, from the Hebrew. There is nothing sufficiently distinctive in the English to make the attribution certain. Nor is there in the long prologue anything that could not have been written by, for example, George Joye. True, some of the familiar Tyndale mannerisms are there, like the hypocrites reading the stories in the Bible as if they were of Robin Hood, serving nothing 'save to feign false descant and jiggling allegories';[103] or like lists—the long sentence that is the twelfth paragraph balances the true prophets and preachers against the Pope

which in sinning against God and to quench the truth of his holy spirit, is ever chief captain and trumpet-blower to set other a-work, and seeketh only his freedom, liberty, privilege, wealth, prosperity, profit, pleasure, pastime, honour and glory, with the bondage, thraldom, captivity, misery, wretchedness, and vile subjection of his brethren: and in his own cause is so fervent, so stiff and cruel, that he will not suffer one word spoken against his false majesty, wily

inventions and juggling hypocrisy to be unavenged, though all
Christendom should be set together by the ears, and should cost be
cared not how many hundred thousand their lives.[104]

Characteristic Tyndale, though the lists might be thought a touch too
full. There are images, like those of the young scholars who must have
leisure to grow 'in the spirit, love and in the deeds therof, as young
children must have time to grow in their bodies',[105] or the startling
simile for Jonah's utter inability to venture into the heathen city of
Nineveh; his own free will had as much power 'as the weakest hearted
woman in the world hath power, if she were commanded, to leap in
to a tub of living snakes and adders'.[106] But in all the prologue, the
ratio of such vivid colouring to run-of-the-mill sentences is slightly
lower than elsewhere in Tyndale. The images of outside 'bark, shell
and . . . hard bone' and inside 'pith, kernel, marrow and all sweetness'
of the second paragraph echo the Genesis prologue, and earlier
Tyndale, but they are ultimately from Luther.

It has been argued that a strong development of the work of
Scripture can be seen in the prologue to Jonah, marking a great change
in Tyndale, in that the third paragraph's 'law . . . gospel . . . example'
represents 'how drastically he had to revise the earlier guide for the
sake of consistency'.[107] Such a change is not in fact obvious. Tyndale's
earliest printed document, the 1525 Cologne New Testament prologue, made clear that the law and the promises had both to be inward,
as they are here. To say that 'the large place accorded to the law in the
prologues to the Pentateuch and to Jonah in fact contradicted the
thoroughly evangelical note of the 1525 Prologue to the New Testament'[108] can be shown to misrepresent all three. What is new, however,
though lightly touched, is the move towards a theme of sanctification,
the need for believers to 'grow' in the Lord like the schoolboys noted
above.

Thomas Cromwell

Now in his mid-forties and newly admitted to the royal council, the
efficient Thomas Cromwell had risen from his feckless father's busi-
nesses as brewer, fuller and blacksmith in Putney, through the profession of law, to become right-hand man of Wolsey—and after that
Cardinal's fall, to give much of his best energies to undoing all that his
master had done. He assumed greater and greater power. Whether the
extraordinary change in English life of the ten years from 1532 is to be
attributed to the powers of the King, or to his henchman Cromwell,
is still debated. The steady shifting of power from Rome to Parliament,

the curbing of the wealth and pride of churchmen, presently the very dissolution of the monasteries in two great stages, all happened. Henry was clever, volatile, unpredictable, passionate, increasingly unwell; Cromwell was cleverer and a well-tuned, well-maintained engine, an ideal administrator in that he could see far ahead as well as make things happen in the present. Anne Boleyn was secretly married to Henry in January 1533, and was crowned Queen on the 1 June 1533. She gave birth to a daughter, Elizabeth, in September, by which time the divorce of Catherine had been through every necessary process.

The tide of England's political life began to turn towards reform. Anne Boleyn influenced her royal lover, as we shall be see in the next chapter when she recommends to him Tyndale's *Obedience* in 1529. Though Tyndale had been denounced in May 1530 as a heretic and perverter of God's word, Henry may have begun on his own account in January 1531 to consider the value of enlisting Tyndale's active support: or the whole scheme may have been Cromwell's, worked through the King. Henry had certainly been impressed by the *Obedience*: its Erastianism (subordinating Church to State) was exactly what he wanted to hear. Henry, on his own, or pressed by Cromwell, asked for contact with Tyndale. In January 1531, Cromwell commissioned one of the English merchant venturers in the Netherlands, an old friend and employee, Stephen Vaughan, to seek Tyndale out and see if he could induce him to return to England.

Such a move was the more surprising after the hostility stirred up by the arrival in London of Tyndale's *Practice of Prelates*. In December 1530 both the Milanese ambassador, and the imperial ambassador, Chapuys, reported in letters the vivid attempts to destroy the book. The Milanese ambassador explained that there were three thousand copies in circulation: the author was one Tindaro or Tyndal, an Englishman in Germany, reported to be *magna doctrinae*, 'of great learning'. Placards, both reported, were put up in prominent places announcing that the universities were in favour of the divorce, and denouncing Tyndale's book. There being no such thing as bad publicity, these had the reverse effect, and stimulated interest in it. Several Lutheran merchants were given bizarre punishments for being found in possession, with a view to dealing. Chapuys told how the merchants, including the author's brother, John Tyndale, had been arrested in mid-November and soon after were led through the main streets of London with mitred caps of pasteboard on their heads which announced their crime, *peccasse contra mandata regis*, 'I have sinned against the commandments of the king', and copies of the book slung round their necks, which they then threw into a prepared fire. Chapuys objected to this performance too, on the correct grounds that it only made a hundred persons talk where one talked before.[109] Foxe says only that John Tyndale was abjured for sending five marks to his brother William beyond the sea, and for receiving and keeping his letters. Foxe had, however, in his papers, a document giving fuller details of what must be the same event, which was printed by Strype. This explains that with John Tyndale were a merchant named Thomas Patmore and a young man. They were apprehended by Stokesley and taken before the Chancellor, More, and put in ward. They went before the Star Chamber, charged with 'receiving of Tyndale's testaments and divers other books, and delivering and scattering the same' throughout the city of London. They confessed, and their punishment was prison until the next market day, when they were 'to ride with their faces to the horse tail, having papers on their heads, and the New Testaments and other books . . . to be fastened thick about them, pinned or tacked to their gowns or cloaks'. They were to throw the books at the standard in Cheap on a 'great fire', and suffer fines: Strype gives the surely incredible sum of £18,840. 10s.[110]

Chapuys also reported that a few days after the placards were put up, they were suddenly withdrawn and destroyed, either because of the free publicity or because the King feared that the author might reply. Though Thomas More, in the preface to the *Confutation*, sneered at the book as containing a fabrication,[111] he is brief and restrained. There seems to have been genuine concern at the power that Tyndale had, with justification.[112] Perhaps the word went out to hold back. Chapuys reported that he had heard on the most trustworthy authority that the King, 'afraid lest the priest Tyndale shall write more boldly against him, and hoping to persuade him to retract what he has already written, has invited him back to England, and offered him several good appointments and a seat in his council.'[113] What had happened to the King's anger over the *Practice*? Someone, probably Cromwell, had had the notion that it would be better for the court, to adapt Lyndon Johnson's phrase, to have Tyndale inside writing out, rather than outside writing in. There is extant a letter to Cromwell, possibly of December 1530, referring to the safe delivery of a letter to Mr Tyndale, which could be from the King to William's brother John demanding his address.

Stephen Vaughan

Stephen Vaughan was a good choice of emissary, as he had done curious errands for Cromwell before.[114] A long and complicated correspondence between the two some time before was about 'an iron chest of very curious workmanship', which Cromwell wanted for his house at Austin Friars, 'of such expense that Vaughan was almost afraid to buy it'.[115] Vaughan was not unsympathetic to reform—the governor of the English House had suspected him of heresy. Now he was the King's factor in the Netherlands and trustworthy. He wrote to the King on 26 January 1531, from Bergen-op-Zoom, reporting that he had done his best to locate Tyndale but failed. He had written three separate letters to Tyndale, to Frankfurt, Hamburg and Marburg, offering, on the King's authority, a safe conduct to England, with other sureties as needed, as he had heard while in England with Cromwell earlier that Tyndale would accept. Tyndale had replied, refusing, on the grounds that England was not safe for him, and suspecting a trap. Vaughan enclosed two letters in Tyndale's own hand, one to Vaughan and the other a copy of a letter sent to someone else on the same quest. Vaughan explained that his search for a copy of Tyndale's *Answer to More* had been unsuccessful.[116] His own letter to the King, and the enclosed reply from Tyndale, were both copied by Vaughan to Cromwell, and to that letter Vaughan added a significant paragraph. 'It is unlikely to get Tyndale into England, when he daily heareth so many things from thence which feareth him. After his book, answering my lord chancellor's book, be put forth, I think he will write no more. The man is of a greater knowledge than the king's highness doth take him for; which well appeareth by his works. Would God he were in England!'[117]

This tells us much. Wherever he was living, he was hearing 'daily' about the situation in England. The burning of Hitton could only have heralded worse, with Longland active through his enormous diocese, Stokesley having replaced Tunstall in London, and More as Chancellor. What was recorded by Foxe can only have been a fraction of what was happening, as news is always selective. Before he replied, there may have been time for Tyndale to know of the arrest of Latimer and Crome, and the rearrest of Bilney and Arthur early in March—all most probably known to him. John Frith had been briefly in England during Lent and returned with information. Tyndale would know how little weight could be given to the promise of a safe conduct. The most trivial, or non-existent, reason could be established by which he would forfeit such a document—the sixteenth-century equivalent of not signing his driving licence. Precisely that happened to Robert Barnes at the end of the year, of whom More wrote in the *Confutation*, 'Yet hath he so demeaned himself, since his coming hither, that he had clearly broken and forfeited his safe conduct, and lawfully might be burned . . .'[118] John Frith retorted that he had seen Barnes's safe conduct in Antwerp, and the only condition on it was that must arrive before Christmas, which he did.[119]

Vaughan knew what Tyndale was writing, and what was said about it, that it was to be the last: correct, if that meant that Tyndale would finish the business with More with that book. After his *Answer*, he never mentioned More again. (*The Supper of the Lord* is not his.) The most significant thing that Vaughan had heard about him, however, was that Tyndale was 'of a greater knowledge' than the King's Highness took him for. This is important. Vaughan had made soundings, writing to people in Frankfurt, Hamburg and Marburg with letters to pass on to him. He had undoubtedly asked around in Antwerp. The answers suggested that Tyndale was a most formidable scholar, opinions backed by his books.

A further letter to Cromwell from Vaughan, on 25 March 1531, announced that he had found a 'rudely scribbled' manuscript copy of Tyndale's *Answer*, and he (Vaughan) was busy copying it out fair, to send to the King: it made 'three quires of paper thoroughly written', that is, over seventy manuscript leaves, and he was getting on as fast as he could. One wonders what of Tyndale he had read before, as he reported on his work in progress, 'No work that ever he made is written in so gentle a style'. Perhaps the common anger at More's *Dialogue* among the reformers was so great that Tyndale's writing seemed 'gentle' by contrast. Or perhaps Vaughan was out of his depth: an idea supported by the folly of sending as specimen current Tyndale work such an unsuitable book. Perhaps he didn't understand the book, because he had a scribe to do the work (it doesn't sound as if he did), for he also says that Tyndale will not publish it until he hears that 'the king's highness will accept and take it', which is wrong, and that Tyndale has written an epistle to the King in the book, which is also wrong; unless he took such an epistle out before printing. For us, Vaughan is tantalising, giving flashes of Tyndale seen through his own, merchant's eyes, at a time when we are hungry for a view of him; he is not quite sure what sort of an animal he is dealing with, except that he has to be greatly respected. England would benefit if he were there. Probably, as Mozley suggests, Vaughan has misunderstood something said to him in Antwerp, conceivably by George Joye, and conceivably misunderstood by Joye himself, about the conditions under which he would stop writing: that is, he would cease polemic work only if the King would permit the free circulation of Scripture in English.

Three and a half weeks later, on 18 April, Vaughan wrote again to the King, enclosing the part of Tyndale's *Answer* that he has finished, and commending it to his majesty. In the rest of his letter, however, he goes on to produce one of the most important documents in the Tyndale story, reproduced here in full. Unexpectedly, he has met Tyndale.

He sent a certain person to seek me, whom he advised to say that a certain friend of mine, unknown to the messenger, was very desirous to speak with me: praying me to take pains to go unto him, to such place as he should bring me. Then I to the messenger, 'What is your friend, and where is he?' 'His name I know not,' said he: but if it be your pleasure to go where he is, I will be glad thither to bring you.' Thus, doubtful what this matter meant, I concluded to go with him, and followed him till he brought me without the gates of Antwerp, into a field lying nigh unto the same: where was abiding me this said Tyndale. At our meeting, 'Do you not know me?' said this Tyndale. 'I do not well remember you,' said I to him. 'My name,' said he, 'is Tyndale.' 'But Tyndale!' said I, 'fortunate be our meeting.' Then Tyndale, 'Sir, I have been exceeding desirous to speak with you.' 'And I with you; what is your mind?' 'Sir,' said he, 'I am informed that the king's grace taketh great displeasure with me for putting forth of certain books, which I lately made in these parts: but specially for the book named *The Practice of Prelates*: whereof I have no little marvel, considering that in it I did but warn his grace of the subtle demeanour of the clergy of his realm towards his person, and of the shameful abusions by them practised, not a little threatening the displeasure of his grace and weal of his realm: in which doing I showed and declared the heart of a true subject, which sought the safeguard of his royal person and weal of his commons, to the intent that his grace, thereof warned, might in due time prepare his remedies against their subtle dreams. If for my pains therein taken, if for my poverty, if for mine exile out of my natural country, and bitter absence from my friends, if for my hunger, my thirst, my cold, the great danger wherewith I am everywhere encompassed, and finally if for innumerable other hard and sharp fightings which I endure, not yet feeling their asperity by reason I hoped with my labours to do honour to God, true service to my prince, and pleasure to his command: how is it that his grace, this considering, may either by himself think, or by the persuasion of others be brought to think, that in this doing I should not show a pure mind, a true and incorrupt zeal and affection to his grace? Was there in me any such mind, when I warned his grace to beware of his cardinal, whose iniquity he shortly after approved [proved] according to my writing? Doth this deserve hatred? Again, may his grace, being a Christian prince, be so unkind to God, which hath commanded his word to be spread throughout the world, to give more faith to the wicked persuasions of men, which, presuming above God's wisdom, and contrary to that which Christ expressly commandeth in his testament, dare say that it is not lawful for the people to have the same in a tongue that they understand, because the purity thereof should open men's eyes to see their wickedness? Is there more danger in the king's subjects than in the subjects of all other princes, which in every of their tongues have the same, under privilege of their sovereigns? As I now am, very death were more pleasant to me than life, considering man's nature to be such as can bear no truth.'

Thus, after a long conversation had between us, for my part making answer as my wit would serve me, which were too long to write, I assayed him with gentle persuasions, to know whether he would come into England: ascertaining him that means should be made, if he thereto were minded, without his peril or danger, that he might do so: and that what surety he would devise for the same purpose, should, by labour of friends, be obtained of your majesty. But to this he answered, that he neither would nor durst come into England, albeit your grace would promise him never so much the surety: fearing lest, as he hath before written, your promise made should surely be broken, by the persuasion of the clergy, which would affirm that promises made with heretics ought not to be kept.

After this, he told me how he had finished a work against my lord chancellor's book, and would not put it in print till such time as your grace had seen it: because he apperceiveth your displeasure towards him, for hasty putting forth of his other work, and because it should appear that he is not of so obstinate mind, as he thinks he is reported unto your grace. This is the substance of his conversation had with me, which, as he spake, I have written to your grace word for word, as near as I could by any possible means bring to remembrance. My trust therefore is, that your grace will not but take my labours in the best part, I thought necessary to be written unto your grace. After these words, he then, being something fearful of me, lest I would have pursued him, and drawing also towards night, he took his leave of me, and departed from the town, and I toward the town, saying I should shortly, peradventure, see him again, or if not, hear from him. Howbeit I suppose he afterward returned to the town by another way: for there is no likelihood that he should lodge without the town. Hasty to pursue him I was not, because I had

❦The Actes off The Apostles.

❦The fyrst Chapter.

In my fyrst treati／se(Deare frende Theo／philus(J have written off all that Jesus began to do ƈd teache／vntill the daye in the whiche he was take vp／after that he thorowe the ho／ly gooſt／had geven comma／undementſ vnto the Apoſt／les／whiche he choſe: to whō alſo he ſhewed hym ſilfe ali／ve／after his paſſion by many tokens／aperynge vnto them fourty dayes ‘ƈd ſpake vnto them off the kyngdom of god／and gaddered them to geo／der／and cōmaunded them／that they ſhulde not departe from Jeruſalē: but to wayte for the pro／mys of the father／wher of ye have herde off me. For Jhon baptiſed wyth water butt ye ſhalbe baptiſed with the holy gooſt／and that wyth in this feawe dayes.

When they were come togedder／they ared of hym／ſayinge: Maſter wilt thou at this tyme re／ſtore agayne the kyngdom of iſrahel？ He ſayde vnto them: Jt is not for you to knowe the tymes or the ſeaſons which the father hath putt in hys awne power: but ye ſhall receave power off the holy gooſt which ſhall come on you. And ye ſhal￠

1. A page from the only complete surviving copy of Tyndale's 1526 Worms New Testament. It is thought that only a few copies were illuminated in this way; it is not known by whom or for what purpose. (Reproduced by kind permission of the Principal of Bristol Baptist College)

2. The view looking south-west across the Vale of Berkeley from Stinchcombe Hill in Gloucestershire, above Tyndale's likely birthplace. Beyond the River Severn can be seen the beginnings of the Welsh hills. (Photo: Tim Davies)

3. The tower of Magdalen College, Oxford, finished shortly before Tyndale arrived at the college. (Photo: Tim Davies)

4 (and frontispiece). The portrait of William Tyndale that hangs in the dining-hall of Hertford College, Oxford. The artist is not known. The appearance is said to belong to a time shortly after Tyndale's death, but there are good reasons for believing it to be a true likeness. What book Tyndale is pointing to is not known. The Latin in the panel at the bottom has been translated thus:

> This picture represents, as far as art could, William Tyndale, sometime student of this Hall [Magdalen] and its ornament, who, after establishing here the happy beginnings of a purer theology, at Antwerp devoted his energies to translating into the vernacular the New Testament and the Pentateuch, a labour so greatly tending to the salvation of his fellow-countrymen that he was rightly called the Apostle of England. He gained a martyr's crown at Vilvoorde near Brussels in 1536, a man, if we may believe even his adversary (the Emperor's Procurator General), learned, pious, and good.

The couplet set under Tyndale's hand has been translated:

> To scatter Roman darkness by this light
> The loss of land and life I'll reckon slight.

(Reproduced by kind permission of the Principal of Hertford College)

5. The first page of Tyndale's uncompleted 1525 Cologne New Testament. It was made in close imitation of Luther's 1522 'September Testament'. The full-page block shows an angel holding the inkpot for St Matthew. The woodcut was used again, slightly cut down, in a work by Rupertus entitled *In Matthaeum* in 1526, also from Peter Quentell's press, which was edited by Cochlaeus, who betrayed Tyndale.

6 (facing page top). A plan of Antwerp just after Tyndale's time. The English quay is at the top right, numbered 3 (barely visible in this reproduction) and the English House is numbered 17 on a crossroads to the right of the centre.

7 (facing page bottom). A sketch of Antwerp harbour by Albrecht Dürer, 1520. (Graphische Sammlung Albertina, Vienna)

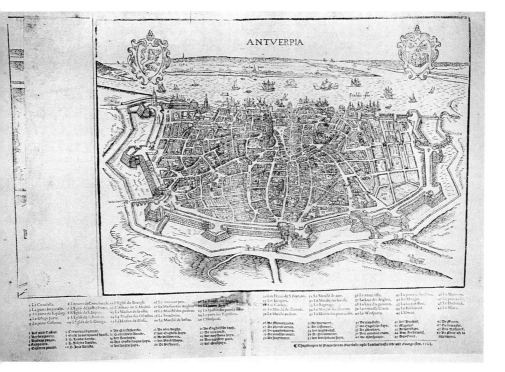

ANTVERPIA

1520 Antورf

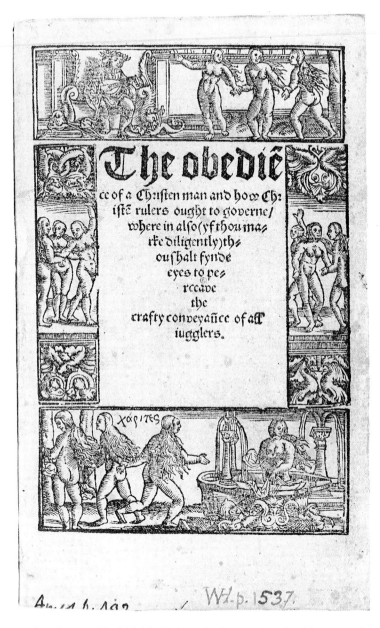

The obedié ce of a Christen man and how Christe rulers ought to governe/ where in also (yf thou marke diligently) thou shalt fynde eyes to perceave the crafty conveyaûce of all iugglers.

8. The title-page of Tyndale's *The Obedience of a Christian Man*, printed by 'Hans Luft of Marburg' (Johannes Hoochstraten in Antwerp) in October 1528. The full title does not properly represent the content. The border is singularly inappropriate. The top panel shows Apollo with his laurel crown, bow and serpent, and a lute instead of a lyre. This would make the three ladies Muses. The bottom panel shows Venus in her bath, and the three ladies are, as the Greek word states, Graces. The two side blocks, clumsily assembled, either make the Muses up to the correct number of nine, or unnecessarily repeat the Graces. (It is possible that all the ladies are Graces, as Apollo does appear with them in earlier manuscript illustrations.) An identical border was used for two books printed in Cologne in 1523 and a further four books printed in Antwerp in the twelve months following *The Obedience*—including biblical commentaries by Erasmus and John Frith. (British Library)

¶ The Gospell of S. Marke.

¶ The fyrste Chapter. ✠

Mat. iij.
a. Lu. iij. a

Mal. iij. a

Esa. xl. a
John. j. c.

The beginnynge of the Gospell of Jesu Christ the sonne of God/as yt is wrytten in the Prophetes: Beholde I sende my messenger before thy face/which shall prepared thy waye before ȳ. The voyce of a cryer in the wildernes: prepare ye the waye of the Lorde/make his pathes streyght.

John bap-
tised.
Mat. iij. a

John dyd baptise in the wyldernes / & preche the baptyme of repentaunce/ for the remission of synnes. And all the londe of Jurie & they of Jerusalem/went out vnto him/& were all baptised of him in the ryver Jordan/ confessynge their synnes.

Mat. iij. e
Luk. iij. c
John. j. d.

John was clothed with cammylles heer/ & with a gerdyll of a skyn a bout hys loynes. And he dyd eate locustes & wylde hony / and preached sayinge: a stronger then I commeth after me/whose shue latchet I am not worthy to stoupe doune and vnlose. I have baptised you with water: but he shall baptise you with the holy goost. ✠

Jesus is
Baptised.
Mat. iij. d
Luk. iij. d

And yt came to passe in those dayes / that Jesus cam from Nazareth/a cyte of Galile:& was baptised of John in Jordan. And assone as he was come out of the water / John sawe heaven open/ and the holy goost descendinge vpon him/lyke a dove. And ther came a voyce

9. The opening of St Mark's Gospel in Tyndale's New Testament of 1534 (actual size). (British Library)

The forme of Aaron with all his apparell.

10. Two pages from Tyndale's Exodus of 1530 (115% of actual size). (British Library)

rpull and bysse.

And they shall make the Ephod: of golde
cyncte, scarlett, purpull ād white twyned bys
with broderdworke, The two sydes shall co
e to gether, clossed vppe in the edges thereof
nd the girdell of the Ephod shalbe of the sa
e workemanshippe ād of the same stuffe: e
en of golde, Iacyncte, scarlete, purpull ād twy
ed bysse,

And thou shalt take two onyx stones and
raue in them the names of the childern of Is
el: sixe in the one stone, and the other sixe in
e other stone: acordinge to the order of the
birth. After the worke of a stonegrauer, euē
sygnettes are grauen, shalt thou graue the. ij
ones with the names of the childern of Isra
, ād shalt make thē to be set in ouches of gol
e. And thou shalt put the two stones apō the
oo shulders of the Ephod, ād they shalbe sto
es off remembraunce vnto the childern off
rael. And Aaron shall bere their names be
rc the Lorde vppon hys two shulders for a
membraunce.

And thou shalt make hokes off golde and
oo cheynes off fine golde: lynkeworke and
rethed, and fasten the wrethed cheynes to
e hokes.

And thou shalt make the brestlappe of en
sample

The Prophecy, &c.

before the Lorde of hoostes: Therfore maye
we saye / that the proude are happie / and that
they which deale with vngodlynesse / are sett
vp: for they tempte God / and yet escape.

But they that feare God / saye thus one
to another: the Lorde consydereth and heareth it. Yee it is before hym a memoryall
boke / wryten for soch as feare the Lorde / &
remembre his name. And in the daye that I
wyll make (sayeth the Lorde of hostes) they
shalbe myne awne possessyon: and I wyll fauoure them / lyke as a man fauoureth hys
awne sonne / that doth him seruyce. Turne
you therfore / and consydre what difference is
betwyrte the ryghtuous and vngodly: betwixte him that serueth God / and hym that
serueth him not.

For marck / the daye commeth that shall
burne as an oue: and all the proude / yee and
all soch as do wickednesse / shalbe straw: and
the daye that is for to come / shal burne them
vp (sayeth þ Lorde of hoostes) so that it shal
leaue them nether rote nor braunch.

Psal.rbiij.a

But vnto you that feare my nam...
þ Sonne of righteousnesse aryse / ...
shalbe vnder his wynges: ye shal go...
multiplie as the fat calues. Ye shal...
downe the vngodly: for they shalbe...
asshes vnder the soles of youre fete,
daye that I shall make / sayeth the L...
hoostes.

Remembre the lawe of Moses ...
uaunt / whych I commytted vnto ...
Oreb for all Israel / wyth the statute...
dinaunces. Beholde / I will sende you ...
the prophet: before the commynge of...
of the greate and fearfull Lorde. He...
turne the hertes of the fathers to t...
childzen / & the hertes of the chyld...
to their fathers / þ I come not ...
and smyte the earth with
cursynge.

¶ The ende of the prophecy of Mala...
and consequently of all the
Prophetes.

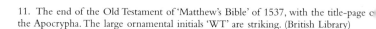

11. The end of the Old Testament of 'Matthew's Bible' of 1537, with the title-page o...
the Apocrypha. The large ornamental initials 'WT' are striking. (British Library)

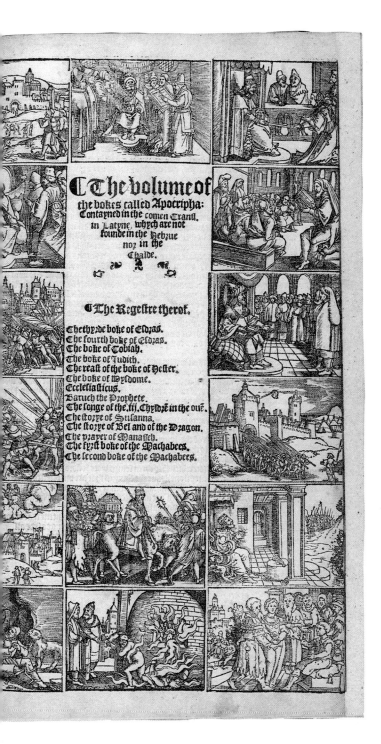

¶ The volume of

the bokes called Apocripha:
Contayned in the comen Tranfl.
in Latyne, whych are not
founde in the Hebrue
noz in the
Chalde.

¶ The Regeſtre therof.

The thyrde boke of Eldzas.
The fourth boke of Eldzas.
The boke of Tobiah.
The boke of Judith.
The reaſt of the boke of Heſter.
The boke of Wyſdome.
Eccleſiaſticus.
Baruch the Prophete.
The ſonge of the .iij. Chyldzē in the oué.
The ſtozye of Suſanna.
The ſtozye of Bel and of the Dzagon.
The pzayer of Manaſſeh.
The fyrſt boke of the Machabees.
The ſecond boke of the Machabees.

he wold caff them. And as Adā called af
ner lioynge beaftes: eos fo are their names.
Adam gape names vnto aff maner careft/
vnto the foules of the ayre/ and vnto aff m
beaftes of the felde. But there was no help
unde vnto Adam to beare him companye

Then the LORde God caft a flomber o
dam/and he flepte. And then he tofe out o
his rybbes/and in ftede ther of he fyffed v
place with flefh. And the LORdeGod ma
the rybbe which he tofe out of Adam/ a w
and brought her vnto Adam. Then fayd
this is once bone of my boones/and flefh o
flefh. This shaff be caffed woman : becauf
was tafe of the man. Fo: this caufe shaff a
leoe father and mother q cleoe vnto his w
they shaff be one flefh. And they were eth
them nafed/both Adam and hys wyfe/ ā
re not afhamed:

The. iij. Chapter

BVt the ferpent was fotyffer tha
the beaftes of the felde which ÿ L
de God had made/and fayd vnt
woman. A h fyr/ that God hath fayd/ ye
not eate of aff maner trees in the garden.
the woman fayd vnto the ferpent/of the fru
the trees in the garden we may eate/ but o
frute of the tree ÿ is in the myddes of the
den (fayd God) fe that ye eate not/ and fe
ÿç touch it not: left ye dye.

12. The story of the Fall in Genesis 3 from Tyndale's Pentateuch of 1530 (115% c
actual size). (British Library)

Then sayd the serpent vnto the woman: tush
e shall not dye: But God doth knowe/ that we
ensoever ye shulde eate of it/ youre eyes shuld
e opened and ye shulde be as/ God and kno=
we both good and evell. And the woman sa=
ye that it was a good tree to eate of and lustie
nto the eyes and a pleasant tre for to make wy=
e. And toke of the frute of it and ate/ and ga=
e vnto hir husband also with her/ and he ate.
And the eyes of both them were opened/ that
hey vnderstode how that they were naked. Th=
n they sowed fygge leves togedder and made
hem apurns.

And they herd the voyce of the LORde God
as he walked in the garden in the coole of the da=
re. And Adam hyd hymselfe and his wyfe also
rom the face of the LORde God/ amonge the
rees of the garden. And the LORde God cal=
ed Adam and sayd vnto him where art thou?
And he answered. Thy voyce Jharde in the
garden/ but J was afrayd because J was na=
ed/ and therfore hyd myselfe. And he sayd: w=
o told the that thou wast naked? hast thou ea=
en of the tree/ of which J bade the that thou
huldest not eate? And Adam answered. The
woman which thou gavest to bere me company
he toke me of the tree/ and Jate. And the LOR
de God sayd vnto the woman: wherfore didest
thou so? And the woman answered/ the ser=
pent deceaved me and Jate,

G and dureth to this daye. Whē Dauid cam to Zikeleg/he sent of his praye vnto the elders of Juda & to his frend/sayig:se there a *blessyng for you/of the spoyle of ye enemyes of ye Lord.He sent to thē of Bethel:to thē of south Ramath:to thē of Gether:to thē of Aroer: to thē of Sephamoth:to thē of Esthamo:to thē of Rachal:to thē of the cyties of ye Jerhamelites:to thē of of ye cyties of ye Kenit:to thē of Haramah:to them of Bozasan:to them of Athach: to thē of Hebrō/& to all places wher Dauid & his men were wont to haunt.

That is a rewarde,

¶ The battell be twixt ye Philistim and Israel Saul kylleth him self/& his chyldrē are slayne in ye battell.

¶ The .rrri. Chapter.

i.Para.r.a.

N Ad as ye Philistim fought agaynst Israel/ye mē of Israel fled awaye from the Philistines/& fell downe deed in mount Gelboe. And ye Philistines folowed after Saul & his sonnes & slew Jonathas / Abinadab and Melchisua Sauls sonn. And ye battell wēt sore agaynst Saul / in so moche ye shoters wt bowes had foūd him/& he was sore wounded of ye shoters. Then sayd Saul vnto his harnesberer:* drawe out thy swerde & thrust me thorow therwith lest these vncircucised come thrust me troughe & make a mocking stocke of me. But his harnesberer wolde not/ for he was sore afrayed. Wherfore Saul toke a swerde & fell vpon it. And when hys harnesberer saw that Saul was deed/ he fell lykewyse vpon hys swerde & dyed with him. And so Saul dyed & his thre sonnes & his harnesberer/& therto all his men/that same daye to geather.

Judic.ir.g. i.Para.r.a.

When the men of Isral ye were of ye other syde ye valeye/& they of the other syde Jordā/ heard ye the men of Israel were put to flight/ & that Saul & his sonn were deed/they left the cyties/& ranne awaye/& the Philistines cam & dwelt in thē.*On the morow whē the Philistines were come to strippe the ye were slayne/they founde Saul & hys thre sonnes lying in mount Gelboe. And they cut of hys heed & stripped him out of his harnesse/& sent into the lād of ye Philistines euery where/ to publisshe in the houses of their Gods & to the people.And they hanged vp his harnesse in ye house of Astharoth/but they hanged vp hys carkasse on the walles of Bethsan. When ye enhabiters of Jabes in Galaad heard therof/ what the Philistines had done to Saul/they arose as manye as were men of warre & wēt all nyght & toke the karkasse of Saul & the karkases of his sonn/frō ye walles of Bethsan & brought the to Jabes &*burnt thē there and toke their bones & buryed them vnder a Tree at Jabes/and fasted seuen dayes.

Para.ri.b

Jere.rrriij.a

¶ The ende of the fyrst boke of Samuel/ which they comēly call ye fyrst of ye Kynges.

The seconde Boke
of Samuel otherwyse called the seconde boke of the Kynges.

¶ Dauid comaundeth to slee ye messenger/that sayde he had kylled Saul. The Lamentacyon of Dauid for Saul and Jonathas.

¶ The fyrst Chapter.

A Fter the deeth of Saul/ whē Dauid was returned frō the slaughter of the Amalekites & had bene two dayes in Zikeleg: Beholde / there cam a man the thyrde daye out of the hoste frō Saul wt his clothes rent & erth vpō his heed.And whē he came to Dauid/he fell to ye erth & dyd obeysaunce. To whō Dauid sayde:whence comest thou? And ye other answered hym: Out of the host of Israel am I escaped.And Dauid sayde to hym agayne: How hath it chaunced:tell me.And he sayde: the people fleed frō the battell:& many of the people are ouerthrowen & deed: and Saul & Jonathas his sonne are deed therto.

And Dauid sayde vnto the young mā that tolde him:how knowest thou that Saul and Jonathas his sonne be deed? and the younge man that tolde him/sayde: I was by chaūce in mount Gelboe.And lo / Saul leaned vpō hys speare / and the charettes and horsemen folowed hym at the heles . And Saul loked backe and called me . And I answered:here am I.And he sayde vnto me: what art thou? and I sayde vnto hym : I am an Amalekite. And he sayde vnto me: come on me & slee me: for anguysshe is come vpō me and my lyfe is yet all in me. And I went on him & slue hym: for I was sure that he coulde not lyue/ after that he was fallen . And I toke the crowne that was vpō his heed and the Braselet that was on his arme and haue brought them vn to my Lorde hyther.

Then Dauid toke hys clothes and *rent thē/& so dyd all the men that were with him. And they mourned/wepte & fasted vntill euē for Saul and Jonathas hys sonne / and for the people of the Lorde / and for the house of Israel/ because they were ouerthrowē wyth the swerde.

a. The rēting of his clothes was a sygne & also of great anger for ye zele of the Lorde/ as in ye Mat.rrvig. And beneth ij.S.and.riij.f

Then sayde Dauid vnto the young mā ye brought him tydyng. Whēce art thou? And he sayde: I am ye sonne of an alyaūt an Amalekite.And Dauid sayde vnto him: How is it that thou wast not afrayed to laye thyne hād on ye Lordes anoynted/to destroye him? And Dauid called one of his young men & sayde: Go to and runne vpō him. And he smote hym ye he dyed. Then sayde Dauid vnto him: b thy bloude vpō thine awne heed:for thine awne mouth

b. This is the maner of speakyng of ye Hebrues

13. The opening of 2 Samuel in 'Matthew's Bible' of 1537. (British Library)

14. The Latin letter written by Tyndale from his prison cell in Vilvorde Castle in the autumn of 1535; a translation appears on p. 379. (Belgian Royal Archives)

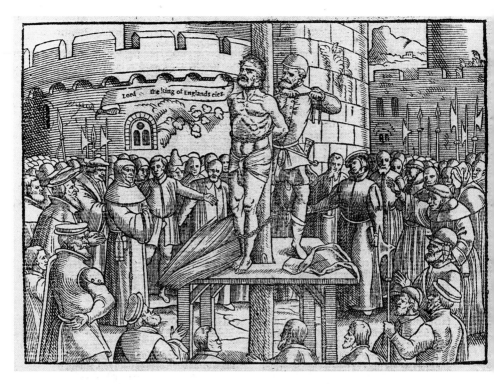

15. The execution of Tyndale, from John Foxe's *Acts and Monuments* of 1563. It is to some extent an artist's impressio and does not tally with an eye-witness account (see p. 383). In the British Library copy reproduced here, the word 'oper has been scratched out of Tyndale's dying prayer; why and by whom are not known. (British Library)

some likelihood to speak shortly again with him: and in pursuing him I might perchance have failed of my purpose, and put myself in danger.

To declare to your majesty what, in my poor judgement, I think of the man, I ascertain [assure] your grace, I have not communed with a man—[120]

At this point the manuscript breaks off.

It has been argued that Henry was exceedingly angry, to the point of tearing the paper so that there is no more. That is fanciful. As it happens, there is enough remaining to be convincing. Vaughan was impressed, and took his work seriously enough to take pains to remember what was said. The long speech of Tyndale which makes most of the first paragraph rings true in tone and content, even to making a sort of tape-recording of the occasion. Vaughan's reply to Tyndale's 'Do you not know me?' is, rather than a blunt 'No. Who are you?', a successful merchant's diplomatic 'I do not well remember you', a courteous social shorthand which authenticates what follows. A late twentieth-century reader might think the long record of his speech incredible, though it does breathe the authentic voice of Tyndale himself. Such a reader would probably have difficulty in remembering yesterday's newspaper headline, so bombarded are our waking hours with unrelated fragments of information. The arts of memory were taught in schools and perfected in universities as part of rhetoric, particularly relating to whole speeches, as in, for example, the methods of Cicero. We might recall that Hamlet, a member of the new university of Wittenberg—not even yet a graduate, as he has been forbidden to return—had no difficulty in accurately recalling from a speech heard 'once' (which implies some time ago), on only one occasion, a dozen lines of rich verse.[121]

That letter reveals a grave, greatly thoughtful, careful, consciously powerful man who is about the highest business, that of opening the King of England's eyes. We owe to Stephen Vaughan almost the only glimpse of him, and we must be grateful. Cromwell's reply, dated sometime in May, shows signs of uncharacteristic agitation. It is most unusually full of crossings-out, insertions above the line and underlinings, and shows the marks of interference. It must have been difficult reading for Vaughan in several senses. His own letter had conveyed a sense of some triumph, and he might have hoped to be congratulated. As it was, Cromwell in his long letter can be watched struggling with the words to express the King's great anger. He found the book

filled with seditious slanderous lies and fantastical opinions . . .
replete with so abominable slanders and lies imagined and only
fained to infect and intoxicate as it seemeth the people . . . the king's
highness therefore hath commanded me to advertise you that his
pleasure is that you should desist and leave any further to persuade
or attempt the said Tyndale to come into this realm . . . [he] is very
joyous to have his realm destitute of such a person . . .[122]

There is a great deal more in that vein, on Tyndale's 'damnable and
detestable heresies . . . venomous and pestiferous works . . . erroneous
and seditious opinions . . .' and so on. It is to be doubted that the King
had looked at the book for himself: the language is familiar enough
from some of his officers. The letter ends with calmer instructions
from Cromwell to Vaughan to continue reporting shipping movements.
And—though this has not survived in the original—a hundred-and-
twenty-word postscript countermanded the King's letter, telling
Vaughan to continue to try persuade Tyndale to return, as 'the king's
royal majesty is so inclined to mercy, pity, and compassion . . .',[123] a
strikingly different picture of the monarch. That postscript of
Cromwell's is copied in Vaughan's next letter of 20 May, from Bergen,
to Cromwell, where he says he has shown it to Tyndale at a second
meeting. It affected him strongly.

For after sight thereof I perceived the man to be exceedingly altered,
and moved to take the same very near unto his heart, in such wise
that water stood in his eyes, and answered, 'What gracious words are
these! I assure you,' said he, 'if it would stand with the king's most
gracious pleasure to grant only a bare text of the scripture to be out
forth among his people, like as is put forth among the subjects of
the emperor in these parts, and of other Christian princes, be it of
the translation of what person soever shall please his majesty, I shall
immediately make faithful promise never to write more, not abide
two days in these parts after the same: but immediately to repair
unto his realm, and there most humbly submit myself at the feet of
his royal majesty, offering my body to suffer what pain or torture,
yea, what death his grace will, so this be obtained. And till that time,
I will abide the asperity of all chances, whatsoever shall come, and
endure my life in as many pains as it is able to bear and suffer.[124]

The conversation was too long for Vaughan to write it all out: but
again we have enough, and in those words a portrait of Tyndale's
single-minded endeavour. Those modern writers who accuse Tyndale
of having a mean tetchiness of spirit cannot have read that letter of

Vaughan's. Not least important is his willingness for someone else's translation to be promoted, just so long as King Henry can act as the Emperor does, and let his people have the Scripture, even in a 'bare text' without explanatory notes. The rest of the letter speaks for itself.

Vaughan met Tyndale a third time, and reported to Cromwell in a letter of 19 June that he had again showed him 'what the king's royal pleasure was, but I find him always singing one note'.[125] That is, he will not promise to stop writing books, or return to England, until the King will grant a vernacular Bible. On the monarch's reception of part of his *Answer*, Vaughan adds a telling sentence: 'If the king's royal pleasure had been to have looked thereon, he should have better judged it than upon the sight of another man.' He knew well enough that Cromwell's confused letter was not giving the King's intemperate response but another man's. Vaughan returned to England for the summer, and, back in the Netherlands in November, wrote twice to Cromwell warmly on Tyndale's behalf, receiving this time no reply.[126] A new emissary was needed, and one of More's friends, Sir Thomas Elyot, was dispatched, this time not to persuade Tyndale, but if possible to apprehend him.

Martyred Scholars

Though it means looking a little ahead, this is a good place to consider the fate of one of Tyndale's close friends: and also Tyndale's lesser, later writing. Tyndale had known Bayfield, and possibly Bainham, from his London days—the circle of 'evangelicals' there was not large. Both had been burned. Their deaths, and those of others, would affect him strongly. The most hard to bear must have been the burning of the young John Frith. Foxe gives several pages to him, beginning, 'Amongst all other chances lamentable, there hath been none a long time which seemed to me more grievous, than the lamentable death and cruel handling of John Frith, so learned and excellent a young man . . .'[127] Foxe here expresses what was a widespread grief in London, in the country as well as in Europe, at the burning of so talented, modest and good a young man. A particularly gifted young Cambridge scholar, one of those brought across in 1525 by Wolsey to add lustre to his new college in Oxford, he had been with Tyndale in Antwerp, and attended the colloquy between Luther and Zwingli in Marburg in 1529 over the nature of the presence of Christ in the Lord's supper. The young Scottish reformer, Patrick Hamilton, had also been in Marburg a little before. After Hamilton's martyrdom, Frith made a translation into English from Latin of a book of his entitled *Divers Fruitful Gatherings of Scripture*, and known to most English-speaking Christians as *Patrick's Places*: it is a collection of Scripture passages on justification by faith. Hamilton, back in Scotland, had been condemned and burned on 19 February 1528. To celebrate that burning, the theological faculty at Louvain joined to send congratulations to the Bishop of St Andrews on the 'worthy deed' in cutting off 'the wicked heretic . . . Believe not that this example shall have place only among you . . . Certainly you have given us great courage'.[128] John Knox, writing his history of the Reformation in Scotland, said that it was he 'at whom our History doth begin'.[129] In July 1529 Frith published a modest octavo under the name of 'Richard Brightwell', from the Antwerp shop of Hoochstraten (another 'Hans Luft of Marburg' volume), entitled *Revelation of Antichrist*, a translation of Luther. At the end of this is joined 'a little treatise' called *Antithesis, where are compared together Christ's acts and our holy father the pope's*, seventy-eight brief records of an action or saying of Christ contrasted in each case with an action or saying of the Pope's, mostly allowed to speak from themselves: it was a form of Protestant preaching sometimes done in pictures.[130] During Lent 1531, Frith paid a short visit to England, and cannot on his return to Tyndale in Antwerp have brought much comfort about English official proceedings. The publication of his masterly *Disputation of Purgatory* in Antwerp in 1531 a little before his arrest had made him a wanted man. By that date the first declaratory publications reaching England from abroad had received confutations, and a new wave of more subtly argued responses appeared, of which Frith's *Purgatory* is one of the finest, answering Rastell, More and Fisher on the subject of purgatory, showing its lack of biblical authority. He had crossed to England again in July, and after strange adventures,[131] was caught and imprisoned in the Tower, where Cromwell ensured for him certain dignities—that is, he was permitted sometimes to go unshackled. He also wrote a great deal, and finely.[132] He received two letters from Tyndale, the first addressing him as 'Jacob' and advising him to enter the controversy over the Sacraments with care. Frith thought he was doing just that, but he died as the first English martyr for stating those very views on the Sacraments, so damnably heretical to the bishops, which were to be the heart of the Anglican doctrine expressed in the Book of Common Prayer. Tyndale's second letter to Frith was by name, shortly before his martyrdom, strengthening him.[133]

Both letters, like so many prison letters of the period, are 'comforting' in the New Testament sense of giving strength, and again characteristically are almost completely made of New Testament phrases. The first includes the paragraph;

> Finally, if there were in me any gift that could help at hand, and aid you if need required, I promise you I would not be far off, and commit the end to God. My soul is not faint, though my body be weary. But God hath made me evil-favoured in this world, and without grace in the sight of men, speechless and rude, dull and slow-witted: your part shall be to supply what lacketh in me; remembering that as lowliness of heart shall make you high with God, even so meekness of words shall make you sink into the hearts of men. Nature giveth age authority, but meekness is the glory of youth, and giveth them honour. Abundance of love maketh me exceed in babbling.[134]

The second letter ends with news—of persecution, of an attempt by George Joye to get for himself a royal commission to translate the whole Bible: 'Out of this is sprung the noise of the new Bible, and out of that is the great seeking for Englsh books at all printers and bookbinders in Antwerp, and for an English priest, that should print. This chanced the ninth of May. Sir, your wife is well content with the will of God, and would not, for her sake, have the glory of God hindered.'[135] John Frith wrote of Tyndale that 'for his learning and judgement in scripture, he were more worthy to be promoted than all the bishops in England'. He commended Tyndale for his 'faithful, clear, innocent heart'.[136] Frith's burning, on 4 July 1531, was like that of Bunyan's Faithful; and it destroyed England's most promising young scholar.

Simon Fish also died in 1531, but of the plague. He was the author of a famous—and notorious—anonymous pamphlet, *A Supplication for Beggars*, a thorough-going piece of anti-clericalism which hardly counts as a Protestant religious tract, though it was attacked by More. The 'beggars' are the outcasts. the lepers, sick, needy, who complain to the King that they are dying of hunger because a different class of holy beggars and vagabonds, bishops, abbots, priests, monks, friars, pardoners and summoners have taken over a kingdom within the kingdom, up to one-third of it, bleeding it white with tithes (the housewife must tithe every tenth egg or be taken as a heretic), probates, mortuaries, pardons and fines. They were impossible to challenge as the instant reponse was accusation of heresy, excommunication, and probably secret murder as Richard Hunne had found—that celebrated Londoner who had stood up to a priests's exaction, and was found murdered in prison. The death of Fish, though he was a different kettle from Frith, was a further loss. (His widow went on to marry Bainham's son.) England seemed a wasp's nest of desperate dispute, with the accusation of heresy stinging, sometimes to death, at any challenge to the system. Tyndale was better where he was.

Biblical Expositions

Stephen Vaughan's last letter about Tyndale, of 14 November 1531, enclosed for the King a copy of 'another book lately put out by Tyndale, being *An Exposition upon the First Epistle of John*', which was published that September. Tyndale's last three books, apart from biblical translations, were all short expository tracts from Antwerp. This on 1 John, printed in 1531, was followed by *An Exposition upon the V, VI, VII chapters of Matthew*, that is, on the Sermon on the Mount. Finally, taken to have been first printed in 1533, *A Brief Declaration of the Sacraments*, of which the first edition has not survived.

John's first Epistle had for some time been precious to the reformers. Tyndale's book is a small octavo from the press of Martin de Keyser, and it is attractive in its exposition of this simple, profound Epistle, which a child could understand and a wise man be baffled by. Tyndale works through the Epistle taking sometimes a sentence, sometimes two or three, and expounds, comments and teaches. Once again, the reader comes away at the end knowing a great deal about what is in the New Testament, and about how it meshes with, and challenges, the individual life of the believer. John was called the apostle of love, but that means righteous love, and the demand for righteousness expressed in John's last three chapters is strong. God is righteous love. In the first two chapters, God is light. The matter suits Tyndale in a lower key: there are no fireworks. A final section expounding 'Little children, beware of images' allows him some extended mockery of the worship of saints ('St White must have a cheese once in a year, and that of the greatest sort: which yet eateth no cheese'[137]): but that leads not to high-flying scorn, but an exposition of the New Testament doctrine of the Sacraments. No doubt the book was written with the same aim as *The Pathway to the Holy Scripture*, which is mentioned, to live alongside the translation of the New Testament, which had been without prologue or glosses. The *Pathway* (possibly written in 1530) is an expansion of the 1525 Cologne prologue, as a further guide to reading Scripture. Here is similar help in understanding the central New Testament theology, expressed by an Apostle more approachable, but in fact no less rigorous, than Paul in Romans. Tyndale seems to have translated the Greek afresh.

Tyndale approached the Sermon on the Mount head on, in the full understanding of all its spiritual demands (in that we might contrast Nicholas Love's *Mirror*, which at this point, after announcing that Jesus sat down and taught, explains the teaching of Augustine at reverent length, with a passage on the necessity of poverty). Tyndale's is a hard-hitting book, written at the top of his bent. It is a rather thicker octavo than the 1 John volume, and it can be dated reasonably clearly to early in 1533, because it is to some extent dependent on Luther's exposition of the same chapters of Matthew, published in the autumn of 1532. He takes large bites at the small texts, allowing himself space.

The prologue sets the tone. It begins: 'Here hast thou dear reader an exposition upon the fifth, sixth and seventh chapters of Matthew, wherein Christ our spiritual Isaac diggeth again the wells of Abraham: which wells the scribes and Pharisees, those wicked and spiteful Philstines, had stopped and filled up with the earth of their false expositons.'[138] The wells of Abraham are the Scripture, which is the kingdom of heaven, which is eternal life, 'and nothing save the knowledge of God the Father and his Son Jesus Christ.' The Law is necessary, but only that we may have salvation by Christ only, through faith. By the fifth page he has found form in leading the reader to the point where Christ (if works are sufficient, and he died in vain) is only 'somewhat more in favour than the other saints be . . . he hath also an higher place in heaven, as the Grey friars and Observants set him, as it were from the chin upward, above St Francis.'[139]

There is much in this book to cherish, not least the running New Testament quotations, intermeshed with existential living, and the directness of the voice.

> Nay, some will say, a man might preach long enough without persecution, yea and get favour too, if he would not meddle with the pope, bishops, prelates, and holy ghostly people that live in contemplation and solitariness, nor with great men of the world. I answer true preaching is salting: and all that is corrupt must be salted: and those persons are of all other most corrupt, and therefore may not be left untouched.[140]

A short and tender passage on marriage stands out:

> Let every man have his wife, and think her the fairest and best conditioned, and every woman her husband so too. For God hath blest thy wife, and made her without sin to thee, which ought to seem a beautiful fairness. And all that ye suffer together the one with the other is blessed also and made the very cross of Christ, and

pleasant in the sight of God. Why should she then be loathsome to
thee, because of a little suffering, that thou shouldest lust after
another, that should defile thy soul and slay thy conscience and
make thee suffer everlastingly?[141]

There are vivid accounts of daily life, as in a sarcastic passage about
exactions,[142] or monks, who had dispensation to make 'their strait
[narrow, strict] rules as wide as the hoods of their cowls'.[143] A snatch
of dialogue between God and a very smoothly plausible Mammon
makes the reader want more.[144] Further, if anyone pleads against
exactions for 'St Edmund's patrimony, St Alban's patrimony, St
Edward's patrimony, the goods of holy church' then 'they [monks] turn
to thorns and briars, and wax at once rougher than a hedgehog: and
will sprinkle them with holy water of their maledictions thick as hail,
and breathe out the lightning of excommunication upon them, and so
consume them to powder'.[145] (One illustration of exaction was omitted
by the Parker Society editor, 'as turning upon a subject too indelicate
for profitable contemplation'.[146]) What Tyndale presents is Christ re-
storing the true meaning of God's commandments, which naturally
draws a sharp line between works resulting from faith and everyone's
experiences of the corrupt practices of the church. Tyndale's final two
tracts were first, *A brief declaration of the sacraments*, apparently found in
manuscript in his papers, and not published in his lifetime. The earliest
known edition was printed in London about 1548. In it, he shows his
affinity with Frith, not least in regarding the Sacraments as among the
'things indifferent', which may be held or rejected without danger of
damnation, the inner faith being what makes the Sacrament of the altar
a rich experience—a view which More furiously denied, and for
which Frith died. The other tract, on a subject Frith had written on
as well (Tyndale's tract was found bound up with Frith's in Frith's own
handwriting) was on the will of a Gloucestershire gentleman, William
Tracy, which, when proved, was found to have used what was later a
common Protestant form, trusting to be saved by the merits of Christ
and not on works, saints or Masses. Tracy, though dead, was pro-
nounced a heretic, his body dug up and burned by the bishop's
chancellor: something only the King's officers could do. It was a *cause
célèbre*. Tyndale's essay was not published until after his own death.

Chapter 9

THE OBEDIENCE OF A
CHRISTIAN MAN

Five months after *The Wicked Mammon*, on 2 October 1528, again from Hoochstraten (again as 'Hans Luft of Marburg'), came Tyndale's next book, more than twice the length, *The Obedience of a Christian Man*. It crossed the sea quickly. Readers would have in their hands—famously in James Bainham's case, in his bosom[1]—a book about five and a half inches by four—like the small Book of Common Prayer, without Psalms, which used to be in church pews, with three hundred-odd pages tightly printed, like all the 'Marburg' series, in the familiar Bastard. A larger edition in small quarto, and thus about twice the page size, was printed in London in 1536, and repeated in 1548. A few more editions followed in the next decades, until in 1572 John Day in London included all Tyndale's writing that was not translation in *The Whole Works of W. Tyndall, John Frith, and Doct. Barnes, three worthy Martyrs . . .* , dated 1573, in double-column folio, with introductory matter from Foxe's *Acts and Monuments*, some tiny variants in the text, and a clamorous host of new marginal notes.

The *Obedience* has three main parts: a thirty-six page preface entitled 'William Tyndale otherwise called Hitchins to the reader', aiming to strengthen faith when both Scripture and those who read it are perscuted. A shorter eight-page section, 'The Prologue unto the Book', explains that he is setting out all obedience that is of God. The book itself is divided into sub-sections, some short like the second, 'The Obedience of Wives unto their Husbands' of a single page, and some very long, like 'The Duty of Kings, and of the Judges and Officers'. It is Tyndale's most important book outside his translations. It was very widely read, and fed into the thinking of many people in the next decades. If we had nothing from Tyndale but his *Obedience*, he would still be of high significance for the time.

Why Tyndale wrote the book is made clear by the title. The reformers were said to have caused the violence in Europe. Thomas

More blamed Luther personally for the Peasants' Wars in Germany and for atrocities at the Sack of Rome.[2] It had to be made clear that the newly-understood teaching of Scripture was that subjects must obey their kings. The reformers were not, as they had maliciously been said to be, stirring up rebellion. Thomas More wrote that Tyndale wrote against obedience to authority, the exact opposite of the truth. Kings and governors must be obeyed, said the reformers, because God has chosen 'to rule the world through them . . . Who so ever therefore resisteth them resisteth God'.

Such political theory is basically Luther's.[3] Rebellion against the magistrate is always wrong: he is ordained of God. Though the duty of the subject is to accept this, he must not carry out evil commands, but if he protests, he is to suffer punishment peacefully. Luther had emphatically asserted this view well before 1525, for example in his *Exposition of the Eighty-second Psalm*.

Tyndale's slant on this fundamental Lutheran doctrine is character-istically his own. He locates that central doctrine of obedience to rulers in the widest and most existential human context—the obedi-ence of children to parents, servants to masters, wives to husbands, even beginning his entire book with the moment of 'your' concep-tion—all of it under God (it was God who found the hour when your parents came together).

Hierarchical order was a familiar enough doctrine in the early sixteenth century, and it emerges in other works of the first three decades. Sir Thomas Elyot, for example, a contemporary of Tyndale, shared, if not his theological beliefs, many of his interests: he translated classical and patristic texts, including Isocrates' *Ad Nicolem* as *The Doctrinal of Princes* in 1534; he wrote an important manual of health (so many of Tyndale's most powerful images of God's work of salvation come from restoration of health after sickness); his Latin-English dic-tionary of 1538 was important.[4] Elyot's *The Book Named the Governor* (1531), essentially a plan for bringing up gentlemen's sons, a treatise on education and politics, says early on 'the discrepance of degrees: whereof procedeth order . . . Take away order from all things, what should then remain? . . . Hath not [God] set degrees and estates in all his glorious works?'[5] Tyndale, working with the doctrine of degree, was not doing anything new. What *was* new, and influential, was first what he interwove into that doctrine of Luther on the wrongfulness of rebellion: after civil war, the English needed a strong monarchy.[6] And secondly, the underpinning of Luther's dogma with such a mass of compelling scriptural quotations and examples.

Throughout, the texture of the writing is thick with detail; the matter is wide-ranging, and the tone is strong. One could even speak of tones, as there is something almost dramatic in the way that individual voices are allowed to speak, though the whole is created by one recognisable mind. For example, the second section, the Prologue, begins with a formally-constructed paragraph of three sentences, in the classical Greek manner 'Forasmuch as . . .', imitating in three sentences the opening of the Gospel of Luke. In contrast, when the temperature of the argument rises, the rhythms and vocabulary of spoken English break through:

> The hallowing, or rather conjuring of churches, chapels, altars, super-altars, chalice, vestments and bells. Then book, bell, candle-stick, organs, chalice, vestments, copes, altar-cloths, surplices, tow-els, basins, ewers, ship, censer, and all manner ornament, must be found them freely: they will not give a mite thereunto. Last of all, what swarms of begging friars are there. The parson sheareth, the vicar shaveth, the parish priest polleth, the friar scrapeth and the pardoner pareth. We lack but a butcher to pull off the skin.[7]

Again, in the heart of his argument about the necessity of having, and knowing, unmediated Scripture, Tyndale writes with the clarity of a good preacher or teacher: 'All the scripture is either the promises and testament of God in Christ and stories pertaining there unto, to strength thy faith, either [or] the law and stories pertaining thereto to fear [frighten] thee from evil doing.'[8] There are other 'speakers', all strong-voiced.

It is obvious that in this book Tyndale attacked the Pope. Yet the impression sometimes given, particularly by modern writers on the period, that Tyndale wrote nothing but anti-papal poison and simply the very notion of a pope drove him to a foaming rage, is not so. (It was More, not Tyndale, who lost control.) Tyndale does not find a pope in the Bible. He does not find everything that stems from the Pope in the Bible. The Bible has to come first. The Pope is a mistake. That is why his analysis of obedience in many places in life is prefaced by the long address to the reader not only defending Scripture in English, but pleading passionately, as with a kind of divine and out-raged disbelief, against those from the Pope down who cannot see that Scripture is the very fountainhead of Christianity, and that that foun-tainhead of Christianity must be available, entire, to everyone, or else Christ died in vain.

The stylistic and rhetorical variety which is characteristic of Tyndale writing at any length is in the *Obedience* permeated by another device. For example, in the early pages he shows that Scripture itself demon-

strates both the inevitability of persecution and the power of God over
the hypocrites who attack God's Word. In his orderly argument, he
builds his sentences, paragraphs and pages out of the bricks of Scripture. Every phrase comes from a mind steeped in both Testaments. His
very first sentence recalls the familiar opening of most of the New
Testament Epistles: 'Grace, peace, and increase of knowledge, in our
Lord Jesus Christ, be with the reader . . .' The next sentence but one
begins 'But much rather be bold in the Lord . . .', echoing Paul in 1
Thessalonians 2 or Philemon, and continues with an 'evident token', as
in 2 Thessalonians 1 and Philippians 1. The reiterated 'of the world'
reflects the familiar phrase throughout John's Gospel and first Epistle.
By the end of the first main paragraph, to sum up his point that the
world is bound to persecute, the scriptural thought has risen in full
Biblical clothes, as it were, and he is quoting John 15: 'If ye were of the
world, the world would love his own. But I have chosen you out of
the world and therefore the world hateth you.'

Scripture in the Obedience

The steady beat of Scripture sounds throughout Tyndale's book. Scripture phrases and echoes are everywhere, and there is hardly a page
without two or three quotations at least. Even in all the stylistic
variety—the sudden moments of awe or beauty, the quick strokes from
common life, the sarcasms, the demonstrations of confusion, the an-
gers, the steady accumulations of rhythmic phrases until the sentence
bursts—even in all these, Scripture is never far away. Indeed, one can
say that God is never far away. The *Obedience* is full of God, as is most
of the work of Tyndale.

Over the next pages Tyndale demonstrates 'the mighty power of
God [which] defendeth the doctrine of God' in a rising rhetoric in
which the scriptural words and phrases, the references to scriptural
stories (the Exodus, the persecution of David) gradually give way to
direct quotation, as if Scripture itself took over the argument. This is
mixed with the ordinary currency of common speech: 'Finally when
they had done all they could, and that they thought sufficient, and
when Christ was in the heart of the earth and so many bills and
poleaxes about him, to keep him down and when it was past man's
help: then holp God.'[9] or 'Who dried up the Red Sea? Who slew
Goliath? Who did all those wonderful deeds which thou readest in the
Bible?'[10] He invites the reader to 'Read the Hebrews the eleventh chap,
for thy consolation', reaching out of the text and making him or her
take up the New Testament. Then, on the reading which which he can

assume has been done, he constructs comment to further strengthen his own argument. For, he says, using Matthew 7, 'If we ask we shall obtain, if we knock he will open, if we seek we shall find . . .' So he makes his own words interactive, as we might put it today, both with Scripture and with the reader's immediate experience of it.

It is thus striking when he uses a voice that is not biblical. Explaining the value of the persecution of the young David in making him a virtuous king, he exclaims 'O that our kings were so nurtured nowadays',

> which our holy bishops teach of a far other manner, saying, your grace shall take your pleasure: ye take what pleasure ye lust, spare nothing. We shall dispense with you: we have power, we are god's vicars. And let us alone with the realm. We shall take pain for you, and see that nothing be well, your grace shall but defend the faith only.[11]

That is appropriately not scriptural language: the point is made with rhetorical neatness, sarcasm and all.

The Structure of the First Part of the Obedience

Tyndale has often been accused of rambling, indeed of writing a sort of formless rhapsody not far from rabbiting on. The 'Forasmuch's, 'Moreover's, 'Finally's', and the regular numbered points, 'First . . . Secondly . . . Thirdly . . .' may, however, suggest more order than he has been credited with. Tyndale would be unusual as an Oxford man trained in late-medieval ways of thought if he were not writing to a scheme. A systematic account of his argument can be found without difficulty. The first part of the Obedience may serve as an example. It divides into three sections:

A. Scripture itself shows that the word of God necessitates persecution.

B. God has the greater power, however, as Scripture demonstrates throughout.

C. It is essential that Scripture be freely available to everyone: they are false who argue against it being in the mother tongue.

Further, to use the last section as a model: that again falls into three sections, here numbered I, II and III, each containing opposed pairs, numbered here 1 and 2, and 3 and 4.

C.I.   1. The children of Israel even in their darkness had the law, the Old Testament, in the mother tongue: how is it that we, who walk in the day, are not allowed to see as well?

2. Moses commanded the children of Israel to give constant attention to Scripture. How can that be any less for us as Christians?

But

3. Laymen are said to be too busy in the world to warrant having Scripture: yet the bishops are busiest in the world.

4. It is feared that laymen would take Scripture too variously: yet the clergy do not teach at all.

★   ★   ★

C.II.   1. Christ and Paul deferred to Scripture. How can we similarly test what someone alleges of them without it?

2. Christ warned of false prophets. Again the only test (in this vital matter) is Scripture.

But

3. We pay clergy to teach God's word; they do not do so.

4. In any case, English is said to be too rude for Scripture: it is not. Hebrew, indeed, goes better into English than into Latin.

★   ★   ★

C.III.   1. What is now preached is theologically wildly various, following fifteen, or indeed numberless, conflicting doctors. How can we judge all those without Scripture?

2. Yet Scripture is said to be so hard that it cannot be understood without the doctors; and particularly Aristotle, who in fact contradicts Scripture.

But

3. What should be taught is the true Scripture, which makes such philosophy harmless: yet confusion is taught.

4. Secular fables which corrupt are permitted.

There is much richness in these pages. Having to understand Scripture by the doctors is, says Tyndale, to measure the meteyard [ruler or tape-measure] by the cloth, a folly even harder when there are many cloths. The section just labelled C.II.4 is a famous plea for Scripture in English. The passage must be quoted in full.

> The sermons which thou readest in the Acts of the apostles, and all that the apostles preached, were no doubt preached in the mother tongue. Why then might they not be written in the mother tongue? As if one of us preach a good sermon why may it not be written? Saint Jerome also translated the bible into his mother tongue. Why may not we also? They will say it cannot be translated into our tongue it is so rude. It is not so rude as they are false liars. For the Greek tongue agreeth more with the English than with the Latin. And the properties of the Hebrew tongue agreeth a thousand times more with the English than with the Latin. The manner of speaking is both one, so that in a thousand places thou needest not but to translate it into the English word for word, when thou must seek a compass in the Latin, and yet shall have much work to translate it well favouredly, so that it have the same grace and sweetness, sense and pure understanding with it in the Latin, and as it hath in the Hebrew. A thousand parts better may it be translated into the English, than into the Latin. Yea and except my memory fail me, and that I have forgotten what I read when I was a child, thou shalt find in the English chronicle how that king Adelstone caused scripture to be translated into the tongue that then was in England, and how the prelates exhorted him thereto.[12]

The sections here labelled C.III.3 and 4 make a fine contrast, and as they give a taste of Tyndale writing movingly and with dignity about what Scripture teaches, and then changing gear, they should be quoted in full. The assurance suggested by the first long-paced sentences contrasts with the later nervy desperation matching current metaphysical controversies.

> By this means then, thou wilt that no man teach another, but that every man take the scripture and learn by himself. Nay, verily, so say I not. Nevertheless seeing that ye will not teach, if any man search for the truth: and read the scripture by himself desiring God to open the door of knowledge to him, God for his truth's sake will and must teach him. Howbeit my meaning is that as a master teacheth his apprentice to know all the points of the meteyard, first how many inches, how many feet, and the half-yard, the quarter and the nail, and then teacheth him to mete other things thereby: even so will I that ye teach the people God's law, and what obedience God requireth of us to father and mother, master, lord, king, and all

superiors, and with what friendly love he commandeth one to love another. And teach them to know that natural venom and birth-poison, which moveth the very hearts of us to rebel against the ordinances and will of God, and prove that no man is righteous in the sight of God, but that we are all damned by the law. And then (when thou hast meeked them and feared them with the law) teach them the testament and promises which God hath made to us in Christ, and how much he loveth us in Christ. And teach them the principles and the ground of the faith, and what the sacraments signify, and then shall the Spirit work with thy preaching, and make them feel. So would it come to pass, that as we know by natural wit what followeth of a true principle of natural reason: even so by the principles of the faith and by the plain scriptures and by the circumstances of the text, should we judge all men's exposition and all men's doctrine, and should receive the best and refuse the worst. I would have you teach them also the properties and manner of speakings of the scripture, and how to expound proverbs and simili-tudes. And then if they go abroad and walk by the fields and meadows of all manner doctors and philosophers, they could catch no harm. They should discern the poison from the honey, and bring home nothing but that which is wholesome.

But now do ye clean contrary. Ye drive them from God's word and will let no man come thereto, until ye have been two years masters of art. First they nosel [nurture] them in sophistry and in benefundatum [something grounded on sure premises]. And there corrupt they their judgements with apparent arguments, and with alleging unto them texts of logic, of natural philautia [self-love], of metaphysic, and moral philosophy, and of all manner books of Aristotle, and of all manner doctors which they never yet saw. Moreover, one holdeth this, another that. One is a real, another a nominal. What wonderful dreams they have of their predicaments, universals, second intentions, quiddities, hecceities and relatives. And whether species fundata in chimera be vera species. And whether this proposition be true non ens est aliquid. Whether ens be equivocum or univocum. Ens is a voice only say some. Ens is univocum saith another and descendeth into ens creatum and into ens increatum per modos intrinsecos. When they have thiswise brawled eight or twelve or more years and after that their judge-ments are utterly corrupt: then they begin their Divinity.

Not at the scripture: but every man taketh a sundry doctor, which doctors are as sundry and as divers, the one contrary unto the other, as there are divers fashions and monstrous shapes, none like another, among our sects of religion. Every religion, every university and almost every man hath a sundry divinity. Now whatseover opinions every man findeth with his doctor, that is his gospel, and that only is true with him, and that holdeth he all his life long, and every man to maintain his doctor withal, corrupteth the scripture and fashioneth it after his own imagination, as a potter doth his clay. Of what text thou provest hell, will another prove purgatory, another limbo patrum, and another the ascension of our lady: and another shall prove of the same text that an ape hath a tail. And of what text the gray friar proveth that our lady was without original sin, of the same shall the black friar prove that she was conceived in original sin. And all this do they with apparent reasons . . .[13]

An eight-page prologue explains that Scripture does not teach disobedience and insurrection. The wickedness of rebellion arises against Christ's express command, as the Gospels show. We have been taught 'even of very babes, to kill a Turk, to slay a Jew, to burn a heretic, to fight for the liberties and right of the church, as they call it . . .' and to believe that if we are slain obeying the pope 'our souls go, nay fly to heaven, and be there ere our blood be cold . . .' So is it any wonder that we think we should fight for 'the true word of God'? Tyndale concludes this prologue with instruction to check what he says against Scripture at every point, and a prayer that the Spirit of God will enable his readers to 'judge what is righteous in his eyes'—the last ten lines are made of New Testament phrases.

The Treatise Proper

Like the author of the Epistle to the Hebrews, Tyndale starts his treatise with 'God . . .' but instead of that Epistle's great historical sweep he begins at the other end of the scale.

The Obedience of all Degrees proved by God's Word and first of Children unto their Elders

God (which worketh all in all things) for a secret judgement and purpose, and for his godly pleasure, provided an hour that thy father and mother should come together, to make thee through them. He was present with thee in thy mother's womb and fashioned thee and breathed life into thee and for the great love he had unto thee, provided milk in thy mother's breasts for thee against thou were born: moved also thy father and mother and all other to love thee to pity thee and to care for thee.

It is a tender beginning. The mountain-ranges of New Testament doctrine that follow in the next 270 pages, the wall-breaking arguments against the corrupt Church, the massivity of the scriptural principles, only come after God 'for a secret judgement and for his godly pleasure' is seen providing for the creation of 'thee' in the womb, and for thy nurture as a child. Tender, and surprising. It is a long way from what he has just been discussing, the plagues of God's vengeance on the hypocrites and erring people, or the idiocies of metaphysical dispute that stand in the way of all laymen having God's word. Yet it neatly places everything that follows in a truly existential frame.

The *Obedience* proper, Tyndale's 'little treatise', has three large sections. The first explains God's law of obedience, from whom no-one is exempt. The second sets out how to rule as father, husband, master, landlord, king or judge. The third discusses signs: true like those Sacraments that are scriptural, or false like the worship of saints; under this heading of the traditional four senses of Scripture—only the first, the literal, can be a true sign. All three sections have balanced sub-sections, themselves several times sub-divided, so that it is possible to draw up a grid showing in detail the process of the thought (see Appendix B).

God's Law of Obedience

God's law of obedience applies to children, wives and servants (though the followers of the pope are able to side-step that law) and, above all, to kings, governors and rulers, who enact God's justice, and themselves give account to God only: no-one is exempt, and certainly not monks, friars, the pope and bishops. The king, even if a tyrant, is minister of God for our welfare. As God's law is only properly kept by spiritual man, so the basis of all obedience to the Law is inward (this section is not surprisingly crammed with reference to Paul). Obedience of the temporal power, the New Testament teaches, is modelled on Christ, Peter and Paul. All things, good or bad, we are to receive from God, including evil rulers. We are not to avenge.

The section, subheaded 'Against the Pope's False Power', begins with a quotation from Matthew 26, Christ's words to Peter, 'Put up thy sword . . .' It is Tyndale's climax to this, main, part of his book, and in spite of what sizzling verbal fireworks the subheading might suggest, it is more than anything a meditation on the implications of many parts of Scripture, quoted or inferred. It is not an artillery barrage. It is an exposition over a dozen pages, schematically worked out, of the

New Testament insistence on the spiritual basis of obedience, incidentally denying the value of resisting rulers.

How to Rule

His next section, the second part of the *Obedience* proper, is set out exactly like the opening of the whole volume. There is no mistaking the sense of fresh beginning. It is announced in a bridge-passage at the end of the previous section as a declaration of 'how the rulers, which God shall vouchsafe to call unto the knowledge of the truth, ought to rule'. Again, he approaches this briefly through the offices of father, husband, master and landlord, for 'God excludeth no degree from his mercy' as he had also noted at the transition to the new part. Then coming quickly to 'The Duty of Kings and of Judges and Officers', he outlines systematically what it means that 'the people are God's, and not theirs'. As he usually does, Tyndale alternates between exposition of what ought to be, from a close and proper reading of Scripture, and what is, waxing eloquent that the only men found able to govern a worldly kingdom should be bishops and prelates 'that have forsaken the world, and are taken out of the world, and appointed to preach the kingdom of God'. High office in the Church should necessitate the preaching of God's word as a full-time occupation.' 'To preach God's word is too much for half a man. And to minister a temporal kingdom is too much for half a man also. Either other requireth an whole man. One therefore cannot well do both. He that avengeth himself on every trifle is not meet to preach the patience of Christ . . .' Bishops and Pope should not 'expound the scriptures carnally and worldly, saying: God spake this to Peter and I am his successor, therefore this authority is mine only', claiming greater power.[14]

Against Fisher

To illustrate such 'philosophy' and 'abuse of the scriptures' in action, with the mocking of God's word, Tyndale has a twenty-three page section attacking the sermon against Martin Luther preached by John Fisher, Bishop of Rochester, on the occasion of the public burning of Luther's books on 11 February 1526 at St Paul's. (The sermon had been printed by T. Berthelet in 1528.) Tyndale makes seven main points, every one of them showing Fisher's erroneous grasp of the Scriptures, and every one showing that Christ, and no other, should be the authority. First, Moses and Aaron cannot, as Tyndale easily shows from the New Testament, 'by a shadow' signify Christ and the Pope, as Fisher said. Second, the Apostles preached Christ, not Peter. In 1 Corinthians 3 when Paul wrote 'all are yours, and ye are Christ's, and Christ is God's', he left out 'Ye are Peter's, or ye are the pope's'. Third, the Apostles were sent on the authority of Christ to preach the Gospel, not what they would imagine, but what he had commanded. 'He said not, I go my way, and lo, here is Peter in my stead . . .' The bishops, as they do not hear Christ's voice, nor see him present, make their own god—'As Aaron made a calf; so the pope maketh bulls'. Fourth, why is Christ's seat, Jerusalem, not as great as Peter's (Rome)? The false apostles ('the shaven nation') have pushed out Christ, and even the emperor and kings, and preach themselves. 'Thus reign they, in the stead of God and man, and have all power under them, and do what they list.' Fifth, Fisher seriously misreads not only Luther's reference to Paul and the Gospel, but Paul more generally. Fisher 'playeth bo-peep with the scripture'. What Fisher is doing is part of the taking away of the authority of Paul, making him subservient to the power of Peter. 'Thereto, *Pasce, pasce, pasce,* which Rochester leaveth without any English, signifieth not poll, sheer and shave'.[15] Sixth, Fisher has claimed Paul's authority for the Church's 'wicked traditions and false ceremonies' which come from outside, using Origen as support: Tyndale remarks that as external authorities Aristotle, Plato and 'even very Robin Hood' are as good. Fisher's false assertion that Martin Luther has killed Christian men, on the grounds that Luther burning the Pope's decretals is a sign that he would burn the Pope, plays straight into Tyndale's hands. 'A like argument (which I suppose to be rather true) I make. Rochester and his holy brethren have burned Christ's testament [Tyndale's own 1526 New Testament]: an evident sign verily that they would have burnt Christ himself also if they had had him.'[16] Finally, Fisher, 'stark mad of pure malice, and so adased in the brains of spite', has turned the Gospel upside-down 'intending to prove that we are justified through holy works, allegeth half a text of Paul of the fifth to the Galatians . . .' Not only is Fisher's Latin at fault—he 'maketh a verb passive of a verb deponent'—but his New Testament theology is plain wrong, as, in a passionate four concluding pages of quotation from Paul and John, and comment, Tyndale makes clear. Faith alone is the root.[17]

The seven points against Fisher add up to one total: the Scriptures show that first must be Christ and faith in him; the institutional Church denies these truths and puts first its own power. To demonstrate not only the error of the Church, but its malice (not only in silencing those who preach God's word, but in actively distorting it),

Tyndale has been comprehensive; he moved from the Old Testament (Moses and Aaron), to the work and theology of Christ, and then the Apostles, and to current Church practices.

It is a grand refutation. Under it Fisher looks not just wrong, but small. It fitted into Tyndale's own larger scheme because at that point he needed a solid illustration of bishops and prelates not only not preaching the word of God, but actively distorting it. He now returns to the point about distortion ('juggling') and develops it to mock the follies in the dense web of church practice. ('What reverence give we unto holy water, holy fire, holy bread, holy salt, hallowed bells, holy wax, holy boughs, holy candles, and holy ashes . . . I say that a steadfast faith . . . bringeth the Holy Ghost . . .') To make the Devil fly, we cast holy water or ring the bells. (Tyndale's margin asks 'why do not the bishops make him flee from shooting of guns.'[18]) The cause of all the practices that he details, as he now comes to show at length, is that the Church is governed by Antichrist. The constant theme in this second main part of the *Obedience* is that kings everywhere should defend their realms against such oppression: there is special reference to questions of faith being judged 'by the manifest and open scriptures, not excluding the lay men'. Many laymen are as wise as the officers, who do not teach at all. 'Is it not a shame that we Christians come so oft to church in vain, when he of four score years old knoweth no more than he that was born yesterday.'[19]

'Though this be madness, yet there's method in't' as Polonius remarked of someone as coolly sane who had similarly a great deal on his mind. As the analysis in Appendix B shows, the process of thought has not by any means been swamped by the power of the emotion. As with Hamlet, it is the ordering of thought and feeling together which produces the power. The following passage comes in a section about the deposition of kings by the church hypocrites; indeed, kings could not be lower, being robbed of 'land, authority, honour and due obedience' by those who make 'narrow consciences at trifles, and at matters of weight none at all'.

Ye blind guides saith Christ ye strain out a gnat and swallow a camel. Matt. xxiii. Do not our blind guides also stumble at a straw and leap over a block making narrow consciences at trifles and at matters of weight none at all? If any of them happen to swallow his spittle, or any of the water wherewith he washeth his mouth ere he go to mass or touch the sacrament with his nose, or of the ass forget to breathe on him, or happen to handle it with any if his fingers which are not anointed, or say Aleluia instead of Laus tibi, domine,

or Ite missa est instead of Benedicamus domino, or pour too much
wine in the chalice, or read the gospel without light, or make not
his crosses aright, how trembleth he? How feareth he? What an
horrible sin is committed? I cry God mercy, saith he and you my
ghostly father. But to hold an whore or another man's wife, to buy
a benefice, to set one realm at variance with another and to cause
twenty thousand men to die on a day is but a trifle and a pastime
with them.[20]

All through this section subheaded 'Antichrist' direct appeal to God's
word is never far away. It is vital that everyone from kings downwards
can call on open Scripture.

Let God's word try every man's doctrine and whomsoever God's
word proveth unclean let him be taken for a leper. One scripture
will help to declare another. And the circumstances, that is to say,
the places that go before and after, will give light unto the middle
text. And the open and manifest scriptures will ever improve the
false and wrong exposition of the darker sentences.[21]

Signs

He now moves into the third main part of his book. He returns not
only to take up the argument of the 'Antichrist' section, but to his
earlier discussion of the organisation of the Church, which can now be
seen as made of false signs—such as that prelates are clothed in red, he
notes sarcastically, because they are 'ready every hour to suffer martyrdom for the testimony of God's word'. Other appurtenances, 'all the
whole pomp of their disguising', are equally false.[22]

First must come discussion of 'the signs which God hath ordained;
that is to say, of the sacraments which Christ left among us for our
comfort . . .' He rightly places 'The sacrament of the body and blood
of Christ' first, and has only to say of it, after quoting Christ's words
'This is my body. . . This is my blood . . . This do in remembrance of
me . . .' that the promise and belief in it is everything. There follow
comments on baptism, wedlock, order (that is, offices), penance, confession, contrition, satisfaction, and absolution, binding and loosing,
confirmation, anoiling (that is, extreme unction) and ceremonies in
general. Only the first and second survive Tyndale's analysis as true
New Testament sacraments. Some, like wedlock, or orders, are ordained of God and of high value (if arranged according to the New
Testament) but cannot be named sacraments because they do not
contain the spiritual promises of God in Christ.

As might be expected, Tyndale's usual tick-tock of Scripture versus current practice is everywhere. His disagreement with Church tradition under the six subheadings begun by penance follows his opening explanation, 'Penance is a word of their own forging to deceive us withal, as many other are'. The Scripture words mean repentance, a changing of mind. He expounds the spiritual, New Testament, meaning of repentance and confession, the latter having nothing to do with 'shrift in the ear'. 'Shrift in the ear is verily a work of satan, and that the falsest that ever was wrought, and that most hath devoured the faith.' A form of it was abandoned by the early Greek church because of 'a little knavery'. Tyndale is careful to spell out over some pages the New Testament authority: '. . . if any man have sinned, yet if he repent and believe the promise, we are sure by God's word that he is loosed and forgiven in Christ. Other authority than this wise to preach, have the priests not.'[23] Only then does he attack the Pope's claim to absolve 'a poena et a culpa', appointing seven years in purgatory for every deadly sin, and then selling relief of that for money. The friars do the same: 'thus is sin become the profitablest merchandise in the world'.

All the promises of God have they either wiped clean out or thus leavened with open lies to stablish their confession withal. And, to keep us from knowledge of the truth, they do all thing in latin.
    They pray in latin, they christen in latin, they bless in latin, they give absolution in latin, only curse they in the English tongue.[24]

Confirmation, again containing no spiritual promise from God in Christ and so again not a sacrament, gives similar power, at parish level, and at Court. 'Last of all cometh the anoiling without promise, and therefore without the spirit and without profit, but altogether unfruitful and superstitious'. Here follow a dozen pages under the running head 'cerem. [ceremonies] in general'. What shows up the follies of local practice is the New Testament teaching that as the margin puts it 'the work saveth not, but the word; that is to say the promise'.

Baptism is called volowing in many places of England, because the priest saith volo say ye. The child was well volowed (say they) yea and our vicar is as fair a volower as ever a priest within this twenty miles. Behold how narrowly the people look on the ceremony. If aught be left out or if the child be not altogether dipt in the water, or if, because the child is sick the priest dare not plunge him into the water, but pour water on his head how tremble they? how quake they? how say ye sir John, say they, is this child christened enough?

Hath it his full christendom? They believe verily that the child is not christened: yea I have known priests that have gone unto the orders again supposing that they were not priests, because that the bishop left one of his ceremonies undone. That they call confirmation, the people call bishoping. They think that if the bishop butter the child in the forehead that it is safe. They think that the work maketh safe, and like wise suppose they of anoiling . . .[25]

Summing up: 'Dumb ceremonies are no sacraments, but superstitiousness . . . Christ's signs speak, and antichrist's be dumb.' Twelve pages follow, 'Of prayer and good deeds, and of the order of love', as he has 'abundantly written in my book of the justifying of faith', that is, *The Parable of the Wicked Mammon*. Here, to clarify 'what the prayers and good works of our monks and friars and of other ghostly people are worth' he will 'speak a word or two'. He expounds, over some pages of close New Testament quotation, how in Christ we are one as good as another, and in all criteria equal, and love is for Christ's sake, 'And to all can nought be added'. For the monks and friars and the rest, however, love is the result of giving money—cupboard-love, or as Tyndale has it 'belly-love'.

'The Four Senses of Scripture'

The *Obedience* closes with a twenty-one page summary of the whole book. But before that comes the longest section of this third part and of the whole volume, an extended essay on 'The Four Senses of the Scripture'. It is not difficult to see why this is here. Before Tyndale finishes, he has to cover himself, as it were, from possible attacks on his own headquarters. His whole book has been about the calamitous errors of the current practices and almost all the beliefs of the Church, in the light of Christ and his promises as set out in the New Testament. These are either abandoned or distorted by the Church. If his reading of the New Testament could be shown to be in error, not in some details so much as in the whole method, then his claim to speak of Christ and his promises is quite invalid. It is characteristic of him to direct his book to a mounting close, and as befits the skills of a great translator, these pages about Bible language and interpretation are the most vividly written in the book.

The system of interpreting every word of the Latin Bible in four different ways went back to the methods of the fathers, and in particular to Origen, over a thousand years before Tyndale, and had been standard ever since; scholars in Tyndale's Oxford were in touch

with some important challenges to the system.[26] Allegorical interpretation is not by any means unknown in both Old and New Testaments,
all the way from some simple sayings of Christ ('I am the vine') to the
dark conceits of the apocalypses found in Daniel, in Mark 13, and
throughout Revelation. The dangers of the Church's method, however, were twofold. It can become a licence to what is little more than
wilder forms of free association, whereby words can mean anything,
according to whim; and it automatically suggests something that suited
the Church very well at the time—that all Scripture is difficult to
interpret, and only the very learned can handle it. (Recollection of
Christ's parables, of the Kingdom for example, or of the Prodigal Son,
refutes that statement at once.)

> Thou shalt understand, therefore, that the scripture hath but one
> sense which is the literal sense. And that literal sense is the root and
> ground of all, and the anchor that never faileth, whereunto if thou
> cleave thou canst never err or go out of the way. And if thou leave
> the literal sense: thou canst not but go out of the way. Never the
> later the scripture useth proverbs, similitude, riddles or allegories as
> all other speeches do, but that which the proverb, similitude, riddle
> or allegory signifieth is ever the literal sense, which thou must
> seek out diligently. As in the English we borrow words and sen-
> tences of one thing and apply them to another and give them new
> significations.[27]

Such use of metaphor he illustrates from common speech, 'Look ere
thou leap', 'Cut not the bough that thou standest upon . . .' Such
common examples soon become barbed. 'When a thing speedeth not
well, we borrow speech and say, the Bishop hath blessed it . . . And of
him that is betrayed and wotteth not how, we say, he hath been at
shrift . . .' (Even more is conveyed by 'she is master parson's sister's
daughter, he is the bishop's sister's son, he hath a cardinal to his
uncle . . .') Scripture uses metaphor, as in 'Christ is a lamb'; but proper
interpretation is not wild, but applies the matter to the basis of Christ
and the faith. The literal sense should bear the allegory as the foundation bears the house. Allegories by themselves prove nothing.

Tyndale illustrates how it should properly be done by interpreting
the incident where Peter cut off Malchus's ear (John 18), and showing
Paul using the same method with the story of Hagar from Genesis. He
continues, in a famous passage:

> And likewise do we borrow likenesses or allegories of the scripture,
> as of Pharaoh and Herod, and of the scribes and Pharisees, to

express our miserable captivity and persecution under antichrist the pope. The greatest cause of which captivity and the decay of the faith and this blindness wherein we now are, sprang first of allegories. For Origen and they of his time drew all the scripture unto allegories. Whose ensample they that came after followed so long, till at the last they forgot the order, and process of the text, supposing that the scripture served but to feign allegories upon. Insomuch that twenty doctors expound one text twenty ways, as children make descant upon plain song. Then came our sophisters with their Anagogical and chopological sense, and with an anti-theme of half an inch, out of which some of them draw a thread of nine days long. Yea thou shalt find enough that will preach Christ, and prove what some ever point of the faith that thou wilt, as well out of a fable of Ovid or any other Poet, as out of St John's gospel or Paul's epistles. Yea they are come into such blindness that they not only say that the literal sense profiteth not, but also that it is hurtful, and noisome and killeth the soul. Which damnable doctrine they prove by a text of Paul, 2 Cor iii where he saith the letter killeth but the spirit giveth life. We must therefore, say they seek out some chopological sense.[28]

('Chopological' is a word of Tyndale's coinage, for ironic effect.)

There follows a precise and Bible-rich explanation of what Paul meant (at root, that 'the letter' means the law) and how Bible stories of many kinds respond to that understanding. The most serious example of false expounding of Scripture is the use of Christ's words to Peter in Matthew 16, 'Thou art Peter, and upon this rock I will build my congregation'. By this and other texts the pope makes himself quite falsely appointed by Christ, empowered to bind and loose, and authorised to fight. Embedded in this exposition is another key principle of the reformers: that the Bible interprets itself; that is to say, that any text has to be judged by the rest of the Bible (which is one of several reasons why More's notion of dealing out little bits to the lay people would not do). 'Now the Scripture giveth record to himself, and ever expoundeth itself by another open text. If the pope then cannot bring for his exposition the practising of Christ or of the apostles and prophets or an open text, then is his exposition false doctrine.'[29] Appeal to 'Fathers, fathers' (the ancient interpreters of Christian doctrine) will not do, as they quarrelled, once they had put God's word to sleep; 'and one pope condemned another's decrees, and were sometime two, yea, three popes at once'.[30] Crying 'miracles, miracles' as support for the false interpretation of Scripture by the

Church will not do either, 'for God hath made an everlasting testament
with us in Christ's blood, against which we may receive no miracles'.
So miracles are either feigned, or if they confirm doctrine contrary
to God's word, they are done of the Devil. This section, and properly
the book, concludes with admonitions as to what New Testament
passages to study when the Pope asserts this or that authority—
above King or Emperor, over 'all the congregation of Christ', as
unrebukeable, against preaching, to burn 'heretics'. Armed always with
God's word 'remember that Christ is the end of all things. He only is
our resting place and he is our peace. Ephesians second chapter.'

Summary

The last twenty pages of the volume are 'A Compendious Rehearsal of
that which goeth before', a summary of the book. He begins, 'I have
described unto you the obedience of children, servants, wives, and
subjects . . .' and continues firmly through all his points, although,
being Tyndale, he cannot make this dull. It is in the nature of a coda
to include fresh material, and here it comes generally in new illustrations. His tendency in these last pages is to gather the material towards 'how they which God made governors in the world ought to
rule if they be christian'. One of the longest new illustrations explains
how

> The king ought to count what he hath spent in the pope's quarrel
> since he was king . . . I doubt not but that will surmount the sum of
> forty or fifty hundred thousand pounds. The king therefore ought to
> make them pay this money every farthing, and fetch it out of their
> mitres, crosses, shrines and all manner treasure of the church, and
> pay it to his commons again . . .[31]

The chronicles will teach the King 'what the popes have done to kings
in time past . . .' If the King will not make them restore their wealth
to the commons for the welfare of the poor, for education and for
defence, then the commons must 'think that God hath blinded the
King for their sins' sake and commit their cause to God' who will
'make a scourge for them'. The tone steadily rises over these last pages
as the evils of the spiritualty, bishops and pope are exposed. The focus
is still on kings being deceived by them, even at the highest level of
international politics: but Tyndale can swoop to everyday reality: 'If a
poor man die and leave his wife and half a dozen young children and
but one cow to find them, that will they have for a mortuary merciless:
let come of wife and children what will.'[32] His very last pages are a

return to straight summarising. There follows 'The table of the book', that is, an index running to fourteen pages.

The Obedience *and the Monarchy*

Henry VIII is said to have praised Tyndale's *Obedience* with the words 'This is a book for me and all kings to read'. Before we look at the romantic story of how he came to have a copy in his hand, and consider the likelihood of that startling remark, we should consider what he might be thought to have meant.

A cursory reading of the *Obedience* has suggested to historians that Tyndale's Lutheran doctrine of non-resistance to princes was offering the monarch absolute, unlimited power. The evidence appears to be in Tyndale's remark, 'Hereby seest thou that the king is in this world without law and may at his lust do right or wrong and shall give accompts, but to God only'. Subjects are wrong to think of rebellious disobedience. Tyndale in all such passages, however, also zooms in on the condition of the king himself before his God (accompts, but to God only). The ruler is under the religious and moral duty to act in accordance with God's law.[33] He has a heavy and particular burden (a heaviness known well to Shakespeare's kings, from Richard II to Henry V and his father: it belongs to kings alone. It is the amoral aspiring usurper like Richard III who is blithe). Tyndale did not offer Henry VIII or anyone else a sovereignty not subject to natural law.[34] The difficulty, of course, is that the monarch won't act according to the Law of God and nothing can be done about it—a difficulty inherent in the whole doctrine of non-resistance. But what later became a Reformation standard to fight under, the principle of the godly prince, one law for a nation, and so on[35] is here adumbrated in Tyndale. And his recognition of the King's own condition alone with his God, as it were, did allow Tyndale to be uninhibited about what 'commmon pestilence' in particular 'all princes' had, i.e. 'women and pride'.

'Imperial Kingship'

Tyndale's *Obedience* was branded as a heretical book. Nevertheless, its influence was widespread, seemingly at all levels. The anonymous *The Institution of a Christian Man* (1537) which strikingly parallels both Tyndale's setting of obedience to princes in a context of more immediate obediences (of children to parents, for example) and his scriptural quotations, even adding more.[36] Ten years later, the first of the official Homilies, published under Edward VI, that of 1547, does the same. (These Homilies were instruments of government, distributed throughout the nation, intended to be read from all pulpits on certain Sundays instead of sermons.) This, *Of Obedience*, sets the idea of the importance of firm kingly rule in a setting of daily life that is recognisably like Tyndale's. It has been shown, to continue the dependence even more remarkably, that part of the end of John Bale's *King John* (?1540) directly reproduces passages from Tyndale's *Obedience*.[37] Bale, another exact contemporary of Tyndale, when he worked for Cromwell before the latter's fall, among other things wrote anti-Catholic plays for Cromwell's itinerant troupe of players. Five of these have survived. Four are in the later medieval form of allegorical morality plays, where abstractions like Mercy or Lust vie for the soul of Man; *King John* is different. Though Dissimulation, Private Wealth and Sedition come on stage, at the centre of the play are portraits of King John, of Stephen Langton and of Cardinal Pandulphus, referred to by Tyndale. In the late 1530s that King, John, was having a good press as a proto-Protestant, a King who stood up against the Pope and all his power, and Bale's central royal figure is dazzlingly effective. After his death, at the close of the play, Imperial Majesty quotes Tyndale's *Obedience*—without acknowledgement, of course, but the source could well have been recognised. Tyndale's book would have been well-known to Cromwell's circle and Tyndale was the first widely-disseminated exponent of these essential political theories in their scriptural base. The influence of Tyndale's general political theory, so reinforced by so much Scripture as it was, can be traced far ahead into Elizabeth's reign and beyond, not least in Shakespeare.

It is said of Tyndale's *Obedience* that in setting out who should obey whom it shows Tyndale's solid maintenance of divine order expressed in the Tudor understanding of degree—that is, that everything in creation had its place in what later writers called 'the great chain of being', from God down through the orders of angels, and then to kings and all levels of subjects, and on down further through the animal kingdom to the lowest forms of organic life—and that this is why it so appealed to the King. Henry VIII needed at that point such learned arguments supporting his sovereignty over everything in England below the angels, by-passing both the Pope and the Holy Roman Emperor.

Certainly, it is true that Tyndale's first section proper begins 'The Obedience of all Degrees proved by God's Word . . .', but the true heart of the book is at a deeper point altogether. From start to finish it is about the Bible, and the neglect and distortion of it by the

institution of the Church. The important part of the title just quoted
is the end, the four words 'proved by God's Word'. Tyndale's *Obedience*
is the first book in English about the political effect of Scripture. Being
about Scripture meant also that it had to be about the necessity under
God of Scripture in the vernacular. That, of course, also appealed to
King Henry in one of his many moods, the one in which he saw
himself, as in the title-page to the Great Bible of 1536, as the giver of
the English Bible to his clamorously grateful subjects.

Anne Boleyn

Henry VIII has been described as captivated by the *Obedience*, an
entrancement which seems unlikely.[29] When it was first printed, Henry
was, however, captivated by the young woman who would be his
second wife, Anne Boleyn. A document of the time, supported from
another source, tells how she took the book to her husband-to-be and
commended it to him.

   This is not the place to attempt in detail an account of the character
of Anne, the extent of her sympathies with the reformers, or even the
reasons for her downfall. All these have been regularly re-considered:
there is continuing sharp debate. A modern historian trying to bring
up a clear picture behind all the unusually strong distortions produced
by factions, then and later, faces serious problems. For a long time we
have had conflict between, at one extreme, a meretricious Anne, a
witch, scheming and adulterous, the hard-faced rival of the old and
saintly Queen Catherine, the instrument of her own ruthlessly ambi-
tious family: a picture which originally came from the gossip-laden
reports of the Holy Roman Emperor's legate at the court, Eustace
Chapuys, a spy at keyholes who, it was said, almost certainly did not
speak or read English, and who was hell-bent on trying to save
Catherine—and the papal power over England. At the other extreme,
we hear of an accomplished, scholarly and even saintly Anne who
loved equally the work of the reform of Christ's church, the Bible in
English, and her husband; who was deeply loved by her husband in
return, and with the birth of their child Elizabeth gave England her
greatest Queen; who was the victim of a swift and vicious plot by the
papal party on the wholly-incredible grounds of frequent adultery; and
who was murdered before the King properly woke up to what was
happening. (It is certainly true that he powerfully regretted her loss.) It
has always been questioned how many, if any at all, of the charges
against her of multiple adultery and incest should be believed. That she
was a witch was understood from a slight deformation in her hand,

and chiefly from the fact that instead of the expected thriving son, so desperately needed, she had a still-born child—and, being punishment by God, that was also proof of her general guilt. Deeper investigation by professional historians stirs a murky pool indeed, of the manufacturing and manipulating of a case against her, probably by court factions, with under all the deepest enigma, the unknowable psychology of the King. Anne's fall remains a mystery. It is unknown how far the King was manipulated by Court factions, and how far he was in charge of the events of her removal, The power-groups that may now be identified drew ultimately on the largest resources. The battalions against Queen Anne included those in Britain and the rest of Europe who still hoped to see Queen Catherine's marriage validated and Princess Mary legitimised: that is, the highest eminences of the imperial Church. Queen Anne's cohorts included those who saw the future of England in King Henry as *Fidei Defensor*, head of an English church controlled from Westminster and Canterbury, not Rome. The importance of the Boleyn family's interest in a handful of busily-writing English exiles can be exaggerated. But Tyndale's book did briefly brush against the power-lines at the very centre of the English court.[38] In the 1530s the Court of Henry VIII was, even for Europe, exceptionally febrile. The task here is to try to find a cool assessment of the likelihood of Tyndale's *Obedience* being read there, rather than just being present, and with what effect.

Foxe tells us that he owns the manuscript which gives the story, which is that Anne Boleyn possessed a copy of the *Obedience*, and lent it to a gentlewoman in her service, Anne Gainsford. Also in her service was a young man, George Zouch, a suitor for the young maid of honour. One day in sport he plucked the book from her, and beginning to read was so charmed with it that he refused to return it, despite her tears. It happened, however, that Dr Richard Sampson, dean of the King's chapel, observed him reading it at service time, and calling the young man, he seized the book and delivered it to the Cardinal: for Wolsey had warned him to keep a watch for unsuitable books, lest they come to the King's reading. When Anne Boleyn asked her maid for the book, the young woman fell on her knees and confessed the truth.

> The lady Anne showed herself not sorry, nor angry with either of the two. But, said she, well, it shall be the dearest book that ever the dean or cardinal took away. The noble woman goes to the king, and upon her knees she desireth the king's help for her book. Upon the king's token the book was restored. And now bringing the book to

him, she besought his grace most tenderly to read it. The king did
so, and delighted in the book. For, saith he, this is a book for me
and all kings to read.[39]

Foxe's manuscript was printed by Strype. Corroboration of the story
in the large part comes from a history of Anne Boleyn published in the
1590s. It was written by George Wyatt, the grandson of Sir Thomas
Wyatt the poet, who tells us that Thomas, as a young man, fell in love
with Anne when she came back from education in France (this was
before King Henry first saw her). Earlier historians have been quick to
find a story of reciprocated passion in Wyatt's poetry, which is as
doubtful a procedure as finding Shakespeare's biography in his sonnets,
and as unhelpful. The Wyatt family home in Kent was not far from
Hever Castle, the Boleyn seat, and it is not unlikely that Thomas and
Anne were childhood friends. Thomas was an automatic target for
scurrilous accusations when Anne fell, and he was briefly imprisoned
on nebulous charges of having had sexual relations with her before and
during her marriage to Henry—charges quickly dropped, but leaving
a stain. Thomas's grandson wrote to give a picture of a wronged
woman, and probably to settle an old score against Wolsey. That story,
which corroborates Foxe, indicates her theological allegiance and the
'secret-police' habits of Wolsey's faction, with Anne herself as the
obvious target of the politicking. In Wyatt's version, the book is not
named but is described as dealing with the 'controversies concerning
religion, and specially of the authority of the pope and his clergy, and
of their doings against kings and states'. Anne Boleyn had read the
book, marking with her nail such places as the king ought to read. Her
maid, finding it lying in a window, began to read it, when her suitor
came in and took it from her. As she was called away to her mistress,
he walked out reading it, and met one of the Cardinal's gentlemen,
who borrowed it and gave it to Wolsey. Anne, hearing of this, went at
once to inform the King, and told him of the places that she had
marked. Scarcely had she left the chamber, when Wolsey entered with
the book in his hand, intending to complain of it, and to use it as a
lever against Anne. But the King's mind was already hardening against
the Cardinal, and finding the marks which Anne had made, he read
the book, and the reading hastened the Cardinal's ruin. (If Foxe's date
is right, then Wolsey, who fell in the late summer of 1528, was already
sliding.)

King Henry fell in love with Anne after had she returned from her
childhood and adolescence abroad, early in May 1527, apparently
attracted at first by her good looks, her musical and dancing abilities,

and her charming conversation—the French Court had trained her well. It has to be remembered that Henry insisted tenaciously for six difficult years that he wanted to marry her. This suggests something deeper than a sudden passion on his part, and it clarifies as well a determination on her part to show that she could be for him someone worth waiting for, as well as an honourable Queen. Recent work on documents giving evidence by contemporaries confirms the picture given by Foxe, Strype and George Wyatt of Anne's commitment to reform, and particularly her concern for the Bible in the vernacular— her copy of Tyndale's 1534 New Testament is in the British Library, and she was said on good authority to have kept an English Bible open in her chamber.[40] She interceded for men considered heretical by Wolsey. She was altogether more active in the cause of reform than has often been stated. That historical seam is rich, and still to be fully mined.

Tyndale's Craft of Rhetoric

Within each subdivision of the *Obedience*, within each paragraph and almost in every sentence there can be found and analysed a kaleidoscope of technical, rhetorical devices. One older picture of Tyndale the polemicist as a naive (but still dangerous) eccentric, pouring out sentences in a torrent of disorganised thoughts, making a rag-bag of subversive rantings, could not be further from the truth. There is passion in his words; but there is also the craftsmanly skill which, as a well-educated man of the time would, knows coolly and exactly how the mechanisms of word-order work. It has taken some centuries for Shakespeare to lose the label of 'child of Nature', wanting art—as if all his plays and poems were poured from on high into a funnel in his head without him having to do anything except write them down. We know a little better now, and can see how his excellent education at the school in Stratford gave him a grounding in great classical literature which grew all his life, and also taught him those schemes and methods of using words to greatest effect that he went on to develop so remarkably. Precisely the same is true of Tyndale, whom we patronise at our peril. Tyndale's education (at Oxford, unlike Shakespeare's) was two generations earlier than Shakespeare's and so without the latter's advantage of the matured Erasmian educational revolution; but the chief point was even then to teach him how to make words work, to whatever effect was needed. The classical systems have long ago disappeared from view, being finally expunged by the sub-Romantic ideas of expression of the self. Yet to understand Tyndale, one must see him working with the late medieval and early humanist methods of rhetoric, as then understood.

This is a huge field—more like a continent—which has never been properly explored. There have been short studies which have touched it, but oddly only in relation to Thomas More and the art of controversy.[41] In such pieces Tyndale's powerful sarcasm is observed (the clergy 'love you so well, that they had rather burn you, than that you should have fellowship with Christ') though not its particular complexity. His pleasure in irony is observed, as in scrupulously polite references, when writing of the machinations of the papacy, to 'our most holy father'; and his text-book uses of logic and analogy, though again not crediting him with subtlety in his disarming claim not to be interested in such things. Tyndale's skill with *reductio ad absurdum* for example when writing of the clergy is obvious—if as they say, every Mass delivers one soul out of purgatory, there are so many priests and so many Masses that even if took ten, purgatory would long ago have been empty. More's slippery tricks—inuendo, shifting the meaning of terms in the middle of the argument, pretending to misunderstand, misquoting, correcting his opponent's grammar to discredit his authority and so on—met a match in the sheer capacity of Tyndale to keep on returning a straight ball. The two men's controversy has been admired for its demonstrations of technique.

Tyndale, however, though a serious player in controversy, was at his rhetorical best elsewhere; and that has had little, if any, attention. Much needs doing in analysing his rhetorical skills as expositor, not to say translator. The *Obedience* might be a place to start, to glance at a fragment of its construction and see what can be learned. Let us take a passage[42] at random and see what happens. We shall use Erasmus's *De copia* in a recent English translation,[43] remembering that the aim is to use the many available methods of varying, and note the technical names that a trained rhetorician would give to the devices. That is not simply labelling, but indicating the rich store of possibilities ready for the craftsman to use. 'How wonderfully were the children of Israel locked in Egypt! In what tribulation, cumbrance, and adversity were they in!' These sentences are *admiratio*, here 'altering the emotional tone, exhibiting in a different attire', as Erasmus puts it in chapter 32. The verb 'locked' is *deflexio*, a kind of metaphor (chapter 16). 'Tribulation, cumbrance and adversity' make *enallage*, where 'variety is gained by a small change in the same word' (chapter 13). 'The land also that was promised them was afar off, and full of great cities, walled with high walls up to the sky, and inhabited with great giants.' 'Full of . . . up to the sky . . . great giants' are *hyperbole*, obviously (chapter

28). 'Walled with high walls up . . .'; the repetiton reproduces the upward movement with decorum, making possibly a form of *tractatio*, strictly of *repetitio* (not in Erasmus). 'Yet God's truth brought them out of Egypt and planted them in the land of the giants.' The metaphor 'planted' is straightfoward *deflexio*, but the subject of 'brought'—'God's truth'—is the extension of metaphor called *catachresis*, which Erasmus says is 'to express a meaning related to its own for which no proper word already exists': one of his illustrations is 'far reaching plan'. 'This was also written for our learning: for there is no power against God's, neither any wisdom against God's wisdom: he is stronger and wiser than all his enemies.' 'Stronger and wiser' make a form of *auxesis*, amplification by using a stronger word than expected. The omission of 'power' after 'God's', and of the verb in the following phrase, make a form of *epanalepsis*, allowing the sense to run on quickly. Out of that grow the clinching comparatives, 'than all his enemies' being not hyperbolic at all.

Perhaps enough has been said. It is time to recognise in Tyndale a confident technical craftsmanship outside controversy—the bulk of his writing, after all.

Chapter 10

SIR THOMAS MORE

More and Religious Controversy[1]

In the late 1520s the English campaign against Luther was running strongly. Attention of churchmen would presently be diverted into the new and different conflicts of the 'King's Great Matter', the divorce and the subsequent break with Rome; but in 1528 in London, and in Oxford and Cambridge, there was a surge of heresy-hunting. With Wolsey working behind the scenes, three men were by then central in the work of resisting Protestantism in England. First was John Fisher, Bishop of Rochester, whose preaching against Luther had been attacked by Tyndale in his *Obedience*. Fisher had written anti-Lutheran tracts in Latin that were widely read outside England. His first famous St Paul's sermon 'against the pernicious doctrine of M. Luther', on the text John 15:26, was printed by Wynkyn de Worde in 1521. His next, five years later, on the text 'thy faith hath saved thee' was at the ceremonial, and celebrated, occasion at St Paul's on 11 February 1526 where at their abjuration Robert Barnes and the five Steelyard merchants carried faggots to the bonfire on which Tyndale's New Testament was burned. That sermon was printed 'in the house of T. Berthelet' in 1526.[2] The second of the three men was Cuthbert Tunstall, Bishop of London, whom we have already seen at work and will meet again. The third was Thomas More, who now for the first time, in June 1529, enters the story of William Tyndale. It is sometimes suggested that Tunstall, wishing to destroy Tyndale, bethought him of his friend Sir Thomas. He then persuaded that reluctant humanist to break new ground and bring his fresh forces to join in the war against the influx of heresy from the continent. In 1529 More did break new ground, in moving from Latin to English.[3] His youthful poems had been in English, and his first published work a translation into English of the *Life of Picus, Earl of Mirandula* from the Latin of Pico's nephew, written around 1510. His *History of King Richard the Third* was written in English in 1513, but not published until 1557: the simultaneous Latin version not until 1566 (by then the English version had been incorporated into Hall's 1548 *Chronicle*, and the unique, highly-coloured, defamatory picture of this King went from there to Shakespeare and into everyone's knowledge). *Four Last Things*, also in English, was written in 1522. By 1529, however, he was a more battle-hardened veteran of the Latin campaign than even Tunstall. To understand what More's entry into Tyndale's life meant, we must first look at the English forces against heresy which More had significantly led for at least the previous eight years.

Since Oxford days under Thomas Linacre, and later with William Grocyn learning Greek, Thomas More had been the central star in England's small constellation of Christian humanist scholars. He had met Erasmus in 1499 when he first visted England, cementing the friendship under his own roof, in correspondence and in joint work (both men, during Erasmus's second visit to England, produced translations of the satirist Lucian). With their mutual high praise, they led the thought of what few English 'intellectuals' there were. Erasmus, on his third visit to England, in 1509, had written for More his most famous book, the *Encomium moriae*: the title puns on his name. The satire caused amusement at this praise of Folly through all Europe. A London lawyer, More had been drawn to the priesthood and shared for a while some of the monastic life of a Carthusian monastery while he was living at Lincoln's Inn. From 1510 to 1518 he had been one of London's two under-sheriffs, going on a delegation to Flanders in 1515 over disputes about the cloth trade, particularly in wool, with further missions to Calais and Bruges. (He may have learned in the workings of the cloth trade details which he could use later in catching heretical books.) Thomas More, on his mission to Bruges, had begun his own most famous book, *Utopia*, printed in Louvain in 1516, with Erasmus in mind. He had been present at the Field of the Cloth of Gold in 1520–21, and was knighted in 1521. Favoured by the King, he had become Speaker of the House of Commons in 1523, and Chancellor of the Duchy of Lancaster in 1525.

We saw above[4] how in January 1521 Cuthbert Tunstall in Worms wrote to Wolsey with news of Luther, particularly of his *De Babylonica captivitate*, and Tunstall's hopes that it could be kept out of England. Late in that January 1521, or early in February, Wolsey probably issued a ban on the sale and possession of Luther's books: the document has not survived but its effects can be plotted.[5] By April 1521, King Henry himself was at work on his book against Luther, the *Assertio septem sacramentorum*, the 'assertion' being of the orthodox theology of there being seven Sacraments, to challenge Luther's heretical declaration in his *Babylonian Captivity* that there were, scripturally, only two. Thomas More's closeness to the King meant that he could not avoid taking part in the most serious controversy of the time—the threat, coming from Luther, to the grip of the Church on the lives of everyone. More himself said that he was involved in the King's own writing against Luther, the *Assertio*.[6] The authorship of that book is a celebrated crux. Henry had begun to write it in April 1521 and had then given up. A month later it was caught up in Wolsey's promulgation in England of the previous year's papal Bull against Luther, *Exsurge Domine*. When Fisher preached his first sermon against Luther at St Paul's on 21 May 1521, he made the first public announcement of the King's attack on Luther. Wolsey, also present, waved to the crowds a copy of his sovereign's unfinished work. The book was published by Pynson on 12 July; it has been thought unlikely that Henry, notoriously incapable of sustained concentration, finished it himself, carefully assembling the orthodox arguments. The book consists of a short section on indulgences, with reference to papal authority, and then in the rest works steadily through the orthodox sacraments in their defence. The likelihood is that it was the work of a commission of theologians, itself set up earlier by Wolsey to promulgate *Exsurge Domine* and attack Luther. Thomas More himself claimed only a minor role 'by his grace's appointment and consent of the makers of the same'.[7] The direction of the book's attack, however, fits with what we know of More's legally-aware lines of argument in his own work. Surprisingly, the book— from the King, or whoever—defends the papacy ambiguously. Though Henry supports the standard line that Church practices not expressly sanctioned by Scripture are part of an oral tradition from Christ himself, even to saying that the gestures used by priests in the Mass had been taught by Christ and handed down, and that the Church could not err, much is revealed by the prudent selection of topics. Some legal mind pointed out to Henry that when kings and popes so easily quarelled there was value in caution. So the assertion of papal power is limited to the matter of indulgences, and the *Assertio*'s lack of precision in defining papal primacy is lost in the smoke of savage denunciations of Luther for his public disobedience and swirling praises for Pope Leo's person.[8] Thomas More was a lawyer-theologian who was with the King every day, and he wrote years later, in 1534, that he had counselled the King to such carefulness. The resulting mixture of legal circumstantiality, theological casuistry and vicious attack on the person of the heretic is characteristic of More later on, on his own. It would not be wrong, it appears, to see More in the *Assertio*.

The task of attacking Luther was international. The works produced in England were part of a cross-Europe traffic in orthodox defence, not to say outrage. The book by the English monarch was important, and ran through six editions in 1521 and 1522 in London, Rome, Strasburg and Antwerp. It was translated into German in 1522. It has been called 'the first widely-selling book against Luther'.[9] To Luther, it was a bad blow. The rush of events since 1517 had led him to believe that European kings would rally to his cause, which was suddenly in danger. Now, and worse, if the English monarch declared himself so strongly against him in this *Assertio*, Henry VIII might be followed by German princes and others on whom he was relying. To Henry himself, the book was good. It was the means of his securing a special religious title from the Pope, something he had wanted for a long time. He sent to Rome twenty-eight signed presentation copies of his book, some printed on vellum for distribution to sovereigns and the more important cardinals, and some on paper for the lesser cardinals and the universities. On Wednesday 2 October 1521 the formal ceremony of presentation to Pope Leo X took place.[10]

Though the Imperial ambassador at Rome wrote to Charles V that it was said that all the learned men in England had a part in its composition,[11] the papal consistory granted Henry the title of *Fidei Defensor* nine days later, and 'Defender of the Faith' has been a title of the British monarch ever since, appearing as 'Fid. Def.' or 'F.D.' on coins even to this day. The consistory approved of the *Assertio*; they cannot have appreciated the artful politics within it.[12] King Henry received loud praise from dignitaries close to the Pope. His book sold well.

Luther read the King's *Assertio* in the spring of 1522, when he was closely involved in Wittenberg in constructive reform, and even more closely applying himself to his translation of the New Testament. He was shocked by the violence of the attacks on him in the book, and dismayed by its translation into German. He replied soon after with a little book which demonstrated his alarm, *Contra Henricum Regem Angliae* printed in Wittenberg a few months later. He had also heard, as he reported later, that Henry's book was known to be by a number of other people: he would have had no doubt that the King's view was official and fully-supported policy. Until twelve months before, he might have expected the interest in him, mixed with scepticism and doubt and some lack of sympathy, among the learned in England, to continue. He would not have expected such vicious opposition, until that was orchestrated by Wolsey following the Bull *Exsurge Domine*. Earlier reponses to Luther in England may be judged by the correspondence of More and Erasmus. In March 1518 Erasmus had sent More a copy of Luther's *Ninety-five Theses*, with a jocular letter including the anti-papal games, and witty satirical diatribes against abuses within the Church, which both of them loved to make.[13] Luther was thought of then as a powerful speaker and writer, a great scholar, even in all his contradictions a great man, but no more, it was imagined, than a new version of a familiar old character, the charismatic prophet, this time with real learning. Thomas More, as Erasmus hinted in a letter to Luther of 30 May 1519, was probably one of the 'great men' in England 'who think the best of your writing', and More himself in his 'Letter to a Monk' of 1519 saw Luther not as a heretic but simply as an extreme Augustinian.[14] Events in Germany steadily darkened the sky; but what turned More to join in the work of the King's *Assertio* against Luther were, specifically, Wolsey's English campaign of fulfilling the tenor of the papal Bull, and Luther's retort in his *Contra Henricum*. A number of Catholic polemicists in Europe presently received royal patronage for their published support of Henry after the *Contra Henricum* (they included Jacob Latomus, who will apppear in Tyndale's story as one of the judges at his trial). The principal English response, however (in Latin, of course), came from Thomas More.

More against Luther

When Henry's *Assertio* came out, Luther was occupied with other things. His temper was shortened both by disputes with German leaders and the ready accessibility of Henry's book, in German, in bookshops. His first answer to Henry, in German, came out on 1 August 1522 as the *Antwort deutsch*: the extended Latin *Contra Henricum*, at the end of September. The world was tough, and the struggle to establish the Word of God was going to be an uphill fight needing many weapons. He called Henry *stolidem regem*, 'stupid king', *stultum regem*, 'dense king': 'he does not come forward with a king's mind, nor with any vein of royal blood but with a slavish and openly immodest, immoderate behaviour like a courtesan' . . . 'with his falsehoods he is more a trivial buffoon than a king'. Luther attacks him for Thomism:[15] Henry has 'a Thomist cranium and plebeian mentality', he is 'this demon of Thomists'. 'Are you not ashamed,' he asks Henry, 'now no longer a king, but a sacreligious brigand . . . ?'[16] Yet there is nothing here particularly foul. The insults are in the language of the comedies of Plautus and Terence, the very stuff of disputation. They may be compared to Henry's own language in his *Assertio*. There he said of Luther that

> the most greedy wolf of hell has surprised him, devoured and swallowed him down into the lowest part of his belly, where he lies half alive and half dead in death: and whilst the pious pastor calls him, and bewails his loss, he belches out of the filthy mouth of the heathen wolf these foul inveighings, which the ears of the whole flock detest, disdain and abhor.[17]

Quite why Luther's *Contra Henricum* has been reported to cross all bounds of decency, bombarding Henry's crown with filth, is mysterious. Of the two disputants, it is Henry who may be felt to be the more offensive. Yet Luther's book has been described as uniquely 'insulting . . . vitriolic . . . obscene. . . .'[18]

In the exchange, the reality of the controversy was revealed. Henry stood for the ancient authorities, the pronouncements of popes and councils, the fathers, custom, tradition, numbers and length of time—and personal abuse of Luther as heretic. Luther fought for *sola scriptura*, the Word of God eternally announcing the good news of God imparting his redemptive self in Christ to man, through Scripture which interprets itself. Luther's best explicit statement of *sola scriptura* had been made in his own *Assertio* of 1520. The implications were more fully worked out in his *De Babylonica captivitate* of 1521 and here now in the *Contra Henricum* of 1522.[19]

What was at issue was a matter of supreme crisis for the Church. Basil the Great a thousand years before had explicitly stated that equal obedience was owed to Scripture and to the secret, oral tradition handed down by the Apostles. By the late Middle Ages this supposed oral tradition had spawned a huge proliferation of ceremonies and practices, always open to attack. Luther's reassertion in his *Contra Henricum* brought Scripture back as the true authority: it was bound to identify, judge and condemn the great influx of new observances and systems.[20] The possibility of partial reform of the Church from inside was swept away by the uprooting force of *sola scriptura*.

Among the replies to Luther was John Fisher's *Assertionis Lutheranae confutatio* printed in Antwerp early in 1523, a book often republished in the following decades. In the course of it Fisher praised the power of Henry's *Assertio*, a neat trick considering that he himself probably had a hand in the writing of it. Fisher did not, however, refer to Luther's *Contra Henricum*. Henry wrote a letter from Greenwich on 20 January 1523 to the Saxon dukes warning them of the dangers Luther was presenting, keeping his dignity by not attempting to reply to

Luther, or even to notice that he had replied, but at the same time making sure that all the German princes knew that Henry was able to riposte. A more subtle answer to Luther was called for, something which would out-Martin Martin in ridicule and at the same time in that medium refute him point by point. The King, of course, in his letter to the Saxon dukes, as everyone immediately agreed, had done absolutely all that could be possibly done with such a flea-bite as Luther had caused. Yet it could just be said at court, perhaps, that there was possibly just room for another champion in the lists—the King does not actually forbid it. There was maybe need for a 'a master of dialogue and dispute, a man who was both fully informed and religiously concerned and . . . not of the spiritual estate.'[21] It is not known if Thomas More was assigned the task, or asked to do it; the result was the two documents which make up his *Responsio ad Lutherum* of 1523.

More's Responsio

In 1523 More had a European reputation as England's leading humanist and friend of Erasmus, and above all as the author of *Utopia*. He was lawyer, statesman and politician, and the head of a family noted for piety and instruction. He was in close attendance on the King in the presentation and execution of correspondence.[22] His increasing involvement in the anti-Lutheran campaign driven by Wolsey meant that to his religious, educational and social concerns of humanist 'good letters' were now added doctrinal strife and polemical warfare.[23] Dispute had always been a method of the schools, close argument mingling with verbal attack: it now took on the techniques of total war. Among friends of More at this time, Erasmus himself was engaged in prolonged and sometimes unpleasant quarrels, and John Fisher was in dispute with Lefèvre d'Étaples over the identity of the three Marys in the Gospels. Thomas More had for some time used his skills of controversy and invective in a number of non-theological disputes. Now he undertook officially the forcible task of responding to Luther.[24]

This is not the place for a detailed account of More's *Responsio*, important as it is both as a document of the English Reformation and as an indicator of More's development as polemicist. The theological arguments are subtly marshalled in the two parts, using Henry's *Assertio* as stalking-horse. More goes further than Henry in asserting the power of the unwritten, rather than scriptural, tradition, and does so in more complex detail—the voice of the lawyer is never far away. He had done various things to prepare himself, reading the Catholic polemicists like Cochlaeus whom he cites, learning from Fisher and from daily life at court, and especially from Thomas Murner, the German polymath enemy of Luther, then around the English court. He read Luther for himself, though not systematically and not much. Four editions of Luther's collected works had been published from 1518 to 1520, but More seems not to have referred to them more than occasionally. His concentration is on what came after 1520, particularly, as might be expected, *De captivitate Babylonica* and *Contra Henricum*. Further Luther material came to him, with appropriate aptness, not from the written Luther canon but from another 'oral tradition', that web of rumours, reported errors and lies so actively fostered by the papal authorities before, during and after the Diet of Worms, and so eagerly responded to, for and against, throughout Germany. Luther made the most fundamental challenge to the western Church for a millenium, and wild and extreme were the stories about him, from all sides. He was god and devil, saint and monster. In the court where Wolsey was Chancellor, More would hear, and read, the hungrily-assembled tales of his unspeakableness (to take one small example, prints of Luther as a hideously deformed monstrous calf) and carefully assemble them for use. Whether or not More was explicitly asked by the King to write an attack, in a way that did not undermine the excellence and adequacy of the King's letter to the Saxon dukes, it is clear that in the winter of 1523 there was at court a larger programme to defend the King's majesty and his *Assertio* and extend the attack on Luther, and More was perfectly placed to write a response.

Because he would need language unseemly for a king or councillor, and because he liked to work that way, More used a *persona*, which gave him more flexibility with which to combine the necessary air of resignation at having to fence with a fool and the most serious dogmatic *gravitas*. He invents a student, Ferdinandus Baravellus, who is attending a Spanish university and happens to visit the uncle of the person with whom he is corresponding, who persuades him to attack such insane ravings of Luther as have not already been so magisterially countered by the King of England, which he does, and the book is the result. So far, so complicated. Thomas More, however, went on to make a second version, with a new *persona*, 'William Ross' (Guilielmus Rosseus), now writing to 'John Carcellius' from outside Rome, and now with a quite new slant. More here moves away from Henry's arguments and on his own account defends at length the position of the Church as superior to Scripture through the power of the un-

written tradition. Fundamental to his method in both, and especially
in the Rosseus version, is the scholastic tradition of verbatim quotation
of one's opponent, humanistically extended by, if possible, giving the
complete text. This is more than the good manners of good letters.
The assumption is that the reader, helped by judicious commentary to
be sure, will see for himself the utter folly of the opponent's case.
Furthermore, an occasional tampering with a text, as More permits
himself in the Rosseus version, will not be visible.[25] Yet this is a work
by Thomas More, and all the complexities of his nature come through,
a pugnacity 'reinforced by an earnestness, a serious devotion . . .
[which] nevertheless treated his opponent with profound repugnance
and invincible hostility. Luther was a heretic and thus was totally evil.'[26]
Heresy infected every part of the heretic, all his doctrines, all his
personal life, and was one with all heretics and heresies of all time. The
truth was also one, so the Church could never compromise on even a
minute point, without causing the whole to crumble at once. In that
clash of absolutes, neither side could respond to the other's arguments.
Instead of the directly personal thrust and counter-thrust of a duel
which even such incensed dramatic opponents as Hamlet and Laertes
make, there can only be blanket bombing. More's bombs are carefully
selected for their purpose, including frequent quotation from Scripture
and classical authors, and (unlike Henry) avoidance of dependence on
patristic authorities, now a useless weapon for attacking Luther. His
high explosives include ribald, Rabelaisian abuse. 'Punning on the
rhetorical and logical distinctions between prior premise and posterior
argument', notes a modern biographer, 'he wrote of Luther

> Since he has written that he already has a prior right to bespatter
> and besmirch the royal crown with shit, we will not have the
> posterior right to proclaim the beshitted tongue of this practitioner
> of posterioristics most fit to lick with his anterior the very posterior
> of a pissing she-mule until he shall have learned more correctly to
> infer posterior conclusions from prior premises.[27]

A study of the anti-Luther material across Europe, even only up to
1523, would show the common violence of the language. But in being
'merry' so filthily (the biographer notes 'a monotonous scatology as
wearing as the talk of small boys in school washrooms'[28]), More digs
far below others. More's book is uniquely disreputable, and worse, in
matter and in spirit.[29] Here, as example and pretty well at random, in
a modern English translation, is Thomas More at the end of the final
paragraph of the Rosseus version: the end of 11:27, before the peroration, and thus effectively the climax of the work.

[Luther] has nothing in his mouth but privies, filth and dung, with which he plays the buffoon . . . he would cast into his mouth the dung which other men would spit out into a basin . . . If he will leave off the folly and rage and the till now too familiar mad ravings, if he will swallow down his filth and lick up the dung with which he has so foully defiled his tongue and his pen . . . to carry nothing in his mouth but bilge-water, sewers, privies, filth and dung . . . we will take timely counsel, whether we wish . . . to leave this mad friarlet and privy-minded rascal with his ragings and ravings, with his filth and dung, shitting and beshitted.[30]

As was intended, More's 1523 *Responsio ad Lutherum* was read throughout Europe, though not everyone knew the identity of the author, even in England. Wolsey's campaign in his home country was gathering force. The theologians from Oxford and Cambridge summoned by him in May 1521 to discuss Luther most probably had a hand in the King's *Assertio*. That meeting resulted immediately in the first bonfires of Luther's books, in Cambridge as well as more famously in London. They parted to return to their cities to kindle anti-Lutheran endeavours by their writing, which they did with enthusiasm over the next years.[31] In London, John Fisher, who was Chancellor of Cambridge as well as Bishop of Rochester, wrote his *Assertionis Lutheranae confutatio*, printed in Antwerp in 1523 as we saw above: this grew out of his May 1521 St Paul's sermon, which became the touchstone of refutations of Luther. Fisher had a European reputation as a scholar: probably at the request of the King, he went on to answer Luther's *Contra Henricum* with his *Defensio regiae assertionis*, written like More's in 1523 but not published until 1525, when his other answer to Luther, the *Sacri sacerdotii defensio* was printed.[32] That book was dedicated to Cuthbert Tunstall, who collaborated in at least four of Fisher's anti-Lutheran polemics. Tunstall brought to Fisher's attention (and caused Fisher's immediate response in his *Convulsio calumniarium*) a recent book by one Ulrich Velenus which argued that St Peter had never been to Rome, 'with catastrophic implications for papal primacy'.[33] Fisher and Tunstall collaborated in other anti-Lutheran ways: in 1524, Wolsey, Warham, Fisher and Tunstall were constituted official censors of the book trade, and there are indications that the latter two did most of the work. They were nominated from Rome as the two delegates from England for a proposed small council to reform the Church.[34] At the Court, the poet John Skelton rebuked the younger unorthodox university men in his *A replication against certain young scholars*. Queen Catherine's confessor produced treatises against Luther on indulgences, and Richard Pace, the King's secretary, translated into Latin Fisher's first sermon against Luther and sent it to Pope Leo X.[35] Such activity was Europe-wide, and Latin texts came in and out of England, a country highly regarded in the campaign after the circulation of the *Assertio* by the powerful English monarch himself. From Erasmus down, major continental scholars enjoyed English patronage or encouragement in writing against Luther.[36] One of them, John Eck (one of Luther's earliest opponents, who in England had been introduced to Henry VIII, Fisher, More and others) wrote in 1525 the single best-selling anti-Lutheran book of the century, the *Enchiridion locorum communum*, a collection of useful quotations and arguments to be used in controversies which had more than one hundred editions.

It seemed that the campaign was being successful, and the second half of the decade would show a decline in Luther's influence in England. Then came the unforeseen. On 1 September 1525, Luther, misled, probably by the King of Denmark, into thinking that King Henry was becoming favourable to his ideas, wrote to Henry to adjust his *Contra Henricum* in that light. He wrote that he had not previously understood that Henry was the sole author, and now offered some reconciliation, largely on his own terms, one of which was that Henry should convert to the gospel.[37] In the same months, John Bugenhagen, Luther's close lieutenant, wrote his *Epistola ad sanctos in Anglia*. He summarised Luther's theology and encouraged English Lutherans to persevere and hope for deliverance.[38] That Christmas Robert Barnes and Hugh Latimer preached the sermons at Cambridge we noticed in a previous chapter.[39] And Cochlaeus in Cologne stumbled upon two Englishmen printing an English New Testament. A new surge against Lutherans in England was called for, and followed. King Henry's reply to Luther was scathing. His techniques and material so agree with More's in the *Responsio* that we can have no doubt that 'King Henry' means Thomas More.[40] In this reply, Luther is ferociously attacked—for marrying a nun, 'his whore', for a long list of heresies, and for insane errors—but not, significantly, for attacking the papacy.

Some time before the spring of 1527, Thomas More replied in Latin to Bugenhagen, this time apparently writing entirely off his own bat. The 'letter' (a monograph) may not even have been sent, and it was not published until 1568. It is powerful polemic. He sees in the Peasants' War in Germany that his earlier predictions of tumult, massacre and rapine from Luther's madness had come true. He knows that the Protestant movement has split into warring camps, and he thrusts mercilessly into the divisions and widens them. He notes the unreliability of Scripture. More first sounds a note that he will ring again and again, that miracles authenticate the Catholic Church and

the heretics never produce any '—this from a humanist scholar who
had earlier scorned the credulity of the masses in their acceptance of
false miracles and foolish wonders'.[41] More is, in this unpublished tract,
at his most theological, attacking the simplicity of the confession,
'Christ is our righteousness', and condemning at length the teaching of
predestination.

In anti-heretical polemic More had learned from Cochlaeus, who
had also written a defence of Henry's *Assertio*, and was setting out to
capitalise his revelation about the English New Testament by dedicating
volumes of his own book to Henry VIII, Wolsey, Fisher, Tunstall and
West. The first three volumes were forwarded in September 1526 by
the charmingly-named English representative in Cologne, Sir John
Wallop. Cochlaeus was corresponding with Fisher, whom he greatly
admired, even to translating sections of his *Confutatio* into German and
publishing them. With many others in Europe, he was a busy bee
gathering and passing on information about the progress of Protestantism in Germany. Apparently he did that for More, who was writing his
Latin 'letter' to Bugenhagen. Significantly for his frame of mind at this
time, More not only failed to publish it, and probably even to send it;
he also failed in a grand attempt to bring Erasmus to write against
heretics.[42]

The Dialogue Concerning Heresies

More needed a new strategy. Early in 1528 he found in his heart two
great tasks. The first 'was to do all he could as a royal councillor to
bring the power of both church and government to bear against the
heretics, to crush them and their beliefs, and if need be to burn heresy
out of England with fire.'[43] The second was a big change of tactics: to
write against heresy in English. That would be an antidote to the
poison affecting all the unlearned innocents who were being led astray
by heretical works in English that were being smuggled in—books like
Tyndale's New Testament. In English, he would reach them to
strengthen their true faith. Having failed to get Erasmus to write
against heresy, More would do it himself, 'put business aside, and rob
himself of time and sleep to defend the most esential thing in his life—
the Catholic Church'.[44] It is suggested that More asked Tunstall to
commission him to write in that new way, and to read heretical books.
Tunstall wrote to More, 'And since you, dearest brother, are distinguished as a second Demosthenes in our native language as well as in
Latin . . . I am sending you their mad incantations in our tongue along
with some of Luther's books . . . you will understand more easily in

what hiding places these twisting serpents lurk . . .'[45] The immediate result was More's *Dialogue Concerning Heresies*, which appeared in June 1529.

It is on that date, and not before, that Sir Thomas More enters the world of William Tyndale. Though both were clever Oxford men, full of later achievement, their paths had not crossed: More was seventeen years older than Tyndale, and moved in that wealthy, mutually flattering, small exclusive circle of English humanism, and then in the politics and high promotion in city and court. By the middle of 1529 and the publication of the *Dialogue* he was weeks away from becoming Lord Chancellor. By contrast, Tyndale was a worker at the coal-face, a linguist and craftsman who was never seduced away to a more comfortable surface job. He was above all a scholar of the Greek Bible, and now of the Hebrew, who had translated the New Testament into a form of English that would live for ever, and published two books about the implication of the scriptural doctrine of justification by faith, one relating it to works, the other to civil obedience. Tyndale might have expected to be attacked, but would not have known by whom, beyond perhaps Tunstall or Fisher. It is very probable that More's attack took him by surprise.

Some writers on More suggest that Tyndale had been wickedly and treasonably taunting the great More, who gathered up his immense and loyal *gravitas* to squash this annoying bug from Germany. Of course More was offended by the English New Testament. He did not need anyone, thank you very much, and certainly not some stray Englishman living abroad, to tell him that 'priest' should be 'senior', that 'church' should be 'congregation' and that 'charity' should be 'love';[46] that there was no purgatory in Scripture, and that five of the seven sacraments were not sacraments at all. In the whirligig of time and fashion, Tyndale is today only known in some powerful intellectual circles as an annoyance to the blessed Saint Thomas, clinging like a burr to the great man's coat, as if Tyndale's life were meaningless without More. Tyndale is indeed, sometimes cited first of all as 'opponent of Sir Thomas More', with the fact that he gave us our English Bible mentioned among the also-rans, as being of little account. That is absurd. Even the modern Catholic English Bible, the Jerusalem Bible in its various revisions, depends greatly on Tyndale's legacy of translation. So we may observe here that More did not enter Tyndale's life until July 1529, when half Tyndale's work was done: and he entered as a trained and experienced assassin. This *Dialogue* sets itself out as a Socratic, humanist debate. It does not come over as anything so rational; its intention is slaughter.

As it first appeared in June 1529, More's *Dialogue* in its four books is a thick folio printed in two columns of forbiddingly heavy black-letter type. The running heads are simply of 'The first book' and so on. There are fairly frequent marginal notes, of the order of 'God will not suffer his church to agree in any damnable error' (II: xii) or 'The Lutherans are the worst heretics that ever sprang in Christ's church' (IV: xvii)—two remarks that could sum up the whole large volume. The first two books deal with saints, pilgrimages, miracles and heretical sects, making ranging shots against Luther and Tyndale. The third book considers whether the Church and Scripture can be considered equal, at chapter 8 moving in to a wholesale attack on Tyndale's New Testament and Lutheran heretics in England, with a long digression on the case of Richard Hunne (popularly said to have been murdered by the Bishop of London). Book four attacks Luther, blaming him for the Peasants' War and atrocities (recounted with relish) at the Sack of Rome.

The device throughout the book is of a debate in which a fictional opponent is allowed to make arguments supporting his case and the author replies and wisely corrects him, many paragraphs beginning 'The author proveth . . .' As is usual with More, the fiction is peculiarly oblique. Just as six years later More will write in the Tower his noble *Dialogue of Comfort Against Tribulation*, of which 'the theme is almost the gravest that the human mind can entertain',[47] the certainty of imminent death, probably with great pain—and pass it off as a supposed English translation of a French version of a Latin dialogue between two Hungarians: so here, even the tremendous work of combating the Lutheran heresy now circulating in England in English, even to the point of (as he saw it) a Lutheran (not Christian) New Testament, is presented because 'a right worshipful friend of mine sent once unto me a secret sure friend of his . . .' This mysterious friend's 'special secret man this bearer' appears as the opponent in the debate, 'the Messenger', a figure no firmer than a straw man. He has picked up popular ideas about reform and the response of the Church to it, and been partly drawn in to a nest of Lutherans at university, and he is troubled by the apparently good cases both against the worship of saints and what goes with them, and for an English Bible. More has no difficulty in proving him wrong, every time, an ease which is helped by the air of the ridiculous which hovers around everything the Messenger says. Thus, for example, the 'insane' notion (as More believes it) that Scripture is sufficient for faith, Luther's *sola scriptura*, is introduced by the messenger telling him 'merrily' of his scorn for all his education, 'Logic he reckoned but babbling . . . Arithmetic meet for merchants,

Geometry for masons . . .' scorning the quadrivium and trivium, because 'man he said hath no light but of holy scripture . . . which he said was learning enough for a Christian man . . .' The Messenger is thus established as a airy-headed nitwit before he has properly begun, and just before he gets to one of the centres of the Protestant claim: 'And as touching any difficulty he said that he found by experience that the best and surest interpretation was to lay and confer one text with another, which fail not among them well and sufficiently to declare themself.'[48] The tone is subtly controlled, suggesting by means of the superficiality of 'as touching any difficulty' and 'he found by experience' that the work of knowing, and using intelligently, the whole Bible, is nothing but the meretricious practice of fools. (To give More his due, however, a sense of the dangers of *sola scriptura* was already apparent in Germany, and would appear later in Germany.)

The form of statement and counter-statement-but-this-time-irrefutably-right suits More's cast of mind, and his technique has been enlarged through a great deal of Latin anti-Lutheran writing. Never far away is More the interrogator, supposedly patient, urbane and receptive but in fact solid iron in the absoluteness of his double conviction that it is impossible for the Church to err even in the slightest way, and all heretics, in all time, are in all ways the Devil, who must be burned away. There is something devious in More's arguing with nothing, with no man, with an interlocutor no more present than a half-collapsed think-balloon. But dialogue with an anonymous small mind does allow him to keep Lutherans in place; they are pathetically trivial except in their power to incite mayhem. (More quite exceeds the mark in blaming Luther for the outrages of the Peasants' War and the atrocities of the Sack of Rome.) And thus the Lutheran Tyndale is given a context which is demeaning. Though his New Testament is not attacked fully until half way through book 3, he is everywhere, and the last pages of the last book are given over to explaining that he is worse than Luther. Though in the first two books Tyndale's *Obedience* is not much referred to in the text, the presence of that book is everywhere in the very subjects of 'debate'—More's insistence on the necessity of images, the worship of saints, pilgrimages, and so on. More's first English work, his address to the mass of his fellow-countrymen (or such as knew of his book, and could afford it) has Tyndale as its subject. It is wrapped up in an apparatus of a mysterious friend and messenger, classsical dialogue with urbane approachability, citizen talk and London hearsay, recent European history, current Church practices. It is driven by outrage at the very notion of heresy embodied in Luther: but Tyndale is the target. More's *Dialogue* was published in

1529, in 1531 and in 1557 (an edition overseen by his nephew William Rastell) and then not again until 1927, when it appeared under the title *A Dialogue Concerning Tyndale*.[49] However much that last title must be regretted as unauthorised, the impulse to call the book by that name must be saluted, for that is what it is.

Physically More's *Dialogue* is a large and forbidding book, a folio of more than a hundred and fifty pages in double columns of the thickest black-letter type. Intellectually it has been described as 'great Platonic dialogue: perhaps the best specimen of the form ever produced in English'.[50] The range of reference is wide, and some of it is interesting. Three matters dominate: the cult of the saints, the Bible in English, and the Church as incapable of error. The discussion is brought to some life by reference in the Platonic manner to time and place, by interruptions, and generally by 'merry tales', colloquialisms, and some high eloquence. The problem arises because those are the only places where the discussion really does come to life. Column after column after column is tedious, because nothing at all valuable or fresh is being achieved. There is no new theological truth, just insistent reiteration that the Church can never be wrong. The Messenger is drawn into the snares, very slowly. All is predictable. More is trying to demonstrate the patience of the Church: he can try the patience of his reader beyond endurance. Here is a passage, as the book fell open:

> I am quod I very glad that it hath been your hap to be there. Not so much for any thing that ye have shewed them of our communication had already, concerning the praying of saints, worshipping of images and relics, and going in pilgrimage, wherein I think ye told them no newelte [novelty], for I doubt not but they could have told you more of the matters them self than ye have heard or could hear of me, as for that I think that among them being as ye say so well learned, ye have either heard somewhat whereby ye be in some part of these matters (that we shall speak of) already satisfied, wherein our business therein may be the shorter, or else ye be the more strongly instructed for the other part whereby our disputation shall be the fuller, and the matters the more plainly touched, for the more ample satisfaction of such as yourself or your master shall hereafter happen to find in any doubt of these things that we shall now touch and treat of.
>
> Indeed quod he somewhat have they showed me their minds therein, as in some part of the matters ye shall hear when we hap to come to them.
>
> That shall I gladly hear quod I, and shape you such answer as my

poor wit will serve me. But yet I pray you be plain with me in one
thing. Were they satisfied and held themself content in those things
that were at last with much work agreed between us?

In good faith quod he to say the truth, all were save one, and he
in all thing save one. And to your great praise and high commenda-
tion, they said that in these matters.

Nay quod I let their praise pass lest you make me too proud. But
I pray you tell me, not which one misliked one thing, but what one
thing it was, and why he misliked it.

Surely quod he for ought that I could bend upon him, he could
never agree that the faith of the church out of scripture, should be
as sure and bind us to the belief thereof, as the words of holy
scripture.

Why quod I if ye remembered well what we said, ye had enough
to prove him that . . .[51]

Plato has a lot to answer for. Reading those four hundred words—and
they are typical of More's usual over-relaxed, rambling, after-dinner
manner—one has to challenge his high reputation earlier in the twentieth century as a great writer of English prose.[52] This passage may be
Sir Thomas treading water: but he does that exercise an awful lot; and
why we do have to watch? Tyndale would have made the point in
nineteen words, perhaps 'They know more of saints, images, relics and
pilgrimages than you. It was disputed that scripture overtopped the
church'.

To add spice to the Bible and the Fathers, More in English brings
in Chaucer and Robin Hood. A kind of citizen comedy sometimes
appears, at its best located in London, like the fatuous story in a
discussion of miracles about the young couple of Walbrook in book 1,
chapter 10; they were wedded and bedded and in under a year
produced a baby (the point is how we take some natural processes for
granted), the jest being in the earthy digressiveness of the teller. The
sudden appearance of a garrulous gossip there is fetching, as is some of
the 'Our London Correspondent' kind of writing about supposed
English heretics like Bilney or Hunne. Sir Thomas is at home with that
manner, and the reader longs for more of it. In the last book his
crescendo of repeated spitting at Luther is not attractive at all (Plato is
now miles behind) and the anecdotes he uses about Luther are anything but charming. He tells well the story of the fake miracle at St
Albans which eventually got into Shakespeare's *King Henry the Sixth
Part Two* (Act 2, scene 1). One reason for such passages of citizen
anecdote might have been to distract attention from the speedy way he

slides over any mention of the gross corruption of the clergy, and is so bleakly unjust in attacking those like Luther (or Tyndale in his *Mammon* or *Obedience*) who dare to raise the matter.

The two—London and Luther—come together in Tyndale. A false, Lutheran, New Testament had arrived in the capital: the very Bible that is being so wrongly elevated above Church practice is corrupt, More insists, and he spells out the objections. He insists that Tyndale deliberately mistranslates, printing 'senior', 'congregation', 'love'—and 'favour' for 'grace'.[53] More's title-page announces that his book treats of images, relics, saints and pilgrimages, 'with many other things touching the pestilent sect of Luther and Tyndale, by the one begone in Saxony and by the other laboured to be brought into England'. Tyndale is introduced on early pages with a tone of sorrow, on the heels of a defensive section about the burning of the New Testament at Paul's Cross, 'late translated in English by master William Huchyn, otherwise called master Tyndall, who was (as men say) well known ere he went over the sea, for a man of right good living, studious and well learned in scripture, and in divers places in England was very well liked and did great good with preaching . . .'[54]

But Tyndale, fatally, was with Luther in Wittenberg, writes More, 'and set certain glosses in the margin, framed for the setting forth of the ungracious sect'. (It must be asked whether More has seen Tyndale's translations for himself, as the only biblical glosses by Tyndale at this date are in the 1525 Cologne fragment, and one has to wear very special spectacles indeed to see much Lutheranism in the expository glosses there: the prologue is a different matter.) Tyndale's heresy—on the basis of those few words, and remarks in his *Mammon* and *Obedience*—is so all-pervasive that his New Testament is far beyond correction. Chapter 10 of the third book is as follows:

> The author sheweth that the translation of Tyndall was too bad to be amended.
>
> But yet he said that the faults might be by some good men amended, and then the book printed again if nothing letted [hindered] but that.
>
> Surely quod I if we go thereto, the faults be as ye see so many and so spread through the whole book, that likewise as it were as soon done to weave a new web of cloth as to sew up every hole in a net, so were it almost as little labour and less to translate the whole book all new, as to make in his translation so many changes as need must ere it were made good, besides this that there would no wise man I trow take the bread which he well wist was of his enemy's

hand once poisoned, though he saw his friend after scrape it never so clean.[55]

A few pages later, More returns to marriage. The Messenger has been foolish enough to say 'it would do well that priests should have wives'. More, delighted, ('Marry, quod I . . .') says that Luther and Tyndale say that and more.

> For Tyndall (whose books be nothing else in effect but the worst heresies picked out of Luther's works and Luther's worst words translated by Tyndall and put forth in Tyndall's own name) doth in his frantic book of obedience (wherein he raileth at large against all popes, against all kings, against all prelates, all priests, all religious, all the laws, all the saints, against the sacraments of Christ's church, against all virtuous works, against divine service, and finally against all things in effect that good is) in that book I say Tyndall holdeth that priests must have wives.[56]

More, of course, does not rail. And 'frantic' is a good word for that sentence, not least in its gross misrepresentation of Tyndale's *Obedience*.[57] The heinous crime is to say that priests should have wives. More sneers at Luther and Tyndale's claim to have understood Paul, in these words:

> . . . there was never none that had either the wit or the grace to perceive that great special commandment this fifteen hundred years, till now that God hath at last by revelation showed this high secret mystery to these two godly creatures Luther and Tyndall, lest that holy friar should have lost his marriage of that holy nun, and Tyndale that good marriage that I think him toward . . .[58]

By now, Tyndale is sodden in heresy, and for the rest of the book his name will recur until it dominates the last pages as someone worse than Luther. It is sorry arguing indeed when More has to return yet again to Luther's marriage (he mentions it under Luther's name a dozen times, and more generally elsewhere) to discredit Tyndale, and even invent a possible wife for Tyndale himself. That is the only mention anywhere in the Tyndale literature, and, as Tyndale was a priest, it is unlikely. More is arguing that the only reason Tyndale supports Paul in 1 Timothy 3:2–4 (given several pages in the *Obedience*) is because he is 'toward . . . some good marriage'. More is demeaning himself. He continues for a dozen columns on the subject of priests and marriage. After a long digression on the case of Hunne, he returns in chapter 16 of the third book to the issue of the English Bible, claiming, wrongly, that there were English Bibles before Wyclif, which could still be lawfully printed. The Messenger is allowed a vehement declaration of the people's dismay at the refusal of the Church to grant an English Bible, allowing More extensive play with the usual arguments that if the common people had it they would get it wrong— especially the Epistle to the Romans, 'containing such high difficulties as very few learned men can very well attain'.[59] (Romans contains the classic exposition of the New Testament doctrine of justification by faith alone.) It is good that the Bible should be translated into English, More explains, 'by some good catholic and well learned man', and then the bishops should undertake to buy copies and break them up and dole out small portions to trusted men, reclaiming them at their death.[60] Book 4, the last, turns most of its attention to Luther, often in highly-coloured exposition of his supposed evil effects, like causing the brutal burning of infants on the spit at the Sack of Rome. Heresy, for More, was bound to hold the hand of sedition and violence. (He does not mention here that according to Hall in his *Chronicle*, he himself had arrested and imprisoned, without accusers or witnesses, 'a great number', and tortured Tewkesbury and Bainham in his own Chelsea house.[61]) The scores of references to Tyndale in the book come to a climax here, as he is woven into the fabric of More's hatred of Luther. The final pages of vituperation show no advance of argument against Tyndale, and include quite basic misrepresentation of what he wrote in *Obedience*.[62] At bottom, Tyndale's offence has been to offer the people Paul in English, and translate four key New Testament words (*presbuteros, ekklesia, agape, metanoeo*) in their correct Greek meanings (senior, congregation, love, repent) instead of priest, church, charity and do penance.

Tyndale's Answer unto Sir T. Mores Dialogue

Although it means anticipating the story a little, it is best to deal here with Tyndale's reply, and More's replies to Tyndale's reply. Tyndale's *Answer* came in 1531, two years after More's *Dialogue*. More's next big reply, his *Confutation of Tyndale's Answer*, was published in 1532, and his *Apology*, devoting a good deal of attention to Tyndale, in 1533.

An Answer unto sir Thomas More's dialogue, made by William Tyndale continues on its title page, *First he declareth what the church is, and giveth a reason of certain words which Master More rebuketh in the translation of the New Testament. After that he answereth particularly unto every chapter which seemeth to have any appearance of truth through all his four books. Awake thou that sleepest, and Christ shall give thee light. Ephesians 5*. In this crisp small quarto volume, Tyndale goes at once to the heart of the matter, and stays there. Scripture is the test of the Church, both its doctrine and its practices. Let the reader judge. In a brief prologue he writes

> Judge therefore reader whether the pope with his be the church, whether their authority be above the scripture, whether all they teach without scripture be equal with the scripture, whether they have erred and not only whether they can . . . Judge whether it be possible that any good should come out of their dumb ceremonies and sacraments into thy soul. Judge their penance, pilgrimages, pardons, purgatory, praying to posts, dumb blessings, dumb absolutions, their dumb pattering, and howling, their dumb strange holy gestures, with all their dumb disguisings, their satisfactions and justifyings.[63]

The book proper begins, 'This word church hath divers significations'. The first is a place where Christians of old heard the word of God and sermon and prayers in their own tongue, unlike the current 'voices without significations and buzzings howlings and cryings as it were the hallooing of foxes or baiting of bears . . .' Next, it is properly a congregation, with an elder not a priest, (Tyndale has moved on from 'senior'), united in love not charity, experiencing favour not grace, knowledge not confession, repentance not penance, going on to tackle the question 'whether the church were before the gospel or the gospel before the church' and 'whether the apostles left aught unwritten that is of necessity to be believed', and 'whether the church can err'. Tyndale hammers home the points, the central ones at issue—and we are still only a few pages in. After the Platonic vapourings of More, however charming they may have been found in places, to read this is to drink at a pure and full spring. Moreover, here is the advance in theology that was so missing in More. On many pages are New Testament doctrines, supported by quotations, like the long exhilarating account of faith in the section 'Whether the church can err or no'.

> . . . Christ's elect church is the whole multitude of all repenting sinners that believe in Christ, and put all their trust and confidence in the mercy of God, feeling in their hearts that God for Christ's sake loveth them, and will be or rather is merciful unto them, and forgiveth them their sins of which they repent: and that he forgiveth them also the motions unto sin, of which they fear lest they should thereby be drawn into sin again. And this faith they have without all respect of their own deservings, yea, and for none other cause than

that the merciful truth of God the father, which cannot lie, hath so promised and so sworn.

And this faith and knowledge is everlasting life, and by this we be born anew and made the sons of God . . . And this faith is the mother of all truth . . . And this faith is the foundation laid of the apostles and prophets . . . And this faith is the rock whereon Christ built his congregation . . . And against the rock of this faith can no sin, no hell, no devil, no lies, nor error prevail.[64]

These pages on faith, like many others, are an anthology of scriptural points. Once again with Tyndale, the reader who opens this book knowing nothing of the New Testament finishes it knowing a lot. The contrast with More's *Dialogue* is obvious: the reader finishes that book knowing a great deal about the amusing, richly stored, clever, long-winded, devious, malevolent mind of Thomas More. As in the *Obedience* especially, Tyndale makes clear that his aim is to show the faults of the Church, to purge not to destroy. He does not want to burn anyone alive, not even Master More. The first part of Tyndale's book is a general survey of New Testament doctrines as travestied, or replaced, by the Pope and his Church. The second is a systematic rebuttal of More's *Dialogue* book by book, and when necessary chapter by chapter and line by line. The points are good. More does not come off well. They are sharply expressed—Tyndale has by some way the better command of English—and often with brevity, like his opening remark about More's book 1: 'In the first chapter, to begin the book withal, to bring you good luck and to give you assay or a taste what truth shall follow, he feigneth a letter sent from no man.'[65] *Touché*! From the fourteenth chapter of the fourth book onwards, Tyndale frequently drops into direct dialogue, as in the following, which is the whole of Tyndale on book 4, the eighth chapter: (the names 'M. More' and 'Tyndale' stand in the margin against the initial letters)

M: What good deed will he do, that believeth Martin [Luther] how that we have no free will to do any good with the help of grace? **T**: O poet [feigner] without shame.

M: What harm shall he care to forbear, that believeth Luther, how God alone, without our will, worketh all the mischief that they do? **T**: O natural son of the father of all lies.

M: What shall he care how long he live in sin that believeth Luther, that he shall after this life feel neither good nor evil, in body nor soul, until the day of doom? **T**: Christ and his apostles taught no other: but warned to look for Christ's coming again every hour:

which coming again because ye believe will never be, therefore have ye feigned that other merchandise.

M: Martin's books be open, if ye will not believe us. **T**: Nay ye have shut them up, and therefore be bold to say what ye lust.

M: They live as they teach, and teach as they live. **T**: But neither teach nor live as other lie on them.[66]

More is speaking his own words as printed in his *Dialogue*. The effect is of his immediate direct presence, unlike the feigned-conversation-with-a-secret-messenger-of-a-non-existent-friend apparatus of More's *Dialogue*. Tyndale's method is a one-to-one duel with rapiers.

In that the reader comes away knowing Church practices in the light of the New Testament the enterprise was valuable. But one can only lament the necessity. Tyndale, as Mozley puts it, 'had in no way meddled with More, and indeed had not hitherto even mentioned his name'.[67] Yet here he was, laid into by More as a man dishonest, evil in intent, an inadequate Grecian to boot, mis-translating the New Testament, out of malice. Tyndale can only have wondered what had happened to the Christian humanist who had been so scathing in *Utopia* about prejudice, the scholar who should have recognised a fine piece of work in his English New Testament, carrying as it did the torch of the Greek and new Latin of his friend Erasmus. By 1530, More had lived in personal service to his King, been Speaker of the House of Commons, and received a knighthood. He had then changed from merely assisting with the controversy with Luther to leading the van. Then within weeks of the publication of the *Dialogue* he 'received the chancellorship of England . . . which no layman had held for hundreds of years' as Mozley puts it.[68] It was hard for the exiled band of English reformers, and their threatened associates in England, not to feel that More had sold himself.

Tyndale's personal anger against More is because of that, and because he is upholding from his position of unique privilege

> the practice of our fleshly spiritualty and their ways by which they have walked above eight hundred years: how they stablish their lies first with falsifying the scripture, then through corrupting with their riches whereof they have infinite treasure in store, and last of all with the sword.[69]

Tyndale's language is strong: it could not be other. It feels more powerful even than More's for two main reasons. The first is that he knows, and he knows that More knows, that one of his premises, at least, was right: the Church was indeed corrupt. More will not admit it. With Erasmus years before, the witty game of mocking the failings of the Church included some recognition that all was very far from well. Tyndale knows his Erasmus, has translated the *Enchiridion*, and knows the tone. Now More simply reiterates through clenched teeth that the Church cannot possibly err. He has sold himself to a lie. 'What shows what faces and contrary pretences are made, and all to establish them in their theft falsehood and damnable lies, and to gather them together for to contrive subtilty, to oppress the truth and to stop the light and to keep all still in darkness.'[70]

Throughout the book, Tyndale has Scripture, strongly quoted, on his side: it is gospel Christianity that is condemning the church. His second strength is rhythmic, with a brilliance that More can rarely manage. Simply to mark the stresses in that last phrase, from 'to oppress the truth . . .' is to watch Tyndale's skill in making running stresses, 'press . . . truth . . . stop . . . light' in order to build to the three long main stresses, 'keep all still', climaxing with the unstressed 'in' and the dactyl 'darkness'. It is speech-based, only slightly heightened, which asks to be spoken aloud, and which arrives at a most satisfying conclusion—as his argument is meant to do. This craftsmanly skill is used throughout his *Answer* to press hard on More's insistence that the Church cannot err. His strength is often in direct relation to Scripture. How do we know what scripture is without the guidance of an infallible Church? Tyndale begins his answer 'Who taught the eagles to spy out their prey? Even so the children of God spy out their father, and Christ's elect spy out their lord, and trace out the paths of his feet and follow. . .'[71] The rhythms of Tyndale's righteous anger can be especially dramatic in the use of imagined figures, as for example in the last pages of his answer to More's first book of his *Dialogue*, where 'little flock' (the phrase is from Luke 12) quietly confesses Christ and is roared at by 'the great multitude' who are violently active against it. All fourteen long paragraphs are worth quoting, but there is space only for the end.

God saith. If thou believe St Johns gospel thou shalt be saved: and not for the bearing of it about thee with so many crosses, or for the observing of any such observances.

God for thy bitter passion, roar they out by and by, what an heretic is this. I tell thee that holy church need to allege no scripture for them for they have the Holy Ghost which inspireth them ever secretly so that they cannot err, whatsoever they say, do, or ordain . . . thou art a strong heretic, and worthy to be burnt. And then he is excommunicate out of the church. If little flock fear not that bug then they go straight unto the king, And it like your grace perilous people and seditious and even enough to destroy your

realm if ye see not to them betimes. They be so obstinate and tough
that they will not be converted and rebellious against God and the
ordinances of his holy church. And how much more shall they so be
against your grace if they increase and grow a multitude. They will
pervert all, and surely make new laws, and either subdue your grace
unto them or rise against you. And then goeth part of little flock to
pot and the rest scatter. Thus hath it ever been, and shall ever be: let
no man therefore deceive himself.[72]

Tyndale made no more reply.[73] He had other things to do. We could
wish that the time he had taken to write his *Answer* had been given to
extending his Hebrew translation, so that he would have gone sooner
beyond Deuteronomy, or later beyond 2 Chronicles into the poetic
books of the Old Testament, which he did not reach before he was
martyred.

More's Confutation of Tyndale's Answer

More could not leave his task. He published early in 1532 the first
three books of his enormous *Confutation*, and a year later the remaining six books (of which the fifth was an attack on Robert
Barnes).

Approaching these half million words in hundreds of grim pages
again, the heart sinks. More has lost all sense of how matters might be
ordered. There is desperation in the very length: the feeling is that
unless he reiterates on almost every page the entire case against
Tyndale, real or imagined, and lashes Tyndale with fury (he is 'a hell-
hound in the kennel of the devil' and scores of similar things, of which
'an abominable beast' is one of the more controlled) then the entire
Church in the western world will collapse at once. Some of the more
highly-coloured parts of the *Dialogue* were unedifying: the *Confutation*
is almost unreadable. What has happened to More's literary judgement?
Not to mention his common sense? Did he not see how damaging it
was to his own cause to write at such length so relentlessly? Even
Nicholas Harpsfield, More's biographer, writing some twenty-five
years later, noted the frantic quality of the pursuit: 'And Tyndall, being
thus brought often times to a bay and utter distress, he scuddeth in and
out like a hare that hath twenty brace of greyhounds after her, and
were afeard at every foot to be snatched up'.[74] The editor of the
modern three-volume Yale edition of the *Confutation* encapsulates
clearly.

More's method of confutation consists in quoting Tyndale's text in gobbets, seldom more than one paragraph at a time and often merely a single sentence, then overwhelming it with a varied barrage of polemical artillery: painstaking logic in isolating and reconstructing premises, copious invention of arguments to bolster the case of the opposition, biblical exegesis, invective and *ad hominem* barbs, patristic documentation, heckling, legalistic analogy, occasional ribaldry, testimony of saints and martyrs, cautionary reference to past heretics, conciliar pronouncements, theological distinctions, mocking repetition, together with countless variations on these practices.[75]

The same editor notes More's scrupulous accuracy in quoting Tyndale,[76] of which More himself boasts, incidentally. The matter does not quite stand up so cleanly, however, and More can be found misrepresenting: perhaps, as that editor generously observes, More is 'suffering from polemical battle fatigue.'[77] More can grossly mistranslate when he wants to. Defending the erroneous doctrine that Church traditions came directly from the Apostles, and thus Christ, and thus were of more authority than mere Scripture, he quotes Paul in 1 Corinthians 11, one of the most familiar passages in all Christendom, at the moment of the words used at the Eucharist. More writes, from the Vulgate, 'Ego enim accepi a domino quod et tradidi vobis'. He then translates it 'For I have received that thing of our Lord by tradition without writing, the which I have also delivered unto you'.[78] The crucial words there are 'without writing'. They do not appear in Paul in Latin, nor Greek, nor anywhere in Paul in Latin nor Greek nor any other language. More has inserted them. So much for saintly accuracy.

Another editor comments on the 'thirty-seven precious pages' at the start of the *Confutation* 'of documentary information and interpretation of the contemporary religious situation in England'. This sounds hopeful. He goes on, however, 'More then draws upon his classified knowledge of the leading English reformers to impugn their motives, expose their cowardice, and identify them as religious and political criminals—thereby deflating any pretensions of heroism.'[79]

The biographer of William Tyndale has to find a means of treating the almost two thousand heavy pages of More's attack on him (one thousand and thirty-four pages in the modern Yale edition of the *Confutation* alone), the mountainous bulk of his writing in English. This particular By-Path Meadow is alluring because it tells us so much about Sir Thomas More, that famous, clever, complicated, mocking

man. Edward Hall in his *Chronicle* of 1548, writing thirteen years after
More's beheading, goes out of his way to stress his habit of mockery:

> I cannot tell whether I should call him a foolish wise man or a wise
> foolishman, for undoubtedly he beside his learning, had a great
> wit, but it was so mingled with taunting and mocking, that it
> seemed to them that best knew him, that he thought nothing to
> be well spoken except he had ministered some mock in the
> communication . . .[80]

Yet this trait in More lost its humanist, Erasmian lightness and went
sour, when he wrote against heretics, from Luther on. He was so
desperate to destroy heresy that what balance he once had was eaten
away. Theologically, his whole attack can be boiled down to his
objection to Tyndale's translation of four or five words: Tyndale translating *ekklesia* as 'congregation', and so on, was of course at root
offensive because More had to defend the orthodox doctrine that the
Church came first and Scripture followed. Why did his literary nature,
at least, so change? The enigma remains fascinating, though By-Path
Meadow has become a bog. One can't escape curious finds: why in the
Confutation does he return so often to Luther's marriage? The reader
comes to feel that whatever More is discussing, he has to come back
to the monk and nun ('friars and nuns creeping to bed together . . .
monk's marriages . . .'[81]). The cause was lechery, he says. He made his
point. He cannot leave it, but goes on and on rubbing the itch of his
obsession, countless times.

Take this passage from Book three of the *Confutation*, typical of the
whole:

> And he [God] shall not send such fond fellows as would be so
> shameless without any miracle showed, to bid all the world believe
> them upon their bare word, in the understanding of holy scripture,
> against all holy saints and cunning doctors of fifteen hundred years
> passed, and bear men in hand that all is open and plain, and prove
> it by nothing else but by that there is no place of holy scripture
> so hard, but that them self can expound it in such wise that it shall
> serve them shameful for jesting and railing against god and all
> good men, against all good works, against all religion, fasting,
> prayer, devotion, saints, ceremonies and sacraments, and to set forth
> vice in boldness of faith, and to praise lechery between friars
> and nuns, and call it matrimony, and thus make mocks of holy
> scripture solemnly, with such open shameless abominable blasphe-
> my, that if the zeal of god were among men that should be, such

railing ribalds that so mock with holy scripture, should at every such exposition have an hot iron thrust through their blasphemous tongues.[82]

The construction of that sentence has got totally got out of hand. So has the scholarship, in that Tyndale most certainly did not 'rail' against God and 'all good men, all good works, all religion . . .' and so on. So, quite dreadfully, has the feeling: the final words are plainly horrific, and suggest a kind of madness.

A biographer of Tyndale has to write about More because, to put it crudely, even beyond the *Dialogue* the name Tyndale appears several times on each one of the thousand pages of the *Confutation*, and many of the *Apology*. Proportion, however, has to be kept. Historians sometimes write as if there were six main documents in More's controversy with Tyndale, three from Tyndale and three from More, rendering them equal.[83] On the one hand, such a summary does not mention the disproportionate lengths of More, whose close on three quarters of a million words against Tyndale stand against Tyndale's eighty thousand in his *Answer*. On the other, such calculation makes the first document in the controversy Tyndale's New Testament, which is downright misleading. The first document has to be More's *Dialogue*, the appearance of which must have surprised Tyndale. The second is Tyndale's *Answer*. The third and fourth are More's *Confutation* and *Apology*. There is no sixth, as the final work in which More is attacked, *The Supper of the Lord*, is not by Tyndale.[84] The puzzle of More's curious nature, is however, a distraction, almost an irrelevance, in the story of William Tyndale. We must register what it is about Tyndale that is of special interest in a chapter on More, and then move on.

First, an oddity. Tyndale is 'a hell-hound in the kennel of the devil', 'a drowsy drudge drinking deep in the devil's dregs', 'a new Judas', 'worse than Sodom and Gomorrah', 'an idolater and devil worshipper, worse than a Mahometan', 'discharging a filthy foam of blasphemies out of his brutish beastly mouth' and much else—but the offensive cloacal imagery used so strikingly against Luther is missing. One wonders why. The idea that the sewer was Luther's own does not explain More's obssessive anality in his Latin: and in any case Luther's most famous remark in that direction has been much mis-treated: he was making the point that redeeming incarnation cannot exclude Christ from the privy.[85] Does it make all the difference that More is writing in English not Latin, his language for all his anti-Luther writing? If so, why? English was a much more informal language, and that fact would lend occasion for amused scatology. There are indeed three small mild remarks in Tyndale's *Practice of Prelates*, and one in the *Obedience*, which his Victorian editor, Henry Walter, had to omit, or not explain, out of modesty.[86] Did More's commission, whether from himself or not, deliberately preclude such methods, or was it something below conscious control? The incessant monks-sleeping-with-nuns references do suggest that he wrote unguardedly. Less superficially, the size and extreme ferocity of More's attacks on him help us to see the height of Tyndale's shadow in 'Establishment' England. Tyndale was a heretic to be greatly feared. Any means, fair or foul, were justified to preserve the Church and the realm from his effects. His books, his followers, he himself, must be burned with proper zeal—something to which More looks forward, appallingly.[87]

The controversy revealed the depth of the chasm between Tyndale and the Church in the early 1530s. Tyndale wrote from the New Testament that the Christian life was an inner thing. Receiving Christ in the heart, through the gift of faith, was a releasing experience, energising the whole being. Everything was transformed for the Christian in that conversion, as all the New Testament made witness. Moreover, a large number of Church practices, in the light of that individual experience, appeared either irrelevant or obstructive. Not so, said More. Faith means belief in the dogmas of the Church formulated, discussed and defended these fifteen hundred years by the fathers; dogmas and practices which were established and secretly handed down by word of mouth from Christ through the Apostles even before Scripture was written. God is only in his Church, which is thus incapable of error. To assert otherwise in any way is literally damnable.

What the controversy does for us today, when we can begin to take it in, is to lay out the two entire tapestries of conflicting belief, spread out on either side. On the level of scholarship, Tyndale was right about Scripture and More was wrong. The doctrine of the secret unwritten tradition superior to Scripture could not survive. Our interest has to be more than historical, however, for before the end of the century public events and new understandings were to change utterly the religious nature of our own land, much of Europe, and presently the larger globe. The changes began just at this point, with Luther's Ninety-five Theses affecting Germany and northern Europe, and Tyndale's Bible addressing the English-speaking world.

The revolution that Tyndale began was not just that, in the teeth of the most ferocious opposition he gave the people the Bible in the mother tongue: the whole New Testament, in all its comprehensiveness and integrity, and half the Old Testament, and so soon after his death the whole word of God available in English. Those deeds opened the gates of the flood of biblical knowledge which has been freely available to us ever since.[88] The records of the burnings, of books and men and women, tell the hard practice of the opposition: More's writings against Tyndale spell out the theory—spill out might be a better verb. It is impossible, writes More over and over again, to understand the Bible without the guidance of the infallible Church. Scripture, explains More, belongs to the Pope and the hierarchy of the Church. It is interpreted by the living voice of the Church, which interprets it and uses it. With that last statement Tyndale eagerly agreed. The difference is that for Tyndale the living voice of the Church is the congregation of believers, as he finds that the New Testament explains that it was from the very beginning, at Pentecost, so soon after the resurrection of Christ. Scripture belongs, writes Tyndale, to the whole body of Christian people, guided by the Holy Spirit in their congregation, and not to a few men or a line of men. Thus it can be reinterpreted in every generation. At that point is revealed a fundamental, irreconcilable difference. Saying that Scripture can be, indeed has to be, reinterpreted in every generation, Tyndale is modern, and is looking forward—and releasing theology. More looks backward. Tyndale can (against Luther) keep the New Testament canon intact, sticking up for the Epistle of James. But he feels free to challenge the attribution of the Epistle to the Hebrews to Paul, in the light of later knowledge, without lessening its authority. More is shocked by that attitude. Yet Tyndale's argument, expressed a few years later in his prologue to Hebrews in his 1534 New Testament, is that as 'it agreeth to all the rest of the scripture'[89] it belongs, whoever wrote it. In that he is right, both in procedure, taking Scripture in its integrity, and in conclusion.

Tyndale angered More in insisting that the Church of their day was not the true Church of Christ, because it had abandoned the teaching of the gospel, and, worse, persecuted those who did preach that gospel. In place of a Church made up of the hearts of men and women redeemed by Christ, Tyndale saw only a contemporary Church containing nothing but a host of outward actions—words in Latin, gestures, rituals, ceremonies, worship of objects, pilgrimages, tithes, and many more. At this point is another irreconcilable division. Tyndale saw an inward Church, More an outward. More made whole countrysides of hay with this, asking how you could meet an invisible Church, and pointing out that Christ's body needs a body. In that he was right. But Tyndale's point would not need to have been made had the very visible Church shown more sign of understanding the necessity of inward spiritual life, and not been so externally, and very visibly, corrupt.

The third irreconcilable clash follows from this. Tyndale argues that works are only of value to God when they come from a believing heart which expresses the gift of faith outwardly as naturally as the tree bears fruit. More insistently mis-reports Tyndale as saying that works are of no value at all. The two men stand on either side of the street and shout at each other. The difference is so great that they can never meet. Yet Tyndale's own deeds bore out his belief. The Church was reformed, by strange ways indeed, and from the outside, in spite of More.

Both men died martyrs, close in time, and curiously honoured in being saved the extremes of torture at their death—More was not disembowelled, and Tyndale was strangled before the flames were lit. But their legacy, in relation to each other, has been totally opposite. More gave us three quarters of a million words of scarcely readable prose attacking Tyndale. Tyndale outraged More by giving us the Bible in English, England's greatest contribution to the world for nearly five hundred years.

Part 4

HEBREW AND THE OLD AND NEW TESTAMENTS

Chapter 11

TYNDALE'S PENTATEUCH

Some time in January 1530 there began to appear in England, smuggled in from Antwerp, copies of a well-made little book, again printed by Hoochstraten of Antwerp (as 'Hans Luft at Marburg' again) the title-page of which simply announced *The first book of Moses called Genesis*, and nothing more. The next page began a prologue with the words 'W.T. To the Reader' so there could be no doubt about its origins. A few glances would have shown that the volume was a printed translation of the first five books of the Old Testament, Genesis, Exodus, Leviticus, Numbers and Deuteronomy, each with a separate prologue, each with a sparse scattering of marginal notes, and one (Exodus) with a dozen full-page pictures. Unlike the 1526 New Testament, *The Wicked Mammon* and *The Obedience*, the body of this volume was printed in Roman type, with only Genesis and Numbers in familiar Bastard black-letter. The differences suggest that each part was printed to be issued and transported to England, separately. This may well turn out to have been part of what happened: of the dozen or so copies of Tyndale's *Pentateuch* that have survived, most are complete. One copy, in the Bodleian, is of Genesis only, and one, in New York, is of everything except Genesis.

A reader in London going, for example, straight to the beginning of the text would find: 'In the beginning God created heaven and earth. The earth was void and empty, and darkness was upon the deep, and the spirit of God moved upon the water. Then God said: let there be light and there was light.' A learned reader would have been used to 'In principio creavit Deus coelum et terram. Terra autem erat inanis et vacua, et tenebrae erant super faciem abyssi, et spiritus Dei ferebatur super aquas. Dixitque Deus: Fiat lux! et facta est lux'. A reader with a manuscript copy of one of the Wycliffite versions made a hundred and fifty years before would have known those words as 'In the first made

God of nought heaven and earth. The earth forsooth was vain within and void, and darknesses were upon the face of the sea: and the Spirit of God was born upon the waters. And God said, Be made light; and made is light.' In the revised slightly later form we call Wyclif B it became 'In the beginning God made of nought heaven and earth. Forsooth the earth was idle and void, and darknesses were on the face of depth: and the Spirit of the Lord was born on the waters. And God said, Light be made, and light was made.'

Tyndale's Genesis was something strikingly new. He was translating not the Latin, but the Hebrew. And he was writing recognisable English. Simply registering the changes in the English language from Chaucer's day to Tyndale's in no way explains the difference between 'Be made light; and made is light' and 'let there be light and there was light'.

To take another example of how new this book was: the reader in 1530 would see that at the end of Genesis, as at several other points, there are pages devoted to 'A table expounding certain words'. Among the unfamiliar words like 'Abrech' or 'Siloh' or 'Zaphnath paenea' is 'Jehovah', with the explanation

> Jehovah is God's name, neither is any creature so called. And is as much to say as one that is of himself, and dependeth of nothing. Moreover as oft as thou seest LORD in great letters (except there be any error in the printing) it is in Hebrew *Jehovah*, thou that art or he that is.

So, early in Exodus 6 is '. . . I am the Lord . . . in my name Jehovah . . .' This was indeed new. In Hebrew, the four-consonant sacred name was not to be spoken, so when the vowel-points were added it was given those of *Adonai* (Lord), indicating that the latter was to be substituted. Renaissance scholars of Hebrew thought that those vowels were to be understood as belonging to the sacred tetragrammaton itself, producing *Jehovah*. (A modern attempt to reconsruct the pronunciation of the tetragrammaton is *Yahweh*.) *Jehovah* was first written in a Latin text of 1516. Fourteen years later, Tyndale incorporated and explained the name in a text designed to be read by ordinary, un-Latined people. This must have been startling. Just as the Vulgate had *nomen meum Adonai*, the Lollard versions of Exodus 6 had 'my name Adonay' and (in Wyclif B) 'my great name Adonai', with, in some texts of the latter, a marginal note: '*Adonay*, that is, tetragrammaton, that signifieth God's being nakedly, without consideration to creature'. (That note must be honoured as an attempt to explain the inexplicable in a few words.) Readers of Tyndale's Genesis in England must have felt that in more than one sense they were meeting the God of the Old Testament for the first time. It is little wonder that the covenant made with that God became so central to the theology of so many of them.

To take a third example from the story of the Fall of Man: Genesis 3 begins in the Vulgate 'sed et serpens erat callidior cunctis animantibus terrae, quae fecerat Dominus Deus. Qui dixit ad mulierem . . .' The earlier Lollard versions had variations on 'But and the adder was feller than any lifers of the earth, the which made the Lord God. The which said to the woman . . .' which is the Vulgate put into English by someone, it must be felt, with a shaky hold on even late fourteenth-century English. The second, Wyclif B, version is better, with roughly 'But and the serpent was feller than all the living beasts of the earth, which the Lord God had made. Which serpent said to the woman . . .' Tyndale's 'But the serpent was subtler than all the beasts of the field which the Lord God had made, and said unto the woman . . .' speaks even to the late twentieth century. This is not only because with minor changes it is taken into the 1611 Authorised Version, and is even recognisably behind such modern versions as the 1989 Revised English Bible: but because, as before, it both translates the original Hebrew instead of the later Latin, and is in a recognisable English. Scholars of the Hebrew text can see the Hebrew forms still present—for example the terse running-on of 'and said', rather than starting a new clause, as the Latin does. Modern speakers of English recognise the vocabulary, syntax and rhythms. 'Serpent' gives no problem. 'Subtler', it could be argued, feels as modern as the Authorised Version's 'more subtle'. 'The beasts of the field', while good modern English syntax ('the state of the economy', 'the collapse of the health service', 'the fall of the government') is in its 'the+noun+of+the+noun' both a fair rendering of the Hebrew grammatical form known as the construct, and an invention of Tyndale's for that form whenever it occurs. It is a matter of the history of the English language that we have that arrangement, the+noun+of+the+noun, so available for a slightly more formal use, making a distinction between 'the Prime Minister's resignation' and 'the resignation of the Prime Minister', between 'Abraham's seed' in John 8:37, and 'the works of Abraham' two verses later. It is a distinction that goes back to Tyndale for its origins.

Yet it is what happens next in Genesis 3 that marks the force of this small book, so new in 1530, so powerful in its impact. The Vulgate has 'Cur praecepit vobis Deus, ut non comederetis de omni ligno Paradisi?' Which in both Lollard versions comes out as 'Why commanded God to you, that ye should not eat of each tree of paradise?'

Tyndale smites between the eyes with 'Ah, sir, that God hath said, ye shall not eat of all manner trees of the garden'. This serpent is not one to ask questions, as the Latin makes him do. He does not demean himself to ask why God has done something: he knows 'that God hath said'. There is even a hint of North Country in the (non-Hebrew) sense of 'that', [Latin *ille*] like saying of someone as 'that Jack, he does go on so'. He introduces himself to the woman with the comic mock courtesy of 'Ah, sir . . .'[1] She, thus flattered and insinuated into, replies with garrulous, and unasked-for, explanation, though no question has been made. 'And the woman said unto the serpent, of the fruit of the trees in the garden we may eat, but of the fruit of the tree that is in the midst of the garden (said God) see that ye eat not, and see that ye touch it not: lest ye die.'

Tyndale, exactly like the Hebrew, is raw, comic and tragic all at once.[2] There is a dreadful human inevitability about all this. Two characters, 'serpent' and 'woman', are present, lightly sketched, but fearfully familiar, and not at all safely hidden behind the screen of a slightly remote language special to 'sacred scripture'. What happens next marks Tyndale's specialness. The Authorised Version, as is well known, has 'And the serpent said unto the woman, Ye shall not surely die'. The Vulgate has 'Dixit autem serpens ad mulierem: Nequaquam morte moriemini', and the Lollard versions, first 'Forsooth the adder said to the woman, Through death ye shall not die', and in Wyclif B, 'Forsooth the serpent said to the woman, Ye shall not die by death'. Tyndale's 'Then said the serpent unto the woman: tush ye shall not die', catches the immediate and sophisticated dismissiveness. This serpent waves away the consequences as being beyond any consideration with a flick of the hand (and the best gloves and an elegant cane, no doubt).[3]

Tyndale's translation then continues to transmit the rawness of the original Hebrew. Where the Authorised Version makes the Fall of Man happen at the end of a longish sentence with (ultimately Latin) subordinate clauses, ('And when . . . and that . . .'), Tyndale understands the force of the Hebrew conjunction *waw* to make successive sentences which give the necessary forward movement of monotonous repetition and therefore tragic inevitability. There are no contingencies of 'when' here.

And the woman saw that it was a good tree to eat of and lusty unto the eyes and a pleasant tree for to make wise. And took of the fruit of it and ate, and gave unto her husband also with her, and he ate. And the eyes of both of them were opened, that they understood how that they were naked.

Scripture as a Whole Book

These opening chapters of Genesis are the first translations—not just the first printed, but the first translations—from Hebrew into English. This needs to be emphasised. Not only was the Hebrew language only known in England in 1529 and 1530 by, at the most, a tiny handful of scholars in Oxford and Cambridge, and quite possibly by none; that there was a language called Hebrew at all, or that it had any connection whatsoever with the Bible, would have been news to most of the ordinary population. Religion was in Latin: the Mass was in Latin; all the other services, like baptism, were in Latin; everything the priest did was in Latin; the Psalms in the Mass were in Latin; the Bible-readings in the services, such as they were, were in Latin; the Bible, when visible, was a big Latin volume; some priests, and most laymen, had only a few words of Latin, if that. The Bible was thought of only by a very few as a whole and complete thing, referring throughout, backwards and forwards, not just to itself from Genesis to Revelation, but also from the Creation to the end of history—an entity.

Now here in 1530 was Genesis, from the Hebrew, in English, in a form that fitted a pocket. Here, instead of 'faciamus ei adjutorium simile sibi' or even, in the first Lollard Bibles, first 'make we help like him' and then, in Wyclif B, 'make we to him and help like to himself', the reader of Tyndale finds 'I will make him an helper to bear him company'. Those stories of Adam and Eve, and of Cain and Abel, of Noah, Abraham and Isaac, Jacob and Esau, Joseph and his brothers, some of which would have been in part familiar in outline, by different routes, from references in sermons, from stained-glass windows, and sometimes from the mystery plays of the guilds, could now be read in full, in a way which made the text speak. So could all the other, less familiar, parts of Genesis. But more importantly, Genesis was followed by the rest of the Pentateuch, so that more of the whole story from Creation to the discovery of the Second Law (the literal meaning of Deuteronomy) was available, and not only the older and newer laws themselves, but a full rounding-out of the meaning of the covenant made by a nation with God, as all five books could be studied complete.

We note again that the interrelation of Bible books was, for the reformers, an essential part of the reading of Scripture. Genesis, of course, had always been understood as standing in a special place, starting as it does with the God-given accounts both of the Creation and the Fall of Man—both of them the very foundation of theology. Moreover, as the first book in the world (as it was thought to be), by the world's first author, Moses, it can express something important

about Scripture, that is, about religion with a book at the heart.
Genesis had always been pre-eminent, and whole libraries of commentary were written, almost on every word, as scholars of Milton are
aware.[4] But in the Hebrew Bible, Genesis is followed by Exodus and
Leviticus, with some narrative (of Moses and Pharaoh, the plagues and
the exodus, principally) but long stretches of given laws, most compre-
hensively in Leviticus. That book is followed by Numbers, introduced
by Tyndale with 'In the second and third book they received the law.
And in this fourth they begin to work and to practise'. The last book
is Deuteronomy, this time introduced by Tyndale with the words:

> This is a book worthy to be read in day and night and never to be
> out of hands. For it is the most excellent of all the books of Moses.
> It is easy also and light and a very pure gospel that is to wete, a
> preaching of faith and love: deducing the love to God out of faith,
> and the love of a man's neighbour out of the love of God.

For Jews, the five books together make up the *Torah* [literally
'teaching'], the Law, that unique relationship between God and his
people, 'the children of Israel'; the point at which everything begins.
For Christian readers, the Law is also the essential starting point, but
now under a new covenant in Christ (the 'New Testament'). In his
teaching, Jesus himself insisted on the keeping of the Law (see Matthew 5, 'I am not come to destroy... but to fulfil...'), though the
significance of his work as well as his words extends far beyond the
children of Israel. That beating heart of Christian theology, Paul's
justification by faith, is located in a body which has been re-born, as
Paul makes clear, from an imprisonment in the God-given Law to the
full daylight of the new God-given redemption in Christ. For the
Christian, Tyndale insisted, it is essential to be able to study the whole
of the Hebrew Law in order to understand what Christ did with it.
Tyndale understood how much Hebrew there is in parts of the New
Testament, and not just when the Gospel writers or Paul or Peter are
quoting the Old. That he had found in the New Testament a
Hebraized Greek is something to which he will return, in the preface
to his revised, 1534, New Testament. Moreover, Tyndale discovered
that Hebrew goes wonderfully into English—better than into Latin,
and better even than Latin goes into English. All that he did in
translating Hebrew rings with that discovery, which is very much his
own, and one which only ignorance and prejudice have prevented the
English nation from properly praising.

Tyndale, and Tyndale alone (with his one or two occasional helpers
in Antwerp like George Joye, or in Hamburg like Miles Coverdale,

whose Hebrew was not more than basic, if that), was engaged in a full-scale work of translating Hebrew into English. His discovery of the happy linguistic marriage of the two languages, though not *quite* as important as Newton's discovery of the principle of universal gravitation, was still of high significance for the history of western Christian theology, language and literature—a high claim, but not difficult to support, though the work on it has largely still to be done: the immense influence of Hebrew forms on the English language has not been properly recognised even now. Not just the Hebrew construct as the+noun+of+the+noun. Nor in that mass of familiar phrases now often thought to be proverbial, like 'let there be light', 'am I my brother's keeper?', 'in the land [of] Nod', 'men of renown', 'the imagination of man's heart', 'every man's hand against him', 'old and well stricken in age', 'turned into a pillar of salt', 'corn . . . in Egypt', 'bring my grey head with sorow unto the grave', 'the fat of the land', 'unstable as water', to take ready examples only from Tyndale's Genesis. The Hebrew method of story-telling even in high moments, in successive phrases linked by 'and', is quite unlike the locking and hanging of clauses, ('When . . .', '. . . who . . .', '. . . that . . .') from Latin or Greek high narrative, and is deep in English narrative.

All Old Testament English versions descend from Tyndale; even of the books of the Old Testament which he did not reach. Miles Coverdale, who first gave us printed in English the second half of the Old Testament, had worked with Tyndale, and imitated him. Coverdale knew less Hebrew than Tyndale, but when he came to translate the great books of poetry that make up the second part of the Old Testament, like Job, the Psalms and the Song of Songs, and all the prophets, using to help him Luther's German version, Pagninus's new Latin version of the Hebrew, Olivetan's French version and the Greek of the Septuagint, he was able to make a Hebrew-into-English that was not too jarring a contrast with Tyndale's work. This can be tested. Coverdale's Psalms, beloved of the Anglican Church in its Prayer Book services until the last decades of the twentieth century, though sometimes clumsy and occasionally dated ('thou hast holp the runagates in his scarceness'), have always felt to be related to those parts of the Old Testament which came through to the Authorised Version from Tyndale, so that a congregation would find the set Old Testament lessons linguistically at least cousins, if not sisters, of Coverdale's Psalms. Tyndale's discovery, which is what it was, that Hebrew and English fitted so well together, he explained in his preface to the *Obedience*. There he was arguing, it may be remembered, that Scripture in Bible times had been in the mother tongue, and that St Jerome translated the Bible into his mother tongue. 'Why may not we also?' In fact, Greek agrees more with the English than with the Latin.

> And the properties of the Hebrew tongue agreeth a thousand times more with the English than with the Latin. The manner of speaking is both one, so that in a thousand places thou needest not but to translate it into the English word for word, when thou must seek a compass [go round about] in the Latin, and yet shall have much work to translate it well-favouredly, so that it have the same grace and sweetness, sense and pure understanding with it in the Latin, and as it hath in the Hebrew. A thousand parts better may it be translated into the English, than into the Latin.[5]

Tyndale quantifies it—'agreeth a thousand times more . . .' 'in a thousand places . . . a thousand parts better . . .' Even allowing for rhetorical devices of *hyperbole* and *repetitio* to strengthen his point, the reader must still find Tyndale's case good. Those words were written by someone who knows the work of translating from Hebrew into English very well indeed. The properties of the languages agree. So similar are they that they work over the same range, and match word for word 'in a thousand places'—that is an indication not just of frequency of occasions when they match, but of the variety of material they can cover together. The Pentateuch starts majestically with the Creation but, as we saw above, soon moves with the story of the Fall into raw dialogue and event. Genesis contains a wide spectrum of Hebrew styles, which a translation has to match, if it is not to flatten everything out to one level. There is narrative, sometimes rich and even novelistic, as in the story of Joseph and his brothers in the last twelve chapters of the book, but often strangely spare as in the story of Cain and Abel in Genesis 4, or of Abraham and the young Isaac in Genesis 22. There are genealogical lists; annal-like chronicles; sections of military history; accounts of religious revelations; details of domestic conflicts; tribal legends, dreams and epic poetry, and much else. The claim that Tyndale is making is that English has the capacity—even in 1530—to match all that. Indeed, he says, compared with Latin it does it not only well, but 'a thousand parts better'.

Tyndale's Pentateuch came out a year or eighteen months after his *Obedience*, but it is clear that when he wrote that book he was already not only well-advanced in Hebrew studies, but an experienced translator. Significantly, that part of his preface to the *Obedience* has strong illustration from the Pentateuch: in the course of reminding of the power of God those persecuted in England for reading the Bible, he writes 'How wonderfully were the children of Israel locked in Egypt! . . . yet God's truth brought them out . . . Who dried up the Red Sea? . . .' Joseph was undeservedly imprisoned, before his triumphs, and the Israelites had forty years of starvation in the desert before they were led into the land 'with rivers of milk and honey'. A paragraph on the sixth page (after advice to read the eleventh chapter of the Epistle to the Hebrews in the New Testament—an example of that command of the whole Bible so important to the reformers) summarises Moses's comforting of the children of Israel, giving a précis of several places in the Pentanteuch, for example Deuteronomy 8. Again it implies a grasp of the whole—not just the Pentateuch either, but the Old Testament historical books and the New Testament, and not just Epistles like Hebrews; for the paragraph ends with quotation from Matthew 7 and 28, and Luke 12, as well as Romans 8. The writer of the *Obedience* was already steeped in Hebrew as well as Greek.

Learning Hebrew

Where did Tyndale learn Hebrew? The straightforward answer is that we do not know. Because so little Hebrew was known in England in the 1520s, he must have learnt it somewhere on the Continent, where Hebrew studies were gathering pace. The strong likelihood is that it was somewhere in Germany. That he knew Hebrew well, and not only well but exceptionally, is something that will be shown below. Those (and they have been many) who have wanted to deny Tyndale any stature at all have claimed that his Hebrew was elementary, and that he relied on recent work by Luther in German and Pagninus in Latin. It will be seen that he used Luther's translations, certainly, and Pagninus, and others: a good translator uses any help he can find. But there can be no doubt at all that Tyndale was a remarkable Hebrew scholar, and, by the standards of Englishmen of the 1520s, astonishing.

First, let us look at the position of Hebrew knowledge in the England that Tyndale knew up to 1525. Though there was such an animal as medieval Hebrew work, in Europe and occasionally in England (Roger Bacon in Oxford in the 1260s knew the language, and recommended its study) Hebrew studies in England only began to expand under Elizabeth and James. Thanks to the recent work of G. Lloyd Jones[6] a good deal is now known about knowledge of Hebrew in those decades. There is little to tell about Hebrew under the first Tudors, however. Though Oxford humanists such as John Colet recognised before the turn of the century that particular 'dark places' in, for example, Genesis 1, would not yield proper understanding unless one were 'versed in the Hebrew tongue, and has the means of consulting Hebrew commentaries',[7] there was not enough sense of the importance of the Hebrew texts for the life of the Christian to drive a study of the language. And though most of the Oxford-and-London humanists were in touch with continental scholars such as Johannes Reuchlin who were great and enthusiastic masters of Hebrew, a personal acquaintance which owed everything to the formative Italian experiences which so many of them had shared, once again the deeps of the new English learning were not sufficiently stirred to make knowledge of Hebrew essential in those early days of the sixteenth century. There was, on the contrary, considerable suspicion, because men like Reuchlin, and Cornelius Agrippa of Cologne (who stayed with Colet in London in 1510), were immersed in the Hebrew Kabbalah, of absorbing interest to intellectuals across Europe, but not what might be called straight exegesis of the Hebrew Scriptures. Kabbalistic teachings were of three kinds: Neoplatonic and Gnostic notions of God as emanation; Jewish apocalyptic ideas; and the offering of techniques 'to enable the reader to discover profound spiritual significance and hidden meanings in the most trivial passages of Scripture'.[8] Such near-magic schemes were deeply attractive in England for a century and beyond (and Agrippa can be plausibly put forward as one of the ultimate sources of Shakespeare's *The Tempest* of 1611). Yet the intoxication with such ideas that the youthful humanists found in Padua and Florence did not survive in the colder climate of England in the first decades of the sixteenth century, where the pressures to reform the Church from inside, to study the Scriptures in the originals, and to revolutionise education, all three being widely-admired ideals of Erasmus, needed knowledge that was far less eccentric.

Corpus Christi College in Oxford was founded in 1517 by Richard Fox, Bishop of Winchester, and first provided for the teaching of Greek. Some time later, it became admired for its 'trilingual library' (that is, in Latin, Greek and Hebrew), though until 1537 it had only one Hebrew book, Reuchlin's *De rudimentis hebraicis* published in Germany in 1506. In Cambridge, St John's College was founded in 1511, and the statutes, drawn up by John Fisher, Bishop of Rochester, included provision for study of the three languages. We may assume that little progress was made, for 'in 1530 he [Fisher] complained of the past neglect of Hebrew and Greek' in the College.[9] There was thus in England as on the Continent, a small but growing recognition that knowledge of Hebrew as well as Greek was valuable, even essential, in understanding the Scriptures: but unlike the continental centres, England, with one exception, did little more significant than make small gestures in Oxford and Cambridge. John Fisher's ability to refer to rabbinic authorities in 1525 in his *Defence of the Sacred Priesthood* suggests that he was using intermediaries, though he later (1535) bequeathed to Christ's College, Cambridge, his personal copies of Bomberg's Hebrew Bible and Pagninus's Hebrew lexicon.[10] The library of the vice-provost of King's College Cambridge contained, when he died in 1521, two Hebrew books. A Franciscan, Richard Brinkley, living in Cambridge 1480–1518, borrowed a copy of the Psalms in Hebrew from the Abbey of Bury St Edmunds in 1502, which suggests, but does not prove, knowledge of Hebrew. Neither Fisher nor Brinkley seems to have taught—and we have to remember Tyndale's long and detailed attack on Fisher's scholarship in the heart of the *Obedience*.

The exception, however, is important. Robert Wakefield studied Hebrew in continental universities, including the trilingual college at Louvain, from 1517. He was even for a while Reuchlin's successor at Tubingen in 1522–3. He became the first salaried lecturer in Hebrew in Cambridge, in 1524, and published his inaugural oration in the same year. It was printed by Wynkyn de Worde, the first book in England to employ Hebrew type. Wakefield's oration, in Latin, is a call to learn Hebrew as the fount of wisdom in order to understand both Testaments. Like Tyndale, he insists that New Testament Greek cannot be understood without seeing the Hebrew in it, though Wakefield's concern is wholly scholarship, and he is quite against translation of any kind. In his oration he refers to three or four English Hebraists, including John Stokesley, though there is not yet any other confirming evidence. His younger brother later became Regius Professor of Hebrew at Cambridge. His successor at Louvain was another Englishman, Robert Shirwood, who had apparently learned some Greek and Hebrew at Oxford even before 1522. All these facts are relevant to William Tyndale: there is clearly room for research.[11]

'They order this matter better in Germany', it might have been said—or the Netherlands, or Italy, or Switzerland, or Spain. The growing understanding of the importance for Christianity of an understanding of Hebrew in Europe may be illustrated by the work of Cardinal Ximenez, who founded in 1498 a new university at Alcala (in Latin, Complutum) near Madrid as, among other things, a centre of biblical scholarship. Like many others, he recognised the poor state of the Vulgate, and by-passed possible international outrage if he had attempted to do something about it, by a grand scheme to reproduce the ancient versions side by side as a trilingual version, with, in the four volumes of the Old Testament, the Vulgate in the centre of the page, the Greek of the Septuagint with an interlinear Latin translation on the inside, and the Hebrew text on the outside with Hebrew roots in the margins. Volumes 1 and 6 of the magnificent completed work, known as the Complutensian Polyglot, included aids to the study of Hebrew, with a Hebrew grammar and dictionary. The whole was finely printed in 1514–17, though it had to wait for authorization by the Pope and was not issued until 1522. Ximenes needed Hebrew manuscripts and Hebrew scholars, and set about getting both, at high cost. He was also Archbishop of Toledo, a centre of Jewish studies, and he was able to establish a centre where at least four Jewish scholars, converts to Catholicism, worked on the Hebrew text. One of them, Alfonso de Zamora, was appointed the first ever professor of Hebrew in 1508.

There was scholarly traffic between Spain and Italy. Hebrew Bibles, in part or entire, had been printed in Italy from the 1470s, sometimes very beautifully—in spite of the technical difficulty of setting the vowel points—and northern Italy had become a centre of Hebrew grammatical studies since that time, attracting, as we have noted, Christian students of the new learning from all over Europe, though not necessarily to further mainstream exegesis of Hebrew Scripture. Christian Neo-Platonists Marsilio Ficino and Pico della Mirandola, the most influential thinkers, knew rabbinic writings, though how far their own Hebrew knowledge went remains a question: they were, however, open to the ideas of their Jewish teachers, and through the visiting humanists effectively conveyed that readiness to northern Europe at the turn of the century.

Pico's most important disicple was the Christian scholar Johannes Reuchlin, who went back to Germany to perfect his Hebrew with learned Jews, and in 1506 published his *De rudimentis hebraicis*, a Hebrew grammar and dictionary of great importance throughout Europe. It was a basic tool of the Reformers, including, we must assume, Tyndale as well as Luther and Melanchthon. Reuchlin's edition of the penitential Psalms in 1512, the first Hebrew text to be printed in Germany, included a translation and commentary especially for students.[12] In doing this work as a Christian, he was showing courage, because as knowledge of the existence of Hebrew spread downwards through geological layers of ignorance and bigotry, so hostility rose and spread. As, on the one hand, the growing appreciation of the Hebrew Scriptures was felt to bring into often moribund European theology and practice new direct links with the God of his people, being an inspiration by the Word itself for the work of reformation from the inside, so, on the other, a monk of Freiburg (where Reuchlin studied) could say in 1521 'Those who speak this tongue are made Jews', and Jewish teachers of Christians were made to fear being accused of destroying their pupils' faith.[13]

> Jerome's Vulgate was the Bible of Christendom, and it was upon the renderings of this version that the Church of Rome based its doctrinal teaching . . . Ignorant and illiterate monks, alarmed at the progress of the new learning, thundered from the pulpit that a new language had been discovered called Greek, of which people should be aware, since it was that which produced all the heresies. A book called the New Testament written in this language was now in everyone's hands, and was 'full of thorns and briers'.[14]

There was also now another language called Hebrew, which was worse.

Reuchlin came under fire from Dominicans in 1510 in what became known as 'the battle of the books'. The Dominicans wanted to burn all Hebrew books supposed to be inimical to the Christian faith. Reuchlin sprang to the defence of the Jews and their right to their own religion, again courageously, and gathered support from all over Europe. One of his supporters was Erasmus, though surprisingly that great sage was at best lukewarm about the importance of Hebrew studies for understanding Scripture: he seems to have had a blind spot, finding Judaism 'totally meaningless'.[15] Recent studies have shown that support for Reuchlin was not as widespread, nor as unambiguous, as had been supposed. Reuchlin was condemned by the Pope (influenced by the Dominicans)—an image of the fear that Hebrew studies was producing. Yet the knowledge of the battle across Europe did stimulate German scholars, in particular, to serious study of Hebrew.

What aids would Tyndale have had in learning Hebrew? Reuchlin's *De rudimentis* with its grammar and dictionary would be the most likely place for him to have begun to learn the language. A printed Hebrew text of Scripture would not have been too hard to come by from a German bookseller. Access to the volumes of the Complutensian Polyglot would have been of great value to him, giving him comparative texts and supporting grammar and dictionary and, for most of the Hebrew Bible, Targums, that is, Aramaic commentaries and paraphrase. For those volumes he would certainly have needed access to a library, in a university or well-equipped monastery—the notion that he did much of his Hebrew work at Wittenberg begins to look a little more attractive. Tyndale was obviously unusually skilled with languages (Buschius said he knew eight) including of course his

own. Whether he was able to make use of Jewish teachers is impossible
to know. That he learned Hebrew to the level of accuracy which has
meant that his Old Testament translations survived not only into the
Authorised Version (by which time Semitic studies had greatly advanced) but to this day, and that he did it in three years, between 1526
and 1529, while seeing other books through the Antwerp presses,
suggests some help. Great minds before him had either never begun
Hebrew (like the Oxford-Cambridge-and-London humanists) or had
started and soon given up (like Erasmus). Teachers at his elbow or not,
there would have been other Jewish helps. In Provence in the late
twelfth century Moses Kimchi wrote a Hebrew grammatical treatise
which was later translated into Latin and used by Christian Hebraists.
His brother David wrote a Hebrew grammar with the aim of simpli-
fying the business of learning the language, and a widely-used dictionary, a 'book of roots'. The latter was certainly greatly influential—for
example on the Italian Sanctes Pagninus who in 1528 published his
Biblia, his own new Latin translation of the Old Testament (from the
Hebrew) and the New (from the Greek)—the first with verse divisions—which became at once a major influence on the European
work of translation of the Bible into the vernacular. Not only did he
challenge the Vulgate with a different Latin version of the Hebrew: he
took great pains to consult and use the comments of medieval rabbis,
particularly David Kimchi, in elucidating problematic Hebrew words
or phrases—with considerable success.[16] As valuable for him were the
comments made by 'Rashi' (1040–1105), so known from the initials of
his name, Rabbi Solomon ben Isaac, known as the greatest of Jewish
Bible commentators. He was immensely learned, and was able to show
that the literal meaning of the Hebrew came first, and next were the
deeper significances of the text as they had been handed down.[17] Now,
Tyndale (or his 'Matthew's' editor John Rogers) certainly knew of him,
as the ascription of a comment as 'Rabbi Salomon' appears in his
margins (for example, in the Third Book of the Kings[18]). It could be
that Tyndale (or Rogers) took this from Pagninus at some points: that
does not greatly matter, except as being evidence that Tyndale (or
Rogers) used Pagninus, which is likely anyway. (In fact, that reading in
'3 Kings 14' shows Tyndale or Rogers consulting 'Rab. Sal.' indepen-
dently.)[19] The point is here to note Tyndale (or Rogers) at home with
such essential medieval Jewish helps.

Tyndale Translating

Before we come to what is undoubtedly the biggest help that Tyndale
had in front of him, Martin Luther's vernacular German translation,

mention should be made of two others. Ulrich Zwingli's biblical commentaries, some of which were published in time to be of use to Tyndale in the Pentateuch, could have been helpful in that they are not only clearly based on a knowledge of the Hebrew text, but they show less a philological interest (valuable as that has been for translators, and interested as Zwingli was in it) than a theological. This was spurred on by needing to make points in the various disputes which so marked the earliest days of the Swiss Reformation, and Zwingli used Greek and Hebrew in the pulpit (to Luther's annoyance). An anonymous French translation of the Old Testament was printed in Antwerp in 1528: it is thought to be by Jacques Lefevre, a Catholic 'internal reformer'; his translation is heavily dependent on the Vulgate and could have been known to Tyndale.

Martin Luther, it seems, came late to Hebrew. He apparently acquired a copy of Reuchlin's *De rudimentis* soon after it came out, in 1507, at the start of his second stay at the University of Erfurt. He seems to have done little with it, lacking a teacher. His first lectures on the Psalms, however, delivered at Wittenberg between 1513 and 1515, though based on the Vulgate, show some support from the Hebrew text, if heavily buttressed by previous commentators. By the time of the second set of lectures on the Psalms, published in 1519, he was showing better mastery of Hebrew. His New Testament in German, published in September 1522, was a landmark not only of scholarship, checked at every point by the considerable Greek scholar who was professor of Greek at Wittenberg, Philip Melanchthon; but also, and especially, of language, which was vernacular German with a special clarity. Five thousand copies of Luther's 'September Bible' were sold within a few weeks; a new edition in December was followed by over a dozen more in two years, and there were said to be over sixty pirated editions in the same time. The press of Hans Luft at Wittenberg became even more significant: it had had enormous print-runs of Luther's pamphlets in the three years before—in 1520, four thousand copies of his address *To the Christian Nobility* were sold within five days.[20] Luther's New Testament was a new kind of landmark.

In the summer of 1523 appeared Luther's Pentateuch, like the New Testament in a fine folio with illustrations by the elder Lucas Cranach, on the way to the complete High German Lutheran Bible published in the autumn of 1534. Luther's Pentateuch is important in the history of vernacular Bibles, being the first from the Hebrew. What is known of the making of it may (or may not) cast light on the making of Tyndale's far more modestly presented Pentateuch—about one-eighth the size, but even more influential.

Luther was heavily dependent on a group of advisers, dead and living. The writing of the fourteenth-century Franciscan Nicholas of Lyra, a great medieval exegete who certainly knew the Hebrew text of Scriptures, had introduced Luther to the writings of Rashi. Luther expressed his great respect for the scholarship of Pagninus and of Sebastian Munster, professor of Hebrew at Basle from 1528, who had also been a Franciscan until his conversion to Protestantism in 1526: he was the translator of Jewish works into Latin, and the author of Semitic studies. Luther took help from Bernard Ziegler, a famous Hebraist from Leipsig, and especially from Matthew Aurogallus, professor of Hebrew at Wittenberg from 1521–8, and afterwards Rector of the university: he had written several books on Hebrew grammar and lexicography. His successor as professor was Caspar Cruciger the elder. The best Hebraist at the time was Andreas Osiander at Nuremberg. All these advised Luther, who called them his 'Sanhedrin'. Their presence demonstrates how far Hebrew studies had come in Germany after Reuchlin's *De rudimentis* of under twenty years before—and how far behind was England.

Was it to Wittenberg that Tyndale went to learn Hebrew? The idea is attractive. He would not, of course, have needed to know personally Osiander or Aurogallus, Ziegler or Cruciger—or even Luther—to have benefited, as he certainly did, from all the help and advice that flowed from those great Hebraists into Luther's Pentateuch, which it is clear Tyndale studied very closely. Nor would he have needed to know Luther personally to have been under the immense debt to his writings which he showed. As we have seen above, from the first moment that Tyndale was in print, in 1525, he was Englishing Luther, though with strong variations of his own.

It might be tempting for a biographer to make a romantic scene in which the two great leaders of reform, Martin Luther and William Tyndale, shared their profoundest insights and enthusiasms. Calling each other 'Martin' and 'William', and therefore necessarily using for 'you' the intimate German form 'du' instead of 'Sie', in this fantasy they also compare notes about the problems raised by some Hebrew *hapax legomenon*. Sadly, the biographer has only imagination to draw on for this intimate scene.

That, as far as has been discovered, the serious influence was all one way, tends to strengthen the probability that if Luther and Tyndale ever met it was at a distance, though there is a thin filament of possibility of something closer at one point. Why, indeed, should Tyndale, a young foreigner from England, virtually alone and without court or ecclesiastical connections, have had any effect on Luther? German Reform was the power-house, and England had nothing in the 1520s to offer. German Hebrew studies led Europe, and at Wittenberg Philip Melanchthon led the world in Greek: in both studies, England was almost invisible. Luther was a political being, and had his own authority: he was able to write directly to kings and emperors. When, on the persuasion of the the ex-king of Denmark, Luther drafted, probably in May of 1525, his slightly more emollient reply to Henry VIII, he claimed to have been misled by false information. J.F. Mozley rather strains to see the influence of Tyndale on Luther here, as being one of the 'trustworthy people' who told Luther that Henry's treatise, 'so far beneath the dignity of the king of England', was not written by Henry, as had been put about, but by 'crafty sophists' around Wolsey, 'the destroyer of your majesty's kingdom'.[21]

Nevertheless, though direct evidence is lacking, Tyndale may have studied Hebrew at Wittenberg. Foxe suggests, vaguely, that he had been there: 'on his first departing out of the realm, Tyndall took his journey into the furthest parts of Germany, as into Saxony, where he had conference with Luther and other learned men in those quarters.'[22] The Elector of Saxony was in favour of reform, and Wittenberg would be a safe, and resource-rich, city, with its university, libraries and famous scholars. Both Cochlaeus and Thomas More put Tyndale with Luther there, though More may be relying on Cochlaeus, who used the idea of being with Luther as a smear. More claims that evidence from interrogated heretics newly returned from Germany shows that Tyndale 'got him to Luther straight' and that 'Hychens was with Luther in Wittenberg' while translating the New Testament. Cochlaeus says that Tyndale and Roye 'had learnt the German tongue at Wittenberg'.[23] These assertions, from enemies, in the primary colours of condemnation, are to be handled with a little care. Cochaleus's remark is in fact strange: why should Tyndale, who could have learned German from native speakers anywhere, even in London in his year there before he sailed for the Continent (and Luther's New Testament was already out) go especially to Wittenberg for the purpose? Perhaps it suggests that Cochlaeus had understood Tyndale as learning *some* language at Wittenberg, and had failed to grasp the importance of Hebrew, which is not at all unlikely.

This is clutching at straws. Tyndale himself answers More's statement with the words 'When he saith Tyndale was confederate with Luther, that is not the truth', which does nothing to clarify the matter.[24] Mozley, however, presented an ingenious argument. He noted that William Roye matriculated at Wittenberg on 10 June 1525 as *Guilhelmus Roy ex Londino*; he then looked for Tyndale's name and failed to find it. He did note, however, the entry on 30 May 1524 with

the name of Matthias von Emersen of Hamburg. Mozley was struck by
the fact that this was the nephew to the widow in Hamburg, Margaret
von Emersen, with whom Tyndale lodged five years later. He postu-
lates that Tyndale sailed from England for Hamburg to stay a few
days with the Emersens, 'who had likely been recommended to him
by a merchant of the Steelyard', and then went with Matthias to
Wittenberg to matriculate there, staying nine or ten months, 'probably
till the end of the winter university term', returning to Hamburg in
April in time to be asking Monmouth for his money, from that city.
There is no evidence for this at all, though Mozley believed that he
had found some in an entry for 27 May 1524 in the Wittenberg
register, 'in close neighbourhood' to the name of Matthias von
Emersen, the entry reading *Guillelmus Daltici*, a name without explanation until 'suddenly it flashed upon me that by reversing the two
syllables of *Tindal* you get *Daltin*, which only differs from *Daltici* by one
letter. The present register is but a copy of the original, and if the
copyist misread the final letter, all becomes clear.'[25] So, Mozley avers,
Tyndale was in Wittenberg for nine or ten months, where he learned
German and almost finished translating the New Testament. Mozley
rightly understands that Tyndale's 1525 New Testament was dependent
for style of presentation, if no more, on Luther's 'September Testament', but the programme he sets Tyndale in Wittenberg feels unnecessarily ravelled. Are we to think, moreover, that Tyndale drank at the
fountainheads of Hebrew scholarship as well as Greek and German in
those 'nine or ten months' in Wittenberg? It is pleasant to think of
Tyndale polishing his first New Testament translation in German-
speaking proximity to Philip Melanchthon, though again we have no
evidence at all. It is probably too tangled, even for a man of Tyndale's
gifts, for him to be thought of as mastering Hebrew among the giants
at the same time.

Something should be said here about the language of Hebrew, and
how the business of learning it from scratch might appear to even a
clever Englishman in the 1520s. The first thing that strikes anyone is
that encountering it linguistically is an alien experience, for someone
versed in the vocabulary, grammar and syntax of the language-families
which include Latin and Greek: Hebrew is a very, very distant
cousin—if related at all. It is not just that the script is unlike Latin or
Greek, including being read from right to left. Most Hebrew words are
built on the basis of a three-consonant form, the 'root' which charac-
terises that group of Middle Eastern languages. (David Kimchi's 'book
of roots' of the early 1200s cleared the ground for Europe's later
understanding of the language.) That consonant-root mutates to pro-

duce all other forms, so that most words can be taken back to the three-consonant root, as, to give a simple example, the verb *yalad* 'bear', gives *yeled* 'child', and even *meyalledet* 'midwife'. Hebrew scripture is all consonants, in many early texts with little space between words: the vowels were added as 'points', dots and bars in significant places around the consonants, at various stages in about the ninth century AD.

Much more significant, however, is a major difference of location. Latin was a widespread Mediterranean language, spoken and written in everyday forms, and capable at the same time of a vast literature. Should a word in an epic be hard to understand, the scholar has available other literature in that language on a colossal scale, and inscriptions, daily records, and so on, in order to find clues to meaning through similar words, or variants. The same is true of Greek, perhaps more strikingly, as difficulties in some great Greek literature, the epics of Homer for example, though so early in composition, respond to knowledge of the widest Greek world, the speaking and writing of the language by people in thousands of square miles of territory and over many centuries. By strong contrast, Hebrew of the biblical period, probably from the thirteenth to the second centuries BC, only exists in the Scriptures. Rabbinic Hebrew was written from about AD 200, but it was not a lineal descendent, and many words had been forgotten in the four-hundred year gap, during which the Jews had been in exile. It is as if English only existed in the works of Shakespeare. Hebrew is equally glorious and limited as Shakespeare—but in fact the analogy breaks down, because Hebrew cannot match the uniquely large vocabulary and syntax of Shakespeare. The range of available roots, especially in Hebrew poetry, is limited. When problems of understanding arise, as they frequently do, they have to be tackled from within the frame, so to speak: there are no documents like laundry-lists. True, the position is not quite so desperate as that, as there are three areas where help can be found: light can be cast by neighbouring languages, like Arabic, sharing systems and roots; explanation can appear in the rabbinic commentaries and expositions known as Midrashim; and help can be found in the translations made in the first centuries AD into Aramaic (the Targums), Latin and above all Greek, the latter translation, known as the Septuagint or LXX (from the legend that seventy scholars produced magically-identical Greek) being especially helpful. Yet it is true that for many *hapax legomena*, words that appear once only (for example, in the descriptions of the Temple furnishings in Exodus, or items of daily life in the prophets) there are no reliable helps at all.

So a Latinist of the 1520s learning Hebrew entered a very unfamiliar world indeed (not unlike a modern theoretical space-scientist leaving his oxygen-based experience to try to understand a world where creatures breathe nitrogen and swim in seas of nitric acid). He would also find himself working from the start solely with the Scriptures: early lessons can never include charming sentences about the family dog or the arrival of the postman. Not only is all ancient Hebrew, from Lesson One, the Word of God: that written Word has, as the later phrase has it, 'many dark places'. As the sixteenth century progressed, knowledge of the Hebrew Scriptures increased greatly. Better Hebrew texts were printed, and the world of Semitic studies widened to allow in light from other languages. Some of the 'dark places' began to be understood—but not all. Some still remain, in spite of the remarkable expansion of better Hebrew texts and comparative linguistics in the twentieth century. As an experiment, one need only compare any two recent English bible translations to see how far we are from certainty, even today.

Tyndale's Hebrew Translation

When translating, Tyndale had in his mind two principles, it is clear. One was to understand the Hebrew text as well as he possiby could, using whatever helps he could find—from the Wittenberg workshops, from Pagninus, from the tradition enshrined in the Vulgate, from the Septuagint. The other was to write something in English that made sense. Both principles seem obvious, but the second has not always been followed. The Hebraists in London who worked for King James from 1607 to 1609 to produce what became from 1611 the Authorised Version, riding on the increase in knowledge of Hebrew, tended to prefer philological accuracy even though the English came out cloudy and, often, supported by extra phrases (printed in italics to show that they were not in the original). The Authorised Version's determination to be literal, especially in the obscurer passages in the prophets, can often defeat understanding ('As for Samaria, her king is cut off as the foam upon the water', Hosea 10; a sentence which appeared as the book fell open, among hundreds similarly foggy in King James's Old Testament). Tyndale set out to be clear. So, peculiar as the Temple furnishings in the later chapters of Exodus (and in Kings and Chronicles) seem, the reader of Tyndale does get *some* picture: and in Leviticus 8 he gives the mysterious Urim and Thummim, symbolic parts of a priest's vesture, as 'light and perfectness'. That is still strange, but it is a step nearer conveying something than Urim and Thummim, and it bears out his constant principle that Scripture is never mumbo-jumbo—a major theme of the *Obedience*. Taking his Genesis on its own, which in a way we are invited to do from the beginning as the title-page of the whole is 'The first book of Moses', and from the end of that book with the fullness of the 'Table expounding certain words' followed by the colophon, the determination to be clear is uninterrupted. Wholly mysterious words like *abrech* in Genesis 41, still unknown, he glosses with alternatives. Other Egyptian words in the Joseph story, like *Zaphnath paenea*, also in 41, he also leaves in and glosses at the end. (The Authorised Version translates the first as 'Bow the knee', one of Tyndale's alternative glosses, but ducks the second, and prints the Hebrew transliteration, as Tyndale does, and as modern versions do.) Tyndale glosses 'ark', ('a ship made flat as it were a chest or coffer'), 'Eden', 'firmament', 'marshal', 'vapour' and a dozen others, feeling free to give doctrinal notes on 'bless', 'curse', 'faith' and 'testament'. At the other end of the scale, he uses colloquial words like 'charmers' for enchanters (Genesis 7), 'courtesy' in Genesis 43 for a moderate quantity ('a courtesy balm, and a courtesy of honey . . .') and 'Esau came from the field and was fainty . . .' (Genesis 25). 'Cain was wroth exceedingly, and loured' in Genesis 4, where the Authorised Version has 'Cain was very wroth, and his countenance fell' and the modern Revised English Bible has 'Cain was furious and he glowered'. Esau 'became a cunning hunter and a tillman', which is a touch more artisan than the Authorised Version 'was a cunning hunter, a man of the field' in Genesis 25. In Genesis 31, Laban says 'Thou wast a fool to do it', which the Authorised Version gives as 'thou hast now done foolishly in so doing' an excellent illustration of what occurs everywhere in the Pentateuch: Tyndale's phrase feels modern and the Authorised Version's archaic. ('In this you behaved foolishly' says a recent version, which has all the excitement of the published proceedings of an investigative tribunal.) In the same chapter, Tyndale is not going to be defeated: where the Authorised Version gives 'Mizpah' (the Hebrew for 'watch-tower'), Tyndale uses 'toot-hill', a West Country word for a hill used as a look-out. With the determination to be clear goes a concern to be interesting, and make variation. The matter became an issue later in the century: should the Hebrew or Greek word always have the same English word, to maintain the sense of the specialness of the Word of God? Tyndale feels free to vary, which can be a relief when the Hebrew is formulaic, as sometimes he makes 'it came to pass' into 'it fortuned'. In the 1530 Genesis, he is able to translate the central Hebrew word *b'rith* as 'testament', 'bond' or 'appointment' as well as 'covenant', with a doctrinal gloss on 'testament' at the end of the book.[26] This freedom speaks clearly for his faith in the power of the

English language: the multiple inflow, from first Germanic (Anglo-Saxon) and then Romance (Norman-French) streams, with Latin added, has always meant that after about 1400 English was rich with near-synonyms, able to take quite subtle shading, as seen for example in the fine differences between 'holy', 'sacred' and 'sanctified'. Tyndale feels this flexibility under his hand, which is one reason why his appeal has remained so strong. Moreover, he knows that in English he can get effects that are difficult in Latin, like the great variation in colouring and tone of narrative. We have seen how in the story of the Fall he was able to match his English to the curious stark comic tragedy of the Hebrew. A richer narrative tone appears in later stories in Genesis, like Isaac's courtship of Rebecca in chapter 24, or of Jacob serving for Rahel in 29: 'And Jacob served seven years for Rahel, and they seemed unto him but a few days, for the love he had to her'—a sentence which went straight to the Authorised Version. (The Revised English Bible's version is unhappy: 'When Jacob had worked seven years for Rachel, and they seemed like a few days because he loved her, he said to Laban, I have served . . .' making the love a parenthesis, the serving subordinate, and the main point 'he said . . .', missing the contrast so strongly present in 'but a few days', and flattening the lilting monosyllables of 'for the love he had to her' to the cruder 'because he loved her'.) There, as so often with Tyndale, it is the arrangement of stresses which helps to catch, and grip, the reader. 'Then Jacob gave Esau bread and pottage of red rice. And he ate and drank and rose up and went his way. And so Esau regarded not his birthright' (Genesis 25). Each sentence is complete, and within each is a rhythmic pattern. The middle one is held together by light-stressed 'and's', allowing four major stresses, 'ate . . . drank . . . rose . . . way', with variations of light stresses before them allowing a sense of rising, from the one word 'drank' to the two of 'rose up' to the three of 'went his way'. What follows is consequence rather than cause: where the Authorised Version has 'thus Esau despised his birthright', Tyndale makes a fresh, flat, statement of fact, 'And so Esau regarded not his birthright'.

Again, note the work of the monosyllables in the pattern of stresses in this, from Genesis 28:

> Jacob departed from Berseba and went toward Haran, and came unto a place and tarried there all night, because the sun was down. And took a stone of the place, and put it under his head, and laid him down in the same place to sleep. And he dreamed and behold there stood a ladder upon the earth, and the top of it reached up to heaven. And see, the angels of God went up and down upon it, yea and the Lord stood upon it and said . . .

After 'Haran', there are only six words that are not monosyllables, 'tarried', 'because', 'behold', 'ladder', 'heaven', 'angels' (and they make a summary of the whole). The second sentence, telling of something ordinary, is a sequence of three phrases beginning with 'and', each of which has runs of light stresses 'And took a stone of the place . . .' to build towards the significant heavier stress on 'And he dreamed'. That 'dream' sentence also builds to the three anapaests (two light stresses and a heavier) of 'and the top/of it reached/up to heaven'. Take out the 'up', as the Authorised Version does, and the effect is of checking the infinite climb of the ladder with a jerk; 'and the top of it reached to heaven'.

It is trebly instructive to note the Revised English Bible here, in showing first how simple Tyndale is, secondly what happens when philological accuracy is dominant, and third how to flatten the life out of language:

> He came to a certain shrine and, because the sun had gone down, he stopped for the night. He took one of the stones there and, using it as a pillow under his head, he lay down to sleep. In a dream he saw a ladder, which rested on the ground with its top reaching to heaven, and angels of God were going up and down on it.

No doubt 'he stopped for the night' is intentionally 'relevant language' and like taking a break on the long drive to the south of France: but is it thought that no-one will at least *understand* 'and tarried there all night', not to mention respond to the richness of the expression? 'Tarried there all night' has a sense of bodily presence which the Revised English Bible phrase loses. Such physicality is one of Tyndale's strengths. It is especially suited to Genesis, where the strong and immediate activity of God or one or more of his angels acts with humans busy being human, sitting, standing, looking, eating and drinking, travelling, quarrelling, sorrowing, being sexual, being in families, or going about their business. Tyndale's ear for the directness of English controls the rhythms of dialogue, in which much is done:

> And she departed and wandered up and down in the wilderness of Berseba. When the water was spent that was in the bottle, she cast the lad under a bush and went and sat her out of sight a great way, as it were a bowshot off: For she said: I will not see the lad die. And she sat down out of sight, and lifted up her voice and wept.
>
> And God heard the voice of the child. And the angel of God called Hagar out of heaven and said unto her: What aileth thee Hagar? Fear not, for God hath heard the voice of the child where

he lieth. Arise and lift up the lad, and take him in thy hand, for I wil make of him a great people. And God opened her eyes and she saw a well of water. And she went and filled the bottle with water, and gave the boy drink. And God was with the lad, and he grew and dwelled in the wilderness, and became an archer. (Genesis 21.)

The last fifth of Genesis, chapters 37–50, in a barely-interrupted sweep tells the story of Joseph and his brethren, a skilfully-told Hebrew narrative which resembles a modern *novella* in its characterisation and development. Tyndale is just as at home here with a long, involved movement as he is in the terse and strange sentences at the beginning of the book ('And the Lord put a mark upon Cain that no man that found him should kill him', Genesis 4). The rhythms keep the long-paced story moving forward, patterns of stresses which express no idealised state of being human: 'Behold this dreamer cometh, come now and let us slay him . . .'; 'And she caught him by the garment saying: come sleep with me . . .'; 'Notwithstanding the chief butler remembered not Joseph, but forgot him . . .' 'And so should ye bring my gray head with sorrow unto the grave . . .' Again, much is told in dialogue, and Tyndale's ear for how people speak, particularly under pressure, makes the story grow from the page: 'Me have ye robbed of my children: Joseph is away, and Simeon is away, and ye will take Beniamin away. All these things fall upon me. Ruben answered his father saying: Slay my two sons, if I bring him not to thee again.' (Genesis 42.)

Tyndale and Luther's Pentateuch

Genesis alone vindicates Tyndale's claim that Hebrew and English marry particularly well. That last passage, 'Me have ye robbed . . .' is Hebrew in English: Hebraists recognise the forms, and it is palpably English in a way that the Authorised Version cannot achieve, with its 'Me have ye bereaved of my children: Joseph is not . . .' The question must now be put: how much of all that Hebrew-into-English in Genesis is Tyndale's own work? Is it not, as has so often been said, cribbed from Luther? The answer, for example, in that passage from Genesis 42, is absolutely not. Here is Luther in the 1523 Pentateuch:

yhr habt mich meyner kinder berawbt, Joseph ist nit mehr furhanden, Simeon ist nicht mehr fur handen, BenJamin wollt yhr hyn nahmen. Es geht alles uber mich. Ruben antwort seynem vatter und sprach, Wenn ich dyr yhn nicht widder bring, so erwurge meyne zween sone.

Transliterated (without intending to be comic), that comes out as

> you have from me my children robbed, Joseph is not more present, Simeon is not more present, Benjamin will you away take, everything goes over me. Ruben answered his father and spoke, If I to you him not again bring, so throttle my two sons.

This does not look like influence, apart possibly from the the verb 'robbed'. 'Joseph ist nit mehr furhanden . . .' cannot in a month of Sabbaths be said to be behind Tyndale's 'Joseph is away. . .' Tyndale's lament 'All these things fall upon me' does not relate at all to Luther's more colloquial 'Es geht alles . . .' Even the Septuagint there is closer to Tyndale, with *ep' emoi egeneto panta tauta*, literally, 'all these things happen to me'. The Vulgate makes a mouthful of everything: 'Absque liberis me esse fecistis, Joseph non est super, Simeon tenetur in vinculis, et Benjamin auferetis; in me haec omnia mala reciderunt!' Translated, 'You have made me to be without my children, Joseph does not survive, Simeon is held in bonds, and you will carry Benjamin away; on me all these evils have fallen!' It is altogether simpler, as well as more sensible, to watch Tyndale working from the Hebrew, which has *oti shikkaltem yosef enennu we-shim'on enennu we-et binyamin tiqqahu 'alay hayu kullana'*, 'me you have bereaved; Joseph is not, and Simeon is not, and Benjamin you will take; on me have been all these (things)'.

Let us take two more brief more examples, to watch the relation between Luther and Tyndale. We saw above the expressiveness of Tyndale's serpent's dismissal of the idea of death in his answer to Eve, 'tush ye shall not die'. Here Luther has 'yhr werdet mit nicht des tods sterben', literally 'you will not die with the death', faintly echoing the Vulgate's 'Nequaquam morte moriemini', that is, 'By no means will you die of death' and the Septuagint's *ou thanato apothaneisthe*, and close to the Hebrew *lo mot temutun*, you will not die a death. Luther, it can be seen, is mainstream: Tyndale is on his own with the Hebrew, expressing the emphasis created by the repetition of the Hebrew root, memorably, where AV reproduced the form of the repetition.[27]

In Genesis 49 is an ancient poem celebrating the tribes, which in places presents considerable difficulty. Much of what Tyndale printed went straight into the Authorised Version, itself a tribute to Tyndale's Hebrew skill. One of the difficulties is with the sentence about Gad, which Tyndale has as 'Gad, men of war shall invade him. And he shall turn them to flight', which is clear. The Authorised Version is less clear, with 'Gad, a troop shall overcome him: but he shall overcome at the last', giving the verbal play on 'overcome' which is in the Hebrew. The Septuagint and the Vulgate do the same. Luther is on a different tack, though keeping some word-play, with 'Gad, geruft, wirt das heer furen, und widder erumb furen', that is, 'Gad cries out, will the Lord lead, and lead about again'—so different that it feels as if Luther is using a different Hebrew text. But the point is clear: Tyndale is again on his own against the Septuagint and Vulgate, and is most certainly not taking that originality from Luther.

The subject demands very much fuller treatment. Gerald Hammond's pioneering book[28] and useful essay[29] (of which some of the illustrations above are independent) show that Tyndale sometimes follows Luther closely in grammar and vocabulary. That is not surprising given the limited nature of the Hebrew grammars and lexicons available. The brief comparisons here, however, have shown Tyndale independent in passages in Genesis, and a strong case begins to emerge for detaching Tyndale from Luther even more firmly as translator of Hebrew.

Tyndale's Genesis: Prologues and Marginal Notes

Tyndale's Genesis has chapter numbers for page-heads, and neither chapter-summaries nor cross-references: the pages look strikingly clean. There are only six marginal notes, all quite independent of Luther's seventy-two. One, half-way through chapter 24, reads 'God blesseth us when he giveth us his benefits: and curseth us, when he taken them away'. Another, in chapter 32, reads 'Prayer is to cleave unto the promises of God with a strong faith and to beseech God with a fervent desire that he will fulfill them for his mercy and truth only. As Jacob here doth'. One marginal note is mildly against the bishops and clergy, towards the end of chapter 24: 'To bless a man's neighbour is to pray for him and to wish him good and not to wag two fingers over him'. Two, in chapters 4 and 9, mention the Pope, with reference to Cain, related to the Pope's absolute power, even over the Crown. The last note, to Pharao's priests in chapter 47, reads

> The blind guides get privileges from bearing with their brethren contrary to Christ's law of love. And of these priests of idols did our compassing ivytrees learn to creep up by little and little and to compass the great trees of the world with hypocrisy, and to thrust the roots of idolatrous superstition into them and to suck out the juice of them with their poetry, till all be sear boughs and no thing green save their own.

This first book of Tyndale's Pentateuch has two prologues. In the first, 'W.T. To the Reader', is that rare and precious passage of autobiography, telling how he came to see the need for an English New Testament, imagined it could be done under the patronage of the Bishop of London, was sent away, and came to realise 'there was no place to do it in all England, as experience doth now openly declare.' The second is a prologue to Genesis, claiming from the start that the use of Scripture is something to appeal to God for help about, with four quotations from Paul's Epistles to make his point. Scripture is to be searched for the Law and the promises, and for examples, good and bad. 'This comfort shalt thou evermore find in the plain text and the literal sense . . .' 'Think', he writes, 'that every syllable pertaineth to thine own self . . .', however inadmissable it might seem at first sight. In the second half, Tyndale gives a summary of the book, with spiritual comments as he goes: 'Note the weakness of his [Jacob's] children, yea and the sin of them, and how God through their own wickedness saved them.' He concludes the prologue

> for . . . learning and comfort, is the fruit of the scripture and cause why it was written. And with such a purpose to read it, is the way to everlasting life, and to those joyful blessings that are promised unto all nations in the seed of Abraham, which seed is Jesus Christ our Lord, to whom be honour and praise for ever and unto God our Father through him. Amen.[30]

Tyndale's Exodus, Leviticus, Numbers and Deuteronomy

The four remaining books of Tyndale's Pentateuch show some differences. Three, Exodus, Leviticus and Deuteronomy, are set in light roman type, making the page look even clearer, though there are a few more marginal notes, set in smaller roman. Exodus has eleven full-page woodcuts (borrowed from another printer, as was common) depicting 'The form of the ark of witness' and similar things felt to benefit from being illustrated. These look like reduced imitations of the large dramatic woodcuts by Lucas Cranach in Luther's Pentateuch. They are bold rather than beautiful. That in chapter 28 shows a fierce, slightly cross-eyed Aaron 'with all his apparel' glaring at the reader, his upper half set against solid-seeming woolly clouds like flying sheep. The word one reaches for is 'striking'.

The prologue to Exodus begins

> Of the preface upon Genesis mayest thou understand how to behave thyself in this book also and in all other books of the scripture. Cleave unto the text and plain story and endeavour thyself to search out the meaning of all that is described thereon and the true sense

of all manner of speakings of the scripture, or proverbs, similitudes and borrowed speech, whereof I entreated in the end of the Obedience, and beware of subtle allegories.

Tyndale discusses at some length Jewish Law as Christians and churchmen encounter it, giving a looser summary of the contents of the book, and in the second half relating the two Testaments, the Old and the New, concluding with passionate paragraphs about how 'blessings or cursings follow the keeping or breaking of the law of Moses'. 'A Christian worketh to make his weak brother perfecter, and not to seek an higher place in heaven.' A thousand-year sinner who repents is his equal—'this thousand years I have prayed, sorrowed, longed, sighed and sought for that which I have this day found, and therefore rejoice with all my might and praise God for his grace and mercy'. The prologue to Leviticus not surprisingly discusses sacrifices and ceremonies, with a strong section warning against false allegories. That to Numbers begins 'In the second and third book they received the law. And in this fourth begin to work and to practise'. Here, in the longest of the prologues, he returns to the business of Church practices, developing at greater length some of the issues of the *Obedience*, particularly what arises with the taking of vows. The prologue to Deuteronomy is the shortest and the brightest, beginning

> This is a book worthy to be read in day and night and never to be out of hands. For it is the most excellent of all the books of Moses [i.e. the Pentateuch]. It is easy also and light and a very pure gospel that is to wete [know], a preaching of faith and love: deducing the love to God out of faith, and the love of man's neighbour out of the love of God.

This he then follows through roughly chapter by chapter. 'The twenty-eighth is a terrible chapter and to be trembled at.' It is the long chapter describing the horrors of severe drought, pestilences and siege. Tyndale sees these as the results of 'the abominations of blindness'. Deuteronomy ends with a brief glossary, as Exodus had begun.

Again, there are only chapter numbers as page-heads throughout the four books, and no cross-references or section letters. There are a few more marginal notes, forty-six in the forty chapters of Exodus, a dozen of only a single word (e.g. 'Gifts'), and all independent of Luther's thirty-seven. Leviticus has twenty-one, Numbers nineteen, all short, Deuteronomy forty all even shorter, including the shortest in chapter 16—the single word 'Why.'

These one hundred and twenty-six marginal notes have often been vilified, usually by those who have not read them: the word has gone down from writer to writer that Tyndale's Pentateuch notes are, at worst (when described by his opponents) scandalous, or at best (when described by modern friends) 'salty'. Here we may straighten the record. Most of the marginal notes are elucidatory like 'By bread understand all food: flesh, fruit, or whatsoever it be' (Leviticus 21), or elevatory like 'Mercy is never denied unto him that repenteth' (Leviticus 26), or scholarly like 'Hence our bells were fetched' (Numbers 10) or 'Hence came holy water' (Numbers 19) or 'This was the manner of the Hebrews to make their officers and of this manner did the apostle make deacons, priests and bishops, without any other ceremony as thou seest in the Acts, and mayst gather of Paul and Timothy' (Numbers 27).

Tyndale the Hebrew scholar is often present. The longest note of all, one of three to Exodus 28, is this:

> Light and perfectness: In Hebrew it is lights and perfectnesses: and I think that the one were stones that did glister and had light in them and the other clear stones as crystal. And the light betokened the light of God's word and the pureness clean living according to the same and was therefore called the example of the children of Israel, because it put them in remembrance to seek God's word and to do thereafter.

Of the one hundred and twenty-six notes, forty are recognisable as coming from the writer of the *Obedience*, alert to the unbiblical elements in Church practices, and the unscriptural power of the Pope. Thus, against the ringing second paragraph of Deuteronomy 6, '. . . these words . . . shall be in thine heart . . .', Tyndale notes 'It is heresy with us for a lay man to look of God's word or to read it', which is both trenchant and true. Against the law in Deuteronomy 19 forbidding one sole witness, Tyndale writes, 'Yes in all matter of heresy against holy church'. Against 'Ye shall put nothing into the word . . .' (Deuteronomy 4) is 'No: nor yet corrupt it with false glosses to confirm Aristotle: but rebuke Aristotle's false learning therewith'. Moses, angry at the rebellion in Numbers 16, saying to the Lord 'Turn not unto their offerings' has the comment 'Can our prelates so say?'

The writer of the *Obedience* at his most anti-papal produces twenty-three notes, across all four books, which mention the Pope. In Exodus 21, the murderer is not immune at the altar; Tyndale comments 'But the pope saith come to mine altar'. Moses praying for his sinful people in Exodus 32 produces the note: 'The pope would curse twenty hundred thousand as black as coals, and send them to hell for to have such a proffer, and would not have prayed as Moses did.' The next note, in the same chapter, has been much observed: 'The pope's bull slayeth more than Aaron's calf, even an hundred thousand for one hair of them', which has the advantage of wit. Just below is 'O pitiful Moses, and likewise O merciful Paul: Rom. 9. And O abominable pope with all his merciless idols'.

Two chapters later, against words about animals for offerings '. . . if thou redeem him not: see thou break his neck', Tyndale has 'That is a good text for the pope'. In Deuteronomy 1, at the Lord saying 'And when I told you ye would not hear', Tyndale has 'Here thou seest the very image of the papists. For they likewise where God's word is, there they believe not and where it is not there they be bold'.

The most notorious note is that to Numbers 23. Balam is quoting Balac the king of Moab, saying 'How shall I curse whom God curseth not and how shall I defy whom the Lord defieth not?', questions which Tyndale answers with 'The pope can tell how'. Such observations are angry. Anyone who believes that that the margins of the Bible are not the place for anger about social and religious practices is not reading that Bible very well.

Tyndale's Achievement

Tyndale, who could match his English to the great varieties of Hebrew in Genesis, is in these four books able to bring alive long stretches of law-giving interspersed with narrative, hardly putting a foot wrong. To turn to Leviticus, for example—not a book one tends to keeps close for spiritual comfort in the small hours. Reading Leviticus in Tyndale, after the Authorised Version, is like seeing a road ahead through a windscreen that has been suddenly wiped. The Authorised Version's 'And the Lord spake unto Moses' is often in Tyndale 'And the Lord talked with Moses.' Chapter 5 opens in the Authorised Version, to take a verse at random, with 'And if a soul sin, and hear the voice of swearing . . .' which gives a sense of some meaning: Tyndale's 'When a soul hath sinned and heard the voice of cursing . . .' is just that bit sharper. In the chapter of sexual prohibitions, 18, instead of the Authorised Version's relentless 'uncover the nakedness of' (or the Revised English Bible's 'have intercourse with') Tyndale has 'uncover' or 'discover' or 'open' or 'unhele' (reveal) the 'secrets' or 'privities': the variation of verbs and nouns gives to a piece of law-giving more sense of bodies doing forbidden things. And when called upon, Tyndale can rise to the grandest heights, 'with a mighty hand and a stretched out arm' in Deuteronomy 4, or the splendid 'and thou shalt love the Lord

thy God with all thine heart, with all thy soul and with all thy might'
of Deuteronomy 6, which not only passed into the Authorised Version,
but soon came to be in daily use in Anglican services.

Some of the dietary laws have always presented problems, and still
do. What exactly are the creatures referred to as unclean, for example
in Leviticus 11? Some of them, like the camel, the hare or the swine
are easy. Later Hebrew scholarship, even by the time of the Authorised
Version, made more precise Tyndale's vivid list of 'The little owl, the
stork, the great owl, the back, the pelican, the pye [magpie], the
heron, the jay... the lapwing and the swallow', though it is clear
enough except for 'back', a word that was familiar enough to him for
him to use, but that did not get into the Oxford English Dictionary.
Tyndale's principle of making sense at all times is obvious. Trouble
comes with the next list, those of creatures with joints above the feet
for jumping, that is, 'The arb... the soleam... the hargol... the
hagab...' They are all varieties of locust, apparently, and are all
transliterations of the Hebrew words. The Vulgate takes from the
Septuagint three very obscure devourer-or-locust-or-serpent words,
and adds 'locusta'. Tyndale, noting the lack of help from the Latin
or Greek, followed Luther, who has 'Arbe... Selaam... Hargol...
Hagab...' Tyndale, unable to write an undifferentiated 'locust' four
times, opted for once for Hebrew mystery, feeling that it was possibly
not the most significant matter for those on the highroad of the
Christian way. There, Tyndale's dependence on Luther in a tight spot
is obvious. But again, until much more is known, it is unwise to over-
stress such adherence. Tyndale's phrase in Exodus 9[verse 20], 'flee to
house' suggests straight and rather thoughtless German-to-English. Yet
the Hebrew there has *el ha-batim*, which means 'to the houses', and
Luther, against the Septuagint and the Vulgate, has 'into the houses'.

In narrative, Tyndale does not waver. The first half of Exodus, to the
giving of the Ten Commandments in chapter 20, is rich with stories,
part of the epic of the oppression of the Israelites in Egypt, the plagues,
the institution of the Passover, the escape over the held-back waters of
the Red Sea, and the wanderings in the wilderness. In Exodus 14,
against the Authorised Version's 'And Moses stretched out his hand over
the sea; and the Lord caused the sea to go back by a strong east wind
all that night, and made the sea dry land, and the waters were divided',
can be set Tyndale's 'When now Moses stretched forth his hand over
the sea, the Lord carried away the sea with a strong east wind that
blew all night, and made the sea dry land and the water divided itself'.
'Carried away the sea' is wonderfully physical, where the Authorised
Version's 'caused the sea to go back' is legal, even, one might say, dry.

The extra verb 'blew' in Tyndale's 'a strong east wind that blew all night' carries forward the sense of a natural event. (There is one moment where the Authorised Version improves on Tyndale, in chapter 11; the death of the firstborn will, says the Lord, afflict the Egyptians from, as Tyndale has it, 'the firstborn of Pharaoh that sitteth upon his seat, unto the firstborn of the maidservant that is in the mill . . .' which becomes 'the firstborn of the maidservant that is behind the mill'.)

There are passages in the Pentateuch which show Tyndale at work with a different kind of Hebrew, in that not only Genesis 49 but Exodus 15, parts of Numbers 23 and 24, and Deuteronomy 32 and 33 are poetry, dating from very early in Israel's history, and therefore full of difficulties for the translator. The principle on which Hebrew poetry was constructed was not properly understood by Gentiles until 1753, when Bishop Lowth called it parallelism ('The Lord is my strength and song/and he is become my salvation'). But Tyndale, himself searching always for variation, must have been alert to what was happening, and his skill as a translator of difficult Hebrew poetry can be demonstrated. We must always lament that he was killed before he could work on the Psalms and Prophets: a drop of balm for that regret is that we do have some poetry from him, and much of it overlaps with what was later in the Psalms, so that we could build a picture of Tyndale as Psalm-translator. The quotation above is from Exodus 15, and Psalm 118, and is Tyndale's, taken through into the Authorised Version in both places. Other passages from Exodus 15 and Deuteronomy 32 have the same history. One phrase that was not transmitted, and has been the subject of misplaced merriment, is early in Exodus 15; the Hebrew refers to the drowning of the Egyptian army in the Red Sea, his chariots and his host, and in the parallel *mibhar salisaw*, that is, 'The choice (pick) of his captains'. The Septuagint has 'chosen horsemen', the Vulgate 'chosen captains'. Luther gives 'auserwelten hawbleut', chosen officers. Tyndale has 'jolly captains'. As long as 'jolly' is redolent of maiden aunts sending hearty birthday cards to middle-class children in the 1930s, to go back no further, it is wildly wrong. Yet in 1530 two current meanings of the word were 'high-hearted, gallant, brave' or 'defiantly bold, arrogant, overbearing', and the combination catches pretty well the specialness, and the self-regard, of the wiped-out officer corps, which make the Authorised Version 'chosen' seem rather dull.

Those meanings of 'jolly' have not survived. An astonishing quality of Tyndale's translations is that so much has not only survived, but has permanently enriched the language. Over and over again it is Tyndale, of all Bible translators of the next centuries, who feels modern.

Beyond that is his gift for coining words, in the Penateuch not only
'Jehovah' as an English word, as we saw above, but 'mercy seat',
'Passover', 'scapegoat' and others, many, like 'scapegoat', still very
much alive and in everyday use, with the added value of being made
a verb, 'to scapegoat'. At one time, it was customary to deny 'mercy
seat' (in Exodus 25 and thereafter) to Tyndale, pointing to Luther
being there first with *Gnaden stuel* for whatever it is that the Hebrew
kapporeth is describing. But Luther's words properly mean 'chair of
grace'; both the Septuagint and the Vulgate have at that place standard
words for 'propitious place'. As the Oxford English Dictionary demonstrates for all three words, Tyndale should not be denied his coinages.

In 1530, Tyndale, it seems, was one of a few Englishman to know
Hebrew beyond, possibly, the merest smattering. He probably learned
Hebrew somewhere in Germany. Within those few years after he left
England, and while producing the first English New Testament from
Greek and writing other books, he learned Hebrew to a level that
meant that what he printed lived for five hundred years, and translated
it into an English still largely as fresh as when he wrote it. When we
think officially of the triumphs of the Tudor age, we remember some
glories of Henry VIII and Elizabeth I as monarchs, we honour the
playwrights and poets, we treasure the painters, musicians and archi-
tects. We have until now completely failed to register the achievement
that is Tyndale's little volume of the Pentateuch.

Chapter 12

THE 1534 NEW TESTAMENT

Here thou hast (most dear reader) the new testament or covenant made with us of God in Christ's blood.

So Tyndale begins his prologue to his revised New Testment, the glory of his life's work, and the first translation with his name on the title-page. The volume is, as usual, pocket size. It is six inches tall, four inches wide, and one and a half inches thick, a small thick book of four hundred pages that sits comfortably in the hand. It is attractive, with pleasing black-letter type and a good deal of white space on each page: the outside margins are an inch wide, and the top and bottom margins are generous. There are simple running-titles of each book across the page tops, some notes and biblical cross-references in the outside margins, and upper-case section-letters in the inside margins. Chapter-numbers, spelled out in roman letters, are inserted without line-spaces, so that the text of every book is continuous, as it should be. These strong but unassuming pages in octavo by the Antwerp printer, Martin de Keyser, are noticeably less dramatic than the grand Lutheran gestures in quarto of Peter Quentell in Cologne, though the prologues, marginal notes and more frequent decorations do make de Keyser's pages look more interesting than Peter Schoeffer's from Worms. Every book now has a prologue, and most books and pro-logues have small decorations at the head. The book of Revelation has twenty-two woodcuts, two-thirds page size: not great art, but full of energy. One of the prologues, to Romans, is almost as long as the Epistle itself. At the back of the book are fifteen pages containing forty Old Testament passages, the extracts read on certain days in the services in Salisbury Cathedral (which 'Sarum use' became the basis of the first Book of Common Prayer in 1549) translated so that worshippers could hear, or use, all the Bible passages in English. Those pages are followed by a further eighteen giving a table of the set readings from Epistles and Gospels throughout the year, again anticipating the Prayer Book. Of the original print-run of three thousand of this book, about a dozen seem to have survived, and are now in libraries in England and America.

The whole book has two prologues. The first, 'W.T. Unto the Reader', begins as above.[1] It then continues: 'Which I have looked over again (now at the last) with all diligence, and compared it unto the Greek, and have weeded out of it many faults, which lack of help at the beginning, and oversight, did sow therein.' Tyndale acknowledges that he has been slow to tackle the revision promised eight years earlier in Worms, but 'now at the last' he has made a thorough job, working again from the Greek. That is as clear a statement as should be needed that, though like all translators he took what help he could from elsewhere, his occupation was with the New Testament in Greek, which meant Erasmus's pioneer work of 1516, now in its fourth edition (Tyndale used the second, 1519, and third, 1522, editions). Detractors of Tyndale who promote his lack of Greek have to go against all his own statements, not to mention the overwhelming evidence from every paragraph on every page. Tyndale's next sentences, the third and fourth in the volume, are:

> If ought seem changed, or not altogether agreeing with the Greek, let the finder of the fault consider the Hebrew phrase or manner of speech left in the Greek words. Whose preterperfect tense and present tense is oft both one, and the future tense is the optative mode also, and the future tense is oft the imperative mode in the active voice, and in the passive ever.

This may seem a strange way to address a ploughboy. Yet the ploughboy, like anyone else, deserves the best, and Tyndale the scholar and craftsman is going to give every reader that. His Hebrew studies and translations, all done since the last New Testament, have given him insight into the Greek such as no other scholar or translator had at that time. The New Testament frequently translates Hebrew words or sentences—Jesus's language after all was Aramaic, a dialect of Hebrew used throughout the region at the time. All New Testament writers translate Hebrew into Greek, as they regularly quote Old Testament texts. Further, the ground of many New Testament ideas is a sometimes subtle alteration to a Hebrew phrase. Even such a Hellenic book as Luke's Gospel is densely permeated by Old Testament echoes. But none of these seems to be what Tyndale has in mind here, which is something subtler. The Hebrew mind of Paul writing in philosophical, theological Greek, Tyndale has noticed, tends to write Greek with a Hebrew accent, as it were. The book of Revelation is in the Jewish tradition of the Apocalypse, and a Christian book in Greek which is essentially Hebrew. And so on. (Tyndale does not himself give these examples, which are two of the more obvious ones.) He has noticed something more pervasive, and that is to do with verbs, and particularly tenses. Hebrew tenses are, one might say, the very marrow of Old Testament religion—Jehovah gave his name, after all, when asked, as 'I am'. The preterperfect tense, notes Tyndale (our perfect tense), as in 'I have commanded' is often in Hebrew the same as the present tense, 'I command', with obvious significance for a religion so built on divinely-controlled history. Similarly, straight futurity often overlaps with the idea of desire or wish ('the optative mode'), as in the English 'I will go into the house of the Lord', or with the imperative in the active voice, 'Obey my commands'; and always with the imperative in the passive voice, 'Be ye obedient to my commands'. Those uses of tense are certainly true of Hebrew. Tyndale has observed that these, and other Hebrew forms, underlie some of the Greek of the New Testament, and has translated accordingly. His fifth sentence, concluding his first paragraph, is 'Likewise person for person, number for number, and an interrogation for a conditional, and such like is with the Hebrews a common usage'. So in English, parallel to his last point, we can say, instead of 'If you go into the house of the Lord, there you will praise him', 'Do you go into the house of the Lord? There will you praise him'. (Tyndale's point in the prologue to the *Obedience*, that Hebrew goes so well into English, is clearly illustrated here, as is most of the matter in this paragraph.)

The first thing we meet in this new volume is Tyndale the working translator, the craftsman. The same was true of the prologue to the Cologne fragment, though not in such immediate detail. His understanding of Greek was now much more advanced. He had not set it aside while he worked on the Hebrew translations and other writing. His work on Greek must have been more than simply the fact that constant reference to the Septuagint while he worked on the Pentateuch kept it alive, though that must have come into it, as the Septuagint has itself a Hebrew flavour to its Greek, understandably. He has gone further, and thought hard not only about the working of the *koine*, the language of Mediterranean life in the first century in which the New Testament is written, but also about particular qualities of that language sometimes visible in the New Testament texts. In attending to this, he can be shown to be well ahead of any other scholar in

Europe, even the foremost professor of Greek, Philip Melanchthon at Wittenberg, as close study of successive editions of Luther's German New Testament can show. He is conscious, too, of being observed at a high level as a translator of Greek, and without rancour makes his technical point to forestall both learned and ignorant criticism—that his understanding of Greek is faulty, or simply that he has changed his mind.

This is a subject for later discussion. We have at this point, however, to utter a cry of grief. It was a scholar of this towering stature, leading all Europe in his knowledge of Greek, matched now by an equal command of Hebrew, uniquely gifted in tuning the sounds of the English language, who had achieved so much but who still had some of his greatest work to do, who was, soon after this, by a vicious, paltry and mean villain tricked into death. It is as if Shakespeare had been murdered by a real-life jealous Iago half-way through his life, and the great tragedies had never been written. Had Tyndale gone on to the poetic books and prophecies of the Old Testament, we should not only have had them in English far surpassing Coverdale's: we should surely also have had even finer tuning of the New Testament, so much of which is directly entwined with those very poems and prophecies. Tyndale's 1534 New Testament is a triumph; but another New Testament, after another eight years or so, would surely have followed. As Tyndale constantly notes, the work of translation never ends.

That indeed is the subject of the second paragraph of his first prologue. He writes, in part:

> If I shall perceive either by myself or by the information of other, that ought be escaped me, or might be more plainly translated, I will shortly after, cause it to be mended. Howbeit in many places, me thinketh it better to put a declaration in the margin, than to run too far from the text. And in many places, where the text seemeth at the first chop hard to be understood, yet the circumstances before and after, and often reading together, maketh it plain enough etc.

His subject is still his absolutely primary one, the craft of translation. He makes here two vital points. The margins are above all explicatory; and hard places yield if put in the context of the whole. Tyndale does not use his margins, as they so often had been used in the long history of biblical texts, for the elaborate exposition of largely allegorical matter growing out of, and away from, the text. Some of his notes are doctrinal, and those are usually keyed into the text with asterisks, but most are to assist the work of translation. And secondly, if not inter-

fered with, the Bible interprets itself. That second point he is about to
return to at full power in a surprising second, additional prologue.

Meanwhile, his third paragraph is a long pair of parallel sentences
explaining that 'false prophets and malicious hypocrites' (he means the
scholastic traditions of the Church, 'the popish doctors of dunces' dark
learning', where 'dunces' refers to Duns Scotus and his followers)
'whose perpetual study is to leaven the scripture with glosses', have by
that means locked up the kingdom of heaven, 'that he which readeth
or heareth it, cannot understand it'. Because of that, he has set out
'(most dear reader) to warn thee before, and to shew thee the right
way in, and to give thee the true key to open it withal'. This key
follows in the next twelve pages, indicated by the marginal note, the
first in the volume, 'The right way into the scripture'. These pages at
first glance contain nothing new, being a summary of the familiar
Tyndalian law-fulfilled-in-the-promises New Testament doctrines, with
references to key chapters in the Gospels and Paul. Yet they feel
noticeably unlike Luther. The Old Testament references are only a
mention of four figures in an aside about openly resisting the spirit of
God 'after the example of Pharaoh, Coza [Cora], Abiram, Balaam,
Judas, Simon Magus and such other', and a later dismissal of Moses.
All but five of the nineteen references, which are in the text, are to
Matthew and Luke: the rest are to John (twice), James (once) and Paul
(three times)—a pattern unlike the usual habits of Luther. Moreover,
there is detectable a subtle shift away from Luther, into something
more closely linked with the idea of covenant—a change which may
relate to that regularising of the Hebrew word *b'rith* to 'covenant' in
the revision of Genesis, which also happened in this year, 1534. It is as
if Tyndale now wants his key to Scripture to be more existentially
related to the daily decisions of the Christian way, and less to raw
doctrine. 'The general covenant wherein all other are comprehended
and included, is this. If we meek ourselves to God, to keep all his laws,
after the example of Christ: then God hath bound himself unto us to
keep and make good all the mercies promised in Christ, throughout all
the scripture.' Three paragraphs later comes: 'For all the promises of the
mercy and grace that Christ hath purchased for us, are made upon the
condition that we keep the law.'

A scholar remarks 'It sounds almost like justification-by-keeping-
law.'[2] The classic reformers' position does return, however, and the
last pages are dominated by 'For faith unfeigned in Christ's blood
causeth to love for Christ's sake'. Yet the ferocious dogmatics of
the Cologne prologue have quite gone. Instead, the ploughboy is
instructed,

Also ye see that two things are required to begin a Christian man. The first is a steadfast faith and trust in almighty God, to obtain all the mercy that he hath promised us, through the deserving and merits of Christ's blood only, without all respect to our own works. And the other is, that we forsake evil and turn to God, to keep his laws and to fight against ourselves and our corrupt nature perpetually, that we may do the will of God every day better and better.

This prologue ends with two pages given to his reasons for translating *metanoeo* as 'repent' and not 'do penance', and a note on 'elders'— 'whether ye call them elders or priests, it is to me all one: so that ye understand that they be officers and servants of the word of God . . .' Then follow brief prologues to the four evangelists, and an erratum.

But the New Testament does not follow. Instead come eight and a half pages headed 'William Tyndale, yet once more to the christian reader'. He goes straight to the point. Before he could get this revision out, George Joye had taken it, altered it, and printed it 'in great number' before Tyndale's began at his own press. Joye's alterations were frequent and serious. 'For throughout Matthew, Mark and Luke perpetually: and oft in the Acts, and sometime in John and also in the Hebrews, where he findeth this word resurrection, he changeth it into the life after this life, or very life, and such like, as one that abhorred the name of the resurrection.' If, says Tyndale, that is right, then he, Tyndale, and everyone else ever heard of, including Jerome, is wrong. Worse, he says, that is not simple error. Joye has been for a long time well known for having strange ideas about the resurrection, and has confused, with serious consequences, the brethren in London. Worst of all, he had not put his name to the book. That last fact Tyndale quite finds outrageous. He is angry, and rightly. Let them all translate Scripture if they will, he says, out of Greek, Latin or Hebrew. 'Or (if they will needs) as the fox when he hath pissed in the gray's [badger's] hole challengeth it for his own, so let them take my translations and labours, and change and alter, and correct and corrupt at their pleasures, and call it their own translations, and put to their own names, and not to play bo-peep after George Joye's manner.' Tyndale has not yet had time to read the whole volume, which has 'I wot not what other change', but, he concludes, so that you (reader) will be able to recognise it, here is the colophon, 'in the end before the Table of Epistles and Gospels' (and thus not at all obvious, incidentally): '(Here endeth the New Testament diligently overseen and correct and printed now again at Antwerp, by me widow of Christopher of Endhoven. In the year of our Lord 1534 in August.)' And thereby hung a tale.

George Joye

It would be pleasant if George Joye had been a more attractive man. As it was, he irritated everyone he met, including, with what must now seem spectacular folly, John Foxe. He was probably about the same age as Tyndale, and had been at Cambridge, where he was recorded as being a Fellow of Peterhouse and skilled in Latin and Greek, from about 1509 to about 1527.[3] As is evident here, little is known for certain of his early life, though he was a priest in Bedfordshire. Unlike Tyndale, however, he was interested in giving defensive accounts of certain points in his life where he felt resentful. One of these, not published until 1531, explains how unsuitably he was treated by everyone early in the winter of 1527. The Prior of Newnham Abbey near Bedford, John Ashwell, decided that Joye had some heretical ideas, and secretly informed the Bishop of Lincoln, John Longland, adding a little gossip; whereupon Joye was summoned to appear before Wolsey at Westminster to answer four charges of heresy. In London he found that two other Cambridge men, Thomas Bilney and Thomas Arthur, were being examined by Wolsey and the bishops.[4] He was perhaps in some danger, but it is the offence to his dignity which comes over in his story. 'I got me to horse when it snowed, and was cold'; he was left hanging about for over a week both in and out of the Cardinal's house, lost his way and found himself in the kitchen, and, worst of all, 'though I saw now and then a Bishop come out', no one recognised him. He was directed to the Bishop of Lincoln's house and again put off, and offered neither supper nor lodging. He decided that he was worthy of better treatment. 'As I went now I thought thus with myself, I am a scholar of Cambridge under only the vice-chancellor's jurisdiction and under the great God the Cardinal, and M. Gascoinge [sic] sent not for me, I will take a breath ere I come to these men again.'

So, after an ambiguous encounter in London the next morning, 'I got me to horse . . . and conveyed myself toward the sea side'. Thus, in December 1527 he fled across the Channel, probably to Antwerp. He remained in exile until 1535, with another period from 1540 to 1548. He died in England in 1553, having managed to quarrel with just about everyone he had ever met. He had apparently, among other works, written some Primers (said to anticipate Cranmer's Prayer Book of 1549), and printed a long and excessively tedious collage of recent commentaries on the book of Daniel. He made the first printed translations into English (from Latin) of the Psalms in 1530 and Isaiah in 1531 (printed by Martin de Keyser in Antwerp, as was also Tyndale's Jonah in the same month as Joye's Isaiah) and Jeremiah in May 1534 (from 'the Widow of Christopher from Endhoven' also in Antwerp. The widow's husband had first been arrested in November 1526 on instructions from Wolsey, for printing heretical books; but the authorities in Antwerp would not proceed against him: in England in 1531, he was imprisoned in Westminster for selling English New Testaments, and died there).

By comparison with Coverdale, the Old Testament translations from various secondary Latin sources (Joye had no Hebrew) are generally not too happy, as even his faithful biographers admit.[5] But he knew his way about printing Scripture in English, and probably already had some sort of connection with the van Endhoven press, who would soon print his Jeremiah. So it was not surprising that that firm approached him, probably in the spring of 1534, and in fact for the second time of asking, to oversee their fourth pirated edition of Tyndale's 1526 Worms New Testament. The first such piracy had been in 1527, the second in 1530 and the third in 1533/4. What Tyndale thought of them is unrecorded. He may not have bothered himself too much. They were inhibitingly chunky, even clumsy, sextodecimos of about 450 pages, set and proof-read by non-English-reading Flemings. Though the demand was so great that Endhoven got quickly through a total of seven thousand copies of his first three editions, no copy of these earlier printings has survived. Such print-runs give a sort of opinion-poll of the expected level of interest in England: van Endhoven may have been motivated by the love of God's word alone, but he (later she) stood to make considerable profit from an investment, and must have gauged the market pretty well.[6] Perhaps Tyndale did not consider these piracies wholly reprehensible. The falseness of the English would be regrettable to him, but not, after all, uncommon. The strain of reading minute print in awkward, fat and tiny sextodecimos; the frequency of printing errors and unevenness of type; not to mention the wildest variations in local spellings—such things must have always made readers at the lower ends of the market (such as students) astute guessers. It is striking both that Tyndale himself never published in smaller form than decent-to-read octavo (though books half the size would have been easier to smuggle) and that he never once mentioned the piracies. What he did attack, loudly and with all the force he could muster, in the most public place he could find, was Joye's silent theological tinkering.

There was much sense in the approach to Joye by the van Endhoven press. Tyndale himself, in his prologue to the Cologne fragment, had made an open invitation to correctors. His attitude at that time can also be judged by his remarks to Vaughan noticed above, to the effect that he, Tyndale, would stop at once all he was doing, and go to England, and 'submit himself at the feet of his royal majesty, if it would stand with the king's most gracious pleasure to grant only a bare text of the scripture to be put forth among his people . . . be it of the translation of what person soever shall please his majesty'.[7]

Tyndale was being slow in producing his own revision and correction, promised in the 1526 volume, though the printers' grapevine in Antwerp must have known that he was about it.

It cannot be known now how much work Joye had to do. He had beside him a Worms copy of the 1526 New Testament. One copy of the resulting Joye/Endhoven piracy has survived, and it is remarkably close to that Tyndale original, with something under a hundred variants, many extremely minor, which is a fair situation in a book set up, even with Joye in attendance, by non-English-reading printers.[8] It may be that Joye, correcting a copy, or proofs, of the third edition, perhaps now at four removes from the original, with each remove sowing fresh errors, found himself faced with a printer's pie of Flemish-English, or Flenglish, and had great labour. Yet however much or little he had to do, he made four strategic blunders, all surely born of a quite unjustified self-conceit. His biographers give the details.[9] They boil down to the following.

First, he had beside him a Vulgate, in order to check Tyndale's accuracy; precisely as if Jerome were after all the true text and Erasmus's Greek text (from which Tyndale worked) a sport. Joye did not have much Greek, and he was, if you please, 'correcting' the work of one of the most formidable Greek scholars of the time. Second, he took it upon himself to make silent substantive changes, like making Jesus say to Peter in Matthew 16, 'Thou art Stone. And upon this same stone . . .' Third, and with breathtaking folly, he 'corrected' Tyndale's theology at that point of importance, the word 'resurrection', changing it in twenty places to 'the life after this life' or whatever: in Tyndale's appalled illustration from John 5, for instance, Joye changed Tyndale's 'resurrection of life' to 'very life'.[10] Finally, all this was done silently, appearing under Tyndale's name on the title-page, without bothering to inform Tyndale, his neighbour, colleague, fellow-exile and Christian brother, that he was doing it.

Tyndale's rejoinder, in that second prologue to his 1534 New Testament, was thunderous. Joye could do what he liked, as long as he signed his own work. Not to have done that was bad enough. But for Joye to make the principal silent 'correction' in that crucial area was elephantine. The English reformers had found no doctrine of purgatory in the Bible, or in the early fathers up to Augustine, and even after. The ablest English reforming theologian, the young John Frith, had published a definitive book three years before, in the summer of 1531, to demonstrate just that point,[11] supported in letters by Tyndale, and then had been only months before Joye's interference in Antwerp burnt at the stake in London, one of the greatest losses to the reformers' cause. Joye added scarcely credible tactlessness to this particular folly. The reformers' point was dynamite. If purgatory went, most of the Church's power and income went with it. And the reformers had themselves to sort out urgently what they now understood from the New Testament about the present state of the souls of the departed, not to mention bodily resurrection.

What is commonly called the quarrel between Tyndale and Joye was exceedingly one-sided. Tyndale made his blast from his New Testament, and dropped the matter. It was Joye who quarrelled. To a new van Endhoven piracy, and now the fifth, he added a self-justifying address.[12] He visited Tyndale, suggesting that they should jointly publish their views. Tyndale declined, in spite of some pestering from Joye. So Joye produced a fresh work, his tendentious and intemperate *Apology*, dated February 1535, where at length and self-righteously he told a long story about himself and Tyndale, and point by point 'answered' Tyndale in dialogue form. He does succeed in one thing: he makes Tyndale seem as petty as himself. He even sneers at Tyndale's Greek. Dialectical argument, serious intellectual debate, is one thing, but that is what the *Apology* is not. It is personal resentment, apparently never-ending, and therefore tedious in the extreme. Having read it, one feels that George Joye has followed one round the house all day like a guest with a grievance, never stopping in telling the tale. Tyndale's majestic silence was right.

What could Tyndale have done? The nearest international copyright mark, and thus appeal, was four hundred and eighteen years away. He put his name on his title-page for the first time, wrote his prologue, indicated the offending volume, and left it at that. He was not stung because of offence to his vanity, or even his purse. The damage was being done to the word of God. It was bad enough having such foolish philology—the Greek word *anastasis* can only mean 'resurrection'— and generally bad work passed off as Tyndale's. His horror was at the evidence that Joye had not understood how Scripture worked. He was wrecking the harmony of the whole, which is both *sui generis* and above all *Dei generis*. Left to itself, he says in a powerful image, the Scriptures will purge themselves of error, as the scum rises to the top of a boiling pot.[13] After all, is that not what is happening now as he writes? The misrepresentation of the Greek word *metanoeo*, which had been powerful in Church practice for the three hundred years before, was being removed by having the whole New Testament in English from the Greek.

New Testament Prologues

Unlike the 1526 New Testament, though like the 1530 Pentateuch, each book of this Testament is introduced by a prologue. Those 'into the four Evangelists showing what they were and their authority' come briefly at the end of 'W.T. Unto the Reader': that to 'St Matthew' is only six and a half lines long. The emphasis is either the writers' presence at what they describe, or in the case of 'Mark' and 'Luke' (only Matthew is 'St') with the first Apostles. 'John' has an appropriate personal tenderness and theological strength. 'Luke' mentions Acts, which is the only book to have no prologue of its own, simply a slightly extended title, 'The Acts of the Apostles, written by Saint Luke Evangelist which was present at the doing of them'.

The picture then changes dramatically. 'A Prologue to the Epistle of Paul to the Romans' is thirty-six pages long, as long as Paul's Epistle. Like the rest of the prologues to the Epistles, it is almost, but not quite, pure Luther, translated from the latter's complete Bible published in Wittenberg some weeks before. Paul's Epistle to the Romans had always been the central document in Christian theology, and for the English reformers its rediscovery in its textual purity, rid of the 'baroque' efflorescence of scholastic commentary, had connected them to a scriptural power-source. Continental reform understood the Epistle to the Romans as the thrusting point of the whole Gospel, integrating both testaments. It was natural for Tyndale to turn to Luther's mature thoughts in that essay on the Epistle, and to feel that there was little he wanted to change or add. It also solved a problem. The prologue to the Cologne New Testament, where Luther on Romans had been very present, in the background if not directly quoted, was in places dogmatically harsh. Tyndale obviously (because that is how it came out) wanted his new prologue to be more comprehensive about the way in to the Christian life: to be offering a key, less to the hard prison of the fact of sin under the law, and more to the effect of the promises in Christ on the everyday Christian way—with some implications for the rather greater sympathy for some value in works than ever Luther would stomach. By making the Romans prologue, and those to the other Epistles, fully Luther, he was freer in his own introduction at the start of the volume.

Yet the prologues to the Epistles (after Romans they are usually just over a page long) are not quite pure Luther. They are subtly reconstructed. Without any signal in the text or margin, five paragraphs from the end of the Romans prologue, from a sentence beginning 'The sum and whole cause of the writings of this epistle, is . . .' Tyndale leaves Luther and writes on his own. The prologue to 1 Corinthians begins with a paragraph of his own. That to Galatians fills out Luther's. That to Hebrews, as we shall see, is a special case. It is not so much now, eight years after leaving Cologne, that Tyndale moves in and out of Luther, as that he can more completely block things out on his own. A study, however brief, of these 1534 prologues can show Tyndale markedly less Lutheran, and moving more to something of his own, something English. Had he lived, he might have gone on to be the architect of a new, more English, Reformation theology with the profoundest effect on the arriving Church of England. That is speculation: but there is a wisp of sad irony in the fact of his being executed on the Continent as a Lutheran at the point when he was a little less in thrall to Luther.

This is clearest in the prologue to the Epistle to the Hebrews—a notoriously problematic text. His essay, of about fifteen hundred words, the longest outside that to Romans, is not Luther (or even Erasmus, as it could have been) translated. Tyndale begins by briskly disposing of the doubts, both ancient and modern, about it being by Paul. The earliest fathers, at least until Jerome in the fourth century, and more recent medieval exagetes, had been divided: the Epistle was apostolic, but might not be by Paul. Of seven scholars who wrote about the Epistle in the twenty years before 1534, though all acknowledge its authority, two, Bullinger and Oecolampadius, argued for Paul as author: two, Titelmans and Erasmus in 1521, were silent on the subject: two, Erasmus in 1516 and Cajetan, were doubtful about Pauline authorship: two, Luther and Bugenhagen, were against Paul (as were, incidentally, Calvin and Beza later, and the translators of the Geneva Bible). Tyndale acknowledges that 'about this epistle there hath ever been much doubting and that among great learned men who should be author thereof'. He notes that it is not like the rest of Paul, and explains the standard crux, that Hebrews chapter 2 (verse 3) is contradicted by Paul in Galatians chapter 1. He leaves that matter to 'other men's judgements'. Tyndale says it is not 'an article of any man's faith . . . a man may doubt of the author'.

He then goes straight to what interests him, that other major issue, the frequent rejection of the whole Epistle 'because of certain texts written therein', particularly in chapter 6, supported by texts in chapters 10 and 12, which have been made to say 'that if a man sin any more after he is once baptised, he can be no more forgiven'; that is, says Tyndale, 'contrary to all the scripture'. This is indeed a notorious point. What is notable is that Tyndale strikes out so strongly on his own, first of all using arguments not traditional in that discussion but absolutely in accord with his principle of using the whole New Testament to comment on, and confirm, itself: and secondly so closely relating that theological issue to the daily life of his readers. To clarify the problematic verses in chapter 6, he takes texts from Matthew, Mark, Luke, John and Peter—authorities indeed—and Paul himself in 2 Timothy, to show that the New Testament shows that it is possible wilfully to cut oneself off from God's light. The passage in chapter 6 says no more than that 'such malicious unkindness' as the Pharisees, for example, showed, 'deserveth that the spirit shall never come more at them to convert them, which I believe to be as true as any other text in all the scripture'. The place in the tenth chapter only needs putting into context, that of the sin of blasphemy of the spirit, worthy of worse punishment under Christ than under Moses, because by the sinner's action in maliciously persecuting the truth, 'the way to mercy is locked up'. And in the twelfth chapter, the text about Esau having no way of being restored to his birthright again, says Tyndale, 'must have a spiritual eye'.

> For Esau in selling his birthright despised not only that temporal promotion that he should have been lord over all his brethren and king of that country: but he also refused the grace and mercy of God and the spiritual blessings of Abraham and Isaac and all the mercy that is promised us in Christ which should have been his seed. Of this ye see that this epistle ought no more to be refused for holy, godly and catholic than the other authentic scriptures.

So, if the Epistle to the Hebrews is authentic Scripture, what is it? Not a work to lay 'the ground of the faith of Christ', says Tyndale: but it builds upon that ground

> pure gold, silver and precious stones, and proveth the priesthood of Christ with scriptures inevitable. However there is no work in all scripture that so plainly declareth the meaning and significations of the sacrifices, ceremonies and figures of the old testament, as this epistle . . .

So much so, in fact, that

if wilful blindness and malicious malice were not the cause, this epistle only were enough to weed out of the hearts of the papists that cankered heresy of justifying of works, concerning our sacraments, ceremonies and all manner traditions of their own inventions.

A final paragraph remains. Tyndale has affirmed that this Epistle is authentic Scripture, judged by the highest criterion, Scripture itself. Now he shows that it has its heart in the right place. The clarity of this brief argument, the force of the point, are not at all what is in the previous discussions of this Epistle. In 1521 Erasmus, for example, had done no more than use medieval arguments in stressing the discontinuity between Old Testament and New. Luther, having argued strongly against Paul as author, reversed the medieval comparatives (that Christ was simply 'more excellent' than the old Law) to stress the new dogma that Christ alone suffices for salvation in each Testament. Tyndale does something different. He knows his English readers, ploughboys and all, and writes to their condition as readers of contraband. Not only is he not going to diminish for them any part of Scripture: he is going to let this Epistle make immediate impact. The author of it knew persecution, 'had been in bonds and suffering for Christ's sake'. He 'driveth all to Christ', and so cared for the distant flock that he wrote this to them, and also sent to them Timothy.

Marginal Notes

Historians sometimes assert that Tyndale's Testament gave such offence because his notes were so outrageously inflammatory, and even because he put in notes at all, as if this were some new thing. Annotation in the margin of a page has a very long history indeed. Tyndale's notes to his 1534 New Testament are not outrageous, being entirely made up of either biblical cross-references, of which there are several on most pages, or single-word indicators like the 'Publicans. Alms. Trumpet. Prayer. Babbling'. which stand in the margin of a page of the Sermon of the Mount. The longer ones, of about twenty words, are expository: 'Prophecy is taken here for the expounding of Scriptures: which in dark places must be expounded that it agree to the open places and general articles of the faith' (Romans 12). If there is inflammation, it is caused by such sound pieces of Paul as 'Justifying cometh by faith' (Romans 3), which is simply indicating what Paul is there saying.

Many more marginal notes arrived when the 1534 New Testament appeared in 'Matthew's Bible', some of them long. The longest, of several hundred words, is to Acts 10, saying that Scripture affirms that by works no man can be saved. The first eight chapters of Romans in 'Matthew's Bible' are heavily annotated, and James even more. By the time of Day's folio of 1573, giving the works of Tyndale, Frith and Barnes (not including Tyndale's translations, of course) annotation had been greatly enlarged again, and Tyndale was made for the first time to comment very largely on his own prologues to all the books (Romans has twice the number, all new) which he did only lightly in his 1534 New Testament. Unfortunately Henry Walter, the editor of the Parker Society editions, chose to follow later versions, so that the prologue to the Epistle to the Hebrews, for example, has seven notes, whereas Tyndale wrote none.

Tyndale's Translation

Tyndale has now settled on 'elder' for *presbuteros*. 'Blessed are the maintainers of peace' in Matthew 5 has become 'Blessed are the peacemakers'—it is not simply familiarity that makes that ring better: the stress on the key word 'peace' is even stronger, and it chimes, rhythmically, with 'comforted', 'righteousness', and 'merciful'. He has solved the problem of the ending of Matthew 6 triumphantly, with a run of Saxon words. Where in 1526 both the Latin 'sufficient' and the slightly clumsy construction did not quite hit firmly ('Each day's trouble is sufficient for the self same day'), he now has 'for the day present hath ever enough of his own trouble', where the English vocabulary and running rhythm come close to making a proverb, excellent for the neat six-word phrase in the Greek. He has reversed the order of 'which would proffer his son a stone if he asked him bread' in Matthew 7 to make 'if his son asked him bread, would he offer him a stone?' to good effect, and done the same with changing 'behold here is a greater than Solomon' to 'and behold a greater than Solomon is here'. In Matthew 8, 'O ye endued with little faith' has become 'O ye of little faith' for the one Greek word *oligopistoi*. John the Baptist has not been expected to be 'a reed wavering with the wind' but 'shaken', a sharper image. The 'yea sir' of Matthew 13 has become 'yea Lord'. 'There is no Prophet without honour . . .' in Matthew 14 has become 'A Prophet is not without honour . . .' which for the context is clearer and stronger. We are fourteen chapters in to Matthew's Gospel, and there are already well over two hundred changes from the 1526 Testament. The whole New Testament has well over five thousand revisions.

Tyndale's claim that his work on the language of New Testament Greek, now on top of his own good knowledge of Hebrew, has shown him the Hebrew lying in some of the Greek, was far ahead of its time, though some work may have been done on it by Melanchthon. New Testament Greek was not classical, literary Greek: it was the working language of the Eastern Mediterranean, and there can be no surprise that Aramaic speakers in Jerusalem, talking about a religion founded on the Hebrew Scriptures, tinged their Greek in that way. When Paul quotes the Old Testament, Tyndale now goes behind the Greek to translate from the Hebrew original. But, striking as that is, it is not what he means in his prologue. We perhaps get closer to it in Hebrews chapter 10, where 'holocausts and sacrifice for sin' has become 'burnt sacrifices and sin-offerings', though that turns out to be close to Wyclif.

In that year, 1534, Tyndale published a new Genesis, with some minor revisions, and one major change, which is in the translation of the Hebrew *b'rith*. Whereas in the 1530 Pentateuch Tyndale went for variation, using 'bond' and 'testament', now he uses 'covenant' throughout. This has been seen as historically significant for the 1530s, showing how the reformers moved to a more legalistic covenant theology. That may be so, though the argument is questionable. What has not been said is that the revision may have been done after Tyndale had worked again on Paul, in, for example, Romans 9 and Ephesians 2, 2 Corinthians 3 and especially Ephesians 4, where the covenant is something made with God 'with his face open' as he now puts it. In 1526, the passage read 'And now the lord's glory appeareth in us all, as in a glass: and we are changed unto the same similitude, from glory to glory, even of the lord—which is a spirit' (Ephesians 4). This is now 'But we all behold the glory of the Lord with his face open, and are changed into the same similitude, from glory to glory, even of the spirit of the Lord.' The covenant is with a God revealing himself and looking directly at us.

Summary

There are too many riches in the 1534 revision for adequate comment.[14] It is the New Testament, as English speakers have known it, until the last few decades of this century. The makers of the Authorised Version, who did some curious things elsewhere, had the wisdom to pass on Tyndale's New Testament as they had received it. Phrase after phrase after phrase is his: 'With God all things are possible', 'In him we live and move and have our being', 'Be not weary in well doing', 'Behold, I stand at the door and knock'—the closeness to proverbs can be felt. Here, to stand for all, is part of John 10:

> I am the good shepherd. The good shepherd giveth his life for the sheep. An hired servant, which is not the shepherd, neither the sheep are his own, seeth the wolf coming, and leaveth the sheep, and flyeth, and the wolf catcheth them, and scattereth the sheep. The hired servant flyeth, because he is an hired servant, and careth not for the sheep. I am that good shepherd, and know mine, and am known of mine. As my father knoweth me: even so know I my father. And I give my life for the sheep: and other sheep I have, which are not of this fold. Them also must I bring, that they may hear my voice, and that there may be one flock, and one shepherd.

Chapter 13

'MATTHEW'S BIBLE'

In 1548, Edward Hall's Chronicle, *The Union of the Two Noble and Illustre Families of Lancaster and York* . . . was published, an account of the history of England from 'The unquiet time of king Henry the Fourth' through eight reigns to 'The triumphant reign of King Henry the VIII'. Though that volume is a primary source for, for example, the history of the Wars of the Roses under Henry VI, Edward IV and Richard III (and was used as such by Shakespeare and others) the account of events under Henry VIII makes nearly half of it.

An entry under 'The XXVII Year of Henry VIII', that is, 1536, immediately after the dry but tragic sentence 'And in February following was queen Anne brought a bed of a child before her time, which was born dead', Hall has a longish paragraph recording the death, and expounding the life, of 'William Tyndale otherwise called Hichyns', giving a recognisably accurate account. His second sentence reads: 'This man translated the New testament into English and first put it in Print, and likewise he translated the v. books of Moses, Josua, Judicum, Ruth, the books of the Kings and the books of Paralipomenon, Nehemias or the first of Esdras, the Prophet Jonas, and no more of the holy scripture.' 'The books of the Kings' are what we call 1 and 2 Samuel and 1 and 2 Kings; 'the books of Paralipomenon' are 1 and 2 Chronicles, and 'Nehemiah' is what we call the books of Ezra and Nehemiah, Ezra in Greek having the later title 'First Esdras'. Since Hall's other facts are correct, and he has no axe to grind at this point, we can take it that he is reporting the truth: particularly as Hall's book was prepared for the press and printed, soon after Hall's death, by Richard Grafton, who was familiar with the work of English Bible translation at the time.

The historical books Joshua to Nehemiah complete the history of the Chosen People begun in the Pentateuch with the creation of

Adam. They continue the story through the entry into the Promised Land, the creation of the kingdoms, the exile in Babylon and the return to Jerusalem, that scriptural saga which is the foundation of all Bible—and much world—history. If Tyndale, having translated these books, thus completing an entity making half the Old Testament, did print them himself, no copies have survived. Having finished his Pentateuch in 1530, however, and revised his Genesis in 1534; having translated and printed Jonah; and having included at the back of his 1534 New Testament forty Old Testament passages, all but six of them from outside the Pentateuch, he was clearly continuing his Hebrew work, which would be the natural thing for him to do.

In 1537 there appeared a large folio Bible, well printed (probably in Antwerp) in double columns of black-letter, and on the title-page

> The Bible, which is all the holy Scripture: In which are contained the Old and New Testaments truly and purely translated into English by Thomas Matthew Esq. Hearken to ye heavens and thou earth give ear: For the Lord speaketh. MD XXXVII. Set forth with the King's most gracious licence.

This is the second complete English Bible, the first of two years before being Coverdale's. That was dedicated to the King: this, by Thomas Matthew, is licensed by him. It is an important volume.

The contents are easily described. The Pentateuch is Tyndale's, with some minor variarions. The New Testament is Tyndale's last revision, the so-called 'G.H.' edition, of his 1534 version. The Old Testament outside the Pentateuch and historical books, that is, that half of the Old Testament made up of Job, the Psalms, Proverbs and so on, and all the prophets, is Coverdale's version without change (as are Ezra and Nehemiah). The historical books from Joshua to 2 Chronicles, however, are very different from Coverdale, and seem to have come from nowhere; except that in the treatment of both Hebrew and English, they match exactly the methods of Tyndale in the Pentateuch. In that little volume, Tyndale's determination to make sense almost at all costs, his interest in variation, and his invention of English formulations like 'men of activity', 'observed dismal days', 'upon high mountains and on high hills and under every green tree' are all quite unlike Coverdale. Now, Tyndale's distinctive signature when he turns Hebrew forms into English is found as much in these historical books as it is in the Pentateuch. Such continuity of idiosyncrasy, with other arguments that can be assembled, make it almost completely certain that the historical books in 'Matthew's Bible' are by Tyndale.

That big book has several remarkable features. One of them is a whole-page frontispiece, showing an appreciative Adam and Eve in Paradise before the Fall: they are surrounded by 'nature naturing'— plants, animals, heavenly bodies, and landscape all busily being themselves, presided over by a benevolent Creator, with no sign of a serpent. Another is the large and heavily-ornamented initials which appear in various places. We shall return to these; but here we note the last of them, the whole-page 'W.T.' at the end of the Old Testament, which may be intended to stand for the larger presence of William Tyndale in the whole.

The King's policy about the Bible in English had been changing, and Cromwell had been able to persuade him to license this book. This volume is generally considered to be the real primary version of our English Bible.[1] 'Thomas Matthew' with his good New Testament names, making this whole Bible, is a fiction, to hide Tyndale's presence. That has been understood from the earliest time. John Bale in 1548, and Foxe in 1563 and 1570, refer to a Bible 'under the name of Thomas Matthew'.[2] Both authorities, further, say that the volume was in fact prepared by Tyndale's friend John Rogers.

This man was the incumbent of a church in London from Christmas 1532 until the autumn of 1534. He then went over to Antwerp to serve the English merchants there, being chaplain to the English House, which made him necessarily close to Tyndale, who was living there, in the months before Tyndale's arrest in May 1535. In the autumn of 1536, after Tyndale's death, he went to look after a parish in Saxony, an indication that while in Antwerp he had gone over to the side of the reformers. He matriculated at the University of Wittenberg in November 1540. He returned to England, and early in Mary's reign was in serious trouble for his reformer's views. In that year he went to the stake, the first of the three hundred or so Protestants burned by Mary. Official documents about him refer to 'John Rogers alias Matthew.'[3]

It seems that he knew Greek and some Hebrew. The long-standing tradition that he both helped Tyndale with translation work in those months in the English House, and, when Tyndale was arrested, took charge of the manuscripts which Tyndale was then preparing for the press, has a good deal in its favour. From May 1535 we must think of Rogers assembling the material for his 'Matthew's Bible', and doing it with skill. The volume opens with twenty preliminary leaves, at first of general aids like the Church calendar and an almanack for the years 1528–57. A page of 'exhortation to the study of the holy Scripture gathered out of the Bible . . .' has the large flourished initials 'IR' at the foot of the page, surely for John Rogers. A three-page dedication 'To the most noble and gracious Prince King Henry the eighth' which mentions with respect Queen Jane, and signed 'Your grace's faithful and true subject Thomas Matthew', has at the foot similar initials 'HR', no doubt for Henricus Rex. Further preliminary pages give summaries of the content of the Bible as a sort of religious encyclopaedia, taken verbatim from the new French Bible printed by Olivetan at Neuchâtel in 1535, and a brief account of world history from the Creation until 1537. Later in the book the title to the section of the prophets has on its verso the elaborate initials 'RG', 'EW', taken to stand for Richard Grafton and Edward Whitchurch, the London printers who financed the publication. (As Grafton saw Hall's Chronicle through the press, what that Chronicle says about Tyndale's work of translating was likely to have been accurate.) The initials 'WT' come at the end of the prophets, and before the Apocrypha, included as biblical, as it had been in Coverdale's Bible.

Rogers acted editorially. There are a few small but noticeable changes to Tyndale's text. The serpent now says to Eve, not the 'Ah, sir . . .' phrase noted above, but 'Yea: hath God said indeed, ye shall . . .' We cannot know whether that was Tyndale's third thoughts (the 1534 revision kept 'Ah sir'), or Rogers's move to more conventional phrasing; we might suspect the latter. There are fifty-seven changes to Genesis, of the order of 'an earring' to 'a golden earring' or 'sip' to 'sup'. About half a dozen are significant, like amending Tyndale's phrase in Genesis 46 'For an abomination unto the Egyptians are all that feed sheep' to 'For the Egyptians abhor all shepherds', which is tidier, but has lost two tiny touches of shading, the noun 'abomination' and the act of feeding sheep. Changing 'springing water' to 'living water' in chapter 26 has again just lowered the force a fraction of what Isaac's servants found when they dug in the valley—but it is more literal. In chapter 24, Rebecca, asked if she will go with this man [Isaac] answered 'Yea'. 'Then', wrote Tyndale, 'they brought Rebecca their sister on the way and her nurse and Abraham's servant'. In 'Matthew's Bible', this is 'So they let Rebecca their sister go with her nurse . . .' Again, it is tidier and more literal, but minutely less human. In chapter 49, Rogers, having access to a better Hebrew text, or better assistance, changes 'the daughters come forth to bear rule' to 'the daughters ran upon the wall', struggling half way towards the modern reading 'the branches climb over the wall'. That alteration, to something completely different, well illustrates the difficulty of ancient Hebrew poetry, and the grasp of even one change must be praised. But what Rogers prints, with daughters running on the wall, makes less sense, is even harder to imagine, than Tyndale's original 'come forth to bear rule', and is thus less likely to be his change.

In all the five books of the Pentateuch there are three hundred and thirty changes from Tyndale's original to 'Matthew's Bible', some, again, being small, like 'brodered' to 'bordered', 'ox' to 'bullock' or 'date trees' to 'palm trees'. But some are significant. In Exodus 28, Tyndale's 'light and perfectness' become 'Urim and Thumin', a sad loss. In Exodus 10, Pharaoh's courtiers lose their pointedness: 'Matthew's Bible' has them saying, of Moses, 'How long shall we be thus evil intreated?' where Tyndale in 1530 had 'How long shall this fellow thus plague us?' Tyndale's active, transitive verb 'plague' hits directly, where the passive, intransitive 'be evil intreated' is more mealy—and avoids what is being pointed at, 'this fellow'. In Tyndale's 1530 Leviticus 20, the Lord says 'If any soul turn unto them that work with spirits or makers of dismal days and go a-whoring after them . . .': this has become 'turn him to enchanters or expounders of tokens'. In Leviticus 25, 'Matthew's Bible' has the familiar 'year of jubilee' each time for the fiftieth anniversary, where Tyndale originally had 'year of horns blowing' or 'trumpet year' or 'horn year', which made some sense. 'Jubilee' is hardly a translation at all. In Numbers, 'Matthew's Bible' restores two omitted sentences; elsewhere it itself omits two of Tyndale's accidental repetitions, in Leviticus 11 and Deuteronomy 1.

The work, as we said, is editorial: there is a sense of bringing better knowledge, and probably better Hebrew texts, to the problems, even only a few years after Tyndale's Pentateuch. It seems that John Rogers's Hebrew was adequate for this, but he would not have been alone in his work, even after Tyndale had been taken away. And he clearly has Coverdale's English Bible in front of him: a notable number of changes, like 'Urim and Thumin' are there in Coverdale. A great deal of work needs to be done on the growth of Hebrew knowledge on the Continent between 1529 and 1535 or 1536 before what Rogers did can be evaluated more exactly. What he did do, triumphantly, was transmit the 200,000 words of Tyndale's Pentateuch, and the even longer New Testament, to a more influential English readership, and guarantee that Tyndale was the maker of most of the English Bible for centuries to come. The three-hundred-odd changes Rogers made dwindle into almost nothing when put in such proportion. Having sampled John Rogers's method as an editor, we can surely approach the historical books, which come to us only through his filter, with near-absolute confidence that what we are getting is Tyndale's work.

The presentation is very different. Tyndale's 1530 Pentateuch is a small light book; the pages are uncluttered, with nothing on them except clean text, some in roman type and all pleasant, and occasional short notes. Even the chapter numbers are unobtrusive. 'Matthew's Bible' of 1537 is a large folio, thick and heavy, the text in strong black-letter in two columns. (Later reprints, of 1549, including unfortunately the one on microfilm, and the last editions of 1551, are smaller folios, where the text is cramped and often difficult to decipher.) Books have ornamental openings. Pages have large-print summary headings ('Saul killeth himself'). Chapters are fully demarcated, with summaries before the chapter-titles, and large upper-case section-letters in the outer margins (verse-numbers were not used in English Bibles until the Geneva translations twenty years later). There is a steady drizzle of marginal notation; cross-references to other books of the Bible, explanatory notes, hands pointing to key passages and some subheadings, for example of the names of kings in the later chapters of 2 Kings and Chronicles. Marginal activity is still only a light rain, however; the general rule that the later in the sixteenth century an edition is made, the heavier is the annotation, holds true, so that from John Day's printings of 1551 onwards, for example, the margins are thick with additional notes, and in some editions of the Geneva Bible after 1599, the small-print annotation of a book like Revelation can smother the pages, driving the biblical text into a corner.

Though the cross-referencing was not by Rogers or Tyndale themselves, as far as can be seen the marginal notes are by one or the other: they are not copied wholesale from another European Bible, a common practice.

Tyndale and the Historical Books

Tyndale, starting with Joshua 1, had in front of him eight books fully flowing with a tide of history from 'The Lord courageth Josua to invade the land of promise' as that chapter-summary puts it, to 'Juda is brought to Babilon', part of the heading to the last chapter of 2 Kings, the whole thing then starting all over again, this time from Adam, often through thickets of tedium, in the two books of Chronicles. The first two books, Joshua and Judges, alternate strong, sometimes startling, narrative with lists, as do the books of Chronicles without the vividness. To carry it all off, Tyndale was first going to need two skills, on the one hand of story-telling, and on the other of making long lists of begetters, tribes or villages even a little bit interesting. Additionally, he would find difficult poetry at length in Judges 5, 2 Samuel 22 and 1 Chronicles 16, and some shorter bursts elsewhere. The challenge is greater than it was in, for example, Genesis, where the older prose had more limited vocabulary and syntax. Here, with Samuel and Kings, a translator is often working with a Hebrew court historian who is alert to subtle nuances of life close to the throne of David or Solomon.

To deal first with the lists. Where he can do it, Tyndale makes variety. So in formulaic accounts of the succession of leaders, he turns the simple Hebrew prepositional phrase *tahtaw* into 'in his room' or 'in his stead' or 'in his place', or the Hebrew noun *mahaloqet* becomes, if only briefly, 'number' or 'host' or 'part' or 'company'. But he has little room for manoeuvre in such places, as shown by the lists in the second half of Joshua or the first nine and the last five chapters of 1 Chronicles, and elsewhere.

Poetry makes the contrary problem: too much is possible. The primary technique has still to be variety, to fix a forceful pair of phrases for the parallelisms ('I will beat them as small as the dust of the earth, and will stamp them as the dirt of the street', 2 Samuel 22): but the ancient Hebrew text can be difficult to make out, and Tyndale's need to be clear gives him a challenge. With his limited aids to translation, he has done well. The Authorised Version's London panel in 1609 had the advantage of seventy years of great advances in the knowledge of Hebrew and establishment of texts, but even so Tyndale's translation of the three long poems gave those scholars some phrases which they could take straight over. 2 Samuel 22 is virtually the same as Psalm 18, which means that we can easily watch Coverdale, who translated the Psalms, at work on the poem, by reference to any Book of Common Prayer.

Here is the Authorised Version, in verses 33–8:

God is my strength and power: and he maketh my way perfect.
He maketh my feet like hinds' feet: and setteth me upon my high places.
He teacheth my hands to war; so that a bow of steel is broken by my arms.
Thou hast also given me the shield of thy salvation: and thy gentleness hath made me great.
Thou hast enlarged my steps under me; so that my feet did not slip.
I have pursued mine enemies, and destroyed them; and turned not again until I had consumed them.

Coverdale, who, it should be recalled, had little Hebrew and worked primarily from the Vulgate, taking help where he could find it, does feel noticeably different:

It is God, that girdeth me with strength of war: and maketh my way perfect.
He maketh my feet like harts' feet: and setteth me up on high.

He teacheth mine hands to fight: and mine arms shall break even a bow of steel.

Thou hast given me the defence of thy salvation: thy right hand also shall hold me up, and thy loving correction shall make me great.

Thou shalt make room enough under me for me to go: that my footsteps shall not slide.

I will follow upon mine enemies, and overtake them: neither will I turn again till I have destroyed them.

Here is Tyndale:

God is my strength in war, and riddeth the way clear before me. And maketh my feet as swift as an hinds', and setteth me fast upon my high hold. And teacheth my hands to fight, that a bow of brass is too weak for mine arms.

And thou hast saved me with thy shield, and keptest me ever in meekness. And thou madest me space to walk in, that my feet should not stumble. I followed mine enemies and destroyed them, and turned not again until I had consumed them.

Tyndale, as usual, is clear. The first sentence sets God my strength in war as the subject, to which everything coheres; certainly 'riddeth the way clear before me' offers a picture in the way that the Authorised Version and Coverdale's 'maketh my way perfect' do not. The Vulgate has 'et posuit immaculatam viam meam' (and sets my way without spot), and Luther 'und macht meine Weg ohne Wandel' (and makes my way without change). Coverdale's and the Authorised Version bow is steel: the Vulgate's is bronze, and Luther's, like Tyndale's, is brass, though Luther cannot make the word-play on 'bow of brass'. Coverdale's 'Thou shalt make room enough under me for me to go' is Luther's 'Du machst unter mir Raum zu geben', and is better than the Authorised Version's 'enlarged my steps under me' (which is the Vulgate's 'Dilatasti gressus meos subtus me', following the Septuagint's 'widen my steps . . .'). The Vulgate's 'infirmata vestigia' (feeble footsteps, which is also the Septuagint's reading) and Luther's 'Knochel . . . gleiten' (ankles . . . to glide) are neither so expressive as as Coverdale's sliding footsteps or slipping feet of the Authorised Version; but they are bettered by Tyndale's 'feet should not stumble', which, instead of feebleness, gliding, sliding or slipping, is for feet, the proper result of having the road cleared in front of you. Finally, the Authorised Version's response to Tyndale's last phrase is to steal it.

Coverdale's switch of tense throughout this Psalm, from past to future, is a legitimate response to the Hebrew by a translator with a little learning, though the future tense is not found in the Psalm in the

Septuagint, Vulgate or Luther—or Tyndale. The dominant tense in the Hebrew of this Psalm is imperfect, which conveys various senses. Coverdale has understand only futurity, which suggest the psalmist reassuring himself that the covenant is still to be fulfilled, as in the earlier 'He shall send down from on high to fetch me: and shall take me out of many waters'. Tyndale, with greater understanding of Hebrew, gives past tenses and so is altogether more forceful, and able to suggest the psalmist saying that because God was doing this to me, he is is still here, and still doing it, as the Hebrew imperfect can convey of such a past: 'He sent from on high and fetched me, and plucked me out of mighty waters'. Tyndale's 'plucked' for the Hebrew *yamsheni* is good (it is the Hebrew word used in Exodus 2 when Pharaoh's daughter names the infant Moses 'because . . . I took him out of the water', as Tyndale has it). 'Plucked' is better than Coverdale's 'shall take', the Septuagint's *proselabeto*, (took hold of), the Vulgate's 'assumpsit' (took up), or Luther's 'zog' (pulled or drew).

Tyndale was executed before he could get to Job, the Psalms, Isaiah or Jeremiah, so we shall never know what he was capable of at those poetic heights: except that we do have those passages in 'Matthew's Bible' that overlap with Psalms; in addition to the 2 Samuel 22/Psalm 18 relationship, 1 Chronicles 16 repeats parts of Psalms 105, 96 and 106. There are also a few Tyndale fragments from the Prophets, which will be discussed at the end of this chapter. Watching Tyndale at work with the most difficult poetry is a good way of evaluating his skill with both Hebrew and English, so we shall look briefly at two more passages in Psalm 18, and at another poem in 'Matthew's Bible', before moving on to Tyndale as story-teller in Judges, Samuel and Kings.

Towards the end of that Psalm there is a passage which in Coverdale runs 'A people whom I have not known shall serve me. As soon as they hear of me, they shall obey me: but the strange children shall dissemble with me. The strange children shall fail, and be afraid out of their prisons'. Coverdale is using Vulgate's 'filli alieni' (and Vulgate is following Septuagint's *huioi allotrioi*, leading to Luther's 'fremden Kinder'); but he makes little sense of what in the Hebrew those 'sons of the aliens' are doing. Perhaps the clearest modern version is the Jerusalem Bible (1966) 'A people I did not know are now my servants, foreigners come wooing my favour, no sooner do they hear than they obey me. Foreigners grow faint of heart they come trembling out of their fastnesses.' The idea in the Hebrew is that these are the smiles of the conquered, who have no choice but to put on a show of deference. Tyndale has 'For the people which I knew not became my servants. And the aliens crouched unto me, and obeyed me at a word. And the

aliens that shrink away shall tremble for fear in their defended places'.
He has a note on 'defended places', 'That is, even where they lurk and
hide themselves although in strongholds'. ('Defended' is literally 'shut
up'.) Tyndale makes immediate sense. One reason for this is that his
verbs are directly physical: 'crouched', 'shrink away', 'tremble'. No
doubt the Jeruslaem Bible's 'come cringing', the Revised English
Bible's 'come fawning' come from a better modern understanding of
the Hebrew. Yet Tyndale's 'crouched unto me' is the most physically
realised, even to the point of being like a moment in a drama:
followed, as it is, by 'obeyed me at a word' it gives immediately a
kinetic effect, a movement, which brings the 'aliens' to life. Yet the
action does not stop there. Coverdale is cloudy: the 'strange children
shall dissemble with me . . . shall fail'. Tyndale follows the movement
through: 'And the aliens that shrink away shall tremble for fear in their
defended places.' (At that point, a modern version has 'foreigners will
be disheartened' as if they can't find luggage trolleys at Heathrow.)

Tyndale's chapter, his version of the Psalm, is packed with verbs of
action—'I wasted them and so clouted them, that they could not arise:
but fell under my feet' (2 Samuel 22). (Coverdale has there, 'I will
smite them, that they shall not be able to stand: but fall under my
feet.') Tyndale's Most High 'hurled' lightning—Coverdale's was 'cast
forth'—and there is no verb supplied in the Hebrew. Coverdale does,
however, have the edge on Tyndale at one point. Where Tyndale has
'Thou art my light, O Lord, and the Lord shall light my darkness',
which is satisfactory, Coverdale has 'Thou also shalt light my candle:
the Lord my God shall make my darkness to be light', which is
followed largely by the Authorised Version.

Finally, two sentences early in the Psalm will again show Tyndale
going for a clarity that can be felt in the body. Coverdale has 'The
sorrows of death compassed me: and the overflowings of ungodliness
made me afraid. The pains of hell came about me: the snares of death
overtook me'. The later Geneva Bible moves understanding on a little:
'The sorrows of death compassed me, and the floods of wickedness
made me afraid. The sorrows of the grave have compassed me about:
the snares of death overtook me.' The Geneva margin for the second
'sorrows' gives: 'Or, cords, or cables'. The Authorised Version's panel
kept a good deal of Geneva, but wisely tried to sharpen Coverdale's
'the overflowings of ungodliness' or Geneva's 'the floods of wickedness'
a little, to read 'the floods of ungodly men'—without much success.
They went to Latin for the last verb, 'the snares of death prevented me'
which has the classical sense of death outstripping someone, which is
correct but heavy and confusing. In the Hebrew, there are two root

images, both concrete, and each with its parallel: massive water, which smothers, and cords, which entrap. The Hebrew shows polysemy, from a basic meaning of being knotted: either rope (probably correct) or writhing in pain. Both water and cords belong by possessives to death: and the two central nouns, Geneva's 'wickedness' and 'the grave', are proper nouns in balance. The Jerusalem Bible recognises this: 'The waves of death encircled me the torrents of Belial burst on me; the cords of Sheol girdled me, the snares of death were before me'. But, philologically accurate as it is, it is unclear, particularly in the last line, though the second line is much to be preferred to top the Revised English Bible's 'and destructive torrents overtook me'.

Tyndale—the first translator from the Hebrew—has: 'For the waves of death have closed me about, and the floods of Belial have feared me. The cords of hell have compassed me about, and the snares of death have overtaken me.' 'Feared' as a transitive verb, and 'compassed me about', have left the language: but of all the versions, only Tyndale preserves that run of parallel concrete nouns and parallel concrete verbs in strong simplicity: waves, floods, cords, snares, and closed about, feared, compassed, overtaken.

The Song of Debora

The fifth chapter of the book of Judges is a heroic song of some antiquity, celebrating the triumph of Debora and Barak over Sisera and the kings of Canaan, saving Israel from oppression. Powerful in itself as early Hebrew poetry, and often puzzling, it also contains unique difficulties caused by the manifest corruption of a great deal of the text beyond restoration. The challenge to a translator here is to make something that has meaning without being too implausible: it is thus a useful testing-ground. In the mid-1530s, Tyndale would have had available his customary Septuagint, Vulgate and Luther texts. For a chapter of such notorious difficulty he might have needed other helps. The new translation from the Hebrew by Santi Pagnini (Sanctes Pagninus), though barbarous Latin, was widely used after its publication in 1528 because in its deliberate literalness it did illuminate the Hebrew text. Tyndale may have had sight of a French version of the Bible by Calvin's cousin, Pierre Robert Olivetan, published in Neuchâtel in February 1535, which used Pagninus, as everyone did, but went back to the original Hebrew as well. (It is not totally impossible that the influence was the other way round, and that Tyndale's Hebrew thinking filtered through to such a reformed text as Olivetan's Bible. There is more work to be done on the interaction of

Hebrew studies among European reformers in the 1530s.) While considering this poem, it may be of value to look forward to the Geneva scholars a quarter of a century later and to King James's London panel a half century after that. Those scholars were tied by having, at the King's command, to base their work on the ill-done, backward-looking, heavily Latinate Bishops' Bible of 1568 partly because it had no marginal notes. They did not do so in many parts of the Bible, and some advanced Hebrew knowledge came through.[4] It might be useful to see if some of their readings supported Tyndale.

From the start, we find that Tyndale, always concerned with the output side of his work, has understood a ringing opening. All the other versions mentioned, including the Hebrew (except Olivetan), put the verb first, and begin with something like 'Then sang Debora and Barak ... on that day, saying ...' Tyndale not only understands that the natural English order is subject + verb, but goes for four heavy chords at the end of the phrase, with 'Then Debora and Barak the son of Abinoam sang the same day: saying ...' (Olivetan by contrast is lyrical, 'Et en ce jour là Deborah et Barak ... chanterent, en disant ...') 'Sang the same day saying' is a trumpet-call. Praise the Lord, writes Tyndale, for the willing ones, 'while other sat still in Israel', an idiosyncratic rendering of the Hebrew unique to Tyndale, who has ignored what other versions give, that is, vengeance (but put the idea in the margin), and gone for the possibility of the Hebrew meaning literally the loosening of hair, suggesting unbuttoned people flopping about. Luther gets the inaction but misses the looseness, with 'da die grossen inn Israel still sassen', (while the great ones in Israel sat still).

'Hear kings and hearken lords, I will sing ...' Tyndale continues, alone taking up the Septuagint's avoidance of ponderous solipsisms, the repeated 'Ego's in the Latin translations, Olivetan's 'moymesme moymesme je chanterai' and Luther's 'Ich will dem HERRN will ich singen', to move the sentence forward to the point of it, 'praise unto the Lord God of Israel'. He is uniquely economical by making the 'hear' verbs do the work, and can finish in seventeen words what Luther and Geneva take twenty-four to do, and the Authorised Version twenty-seven. Tyndale seems to have felt that to reproduce the repetition that is in the Hebrew would get in the way of being intelligible, to him paramount.

Presently, according to Tyndale, when the Lord came 'the earth trembled, and the heaven rained and the cloud dropped water'. The Hebrew 'rain' word is the same both times, as it is in the Septuagint, Vulgate, Pagninus, Olivetan and Luther—and the Authorised Version.

But Tyndale loves variation; and Geneva took over his phrase. Then in the Hebrew the mountains 'flowed', as they did in the other versions (Luther, 'Die berge flossen'). But Tyndale, on his own, has 'the mountains melted', pleasingly alliterative for high poetry, but also more physical: flowing mountains are one thing; melting mountains, which are only then able to flow, make a stronger image (one used by the 1966 Jerusalem Bible).

Already, three sentences in, we can see Tyndale not only striking out on his own in interpreting the Hebrew, but uniquely making the English sing. It might be tedious to go in this way through every word and phrase of Judges 5, though it would continue to be instructive, especially in the matter of Tyndale's determination to be clear; but it is worth looking at a few of the song's especially teasing moments, or at particular felicities of Tyndale—as in the very next sentence: 'In the days of Samgar' says the Hebrew, 'the highways ceased'; the other versions agree; Luther has 'waren vergangen die wege' (literally 'were passed away the ways') which is not very sharp. Tyndale sees the scene physically, and has 'the high ways were unoccupied' (taken up by Geneva and the Authorised Version), and supports it with a long marginal note giving a picture of the kinds of ordinary people, 'husbandman nor citizen . . . nor wayfaring man . . . nor plowman' who dare not 'peep out of his city, town or village' for fear of being 'straightway snatched up of the thieves' (a note summarised by Geneva).

Then Tyndale has 'God chose new fashions of war, for when they had war at their gates'. The Jerusalem Bible, for the same impossible Hebrew, has, 'Those that should stand for God were dumb' and the Revised English Bible 'They chose new gods and consorted with demons.' That makes a good indication of the extent of the problem—and so much for the literal inspiration of Scripture! At this point the ancient versions differ completely, and the most sophisticated modern interpreters are poles apart. The problem is partly the familar one of vocabulary, deciding what Hebrew root is dominant or present; and partly that as Hebrew lacks case-endings, there can be real doubt about subjects and objects, as here around the verb 'chose'. The Septuagint has 'They chose new gods', the Vulgate 'The Lord chose new wars', Pagninus 'Who chose new gods', Luther 'A new [thing] has God chosen', and Olivetan 'He has chosen new gods'. Tyndale, sensing that the Vulgate's grammar is right but its sense wrong, as the triumph was not in having new wars but in the newness in the war being fought, made out of his own head something that is appropriate and clear, 'God chose new fashions of war', which the most modern commentators think is the right way round, with the right subject of 'chose', 'God', and the right adjective, 'new', though what is new is debatable. The other way, with new gods being chosen, allowed a scholar to suggest, via a Babylonian parallel, that the Hebrew for gates (*she'arim*) should instead be construed as demons (*se'irim*); hence the Revised English Bible's reading.[5]

Geneva, followed by the Authorised Bible, then has 'Praise (bless) ye the Lord: Speak, ye that ride on white asses . . . and walk by the way', though there is complete disagreement about the middle phrase. The ancient versions and the mediaeval Hebrew commentators agreed about the white asses, though fancifully, with words like 'shining': Luther has them simply as 'schonen eselyn', (beautiful asses). Tyndale both economises by putting the 'praise' and 'speak' verbs together 'Bless the Lord ye that ride . . .' and then alone suggests that the asses are more than white or beautiful, but 'goodly', with a sense of specialness.[6] Modern scholarship understands them as tawny asses, much sought after in the Arab world, [7] making Tyndale's shot a good one. What the Hebrew *middin* that follows means is uncertain. Geneva does what Tyndale so rarely does, and ducks the issue, giving 'ye that dwell by Middin'. The ancient versions and Luther give 'sit in judgement', taking the possibility of one Hebrew root; another root gives the sense of fine drapes or a carpet, leading also to the notion of sitting, and supporting the idea of an original sequence about those who ride, those who walk, and those who sit. Tyndale is sensible as well as economical, making a division between the wealthy-with-governors and the ordinary wayfarers: 'Bless the Lord ye that ride on goodly asses and sit in judgement. And ye that walk by the ways make ditties.' 'Making ditties' at the end parallels 'bless' at the beginning, and points up Luther's verb 'tichtet', beyond the Septuagint's 'meditate' and the Vulgate's 'speak'. 'Ditty' has, since the seventeenth century, lost its force as meaning a high composition: for four hundred years before that it had an honourable place. Shakespeare's Rosalind refers to 'no great matter in the ditty', and Sir Thomas Browne wrote of a friend 'to be with Christ was his dying ditty'.[8] The word gives Tyndale a rhythm, so that each unit, made of monosyllables, ends with a dysyllable—'asses', 'judgement', 'ditties'.

Two more illustrations from this baffling and absorbing poem. Tyndale follows his 'ditties' with 'Now the archers did cry, where men draw water'—not a common remark, but picturable as a scene. The Hebrew has 'from the sound of the archers'. The chief problem is the 'from'; the ancient versions give different treatments with different results. The Septuagint omits 'from', and Tyndale takes that further, turning the noun 'sound' into a verb, 'did cry'. That is good work, and at the time unique to him. True, he has suppressed the sense of 'from' in the Hebrew: but the Authorised Version, who did not, had then to introduce fresh words. Time would fail to tell of the tangles produced by most other versions before this century. We note only the Authorised Version, whose scholars had to import a string of italics to indicate what was not in the Hebrew, and even then made something elephantine: '*They that are delivered* from the noise of archers in the places of drawing water . . .' (The end of the story is that by the late twentieth century the archers had disappeared altogether, scholars giving something like 'Louder than the shouts of those distributing water', and the Revised English Bible has 'Hark the sound of the merrymakers at the places where they draw water'. Let us continue to thank God for Tyndale.)

One final example. Between marginal section-letters C and D, Tyndale has 'But the silver that they coveted, they carried not away'. All the ancient and sixteenth-century versions agree that the enemy (the Canaanites) failed in their intention of despoiling the Israelites, to the point that, as the Geneva margin has it, 'They won nothing, but lost all'. Tyndale uniquely shades in the notion of coveting. This shows his alertness to a word-play in the Hebrew, where the word for the expected loot, *kessef* ('silver'), also carries a sense of being pale with desire. Bringing that notion to the enemy kings' military attacks—they are, as it were, swooning with desire for the spoil—adds to the sense of the futility of their action, making their defeat that much more strong. Not only did they take neither prisoners nor spoil: they suffered a peculiar disappointment. In this, Tyndale shows that when he needs an effect, he can draw on his own independent, and considerable, knowledge of Hebrew.

Story-Telling

Long stretches of the historical books tell stories, and very fine ones, of the heroes, heroines and villains whose actions filled the imaginations of men and women in the middle east, Europe and America until well into the present century. Here are leaders like Gideon, Jephthah and Samson, kings as richly depicted as Saul, David and Solomon, prophets as heterodox as Elijah and Elisha, and passing presences like Rahab, Jonathan, Abigail, Absalom, Naaman, Jezebel or Jehu; stories that are heroic, when 'Little David overcometh the great Goliath', mysterious, like the walls of Jericho falling down at a shout, touching, as the love of Ruth, or shocking, of the unnamed victim ('the Levite's

wife') of gang-rape; deeds that haunt the consciences of royal generations, like David's adultery with Bathsheba, or fill the mind with
opulence, like Solomon receiving the Queen of Sheba.

Tyndale's first task is to keep the narrative drive. Like a novelist, he
must not allow the pace to drop. Sometimes the story is a sentence
long: 'He went down and slew a lion in a pit in a time of snow' (2
Samuel 23). At the other extreme, Tyndale has to keep going the
account of David as king over three books (1 and 2 Samuel, 1 Kings)
and then over two more (1 and 2 Chronicles). His second concern is
not to get in the way of the Hebrew, which knows very well how to
deal with history, as the very religion it expresses is the relationship
between a unique God and his chosen people, expressed as a story.
Thirdly, he must, as always, write clear English.

> And when he [Gideon: Tyndale calls him Gedeon] had brought
> down the people unto the water, the Lord said unto Gedeon: As
> many as lap the water with their tongues, as dogs do, them put by
> themselves, and so do them that kneel down upon their knees to
> drink. And the number of them that put their hands to their mouths
> and lapped, were three hundred men. And all the remnant of the
> people knelt down upon their knees to drink water. And the Lord
> said unto Gedeon, with the three hundred men that lapped I will
> save you, and deliver the Madianites into thine hand. And all the
> other people shall go every man unto his own home (Judges 7).

That is as clear as one can get. Like the Hebrew, it is five sentences
beginning with 'And'. Geneva and the Authorised Version introduce
'So' and 'but' and sprout italics and other extra words and make it
confusing. Tyndale is direct and economical: his 'as dogs do' is better
than the Authorised Version's 'as a dog lappeth'. He knows, unlike the
others, that he needs a finite verb 'put' and the hand-movement before
the mouth-movement, so that his 'put their hands to their mouths and
lapped' is head and shoulders above Geneva and the Authorised Version's 'that lapped, *putting* their hand to their mouth'.

Or, from the end of 2 Samuel 18,

> And the king [David] said to Chusi: is the lad Absalom safe? And
> Chusi answered: the enemies of my lord the king and all that rise
> against thee, to have thee [Hebrew: for evil], be as thy lad is. And
> the king was moved and went up to a chamber over the gate and
> went And as he went thus he said: my son Absalom, my son, my
> son, my son Absalom, would to God I had died for thee, Absalom
> my son, my son.

After 'rise against thee', Luther has 'die sich wider dich auflehnen ubel zu thun' (literally 'who themselves against you rebel evil to do'). The Authorised Version follows Geneva with the brief 'to do *thee* hurt', which might be thought adequate; except that Tyndale does it in three words against Luther's eight, with simply 'to have thee'. The first three 'son's are, in the Septuagint, 'child'. Tyndale, like the Hebrew—and the Vulgate and Luther—understands the cumulative force of the one word 'son'. Moreover, he expands the Hebrew's five to six, legitimately, for an effect in English. It is a matter of rhythm. After 'And as he went/thus he said', with its repeated double stress either side of 'he' (As . . . went/thus . . . said), Tyndale makes a further balance, giving 'Absalom, my son, my son', twice. The force of that further double repetition (of 'Absalom', and of 'my son' twice in each case) is painful enough for a father in sudden and desperately pointed grief. But between the pairs he puts 'would to God I had died for thee'— English, unlike all the other languages considered here, giving him monosyllables for that cry—and prefaces it with the variant 'my son Absalom'. Moreover, in the monosyllabic phrase he is more alert to rhythm than his successors, for the running emotion of two triplets and a final doublet is extremely forceful: 'would to God/I had died/for thee'. Geneva and the Authorised Version change the punctuation and thus the phrasing, add 'O' to the two outer 'Absalom's' to make a quite different rhythm dominated by those two wordless cries, and lose the first triplet altogether with a jolting double stress, 'would God/I had died/for thee'. It is a different effect. Geneva and the Authorised Version are more baroque: Tyndale is more simple and economical and thus, it might be felt, more movingly human.

Court intrigues intensify as the monarchy has more to lose, from the anointing of the first King of Israel, Saul, in 1 Samuel, to his successor David in 1 and 2 Samuel and 1 Kings, and especially in the great age of David. The story-telling develops sophisticated nuances. While 'the young virgin Abisag keepeth David in his extreme age', as the headnote to the first chapter of 1 Kings has it, 'Adoniah occupieth the realm, unwitting to his father'. Bathsheba (David's wife) and Nathan the prophet agree that David had sworn that Bathsheba's son Solomon should succeed him, and successfully get the old King to intervene and restore Solomon. But that leaves Adoniah, the fourth son of those with different mothers born to David in Hebron, who after the death of Absalom had considered himself, and been considered by the people, David's heir, with a grievance. Though he has Joab, the old army commander-in-chief, on his side, the party of Bathsheba and Nathan has with them Benaiah, the captain of the king's bodyguard and thus

the only courtier with soldiers instantly available. As the story has
survived in the Hebrew, it is a little odd, for the last person Adoniah
would go to declare rebellion (taking the now-dead king's concubine
was an insult to Solomon and an immediate challenge to the throne)
would be Bathsheba; but that is not Tyndale's problem. His concern is
to catch the quality of over-ripe explosive lurking in every move and
speech. As sentence succeeds sentence, in the elaborate court ritual,
somebody's death is nearer.

> After that, Adoniah the son of Hagith came to Bethsabe the mother
> of Salomon. And she said: Betokeneth thy coming peace? And he
> said: it betokeneth peace. Then said he, I have a matter to show
> thee. And she said, say on. And he said: thou knowest that the
> kingdom was mine, and that all Israel put their eyes on me, that I
> should reign, howbeit the kingdom was turned away and given to
> my brother, for it was appointed him of the Lord: and now I ask a
> petition of thee, wherefore deny me not. And she said unto him: tell
> me what it is. Then he said: speak I pray thee, unto Salomon the
> king (for he will not say thee nay) that he give me Abisag the
> Sunamite to wife. And Bethsabe said: well, I will speak for thee unto
> the king.
>   And thereupon Bethsabe went unto king Salomon to speak unto
> him for Adoniah. And the king rose up against her and bowed
> himself unto her, and sat him down on his seat. And there was a seat
> set for the king's mother, and she sat on his right side. Then she said:
> I must desire a little petition of thee: say me not nay. And the king
> said unto her: Ask on my mother: for I will not say thee nay. And
> she said: let Abisag the Sunamite be given to Adoniah thy brother to
> wife. And King Salomon answered and said unto his mother: why
> doest thou ask Abisag the Sunamite for Adoniah? but rather ask for
> him the kingdom, seeing he is mine elder brother: Even for him ask
> it and for Abiathar the priest, and for Joab the son of Zaruiah. Then
> king Salomon sware by the Lord saying: God do so to me and so
> thereto if Adoniah have not spoken this word against himself. Now
> therefore as surely as the Lord liveth whuch hath stablished me and
> set me on the seat of David my father, and which hath made me an
> house as he promised me, Adoniah shall die this day. And king
> Salomon sent by the hand of Banaiah the son of Jehoiada, and smote
> him that he died (1 Kings 2).

Tyndale's trick is to favour concrete nouns and verbs. Geneva and
Authorised Version's 'Comest thou peacably?' is here 'Betokeneth'
(Tyndale's flourish at the opening of courtly manoeuvres) 'thy coming'
(noun) 'peace?' (noun). 'Somewhat' in the Authorised Version is here 'a

matter', even better than Geneva's 'suit' which plays the card too soon. Geneva and the Authorised Version's 'set their faces' is in Tyndale the more concrete 'put their eyes'. The kingdom in the later versions 'is (become) my brother's': in Tyndale it 'was . . . given to my brother'. The next six sentences of Tyndale, with tiny changes, go directly into Geneva and the Authorised Version, ending with the queen-motherly 'Well, I will speak for thee unto the king'. (That very English 'Well', though the ancient versions have 'Good', and Luther 'Wohl', is far more pregnant with thought than them, to the point of being sinister.) The very matter-of-factness of Tyndale's 'there was a seat set . . .' increases the tension. (In Geneva and the Authorised Version Solomon 'caused a seat to be set'.) Seated on the king's right, she then speaks. Whereas Adoniah had asked her 'a petition', it is here in the Hebrew 'a little petition' as Tyndale has it: in Geneva 'a small request' and in the Authorised Version 'one small petition'. Tyndale's run of 'i' sounds and the light rhythm, 'a little petition' catches the queen-mother's nervous-ness with her powerful son, where the Authorised Version thumps the stresses more heavily. Yet it is Tyndale's treatment of the verb which catches the imagination. The Hebrew and all earlier versions have Bathsheba begging, or requesting: it is Tyndale who makes her 'desire' the little petition—and even better, by bringing in a modal verb which cannot be in the Hebrew, 'must desire'. Bathsheba, with that, is not speaking for herself.

The rest of the story, as the final explosion happens, is, in Geneva and Authorised Version, almost entirely told in Tyndale's words: except that where at the swift end the Authorised Version takes the Hebrew idiom and says that Benaiah 'fell upon him that he died', Tyndale, followed by Geneva, not only makes it English but kills him with one dark verb, 'smote'.

The stories of Elijah and Elisha in 1 and 2 Kings as told by Tyndale are Hebrew narratives in English at their greatest. It is a particularly fine experience to read them aloud—and reading, for much more than a century after Tyndale, meant just that. The Second Book of Kings 4, mostly the story of Elisha with the Shunamite woman, was very properly taken through with only small changes into Geneva and the Authorised Version. The same is true of the accounts in 1 Kings 18 and 19 of Elijah on Mount Carmel and then on Horeb, and they show Tyndale at his very best.

1 Kings Chapters 17, 18 and 19

In 897 BC, King Ahab had brought a religious crisis to Israel by marrying Jezebel, a daughter of the King of Tyre and the Sidonians, who had been a priest of Baal and a murderer. Jezebel persuaded her husband to build a temple to Baal in Samaria, and cruelly set about eradicating the worship of Jehovah in Israel, murdering his prophets and persecuting his worshippers to the point where Israel's national religion could have been wiped out. Jezebel almost succeeded in forcibly replacing it by the worship of Baal and Astarte. Elijah is suddenly there. He has no history, beyond being a native of Thisbe in Gilead. His story suddenly begins '. . . said unto Ahab'. God is sending drought (the implication is to chasten the people). He goes east and for a while nature supports him.

From the beginning, Tyndale's ear for English rhythms is keen— compare his 'there shall be neither dew nor rain these years, save as I appoint it' with the Authorised Version's 'there shall not be . . . but according to my word': Tyndale's dactyl stresses 'save as/I app/oint it' have an authority in English which the Authorised Version's phrase, though it chimes with the ancient versions, does not have; the Septuagint gives 'that if but according to the word of my mouth'; Luther simply has 'I say it then'. Tyndale saves 'according to the word of the Lord which he spake through Eliah' for the end of the story of the feeding of the Sarephtha household, and there, like Luther, he omits the intrusive phrase in the ancient versions, 'spake by the hand of Eliah'.

Again, though Geneva and the Authorised Version take over 'what have I to do with thee, O thou man of God?' Tyndale's rhythm is later lost in both. Tyndale, alone unlike the ancient versions, puts the verbs 'thought on' and 'slain' last, making her cry come to a climax on 'slain'. Geneva and the Authorised Version's 'to call my sin to remembrance and to slay my son' is cluttered after Tyndale's 'that my sin should be thought on and my son slain'. (Admittedly, the German verbs are last in Luther; but instead of 'my son slain' Luther has 'mein Sohn getodted wurde', which is hardly Tyndale's single stroke.)

The exasperated reluctance of Abdiah (it is Luther who gives the Authorised Version's form 'Obadiah') at the beginning of chapter 18 makes a human start from which the narrative can climb, but it also gives an important indirect view of Eliah. Ahab and Abdiah are scouring the stricken land for any grass for fodder and for Eliah (for news of the end of the drought), and Eliah is known for disappearing: 'the spirit of the Lord shall carry thee away whither I shall not know'. Eliah is a Bedouin of the former desert time, with the austerity of morals and belief in the older, purer religion which Israel needs, and is in awe of. Abdiah's credentials are excellent, so Eliah will not let him down by vanishing in a whirlwind. Tyndale moves the chess pieces one at a time, 'Abdiah went to Ahab', 'Ahab went against Eliah', 'Ahab saw Eliah', varying the verbs for each move, where Geneva and the Authorised Version repeat 'went to meet' (Tyndale's favourite 'went against' for 'meet' has been lost). This is preparatory to the superb exchange, so well-wrought that it feels proverbial, 'art thou he that troubleth Israel? And he said: it is not I that trouble Israel, but thou and thy father's house . . .' Tyndale does not let the rhythm drop, then making 'ye have' refer to the royal house and 'hast' to Ahab alone. By inserting a comma and 'thou' before 'hast', the Authorised Version breaks the phrase linking 'forsaken' and 'followed' into two.

The same is true of Eliah's challenge on Carmel, again a semi-proverbial gift from Tyndale: 'why halt ye between two opinions?' The ancient versions agree on 'halt' (be lame), but differ on the next part. The Septuagint has them limping 'between both your hollow-parts-of-the-knee'; the Vulgate and Luther are frankly boring, with 'in two parts' and 'on both sides' respectively. 'Between two opinions', with its assonance (be-tween, op-in) as well as its scorn, is Tyndale's own. The people, far from religious fervour, have reduced the choice between Baal and Jehovah to 'opinions'. Geneva and the Authorised Version rightly stole it, but almost spoiled it by changing the cutting 'why?' to the more pleading 'how long halt ye . . . ?'

'If the Lord be very God, follow him: or if Baal be he follow him.' These, as Eliah will show, are anything but matters of opinion. The Authorised Version's 'the people answered him not a word' is fine, and supported by Septuagint and Vulgate (and Luther's 'answered him nothing'). But Tyndale has noticed that numbers follow, 'Baal's proph-ets are four hundred and fifty', so the slight touch of the three stresses with the number in the middle, 'not one word' is effective. The energy of the English prose in the next three paragraphs is wonderful. Of course it reflects the Hebrew, but for a moment let us simply consider it as writing of the mid-1530s in English. The variety and colour in the sentence-patterns (including parentheses), the clash of two sides in the drama of the conflict, the desperate squeals of the four hundred and fifty prophets, 'O Baal hear us' and the full-voiced mockery of Eliah are just the start of it. No-one else in the 1530s is writing English with this colour and this control. The first paragraph divides into two, the first more prosaic, ending 'But there was no voice nor answer'. The second becomes frantic, with 'leapt about', 'call loud . . . And they cried loud . . . and cut themselves . . . with knives and lances, till the blood flowed on them', ending with an extension of the earlier phrase 'But there was neither voice nor answer nor any that regarded them', after five running light stresses 'But there was

'neither', come Tyndale's four final thumps which seal every exit—
'neither voice/nor answer/nor any/that regarded'. One small touch
must not pass unseen: The priests of Baal mutilate themselves. 'According to their use' has the Septuagint; 'rite' says the Vulgate; 'after their
way' writes Luther. Tyndale, with the disdain of a shocked observer,
will not dignify their actions with 'use', 'rite' or 'way', but writes 'as
their manner was'.

The climax of the story is Tyndale's, in Geneva and the Authorised
Version, except that Tyndale begins 'And there fell fire from the Lord'
which is more mysterious than the other two versions' 'Then the fire
of the Lord fell', which assumes an understanding of what 'the fire of
the Lord' is. And Tyndale's 'gutter' is Geneva's 'ditch' which is the
Authorised Version's 'trench'. Much could be noted. We move on to
Eliah on Horeb, and the repeated, almost proverbial, 'What doest thou
here, Eliah?', which Tyndale gave to us, after the Vulgate's 'Quid hic
agis, Elia?'. The repeated 'But the Lord was not in the wind/earth-
quake/fire', reflects the original Hebrew and all versions. What Tyndale
made new is what comes next. 'And after the fire, came a small still
voice'. The Hebrew—like the whole experience—is enigmatic. How
can the Lord be in wind, earthquake or fire? Moreover, the most
inscrutable, and the most haunting, is the Hebrew phrase literally
meaning 'a sound of gentle stillness'. The Septuagint has a 'a thin gentle
sound', the Vulgate has 'sibilus aurae tenuis' ('a thin gentle whisper')
and Luther 'ein stilles sanftes Sausen' ('a still, gentle, whistle'). Luther
may have given to Geneva and the Authorised Version the idea of
putting 'still' first, though Geneva goes on 'and soft voice' and the
Authorised Version 'small voice': but Tyndale first gave us smallness,
stillness, and voice. That noun is vital, for it can be spoken to, and it
can go on to make very specific commands. Because of the familiar
order, the Authorised Version has been credited with the phrase: it is
Tyndale's.

Tyndale's Signature

We noted earlier Tyndale's characteristic signature on his translation of
Hebrew words and phrases. The presence of these idiosyncrasies in
both the Pentateuch and 'Matthew's Bible' is one of the reasons why
we can be almost certain that the latter is his work. To take one
obvious example, the musical instrument which in Hebrew is *toph*
Tyndale consistently translates as 'timbrel', and the word occurs in
Genesis and Exodus, and five times in 'Matthew's Bible': Coverdale,
from Ezra on, calls it a 'tabret'.

It is invariably Tyndale's version of the Hebrew that feels clear and direct, as against the deliberately more ornamented and Latinate Authorised Version, and even against the most modern versions such as the Revised English Bible. So it can be a surprise when part of that characteristic use is of unusual words, which either came from a pool of English vocabulary that was local and did not get into the wider more generally received language, or did not survive in time. The compilers of the Oxford English Dictionary took examples from Tyndale, but they made their main early source Coverdale's Bible or, more surprisingly, the 1568 Bishops' Bible, when a more thorough trawl of Tyndale and the Geneva Bible in the latter's various developments between 1560 and 1599 would have turned up more words. As a result, some English words in Tyndale's translations from Hebrew are not in the Dictionary at all. One, from the Pentateuch, is the noun 'back' in the sense of a large water-fowl (Leviticus 11). Another is the mysterious classical-sounding 'ixion' for a kind of kite in Deuteronomy 14. What a 'hart-goat' is in the same chapter is not now known. 'Perleyed' for small-eyed in Leviticus 21, a delightful formation, is not found in the Dictionary (even under 'pearl' or 'purl'). These belong to fauna in the Pentateuch's dietary laws. 'Ratten', however, for something moist and unpleasant, like pus, is in Judges 15: Samson takes as a weapon 'a jaw bone of a ratten ass'. 'Cast no perils' in Judges 18, meaning 'aware of no dangers', seems not to be recorded. 'Bidden' in the sense of 'remained' in 2 Samuel 14 is not recorded in that form. The most interesting and strange of these words is 'fellowship'. Tyndale uses it in a sense familiar to modern ears, as for example in Judges 14, 'they brought thirty companions to bear fellowship'. But it also occurs eight times, in both the Pentateuch and the historical books, in a sense not recorded in the Oxford English Dictionary, where Tyndale has it for the Hebrew particle *na*, which, when added to an imperative, indicates exhortation, and is commonly rendered 'I pray thee'. It can also indicate urgency, adding 'now'. In 1 Samuel 26, Abisai and David come across Saul 'sleeping within a round bank and his spear pitched in the ground at his head'. Abisai says 'God hath closed in thine enemy unto thine hand this day. Now therefore let me smite him a fellowship with my spear to the earth . . .' David forbids it, telling Abisai 'Now then take a fellowship the spear that is at his head . . .' There are similar uses in Numbers 20 and 22, Judges 9, 1 Kings 14, 2 Kings 2 and 2 Kings 9. The Oxford Dictionary nowhere records 'fellowship' in that sense. Even if it represents a dialect form, perhaps from his native Gloucestershire, Tyndale must have felt confident that it would be understood widely. On more than several occasions,

Tyndale offers the first recorded use of a word or phrase. 'A lusty blood', for a vigorous roisterer, the Dictionary gives first in 1562, and not to Tyndale in 2 Samuel 13. 'Adjured' in 1 Samuel 14 is given first to Coverdale in 1539, though it is in Tyndale here in 1537 (however, the Dictionary is right in saying it is translating the Latin *adjurare*). 'Field-devils', of 2 Chronicles 11, taken from Luther's *feldteufel* as a translation of the Hebrew *sairim* ('satyrs' in the Authorised Version) is given to Coverdale in 1535, which may be correct, though Tyndale's manuscript translation of 2 Chronicles cannot be later than May 1535. 'Siled' for 'ceiled' at 1 Kings 6 is in a similar position. We do not know how much traffic there was between Tyndale and Coverdale. 'Bush' as 'a bushy head of hair', which Tyndale uses in the headnote to 2 Samuel 14 for Absalom's hair, is given a first biblical use by the Dictionary to the Douay Bible of 1609. A good deal of work needs to be done on Tyndale's proper importance as first user, as well as maker, of words.

Sometimes the physicality of Tyndale's words glows in what some might think an unbiblical way. The young David, when we first meet him in 1 Samuel 16, is 'brown with goodly eyes'. Tyndale's sentence for Absalom's 'goodliness' in 2 Samuel 16 was taken by King James's revisers: 'from the sole of his foot to the top of his head there was no blemish in him.' The men of the house of David were not only charismatic leaders; they were good-looking. The woman of Thekoa brought before King David in 2 Samuel 14 reports a (fictitous) plot to have her only remaining son killed, which will deprive her of succession—as she puts it, it will 'quench my sparkle', a particularly Tyndalian way of making the idea of something only just alive, a coal or an ember, belong to the person. Several times men 'sleep with' women in the modern sense. Solomon, indeed, 'fell in love with' many women, also in the modern sense. 'Flaggy' for creatures having no firmness (1 Samuel 15) and 'fainty' (in several places from Genesis 25 on) which speaks for itself, are words we should not have lost.

One key to Tyndale's genius is that his ear for how people spoke was so good. The English he was using was not the language of the scribe or lawyer or schoolmaster; it really was, at base, the spoken language of the people. In this he was unlike all other Bible translators, in English certainly. To give an example. David, as we saw, was 'brown with goodly eyes'. The comment speaks down the centuries: the young man was a looker, and one can hear someone saying it. The whole sentence is 'And he was brown with goodly eyes, and well favoured in sight'. By contrast, this is what Authorised Version has: 'Now he *was* ruddy, *and* withal of a beautiful countenance, and goodly to look to.' That is the sort of sentence that gets the Bible a bad name.

No one, ever, spoke that, or could do, with a straight face. As a sentence, all it can do is live in a big book on a brass lectern and be read out on one of the Sundays after Trinity. Again, where in Tyndale in 1 Kings 11 Solomon 'loved many outlandish women' (that is, foreign, from the outlands, and therefore not what the King of God's chosen people should do, as it muddied the religion) in Authorised Version he loved 'many strange women', which is acceptable as well, as long as we keep out of both versions the jocular modern senses. The historian then lists the women; not only, Tyndale says, 'Pharaoh's daughter', but daughters of 'the Moabites, Ammonites, Edomites, Zidonites and Hethites'. Tyndale goes on, 'Nevertheless to such Salomon clave and fell in love with them'. There, the Authorised Version has 'Solomon clave unto these in love', which again takes away both the natural fixing in the person and the spoken phrase. Tyndale's rhythm extends the compulsive behaviour of 'clave' to the fluidity of emotion, much more problematic in a king.

One final example: in 2 Samuel 13, Tyndale has Amnon, crafty-sick and disastrously lustful for his half-sister Thamar (Tamar) say to King David, who has come to visit him, 'let Thamar my sister come and make me a couple of fritters in my sight, that I may eat of her hand'. What could be more harmlessly brotherly than that spoken 'couple of fritters'? What she shall prepare is a mystery, as the Hebrew word occurs only here. The Authorised Version makes something a little more formal of the snack with 'a couple of cakes', missing the pretend-casualness of Amnon, who is 'frittering' his need. 'A couple of fritters' is a spoken phrase where 'a couple of cakes' is not quite. But the Authorised Version is well ahead of the Revised English Bible, which makes a language not spoken on this earth, with 'Sir, let my sister Tamar come and make breadcakes in front of me, and serve them to me with her own hands'. What can 'breadcakes' possibly be ? And whoever actually said 'in front of me . . .' and so on with the necessary casualness? They sound like someone trying to learn a script.

Part 5

MARTYR

Chapter 14

ENTER HENRY PHILLIPS

In the spring of 1535 Tyndale was living with Thomas Poyntz and his wife in the English House in Antwerp, contentedly it seems. He was making further minor revisions to his 1534 New Testament. He had probably almost finished the Old Testament historical books, Joshua to 2 Chronicles, and was now looking ahead to the continuation of 2 Chronicles in the shorter books now called Ezra, Nehemiah and Esther. He might also have seen even further ahead, to the massive ranges of poetic heights of the books of Job and the Psalms.

His Hebrew was now as good as his Greek, if not even better. It appears that he had whatever help it was that he needed, in both someone to assist, and the necessary books. He would have increasingly felt not only able to finish the Old Testament, and thus the whole Bible, but safe to do that work. In Thomas Poyntz he had a good, shrewd, friend and loyal sympathiser. True, at the court in Brussels twenty-four miles away the power of the Emperor Charles was felt as he became still more hostile to King Henry VIII over his behaviour towards his aunt, Catherine: at that time to be English and abroad was not to be popular. Yet the city fathers of Antwerp would not want to risk disturbing their good relations with the profitable English merchants by intruding into the English House without extremely strong cause. Antwerp was in many ways becoming a place of freedom and tolerance. The rest of the Bible lay ahead of him. Tyndale might well have had high hopes.

Malice, self-pity, villainy and deceit were about to destroy everything. These evils came to the English House, wholly uninvited, in the form of an egregious Englishman, Henry Phillips. This young man came of a good family, and had recently become bachelor of civil law at Oxford. His father was a landowner, with property in the West Country: three times Member of Parliament, and twice sheriff, he held a position of profit and authority as 'customer' of the port of Poole. He was sufficiently grand to have been invited to join in the celebrations in London of the wedding of Queen Anne in 1533. Henry was the third son, and he may have been intended for the Church: certainly he had senior ecclesiastical patrons in the West Country.

Some time between leaving Oxford in February 1533 and the spring of 1535 that son, Henry, fell into extreme disgrace and poverty. He was entrusted by his father with a sum of money for someone in London. He stole it. Then he gambled with it, and lost it all. Not daring to go home, for the next few years he approached his patrons for rescue, to no avail. He wrote letters to his father, his mother, to two brothers and to two brothers-in-law, as well as to his patrons: the letters are extant, and their tone is not healthy.[1] He is both fawning and full of self-pitying complaint. (J.F. Mozley reports contemporary records that he held profitable benefices in Exeter, and comments 'they must have run dry by the time he went oversea'.)[2] Most of the letters were written abroad.

For he then appeared close to Antwerp, in Louvain, a strong centre of Roman Catholic thought, antagonistic to the Reformation. And he suddenly had money: not enough to keep him for the rest of his life, which is what he so desperately sought, but sufficient to enable him to live comfortably and execute a scheme. Someone in London paid him well to carry out a secret operation. It most certainly was not the English government. Henry Phillips detested King Henry and all his works, and was notorious for saying so frequently. English agents on the Continent, when they mentioned Phillips, did so as a traitor and a rebel. Whoever it was in London who employed him, knew his extreme poverty, his whining desperation, his hatred of Lutheranism (and possibly his treasonable hostility to the King), and saw a useful, and no doubt disposable, tool. His covert mission was to find a means to break the security of the English House at Antwerp, and arrest William Tyndale.

What happened is best told by Foxe:

William Tyndale, being in the town of Antwerp, had been lodged about one whole year in the house of Thomas Pointz an Englishman, who kept there a house of English merchants: about which time came thither one out of England, whose name was Henry Philips, his father being customer [customs officer] of Poole, a comely fellow, like as he had been a gentleman, having a servant with him: but wherefore he came, or for what purpose he was sent thither, no man could tell.

Master Tyndale divers times was desired forth to dinner and supper amongst merchants: by means whereof this Henry Philips became acquainted with him, so that within short space Master Tyndale had a great confidence in him, and brought him to his lodging, to the house of Thomas Pointz: and had him also once or twice with him to dinner and supper, and further entered such friendship with him, that through his procurement he lay in the same house of the said Pointz: to whom he showed moreover his books, and other secrets of his study, so little did Tyndale then mistrust this traitor.

But Pointz, having no great confidence in the fellow, asked Master Tyndale how he came acquainted with this Philips. Master Tyndale answered that he was an honest man, handsomely learned, and very conformable. Then Pointz, perceiving that he bare such favour to him, said no more, thinking that he was brought acquainted with him by some friend of his. The said Philips, being in the town three or four days, upon a time desired Pointz to walk with him forth of the town to show him the commodities thereof, and in walking together without the town, had communication of divers things, and some of the king's affairs: by which talks Pointz as yet suspected nothing, but after, by the sequel of the matter, he perceived more what was intended.

Phillips made sure that Pointz knew he had money, for a purpose Pointz could not fathom. Phillips went to the Court at Brussels, at that time very hostile to England, where he was later traitorous to King Henry. He came back with

that procurer-general, who is the emperor's attorney, with certain other officers, as after followeth: which was not done with small charges and expenses, from whomsoever it came.

Within a while after, Pointz sitting at his door, Philips's man came unto him, and asked him whether Master Tyndale were there, and said, his master would come to him: and so departed: but whether his Master Philips were in the town or not, it was not known: but at that time Pointz heard no more, either of the master or of the man. Within three or four days after, Pointz went forth to the town of Barrois, being eighteen English miles from Antwerp, where he had business to do for the space of a month or six weeks: and in the time of his absence Henry Philips came again to Antwerp, to the house of Pointz, and coming in, spake with his wife, asking her for Master Tyndale, and whther he would dine there with him: saying, 'What good meat shall we have?' She answered, 'Such as the market

will give.' Then went he forth again (as it is thought) to provide, and
set the officers whom he brought with him from Brussels, in the
street, and about the door. Then about noon he came again, and
went to Master Tyndale, and desired him to lend him forty shillings:
'for,' said he 'I lost my purse this morning, coming over at the
passage between this and Mechlin.' So Master Tyndale took him
forty shillings, which was easy to be had of him, if he had it: for in
the wily subtleties of this world he was simple and inexpert.

Then said Philips, 'Master Tyndale! you shall be my guest here this
day.' 'No,' said Master Tyndale, 'I go forth this day to dinner, and you
shall go with me, and be my guest, where you shall be welcome.' So
when it was dinner-time, Master Tyndale went forth with Philips,
and at the going forth of Pointz's house, was a long narrow entry, so
that two could not go in a front. Master Tyndale would have put
Philips before him, but Philips would in no wise, but put Master
Tyndale before, for that he pretended to show great humanity. So
Master Tyndale, being a man of no great stature, went before, and
Philips, a tall comely person, followed behind him: who had set
officers on either side of the door upon two seats, who, being there,
might see who came in the entry: and coming through the same
entry, Philips pointed with his finger over Master Tyndale's head
down to him, that the officers who sat at the door might see that it
was he whom they should take, as the officers that took Master
Tyndale afterwards told Pointz, and said to Pointz, when they had
laid him in prison, that they pitied to see his simplicity when they
took him. Then they took him, and brought him to the emperor's
attorney, or procurer-general, where he dined. Then came the
procurer-general to the house of Pointz, and sent away all that was
there of Master Tyndale's, as well his books as other things: and from
thence Tyndale was had to the castle of Filford, eighteen English
miles from Antwerp, and there he remained until he was put to
death.[3]

Tyndale was arrested on or near 21 May 1535. Vilvorde castle, six
miles north of Brussels and about the same distance from Louvain, had
been built in 1374 as an exceptionally secure refuge (it fell into ruin by
the eighteenth century and disappeared). Mozley comments: 'Within
this gloomy stronghold Tyndale would be safe enough, far away from
the turbulent and free-thinking city of Antwerp, where the rulers
winked at the advance of Lutheranism.'[4] Among the archives at Brussels, under the heading 'Account of the confiscated goods of the
Lutherans and heretical sects', is included payment to the lieutenant of

the castle for the money expended by him in the 'keeping of a certain prisoner, named William Tintalus, Lutheran . . . for a year and one hundred and thirty-five days . . .' Foxe reported that the procurer-general went to 'the house of Poyntz, and sent away all that was there of Master Tyndale's, as well his books and other things': Tyndale's sixteen months in prison in Vilvorde were paid for, by the sale of at least some of his confiscated books and other items. We cannot know what manuscripts of translations were removed and destroyed. The completed Old Testament historical books must have been hidden or already sent somewhere else, for them to have survived as they did.

What was Tyndale's crime? For what was he arrested, imprisoned for so long, and eventually condemned to death? Phillips, Foxe explains, had so ingratiated himself with the Court at Brussels by his declared hatred of King Henry that he was able to arrange for 'the procurer-general, which is the emperor's attorney' no less, to go with him, with other officers, to Antwerp to arrest Tyndale. In other words, the charge was heresy, with not agreeing with the Holy Roman Emperor—in a nutshell, being a Lutheran. A letter from Cromwell's godson, Thomas Theobald (whom the Secretary often used as his emissary abroad) both sharpens and extends the matter. In July 1535 Theobald wrote at length to Cranmer, now Archbishop of Canterbury, from Antwerp, partly about his stay with two English black friars in nearby Louvain (one of them Latimer's old enemy):

> All succour that I can perceive them to have, is only by him which hath taken Tyndale, called Harry Phillips, with whom I had long and familiar communication; for I made him believe that I was minded to tarry and study at Louvain. I could not perceive the contrary by his communication, but that Tyndale shall die, which he doth follow [urge] and procureth with all diligent endeavour, rejoicing much therein . . .

From what is known of Phillips's character, some of this joy must have been almost psychopathic: but no doubt also he was to have been paid by results. '. . . saying that he had a commission out also for to have taken Dr Barnes and George Joye with other.'[5]

Phillips seems to have convinced the procurer-general that he could personally arrange for the arrest of the three leaders of English Lutheranism abroad, Tyndale, Barnes and Joye, all in Antwerp. But Barnes had not been in Antwerp for three years. True, in the early spring of 1535 he went to Hamburg, and paid a flying visit to Melanchthon in Wittenberg before returning to London in May: he could have called at Antwerp on his way back. In that case Phillips's intelligence must have been remarkably good. George Joye fled to Calais and relative safety—but only, it appears, after Tyndale's arrest. Theobald's letter to Cranmer explains that he was able to check with Phillips the unpleasant rumour in Antwerp and in England that Joye had helped Phillips in the taking of Tyndale, to which Phillips replied that he did not know Joye, and had never met him. 'This I do write, because George Joye is greatly blamed and abused among merchants and many other, that were his friends, falsely and wrongfully.'[6]

Joye's flight to Calais supports another report. A London merchant named George Collins wrote briefly to another London merchant from Antwerp on 1 May 1525, mentioning that 'the stadholder of Barrow [i.e. Bergen-op-Zoom] spake with Mr Flegge in the church' (Mr Flegge was another member of the English merchant venturers' company). The stadholder said, 'Mr Flegge, there is commission come from the procurer-general of Brussels to take three Englishmen, whereof one is Dr Barnes . . . whereof he willeth Mr Flegge to give Mr Doctor warning . . .' Mr Flegge was so grateful that he forgot to ask who the other two were. But George Collins's letter concludes, 'I pray you, show Mr Doctor hereof', implying that Barnes was there in London. Collins promises to give the other two names in his next letter, which has not survived.[7]

So word was out about Phillips's activities some weeks ahead of the events. The procurer-general sent to Bergen, it seems, in case one of the three heretics turned up there. George Joye, however, stayed in Antwerp long enough for the unpleasant rumour about him assisting with Tyndale's arrest to have had some substance: and Tyndale made no attempt to escape. Mozley's comment is wise: 'More likely the reformers were well hardened in perils and alarms, and having friends upon the town council were confident of receiving timely warning, should the procurer-general send to Antwerp an order for their arrest.'[8] They had, of course, reckoned without Phillips, who had, Judas-like, shared the sop with Tyndale at supper-time.[9] And Tyndale had more to lose by flight than Joye, having a considerable apparatus of Greek and Hebrew translation about him, and probable arrangements with printers.

Knowing instantly of Tyndale's arrest, the English merchants acted promptly. They wrote at once ('incontinent' is Foxe's word) to the Court at Brussels, and apparently to the English government. Their anger must have been great. Not only was Tyndale a treasured fellow-Christian and fellow-Lutheran (to some of them, at least) and certainly fellow-businessman: their corporate diplomatic privilege had been wickedly abused. Their ire was so well-known that Henry Phillips was, as is the manner with bullies, frightened. Theobald's letter to Cranmer from Antwerp, quoted above, contains the following:

> This said Phillips is greatly afraid (in so much as I can perceive) that the English merchants that be in Antwerp will lay watch to do him some displeasure privily. Whereof of truth he hath sold his books in Louvain, to the value of twenty marks' worth sterling, intending to go hence to Paris: and doth tarry here upon nothing but of the return of his servant, which he hath long since sent to London with letters; and by cause of his long tarrying he is marvellously afraid lest he be taken, and come into Mr Secretary's handling with his letters.[10]

Henry Phillips was afraid of attack from two quarters; from the enraged Antwerp English merchants on one side, but even more from the English government on the other. The letters his servant carried, to whomever they were, would have been fatal to Phillips if they had come to the eyes of Cromwell. They would have reported the success of his mission, and probably asked for more money. Foxe says that after the betrayal Phillips 'procured and received more [money], wherewith to follow the suit'.[11] Not only was Phillips a known traitor, his loud mouth notorious: what he had contracted with someone in London to do he had fulfilled, in arresting and imprisoning an English citizen, Tyndale, on behalf of the King's enemy, or at least not friend, the Emperor—not to mention promising that enemy's officer that he would catch for him all three English heretics.

Theobald's letter to Cranmer contains this:

> He raileth at Louvain and in the queen of Hungary's court most shameful against our king his grace and others. For, I being present, he called our king his highness *tyrannum, expilatorem respublicae* [tyrant, spoiler of the commonwealth], with many other railing words, rejoicing that he trusteth to see the emperor to scourge his highness with his council and friends.[12]

How far Phillips's indiscretions were from his own foolish nature, and how far they were to maintain his image as someone deserving support by the emperor's powers, to enable him to fulfil his contract with his employer in London and thus receive money is uncertain. The truth was probably a mixture of the two.

Who was this secret employer? There is no direct evidence, but several clues. Foxe says that there were great persons in the Church behind Phillips. Thomas Poyntz in a letter to his brother says the same.

Theobald's letter to Cranmer includes the sentence 'Either this Philips hath great friends in England to maintain him here, or else, as he showed me, he is well beneficed in the bishopric of Exeter.' Had be been so 'well beneficed', of course, he would have paid his debt to his father long before. Edward Hall in his Chronicle, under the twenty-seventh year of King Henry the VIII, towards the end of his long paragraph about Tyndale and his death, remarks 'he was at Antwerp this year by one Phillips an Englishman and then a scholar at Louvain, betrayed and taken, and as many said, not without the help and procurement of some bishops of this realm . . .' Mozley, while recognising that no-one can now be named, declares that

> suspicion rests upon Stokesley. He was bishop of the capital city; he it was that was most active with Thomas More in the examination of Lutherans in 1531, when special enquiries were made about the lodging and appearance of Tyndale. It was his servant, John Tisen, an old pupil of Tyndale and therefore able to recognise him, who was seen in Antwerp about January 1533, but who kept away from the society of Englishmen. Another servant of his, a public notary, visited Antwerp for two weeks in the following July . . . All this, together with the cruelty of his character, his zeal for persecution, his boasts on his deathbed of the number of heretics whom he had robbed of life, makes it reasonable enough to see in him the chief backer, if not the prime engineer, of the plot which destroyed Tyndale.[13]

If this is correct, then Phillips must have been told to be extremely careful about secrecy. No holds, in the 1530s, were barred, and Sir Thomas More had used a traitor, Holt, in his accusation of John Frith: but even so Phillips could have brought upon certain bishops, and the Bishop of London no less, something more than royal displeasure. Phillips was known to Cromwell as a persistent enemy of the State: and to the Secretary's agents 'his betrayal of Tyndale, when mentioned at all, is made an aggravation of his offences'.[14]

Not that the English government was sufficiently outraged to do all it could to rescue Tyndale, in spite of strong appeals, as we shall see. The climate was wrong for King Henry, or Cromwell, to be able to ask for concessions from Charles, of any kind at all. Henry had been excommunicated, and even beyond the personal offence to the Emperor of his divorce from Catherine and marriage to Anne, were his more recent moves to take the English Church completely from away from Rome and his increasing manoeuvres against the ancient power-bases, the monasteries. Opposition to these acts in England had been stifled by the executions of Bishop John Fisher and Sir Thomas More. And those were more than offset by his continued burning in London of Lutheran, or supposed Lutheran, heretics. Henry was not interested in reform. It is just possible that if everyone had acted more vigorously, Tyndale might have been rescued. Thomas Poyntz wrote in a letter to his brother in England that 'I think that if Walter Marsh, now being governor of the English house, had done his duty effectually here at this time, there would have been a remedy found for this man. There be many men care not for a matter, so as they may do aught to make their actions seem fair, in avoiding themselves, that they be not spied'.[15] Cromwell, though appealed to and sympathetic to the cause, took his time to think out what might be done, and probably lost an opportunity. Henry Phillips, who had no scruples at all where fulfilling his contract and getting paid were concerned, lost no opportunities to hasten the end, as we shall see.

The one person who can never be accused of dragging his feet, even at cost to his own liberty and fortune, was Thomas Poyntz. He had been away on business in Bergen-op-Zoom when Phillips, choosing just such a time, trapped Tyndale. For that he must have blamed himself, because as Foxe reports, from personal knowledge of Poyntz, he had been from the first suspicious of Phillips. He must no doubt have moved the English merchants to action 'incontinently' on Tyndale's behalf, appealing to the court at Brussels; and wished afterwards that the governor of the English House had been less cautious. After nothing had happened over some weeks, he heard that Thomas Theobald was coming, he who had such high contacts (Secretary, Archbishop) in England. He was also intimate with the English House (his own banker, Thomas Leigh, was a member of it): it was his letter to Cranmer that we have already quoted. But nothing came of that either. So Poyntz decided to move on his own initiative. On 25 August 1535 he wrote to his elder brother John, lord of the manor of North Ockenden in Essex, who had for years been in the royal household, hoping that thereby some strings might be pulled, as the matter greatly concerned the King, he believed. He believes that the King has already acted, but does not now know that his actions were blocked by a conspiracy in Brussels.

For whereas it was said here the king had granted his gracious letters in the favour of one William Tyndale, for to have been sent hither: the which is in prison and like to suffer death, except it be through his gracious help: it is thought those letters be stopped. This man was lodged with me three quarters of a year, and was taken out of my house by a sergeant-of-arms, otherwise called a door-warder, and the procurer-general of Brabant: the which was done by procurement out of England, and, as I suppose, unknown to the king's grace till it was done. For I know well, if it had pleased his grace to have sent him a commandment to come to England, he would not have disobeyed it, to have put his life in jeopardy [i.e. even at the risk of his life] . . .

And by the means that this poor man, William Tyndale, hath lain in my house three quarters of a year, I know that the king has never a truer hearted subject to his grace this day living . . .

But and it would please the king's highness to send for this man, so that he might dispute his articles with them at large, which they lay to him, it might, by the mean thereof, be so opened to the court and the council of this country, that they would be at another point with the bishop of Rome within a short space. And I think he shall shortly be at a point to be condemned: for there are two Englishmen at Louvain that do and have applied it sore, taking great pains to translate out of English into Latin in those things that may make against him, so that the clergy here may understand it, and to condemn him, as they have done all others, for keeping opinions contrary to their business, the which they call the order of holy church.

Brother, the knowledge that I have of this man causes me to write as my conscience bids me: for the king's grace should have of him at this day as high a treasure as of any one man living, that has been of no greater reputation. Therefore I desire you that this matter may be solicited to his grace for this man, with as good effect as shall lie in you, or by your means to be done, for in my conscience there be not many perfecter men this day living, as knows God.[16]

John Poyntz forwarded this letter to Cromwell on 21 September. Three weeks before, however, Cromwell had asked the King's permission to write to two leading privy councillors in Brabant 'for Tyndale', and received it. The letters were written, apparently recognising that Tyndale's arrest was because of his transgression of the laws of the Low Countries, but asking as a matter of grace for Tyndale to be released and sent to England. They were sent to Stephen Vaughan in London, who received them on 4 September. Vaughan in turn passed them on to the merchant George Collins whose letter is quoted above, and he gave them to that same Robert Flegge mentioned in that letter, in Antwerp. Flegge received them on 10 September, and then on the 22 wrote himself to Cromwell, enclosing the replies. The simple request had become tangled.

Foxe goes into great and confusing detail about what happened. To summarise: two privy councillors were addressed by Cromwell, the Marquis of Bergen-op-Zoom and the Archbishop of Palermo. The Marquis had just, two days before, left on a diplomatic mission (escorting the eldest daughter of the King of Denmark to be married) to Germany. So Flegge sent after him Thomas Poyntz with the letter, with one of his own asking the Marquis to appoint a deputy at the Brussels court. Poyntz was not well received, the Marquis complaining that his countrymen had recently been burned at Smithfield: but he agreed that Poyntz should ride on with him to Maastricht. There the Marquis gave Poyntz a more kindly reception, and letters, one of which appointed the Archbishop of Palermo as his proxy in Brussels, with his own opinion, one was to the merchant venturers in Antwerp, and one was to Cromwell. Poyntz rode to Brussels and delivered the letters from England and the letters from the Marquis to the council there, and took the immediate replies to Antwerp. There the merchants sent him off to England with the Brussels letters. Foxe writes: '. . . and he, very desirous to have Master Tyndale out of prison, let [hindered] not to take pains, with loss of time in his own business and occupying: but diligently followed with the said letters, which he there delivered to the council, and was commanded by them to tarry until he had other letters . . .' which was not until the end of October. He then returned to Brussels and delivered them to the Emperor's council, and waited there three or four days for replies. He was then told that Tyndale was to have been released to him.

But Henry Phillips saw his scheme going wrong and his payment lost, for if Tyndale were alive, in England, and talking to Cromwell and even the King he, Phillips, could be seriously damaged. So he stepped in and announced that Thomas Poyntz, who up to then had been only a visiting English messenger at the court, was 'a dweller in the town of Antwerp, and there had been a succourer of Tyndale, and was one of the same opinion' and that his whole embassy to the court was from him alone and no one else (implying that the goverment letters from England were worthless). So the procurer-general arrested Poyntz, and imprisoned him. Foxe gives great detail about Poyntz's ruinous experiences, too long and too rambling to quote here (Poyntz was never good at expressing himself, and Foxe is clearly following an original document). Again in a nutshell, Poyntz was kept under house-arrest in Brussels while a case was built against him. The procurer-general spent five or six days of inquisition with him, examining him on more than a hundred articles, eventually drawing up twenty-three or twenty-four articles against him which were given to the commissioners, who then appeared every eight days to continue the process of prosecution and hearing Poyntz's defence—the latter hamstrung by restrictions of communication placed on him, as well as his own strategies of delay. This went on from the beginning of November to at least the end of January, and whenever the commissioners came to Poyntz 'that traitor Phillips accompanied them to the door, in following the process against him, as he also did against Master Tyndale, as they who had Poyntz in keeping showed him'.[17]

Attempts to get the English merchants at Antwerp to help with release on bail failed miserably: he was then asked to find sureties for the cost of his own imprisonment. At that point it dawned on Poyntz that his life was in danger: he had been a prisoner in Brussels for twelve or thirteen weeks. If he stayed, he would be put to death. If he tried to escape and was caught, he would be put to death. He was clearly about to be transferred to a stronger prison. That night he escaped and at dawn slipped out of Brussels. A hue and cry was raised, and horsemen were sent after him. But he knew the lie of the land, and got away, and came to England. (His gaoler was heavily fined.) He was banished from the Netherlands. His wife refused to join him in England. His business and his domestic arrangements were both in ruins, and neither recovered. Twelve years later, in 1547, on his brother's death, he succeeded to the ancestral manor of North Ockenden, but was said to be too poor to live there. He died in 1562.

No record exists of what he did in England to continue to try to rescue Tyndale. Stephen Vaughan wrote from the Low Countries on 13 April 1536 to Cromwell, adding a postscript 'If now you send me but your letter to the privy council, I could deliver Tyndale from the fire, so it come by time, for else it would be too late'. Cromwell did nothing. Mozley considers that had Tyndale been released from Vilvorde and arrived in England, his plainness of speech and refusal to compromise would have guaranteed that he would have been burned. 'He was too prominent a man to be overlooked, and he had bitter and powerful foes. His radical opinions, his outspoken nature, his outstanding abilities would soon have brought him into trouble. He could not hedge nor trim, nor speak with a double voice.'[18] It cannot now be known. Many were burned in the next four years, including Doctor Barnes.

Henry Phillips outlived Tyndale, being last heard of in Venice in 1542. After Poyntz's escape, he seems to have used the security of

Louvain for even more extreme railings against the King, even, it was reported, imprisoning English students there. King Henry reached into Europe with demands for his arrest, but he arrived in Rome early in May 1536, claiming to be a kinsman of Sir Thomas More, and being taken up by a cardinal. But the English ambassadors at the papal Court informed the cardinal that Phillips was a scoundrel and a traitor, and he was rejected. In Paris the same happened, and an old Oxford friend helped him 'al to ragged and torn' with clothes and lodging, and was said to have been robbed for his pains. He returned to London, where he wrote twice to his mother, and then fled again to Louvain, writing from there the other unattractive letters noticed above. He next appears, still in Louvain in the summer of 1537, 'trying to insinuate himself in the entourage of cardinal Pole' as Mozley puts it.[19] He complained that he was in danger from the English ambassador who was watching to entrap him, as if when he did that, precisely, to Tyndale, it somehow did not count. In January 1538 he wrote from Louvain 'a cringing letter' (Mozley's words) to his old patron, the chancellor of Exeter, now complaining that he is so poor that he has had to take service with the imperial army—would his patron kindly reconcile him to his parents so that he can get back to the muses where he belongs? He arrived in Italy in the autumn of 1538 as a Swiss soldier, having walked from Flanders; he went to Cardinal Pole for help, but was suspected of intending to murder him, and was forbidden to enter Venetian territory. He was then destitute and in great distress and sold his clothes and turned up again in Flanders. There early in 1539 he gave himself up to the English ambassador, to be sent to England, apparently on the promise of a pardon from the King himself, but had second thoughts and escaped, and was afterwards accused of robbing his captor. His extradition was demanded. Early in April he was included in a parliamentary act of attainder against traitors. Next year he was back in the Low Countries, 'once more in trouble and difficulty' as Mozley says. The last word of him was in the summer of 1542. He was seized in Vienna as a traitor to both the kings of Vienna and Hungary, and was threatened with losing his eyes or his life. Foxe reports a rumour that 'he was consumed at last with lice'.[18] Mozley's words must stand as epitaph:

We take our leave of him, disowned by his parents, cast aside by his friends, denounced by his country, shunned by the very party for whose sake he had marred his life, mistrusted by all, valued only as a tool, friendless, homeless, hopeless, desitute, fated to go down in history as the author of one perfidious deed.[20]

Chapter 15

TRIAL AND EXECUTION

Early in August 1536, when Tyndale had been in his cell at Vilvorde for four hundred and fifty days, he was formally condemned as a heretic, degraded from the priesthood, and handed over to the secular authorities for punishment—that is, burning at the stake. All these were public events. The condemnation for heresy, including the reading out of the articles of guilt, could have been in private, but was probably in public. In the case of a priest, and the degradation that followed, the prisoner was led on to a high platform, on which the bishops were prominent, in his priestly vestments. The anointing oil was symbolically scraped from his hands, the bread and wine of the Mass placed there and removed and the vestments ceremonially stripped away. William Tyndale, suffering this, no longer a priest, would find the secular officer waiting alongside to receive him.

This man was again the procurer-general, who had been Tyndale's— and Poyntz's—accuser throughout. This officer's ruthlessness in the hunting down of heretics was encouraged by the fact that he received a proportion of the confiscated property of his victims. He also received a fee for his services: for the destruction of Tyndale it was £128, a large sum, and by a long way the highest payment to those involved in Tyndale's case. The holder of the position in those years was Pierre Dufief, a magistrate of evil reputation, widely known in the Low Countries for his cruelty. He was assiduous, attending the private examinations of the prisoners, reading (in Poyntz's case) the defendant's letters, arranging for victims to be tortured in search of fresh evidence, even sitting in the seat of justice and acting as judge, sending prisoners to the flames. And always at his elbow, of course, was Henry Phillips. While a formal accusation was being prepared, those first weeks of Tyndale's imprisonment would have been punctuated by long visits from the procurer-general and a notary, as a formal accusation was prepared. Tyndale would have first been sworn, and then questioned about his life and beliefs, and especially about the evidence found in his house of his Lutheran ideas—among others, books by Luther himself, in German, and by Tyndale himself, in English. The translation, or at the least description, of the latter into Latin must have been one of the reasons why the preparation of Tyndale's case took so long. All that preliminary work was done by the procurer-general himself. After some time the regent appointed commissioners to try the case, and from that time one or more would always be present at an examination. They were not a legal tribunal, but something quite separate: the courts of justice in cases of heresy were overruled.

The commissioners who tried Tyndale seem to have been seventeen in number; three theologians; then William de Caverschoen, the secretary to the inquisitor-apostolic of the Low Countries, de Lattre; then four lawyers, members of the privy council; and nine others. Probably because Tyndale was a foreigner, and no-one could speak English, and few Latin, a smaller number of commissioners seems to have been involved: Dufief, the procurer-general; the four lawyer privy-councillors, of whom one, Godfrey de Mayers, seems to have been most significant; de Caverschoen, the inquisitor's secretary; and the three theologians. Two of these were leaders of European Catholic divinity, both at Louvain. Latomus, or James Masson, was a scholastic of the greatest brilliance, then about sixty, 'a tiny little man' as Mozley describes him,[1] dedicated to opposition to humanism and Lutheranism, an opponent even of Erasmus (who admired him) as well as Luther. Enchusanus, or Ruard Tapper, was, like Latomus, professor at Louvain, and also chancellor of the university, and just becoming dean of St Peter's, the main church in Louvain. He was politically more powerful than Latomus, and had already a dozen years of experience as theological assessor at such heresy trials: he later became a venerated, and at the same time especially cruel, Church leader.

In netting Tyndale, the heresy-hunters had their largest catch. Tyndale was a particularly learned scholar, and a leader of European Lutherans. He was also extremely important in England—had not Sir Thomas More, no less, expended gallons of ink in attacking him? Tyndale was almost single-handedly spreading the heresy of Lutheranism in London and across England, with his books and especially his translations. The case against him would have to be extremely thorough, and the accusations widely known, so that with his destruction would fall a keystone of European heresy. This was no simple, deluded anabaptist: this was a learned enemy and politician who was a 'mighty opposite' to the leaders of the Catholic Church, from the Pope himself

down. His inquisition by the theologians would have been frequent
and intense as well as implacable. Latomus certainly, and possibly
Enchusanus as well, met Tyndale face to face in his cell, and conversed.
All this time, passages from Tyndale's English works were being translated into Latin—Mozley suggests by Henry Phillips.[2] In case he was
needed, Phillips was always outside the door of Tyndale's cell when the
commissioners visited. He shuttled between Louvain, Brussels and
Vilvorde, his life dedicated wholly to the destruction of Tyndale.[3]

The process of preparing accusations would have begun as soon
as Tyndale was arrested in May, and would have gone on slowly
through the summer as the translation work continued. In September,
Cromwell's intervention brought matters to a halt, for some weeks.
Letters of request from the secretary of a powerful monarch for the
release of one of his countrymen had to be taken seriously. The
commissioners, and the privy council in particular, must have thought
hard. It seems likely that they had decided to stop the work of
preparation and release Tyndale to the waiting Poyntz. Henry Phillips's
action in getting Poyntz—another of King Henry's loyal subjects—
arrested and imprisoned seems desperate enough to suggest that. And
then the procurer-general's attention was distracted in the business of
ensuring the conviction of that other English Lutheran, Poyntz, a quite
unexpected second catch, demanding frequent visitation (with Henry
Phillips alongside) until his escape in early February 1536. We must
believe that the preparations for the accusation of Tyndale did not
properly resume until 1536.

He was offered his own notary and a procurer. He declined the
offer, preferring to make his own answer, which, Foxe shrewdly
observes, will never be published.[4] 'The great hour was come', wrote
Mozley, 'Not for him to play for time, or to help himself with the
subtleties and evasions of the law'.[5] The biblical truths he had lived by
for a dozen years of dangerous exile in poverty, which had driven his
work of translating and writing with absolute dedication and total
integrity (no wonder Henry Phillips hated him with such virulence)
were not a matter of legal quibbles in an irregular court in a local spot
in the Low Countries, but Scripture itself, the word of God himself.
'There was much writing, and great disputation to and fro between
him and them of the university of Louvain . . . in such sort, that they
all had enough to do, and more than they could well yield, to answer
the authorities and testimonies of the Scripture, whereupon he most
pithily grounded his doctrine.'[6]

That is all that Foxe reports; but Latomus kept a record, this was a
significant trial, and worthy of his highest abilities. The result was three

books, no less, now in a rare volume printed after his death and dedicated to Enchusanus. There he tells posterity that while Tyndale was in prison for Lutheranism, he, Tyndale, wrote a book on *Sola fides justificat apud Deum*, that is, faith alone justifies before God. That book has not survived, though it is not hard to reconstruct, both from knowledge of what Tyndale had written before and the way that Latomus replies. Though we might be tempted to lament the loss of another book from Tyndale, we might do better to rejoice in Latomus's dignified Latin. Sir Thomas More wrote in controlled Latin, the European language of the study and the library, except for his attacks on Luther and Tyndale, when he used a sort of effluent English, as if they belonged to what had to be poured away from the common household. Latomus, greater theologian by far than More, and with more power, responded to Tyndale as to a great scholar. The issue is at root the familiar dogmatic one—salvation by faith alone, as Tyndale, following Luther, following Paul, maintained: or salvation by works, as the Church, understandably, insisted. Latomus is in his way respectful, enjoying dialectic rather than More-like abuse. In a foreword to his three books he reported that Tyndale's response to his reply (that is, Latomus's first book, in which he simply removed Tyndale's key to understanding Scripture and substituted another), was not to acknowledge his error, as he should have done, but to prefer 'to make a show of replying'.[7] Latomus of course had all the truth, and Tyndale in not seeing that was being merely vexatious. For all Latomus's obvious pleasure in the learned disputation, this was a match in which the result had been decided beforehand. There was no way in the world by which Tyndale could win. Latomus ended his foreword by saying that he had feared all along that all the labour he undertook in writing his replies would not in the end profit Tyndale, but he hoped that others might be helped. Latomus's first book, of seven close-printed folio pages, after covering the ground of Christian belief which Tyndale and he have in common, goes to the problem of faith and works, and makes some shrewd debating points. Tyndale replied, in writing and at length. The document is lost, but we can see that it was a vigorous as well as lengthy answer from the tone of Latomus's second book, of eighteen close-printed folio pages, written in reply. We can assume, too, that it was, for all its length, ordered in contruction and with frequent reference to the New Testament. To show how absurd he is, Latomus quotes Tyndale back at him, and reveals just those qualities—which were present in Latomus's writing as well, of course. Latomus's third book replies to Tyndale's request for a written statement of Latomus's position on matters of Church practice, a list familiar to readers of the *Obedience*: the sacraments, the order of priests and the power of the keys, vows, fasting, images, worship of saints, the authority of the Pope. Latomus replies with many pages of logical arguments and appeals to the Fathers (Latomus can never understand how Tyndale can desert the Fathers for upstarts like Luther and Melanchthon), but of course quite fails to address the real abuses which are Tyndale's, and increasingly all Europe's, cry.

Foxe, in the life of Tyndale prefixed to Day's folio of 1573 writes:

> There [at Vilvorde] he remained more than a year and a half; and in the meantime came unto him divers lawyers and doctors in divinity, as well as friars and other, with whom he had many conflicts. But at the last Tyndale prayed that he might have some English divines come unto him . . . And then was sent unto him divers divines from Louvain, whereof some were Englishmen: and after many examinations at the last they condemned him.[8]

Clearly it was not just Latomus who disputed with him: indeed, Foxe gives a picture of a somewhat crowded cell, and a possibly exasperated Tyndale. No doubt Enchusanus had to have his say with 'Tindalus', at length to match Latomus's at least—was not he, though younger and more energetic, actually senior to Latomus, and with much more experience of these things? Foxe tells of 'divers lawyers' as well—the spirit groans at that 'divers', and what they must have brought with them. Friars, also, would not be all that welcome: even the English friars Roye and Joye and Barlow had not been the most stable of men. Probably Tyndale longed to hear an English voice. English was his mother tongue, in which in its common use he excelled beyond most. These power-wielding visitors would fill the day with spoken Latin, and his warders were Flemings. So even hostile Englishmen from Louvain—there were plenty to choose from at that time, refugees from England who were escaping Henry's anti-papal stance—might have brought a touch of relief. The control at Vilvorde was clearly strict: Thomas Poyntz, when he was at liberty, could not see him. Henry Phillips, though a prime mover, did not, it seems, enter Tyndale's cell, always stopping at the door, his leering shadowy presence no doubt horrifying in its total hatred. Almost any Englishman might have been welcome after knowledge of him. Yet, consciously or not, Foxe does give a sense of cause rather than sequence alone: the visiting Englishmen are followed swiftly in that last sentence by 'many examinations' and 'at the last they condemned him'.

There were lulls in the storms of visiting divines and lawyers, as was common in such examinations. One such seems to have happened in

September 1535, when Tyndale, with requests to make, found no-one calling who could carry a message, and had himself to write a letter. This is the one thing written by Tyndale in that year and a half in Vilvorde which has survived. It was unknown to Foxe. It rested unread in the archives of the Council of Brabant for three centuries. It is written in Latin signed 'W. Tindalus', and addressed to someone in authority and undated. Mozley's guess of the date is convincing, as is his support for the recipient being the Marquis of Bergen-op-Zoom, the privy-councillor to whom Cromwell wrote, who was also the governor of Vilvorde Castle. Mozley gives the Latin text, and his translation is well known:

> I believe, right worshipful, that you are not unaware of what may have been determined concerning me. Wherefore I beg your lordship, and that by the Lord Jesus, that if I am to remain here through the winter, you will request the commissary to have the kindness to send me, from the goods of mine which he has, a warmer cap; for I suffer greatly from cold in the head, and am afflicted by a perpetual catarrh, which is much increased in this cell; a warmer coat also, for this which I have is very thin; a piece of cloth too to patch my leggings. My overcoat is worn out; my shirts are also worn out. He has a woollen shirt, if he will be good enough to send it. I have also with him leggings of thicker cloth to put on above; he has also warmer night-caps. And I ask to be allowed to have a lamp in the evening; it is indeed wearisome sitting alone in the dark. But most of all I beg and beseech your clemency to be urgent with the commissary, that he will kindly permit me to have the Hebrew bible, Hebrew grammar, and Hebrew dictionary, that I may pass the time in that study. In return may you obtain what you most desire, so only that it be for the salvation of your soul. But if any other decision has been taken concerning me, to be carried out before winter, I will be patient, abiding the will of God, to the glory of the grace of my Lord Jesus Christ: whose Spirit (I pray) may ever direct your heart. Amen W. Tindalus[9]

If the Marquis is the recipient, then the comissary must be the procurer-general, the more likely because he had seized Tyndale's goods at his arrest, and would be holding the 'warmer cap . . . warmer coat . . . piece of cloth . . . warmer night caps . . . woollen shirt . . . leggings of thicker cloth . . .', and also the 'lamp . . . Hebrew bible, Hebrew grammar, and Hebrew dictionary . . .' Mozley's comment on the letter deserves quotation:

A noble dignity and independence breathe through it. There is no touch of flattery, much less of cringing, yet it is perfectly courteous and respectful. Tyndale accepts his present plight with an equal mind, though he will lighten the burden as far as he can. But through it all, his chief thought is for the gospel which is committed to him.[10]

'An equal mind' is an apt phrase. Mozley does not make the contrast, but Sir Thomas More in Chelsea comes to mind, also alone through the dark hours, but using them to pour out venom from a mind (and body) disturbed, writing above (possibly tortured) prisoners held in the cellars.

Whether or not the requests were granted is unknown. The tradition that they were, and that Tyndale spent heroic hours through the long nights of winter in his damp and chilly cell translating Joshua to 2 Chronicles, is pure sentiment. It is also absolutely unlikely. On the one hand, Poyntz did not paint such a picture for Foxe, though he mentioned other manuscripts left behind at Tyndale's death. On the other, the most elementary understanding of the work of translating those books shows that he used a great deal more apparatus than the three books he requested. Another romance would be harder still to bear—that he had already progressed even beyond Ezra-Nehemiah and Esther, and was, in those lonely nights of intense suffering, perhaps feeling himself abandoned by his God, now translating the next book, the first extended poetic outburst he would have encountered, the so-appropriate book of Job. What would we not give for Tyndale's Job! Intense as it is, moreover, Job is not a long book compared, for example, to the five books of the Pentateuch. So perhaps he had gone further, and was busy translating the Psalms, smuggling them out to Miles Coverdale . . . Tyndale's life, like Shakespeare's, attracts sentimental speculation. It is so likely as to be certain that Tyndale would not have had in Vilvorde access to his translator's normal structure of aids; Septuagint, Vulgate, Luther, Jewish commentaries, other published vernacular versions, and a clutch of dictionaries, not to mention friends or employees to act as readers, checkers or scribes. No. By September he would not have touched the Hebrew language since late May, over a quarter of a year. For anyone who has had to learn their Hebrew as an adult with painful application, that is an alarming interval. Learn Latin, it is said, and it stays with one for life: Greek needs keeping up weekly. Learn Hebrew later in life, however, and without doing something with it daily, it begins to slip. Tyndale cannot have been younger than thirty-four when he began to learn it, seven years before. If he received the three volumes, he may have looked ahead to the poetry, and to the great prophecy of Isaiah and Jeremiah, and made notes for a hoped-for future: but the main aim would be to keep the language going.

There is no word of any amelioration at all. That autumn, Cromwell's merciful attempt failed, and, thanks entirely to Henry Phillips, Tyndale's situation had been made very much worse, as the only free agent who might have done something on his behalf, Thomas Poyntz, was himself in prison, held by the very procurer-general who was his own enemy. We could not blame Tyndale for despairing. Yet Foxe records something else. In a manner reminiscent of the Apostles in the Acts, and to be glimpsed at the conclusion of some of Paul's Epistles, Tyndale was affecting his very gaolers and enemies. Foxe writes

Such was the power of his doctrine, and the sincerity of his life, that during the time of his imprisonment, (which endured a year and a half), it is said, he converted his keeper, the keeper's daughter, and others of his household. Also the rest that were with Tyndale conversant in the castle, reported of him, that if he were not a good Christian man, they could not tell whom to trust.[11]

Edward Hall joins Foxe in telling of something more surprising still. Hall writes: 'But yet this report did the Procurator general there (which we call here the Lieutenant) make of him, that he was, homo doctus, pius et bonus, that is to say, learned, godly, and good.'[12] That is the dreaded Pierre Dufief. It would seem that, by a recognisable human characteristic, the closer people came to an enemy the less did they foam with hatred. It appears particularly true of William Tyndale. Sir Thomas More was separated by much land and sea all the time he was writing against him. A great doctor of divinity who met him, like Latomus, wrote with respect, in a tone of more-in-sorrow-than-in-anger. And even the procurer-general expressed admiration.

None of this would stop the cold machinery of law. Tyndale was condemned as a heretic in August 1536, and probably the same day suffered degradation from the priesthood. His execution was now certain, by burning at the stake. An agent of Cromwell called John Hutton wrote to the Secretary on 12 August 1356:

So it is that as the tenth day of this present the procurer-general, which is the emperor's attorney for these parts, dined with me here in the English house: who certified to me that William Tyndale is

degraded, and condemned into the hands of the secular power, so
that he is very like to suffer death this next week: and as to the
articles on which he is condemned, I cannot as yet obtain, albeit I
have a grant [promise]: which once obtained shall be sent to your
lordship by the first. There was also another Englishman with
Tyndale, judged the same time to return into his habit of St Francis's
order, paying the charges of his imprisonment.[13]

That Tyndale was degraded before 10 August is confirmed by the
record of payments to Pierre Dufief to defray the costs of arranging it,
including the hiring of carriages and payments to 'serjeants and servants of the town', the 'unhallowing' having taken place 'by the bishop
suffragan and the two prelates assisting him: while other ecclesiastics
and laymen were present . . . in the town of Vilvorde'.[14] Another
record, appointing Ruard Tapper to stand for James de Lattre, inquisitor apostolic of the Low Countries, narrows the date to between 5 and
9 August, according to Mozley.[15] During those dates, and for the
degradation of William Tyndale, Mozley notes further, 'a brilliant
galaxy of stars assembled in the little town of Vilvorde'.

But the execution did not follow. The delay probably represents
anxiety in the council about the possible political dangers in taking the
life of a prominent Englishman for whom Cromwell had pleaded.
Cromwell can hardly have made another last-minute gesture, for his
assumption on reading Hutton's letter would have been that Tyndale
was already dead. The sensible thing for the council would be not to
act without the Emperor's express permission, and as he was fighting
a war in south-east France, that permission would take a week or two
to receive. Meanwhile we may assume the maintaining of another
custom, that of sending 'relays of priests and monks' to work 'upon the
weakness or weariness of a condemned man' as Mozley puts it:[16] 'the
unwelcome visitors were ruthless in their attentions, so zealous were
they by hook or crook to snatch a soul from the everlasting fire.'

Two months after the degradation, early in the morning of one of
the first days of October 1536, Tyndale was executed. Tradition has it
that it was the sixth of the month, and the Anglican Church has always
commemorated his death on that day. We have only Foxe's meagre
account of what happened. He was not burned alive, a fiercer punishment reserved for lesser creatures. He was strangled at the stake, and his
dead body then burned.

At last, after much reasoning, when no reason would serve, although
he deserved no death, he was condemned by virtue of the emperor's
decree . . . and, upon the same, brought forth to the place of ex-

ecution, was there tied to the stake, and then strangled first by the hangman, and afterwards with fire consumed, in the morning at the town of Vilvorde, A.D. 1536: crying thus at the stake with a fervent zeal, and a loud voice, 'Lord! open the king of England's eyes'.[17]

We have, however, eye-witness accounts of two such executions, one in Brussels and one in Louvain, recorded by Enzinas, a Spaniard arrested at Brussels seven years later for translating the New Testament into Spanish. From it we can reconstruct Tyndale's last hour. We are to imagine a large crowd held back by a barricade. In the middle of the circular space two great beams were raised in the form of a cross, with at the top iron chains, and a rope of hemp passing through holes in the beams. Brushwood, straw and logs were heaped ready nearby. At a set time, the procurer-general and his colleagues on the commission came and sat on prepared chairs within the circle. The crowd parted to let the guards bring the prisoner through the barricade. As they crossed the space and approached the cross, the prisoner was allowed a moment to pray, with a last appeal for him to recant. Then he alone moved to the cross, and the guards busily knelt to tie his feet to the bottom of the cross. Around his neck the chain was passed, with the hempen noose hanging slack. The brushwood, straw and logs were packed close round the prisoner, making a sort of hut with him inside. A scattering of gunpowder was added. The executioner went to stand behind the cross, and looked across at the procurer-general. It is at this moment, most probably, that Tyndale cried 'Lord, open the king of England's eyes'. When the procurer-general was ready, he gave the signal, and the executioner quickly tightened the hempen noose, strangling Tyndale. The procurer-general watched Tyndale die, and as soon as he judged him dead, he reached for a lighted wax torch being held near him, took it and handed it to the executioner, who touched off the straw, brushwood and gunpowder.

Foxe reports that on the morning of his execution Tyndale wrote a letter to the keeper of the castle, and shortly after his death the keeper went to Antwerp with it, and took it to the house 'of the aforesaid Poyntz' (who was of course by then in England). Foxe, the dedicated archivist, regrets that he hasn't seen that letter, nor 'his examinations and other his disputations' [those would be the examinations before the commissioners and the disputations with the professors of Louvain] which he hears are still in the keeper's family, 'in the hands of the keeper's daughter'.[18] But he knows (and reports in his 1563 edition), as he must have heard from Poyntz's wife, that on that occasion in her house the keeper spoke warmly of Tyndale, comparing his behaviour in prison to that of the Apostles. For Poyntz's wife, that experience in her rooms must have faintly sweetened the bitter memory of having entertained there the appalling Henry Phillips. Cromwell's agent John Hutton wrote from Brabant on 13 December, over two months later, of the general scene: 'They speak much of the patient sufferance of Master Tyndale at the time of his execution.' In 1550, Roger Ascham, tutor to that Princess Elizabeth who in eight years would be Queen, rode through Vilvorde. 'At the town's end is a notable solemn place of execution, where worthy William Tyndale was unworthily put to death.'[19]

Appendix A

THE SCHEME OF
THE PARABLE OF THE WICKED
MAMMON, 1528

(Numbers in parentheses refer to pages in PS.)

I. Faith comes first and alone justifies
  A. Faith alone brings life: the law, death (46)
    1. God cannot but fulfil his promises
    2. Paul and Christ declare goodness necessary before good works result
    3. The law cannot justify, only the promises
  B. Scripture enjoins good works (52)
    1. Matthew 25, 'I was an hungred . . .'
    2. These only come from faith
    3. Scripture ascribes both faith and works to God only
  C. The outward works show the inward goodness (56)
    1. Righteousness is by faith, shown by works: profit is not to result
    2. Eternal life follows faith and good living, and cannot be earned: God (not saints) receives us in heaven
    3. God (not saints) receives us in heaven: works should be aimed at the poor, nor the saints

II. Mammon and the unrighteous steward
  A. What the word Mammon means (67)
    1. Riches, temporal goods
    2. Superfluity, above necessity
    3. Abundance, plenteousness
  B. What 'unrighteous mammon' is (69)
    1. Not got unrighteously
    2. In unrighteous use
    3. Not to our neighbour's need

C. Why we should follow the unrighteous steward? (70)
1. Example of wisdom and diligence
2. As sinful Adam is a figure of Christ
3. God sends his Spirit even to us, naturally damned, to his elect, who do not question, but believe Scripture: copious illustration from the Gospels and Paul about the true place of works

III. What are good works?
A. Whereof good works serve (90)
1. (For us) Fasting and watching
2. (For us and others) Prayer
3. (For others) Alms
B. Works are natural (100)
1. But are nothing without the word
2. But beware of zeal
3. We should be to the poor as Christ to us
C. The world does not understand God (107)
1. Socrates, Plato and Aristotle confuse
2. All is from God
3. Understanding Scripture leads to keeping commandments: copious illustration from the New Testament

THE STRUCTURE OF
THE OBEDIENCE OF A CHRISTIAN MAN

As a demonstration of the process of thought, here is the scheme of the first pages of the *Obedience* proper, after the Preface and Prologue. (Numbers in parentheses refer to pages in PS.)

God's Law of Obedience

1. Children (168)
    a. Original duty
        (i) Made through parents
        (ii) So under their authority
        (iii) Obedience to them is to God
    b. Everyday effects
        (i) Disobedience punished by elders
        (ii) If not, by God
        (iii) marriages should respect elders
            a) but can be broken by prelate
            b) and can be bought off by pope

2. Wives (171)
    a. equal until married, then weaker vessels
    b. follow examples of obedience of holy wives
    c. husband in the stead of God

3. Servants (172)
    a. Paul and Peter enjoin obedience
    b. Master's commandments are God's
    c. Monk, friar and priest exempt from all obedience

4. Subjects to Kings, Princes and Rulers (173)

Introduction: Romans 13 (verses 1–10)

    A. God's law forbids all vengeance but his own (174)
        1. Kings, governors and rulers enact God's justice

a. Requirement of obedience is universal
    (i) law-keeping brings prosperity
    (ii) law-breaking brings curses
b. Avenging a superior is taking God's work: it is unlawful to kill a king
    (i) 1 Sam 24, David and Saul
    (ii) 1 Sam 26, David and Saul

'He that judgeth the king judgeth God;
and he that layeth hands on the king layeth hand on God;
and he that resisteth the king resisteth God, and damneth God's law and ordinance.
If the subjects sin, they must be brought to the king's judgement.
If the king sin, he must be reserved unto the
        judgement,
        wrath,
        and vengeance of God.
And as it is to resist the king,
    so it is to resist his officer, which is set, or sent, to execute the king's command.'

    (iii) 2 Kings 1 } killing to please David, not God
    (iv) 2 Kings 4 }
    (v) Luke 13 and Matthew 22: not to resist even a heathen prince
2. Kings, outside the law, give accounts to God only
    a. no one exempt: not monks, friars, pope, bishops
        (i) those who resist
            or seek exemption
            cause the evil
        (ii) do well, and receive praise

'With good living ought the spritualty to rid themselves from fear of the temporal sword:
and not with craft
    and with blinding the kings
    and bringing the vengeance of God upon them
    and in purchasing licence to sin unpunished.'

    b. the king is minister of God for our welfare
        (i) even if a tyrant
            (a) a tyrant is better than a shadow
            (b) an effeminate king is worse — see the English chronicles
        (ii) princes are to be feared, being ordained to punish evil-

doers: even the spiritualty, claiming sanctuary for themselves and criminals, should fear

B. God's law is properly only kept by spritual man (181)
    1. Mankind has three natures
        a. beastly: those who rise against princes and rulers; like those
            who worshipped the golden calf, before whom Moses
            broke the tables of the law
        b. receive the law, but as worldly not spiritual; such look for
            reward
        c. spiritual; have law in their hearts
    2. Human variableness comes from natural blindness: erring wit
        leads to erring will, shown by
        a. persuasion can reverse beliefs
        b. erring leads to captivity not freedom: only Christ makes
            free
        c. everything is sin which does not come from God
            (i) pride: when Lucrece lost her chastity, her glory,
                 she had nothing
            (ii) 'Of like pride are all the moral virtues of Aristotle,
                 Plato and Socrates . . .'
            (iii) the supposed merit of saints
    3. Kings ordained to take vengeance on evil-doers and make others
        fear
        a. Not ordained to fight each other at the behest of the pope
        b. Nor that bishops should wield the temporal sword; they
            neither preach God's word nor permit it

Conclusion: The pope has usurped the power of emperor and kings,
demonstrated from recent European history.

C. The basis of obedience is spiritual: the New Testament denies
    the resisting of temporal rulers (188; 'Against the Pope's False
    Section')
    1. Outward.
        a. Christ as well as Peter were under the temporal sword:
            Matthew 26, Galatians 4, Matthew 3
            there are no exemptions for bishops and kings
        b. Christ and Peter both paid tribute: Matthew 17
            (i) But prelates pay nothing—until called to fight in
                 the pope's quarrel
            (ii) That Peter paid the tribute does not make him the
                 greatest apostle
        c. Paul preached obedience from conscience
            (i) your own
            (ii) your neighbour's, the weaker brother: we are to
                 share burdens

     (a) out of Christian love
  but (b) the spiritualty rob
    (iii) because officers are God's ministers

2. Inward: the law is spiritual
  a. it is not fulfilled in the deed
  b. faith makes the love which keeps the law
  c. justification is the forgiveness of sins
     and the favour of God, who will avenge for us

3. The law terrifies, as a king is to be feared
  a. rulers are the gift of God
  b. evil rulers are because of our wickedness
    (i) bad in all degrees
    (ii) through the particular wickedness of prelates, to punish us
    (iii) through false miracles

4. We are to receive all things, good or bad, of God
  a. not avenge
  b. not resist evil rulers
    (i) it produces more bondage
    (ii) God is faithful and will take them away
    (iii) Christ was passive, as Christian men should find bitter medicines wholesome
  c. persecution makes us feel the working of God's Spirit (198)
    [*marginal note*: The greatest sinner is righteous in Christ and the promises. And the perfectest and holiest is a sinner in the law and the flesh.]

Appendix C

ONE SENTENCE FROM ISOCRATES' *PANEGYRICA*

One sentence from Isocrates' *Panegyrica*, reproduced from G.A. Kennedy, *Classical Rhetoric in its Christian and Secular Tradition from Ancient to Modern Times* (Chapel Hill, 1980), p. 36.

Love of wisdom, then,
    which has helped us *to discover*
        and helped *to establish* all that makes Athens great,
    which *has educated* us *for practical affairs*
        and made gentle our relations with each other,
    which *has distinguished* misfortunes of ignorance
                from those of necessity
   and *taught* us to guard against the former
         and bear up against the latter,
[this love of wisdom] OUR CITY *made* manifest
           and honored Speech,
                which all *desire*
                   and *envy* those who know,
           recognizing, on the one hand
              that this is the natural feature distinguishing us from all animals
                and that through the advantage it gives us we excel them in all other things,
       and seeing, on the other hand,
             that in other areas fortune is troublesome
                    so that in those areas the wise fail
                       and the ignorant succeed,
       and that there is no share of noble and artistic speech to the wicked,
           but *it is* the product of a well-knowing soul,
       and that the wise and those seemingly unlearned most *differ* from each other in this
       and that those *educated* liberally, right from the start, are not *recognized*
               by courage and wealth and such benefits,
               but most by what has been said,
       and that those who *use* speech well are not only *powerful* in their own cities,
                but also honored among other men;
   and
to such an extent had OUR CITY outstripped the rest of mankind in wisdom and speech
    that her students have become the teachers of others,
      and she has made the name of the Hellenes seem no longer that of a people,
               but that of an intelligence,
   and that those rather are called Greeks
        who share our education
        than those who share our blood.

NOTES

Abbreviations

CWM   *The Complete Works of St Thomas More, New Haven and London, 1969–*

EETS   Early English Texts Society

Foxe   *The Acts and Monuments of John Foxe* ed. by Josiah Pratt and John Stoughton, 8 vols, 1877

L&P   *Letters and Papers, Foreign and Domestic, of the Reign of Henry VIII* ed. by J.S. Brewer, J. Gairdner, R.H. Brodie, et al. (21 vols, 1862-1932)

PS   [Tyndale] *Doctrinal Treatises* . . . (1848); *Expositions* . . . and *The Practice of Prelates* (1849); *Answer to More* . . . (1850), edited for the Parker Society by Henry Walter

NOTE TO INTRODUCTION

1. See for example Mozley (1940) and Davis.

NOTES TO CHAPTER 1

1. For fuller details of the various family branches, see Greenfield and also Mozley, pp. 1–6; corrected by Overy and Tyndale.
2. Demaus, p. 23.
3. Sturge, pp. 3–4; Merriman, vol. 1, p. 3; Marius, p. 5.
4. See the statistics in Hoyle, especially pp. 138, 146. I am grateful to Dr J.H. Bettey of the University of Bristol for help in interpreting the figures.
5. Demaus, pp. 24–5.
6. Hoyle, p. 138.
7. See Finucane.
8. I have found myself in small towns in North America, for example, unfamiliarly cut off from anything resembling a view of the larger world, because the entire interest of the news media has been intensely local and selective. Young Tyndale was in many ways to be envied his upbringing within the flowing currents of Northern Europe. Within Gloucestershire, evidence of considerable travel even at the humblest level is found in the records of Bishop Hooper's investigation: see Price, pp. 92–4.
9. PS, p. 149.
10. See Keynes, p. 144 and n. 15; and

Willelmi Malmesbiriensis Monachi De Gestis Regum Anglorum Libri Quinqui, ed. W. Stubbs; I, Rolls Ser. (London 1887–9), *passim.* It has been thought that Tyndale made a mistake for Alfred. Alfred, however, did not translate any part of the Bible himself except Psalms 1–50. Almost at the end of the long Prologue to the Wycliffite Bible is a reference that puts together Bede and that translation by Alfred, which could have led to confusion. See Forshall and Madden, vol. 1, p. 59.

11. See Johnson, p. 19.
12. An estimate based on the figures in Rollison, p. 3. For much in the following paragraphs I am indebted to this excellent study.
13. Rollison, p. 9.
14. Rollison, p. 86.
15. Rollison, p. 27.
16. That name crops up in the sixteenth century in the Forest of Dean area, across the Severn a little to the north, and probably started as de Monmouth. I am grateful to Joan Johnson for this information. Foxe calls him 'Mummuth', very likely a phonetical spelling for a local pronunciation: Foxe appears to be writing as his informant talks.
17. Dickens (1989), pp. 59–60; and Smeeton p. 41, though Berkeley Castle is not just outside the Gloucestershire border.
18. J.F. Davis, p. 2 and passim.
19. It is interesting that from the middle of the seventeenth century the phrase 'man of the cloth' should have come to signify a clergyman or minister: naturally that phrase refers to his distinctive dress, but one wonders if there might be a residual sense of the link between clothworking and faith.
20. Rollison, pp. 67–9.
21. OED defines 'toot-hill' as 'a natural or artificial hill or mound used as a look-out place'. A 'toot', as 'an isolated conspicuous hill suitable as a place for observation' is noted as chiefly south-western. I must also point out here that theories of Tyndale as a philological reformer, specially producing a version of his last New Testament in the Gloucestershire dialect of the ploughboy, are very wide of the mark. The idea came from the article by Roach. The argument is based on the exceptionally strange spelling in a Tyndale New Testament printed in Antwerp in 1535 (e.g. faether, broether). Like the five Christopher van Endhoven Tyndale New Testaments between 1530 and 1535 (see below, p. 323), this is undoubtedly a piracy, set up, like them, by Flemish compositors without the benefit of proper proof-reading. On the other hand, it must also be said that the analysis of Gloucestershire forms in the regularly printed works of Tyndale is work still waiting to be done.
22. *Tyndale's Old Testament*, ed. Daniell, 1992, pp. xxii, xxx–xxxvii.
23. My point here is extended from the excellent quotation from Rollison, p. 92.
24. Smeeton in his interesting book detaches Tyndale far too eagerly from Luther: it is not for nothing that Smeeton's book began as a thesis at Louvain, a university opposed to Luther since Luther's own time.
25. PS, pp. 304–5.
26. Matthew 7.
27. See, for example, Pantin, pp. 81–114.
28. Owst, pp. 41–6.
29. Rollison, p. 71.
30. I am grateful to Enid Brain of Wotton-under-Edge for this information.
31. The point is made by Rollison, p. 94.

32. Sidney, p. 133.
33. See Brook.
34. Sidney, p. 113.
35. Not even in King, a book which did much to stimulate new interest.
36. See for example in the *Obedience*, PS, pp. 220, 328.
37. See *Obedience*, PS, p. 307.
38. See Brownell, pp. 554–70; and Daniell, pp. 134–51.
39. Justifiably: see below, pp. 143–4.

NOTES TO CHAPTER 2

1. See Emden, pp. 567–9; also Foster, where he appears as 'Tyndale, William (or Hitchins)'. The same source makes him 'Canon of Cardinall College' [i.e. Christ Church] 1525' as well as translator of the New Testament. It must be assumed that, at the least, about 'Cardinall College', Foster's date is wrong, if not his information. By 1525 Tyndale was firmly abroad, with already not the most orthodox reputation to be suitable for Wolsey's college. For details of the early years of Magdalen Hall see Stanier, passim.
2. Stanier, p. 9.
3. White, p. xvi.
4. Stanier, p. 22.
5. Stanier, p. 23.
6. See Stanier, p. 25: and Hamilton, pp. 100–143.
7. Stainer, pp. 31–6.
8. Stanier, pp. 38–43.
9. Stanier, p. 41.
10. Baldwin's classic *William Shakspere's Small Latine and Lesse Greeke*, 1, pp. 75–164, gives a thorough account of grammar school curricula, 1509–50.
11. Stanier, pp. 46–7.
12. *Tyndale's Old Testament*, ed. Daniell, p. 17.
13. Wood (1786–90), II, p. 721.
14. Stanier, pp. 49–53; see also

Jacobsen, pp. 119–20.
15. Wood (1813–20), I, p. 29.
16. Jacobsen, p. 129.
17. See *Dictionary of National Biography*, VI, p. 348.
18. Stanier, p. 59.
19. 'Duns Scotus' Oxford'.
20. See Fletcher, passim.
21. Fletcher, p. 343.
22. Fletcher, pp. 344–5.
23. For comprehensive accounts see Evans, pp. 485–538.
24. See M.B. Parkes, 'The Provision of Books' in Catto and Evans, p. 407.
25. Parkes, p. 473.
26. Fletcher, pp. 322–3.
27. Fletcher, p. 323, gives the curriculum as follows: 'for grammar the first or second parts of Priscian's *Institutiones grammaticae* for one term; for rhetoric Aristotle's *Rhetorica*, or the fourth book of the *Topics* of Boethius, or the *Nova rhetorica* (the psuedo-Ciceronian *Rhetorica ad Herrenium*), or Ovid's *Metamorphoses*, or Virgil's poetry for three terms; for logic Aristotle's *Perihermeneias*, the first three books of the *Topics* of Boethius or Aristotles's *Prior Analytics* or Aristotle's *Topics* for three terms; for arithmetic Boethius's *Arithmetica* (*Ars metrica*) for one term; for music Boethius's *Musica* for one term; for geometry Euclid, with Alhazen (Ibn al-Haytham) or Witelo on perspective, for two terms; for astronomy the *Theorica planetarum* or Ptolemy's *Almagest* for two terms.'
28. Fletcher, pp. 323–4, gives 'for natural philosophy Aristotle's *Physics* or other relevant Aristotelian or pseudo-Aristotelian works for three terms; for moral philosophy Aristotle's *Ethics* or *Economics* or *Politics* for three terms; for metaphysical philosophy Aristotle's *Metaphysics* for two terms.'
29. Fletcher, p. 324.
30. Fletcher, p. 325, and esp. pp.

338–45.

31. Catto, p. 265.
32. Catto, p. 266.
33. Smeeton, pp. 162–7.
34. Catto, p. 267.
35. Pecock, pp. 460–6.
36. Catto, pp. 275–8.
37. Catto, p. 278.
38. Catto, p. 780.
39. Weiss (1964), and idem (1957) chapters vii, ix and x.
40. Catto, p. 265.
41. Since Origen in the third century, it had been automatic in the Church, much influenced by Augustine, to treat every sentence and often every word, of the Latin scripture as allegorical. On top of the first meaning, the literal, were piled the allegorical (e.g. animals, suggesting virtues); the tropological or moral, suggesting tropes (figures) of morality; and the anagogical (from the Greek word meaning to rise), that is elevatory, especially to future glory. Thus, in the famous example Jerusalem means literally the city of the Jews: allegorically, the church of Christ; tropologically the human soul; and anagogically the heavenly city.
42. See Gleason, passim.
43. Seebohm, p. 20.
44. Gleason, p. 59.
45. Gleason, p. 59.
46. Gleason, pp. 67–92.
47. Gleason, pp. 118–21.
48. Colet (1869), p. 107; Gleason, p. 92.
49. Gleason, p. 11.
50. Duhamel, p. 494.
51. Gleason, p. 67.
52. Schwarz, pp. 120–21. 'There is no evidence that while in England he [Erasmus] fully comprehended the significance of Greek for theological studies ... How could he judge of the value of Greek before he knew the language and before he himself had found out the discrep-ancies between the Latin text of the Vulgate and the Greek Bible? Nobody was able to assist him in ariving at this idea which was contrary to all tradition.'
53. Schwarz, pp. 120–38, 141, 161.
54. Gleason, pp. 121, et. seq.
55. Catto, p. 279.
56. Gleason, p. 159.
57. See E.W. Hunt, pp. 64–5.
58. Foxe, IV, p. 246.
59. Gleason, p. 236, et. seq.
60. PS, p. 291.
61. PS, p. 206.
62. PS, p. 179.
63. PS, p. 315.
64. Idem.
65. Foxe, V, pp. 114–15.
66. CWM, VI, i, 28.
67. Hall's Chronicle, p. 818.
68. See below, p. 368.
69. For an account of such amplificatio in the opening scene of Hamlet, see Trousdale, pp. 52–5.
70. Jones, p. 13.
71. Shakespeare, Comedy of Errors, 5, i, 62–7.
72. Jacobsen, pp. 111–15.
73. See below, pp. 247–9.
74. See in Obedience, PS, p. 316; in Answer to More, PS, pp. 16, 135, 213; and in Preface to Genesis, Tyndale's Old Testament, ed. Daniell, pp. 4–5.
75. PS, pp. 304–5. See above, pp. 16–18.
76. Erasmus (1963), p. 30.
77. Bone, pp. 50–68.
78. Davis, p. 23.
79. Baldwin, II, pp. 1–238 gives a full account of the study of rhetoric in sixteenth-century grammar schools, especially using Ad Herennium, Erasmus and Quintilian.
80. Figures from a survey, The First Printed Catalogue of the Bodleian Library 1605, a Facsimile, Oxford, 1986.
81. Puttenham, p. 5.
82. See below, pp. 87–90.
83. 'To the Lady Margaret Ley'.

NOTES TO CHAPTER 3

1. Foxe, V, p. 115.
2. Ibid., p. 415.
3. Dickens (1989), p. 91.
4. Dickens wisely says there is 'no certainty' about it, p. 93.
5. Foxe, V, p. 415.
6. See n. 31, below.
7. Dickens (1989), p. 91.
8. Dickens (1989), p. 102.
9. Bainton, p. 101; Faludy, pp. 135–42.
10. Marius, p. 252.
11. Foxe, IV, p. 617.
12. See below, p. 394 n.1.
13. See Catto and Evans, p. 265, and CWM, XV, pp. 133, 137, 143.
14. Answer to More, PS, pp. 75–6.
15. Foxe, V, p. 415.
16. Ibid., p. 115.
17. Hoyle, pp. 2, 3, 4, 6, 7, 12, 21, 22, 23, 34.
18. See above, p. 11.
19. L&P, VIII, p. 989. See Starkey, pp. 118–21.
20. Fraser, p. 186.
21. Mozley (1937), p. 25.
22. Ibid., p. 21.
23. Demaus, p. 61.
24. Foxe, V, p. 117.
25. E.W. Hunt, pp. 82–3.
26. See Fisher, I, pp. 311–48, for the organisation of the 'sermon made against the pernicious doctrine of Martin Luther'.
27. Deanesly, The Lollard Bible, p. 296.
28. See below, p. 129. The phrases here have been chosen at random: they are all from the revision of the Wyclif Bible, and they all strike chords of familiarity from the literature of the period. A systematic study remains to be undertaken.
29. See below chap. 4, pp. 94–100.
30. Mozley (1937), p. 22.
31. The Oxford bookseller John Dorne's records of his sales in 1520 show that one-ninth of his whole sales was of Erasmus. One customer out of every seven came to buy one of his books. See Lindsay, p. 22. Though no bookseller is recorded in Bristol until Eliazer Edgar in 1620, Richard Webb of Chipping Sodbury, servant of Hugh Latimer, is mentioned by Foxe (IV, p. 127). He was said to be in touch with a London booseller, Robert Necton, and to have distributed heretical books in Bristol. Necton later died in prison. Thomas More refers to heretical books being scattered abroad in Bristol at the time, CWM, VIII, ii, pp. 813–14.
32. Translated Erasmus (1963), p. 23.
33. Demaus, p. 66.
34. Foxe Actes and Monuments (1563), pp. 513–14.
35. CWM, XV, p. xxviii.
36. Erasmus (1981), p. 27; I have modernised the spelling.
37. Tyndale's New Testament, ed. Daniell, p. 287. The idea recurs in 2 Corinthians 10 (p. 269) and 1 Thessalonians 5 (p. 303).
38. Erasmus (1981), p. 191.
39. See DeMolen, p. 13.
40. Erasmus (1981), pp. xxii–xxiii.
41. Ibid., p. 87.
42. Ibid., p. 101.
43. Ibid., pp. 115–16.
44. Quoted in Mozley (1937), p. 34.
45. The Poems of Alexander Pope, a one-volume edition of the Twickenham text with selected annotations, ed. by John Butt (1963), pp. 165–6.
46. Faludy, p. 95.
47. Erasmus (1981), p. 91. for Dürer, see Panofsky, pp. 151–4, and pl. 207.
48. Rhodes, p. 24.
49. For further illustration of Erasmus being disturbingly ambiguous, see Rhodes, p. 24.
50. Faludy, frontispiece and pls 9, 12.
51. Erasmus (1981), p. 5.
52. 'A Letter from Capt. Gulliver to his Cousin Sympson', prefacing Gulliver's Travels.

53. Erasmus (1981), p. liii.
54. Ibid.
55. Thomas Tusser, the author of the verse *A Hundred Points of Good Husbandry* (1557) complained that Udall gave him fifty-three stripes when he was a new boy at Eton 'for fault but small, or none at all'. See White, p. xiii.
56. See Edgerton, p. 79.
57. Ibid.
58. Erasmus (1981), p. li, referring to Gee, pp. 43–59. There are suggestive references in Mozley (1944), pp. 97–107. See also Devereux, pp. 255–9.
59. See Madan, pp. 71–178.
60. See Rhodes, passim.
61. '. . . Erasmus (whose tongue maketh of little gnats great elephants and lifteth up above the stars whosoever giveth him a little exhibition) . . .'; *Tyndale's Old Testament*, ed. Daniell, p. 4.
62. *L&P*, IV, no. 4282.
63. *Tyndale's Old Testament*, ed. Daniell, p. 4.
64. Foxe, 1563, p. 514.
65. *Tyndale's Old Testament*, ed. Daniell, p. 4.
66. *CWM*, VI, i, p. 424.
67. PS, p. 213.
68. Foxe, V, pp. 116–17.
69. Mozley (1937), p. 32.
70. As, for example, in translating the Greek *metanoeō* ('turn the mind'), as *poenitentiam ago*; as in Acts 2:38 'do penance'; a radical change.
71. Mozley (1937), p. 33.
72. Price, pp. 77, 99, 122. See also the statistics listed in an anonymous article in *English Historical Review*, 19 (1904), pp. 98–121.
73. Price, p. 101.
74. Ibid., pp. 142, 145. For a different view see Bowker, especially pp. 127–31.
75. See Heath, pp. 73–5.
76. Foxe, *Acts and Monuments* (1563), p. 514: and IV, p. 117.

NOTES TO CHAPTER 4

1. *Tyndale's Old Testament*, ed. Daniell, p. 4.
2. A celebrated difficulty. Erasmus does, however, praise Tunstall in his first *Apology against Lee* of March 1520, 'Cuthbertus Tunstallus unum exemplar sat emendatum', Cuthbert Tunstall provided one sufficiently faultless exemplar; see Rummel. Erasmus's letters contain several flattering remarks, including Tunstall in the phrase 'two of the best scholars in the whole of England', Epistle 332, to Pieter Gillis.
3. See Sturge, pp. 8–14.
4. Ibid., p. 55.
5. Mozley (1937), p. 43.
6. Sturge, p. 25.
7. Thomas More, *Utopia*, tr. Paul Turner (Harmondsworth, 1965), p. 37.
8. Ibid., p. 33.
9. *Tyndale's Old Testament*, ed. Daniell, p. 5.
10. *Practice of Prelates*, PS, p. 337. Mozley (1937), p. 41, notes George Constantine speaking of Tunstall's 'stillness, soberness and subtlety'.
11. Sturge, p. 79.
12. Sturge, p. 84.
13. Mozley (1937), pp. 37–8.
14. See Hall, p. 580, possibly; and Fraser, pp. 58–9.
15. Dixon, pp. 8–9.
16. This is the earliest date, generally accepted, for the establishment of the School on the outskirts of Athens. It survived until dissolution by Justinian AD 529.
17. It is a matter of astonishment to me that Tyndale has been usually accused of formlessness, with his original works described as 'rambling'. See note 6 to chap. 7, below.
18. Dr Martin Kauffmann, Assistant Librarian, Bodleian Library, communicated privately.

19. Dr B.C. Barker-Benfield, Bodleian Library, communicated privately. See R.W. Hunt, pp. 317–45; and Hutter, pp. 108–13.
20. Jacobsen, pp. 47–56.
21. Isaiah 32.4. The Wyclif Bible, exists in both word-for-word and sense-for-sense forms.
22. Workman, p. 8.
23. Chapman, vol. 1, p. 507; Quoted in Jacobsen, p. 147.
24. See Barnstone, passim., and Binns, esp. pp. 21–11.
25. Genesis 22; Luke 7.
26. *Tyndale's Old Testament*, ed. Daniell, p. 5.
27. Black, p. 424.
28. *The New Testament of Jesus Christ, translated faithfully into English, out of the authentical Latin* . . . (Rheims, 1582), sig. a, iii.
29. The work of J.J. Scarisbrick in *The Reformation and the English People* (1984), and Christopher Haigh, *The English Reformation Revised* (1987), is prominent. Eamon Duffy's *The Stripping of the Altars* (1992) is discussed below. Note also the review by Patrick Collinson in the *Times Literary Supplement*, 27 October 1993, pp.14–15, of Haigh's *English Reformations: Religion, Politics and Society under the Tudors* (1993).
30. Duffy, p. 80.
31. See Herbert, p. xxix; and Butterworth, passim.
32. Deanesly, *The Lollard Bible*, pp. 323–5. Lollards were deceived into possessing copies, imagining it to be a life of Christ in English. In one manuscript the section on the sacrament of the altar is scratched through, and a marginal note adds 'Do not believe this foolishness'.
33. See Deanesly, 'Vernacular Books', pp. 354–5.
34. Duffy, p. 80.
35. Duffy, p. 80.
36. Duffy, p. 79. There is much to be challenged in the tradition-centred dogmatism of this book. Duffy's excellent, and indeed moving, brief account of the meaning of the Mass, for example, on p. 91, is fine, except that like the whole long book it simply takes for granted that Christianity is the rituals of late mediaeval peasants. Duffy notes on p. 169 of a saint 'By the mid-1530s the altar on which she stood was no longer referred to as Jesus' altar but St Sidwell's altar . . .': an expected comment on the perversion of Christianity that this represents is not made. What he calls 'the intensity and scope of the Henrician assault on popular religion' (as on p. 415) allows virtually no room in his book for even mention of what was taking its place, and doing so with a popular force which would eventually lead to England being under Elizabeth and for the following four and a half centuries, even until today, a Protestant land, thanks largely to the ministry of the Word, the scripture-gospel. He finds that at the local level, throughout the kingdom 'the unmistakable evidence of prompt compliance with the Tudor reform' is a problem (p. 479): there could be a simple explanation.

He omits any possibility of any other source of Christian belief, like personal faith in a justifying God in Christ understood through private reading of the New Testament. Erasmus is mentioned twice only, for the composition of a prayer for the church, no longer existent. The very few references to Bible-reading, as on p. 420, are made as to something rather ridiculously aberrant. A cruelly wayward remark on p. 480 shows the fanaticism with which Duffy wants to exclude the Bible. 'At the heart of the Edwardine reform was the necessity of destroying, of cutting, hammering, scraping, or melting into a deserved oblivion the monuments of popery, so that the doctrines they embodied might be forgotten.' No. At the heart of the Edwardine reform was the Bible given to the people in English. During Edward VI's short reign forty versions of the New Testament or whole Bible were printed in London. That is not mentioned. Duffy refers to 'the locust years of Edward' (p. 503). On p. 530 he writes, of Mary's reign, 'Bible-reading or the possession of Bibles was never condemned by the regime'. To take it no further, under Mary, no Bible was printed in England, and some existing printings were destroyed. Duffy's last elegiac remarks about Protestantism being 'a relentless torrent carrying away the landmarks of a thousand years' (p. 593) might have also noted the collective sigh of relief that accompanied the removal of a thousand-year-old wall built by the Church between the people and the Bible. Tyndale, as might be expected, gets only two, passing, mentions in this book, the main one a quotation lacking even the dignity of reference in a volume crammed with careful annotation.

37. Duffy, p. 4.
38. Ibid.
39. Ibid., p. 7.
40. Dickens (1966), p. 51.
41. Bennett, p. 188.
42. Ibid., p. 181. See Steinberg, p. 45.
43. *Tyndale's Old Testament*, ed. Daniell, p. 5.
44. Foxe, V, p. 118.
45. Foxe, IV, p. 679.
46. Reprinted from the Foxian MSS by Strype (1821), I, ii, pp. 363 *et. seq.* Monmouth's will is the following document.
47. 'Sodden meat' implies simple food, boiled or simply cooked, as op-

posed to meat enriched by roasting or with tasty sauces. 'Single beer' was once-boiled, therefore less concentrated and cheaper. I am grateful to Joan Johnson for this illumination.
48. Foxe, IV., pp. 617–18, 753. Strype (1821), l. ii., p. 364.
49. Mozley (1937), p. 45.
50. Brigden, p. 105.
51. Latimer, vol. 1, p. 440.
52. Romans 12:20. Interestingly, Foxe quotes no known source for his phrase 'heap hot coals': Tyndale later gave 'heap coals of fire', accurate to the Greek. The Wyclif versions are a long way off, with 'gather together coals', following the Vulgate.
53. Foxe, IV, pp. 618–19.
54. PS, pp. 111, 168.
55. Gleason, pp. 5, 235–7, 341, 379.
56. Quoted by Brigden, p. 109.
57. Brigden, p. 109.
58. C.S. Meyer, p. 189
59. Brigden, p. 109 and passim.

NOTES TO CHAPTER 5

1. Mozley (1937), p. 48.
2. PS, pp. 37–8.
3. Printed in Arber, pp. 20–24, and Pollard, pp. 99–110.
4. See, for example, Gruber.
5. See Mozley (1937), pp. 71–2.
6. I am grateful to Vanessa Champion-Smith for her observations here.
7. Sig. A.ii.v.
8. Sig. B.i.
9. Sig. A.iv.
10. Sig. A.iv.v.
11. All sig. B.
12. Sig. A.iii.v.
13. Sig. A.iv. v.–B
14. Sig. B—B.v.
15. Sig. A.iii.v.
16. Sig. B.2.
17. Attempts to find a parallel passage in Luther have been fruitless. That

does not mean that it will not be found. A big part of the problem is the sheer bulk of Luther's writing even before 1525. A further unfortunate obstacle has been the difficulty of seeing all the volumes of the great Weimar edition together, in the British Library or the Bodleian. I am most grateful to Dr Stephen Ickert of Mansfield College Oxford for spending valuable time in the hunt.

18. For the best analysis there is of Roye's *Brief Dialogue*, see Hume (1967).

NOTES TO CHAPTER 6

1. Johnson (1929), pp. 357–80.
2. *The Good News Bible.*
3. *Revised English Bible.*
4. Wolf, p. 34.
5. *An exposition of the seventh chapter of the first epistle to the Corinthians* [Antwerp, 1529] sig. Cii. r. For Roye as translator of this, and Erasmus's *Paraclesis* bound with it, see Hume (1961), pp. 138–56.
6. See below, pp. 158–9.
7. For a discussion of the 'majesty' of scripture see Norton, pp. 102 et. seq.
8. I am indebted for this account of Roye's *Brief Dialogue* to Hume (1961), pp. 80–90.
9. Ibid., p. 110.
10. Ibid., p. 155.
11. Westcott, p. 158.
12. Largely fulfilled in the 1534 revision.
13. A letter from Robert Ridley, Tunstall's chaplain, to Henry Gold, Archbishop Warham's chaplain, on 24 February 1527 mentions it by name, and thus helps to fix the date. Pollard, p. 122.
14. It should be noted that the Parker Society edition prints the expanded version from 'Matthew's Bible', and is not reliable. A facsimile of the

original was published in 1975 by Theatrum Orbis Terrarum, Amsterdam.

15. Hume (1961), pp. 39–40.
16. Ibid., pp. 39–58 gives the best comparison of the versions.
17. Ibid., p. 48.
18. Sig. B.2–B.2v.
19. Sig. B.6.
20. Hume (1961), p. 53.
21. *Ausslegung deutsch des Vatter unnser fur die Eynfeltigen Leyen* (Wittenberg, 1519).
22. Sig. C.ii.v–C.iii.
23. See Pollard, p. 122.
24. Mozley (1937), pp. 69–74.
25. See below, pp. 191–3.

NOTES TO CHAPTER 7

1. Kronenberg, pp. 139–63.
2. The other nine are: Tyndale's *Obedience of a Christian Man*, 2 October 1528; Erasmus's *Exhortation* and Luther on 1 Corinthians 7, 20 June 1529 (probably translated by Roye); John Frith's *Revelation of Antichrist*, 12 July 1529; Tyndale's Pentateuch, 17 January 1530; Barlowe's *Proper Dialogue*, 1530; *A compendious old treatise* 1530; the latter two reprinted, 1530; the Examinations of Thorpe and Oldcastle, 1530; Tyndale's *Practice of Prelates*, 1530. See *CWM, VIII*, pp. 1065–91.
3. Kronenberg, pp. 156–9.
4. Kronenberg (1967), pp. 81–94.
5. Clebsch, pp. 230–31.
6. Clebsch, p. 307, in an astonishing phrase, calls Tyndale's Bible translations 'prized verbiage'. How he could bring himself to read the rest one cannot imagine. And see Mozley (1937), p. 128, 'the book shows little order or arrangement'.
7. Weimar, X, pp. 283–92. For this section of this chapter I am much indebted to Hume (1961), pp. 59–78.
8. Ibid., p. 60.

9. Sig. B.2. PS, p. 50.
10. Sig. B.4v. PS, pp. 53–4.
11. Sig. B.2v–B.3. PS, pp. 51–2.
12. Sig. B.3v. PS, p. 53.
13. Sig. C.6. PS, p. 65.
14. See above, p. 98.
15. Hume (1961), pp. 68–9.
16. Sig. B.7v–B.8. PS, pp. 56–8.
17. Hume (1961), p. 71.
18. Sig. F.1. PS, p. 90.
19. Sig. F.1v. PS, pp. 90–91.
20. Sig. F.7v. PS, p. 100.
21. Sig. F.7v–G.1. PS, pp. 100–2.
22. Hume, p. 73.
23. PS, p. 102.
24. Foxe gives a 'brief table or catalogue of all such as were forced to abjure in king Henry's days, after the first beginning of Luther'. The list of just over 100 names, which sometimes also gives trades, includes a shipwright, eight tailors, a butcher, a pointer, a bricklayer, a draper, a glazier, a scrivener's servant, a servant, and a shoemaker (IV, pp. 585–6). Strype refers to a tallow-chandler, a pointmaker, a weaver, and three husbandmen (Strype, I, ii, pp. 116–17). Foxe's bricklayer had been imprisoned 'for charging a priest with a lie, that preached at Paul's cross that the blood of Christ was not sufficient for man's redemption without works'.
25. PS, p. 48.
26. Sig. A.5. PS, pp. 43–4.
27. Kronenberg, p. 140.
28. Avis (1973), p. 234.
29. Avis (1972), pp. 180–7.
30. Kronenberg, p. 149.
31. Kronenberg, pp. 153–8.
32. *CWM*, VI, i, pp. 291, 424.
33. Foxe, V, pp. 32–41, noting in particular Patwell and Medwell, pp. 570–7.
34. Foxe, IV, p. 688.
35. Strype, I, i, p. 116.
36. 'In the porter's lodge, hand, foot and head in the stocks, six days without release; then he was carried to Jesu's tree, in his privy garden, where he was whipped, and also twisted in his brows with small ropes, that the blood started out of his eyes; and yet would not accuse no man. Then he was let loose in the house for a day, and his friends thought to have him at liberty the next day. After this, he was sent to be racked in the Tower...' Foxe, IV, p. 689.
37. PS, p. 100.
38. Foxe, IV, p. 692.
39. Foxe, V, pp. 570–7.
40. PS, p. 62.
41. Foxe, V, p. 570.
42. Marius, p. 339.

NOTES TO CHAPTER 8

1. The near-perfect copy has been owned by Bristol Baptist College, and is now on deposit in the British Library: the defective one is in St Paul's Cathedral library.
2. Roye and Barlowe passim, and the English edition of Henry VIII's reply to Luther printed in February 1527: see Mozley (1937), p. 114.
3. 'Monicio ad tradendum libros noui testamenti in idiomate vulgare, translatos per fratrem Martinum Lutherum at eius ministrum Willmum Tyndall alias Hochyn et fratrem Willmum Roy.' Quoted Sturge, p. 132.
4. Not 2,000 copies burned, as Richard Rex has it. Rex is scornful of those who misread Cochlaeus to produce Peter Quentell as the Cologne printer, but himself misreads Cochlaeus here.
5. The figure of 6,000 copies comes from the report by Cochlaeus of his conversation with the Cologne printers: Tyndale's original request there was for that number, and the same might be assumed from Worms. Pollard, p. 104.

6. Pollard, p. 125; for Hackett, see Pollard, pp. 135–49.

7. We cannot be quite sure what this means: 'with the glosses joined' can only mean the Cologne sheets, unless, as is extremely unlikely, the Endhoven piracy had acquired glosses from somewhere. We cannot be surprised if the descriptions are inaccurate, however: the printed English New Testament was a new animal, not in any bestiary. Pollard, pp. 153–4.

8. Mozley (1937), p. 119.

9. Foxe, IV, p. 621.

10. Quoted Dickens (1989), p. 102.

11. Sturge, pp. 137–9.

12. Mozley (1937), p. 121.

13. I am grateful to Sue Thurgood for constructing an outline.

14. Foxe, V, p. 42.

15. Foxe, IV, p. 671.

16. Ibid., p. 768. n. 681, l. 32.

17. Ibid., p. 681.

18. Ibid., p. 685.

19. Foxe, V, p. 42.

20. Sturge p. 139 and Hume, CWM, VIII, iii, pp. 1079–80.

21. Strype (1821), I, ii, pp. 60–5.

22. Foxe, V, p. 26, et. seq.

23. Ibid., p. 29.

24. Mozley (1937), pp. 121–2.

25. Sturge, p. 141.

26. See above, pp. 51–2.

27. Foxe, IV, p. 617; vol. V, p. 5.

28. Ibid., p. 688.

29. see above, pp. 171–3. For More's reply to all such charges see his Apology (EETS, 1930) pp. 131–4, and Chambers, pp. 274–82. Chambers's defence of More's alleged violence is surprisingly weaselly: he nowhere mentions John Tewkesbury. Even Marius, who does (pp. 405–6) reports little more than More's detestation of Tewkesbury, and goes quickly on to Bainham (see below, p. 183), saying that Foxe's story of the latter's torture 'is universally doubted today', which is true only on a limited understanding of 'universally'. Marius does however quote More against himself, and allows the full horror of what More was doing.

30. Foxe, IV, pp. 694–5.

31. Ibid., pp. 582–3.

32. Answer, PS, p. 113: e.g. Practice, PS, p. 340.

33. CWM, VIII, i, p. 15.

34. The Works of Charles and Mary Lamb, ed. E.V. Lucas (1912), vol. 1. p. 203.

35. Mozley (1937), p. 229.

36. Sturge, p. 110; 'valued at fully two and half times that of London'.

37. Foxe, IV, pp. 583–5.

38. Foxe, V, pp. 29–31.

39. Ibid., pp. 32–8.

40. Mozley (1937) writes 'in two and a quarter years there had been ten martyrdoms', p. 245.

41. Lines 176–96. See Skelton, pp. 379, 516.

42. Ibid., pp. 516–17.

43. CWM, VIII, i, p. 25.

44. Ibid., i, p. 17.

45. Foxe, IV, pp. 702.

46. Ibid., p. 698.

47. Ibid., p. 704.

48. Quoted in Marius, p. 406; he observed of that remark that 'we can feel the thud of vindictive triumph in his sentence upon them'.

49. Avis (1973), pp. 234–40.

50. Avis (1972), p. 184.

51. Schuster, in CWM, 8, iii, pp. 1156–7.

52. Steinberg, p. 74.

53. Febvre and Martin, p. 218. Erasmus's amazing figure of 24,000 is only a boast.

54. Darlow and Moule, p. 1.

55. See C. Haigh, in Past and Present (1993) and Historical Journal, 25 (1982); and Scarisbrick. For a spirited contrary view see Dickens (1987), pp. 187–222, an important study.

56. Gwyn, p. 499.
57. See Fines, *Biographical Register of Early English Protestants . . . 1525–1558*, 1. (Sutton Courtenay, 1980): 11. (West London Institute of Higher Education, 1987.)
58. Scarisbrick, p. 136.
59. Foxe, V, p. 416.
60. Ibid., p. 417.
61. *L&P*, iii, p. 1275; a vivid account of the earlier, 1521 burning, is given in Meyer, pp. 185–7.
62. Gwyn, p. 488.
63. Mozley (1937), p. 112.
64. Sturge, p. 132.
65. Ibid.
66. Gwyn, p. 490.
67. Mozley (1937), p. 115.
68. Gwyn, pp. 488–9.
69. Mozley's date, ingeniously calculated on pp. 116–17.
70. Mozley (1937), p. 114.
71. PS, p. 337.
72. Meyer, p. 179.
73. Meyer, p. 180.
74. Meyer, p. 181.
75. Meyer, p. 182.
76. Meyer, p. 184.
77. See, for example, Sturge, p. 133 'the notes which the translator had, in some copies, added'.
78. *Tyndale's Old Testament*, ed. Daniell, p. 3.
79. A curious note follows the record of the monition to the booksellers in Tunstall's own Episcopal Register. Tunstall has inserted 'an extract from an old book in the library of the Dominican Friars in London, to the effect that when certain Greeks, who had come to England from Constantinople about 460, were asked if the Greek populace understood the Scriptures read or recited in their hearing, replied that they did not, since their speech was quite distinct from the Greek in which the divine records were contained' (Sturge, p. 133). Tunstall is obviously troubled. Erasmus in his

Paraclesis to his *Novum instrumentum* had pleaded for everyone to know the Scriptures, as if that was part of his intention in producing his book. Tunstall cannot have forgotten that.
80. Strype (1821), I, i. p. 492.
81. Foxe, V, pp. 213–14.
82. Mozley (1937), p. 116–17. Arber's *English Reprints*, p. 46.
83. Hall, pp. 762–3.
84. Mozley (1937), p. 149.
85. See above, pp. 170–71.
86. Quoted Mozley (1937), p. 146.
87. Mozley (1953), p. 2.
88. Ibid., p. 3.
89. See above p. 109.
90. There is a curious anticipation of that play. Tyndale writes '. . . the old king of Denmark, with his son, a goodly prince if he had lands, shall never come in Denmark again . . .' That old king had lost all his lands, and he was superseded not by his son but by his uncle. PS, p. 334 and note.
91. PS, p. 256.
92. PS, p. 265.
93. PS, p. 291.
94. PS, p. 293.
95. PS, p. 309.
96. PS, p. 245.
97. PS, p. 245.
98. *Tyndale's Old Testament*, ed. Daniell, p. 492.
99. Ibid., p. 494.
100. Ibid., p. 643.
101. *CWM*, VIII, i, p. 9 (modernised).
102. Quoted Mozley (1937), p. 200.
103. *Tyndale's Old Testament*, ed. Daniell, p. 629.
104. Ibid., p. 631.
105. Ibid., p. 631.
106. Ibid., p. 632.
107. Clebsch, p. 164. Clebsch here, as elsewhere, can be seen to be supporting his thesis, which is that Tyndale especially, and other English reformers as well, moved in fifteen years to a much more legal-

istic theology, more on the lines of American Puritanism of many decades later. Not everyone finds that to be so.

108. Ibid., p. 165.
109. See *CWM*, VIII, iii, pp. 1220–21, and Mozley (1937), p. 170.
110. Strype (1812), p. 116.
111. *CWM*, VIII, i, p. 9.
112. See, for example, the effect the book had on John Bale: Pineas, 'William Tyndale's Influence on John Bale's Polemic Use of History', pp. 79–96; and Fairfield, pp. 55–6, 192 n. 13.
113. Quoted Mozley (1937), p. 171.
114. See Richardson, passim.
115. Merriman, I, p. 85.
116. Mozley (1937), p. 188.
117. Mozley (1937), p. 189.
118. *CWM*, VIII, i, pp. 10–11.
119. Mozley (1937), p. 191.
120. Mozley (1937), pp. 192–5.
121. Shakespeare, *Hamlet*, II, ii, pp. 428–58.
122. Merriman, I, pp. 336–7.
123. Mozley (1937), p. 198.
124. Ibid., p. 198.
125. Mozley (1937), p. 200.
126. Merriman, I, p. 101.
127. Foxe, V, p. 3.
128. Quoted Mozley (1937), p. 326, in the conext of the three members of that faculty who were deputed to try Tyndale in 1535.
129. Clebsch, p. 82.
130. Hume (1961), pp. 260–71. Lucas Cranach made thirteen pairs of woodcuts on the theme.
131. Recounted well in Mozley (1937), pp. 245–6.
132. See Hume (1961), passim, but esp. pp. 321–60. Similarly Mozley (1937), but esp. pp. 245–60.
133. Printed in Foxe V, pp. 130–4, and by Mozley (1937), pp. 248–51, 257–60.
134. Foxe, V, p. 134.
135. Foxe, V, p. 132.
136. Foxe, V, p. 130.

137. PS, p. 216.
138. PS, p. 3.
139. PS, p. 5.
140. PS, p. 32.
141. PS, p. 51.
142. PS, p. 59.
143. PS, p. 97.
144. PS, pp. 104–6.
145. PS, p. 124.
146. PS, p. 125.

NOTES TO CHAPTER 9

1. See above, p. 185.
2. *CWM*, VI, i, pp. 368–72.
3. Allen, p. 16.
4. See Lehmberg.
5. Sig. A.2–A.2v. See Shakespeare, *Troilus and Cressida*, I, iii, pp. 109–110.
6. Hume (1961), p. 167.
7. PS, p. 238. Something that needs saying here is that, though we should be grateful to the Rev. Henry Walter for his Parker Society edition of 1848, without which many scholars and general readers would have known nothing of the *Obedience*, he did Tyndale several disservices. One was subtly varying the rhythm of most of Tyndale's sentences by sprinkling commas and semi-colons liberally. Adding many marginal notes from Day's edition has given an impression of a level of marginal activity which is not Tyndale's. The modern reader should be warned that many marginal notes that Walter marks 'W.T.' are not in the earliest editions, those that we may assume Tyndale oversaw. The Bible cross-references in the margin are entirely Walter's own. The worst that Walter did was to interfere with the running-heads by promoting most of the modestly-printed small sub-headings in the text to the tops of pages.

8. PS, p. 310.
9. PS, p. 134.
10. PS, p. 134.
11. PS, pp. 136–7.
12. PS, p. 134.
13. PS, pp. 156–9.
14. PS, pp. 207.
15. The final commands of Christ to Peter in John 21 'Feed my lambs . . . feed my sheep'. Similarly, see PS, p. 257: under 'Of Order', Christ commandeth Peter in the last chapter of John, 'Feed my sheep', not 'Shear thy flock'.
16. PS, p. 221.
17. PS, pp. 221–2.
18. PS, pp. 225–6.
19. PS, p. 241.
20. PS, pp. 247–8.
21. PS, p. 250.
22. PS, pp. 251–2.
23. PS, pp. 270.
24. PS, pp. 272.
25. PS, pp. 276–7.
26. See above, pp. 32–40.
27. PS, p. 304.
28. PS, pp. 307–8.
29. PS, p. 320.
30. John XXIII, Gregory XII and Benedict XIII, between 1378 and 1429.
31. PS, p. 335.
32. PS, p. 338.
33. Hume (1961), p. 172.
34. Ibid., p. 173.
35. Duffield, p. xxxi.
36. *The Institution of a Christian Man*, p. 148.
37. See Rainer Pineas, 'William Tyndale's Influence on John Bale's Polemical Use of History', pp. 79–96; and the same author's 'William Tyndale's Use of History as a Weapon of Religious Controversy', pp. 121–41; Fairfield; and esp. McCusker and Walker (1991).
38. See Ives (1972) and (1986), Steve W. Haas, 'Henry VIII's *Glasse of Truthe*', *History*, n.s., 64 (1979), pp.

353–62; and Warnicke (1985). For more recent contributions to the debate: Warnicke (1989), Dowling (1991), Bernard (1991), Ives and Bernard (1992). Dowling (1984) is recommended.
39. Quoted Mozely (1937), p. 143.
40. Dowling (1984), p. 33.
41. See Rainer Pineas, 'William Tyndale: Controversialist', pp. 117–32, and 'More versus Tyndale: A Study of Controversial Technique', pp. 144–50.
42. PS, p. 134.
43. Erasmus (1963).

NOTES TO CHAPTER 10

1. See the monograph by John M. Headley which prefaces *CWM*, V, ii, pp. 715–859.
2. See Mayor, pp. 311–48, 429–76.
3. See Doyle-Davidson; the same volume contains Joseph Delcourt's 'Some Aspects of Sir Thomas More's English', pp. 326–42.
4. See p. 192.
5. See Rex, p. 86, n. 3.
6. Marius, pp. 278–80.
7. See Rex, pp. 86–9.
8. Marius, p. 278.
9. Rex, p. 99.
10. *CWM*, V, ii, pp. 718–19.
11. Rex, p. 88.
12. Marius, pp. 276–80.
13. Ibid., pp. 269–70.
14. Ibid., p. 270.
15. Thomism is the systematic expression of the doctrines of Thomas Aquinas, felt by Luther to be dry intellectualism with no Christian content.
16. I am grateful to Vanessa Champion-Smith for the translation.
17. From the anonymous English translation of 1687, p. 129.
18. Marius, p. 280.
19. *CWM*, V, ii, pp. 732, 734.
20. Ibid., p. 734.

21. Ibid., p. 731.
22. Ibid., p. 775.
23. Ibid., p. 776.
24. Ibid., pp. 777–81.
25. Ibid., p. 810.
26. Ibid., p. 811.
27. Marius, p. 281.
28. Ibid., p. 282.
29. It is analysed well by Marius, pp. 280–7.
30. CWM, V, i, p. 683. English trans. by Sister Scholastica Mandeville. Doyle-Davidson wrote 'Ever since his death he [More] has been ... a popular favourite, beloved of all for his sweetness and nobility of character...' (Sylvester and Marc'hadour, p. 356). These qualities of More (which some would dispute) do not appear in his Latin controversies.
31. Rex, pp. 89–95.
32. Ibid., pp. 95–6.
33. Ibid., p. 96.
34. Ibid., pp. 96–7. The English edition of Henry's answer to Luther, dated March 1527, attacks Tyndale as being instigated by Luther: see Pollard, pp. 117–18.
35. Ibid., p. 98.
36. Ibid., p. 100.
37. Marius, p. 325.
38. Rex, p. 101.
39. Above, p. 53.
40. For details, see Marius, p. 326.
41. Marius, p. 327; a useful account of the letter is Marius, pp. 326–31.
42. Ibid., pp. 330–38.
43. Ibid., p. 338.
44. Ibid., p. 338.
45. English Historical Documents V, pp. 828–9.
46. I owe this phrase to Patrick Collinson.
47. Lewis, p. 178.
48. CWM, VI, i, pp. 33–4.
49. Ibid., ii, p. 548.
50. Lewis, p. 172.
51. CWM, VI, i, pp. 247–8
52. Lewis, pp. 165, 662–3. The classic

account is Chambers; see also Delcourt.
53. CWM, VI, i, pp. 285–90.
54. Ibid., p. 28.
55. Ibid., pp. 292–3.
56. Ibid., p. 303.
57. Even CWM acknowledges this, VI, ii, p. 687.
58. CWM, VI, i, p. 304.
59. CWM, VI, ii, p. 343.
60. CWM, VI, i, p. 341.
61. Mozley (1937), p. 217; and see Hall, p. 817, where More is 'a great persecutor'.
62. CWM, VI, i, p. 425 and VI, ii, 425 nn. 15–17. Other examples might be found.
63. PS, pp. 9.
64. PS, pp. 30–1.
65. PS, p. 78.
66. PS, pp. 188–9.
67. Mozley (1937), p. 219.
68. Ibid., p. 221.
69. PS, 3. p. 9. The passage immediately follows the section from the end of the preface quoted above.
70. PS, p. 10, four sentences from the end of the preface.
71. Quoted in Mozley (1937), p. 221. The echo is partly of Job 39.
72. PS, p. 110.
73. There are remarks against More in The Supper of the Lord, but this is not now taken to be by Tyndale. See Anthea Hume in CWM, VIII, ii, p. 1083.
74. Harpsfield, pp. 117–8. The Yale editor notes 'Actually Harpsfield is reproducing More's own comment on Tyndale's frantic efforts to escape the argument that scripture needed the church to establish its validity.' CWM, VIII, iii, p. 1261 n. 1.
75. CWM, VIII, iii, p. 1260.
76. Ibid., p. 1260.
77. CWM, VIII, iii, p. 1552 n. 234/10. It is a somewhat two-edged excuse, as More is himself responsible for the inordinate length of the battle. And More is certainly not

above using hearsay as evidence, noted on p. 1625. Other misrepresentations can be found noted on *CWM*, VIII, iii, pp. 1476, 1507, 1550, 1620-1, 1647-8, 1664, and 1681. There may well be more. It is possibly significant, for example, that the Yale editors can give a note on the Protestant martyr Tewkesbury which omits all mention of More's part in his interrogation, imprisonment in his Chelsea house, and torture there, as detailed by Foxe. See also Mozley (1937), pp. 230-2.

78. Quoted by Rainer Pineas in 'More versus Tyndale', p. 149. *CWM*, XI, p. 127; VI, ii, passim, and 148, 508.

79. *CWM*, VIII, iii, p. 1256.

80. *Hall's Chronicle,* p. 817.

81. *CWM*, VIII, i, pp. 140-41.

82. *CWM*, VIII, i, pp. 338.

83. See, for example, Schuster, *CWM*, VIII, iii, p. 1254.

84. See above n. 73.

85. See Oberman, pp. 155-6.

86. The first, on PS, p. 282, has in the original the pope saying 'don't kiss my feet only, but my "N" also'. In the second, on PS, p. 300, the omitted words are [of the Venetians] 'and that (as Erasmus sayeth) they shite as easily as before (with reverence to the holy course I speak it) and . . .' The third, on PS, p. 337, about the clergy, omits 'For their Arses were upon thorns till the loan was forgiven, for fear of after clapps'. In the *Obedience*, PS, p. 285, Tyndale has, of the bishops, 'To preach is their duty only, and not to offer their feet to be kissed . . .'. Walter's footnote reads 'A coarse expression, originating with the once popularly credited story of Pope Joan, is here omitted'. The omitted words are, after 'feet', 'or testicles or stones to be groped'.

87. Quoted Mozley (1937), p. 227.

88. Until possibly 1994. Just before writing these words, I heard a report that one effect of the privatisation of the centre of Basingstoke in Hampshire has been that the new owners, the Prudential insurance company, would not allow a Salvation Army major, as part of his open-air service, to read the Bible there.

89. *Tyndale's New Testament*, ed. Daniell, p. 347.

NOTES TO CHAPTER 11

1. Tyndale's 'Ah syr' might be 'Ah, sure . . .' or 'Ah, surely . . .' (implying something fixed and agreed with) or even 'Ah, it is sure that God hath said . . .', which is fairer for the Hebrew. But none of those are what Tyndale wrote, and kept in the later 1543 revision. Moreover, I have been unable to find any form of 'sure' appearing as 'syr'. The editor of 'Matthew's Bible' changed the reading to 'yea: hath God said indeed, ye shall . . .'

2. I owe the description to Gerald Hammond.

3. Tyndale's use of 'Tush' is interesting, in that it is now a little hard to hear its register. Is Tyndale's serpent using some coarser demotic dismissal, as today someone might say 'Crap, it won't happen'? Or is it a word belonging to a higher level altogether, suggesting that the serpent is trying to speak from some lofty position? In the opening lines of *Hamlet* (I.i.30) the scholar Horatio, dismissing soldiers' talk of a dreaded apparition as 'fantasy', says 'Tush, tush, 'twill not appear'. That was in 1600. Some ten years earlier, Shakespeare made the young and aspiring adventurer Petruchio conclude his fanciful dismissal of dangers with 'Tush, tush,

fear boys with bugs' (*The Taming of the Shrew*, I.ii.207), and the drunk and scheming villain Borachio in *Much Ado About Nothing* (III.iii.130) struggles to dismiss his companion's attempts at learned wit with 'Tush, I may as well say the fool's the fool'. OED's definition as 'An exclamation of impatient contempt or disparagement', with an earliest recorded use of about 1440, helps, but not with the register.

4. See Williams.
5. PS, pp. 148–9.
6. Lloyd Jones, passim.
7. Ibid., p. 90.
8. Ibid., p. 21.
9. Ibid., p. 21.
10. Ibid., p. 96.
11. See Lloyd Jones, pp. 181–9. Lloyd Jones has edited a modern edition of Wakefield's oration, *On the Three Languages* [1524] (Binghampton, NY: Medieval and Renaissance Texts & Studies, and The Renaissance Society of America, 1989).
12. Lloyd Jones, p. 25.
13. Hall, p. 43.
14. Lloyd Jones, p. 26.
15. Ibid., p. 32.
16. For examples see Lloyd Jones, pp. 41–2.
17. See Pearl, passim.
18. *Tyndale's Old Testament,* ed. Daniell, p. 486.
19. Tyndale's 'Rab. Sal.' reading, at what is now 1 Kings 14:24, is 'stews of male children', where Pagninus has 'scortator', whoremonger or fornicator.
20. See Steinberg, p. 144.
21. See Mozley (1937), pp. 55–6.
22. Quoted in Ibid., pp. 51–2.
23. Ibid.
24. Ibid., p. 52.
25. Ibid., pp. 52–3.
26. Something has been made of Tyndale's understanding of 'covenant'. See Moller, and also McGiffert.
27. I am grateful to Dr Michael Weitzman for help here.
28. Hammond (1982).
29. Hammond (1980), in part replying to Karpman.
30. For the passage added to this prologue in the 1534 revision, see *Tyndale's Old Testament*, ed. Daniell, pp. 10–11.

NOTES TO CHAPTER 12

1. The Parker Society edition is misleading here, as Walter prints the version from Day's 1573 folio, which could not possibly have warrant from Tyndale, calling this 'Prologue upon the Gospel of Matthew'. Westcott was deceived by this into remarking on 'his Prologue to St Matthew, which is an extended essay' (p. 149).
2. Hume (1961), p. 431.
3. See Butterworth and Chester, pp. 19–20.
4. Ibid., pp. 38–45: and see Hume (1961) p. 286.
5. Butterworth and Chester, passim.
6. The figures are from *An Apology*, pp. 20–21.
7. Mozley (1937), p. 198.
8. See Butterworth and Chester, pp. 154–63, 269–72.
9. Ibid., pp. 154 et seq.
10. *Tyndale's New Testament*, ed. Daniell, p. 14.
11. Frith (1531).
12. Butterworth and Chester, pp. 170–4.
13. *Tyndale's New Testament*, ed. Daniell, p. 14.
14. Some comment will be found in the introduction to *Tyndale's New Testament*, ed. Daniell, pp. vii–xxxi.

NOTES TO CHAPTER 13

1. Darlow and Moule, p. 18.
2. See Mozley (1937), p. 355.
3. See Chester, pp. 113, 418–24.
4. Hammond, passim.
5. See Soggin, p. 87.
6. 'Matthew's Bible' has this as 'godly', which I reproduced in my *Tyndale's Old Testament*. I now believe that I should have given a footnote saying it was properly 'goodly'; for 'godly asses' makes an oxymoron surely unimaginable to Tyndale.
7. Soggin, p. 87.
8. *As You Like It*, V. iii. 36; Browne, para. 25.

NOTES TO CHAPTER 14

1. See *L&P*, IX, 1138 et. seq.
2. Mozley (1937), p. 299.
3. Foxe, V, pp. 121–3.
4. Mozley (1937), p. 302.
5. Mozley (1937), p. 304.
6. Ibid., pp. 304–5.
7. Ibid., pp. 307–8.
8. Ibid., p. 307.
9. John 13.
10. Mozley (1937), p. 305.
11. Foxe, V, pp. 124–9.

12. Mozley (1937), p. 305.
13. Ibid., pp. 300–1.
14. Ibid., p. 301.
15. Ibid., p. 311.
16. Ibid., p. 311.
17. Ibid., p. 317.
18. Ibid., p. 320.
19. Ibid., p. 322.
20. Ibid., p. 323.

NOTES TO CHAPTER 15

1. Mozley (1937), p. 325.
2. Ibid., p. 327.
3. See Foxe, V, p. 128.
4. Ibid., p. 127.
5. Mozley (1937), p. 328.
6. Foxe, V, p. 128.
7. Mozley (1937), p. 329.
8. Ibid., p. 333.
9. Ibid., pp. 333–5.
10. Ibid., pp. 335–6.
11. Foxe, V, p. 127.
12. Hall, p. 818.
13. Mozley (1937), p. 338.
14. Ibid., p. 338.
15. Ibid., p. 338.
16. Ibid., p. 340.
17. Foxe, V, p. 127.
18. Ibid., p. 128.
19. Mozley (1937), pp. 341–2.

BIBLIOGRAPHY

Unless otherwise stated, the place of publication is London.

Allen, J.W. *A History of Political Thought in the Sixteenth Century*, 1928

An Apology made by George Joy, to satisfy, if it may be, W. Tindale, 1535, ed. E. Arber, *The English Scholar's Library*, 13, Birmingham, 1882

Arber, E. *The First Printed English New Testament*, 1871

—— *English Reprints No. 28* (1871), *Roye and Barlow: Rede Me And Be Not Wroth*

Avis, F.C. 'Book Smuggling into England during the Sixteenth Century', *Gutenberg Jahrbuch*, 1972, pp. 180–87

—— 'England's Use of Antwerp Printers, 1500–1540', *Gutenberg Jahrbuch*, 1973, pp. 234–40

Bainton, R.H. *Erasmus of Christendom*, New York, 1969

Baldwin, T.W. *William Shakespeare's Small Latine and Lesse Greeke*, Urbana, 1944

Bale, J. *King John*, ?1540

Barnstone, W. *The Poetics of Translation: History, Theory, Practice*, New Haven and London, 1993

Baumer, F. Le Van *The Early Tudor Theory of Kingship*, New York, 1966

Bennett, H.S. *English Books and Readers 1475 to 1557*, Cambridge, 1969

Bernard, G.W. 'The Fall of Anne Boleyn', *English Historical Review*, 106, 1991, pp. 584–610

—— 'The Fall of Anne Boleyn: A Rejoinder', *English Historical Review*, 107, 1992, pp. 665–74

[The Bible]

The Holy Bible . . . John Wycliffe . . ., eds J. Forshall and F. Madden, Oxford, 1850

Coverdale's Bible, 1535

Matthew's Bible, 1537

Great Bible, 1539

Geneva Bible, 1560

Bishop's Bible, 1568

Rheims New Testament, 1582

Authorised Version, 1611

New English Bible, 1961, 1970

Good News Bible, The, or *The Bible in Today's English Version*, 1966, 1976

Revised English Bible, 1989

Binns, J. *Intellectual Culture in Elizabethan and Jacobean London*, 1990

Black, M.H. 'The Printed Bible', *The Cambridge History of the Bible: The West from the Reformation to the Present Day*, Cambridge, 1963, pp. 408–75

Bone, G. 'Tindale and the English Language', in S.L. Greenslade (ed.), *The Work of William Tindale*, 1938, pp. 50–68

Bowker, M. *The Henrician Reformation* (1984)

Brigden, S. *London and the Reformation*, Oxford, 1989

Brook, S. *The Language of the Book of Common Prayer*, 1975

Browne, Sir T. *A Letter to a Friend*, 1656

Brownell, M.R. 'Ears of an Untoward Make', *Musical Quarterly*, 62, no. 4, 1976, pp. 554–70

Bruce, F.F. *The English Bible: A History of Translations*, 1961

Butt, J. (ed.) *The Poems of Alexander Pope*, 1963

Butterworth, C.C. *The English Primers (1529–1545): Their Publication and Connection with the English Bible and the Reformation in England*, Philadelphia, 1953

Butterworth, C.C., and Chester, A.G. *George Joye, 1495?–1553*, Philadelphia, 1962

Buxton, J., and Williams, P. (eds) *New College Oxford 1379–1979*, Oxford, 1979

Cameron, E. *The European Reformation*, Oxford, 1991

Catto, J.I. 'Theology after Wycliffism', in J.I. Catto and R. Evans (eds), *The History of the University of Oxford, II: Late Medieval Oxford*, Oxford, 1992, pp. 263–80

Catto, J.I., and Evans, R. (eds) *The History of the University of Oxford, II: Late Medieval Oxford*, Oxford, 1992

Chambers, R.W. *Thomas More*, 1935.

Chapman, G. *Seven Books of the Iliad's of* (1598), ed. Nicoll

Chester, J.L. *John Rogers*, 1861

Clebsch, W.A. *England's Earliest Protestants 1520–1535*, New Haven and London, 1964

Colet, J. *Two Treatises on the Hierarchies of Dionysius*, ed. J.H. Lupton, 1869

Cottret, B. 'Traducteurs et divulgateurs clandestins de la Reforme dans l'Angleterre henricienne, 1520–1535', *Revue d'histoire moderne et contemporaine*, 28, 1981, pp. 464–80

Daniell, D. 'Pope, Handel and Swift', in E. Maslen (ed.), *The Timeless and the Temporal: Writings in Honour of John Chalker by Friends and Colleagues*, Queen Mary and Westfield college, University of London, 1993, pp. 134–51

Darlow, T.H., and Moule, H.F. (eds), rev. by A.S. Herbert, *Historical Catalogue of Printed Editions of the English Bible 1525–1962*, 1968

Davis, J.F. *Heresy and Reformation in the South-East of England, 1520–1559, Royal Historical Society Studies in History*, series no. 34, 1983

Davis, N. *William Tyndale's English Controversy: The Chambers Memorial Lecture Delivered at University College London 4 March 1971*, UCL, 1971

Deanesly, M. *The Lollard Bible and other Medieval Biblical Versions*, Cambridge, 1920

—— 'Vernacular Books in England in the Fourteenth and Fifteenth Centuries', *Modern Language Review*, XV, 1920, pp. 349–58

Delcourt, J. 'Some Aspects of Sir Thomas More's English', in R.S. Sylvester and G.P. Marc'hadour (eds), *Essential Articles for the Study of Sir Thomas More*, Hamden, Conn., 1977, pp. 326–42

Demaus, R., rev. by Lovett, R., *William Tindale: A Biography*, 1904

DeMolen, R.L. (ed.) *Essays on the Works of Erasmus*, New Haven and London, 1978

Devereux, E.J. 'Some Lost Translations of Erasmus', *The Library*, 5th series, XVII, 1962, pp. 255–9

—— *Thomas Cromwell and the English Reformation*, 1959

—— *Reformation and Society in Sixteenth-century Europe*, 1966

—— *The English Reformation*, 2nd ed., 1989

Dickens, A.G. 'The Early Expansion of Protestantism in England 1520–1558', *Archiv fur Reformationsgeschichte*, LXXVIII, 1987, pp. 187–222

—— *The English Reformation*, 1964: 2nd ed. 1989

—— *Reformation and Society in Sixteenth-Century Europe*, 1966

—— *Thomas Cromwell and the English Reformation*, 1959

Dixon, P. *Rhetoric*, 1971

Dowling, M. 'Anne Boleyn and Reform', *Journal of English History*, 35, 1984, pp. 30–46

—— 'A Woman's Place? Learning and the Wives of Henry VIII', *History Today*, June 1991, pp. 38–42

Doyle-Davidson, W.A.G. 'The Earlier English Works of Sir Thomas More' in R.S. Sylvester and G.P. Marc'hadour (eds), *Essential Articles for the Study of Thomas More*, Hamden, Conn., 1977, pp. 356–74

Duffield, G.E. (ed.) *The Work of William Tyndale*, 1964

Duffy, E. *The Stripping of the Altars*, New Haven and London, 1992

Duhamel, P.A. 'The Oxford Lectures of John Colet', in *Journal of History of Ideas*, XIV, 1953, pp. 493–510

Edgerton, W.L. *Nicholas Udall*, New York, 1965

Edwards, B.H. *God's Outlaw*, Welwyn, Herts, 1976

Eisenstein, E. *The Printing Press as an Agent of Change: I*, 1979

Emden, A.B. *Biographical Register of the University of Oxford, AD 1501–1540*, Oxford, 1974

English Historical Documents: V, 1485–1558, ed. C.H. Williams, 1967

Erasmus of Rotterdam, Desiderius *On Copia of Words and Ideas (De utraque verborem ac rerum copia)*, trans. and intro. by D.B. King and H.D. Rix, Milwaukee, Wis., 1963

—— *Erasmus: Enchiridion Militis Christiani: An English Version*, ed. A.M. O'Donnell, Oxford, 1981

Evans, T.A.R. 'The Number, Origins and Careers of Scholars', in J.I. Catto and R. Evans (eds) *The History of the University of Oxford, II: Late Medieval Oxford*, Oxford, 1992, pp. 485–538

Fairfield, L.P. *John Bale: Mythmaker for the English Reformation*, West Lafayette, 1976

Faludy, G. *Erasmus of Rotterdam*, 1970

Febvre, L., and Martin, Henri-Jean *The Coming of the Book: The Impact of Printing 1480–1800*, 1976

Fines, J. *Biographical Register of Early English Protestants: 1525–1558*, I, 1980; II, 1987

Finucane, R.C. *Miracles and Pilgrims: Popular Beliefs in Medieval England*, 1977

Fisher, John *The English Works of John Fisher*, ed. J.E.B. Mayor, 1876

Fletcher, J.M. 'Developments in the Faculty of Arts 1370–1520', in J.I. Catto and R. Evans (eds) *The History of the University of Oxford, II: Late Medieval Oxford*, Oxford, 1992, pp. 315–45

Forshall, J., and Madden, F. (eds) *The Holy Bible . . . John Wycliffe . . .* , Oxford, 1850

Foster, J. *Alumni Oxoniensis, 1500–1714*, 1968

Foxe, John *The Acts and Monuments of John Foxe*, 8 vols, 4th edn, ed. rev. and corrected by J. Pratt; intro. by J. Stoughton, 1877

Fraser, A. *The Six Wives of Henry VIII*, 1992

Frith, J. *Antithesis, where are compared together Christ's acts and our holy father the pope's*, 1529

—— *Revelation of Antichrist*, 1529

—— *Divers Fruitful Gatherings of Scripture concerning faith and works*, 1529

—— *A Disputation of Purgatory . . .* , Antwerp or London, 1531

Gee, J.A. 'John Byddell and the First Publication of Erasmus' *Enchiridion* in English', *English Literary History*, IV, 1937, pp. 43–59

Gleason, J.B. *John Colet*, Berkeley, 1989

Greenblatt, S. *Renaissance Self-fashioning: From More to Shakespeare*, Chicago, 1980

Greenfield, B.W. *Genealogy of the Family of Tyndale* . . . , privately printed, 1843

Greenslade, S.L. *The Work of William Tindale*, 1938

Gruber, L.F. *The Truth about . . . Tyndale's New Testament*, St Paul, Minn., 1917

Gwyn, P. *The King's Cardinal: The Rise and Fall of Thomas Wolsey*, 1990

Haigh, C. *The English Reformation Revised*, 1987

—— *English Reformations: Religion, Politics and Society under the Tudors*, 1993

Hall, B. 'Biblical Scholarship: Editions and Commentaries', *The Cambridge History of the Bible: The West from the Reformation to the Present Day*, Cambridge, 1963, pp. 38–93

Hall's Chronicle: Containing the History of England . . . , 1809

Hamilton, S.G. *Hertford College*, 1903

Hammond, G. 'William Tyndale's Peutateuch: Its Relation to Luther's German Bible and the the Hebrew Original', *Renaissance Quarterly*, 33, 1980, pp. 351–85

—— *The Making of the English Bible*, Manchester, 1982

Harpsfield, N. *The Life and Death of Sir Thomas More*, ed. E.V. Hitchcock, 1932

Heath, P. *The English Parish Clergy on the Eve of the Reformation*, 1969

Herbert, A.S. 'Scripture Translations and Scripture Printing before 1525', in T.H. Darlow and H.F. Moule (eds), *Historical Catalogue of Printed Editions of the English Bible, 1525–1962*, 1968, pp. xxvi–xxxi

Hoyle, R.W. *The Military Survey of Gloucestershire, 1522*, Bristol: Bristol and Gloucestershire Archaeological Society, 1993

Hume, A. 'A Study of the Writings of the English Protestant Exiles, 1525–35', unpub. PhD thesis, University of London, 1961

—— 'Roye's Brief Dialogue, *Harvard Theological Review*, 60, 1967, pp. 307–21

—— 'English Protestant Books Printed Abroad, 1525–1535: An Annotated Bibliography', in *CWM*, VIII, ii, pp. 1063–91

Hunt, E.W. *Dean Colet and His Theology*, 1956

Hunt, R.W. 'The Medieval Library', in J. Buxton and P. Williams (eds), *New College Oxford 1379–1979*, Oxford, 1979, pp. 317–45

Hutter, I. 'Cardinal Pole's Greek Manuscripts in Oxford', in A.C. de la Mare and B.C. Barker-Benfield (eds), *Manuscripts at Oxford: An Exhibition in Memory of Richard William Hunt (1908–1979)*, Oxford, 1980, pp. 108–13

The Institution of a Christian Man in Formularies of Faith (1537), put forth by authority during the Reign of Henry VIII, ed. C. Lloyd, 1825.

Isocrates, with Eng. trans. by George Norlin 3 vols, Loeb Classical Library, 1928

Ives, E.W. *Faction at the Court of Henry VIII*, 1972

—— *Anne Boleyn*, Oxford, 1986

—— 'The Fall of Anne Boleyn Reconsidered', *English Historical Review*, 107, 1992, pp. 651–64

Jacobsen, E. *Translation: A Traditional Craft*, Copenhagen 1958

Jarrott, C.A.L. 'Erasmus's Annotations and Colet's Commentaries on Paul: A Comparison of Some Theological Themes', in R.L. De Molen (ed.), *Essays on the Works of Erasmus*, New Haven and London, 1978, pp. 125–43

Johnson, A.F. 'The Classification of Gothic Types', *Transactions of the Bibliographical Society*, LX, 1929, pp. 357–80

Johnson, J. *Tudor Gloucestershire*, Gloucester, 1985

Jones, E. *The Origins of Shakespeare*, Oxford, 1977

Karpman, D.M. 'William Tyndale's Response to the Hebraic Tradition', *Studies in the Renaissance*, 14, 1967, pp. 110–30

Kennedy, G.A. *Classical Rhetoric and Its Christian and Secular Tradition from Ancient to Modern Times*, Chapel Hill, 1980

Keynes, S. 'King Athelstan's Books', in M. Lapidge and H. Gneuss (eds), *Learning and Literature in Anglo-Saxon England: Studies Presented to Peter Clemoes on the Occasion of his Sixty-fifth Birthday*, Cambridge, 1985

King, J.N. *English Reformation Literature: The Tudor Origins of the Protestant Tradition*, Princeton, 1982

Knox, D.B. *The Doctrine of Faith in the Reign of Henry VIII*, 1961

Kohls, E.W. 'The Principal Theological Thoughts in the *Enchiridion Militis Christiani*', in R.L. DeMolen (ed.), *Essays on the Works of Erasmus*, New Haven and London, 1978, pp. 61–82

Kronenberg, M.E. 'Forged Addresses in Low Country Books in the Period of the Reformation', *The Library*, 5th ser., II, 1967, pp. 81–96

—— 'Notes on English Printing in the Low Countries (Early Sixteenth Century)', *The Library*, 4th ser., 1, 1929, pp. 139–63

Latimer, H. 'Seventh Sermon on the Lord's Prayer' [1552], in G.E. Corrie (ed.), *Sermons*, 2 vols, Cambridge, 1844–5

Lehmberg, S.E. *Sir Thomas Elyot: Tudor Humanist*, Austin, Tex., 1960

Letters and Papers, Foreign and Domestic, of the Reign of Henry VIII, ed. J.S. Brewer, J. Gairdner, R.H. Brodie, et al., 21 vols, 1862–1932

Lewis, C.S. *English Literature in the Sixteenth Century, Excluding Drama*, 1954

Lindsay, T.M. 'Englishmen and the Classical Renascence', in *The Cambridge History of English Literature: III*, Cambridge, 1909, pp. 1–24

Lloyd Jones, G. *The Discovery of Hebrew in Tudor England: A Third Language*, Manchester, 1983

Lucas, E.V. (ed.) *The Works of Charles and Mary Lamb*, 1912

Lupton, L. *The History of the Geneva Bible, XVIII, Part 1: Tyndale the Translator*, 1986

—— The History of the Geneva Bible, XIX, Part 2: Tyndale the Martyr, 1987

[Luther, M.] D. Martin Luthers Werke: Kritische Gesamtaufgabe, Weimar, 58 vols, 1883

McConica, J.K. English Humanists and Reformation Politics under Henry VIII and Edward VI, 1965

McCusker, H. John Bale: Dramatist and Antiquary, Bryn Mawr, 1942

McCusker, H., and Walker, G. Plays of Persuasion: Drama and Politics at the Court of Henry VIII, Cambridge, 1991

McGiffert, M. 'William Tyndale's Conception of Covenant', Journal of Ecclesiastical History, 32, 1981, pp. 167–84

Madan, F. (ed.) 'The day-book of John Dorne', Oxford Historical Society, Collecteana, vol. V, 1885, pp. 71–178

[Malmesbury, William of] Willelmi Malmsbiriensis monachi de gestis regum Anglorum libri quinque, ed. W. Stubbs, Rolls Series 1, 1887–9

De la Mare, A.C., and Barker-Benfield, B.C. (eds), Manuscripts at Oxford: An Exhibition in Memory of Richard William Hunt (1908–1979), Oxford, 1980

Marius, R. Thomas More: A Biography, 1985

Mayor, J.E.B. English Works of John Fisher, 1876, repr. 1935

Merriman, T.B. Life and Letters of Thomas Cromwell, 1902

Meyer, C.S. 'Henry VIII Burns Luther's Books, 12 May 1521', Journal of Ecclesiastical History, 9, 1958, pp. 173–87

Moller, J.G. 'The Beginnings of Puritan Covenant Theology', Journal of Ecclesiastical History, 14, 1963, pp. 46–67

[More Thomas] The Complete Works of St Thomas More, V, ed. J.M. Headley, New Haven and London, 1969

—— The Complete Works of St Thomas More, VIII, eds L.A. Schuster, R.C. Marius, J.P. Lusardi and R.J. Schoeck, New Haven and London, 1973

—— The Complete Works of St Thomas More, VI, eds T.M.C. Lawler, G. Marc'hadour and R.C. Marius, New Haven and London, 1981

Mozley, J.F. William Tyndale, 1937

—— John Foxe and his Book, 1940

—— 'The English Enchiridion of Erasmus, 1533', Review of English Studies, XX, 1944, pp. 97–107

—— Coverdale and his Bibles, 1953

Norton, D. A History of the Bible as Literature, I, Cambridge, 1993

Oberman, H.A. Luther: Man between God and Devil, New Haven and London, 1989

Overy, C., and Tyndale, A.C. 'The parentage of William Tyndale, alias Huchyns, Translator and Martyr', in Transactions of the Bristol and Gloucestershire Archaeological Society, LXXIII, 1954, pp. 208–15

Owst, G.R. Literature and Pulpit in Medieval England, Cambridge, 1933

Panofsky, E. *The Life and Art of Albrecht Dürer*, Princeton, NJ, 1955

Pantin, W.A. 'A Medieval Collection of Latin and English Proverbs and Riddles, from the Rylands Latin MS. 394', in *The Bulletin of the John Rylands Library*, XIV, 1930, pp. 81–114

Parkes, M.B. 'The Provision of Books', in J.I. Catto and R. Evans (eds), *The History of the University of Oxford, II: Late Medieval Oxford*, Oxford, 1992

Pearl, C. *Rashi*, 1988

Pecock, R. *The Rule of Christian Religion*, ed. W.C. Greet, Early English Texts Society, Oxford, 1927

Pineas, R. 'William Tyndale's Influence on John Bale's Polemical Use of History', *Archiv fur Reformationsgeschichte*, 53, 1962, pp. 79–96

—— 'Willam Tyndale's Use of History as a Weapon of Religious Controversy', *Harvard Theological Review*, 55, 1962, pp. 121–41

—— 'More versus Tyndale: A Study of Controversial Technique', *Modern Language Quarterly*, 24, 1963, pp. 144–50

—— 'William Tyndale: Controversialist', *Studies in Philology*, LX, April 1963, pp. 117–32

Pollard, A.W. *Records of the English Bible*, Oxford, 1911

Price, F. Douglas 'Gloucester Diocese under Bishop Hooper, 1551–3', *Transactions of the Bristol and Gloucestershire Archaeological Society*, LX, 1938, pp. 51–151

Prickett, S. (ed.) *Reading the Text: Biblical Criticism and Literary Theory*, Oxford, 1991

Puttenham, G. *The Arte of Englishe Poesie*, eds G.D. Willcock and A. Walker, Cambridge, 1936

Rabil, A. (Jr) 'Erasmus's *Paraphrases of the New Testament*', in R.L. DeMolen (ed.), *Essays on the Works of Erasmus*, New Haven and London, 1978, pp. 145–61

Rex, R. 'The English Campaigns against Luther in the 1520's', *Transactions of the Royal Historical Society*, 5th series, XXXIX, 1989, pp. 85–106

Rhodes, J.T. 'Erasmus and English Readers of the 1530s', *Durham University Journal*, 71, n.s., 40, 1979, pp. 17–25

Richardson, W.C. *Stephen Vaughan, Financial Agent of Henry VIII: A Study of Financial Relations with the Low Countries*, Baton Rouge, 1953

Roach, T. 'Tyndale's New Testament and the Gloucestershire Dialect', *Gloucestershire Notes and Queries*, CCCCII, 1881, pp. 408–9

Rollison, D. *The Local Origins of Modern Society: Gloucestershire 1500–1800*, 1992

Rummel, E. *Erasmus' Annotations on the New Testament: From Philologist to Theologian*, Toronto, 1986

Scarisbrick, J.J. *The Reformation and the English People*, 1984

Schuster, L.A. 'Thomas More's Polemical Career, 1523–1533', in *CWM*, VIII, iii, pp. 1135–267

Schwarz, W. *Principles and Problems of Biblical Translation: Some Reformation Controversies and their Background*, Cambridge, 1955

Seebohm, F. *The Oxford Reformers John Colet, Erasmus and Thomas More: Being a History of Their Fellow-work*, 1867

Sidney, Sir P. *An Apology for Poetry*, ed. G. Shepherd, 1965

Skelton, J. *The Complete Poems*, ed. J. Scattergood, 1983

Smeeton, D.D. *Lollard Themes in the Reformation Theology of William Tyndale*, VI of *sixteenth-century Essays and Studies*, ed. C.G. Nauert, Kirksville, Mo., 1984

Soggin, J.A. *Judges: A Commentary*, 1979

Stanier, R.S. *Magdalen School: A History of Magdalen College School*, Oxford, 1940

Starkey, D. (ed.) *Henry VIII: A European Court in England*, 1991

Steele, R. 'Notes on English Books Printed Abroad, 1525–1548', *Transactions of the Bibliographical Society*, XI, 1911, pp. 189–236

Steinberg, S.H. *Five Hundred Years of Printing*, 3rd edn, 1974

Strype, J. *Memorials of Archbishop Cranmer*, 2 vols, 1812

—— *Ecclesiastical Memorials* . . . , 3 vols, 1821

Sturge, C. *Cuthbert Tunstall: Churchman, Scholar, Statesman, Administrator*, 1938

Sylvester, R.S., and Marc'hadour, G.P. (eds) *Essential Articles for the Study of Thomas More*, Hamden, Conn., 1977

Trapp, J.B. 'Erasmus, Colet and More: The Early Tudor Humanists and their Books', *The Panizzi Lectures 1990*, 1991

Trousdale, M. *Shakespeare and the Rhetoricians*, 1982

Tyndale, William *The Beginning of the New Testament Translated by William Tyndale 1525. Facsimile of the Unique Fragment of the Uncompleted Cologne Edition*, ed. A.W. Pollard, Oxford, 1926

—— [*The New Testament*], Worms, 1526

—— *A Compendius Introduction. . . . unto the epistle of Paul to the Romans*, Worms, 1526

—— [*The Parable of the Wicked Mammon*], Antwerp, 1528

—— *The Obedience of a Christian Man* . . . , Antwerp, 1528

—— [*The Pentateuch*], Antwerp, 1530

—— *The Practice of Prelates*, Antwerp, 1530

—— *A Pathway to the Holy Scripture*, 1530

—— *The Prophet Jonas* . . . , Antwerp, 1531

—— *An Answer to Sir Thomas More's Dialogue* . . . , Antwerp, 1531

—— *The Exposition of the First Epistle of St John*, Antwerp, 1531

—— *An Exposition upon the V, VI, VII Chapters of Matthew*, Antwerp, 1533

—— *The New Testament*, Antwerp, 1534

—— *The First Book of Moses called Genesis*, Antwerp, 1534

—— *The New Testament*, Antwerp, 1535

—— *The Testament of Master W. Tracie Esquire*, Antwerp, 1535

—— *A Brief Declaration of the Sacraments*, London, *c.* 1548

—— *Doctrinal Treatises and Introductions to Different Portions of the Holy Scriptures*, ed. H. Walter, The Parker Society, Cambridge, 1848

—— *Expositions and Notes on . . . The Holy Scriptures . . . together with The Practice of Prelates*, ed. H. Walter, The Parker Society, Cambridge, 1849

—— *An Answer to Sir Thomas More's Dialogue . . .* , ed. H. Walter, The Parker Society, Cambridge, 1850

Tyndale's New Testament modern-spelling edition with an Introduction by David Daniell, New Haven and London, 1989

Tyndale's Old Testament, a modern-spelling edition with an Introduction by David Daniell, New Haven and London, 1992

Wakefield, R. *On the Three Languages* [1524], ed. G. Lloyd Jones, Binghampton, NY: Medieval and Renaissance Texts and Studies, and the Renaissance Society of America, 1989

Walker, G. *John Skelton and the Politics of the 1520s*, Cambridge, 1988.

—— *Plays of persuasion: Drama and Politics at the Court of Henry VIII*, Cambridge, 1991

Warnicke, R.M. 'The Fall of Anne Boleyn: A Reassessment', *History*, n.s., 70, 1985, pp. 1–15

—— *The Rise and Fall of Anne Boleyn*, Cambridge, 1989

Weiss, R. *Humanism in England During the Fifteenth Century*, Oxford, 1957.

—— *The Spread of Italian Humanism*, 1964

Westcott, B.F. *A General View of the History of the English Bible*, 3rd ed., rev. W.A. Wright, 1905

Wheeler Robinson, H. (ed.) *The Bible and its Ancient and English Versions*, 1940

White, B. *The Vulgaria of John Stanbridge and the Vulgaria of Robert Whittington*, Early English Texts Society, 187, Oxford, 1932

Whiting, B.J. and H.W. *Proverbs, Sentences and Proverbial Phrases from English Writings mainly before 1500*, Cambridge, Mass., 1968

Williams, A. *The Common Expositor: An Account of the Commentaries on Genesis, 1527–1633*, Chapel Hill, North Carolina, 1948

Wolf, A. *William Roye's 'Dialogue between A Christian Father and his stubborn Son'*, Vienna, 1874

Wood, A. *à The History of Antiquities of the Colleges and Halls of the University of Oxford [Annals]*, ed. J. Gutch, 2 vols, 1786–90

—— *Athenae Oxonienses*, ed. P. Bliss, 4 vols, 1813–20

Workman, S.K. *Fifteenth Century Translation as an Influence on English Prose*, Princeton, 1940

INDEX